Charles Seymour Robinson

Songs of the Church

Hymns and Tunes for Christian Worship

Charles Seymour Robinson

Songs of the Church
Hymns and Tunes for Christian Worship

ISBN/EAN: 9783337289744

Printed in Europe, USA, Canada, Australia, Japan

Cover: Foto ©Thomas Meinert / pixelio.de

More available books at **www.hansebooks.com**

Songs of the Church:

OR,

HYMNS AND TUNES

FOR

CHRISTIAN WORSHIP.

A. S. BARNES & CO.,

NEW YORK AND CHICAGO

1876.

PUBLISHERS' NOTE.

THIS work is adapted especially to PRESBYTERIAN AND CONGREGATIONAL CHURCHES. The Form of Government of the Presbyterian Church,—the Directory for Membership,—and the Book of Discipline, will be found in the Presbyterian edition. An edition of this work is also printed without a Form of Government, so that it may be adapted to *any* denomination. Any Church wishing the introduction of their own plan of Government, or Form of Admission or Confession of Faith, can secure it, at a slight additional expense, upon application to the publishers.

Entered, according to Act of Congress, in the year 1862, by
A. S. BARNES & BURR,
In the Clerk's Office of the District Court of the United States, for the Southern District of New York

PREF·ACE.

THE HISTORY and purpose of the following Collection of Hymns and Tunes may be sufficiently set forth in a few words.

It has been prepared by a PASTOR; for the use, primarily, of the church to which it is his privilege to minister, in their public and private worship of almighty God. The Book is now offered to the Christian public, in the thought that what has thus been compiled for one congregation may, perhaps, be found acceptable and useful in others like it.

It is designed for use not only in the services of the Sanctuary, but also in the Social Meetings of Christians, in the Sabbath-School Concerts, and in the Family; to be a book, if God and his people shall honor it so far, familiar in the Home as well as in the Church; which children with their parents shall love and study; and by which all shall be aided and taught to take part more joyfully in the worship of the Redeemer.

In the selection of HYMNS for this so wide and comprehensive use, the compiler has intended to follow but one supreme rule; namely, to take those which have been most precious to himself in his own Christian experience and life, and those which have been found most helpful in his efforts as a pastor, to impress upon men the truths of the Gospel, and to quicken and edify the Church of God. They have not, by any means, therefore, been chosen solely for their value as lyrical compositions. The spiritual power of a hymn resides in the Christian thought or feeling which it musically utters. The rhythmical form is plainly and wholly subordinate to this; though, where this primary element of power is indisputably present, it is true, of course, the more perfect the form, the better is the hymn.

Regard has been had, however, especially in deciding between hymns of otherwise equal merit, to the tender and holy associations connected with some, to the exclusion of others; and to the fact that occasionally those, whose esthetic value is least apparent, have yet vindicated their right to a permanent place in such collections, by the hold they have gained on the affections of the Church at large.

Of hymns, which have not heretofore been in general use, whose worth has not, therefore, been subjected to an equal test with those of the older lyrists, it has, in like manner, been his aim, to take from the mixed multitude before him only those which most clearly contain, and sweetly express, the truths, the admonitions, and the cheerful promises of our holy Faith. And yet he has endeavored to bear in mind the fact, that

that may be quickening and inspiring to one person which is not to another; or to any person in a particular mood of feeling, while in a different mood he would be entirely unmoved by it. Occasionally both modern and ancient hymns have been omitted, however, and sometimes with regret, simply because, in the necessary want of room for all, some selection must be made.

He has also attempted to introduce more hymns, and render those in common use more available, by reducing the number of stanzas printed, so as to allow them in most cases to be sung in their entireness, without destroying the symmetry of the parts of public worship. It is customary for pastors to omit certain stanzas in giving out hymns for singing; not a few books found in our pulpits are scored with brackets introduced, either penciled or printed. Why, then, not exclude this useless bulk at once, and take the room for that which is needed?

Frequently a composition, even of our most venerated lyrists, runs endlessly on into seven, eight, and ten stanzas. Some rejection is, of course, here inevitable. And it sometimes happens that, while several stanzas of an established hymn are vigorous and in all respects excellent, others, usually combined with them, are weak and ineffective. The thought or the feeling toils through them as if burdened, instead of singing itself, as it did in the rest, joyfully heavenward.

In preparing this Collection, in order to avoid enlarging it beyond limits as to size, and at the same time to secure the greatest range and variety in the selections, it has been deemed wise to omit at the outset from the longer hymns those parts which, for any reason, are least likely to be used, and to print only those which are really rich in the moving and musical expression of the truth. It will be observed, that, although for symmetry and convenience no separation as to arrangement or numbering has been adopted, to distinguish between Hymns and what are technically called Psalms, yet the best versions of these latter have been carefully and lovingly sought from every source, that each of the old songs of inspiration might, if possible, have its representative here.

And yet it ought to be said, that, in both the alteration and abridgment of hymns, the compiler of this book has allowed himself but very little liberty. Even when it seemed to him, that certain slight verbal changes would be real and great improvements, he has, in most instances, declined to make them on his own unsupported decision. He has, however, usually accepted the alterations which have heretofore been made, the practical adoption of which among the churches has given them familiarity and authority. And not unfrequently he has reproduced the amendments appearing in only a few of the previous collections, but which his own judgment and taste decidedly approved. As almost no one of his predecessors has been content to leave what he found, precisely as he found it, but in all hymn-books alterations and abridgments have been freely made, each compiler adopting or rejecting at will those which each other compiler suggested, now it remains only for any one that comes after to pick his own path through the chaos thus produced, and try to be as judicious as he can. As for a fixed standard, there is none.

No hesitation has been felt by the present compiler in availing himself, as those before him have constantly done, of any suggestions left in his way, when they seemed to him to have intrinsic value. Pains have been taken to preserve the essential completeness of every hymn. And while, no doubt, some worshipers will miss stanzas to which they have been accustomed and, perhaps, attached, and will meet now and then expressions which are novel, yet it is hoped with all earnestness, and confidently believed, that no true and healthful Christian sensibility will be startled with a sense of loss, or repelled by any changes that have been allowed. It is proper to add, that, although ministers and churches will find here nearly all they have most valued and most used, yet in a few cases stanzas have been quietly dropped, which the editor would gladly have retained, but which the mechanical requirements of the page constrained him to exclude.

An ARRANGEMENT of the hymns according to subjects has been attempted in this Collection. No one without experience can at all appreciate the difficulty which falls in the way of an exact accomplishment of a purpose like this, when at the same time the tunes are to be adapted for singing. It has not been possible even here, to carry it out in every instance. Some of our best hymns have really more than one subject, and could easily find themselves at home under quite diverse headings. And in a few cases, for the sake of a familiar adaptation, or a more than usually excellent new one, a hymn has been taken from its proper place, and will have to be sought in the general Index. Yet it is believed, that even the extent to which this plan has been carried will ensure essential convenience.

The MUSICAL ARRANGEMENTS and adaptations have been mostly under the care of Mr. JOSEPH P. HOLBROOK, of Cleveland, Ohio; whose faithfulness and taste are alike evidenced by the skill with which the work has been done. The few pieces of his own composition, with which the Collection is enriched, will be found among the best it contains. And this part of the Book has been also carefully supervised by two gentlemen in that congregation for which it was at first prepared, of large experience in the conduct of Church Choirs, and specially skilled in sacred song: Hon. CYRUS P. SMITH and THOS. S. NELSON, Esq. To all of these gentlemen the compiler desires to make his sincere acknowledgments.

The plan here adopted has had for its purpose the settlement in some measure of that annoying difference of opinion which holds place in many quarters, concerning Artistic and Congregational Singing. A compromise has been attempted on this point. Two thirds of the Hymns are set to music, one third left free. But these latter are arranged in the same order, and contain the same variety of subjects as the others. It is proposed that in each service two hymns shall be given out in Part I., and one in Part II. This one the Choir are at liberty to adapt to any tune, in the Collection or out of it, at their own pleasure. The other two they are expected to lead the Congregation in singing to the music set. Some of the music, however, in Part I. will be found better adapted to Choir use, and Home use, than to the promiscuous worship of the Sanctuary, or the simpler service of a prayer-meeting. Some discrimination must be exercised by Pastors, and by Choristers also, in this particular.

In most cases a choice of Tunes is allowed. A known or old piece has been printed opposite a new or fresher one. It does not follow that a hymn standing under a tune is always to be sung to it. Mechanical reasons may have located it there, when the fitter music for its sentiment will be found on the other page. And sometimes a tune strictly belonging to the Choir has been placed near a hymn of merit, to avoid repeating the hymn in Part II. It is apparent at a glance, however, that this double adaptation could not be carried out perfectly without a large multiplication of hymns of the same metre upon a specific theme. But it is hoped that the attempt has been so far successful as to give frequent convenience. And since the Book in its two forms is intended for the Lecture Room as well as the Sanctuary, this choice of tunes will give opportunity for a little more variety, the Chorister selecting one tune, and the Leader in the prayer-meeting quite possibly using the other.

THE THEORY of choice in the musical adaptations has been simply this;—what the churches at large love, it is hoped they will find here. Tunes which have a melody—a fascination, a magnetism, call it what one will—have been preferred. Musical structure makes no difference. For all time critics have grown violent, and yet the people sung on. The compiler has had no disposition to defy the critics, but he has desired to keep the people singing on, by every means within his reach.

AND NOW, at the conclusion of his self-imposed task, looking back over the many months which have been almost absorbed by it, the undersigned offers his fervent and grateful thanks to God for the kindness which has permitted him to begin, and at last to end it, and for the grace which has made it all to him a labor of love and Christian joyfulness, bringing its own reward in its hand.

He presents the humble result, of what has been to him very serious labor, to his own beloved people, and the Church at large, with unaffected pleasure, in the simple hope that it may be used by our divine Redeemer in building up his chosen in the most holy faith; and that it may be so accompanied by the grace of the Spirit—would that it might be even so honored!—as to be as the sound of silver bells calling those who know not our Lord to his most joyful feasts of love. So may it advance, in its own measure, the worship of our KING, till our eyes shall see Him in his beauty and behold the land that is very far off!

CHAS. S. ROBINSON.

TABLE OF CONTENTS.

		PAGE
I.—PREFACE		3

	PART I.	PART II.
II.—PUBLIC WORSHIP:		
1. OPENING OF SERVICE	1	279
2. GENERAL PRAISE	18	282
3. CLOSE OF SERVICE	29	287
III.—THE SCRIPTURES	32	283
IV.—GOD: BEING, ATTRIBUTES, PROVIDENCE	86	289
V.—JESUS CHRIST:		
1. ADVENT	46	294
2. LIFE AND CHARACTER	49	295
3. SUFFERINGS AND DEATH	52	297
4. RESURRECTION AND ASCENSION	55	298
5. ADORATION	56	299
VI.—HOLY SPIRIT: ADORATION, INVOCATION	64	301
VII.—WAY OF SALVATION:		
1. LOST STATE OF MAN	70	302
2. ATONEMENT AND PARDON	76	303
3. INVITATION AND WARNING	78	305
4. REPENTANCE AND RECEPTION OF CHRIST	92	307
VIII.—CHRISTIAN:		
1. CONFLICT WITH SIN	106	310
2. ENCOURAGEMENTS	124	316
3. LOVE FOR THE SAVIOUR	136	320
4. GRACES	160	325
5. PRIVILEGES	170	327
6. DUTIES	176	330
7. AFFLICTIONS	182	331
IX.—THE CHURCH:		
1. INSTITUTIONS	192	335
2. ORDINANCES	195	336
3. PROGRESS AND MISSIONS	206	339
4. SABBATH SCHOOL	218	
5. SOCIAL MEETINGS	227	
X.—DEATH AND JUDGMENT	244	343
XI.—HEAVEN	262	349
XII.—MISCELLANEOUS: FEASTS, FASTS, SAILORS, ETC.	272	352
XIII—DOXOLOGIES		856
XIV.—SELECTIONS FOR CHANTING		858
XV.—TUNES FOR THE CHOIR		871
XVI.—GENERAL INDEX OF TUNES		381
XVII.—METRICAL INDEX		383
XVIII.—TABLE OF FIRST LINES		385
XIX—INDEX OF SUBJECTS		393

PUBLISHERS' ADVERTISEMENT.

PART FIRST.

FOR THE CONGREGATION.

SABBATH. 7s. 6 lines.

Dr. L. Mason.

1. Safe - ly through an - oth - er week, God has brought us on our way; Let us
now a blessing seek, Waiting in his courts to - day: Day of all the week the best, Emblem
of e - ter-nal rest, Day of all the week the best, Emblem of e - ter - nal rest.

1.

2 While we seek supplies of grace,
    Through the dear Redeemer's name,
Show thy reconciling face—
    Take away our sin and shame;
From our worldly cares set free,—
May we rest this day in thee.

3 Here we come thy name to praise;
    Let us feel thy presence near:

May thy glory meet our eyes,
    While we in thy house appear:
Here afford us, Lord, a taste
Of our everlasting rest.

4 May the gospel's joyful sound
    Wake our minds to raptures new;
Let thy victories abound,—
    Unrepenting souls subdue:
Thus let all our Sabbaths prove,
Till we rest in thee above. .

SPOHR. L. M.

Arranged from Spohr.

1. Thine earthly Sab-baths, Lord, we love; But there's a no - bler rest a - bove!

To that our long - ing souls as - pire, With cheer - ful hope and strong de - sire.

2.

2 No more fatigue, no more distress,
Nor sin, nor death, shall reach the place;
No groans shall mingle with the songs
That warble from immortal tongues.

3 No rude alarms of raging foes;
No cares to break the long repose;
No midnight shade; no clouded sun;
But sacred, high, eternal noon.

4 Soon shall that glorious day begin,
Beyond this world of death and sin;—
Soon shall our voices join the song
Of the triumphant, holy throng.

3.

1 Another day has passed along,
And we are nearer to the tomb,
Nearer to join the heavenly song,
Or hear the last eternal doom.

2 Sweet is the light of Sabbath eve,
And soft the sunbeams lingering there;
For these blest hours, the world I leave,
Wafted on wings of faith and prayer.

3 The time how lovely and how still;
Peace shines and smiles on all below—
The plain, the stream, the wood, the hill—
All fair with evening's setting glow.

4 Season of rest! the tranquil soul
Feels the sweet calm, and melts to love—
And while these sacred moments roll,
Faith sees the smiling heaven above.

5 Nor will our days of toil be long,
Our pilgrimage will soon be trod;
And we shall join the ceaseless song—
The endless Sabbath of our God.

4.

1 My opening eyes with rapture see
The dawn of thy returning day;
My thoughts, O God, ascend to thee,
While thus my early vows I pay.

2 Oh, bid this trifling world retire,
And drive each carnal thought away;
Nor let me feel one vain desire—
One sinful thought through all the day.

3 Then, to thy courts when I repair,
My soul shall rise on joyful wing,
The wonders of thy love declare,
And join the strains which angels sing.

5.

1 Come, gracious Lord, descend and dwell,
By faith and love, in every breast;
Then shall we know, and taste, and feel
The joys that cannot be expressed.

2 Come, fill our hearts with inward strength,
Make our enlargèd souls possess,
And learn the height, and breadth, and
length
Of thine eternal love and grace.

3 Now to the God whose power can do
More than our thoughts and wishes know,
Be everlasting honors done,
By all the church, through Christ, his Son.

MIGDOL. L. M.   DR. L. MASON.

1. Sweet is the work, my God, my King, To praise thy name, give thanks, and sing, To show thy love by morning light, And talk of all thy truth at night.

6.

2 Sweet is the day of sacred rest;
No mortal care shall seize my breast;
Oh! may my heart in tune be found,
Like David's harp of solemn sound!

3 My heart shall triumph in my Lord,
And bless his works and bless his word;
Thy works of grace, how bright they
shine!
How deep thy counsels! how divine!

4 Lord, I shall share a glorious part,
When grace hath well refined my heart,
And fresh supplies of joy are shed,
Like holy oil to cheer my head.

5 Then shall I see, and hear, and know
All I desired or wished below;
And every power find sweet employ,
In that eternal world of joy.

7.

1 How pleasant, how divinely fair,
O Lord of hosts, thy dwellings are!
With long desire my spirit faints,
To meet th' assemblies of thy saints.

2 My flesh would rest in thine abode,
My panting heart cries out for God;
My God, my King, why should I be
So far from all my joys and thee?

3 Blest are the saints who sit on high
Around thy throne of majesty;
Thy brightest glories shine above,
And all their work is praise and love.

4 Blest are the souls that find a place
Within the temple of thy grace;
There they behold thy gentler rays,
And seek thy face, and learn thy praise.

5 Blest are the men whose hearts are set
To find the way to Zion's gate;
God is their strength, and through the
road
They lean upon their helper, God.

6 Cheerful they walk with growing strength,
Till all shall meet in heaven at length;
Till all before thy face appear,
And join in nobler worship there.

8.

1 ANOTHER six days' work is done,
Another Sabbath is begun;
Return, my soul! enjoy thy rest,
Improve the day thy God has blessed.

2 Oh! that our thoughts and thanks may
rise,
As grateful incense to the skies;
And draw, from heaven, that sweet repose,
Which none, but he that feels it, knows.

3 This heavenly calm, within the breast,
Is the dear pledge of glorious rest,
Which for the church of God remains—
The end of cares, the end of pains.

4 In holy duties, let the day,
In holy pleasures, pass away;
How sweet a Sabbath thus to spend,
In hope of one that ne'er shall end.

MARLOW. C. M.

Arranged by Dr. L. Mason.

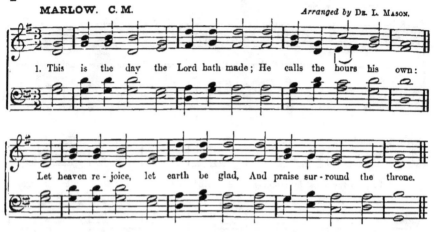

1. This is the day the Lord hath made; He calls the hours his own:

Let heaven re - joice, let earth be glad, And praise sur - round the throne.

9.

2 To-day he rose, and left the dead,
And Satan's empire fell;
To-day the saints his triumph spread,
And all his wonders tell.

3 Hosanna to th' anointed King,
To David's holy Son:
Help us, O Lord! descend, and bring
Salvation from thy throne.

4 Blest be the Lord who comes to men
With messages of grace;
Who comes, in God his Father's name,
To save our sinful race.

5 Hosanna in the highest strains
The church on earth can raise;
The highest heavens, in which he reigns,
Shall give him nobler praise.

10.

1 Blest morning! whose young dawning
rays
Beheld our rising God;
That saw him triumph o'er the dust,
And leave his dark abode.

2 In the cold prison of a tomb
The great Redeemer lay,
Till the revolving skies had brought
The third, th' appointed day.

3 Hell and the grave combined their force
To hold our God, in vain;
The sleeping conqueror arose,
And burst their feeble chain.

4 To thy great name, almighty Lord,
These sacred hours we pay,
And loud hosannas shall proclaim
The triumph of the day.

5 Salvation and immortal praise
To our victorious King!
Let heaven and earth, and rocks and seas,
With glad hosannas ring.

11.

1 Early, my God, without delay,
I haste to seek thy face;
My thirsty spirit faints away,
Without thy cheering grace.

2 I've seen thy glory and thy power
Through all thy temple shine;
My God, repeat that heavenly hour,
That vision so divine.

3 Not all the blessings of a feast
Can please my soul so well,
As when thy richer grace I taste,
And in thy presence dwell.

4 Not life itself, with all its joys,
Can my best passions move,
Or raise so high my cheerful voice,
As thy forgiving love.

5 Thus, till my last expiring day,
I'll bless my God and King;
Thus will I lift my hands to pray,
And tune my lips to sing.

CHURCH. C. M.

J. P. HOLBROOK.

1. My soul, how love-ly is the place, To which thy God re-sorts! 'Tis heaven to see his smil-ing face, Though in his earth-ly courts.

12.

2 There the great Monarch of the skies
His saving power displays;
And light breaks in upon our eyes,
With kind and quickening rays.

3 With his rich gifts, the heavenly Dove
Descends and fills the place;
While Christ reveals his wondrous love,
And sheds abroad his grace.

4 There, mighty God! thy words declare
The secrets of thy will;
And still we seek thy mercy there,
And sing thy praises still.

13.

1 FAR from the world, O Lord, I flee,
From strife and tumult far;
From scenes where Satan wages still
His most successful war.

2 The calm retreat, the silent shade,
With prayer and praise agree;
And seem by thy sweet bounty made
For those who follow thee.

3 There, if thy Spirit touch the soul,
And grace her mean abode,
Oh! with what peace, and joy, and love,
She communes with her God.

4 There, like the nightingale, she pours
Her solitary lays;
Nor asks a witness of her song,
Nor thirsts for human praise.

5 Author and Guardian of my life!
Sweet source of light divine,
And—all harmonious names in one—
My Saviour, thou art mine!

6 What thanks I owe thee, and what love,
A boundless, endless store—
Shall echo through the realms above,
When time shall be no more.

14.

1 FREQUENT the day of God returns
To shed its quickening beams;
And yet how slow devotion burns;
How languid are its flames!

2 Accept our faint attempts to love,
Our frailties, Lord, forgive;
We would be like thy saints above,
And praise thee while we live.

3 Increase, O Lord, our faith and hope,
And fit us to ascend
Where the assembly ne'er breaks up,
The Sabbath ne'er shall end;—

4 Where we shall breathe in heavenly air,
With heavenly lustre shine,
Before the throne of God appear,
And feast on love divine;—

5 Where we, in high seraphic strains,
Shall all our powers employ;
Delighted range th' ethereal plains,
And take our fill of joy.

WARWICK. C. M.   STANLEY.

1. A - rise, O King of grace! a - rise, And en - ter to thy rest;

Lo! thy church waits with long - ing eyes, Thus to be owned and blest.

15.

2 Enter, with all thy glorious train,
  Thy Spirit and thy word;
All that the ark did once contain,
  Could no such grace afford.

3 Here, mighty God! accept our vows,
  Here let thy praise be spread;
Bless the provisions of thy house,
  And fill thy poor with bread.

4 Here let the Son of David reign,
  Let God's Anointed shine;
Justice and truth his court maintain,
  With love and power divine.

5 Here let him hold a lasting throne;
  And as his kingdom grows,
Fresh honors shall adorn his crown,
  And shame confound his foes.

16.

1 With joy we hail the sacred day
  Which God hath called his own;
With joy the summons we obey
  To worship at his throne.

2 Thy chosen temple, Lord, how fair!
  Where willing votaries throng
To breathe the humble, fervent prayer,
  And pour the choral song.

3 Spirit of grace! Oh, deign to dwell
  Within thy church below;
Make her in holiness excel,
  With pure devotion glow.

4 Let peace within her walls be found;
  Let all her sons unite,
To spread with grateful zeal around
  Her clear and shining light.

5 Great God, we hail the sacred day
  Which thou hast called thine own;
With joy the summons we obey
  To worship at thy throne.

17.

1 Lord, in the morning thou shalt hear
  My voice ascending high;
To thee will I direct my prayer,
  To thee lift up mine eye.

2 Up to the hills where Christ is gone,
  To plead for all his saints,
Presenting at his Father's throne
  Our songs and our complaints.

3 Thou art a God before whose sight
  The wicked shall not stand;
Sinners shall ne'er be thy delight,
  Nor dwell at thy right hand.

4 But to thy house will I resort
  To taste thy mercies there;
I will frequent thy holy court,
  And worship in thy fear.

5 Oh, may thy Spirit guide my feet
  In ways of righteousness!
Make every path of duty straight,
  And plain before my face.

COLMAN. C. M.

Geo. Kingsley.

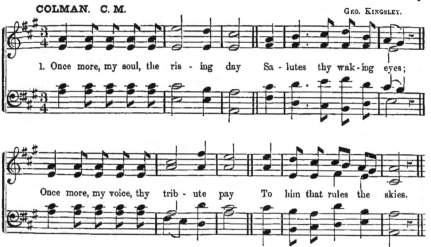

1. Once more, my soul, the ris - ing day Sa - lutes thy wak - ing eyes;

Once more, my voice, thy trib - ute pay To him that rules the skies.

18.

1 Once more, my soul, the rising day
Salutes thy waking eyes;
Once more, my voice, thy tribute pay
To him that rules the skies.

2 Night unto night his name repeats,
The day renews the sound,
Wide as the heaven on which he sits,
To turn the seasons round.

3 'Tis he supports my mortal frame;
My tongue shall speak his praise;
My sins would rouse his wrath to flame,
And yet his wrath delays.

4 Great God, let all my hours be thine,
While I enjoy the light;
Then shall my sun in smiles decline,
And bring a pleasant night.

19.

1 How did my heart rejoice to hear
My friends devoutly say:
"In Zion let us all appear,
And keep the solemn day."

2 I love her gates, I love the road;
The church, adorned with grace,
Stands like a palace built for God,
To show his milder face.

3 Up to her courts, with joys unknown,
The holy tribes repair;
The Son of David holds his throne,
And sits in judgment there.

4 He hears our praises and complaints;
And, while his awful voice
Divides the sinners from the saints,
We tremble and rejoice.

5 Peace be within this sacred place,
And joy a constant guest!
With holy gifts and heavenly grace
Be her attendants blest!

6 My soul shall pray for Zion still,
While life or breath remains:
There my best friends, my kindred dwell;
There God, my Saviour, reigns.

20.

1 Come, ye that love the Saviour's name,
And joy to make it known;
The Sovereign of your hearts proclaim,
And bow before his throne.

2 Behold your King, your Saviour, crowned
With glories all divine;
And tell the wondering nations round,
How bright those glories shine.

3 When in his earthly courts we view
The beauties of our King,
We long to love as angels do,
And with their voice to sing.

4 Oh, for the day—the glorious day!
When heaven and earth shall raise
With all their powers the raptured lay,
To celebrate thy praise.

HYMN. C. M.   MODERN HARP.

1. Come, thou de-sire of all thy saints, Our hum-ble strains at - tend,

While, with our prais - es and com-plaints, Low at thy feet we bend.

21.

2 How should our songs, like those above,
    With warm devotion rise!
   How should our souls, on wings of love,
    Mount upward to the skies!

3 O Lord, thy love alone can raise
    In us the heavenly flame;
   Then shall our lips resound thy praise,
    Our hearts adore thy name.

4 Dear Saviour, let thy glory shine,
    And fill thy dwellings here,
   Till life, and love, and joy divine
    A heaven on earth appear.

22.

1 BLEST day of God! most calm, most bright,
    The first and best of days;
   The laborer's rest, the saint's delight,
    The day of prayer and praise.

2 My Saviour's face made thee to shine;
    His rising thee did raise;
   And made thee heavenly and divine
    Beyond all other days.

3 The first-fruits oft a blessing prove
    To all the sheaves behind;
   And they who do the Sabbath love,
    A happy week will find.

4 This day I must to God appear;
    For, Lord, the day is thine;
   Help me to spend it in thy fear,
    And thus to make it mine.

23.

1 THE bird let loose in Eastern skies,
    Returning fondly home,
   Ne'er stoops to earth her wing, nor flies
    Where idle warblers roam.

2 But high she shoots through air and light,
    Above all low delay,
   Where nothing earthly bounds her flight,
    Nor shadow dims her way.

3 So grant me, Lord, from every snare
    Of sinful passion free,
   Aloft through faith's serener air
    To hold my course to thee.

4 No sin to cloud, no lure to stay
    My soul, as home she springs;
   Thy sunshine on her joyful way,
    Thy freedom in her wings.

24.

1 WEARIED with earthly toil and care,
    The day of rest how sweet!
   To breathe the Sabbath's holy air,
    And sit at Jesus' feet.

2 Fain would I lay the burden down,
    That wounds me with its weight,
   To gaze awhile at yonder crown,
    And press toward heaven's gate.

3 I ask a foretaste of the peace,
    The rest, the joy, the love,
   Which, when their earthly Sabbaths cease,
    Await the saints above.

BEMERTON. C. M.

GREATOREX COLL.

1. Lord, when we bend be - fore thy throne, And our con - fess - ions pour,

Oh, may we feel the sins we own, And hate what we de - plore.

25.

2 Our contrite spirits pitying see;
　True penitence impart;
　And let a healing ray from thee
　Beam hope on every heart.

3 When we disclose our wants in prayer,
　May we our wills resign;
　Nor let a thought our bosom share,
　Which is not wholly thine.

4 Let faith each meek petition fill,
　And waft it to the skies;
　And teach our hearts 'tis goodness still
　That grants it or denies.

26.

1 SPIRIT of truth! on this thy day,
　To thee for help we cry,
　To guide us through the dreary way
　Of dark mortality.

2 We ask not, Lord, the cloven flame,
　Or tongues of various tone;
　But long thy praises to proclaim
　With fervor in our own.

3 No heavenly harpings soothe our ear,
　No mystic dreams we share;
　Yet hope to feel thy comfort near,
　And bless thee in our prayer.

4 When tongues shall cease, and power de-
　cay,
　And knowledge empty prove,
　Do thou thy trembling servants stay,
　With faith, and hope, and love.

27.

1 GOD of the sun-light hours, how sad
　Would evening shadows be,
　Or night, in deeper sable clad,—
　If aught were dark to thee!

2 How mournfully that golden gleam
　Would touch the thoughtful heart,
　If, with its soft, retiring beam,
　We saw thy love depart.

3 But, tho' the gathering gloom may hide
　Those gentle rays awhile,
　Yet they who in thy house abide,
　Shall ever share thy smile.

4 Then let creation's volume close
　Though every page be bright;
　On thine, still open, we repose
　With more intense delight.

28.

1 O GOD! by whom the seed is given,
　By whom the harvest blessed;
　Whose word, like manna showered from
　heaven,
　Is planted in our breast,—

2 Preserve it from the passing feet,
　And plunderers of the air,
　The sultry sun's intenser heat,
　And thorns of worldly care.

3 Though buried deep, or thinly strown,
　Do thou thy grace supply;
　The hope in earthly furrows sown,
　Shall ripen in the sky.

ST. THOMAS. S. M.   WILLIAMS.

1. Come, we who love the Lord! And let our joys be known:

Join in a song of sweet ac - cord, And thus sur - round the throne.

29.

1 COME, we who love the Lord,
  And let our joys be known;
Join in a song of sweet accord,
  And thus surround the throne.

2 Let those refuse to sing
  Who never knew our God;
But children of the heavenly King
  May speak their joys abroad.

3 The men of grace have found
  Glory begun below;
Celestial fruits on earthly ground
  From faith and hope may grow.

4 The hill of Zion yields
  A thousand sacred sweets
Before we reach the heavenly fields
  Or walk the golden streets.

5 Then let our songs abound,
  And every tear be dry;
We're marching thro' Immanuel's ground
  To fairer worlds on high.

30.

1 WELCOME, sweet day of rest,
  That saw the Lord arise!
Welcome to this reviving breast,
  And these rejoicing eyes!

2 The King himself comes near,
  And feasts his saints to-day;
Here may we sit, and see him here,
  And love, and praise, and pray.

3 One day, amid the place
  Where my dear Lord hath been,
Is sweeter than ten thousand days
  Within the tents of sin.

4 My willing soul would stay
  In such a frame as this,
And sit and sing herself away
  To everlasting bliss.

31.

1 AWAKE, and sing the song
  Of Moses and the Lamb;
Wake, every heart and every tongue
  To praise the Saviour's name.

2 Sing of his dying love;
  Sing of his rising power;
Sing—how he intercedes above
  For those whose sins he bore.

3 Ye pilgrims! on the road
  To Zion's city, sing!
Rejoice ye in the Lamb of God,—
  In Christ, th' eternal King.

4 Soon shall we hear him say,—
  "Ye blessed children! come;"
Soon will he call us hence away,
  And take his wanderers home.

5 There shall each raptured tongue
  His endless praise proclaim;
And sweeter voices tune the song
  Of Moses and the Lamb.

WRIGHT. S. M.   J. P. HOLBROOK.

1. Sweet is the work, O Lord, Thy glo - rious name to sing;

To praise and pray— to hear thy word, And grate - ful of - ferings bring.

32.

2 Sweet, at the dawning light,
  Thy boundless love to tell;
And when approach the shades of night,
  Still on the theme to dwell.

3 Sweet, on this day of rest,
  To join, in heart and voice,
With those who love and serve thee best,
  And in thy name rejoice.

4 To songs of praise and joy
  Be every Sabbath given,
That such may be our blest employ
  Eternally in heaven.

33.

1 Behold, the morning sun
  Begins his glorious way;
His beams through all the nations run,
  And light and life convey.

2 But where the Gospel comes,
  It spreads diviner light;
It calls dead sinners from their tombs,
  And gives the blind their sight.

3 How perfect is thy word!
  And all thy judgments just!
Forever sure thy promise, Lord,
  And we securely trust.

4 My gracious God, how plain
  Are thy directions given!
Oh, may I never read in vain,
  But find the path to heaven.

34.

1 O thou above all praise,
  Above all blessing high,
Who would not fear thy holy name,
  And laud, and magnify!

2 Oh, for the living flame
  From thine own altar brought,
To touch our lips, our souls inspire,
  And wing to heaven our thought!

3 God is our strength and song,
  And his salvation ours;
Then be his love in Christ proclaimed
  With all our ransomed powers.

35.

1 How charming is the place
  Where my Redeemer, God,
Unvails the beauty of his face,
  And sheds his love abroad!

2 Not the fair palaces,
  To which the great resort,
Are once to be compared with this,
  Where Jesus holds his court.

3 Here, on the mercy-seat,
  With radiant glory crowned,
Our joyful eyes behold him sit
  And smile on all around.

4 Give me, O Lord, a place
  Within thy blest abode,
Among the children of thy grace,
  The servants of my God.

LISCHER. H. M.   *Arranged by* Dr. L. Mason.

{ To God the Father's throne Your highest honors raise; }
{ Glo-ry to God the Son; To God the Spirit praise; } With all our powers, E-ter-nal King,

Thy name we sing, While faith adores—Thy name   we   sing,   While faith a - dores.

Thy name we sing, While faith a - dores.

36.

1 WELCOME, delightful morn,
   Thou day of sacred rest!
 I hail thy kind return ;—
   Lord, make these moments blest :
From the low train | I soar to reach
Of mortal toys, | Immortal joys.

 2 Now may the King descend
   And fill his throne of grace ;
 Thy sceptre, Lord, extend,
   While saints address thy face :
Let sinners feel | And learn to know
Thy quickening word, | And fear the Lord.

 3 Descend, celestial Dove,
   With all thy quickening powers ;
 Disclose a Saviour's love,
   And bless the sacred hours :
Then shall my soul | Nor Sabbaths be
New life obtain, | Enjoyed in vain.

37.

1 AWAKE, ye saints, awake !
   And hail this sacred day ;
 In loftiest songs of praise
   Your joyful homage pay :
Come bless the day that God hath blest,
The type of heaven's eternal rest.

 2 On this auspicious morn
   The Lord of life arose ;
 He burst the bars of death,
   And vanquished all our foes ;
And now he pleads our cause above,
And reaps the fruit of all his love.

 3 All hail, triumphant Lord !
   Heaven with hosannas rings,
 And earth in humbler strains
   Thy praise responsive sings :
Worthy the Lamb that once was slain,
Through endless years to live and reign !

38.

1 UPWARD I lift mine eyes,
   From God is all my aid ;
 The God who built the skies,
   And earth and nature made :
God is the tower | His grace is nigh
To which I fly; | In every hour.

 2 My feet shall never slide,
   Nor fall in fatal snares,
 Since God, my guard and guide,
   Defends me from my fears :
Those wakeful eyes | Shall Israel keep
That never sleep, | When dangers rise.

 3 No burning heats by day,
   Nor blasts of evening air,
 Shall take my health away,
   If God be with me there :
Thou art my sun, | To guard my head
And thou my shade, | By night or noon.

 4 Hast thou not given thy word
   To save my soul from death ?
 And I can trust my Lord
   To keep my mortal breath :
I'll go and come, | Till from on high
Nor fear to die, | Thou call me home.

WARE. L. M.   KINGSLEY.

1. God of my life! thro' all my days, I'll tune the grate-ful notes of praise;
The song shall wake with opening light, And war-ble to the si - lent night.

39.

2 When anxious cares would break my rest,
And griefs would tear my throbbing breast,
The notes of praise ascending high,
Shall check the murmur and the sigh.

3 When death o'er nature shall prevail,
And all the powers of language fail,
Joy thro' my swimming eyes shall break,
And mean the thanks I cannot speak.

4 But oh! when that last conflict 's o'er,
And I am chained to earth no more,—
With what glad accents shall I rise
To join the music of the skies!

5 Then shall I learn th' exalted strains,
That echo through the heavenly plains,
And emulate, with joy unknown,
The glowing seraphs round thy throne.

40.

1 High in the heavens, eternal God!
Thy goodness in full glory shines;
Thy truth shall break through every cloud
That vails and darkens thy designs.

2 Forever firm thy justice stands,
As mountains their foundations keep:
Wise are the wonders of thy hands;
Thy judgments are a mighty deep.

3 My God, how excellent thy grace!
Whence all our hope and comfort springs;
The sons of Adam, in distress,
Fly to the shadow of thy wings.

4 From the provisions of thy house
We shall be fed with sweet repast;
There, mercy like a river flows,
And brings salvation to our taste.

5 Life, like a fountain rich and free,
Springs from the presence of my Lord;
And in thy light our souls shall see
The glories promised in thy word.

41.

1 Lord God of Hosts, by all adored!
Thy name we praise with one accord;
The earth and heavens are full of thee,
Thy light, thy love, thy majesty.

2 Loud hallelujahs to thy name
Angels and seraphim proclaim;
Eternal praise to thee is given
By all the powers and thrones in heaven.

3 Th' apostles join the glorious throng,
The prophets aid to swell the song,
The noble and triumphant host
Of martyrs make of thee their boast.

4 The holy church in every place
Throughout the world exalts thy praise;
Both heaven and earth do worship thee,
Thou Father of eternity!

5 From day to day, O Lord, do we
Highly exalt and honor thee;
Thy name we worship and adore,
World without end, forevermore.

OLD HUNDRED. L. M.

1. Be - fore Je - ho - vah's aw - ful throne, Ye na - tions, bow with sa - cred joy;

Know that the Lord is God a - lone, He can cre - ate, and he de - stroy.

42.

2 His sovereign power, without our aid,
Made us of clay, and formed us men;
And when, like wandering sheep, we strayed,
He brought us to his fold again.

3 We are his people, we his care,
Our souls, and all our mortal frame:
What lasting honors shall we rear,
Almighty Maker, to thy name!

4 We'll crowd thy gates with thankful songs;
High as the heavens our voices raise;
And earth, with her ten thousand tongues,
Shall fill thy courts with sounding praise.

5 Wide as the world is thy command,
Vast as eternity thy love;
Firm as a rock thy truth must stand,
When rolling years shall cease to move.

43.

1 JEHOVAH reigns; his throne is high;
His robes are light and majesty;
His glory shines with beams so bright,
No mortal can sustain the sight.

2 His terrors keep the world in awe;
His justice guards his holy law;
Yet love reveals a smiling face;
And truth and promise seal the grace.

3 Through all his works his wisdom shines,
And baffles Satan's deep designs;
His power is sovereign to fulfill
The noblest counsels of his will.

4 And will this glorious Lord descend
To be my Father and my Friend?
Then let my songs with angels join;
Heaven is secure, if God be mine.

44.

1 FROM all that dwell below the skies,
Let the Creator's praise arise:
Let the Redeemer's name be sung,
Through every land, by every tongue.

2 Eternal are thy mercies, Lord!
Eternal truth attends thy word:
Thy praise shall sound from shore to shore,
Till suns shall rise and set no more.

45.

1 ALL people that on earth do dwell,
Sing to the Lord with cheerful voice;
Him serve with fear, his praise forth tell,
Come ye before him and rejoice.

2 The Lord, ye know, is God indeed,
Without our aid he did us make;
We are his flock, he doth us feed,
And for his sheep he doth us take.

3 Oh, enter, then, his gates with praise;
Approach with joy his courts unto:
Praise, laud, and bless his name always,
For it is seemly so to do.

4 For why? the Lord our God is good,
His mercy is for ever sure;
His truth at all times firmly stood,
And shall from age to age endure.

LONG. L. M.   J. P. HOLBROOK.

1. Loud hal-le - lu-jahs to the Lord, From distant worlds where creatures dwell! Let heaven begin the sol - emn word, And sound it dreadful down to hell, And sound it dread-ful down to hell.

46.

1 Loud hallelujahs to the Lord,
From distant worlds where creatures dwell!
Let heaven begin the solemn word,
And sound it dreadful down to hell.

2 Wide as his vast dominion lies,
Make the Creator's name be known;
Loud as his thunder shout his praise,
And sound it lofty as his throne.

3 Jehovah—'t is a glorious word!
Oh, may it dwell on every tongue :
But saints who best have known the Lord,
Are bound to raise the noblest song.

4 Speak of the wonders of that love
Which Gabriel plays on every chord :
From all below, and all above,
Loud hallelujahs to the Lord !

47.

1 What equal honors shall we bring
To thee, O Lord our God, the Lamb,
When all the notes that angels sing
Are far inferior to thy name ?

2 Worthy is he who once was slain,
The Prince of Peace, who groaned and
died ;
Worthy to rise, and live, and reign
At his almighty Father's side.

3 Blessings forever on the Lamb,
Who bore the curse for wretched men :
Let angels sound his sacred name,
And every creature say, Amen !

48.

1 With glory clad, with strength arrayed,
The Lord, that o'er all nature reigns,
The world's foundation strongly laid,
And the vast fabric still sustains.

2 How sure established is thy throne !
Which shall no change or period see ;
For thou, O Lord, and thou alone,
Art God from all eternity.

3 The floods, O Lord, lift up their voice,
And toss the troubled waves on high ;
But God above can still their noise,
And make the angry sea comply.

49.

1 Give to the Lord, ye sons of fame,
Give to the Lord renown and power ;
Ascribe due honors to his name,
And his eternal might adore.

2 The Lord proclaims his power aloud,
O'er all the ocean and the land ;
His voice divides the watery cloud,
And lightnings blaze at his command.

3 The Lord sits Sovereign on the flood ;
The Thunderer reigns forever King ;
But makes his church his blest abode,
Where we his awful glories sing.

4 In gentler language, there the Lord
The counsels of his grace imparts :
Amid the raging storm, his word
Speaks peace and courage to our hearts.

EVENING HYMN. L. M.   TH. TALLIS.

1. Glo-ry to thee, my God, this night, For all the bless-ings of the light:

Keep me, oh, keep me, King of kings! Be-neath the shad-ow of thy wings.

50.

1 GLORY to thee, my God, this night,
For all the blessings of the light:
Keep me, oh, keep me, King of kings!
Beneath the shadow of thy wings.

2 Forgive me, Lord! through thy dear Son,
The ill which I this day have done;
That with the world, myself, and thee,
I, ere I sleep, at peace may be.

3 Teach me to live, that I may dread
The grave as little as my bed;
Teach me to die, that so I may
Rise glorious at thy judgment day.

4 Be thou my guardian while I sleep,
Thy watchful station near me keep;
My heart with love celestial fill,
And guard me from th' approach of ill.

5 Lord, let my soul forever share
The bliss of thy paternal care!
'T is heaven on earth, 't is heaven above,
To see thy face, and sing thy love.

6 Praise God, from whom all blessings flow;
Praise him, all creatures here below;
Praise him above, ye heavenly host;
Praise Father, Son, and Holy Ghost!

51.

1 THE Lord is King! lift up thy voice,
O earth, and all ye heavens, rejoice!
From world to world the joy shall ring:
The Lord omnipotent is King!

2 The Lord is King! who then shall dare
Resist his will, distrust his care?
Holy and true are all his ways:
Let every creature speak his praise.

3 The Lord is King! exalt your strains,
Ye saints, your God, your Father reigns;
One Lord, one empire, all secures:
He reigns,—and life and death are yours.

4 Oh, when his wisdom can mistake,
His might decay, his love forsake,
Then may his children cease to sing,—
The Lord omnipotent is King!

52.

1 Now to the Lord a noble song!
Awake, my soul! awake, my tongue!
Hosanna to th' eternal name,
And all his boundless love proclaim.

2 See where it shines in Jesus' face,—
The brightest image of his grace!
God, in the person of his Son,
Hath all his mightiest works outdone.

3 Grace!—'tis a sweet, a charming theme:
My thoughts rejoice at Jesus' name:
Ye angels! dwell upon the sound;
Ye heavens! reflect it to the ground.

4 Oh! may I reach that happy place,
Where he unvails his lovely face,
Where all his beauties you behold,
And sing his name to harps of gold.

OCTAVIUS. L. M.

Root & Sweetser's Coll.

1. Praise ye the Lord—let praise em - ploy, In his own courts, your songs of joy;

The spa - cious fir - ma - ment a - round Shall e - cho back the joy - ful sound.

53.

2 Recount his works in strains divine,
His wondrous works—how bright they
shine!
Praise him for his almighty deeds,
Whose greatness all your praise exceeds.

3 Awake the trumpet's piercing sound,
To spread your sacred pleasures round;
In praise awake each tuneful string,
And to the solemn organ sing.

4 Let all, whom life and breath inspire,
Attend, and join the blissful choir;
But chiefly ye, who know his word,
Adore, and love, and praise the Lord!

54.

1 Awake, my tongue, thy tribute bring
To Him who gave thee power to sing:
Praise him, who is all praise above,
The source of wisdom and of love.

2 How vast his knowledge! how profound!
A depth where all our thoughts are
drowned!
The stars he numbers, and their names
He gives to all those heavenly flames.

3 Through each bright world above, behold
Ten thousand thousand charms unfold;
Earth, air, and mighty seas combine,
To speak his wisdom all divine.

4 But in redemption, oh, what grace!
Its wonders, oh, what thought can trace!
Here wisdom shines forever bright:
Praise him, my soul, with sweet delight.

55.

1 Bless, O my soul, the living God;
Call home thy thoughts that rove abroad:
Let all the powers within me join
In work and worship so divine.

2 Bless, O my soul, the God of grace;
His favors claim thy highest praise:
Why should the wonders he hath wrought
Be lost in silence and forgot?

3 'T is he, my soul, that sent his Son
To die for crimes which thou hast done;
He owns the ransom, and forgives
The hourly follies of our lives.

4 Let every land his power confess;
Let all the earth adore his grace:
My heart and tongue with rapture join,
In work and worship so divine.

56.

1 The floods, O Lord, lift up their voice,
The mighty floods lift up their roar;
The floods in tumult loud rejoice,
And climb in foam the sounding shore.

2 But mightier than the mighty sea,
The Lord of glory reigns on high:
Far o'er its waves we look to thee,
And see their fury break and die.

3 Thy word is true, thy promise sure,
That ancient promise, sealed in love;
Here be thy temple ever pure,
As thy pure mansions shine above.

DOWNS. C. M.   Dr. L. Mason.

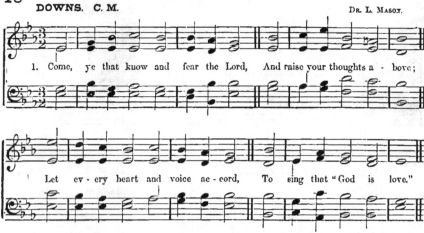

1. Come, ye that know and fear the Lord, And raise your thoughts a - bove;

Let ev - ery heart and voice ac - cord, To sing that "God is love."

57.

2 This precious truth his word declares,
  And all his mercies prove;
  Jesus, the gift of gifts, appears,
  To show that "God is love."

3 Behold his patience, bearing long
  With those who from him rove;
  Till mighty grace their hearts subdues,
  To teach them—"God is love."

4 Oh, may we all, while here below,
  This best of blessings prove;
  Till warmer hearts, in brighter worlds,
  Proclaim that "God is love."

58.

1 What shall I render to my God,
  For all his kindness shown?
  My feet shall visit thine abode,
  My songs address thy throne.

2 Among the saints that fill thy house,
  My offering shall be paid;
  There shall my zeal perform the vows
  My soul in anguish made.

3 How much is mercy thy delight,
  Thou ever-blessed God!
  How dear thy servants in thy sight—
  How precious is their blood!

4 How happy all thy servants are!
  How great thy grace to me!
  My life, which thou hast made thy care,
  Lord! I devote to thee.

5 Now I am thine—for ever thine;
  Nor shall my purpose move;
  Thy hand hath loosed my bonds of pain,
  And bound me with thy love.

6 Here, in thy courts, I leave my vow,
  And thy rich grace record;
  Witness, ye saints! who hear me now,
  If I forsake the Lord.

59.

1 Glory to God the Father be,
  Glory to God the Son,
  Glory to God the Holy Ghost—
  Glory to God alone!

2 My soul doth magnify the Lord,
  My spirit doth rejoice
  In God, my Saviour and my God;
  I hear his joyful voice.

3 I need not go abroad for joy,
  Who have a feast at home;
  My sighs are turnéd into songs,
  The Comforter is come!

4 Down from on high the blessed Dove
  Is come into my breast,
  To witness God's eternal love;
  This is my heavenly feast.

5 Glory to God the Father be,
  Glory to God the Son,
  Glory to God the Holy Ghost—
  Glory to God alone!

MANOAH. C. M.

GREATOREX COLL.

1. Be - gin, my tongue, some heaven-ly theme, And speak some bound-less thing:

The might - y works, or might - ier name, Of our e - ter - nal King.

60.

1 BEGIN, my tongue, some heavenly theme,
   And speak some boundless thing :
   The mighty works, or mightier name,
   Of our eternal King.

2 Tell of his wondrous faithfulness,
   And sound his power abroad ;
   Sing the sweet promise of his grace,
   And the performing God.

3 His very word of grace is strong,
   As that which built the skies ;
   The voice that rolls the stars along
   Speaks all the promises.

4 Oh, might I hear thy heavenly tongue
   But whisper, "Thou art mine !"
   Those gentle words should raise my song
   To notes almost divine.

61.

1 AWAKE, my heart, arise my tongue,
   Prepare a tuneful voice ;
   In God, the life of all my joys,
   Aloud will I rejoice.

2 'T is he adorned my naked soul,
   And made salvation mine ;
   Upon a poor polluted worm
   He makes his graces shine.

3 And, lest the shadow of a spot
   Should on my soul be found,
   He took the robe the Saviour wrought,
   And cast it all around.

4 How far this heavenly robe exceeds
   What earthly princes wear !
   These ornaments, how bright they shine !
   How white the garments are !

5 The Spirit wrought my faith, and love,
   And hope, and every grace ;
   But Jesus spent his life to work
   The robe of righteousness.

6 Strangely, my soul, art thou arrayed,
   By the great sacred Three !
   In sweetest harmony of praise,
   Let all thy powers agree.

62.

1 COME, shout aloud the Father's grace,
   And sing the Saviour's love ;
   Soon shall we join the glorious theme,
   In loftier strains above.

2 God, the eternal, mighty God,
   To dearer names descends ;
   Calls us his treasure and his joy,
   His children and his friends.

3 My Father, God ! and may these lips
   Pronounce a name so dear ?
   Not thus could heaven's sweet harmony
   Delight my listening ear.

4 Thanks to my God for every gift
   His bounteous hands bestow ;
   And thanks eternal for that love
   Whence all those comforts flow.

SILVER STREET. S. M.   I. Smith.

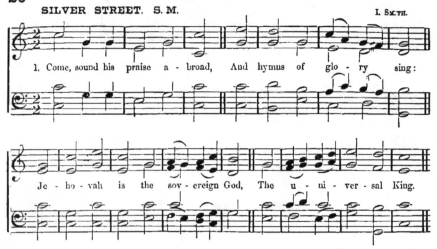

1. Come, sound his praise a - broad, And hymns of glo - ry sing:
Je - ho - vah is the sov - ereign God, The u - ni - ver - sal King.

63.

2 He formed the deeps unknown;
  He gave the seas their bound;
The watery worlds are all his own,
  And all the solid ground.

3 Come, worship at his throne,
  Come, bow before the Lord:
We are his work, and not our own,
  He formed us by his word.

4 To-day attend his voice,
  Nor dare provoke his rod;
Come, like the people of his choice,
  And own your gracious God.

64.

1 Raise your triumphant songs
  To an immortal tune;
Let the wide earth resound the deeds
  Celestial grace has done.

2 Sing—how eternal love
  Its chief beloved chose,
And bade him raise our ruined race
  From their abyss of woes.

3 His hand no thunder bears,
  No terror clothes his brow,
No bolts to drive our guilty souls
  To fiercer flames below.

4 'T was mercy filled the throne,
  And wrath stood silent by,
When Christ was sent, with pardons, down
  To rebels doomed to die.

5 Now, sinners! dry your tears;
  Let hopeless sorrow cease;
Bow to the sceptre of his love,
  And take the offered peace.

6 Lord! we obey thy call;
  We lay an humble claim
To the salvation thou hast brought,
  And love and praise thy name.

65.

1 To God the only wise,
  Our Saviour and our King,
Let all the saints below the skies
  Their humble praises bring.

2 'T is his almighty love,
  His counsel and his care,
Preserves us safe from sin and death,
  And every hurtful snare.

3 He will present our souls,
  Unblemished and complete,
Before the glory of his face,
  With joys divinely great.

4 Then all the chosen seed
  Shall meet around the throne,
Shall bless the conduct of his grace,
  And make his wonders known.

5 To our Redeemer God
  Wisdom and power belongs,
Immortal crowns of majesty,
  And everlasting songs.

STATE STREET. S. M.

WOODMAN.

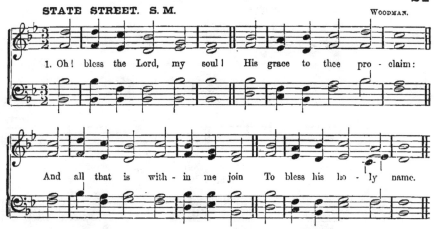

1. Oh! bless the Lord, my soul! His grace to thee proclaim:

And all that is with-in me join To bless his ho-ly name.

66.

2 Oh! bless the Lord, my soul!
  His mercies bear in mind:
  Forget not all his benefits:
  The Lord to thee is kind.

3 He will not always chide;
  He will with patience wait;
  His wrath is ever slow to rise,
  And ready to abate.

4 He pardons all thy sins,
  Prolongs thy feeble breath;
  He healeth thy infirmities,
  And ransoms thee from death.

5 Then bless his holy name,
  Whose grace hath made thee whole;
  Whose loving-kindness crowns thy days;
  Oh! bless the Lord, my soul!

67.

1 Now let our voices join
  To raise a sacred song;
  Ye pilgrims! in Jehovah's ways,
  With music pass along.

2 See—flowers of paradise,
  In rich profusion, spring;
  The sun of glory gilds the path,
  And dear companions sing.

3 See—Salem's golden spires,
  In beauteous prospect, rise;
  And brighter crowns than mortals wear,
  Which sparkle through the skies.

4 All honor to his name,
  Who marks the shining way,—
  To him who leads the pilgrims on
  To realms of endless day.

68.

1 Thy name, almighty Lord!
  Shall sound through distant lands;
  Great is thy grace, and sure thy word,
  Thy truth forever stands.

2 Far be thine honor spread,
  And long thy praise endure,
  Till morning light and evening shade
  Shall be exchanged no more.

69.

1 Lord, in this sacred hour
  Within thy courts we bend,
  And bless thy love, and own thy power,
  Our Father and our Friend.

2 But thou art not alone
  In courts by mortals trod;
  Nor only is the day thine own
  When man draws near to God.

3 Thy temple is the arch
  Of yon unmeasured sky;
  Thy Sabbath, the stupendous march
  Of grand eternity.

4 Lord, may that holier day
  Dawn on thy servants' sight;
  And purer worship may we pay
  In heaven's unclouded light.

BENEVENTO. 7s. Double.

S. WEBBE.

1. While, with cease-less course, the sun Hast-ed through the for-mer year,

Ma-ny souls their race have run, Nev-er more to meet us here:

D. s. We a lit-tle long-er wait, But how lit-tle—none can know.

Fixed in an e-ter-nal state, They have done with all be-low;

70.

New Year's Morning.

2 As the wingèd arrow flies
   Speedily the mark to find ;
As the lightning from the skies
   Darts, and leaves no trace behind,—
Swiftly thus our fleeting days
   Bear us down life's rapid stream ;
Upward, Lord, our spirits raise,
   All below is but a dream.

3 Spared to see another year,
   Let thy blessing meet us here ;
Come, thy dying work revive,
   Bid thy drooping garden thrive :
Sun of Righteousness, arise !
   Warm our hearts and bless our eyes ;
Let our prayer thy pity move,
   Make this year a time of love.

4 Thanks for mercies past receive,
   Pardon of our sins renew ;
Teach us henceforth how to live,
   With eternity in view :
Bless thy word to old and young,
   Fill us with a Saviour's love ;
When our life's short race is run,
   May we dwell with thee above.

71.

1 Let us with a joyful mind
Praise the Lord, for he is kind,
For his mercies shall endure,
Ever faithful, ever sure.
Let us sound his name abroad,
For of gods he is the God
Who by wisdom did create
Heaven's expanse and all its state ;

2 Did the solid earth ordain
How to rise above the main ;
Who, by his commanding might,
Filled the new-made world with light :
Caused the golden-tressèd sun
All the day his course to run ;
And the moon to shine by night,
'Mid her spangled sisters bright.

3 All his creatures God doth feed,
His full hand supplies their need ;
Let us therefore warble forth
His high majesty and worth.
He his mansion hath on high,
'Bove the reach of mortal eye ;
And his mercies shall endure,
Ever faithful, ever sure.

ONIDO. 7s. Double.

Arr. from PLEYEL. DR. L. MASON.

1. Lord of earth! thy forming hand Well this beauteous frame hath planned, Woods that wave, and

hills that tower, O-cean roll-ing in his power: Yet a- mid this scene so fair, Should I

cease thy smile to share, What were all its joys to me? Whom have I on earth but thee?

72.

2 Lord of heaven! beyond our sight
Shines a world of purer light;
There in love's unclouded reign
Parted hands shall meet again:
Oh, that world is passing fair!
Yet, if thou wert absent there,
What were all its joys to me?
Whom have I in heaven but thee?

3 Lord of earth and heaven! my breast
Seeks in thee its only rest:
I was lost; thy accents mild
Homeward lured thy wandering child.
Oh! should once thy smile divine
Cease upon my soul to shine,
What were earth or heaven to me?
Whom have I in each but thee?

73.

1 Holy, holy, holy Lord
God of Hosts! when heaven and earth,
Out of darkness, at thy word
Issued into glorious birth,

All thy works before thee stood,
And thine eye beheld them good,
While they sung with sweet accord.
Holy, holy, holy Lord!

2 Holy, holy, holy! thee,
One Jehovah evermore,
Father, Son, and Spirit! we,
Dust and ashes, would adore:
Lightly by the world esteemed,
From that world by thee redeemed,
Sing we here with glad accord.
Holy, holy, holy Lord!

3 Holy, holy, holy! all
Heaven's triumphant choir shall sing,
While the ransomed nations fall
At the footstool of their King:
Then shall saints and seraphim,
Harps and voices, swell one hymn,
Blending in sublime accord,
Holy, holy, holy Lord!

LYONS. 10s & 11s.   HAYDN.

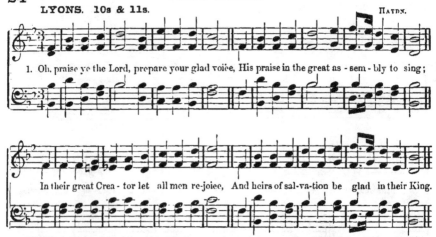

1. Oh, praise ye the Lord, prepare your glad voice, His praise in the great as-sem-bly to sing;

In their great Crea-tor let all men re-joice, And heirs of sal-va-tion be glad in their King.

74.

2 Let them his great name devoutly adore ;
In loud-swelling strains his praises express,
Who graciously opens his bountiful store,
Their wants to relieve, and his children to
bless.

3 With glory adorned, his people shall sing
To God, who defence and plenty supplies ;
Their loud acclamations to him, their
great King,
Through earth shall be sounded, and
reach to the skies.

75.

1 Oh, worship the King all-glorious above,
And gratefully sing his wonderful love ;
Our Shield and Defender, the Ancient
of days,
Pavilioned in splendor, and girded with
praise.

2 Oh, tell of his might, and sing of his
grace,
Whose robe is the light, whose canopy
space ;
His chariots of wrath the deep thunder-
clouds form,
And dark is his path on the wings of the
storm.

3 Thy bountiful care what tongue can recite ?
It breathes in the air, it shines in the
light,

It streams from the hills, it descends to
the plain,
And sweetly distills in the dew and the
rain.

4 Frail children of dust, and feeble as frail,
In thee do we trust, nor find thee to
fail ;
Thy mercies how tender ! how firm to the
end !
Our Maker, Defender, Redeemer, and
Friend.

76.

1 Ye servants of God ! your Master pro-
claim,
And publish abroad his wonderful name ;
The name all-victorious of Jesus extol ;
His kingdom is glorious, he rules over
all.

2 Salvation to God, who sits on the throne,
Let all cry aloud, and honor the Son :
The praises of Jesus the angels proclaim,
Fall down on their faces, and worship the
Lamb !

3 Then let us adore, and give him his right,
All glory and power, and wisdom and
might ;
All honor and blessing, with angels
above,
And thanks never ceasing, for infinite
love.

WILMOT. 8s & 7s. WEBER.

1. Praise the Lord! ye heavens, a - dore him; Praise him, an - gels in the height;

Sun and moon, re - joice be - fore him; Praise him, all ye stars of light!

77.

2 Praise the Lord—for he hath spoken;
   Worlds his mighty voice obeyed;
Laws which never shall be broken,
   For their guidance he hath made.

3 Praise the Lord—for he is glorious;
   Never shall his promise fail;
God hath made his saints victorious,
   Sin and death shall not prevail.

4 Praise the God of our salvation,
   Hosts on high his power proclaim;
Heaven and earth, and all creation,
   Laud and magnify his name!

78.

1 Blest be thou, O God of Israel,
   Thou, our Father, and our Lord!
Blest thy majesty forever!
   Ever be thy name adored.

2 Thine, O Lord, are power and greatness,
   Glory, victory, are thine own;
All is thine in earth and heaven,
   Over all thy boundless throne.

3 Riches come of thee, and honor,
   Power and might to thee belong;
Thine it is to make us prosper,
   Only thine to make us strong.

4 Lord, to thee, thou God of mercy,
   Hymns of gratitude we raise;
To thy name, forever glorious,
   Ever we address our praise!

79.

1 May the grace of Christ, our Saviour,
   And the Father's boundless love,
With the holy Spirit's favor,
   Rest upon us from above.

2 Thus may we abide in union
   With each other and the Lord,
And possess, in sweet communion,
   Joys which earth can not afford.

80.

1 I would love thee, God and Father!
   My Redeemer, and my King!
I would love thee; for, without thee,
   Life is but a bitter thing.

2 I would love thee; every blessing
   Flows to me from out thy throne:
I would love thee—he who loves thee
   Never feels himself alone.

3 I would love thee; look upon me,
   Ever guide me with thine eye:
I would love thee; if not nourished
   By thy love, my soul would die.

4 I would love thee; may thy brightness
   Dazzle my rejoicing eyes!
I would love thee; may thy goodness
   Watch from heaven o'er all I prize.

5 I would love thee, I have vowed it;
   On thy love my heart is set:
While I love thee, I can never
   My Redeemer's blood forget.

RIGHINI. 6s & 4s.   *Arranged by* Geo. Kingsley.

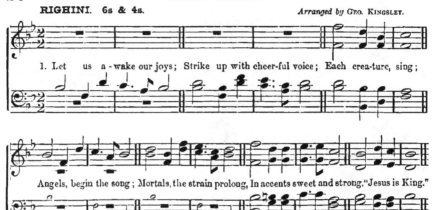

1. Let us a-wake our joys; Strike up with cheer-ful voice; Each crea-ture, sing;

Angels, begin the song; Mortals, the strain prolong, In accents sweet and strong, "Jesus is King."

81.

2 Proclaim abroad his name;
Tell of his matchless fame;
  What wonders done;
Above, beneath, around,
Let all the earth resound,
'Till heaven's high arch rebound,
  " Victory is won."

3 He vanquished sin and hell,
And our last foe will quell;
  Mourners, rejoice:
His dying love adore;
Praise him, now raised in power;
Praise him for evermore,
  With joyful voice.

4 All hail the glorious day,
When, through the heavenly way,
  Lo, he shall come,
While they who pierced him wail;
His promise shall not fail;
Saints, see your King prevail:
  Great Saviour, come!

82.

1 Sing, sing his lofty praise,
Whom angels can not raise,
  But whom they sing;
Jesus, who reigns above,
Object of angels' love,
Jesus, whose grace we prove,
  Jesus, our King.

2 Rich is the grace we sing,
Poor is the praise we bring,
  Not as we ought;

But when we see his face,
In yonder glorious place,
Then shall we sing his grace,
  Sing without fault.

83.

1 Come, thou almighty King,
Help us thy name to sing,
  Help us to praise:
Father! all-glorious,
O'er all victorious,
Come, and reign over us,
  Ancient of Days!

2 Come, thou incarnate Word!
Gird on thy mighty sword;
  Our prayer attend:
Come, and thy people bless,
And give thy word success;
Spirit of holiness!
  On us descend.

3 Come, holy Comforter!
Thy sacred witness bear,
  In this glad hour:
Thou, who almighty art,
Now rule in every heart,
And ne'er from us depart,
  Spirit of power!

4 To the great One in Three,
The highest praises be,
  Hence evermore!
His sovereign majesty
May we in glory see,
And to eternity
  Love and adore.

ITALIAN HYMN. 6s & 4s.

GIARDINI.

1. Praise ye Je - ho - vah's name; Praise thro' his courts pro-claim; Rise and a - dore;

High o'er the heav'ns above, Sound his great acts of love, While his rich grace we prove, Vast as his power.

84.

1 PRAISE ye Jehovah's name;
Praise through his courts proclaim;
  Rise and adore;
High o'er the heavens above,
Sound his great acts of love,
While his rich grace we prove,
  Vast as his power.

2 Now let the trumpet raise
Sounds of triumphant praise,
  Wide as his fame;
There let the harp be found;
Organs, with solemn sound,
Roll your deep notes around,
  Filled with his name.

3 While his high praise ye sing,
Shake every sounding string;
  Sweet the accord!
He vital breath bestows;
Let every breath that flows,
His noblest fame disclose;
  Praise ye the Lord.

85.

1 GLORY to God on high!
Let heaven and earth reply;
  Praise ye his name;
His love and grace adore,
Who all our sorrows bore;
And sing forevermore,
  " Worthy the Lamb."

2 Ye who surround the throne,
Cheerfully join in one,
  Praising his name;

Ye who have felt his blood
Sealing your peace with God,
Sound his dear name abroad:
  " Worthy the Lamb."

3 Soon must we change our place;
Yet will we never cease
  Praising his name;
To him our songs we'll bring,
Hail him our gracious King,
And through all ages sing,
  " Worthy the Lamb."

86.

1 THOU! whose almighty word
Chaos and darkness heard,
  And took their flight,—
Hear us, we humbly pray,
And, where the gospel's day
Sheds not its glorious ray,
  " Let there be light!"

2 Thou! who didst come to bring
On thy redeeming wing,
  Healing and sight,—
Health to the sick in mind,
Sight to the inly blind,—
Oh! now to all mankind,
  " Let there be light!"

3 Spirit of truth and love,
Life-giving holy Dove!
  Speed forth thy flight:
Move on the waters' face,
Bearing the lamp of grace,
And, in earth's darkest place,
  " Let there be light!"

HEBRON. L. M.   Dr. L. Mason.

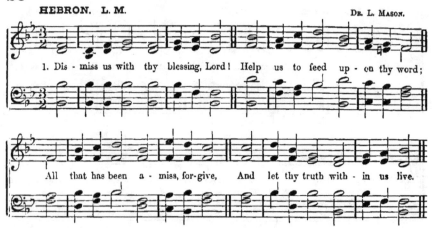

1. Dis - miss us with thy blessing, Lord! Help us to feed up - on thy word;

All that has been a - miss, for-give, And let thy truth with - in us live.

87.

1 Dismiss us with thy blessing, Lord!
  Help us to feed upon thy word;
  All that has been amiss, forgive,
  And let thy truth within us live.

2 Though we are guilty, thou art good;
  Wash all our works in Jesus' blood;
  Give every burdened soul release,
  And bid us all depart in peace.

88.

1 Ere to the world again we go,
  Its pleasures, cares, and idle show,
  Thy grace, once more, O God, we crave,
  From folly and from sin to save.

2 May the great truths we here have heard,
  The lessons of thy holy word—
  Dwell in our inmost bosoms deep,
  And all our souls from error keep.

3 Oh! may the influence of this day
  Long as our memory with us stay,
  And as a constant guardian prove,
  To guide us to our home above.

89.

1 Lord! may thy truth, upon the heart
  Now fall, and dwell as heavenly dew,
  And flowers of grace in freshness start
  Where once the weeds of error grew.

2 May prayer now lift her sacred wings,
  Contented with that aim alone
  Which bears her to the King of kings,
  And rests her at his sheltering throne.

90.

1 While now upon this Sabbath eve,
  Thy house, Almighty God, we leave,
  'T is sweet, as sinks the setting sun,
  To think on all our duties done.

2 Oh! evermore may all our bliss
  Be peaceful, pure, divine, like this;
  And may each Sabbath, as it flies,
  Fit us for joys beyond the skies.

91.

1 Lord, now we part in thy blest name,
  In which we here together came;
  Grant us our few remaining days
  To work thy will, and spread thy praise!

2 Teach us in life and death to bless
  Thee, Lord, our strength and righteousness:
  And grant us all to meet above;
  There shall we better sing thy love.

3 To God the Father, God the Son,
  And God the Spirit, three in one,
  Be honor, praise, and glory given,
  By all on earth, and all in heaven.

WEBER. 7s.   *Arranged from* WEBER.

1. Soft-ly fades the twi-light ray Of the ho-ly Sab-bath day;

Gen-tly as life's set-ting sun, When the Chris-tian's course is run.

92.

2 Night her solemn mantle spreads
  O'er the earth as daylight fades;
  All things tell of calm repose
  At the holy Sabbath's close.

3 Peace is on the world abroad;
  'Tis the holy peace of God—
  Symbol of the peace within,
  When the spirit rests from sin.

4 Still the Spirit lingers near,
  Where the evening worshiper
  Seeks communion with the skies,
  Pressing onward to the prize.

5 Saviour! may our Sabbaths be
  Days of peace and joy in thee,
  Till in heaven our souls repose,
  Where the Sabbath ne'er shall close.

93.

1 For a season called to part,
  Let us now ourselves commend,
  To the gracious eye and heart
  Of our ever-present Friend.

2 Jesus! hear our humble prayer;
  Tender Shepherd of thy sheep!
  Let thy mercy and thy care
  All our souls in safety keep.

3 Then, if thou thy help afford,
  Joyful songs to thee shall rise,
  And our souls shall praise the Lord,
  Who regards our humble cries.

94.

1 Now may he who from the dead
  Brought the Shepherd of the sheep,
  Jesus Christ, our king and head,
  All our souls in safety keep.

2 May he teach us to fulfill
  What is pleasing in his sight;
  Make us perfect in his will,
  And preserve us day and night!

3 To that great Redeemer's praise,
  Who the covenant sealed with blood,
  Let our hearts and voices raise
  Loud thanksgivings to our God.

95.

1 For the mercies of the day,
  For this rest upon our way,
  Thanks to thee alone be given,
  Lord of earth and King of heaven!

2 Cold our services have been,
  Mingled every prayer with sin:
  But thou canst and wilt forgive;
  By thy grace alone we live.

3 While this thorny path we tread,
  May thy love our footsteps lead;
  When our journey here is past,
  May we rest with thee at last.

4 Let these earthly Sabbaths prove
  Foretastes of our joys above;
  While their steps thy children bend
  To the rest which knows no end.

GREENVILLE. 8s, 7s & 4s.   Rousseau.

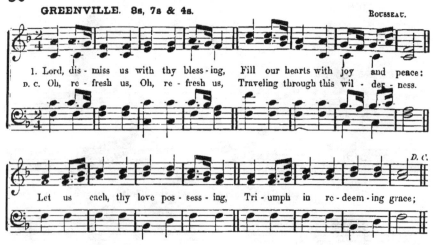

1. Lord, dis - miss us with thy bless - ing, Fill our hearts with joy and peace:
D. C. Oh, re - fresh us, Oh, re - fresh us, Traveling through this wil - der - ness.

Let us each, thy love pos - sess - ing, Tri - umph in re - deem - ing grace;

96.

1 LORD, dismiss us with thy blessing,
     Fill our hearts with joy and peace :
Let us each, thy love possessing,
     Triumph in redeeming grace ;
         Oh, refresh us,
     Traveling through this wilderness.

2 Thanks we give and adoration,
     For thy gospel's joyful sound;
May the fruits of thy salvation
     In our hearts and lives abound ;
         May thy presence,
     With us evermore be found.

3 So, whene'er the signal's given
     Us from earth to call away,
Borne on angels' wings to heaven,
     Glad the summons to obey,
         May we ever
     Reign with Christ in endless day.

97.

1 COME, thou soul-transforming Spirit,
     Bless the sower and the seed :
Let each heart thy grace inherit,
     Raise the weak, the hungry feed :
         From the gospel
     Now supply thy people's need.

2 Oh ! may all enjoy the blessing,
     Which thy word's designed to give ;
Let us all, thy love possessing,
     Joyfully the truth receive ;
         And forever
     To thy praise and glory live.

98.

1 GENTLY, Lord ! oh, gently lead us,
     Through this lonely vale of tears ;
Through the changes thou 'st decreed us,
     Till our last great change appears :
When temptation's darts assail us,
     When in devious paths we stray,
Let thy goodness never fail us,
     Lead us in thy perfect way.

2 In the hour of pain and anguish,
     In the hour when death draws near,
Suffer not our hearts to languish,—
     Suffer not our souls to fear ;
And, when mortal life is ended
     Bid us on thy bosom rest,
Till, by angel-bands attended,
     We awake among the blest.

99.

1 GOD of our salvation, hear us ;
     Bless, Oh ! bless us, ere we go ;
When we join the world, be near us,
     Lest we cold and careless grow :
         Saviour, keep us,
     Keep us safe from every foe.

2 As our steps are drawing nearer
     To our best and lasting home,
May our view of heaven grow clearer;
     Hope more bright of joys to come ;
         And when dying,
     May thy presence cheer the gloom.

LAST BEAM. P. M.   HYMN **100.**

1. Fad - ing, still fad - ing, the last beam is shining; Fa - ther in heav - en! the
2. Fa - ther in heav - en! oh! hear when we call, Hear, for Christ's sake, who is

day is de - clining, Safe - ty and in - no - cence fly with the light, Temp-ta - tion and
Sa - viour of all; Fee - ble and faint-ing we trust in thy might, In doubt - ing and

dan - ger walk forth with the night; From the fall of the shade till the morning bells
dark - ness thy love be our light; Let us sleep on thy breast while the night ta - per

chime, Shield me from dan - ger, save me from crime. Fa-ther, have mer-cy, Fa-ther, have
burns, Wake in thy arms when morn - ing re - turns. Fa-ther, &c.

mer - cy, Fa - ther, have mer - cy thro' Je-sus Christ our Lord.   A - men.

UXBRIDGE. L. M.

DR. L. MASON.

1. God, in the gos-pel of his Son, Makes his e-ter-nal coun-sels known,

Where love in all its glo-ry shines, And truth is drawn in fair-est lines.

101.

1 God, in the gospel of his Son,
Makes his eternal counsels known,
Where love in all its glory shines,
And truth is drawn in fairest lines.

2 Here, sinners of an humble frame
May taste his grace, and learn his name;
May read, in characters of blood,
The wisdom, power and grace of God.

3 Here, faith reveals, to mortal eyes,
A brighter world beyond the skies;
Here, shines the light which guides our
way
From earth to realms of endless day.

4 Oh! grant us grace, almighty Lord!
To read and mark thy holy word,
Its truths with meekness to receive,
And by its holy precepts live.

102.

1 The heavens declare thy glory, Lord!
In every star thy wisdom shines;
But when our eyes behold thy word,
We read thy name in fairer lines.

2 The rolling sun, the changing light,
And nights and days thy power confess,
But the blest volume thou hast writ,
Reveals thy justice and thy grace.

3 Sun, moon, and stars, convey thy praise
Round the whole earth, and never stand:
So, when thy truth began its race,
It touched and glanced on every land.

4 Nor shall thy spreading gospel rest,
Till through the world thy truth has run;
Till Christ has all the nations blessed
That see the light, or feel the sun.

5 Great Sun of righteousness, arise!
Bless the dark world with heavenly light:
Thy gospel makes the simple wise,
Thy laws are pure, thy judgments right.

6 Thy noblest wonders here we view,
In souls renewed, and sins forgiven;
Lord, cleanse my sins, my soul renew,
And make thy word my guide to heaven.

103.

1 The starry firmament on high,
And all the glories of the sky,
Yet shine not to thy praise, O Lord,
So brightly as thy written word.

2 The hopes that holy word supplies,
Its truths divine and precepts wise,
In each a heavenly beam I see,
And every beam conducts to thee.

3 Almighty Lord, the sun shall fail,
The moon forget her nightly tale,
And deepest silence hush on high
The radiant chorus of the sky;

4 But fixed for everlasting years,
Unmoved, amid the wreck of spheres,
Thy word shall shine in cloudless day,
When heaven and earth have passed away.

WILLINGTON. L. M.

GREATOREX COLL.

1. I love the sa-cred Book of God! No oth-er can its place sup-ply;

It points me to his own a - bode, It gives me wings, and bids me fly.

104.

1 I LOVE the sacred Book of God!
No other can its place supply;
It points me to his own abode,
It gives me wings, and bids me fly.

2 Sweet Book! in thee my eyes discern
The very image of my Lord;
From thine instructive page I learn
The joys his presence will afford.

3 In thee I read my title clear
To mansions that will ne'er decay ;—
Dear Lord, oh, when wilt thou appear,
And bear thy prisoner away!

4 While I am here, these leaves supply
His place, and tell me of his love;
I read with faith's discerning eye,
And gain a glimpse of joys above.

5 I know in them the Spirit breathes
To animate his people here ;
Oh, may these truths prove life to all,
Till in his presence we appear!

105.

1 Now let my soul, eternal King,
To thee its grateful tribute bring ;
My knee with humble homage bow,
My tongue perform its solemn vow.

2 All nature sings thy boundless love,
In worlds below, and worlds above ;
But in thy blessed word I trace
Diviner wonders of thy grace.

3 Here what delightful truths I read !
Here I behold the Saviour bleed ;
His name salutes my listening ear,
Revives my heart and checks my fear.

4 Here Jesus bids my sorrows cease,
And gives my laboring conscience peace ;
Here lifts my grateful passions high,
And points to mansions in the sky.

5 For love like this, oh, let my song,
Through endless years, thy praise pro-
long ;
Let distant climes thy name adore,
Till time and nature are no more.

106.

1 UPON the Gospel's sacred page
The gathered beams of ages shine ;
And, as it hastens, every age
But makes its brightness more divine.

2 On mightier wing, in loftier flight,
From year to year does knowledge soar ;
And, as it soars, the Gospel light
Adds to its influence more and more.

3 More glorious still as centuries roll,
New regions blessed, new powers un-
furled,
Expanding with th' expanding soul,
Its waters shall o'erflow the world—

4 Flow to restore, but not destroy ;
As when the cloudless lamp of day
Pours out its floods of light and joy,
And sweeps the lingering mist away.

KNOX. C. M.

1. How precious is the book divine, By inspiration given!

Bright as a lamp its doctrines shine To guide our souls to heaven.

107.

1 How precious is the book divine,
  By inspiration given!
Bright as a lamp its doctrines shine
To guide our souls to heaven.

2 O'er all the strait and narrow way
  Its radiant beams are cast;
A light whose never-weary ray
Grows brightest at the last.

3 It sweetly cheers our drooping hearts,
  In this dark vale of tears;
Life, light, and joy, it still imparts,
And quells our rising fears.

4 This lamp, through all the tedious night
  Of life, shall guide our way,
Till we behold the clearer light
Of an eternal day.

108.

1 Thou lovely Source of true delight,
  Whom I unseen adore!
Unvail thy beauties to my sight,
That I may love thee more.

2 Thy glory o'er creation shines;
  But in thy sacred word,
I read in fairer, brighter lines,
My bleeding, dying Lord.

3 'T is here, whene'er my comforts droop,
  And sins and sorrows rise,
Thy love with cheerful beams of hope,
My fainting heart supplies.

4 Jesus, my Lord, my life, my light,
  Oh! come with blissful ray;
Break radiant through the shades of
    night,
And chase my fears away.

5 Then shall my soul with rapture trace
  The wonders of thy love;
But the full glories of thy face
Are only known above.

109.

1 How shall the young secure their hearts,
  And guard their lives from sin?
Thy word the choicest rules imparts
To keep the conscience clean.

2 When once it enters to the mind,
  It spreads such light abroad;
The meanest souls instruction find,
And raise their thoughts to God.

3 'T is like the sun, a heavenly light,
  That guides us all the day;
And, through the dangers of the night,
A lamp to lead our way.

4 Thy precepts make me truly wise;
  I hate the sinner's road;
I hate my own vain thoughts that rise,
But love thy law, my God!

5 Thy word is everlasting truth;
  How pure is every page!
That holy book shall guide our youth,
And well support our age.

YORK. C. M.

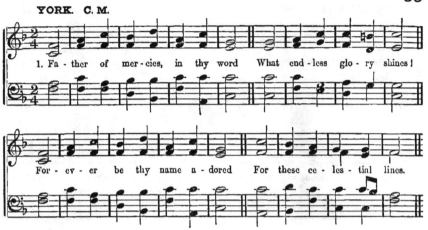

1. Fa - ther of mer - cies, in thy word What end - less glo - ry shines!

For - ev - er be thy name a - dored For these ce - les - tial lines.

110.

2 Here my Redeemer's welcome voice
  Spreads heavenly peace around;
And life and everlasting joys
  Attend the blissful sound.

3 Oh, may these heavenly pages be
  My ever dear delight;
And still new beauties may I see,
  And still increasing light!

4 Divine Instructor, gracious Lord!
  Be thou forever near;
Teach me to love thy sacred word,
  And view my Saviour there.

111.

1 A GLORY gilds the sacred page,
  Majestic, like the sun;
It gives a light to every age;—
  It gives, but borrows none.

2 The hand that gave it, still supplies
  The gracious light and heat;
Its truths upon the nations rise,—
  They rise, but never set.

3 Let everlasting thanks be thine,
  For such a bright display,
As makes a world of darkness shine
  With beams of heavenly day.

4 My soul rejoices to pursue
  The steps of him I love,
Till glory breaks upon my view,
  In brighter worlds above.

112.

1 ALMIGHTY God! thy word is cast,
  Like seed into the ground;
Let now the dew of heaven descend,
  And righteous fruits abound.

2 Let not the foe of Christ and man
  This holy seed remove;
But give it root in every heart,
  To bring forth fruits of love.

3 Let not the world's deceitful cares
  The rising plant destroy;
But let it yield, a hundredfold,
  The fruits of peace and joy.

4 Oft as the precious seed is sown,
  Thy quickening grace bestow,
That all, whose souls the truth receive,
  Its saving power may know.

113.

1 BLEST are the souls that hear and know
  The gospel's joyful sound;
Peace shall attend the path they go,
  And light their steps surround.

2 Their joy shall bear their spirits up
  Through their Redeemer's name;
His righteousness exalts their hope,
  Nor Satan dares condemn.

3 The Lord, our glory and defence,
  Strength and salvation gives;
Israel, thy King forever reigns,
  Thy God forever lives.

JUDGMENT. L. M.   J. N. PATTISON.

1. Fa-ther of heaven! whose love pro-found A ran-som for our souls hath found,—

Be-fore thy throne we sin-ners bend; To us thy pard'ning love ex-tend.

114.
Trinity.

2 Almighty Son—incarnate Word—
Our Prophet, Priest, Redeemer, Lord!
Before thy throne we sinners bend;
To us thy saving grace extend.

3 Eternal Spirit! by whose breath
The soul is raised from sin and death,—
Before thy throne we sinners bend;
To us thy quickening power extend.

4 Jehovah!—Father, Spirit, Son!—
Mysterious Godhead—Three in One!
Before thy throne we sinners bend;
Grace, pardon, life to us extend.

115.
Immensity.

1 WITH deepest reverence at thy throne,
Jehovah, peerless and unknown!
Our feeble spirits strive, in vain,
A glimpse of thee, great God! to gain.

2 Who, by the closest search, can find
Th' eternal, uncreated mind?
Nor men, nor angels can explore
Thy heights of love, thy depths of power.

3 We know thee not; but this we know,
Thou reign'st above, thou reign'st below:
And though thine essence is unknown,
To all the world thy power is shown.

4 That power we trace on every side;
Oh! may thy wisdom be our guide!
And while we live, and when we die,
May thine almighty love be nigh.

116.
Trinity.

1 O HOLY, holy, holy Lord!
Bright in thy deeds and in thy name,
Forever be thy name adored,
Thy glories let the world proclaim!

2 O Jesus! Lamb once crucified
To take our load of sins away,
Thine be the hymn that rolls its tide
Along the realms of upper day!

3 O Holy Spirit! from above,
In streams of light and glory given,
Thou source of ecstasy and love,
Thy praises ring through earth and
     heaven!

4 O God triune! to thee we owe
Our every thought, our every song;
And ever may thy praises flow
From saint and seraph's burning tongue!

117.
Being.

1 THERE is a God!—all nature speaks,
Through earth, and air, and seas, and skies;
See—from the clouds his glory breaks,
When the first beams of morning rise.

2 The rising sun, serenely bright,
O'er the wide world's extended frame,
Inscribes, in characters of light,
His mighty Maker's glorious name.

3 Ye curious minds, who roam abroad,
And trace creation's wonders o'er,
Confess the footsteps of your God;—
And bow before him—and adore.

SEASONS. L. M.

PLEYEL.

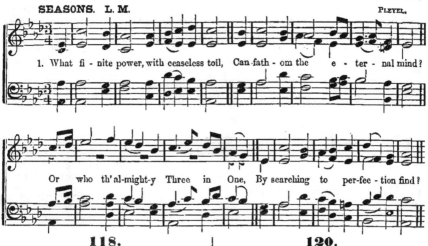

1. What fi - nite power, with ceaseless toil, Can fath - om the e - ter - nal mind?

Or who th' al-might-y Three in One, By searching to per-fec - tion find?

118.
Infinity.

2 Angels and men in vain may raise,
Harmonious, their adoring songs;
The laboring thought sinks down oppressed,
And praises die upon their tongues.

3 Yet would I lift my trembling voice,
A portion of his ways to sing;
And mingling with his meanest works,
My humble, grateful tribute bring.

119.
Omniscience.

1 LORD, thou hast searched and seen me
through :
Thine eye commands, with piercing view,
My rising and my resting hours,
My heart and flesh with all their powers.

2 My thoughts, before they are my own,
Are to my God distinctly known ;
He knows the words I mean to speak,
Ere from my opening lips they break.

3 Within thy circling power I stand ;
On every side I find thy hand :
Awake, asleep, at home, abroad,
I am surrounded still with God.

4 Amazing knowledge, vast and great!
What large extent! what lofty height!
My soul, with all the powers I boast,
Is in the boundless prospect lost.

5 Oh! may these thoughts possess my breast,
Where'er I rove, where'er I rest,
Nor let my weaker passions dare
Consent to sin, for God is there.

120.
Long-suffering.

1 GOD of my life, to thee belong,
The grateful heart, the joyful song ;
Touched by thy love, each tuneful chord
Resounds the goodness of the Lord.

2 Yet why, dear Lord, this tender care ?
Why does thy hand so kindly rear
A useless cumberer of the ground,
On which so little fruit is found ?

3 Still let the barren fig-tree stand,
Upheld and fostered by thy hand ;
And let its fruit and verdure be
A grateful tribute, Lord, to thee.

121.
Sovereignty.

1 MAY not the sovereign Lord on high
Dispense his favors as he will,
Choose some to life, while others die,
And yet be just and gracious still ?

2 What if he means to show his grace
And his electing love employs
To mark out some of mortal race,
And form them fit for heavenly joys ?

3 Shall man reply against the Lord,
And call his Maker's ways unjust,
The thunder of whose dreadful word
Can crush a thousand worlds to dust ?

4 But, O my soul! if truth so bright
Should dazzle and confound thy sight,
Yet still his written will obey,
And wait the great decisive day.

ROCKINGHAM. L. M.   Dr. L. Mason.

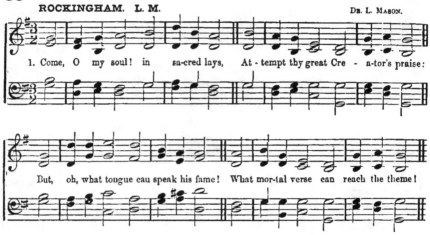

1. Come, O my soul! in sa-cred lays, At-tempt thy great Cre - a-tor's praise:

But, oh, what tongue can speak his fame! What mor-tal verse can reach the theme!

122.
Perfections.

2 Enthroned amid the radiant spheres,
He glory, like a garment, wears;
To form a robe of light divine,
Ten thousand suns around him shine.

3 In all our Maker's grand designs,
Almighty power, with wisdom, shines;
His works, thro' all this wondrous frame,
Declare the glory of his name.

4 Raised on devotion's lofty wing,
Do thou, my soul, his glories sing;
And let his praise employ thy tongue,
Till listening worlds shall join the song!

123.
Omnipresence.

1 Thou, Lord, who rear'st the mountain's height,
And mak'st the cliffs with sunshine bright,
Oh grant that we may own thy hand
No less in every grain of sand!

2 With forests huge, of dateless time,
Thy will has hung each peak sublime;
But withered leaves beneath the tree
Have tongues that tell as loud of thee.

3 Teach us that not a leaf can grow
Till life from thee within it flow;
That not a grain of dust can be,
O Fount of being! save by thee;

4 That every human word and deed,
Each flash of feeling, will, or creed,
Hath solemn meaning from above,
Begun and ended all in love.

124.
Mystery.

1 Wait, O my soul! thy Maker's will;
Tumultuous passions, all be still!
Nor let a murmuring thought arise;
His ways are just, his counsels wise.

2 He in the thickest darkness dwells,
Performs his work, the cause conceals;
But, though his methods are unknown,
Judgment and truth support his throne.

3 In heaven, and earth, and air, and seas,
He executes his firm decrees;
And by his saints it stands confessed,
That what he does is ever best.

4 Wait, then, my soul! submissive wait,
Prostrate before his awful seat;
And, 'mid the terrors of his rod,
Trust in a wise and gracious God.

125.
Majesty.

1 Kingdoms and thrones to God belong;
Crown him ye nations, in your song;
His wondrous names and powers rehearse;
His honors shall enrich your verse.

2 He shakes the heavens with loud alarms;
How terrible is God in arms!
In Israel are his mercies known,
Israel is his peculiar throne.

3 Proclaim him King, pronounce him blest;
He's your defence, your joy, your rest;
When terrors rise, and nations faint,
God is the strength of every saint.

LOUVAN. L. M.

V. C. TAYLOR.

1. Lord, how mys-te-rious are thy ways! How blind are we! how mean our praise!
Thy steps, can mor-tal eyes ex-plore? 'Tis ours to won-der and a-dore.

126.
Incomprehensible.

1 LORD, how mysterious are thy ways!
How blind are we! how mean our praise!
Thy steps, can mortal eyes explore?
'Tis ours to wonder and adore.

2 Great God! I would not ask to see
What in my coming life shall be;
Enough for me if love divine,
At length through every cloud shall shine.

3 Are darkness and distress my share?
Then let me trust thy guardian care;
If light and bliss attend my days,
Then let my future hours be praise.

4 Yet this my soul desires to know,
Be this my only wish below,
That Christ be mine;—this great request
Grant, bounteous God, and I am blest!

127.
Perfections.

1 THE Lord! how wondrous are his ways!
How firm his truth! how large his grace!
He takes his mercy for his throne,
And thence he makes his glories known.

2 Not half so high his power hath spread
The starry heavens above our head,
As his rich love exceeds our praise,
Exceeds the highest hopes we raise.

3 Not half so far has nature placed
The rising morning from the west,
As his forgiving grace removes
The daily guilt of those he loves.

4 How slowly doth his wrath arise!
On swifter wings salvation flies:
Or, if he lets his anger burn,
How soon his frowns to pity turn!

5 His everlasting love is sure
To all his saints, and shall endure;
From age to age his truth shall reign,
Nor children's children hope in vain.

128.
Omnipresence.

1 LORD of all being! throned afar,
Thy glory flames from sun and star;
Centre and soul of every sphere,
Yet to each loving heart how near!

2 Sun of our life, thy quickening ray
Sheds on our path the glow of day;
Star of our hope, thy softened light
Cheers the long watches of the night.

3 Our midnight is thy smile withdrawn;
Our noontide is thy gracious dawn;
Our rainbow arch thy mercy's sign;
All, save the clouds of sin, are thine!

4 Lord of all life, below, above,
Whose light is truth, whose warmth is love,
Before thy ever-blazing throne
We ask no lustre of our own.

5 Grant us thy truth to make us free,
And kindling hearts that burn for thee,
Till all thy living altars claim
One holy light, one heavenly flame!

BRATTLE STREET. C. M. Double.   PLEYEL.

While thee I seek, pro-tect-ing Power! Be my vain wish - es stilled;
And may this con - se - crat - ed hour   -   -   -   -   With

bet - ter hopes be filled. 2. Thy love the power of thought bestowed! To thee my thoughts would

soar; Thy mer - cy o'er my life has flowed; That mer - cy I a - dore.

129.
Providence.

3 In each event of life, how clear
    Thy ruling hand I see!
Each blessing to my soul more dear,
    Because conferred by thee.

4 In every joy that crowns my days,
    In every pain I bear,
My heart shall find delight in praise,
    Or seek relief in prayer.

5 When gladness wings my favored hour,
    Thy love my thoughts shall fill;
Resigned, when storms of sorrow lower,
    My soul shall meet thy will.

6 My lifted eye, without a tear,
    The gathering storm shall see;
My steadfast heart shall know no fear;
    That heart shall rest on thee.

130.
Providence.

1 When all thy mercies, O my God!
    My rising soul surveys,

Transported with the view, I'm lost
    In wonder, love, and praise.

2 Unnumbered comforts on my soul
    Thy tender care bestowed,
Before my infant heart conceived
    From whom those comforts flowed.

3 When in the slippery paths of youth
    With heedless steps I ran,
Thine arm, unseen, conveyed me safe,
    And led me up to man.

4 Ten thousand thousand precious gifts
    My daily thanks employ;
Nor is the least a cheerful heart,
    That tastes those gifts with joy.

5 Through every period of my life,
    Thy goodness I'll pursue;
And after death, in distant worlds,
    The glorious theme renew.

6 Through all eternity, to thee
    A joyful song I'll raise:
But oh! eternity's too short
    To utter all thy praise!

131.
Beneficence.

1 When morning's first and hallowed ray
Breaks, with its trembling light,
To chase the pearly dews away,
Bright tear-drops of the night—

2 My heart, O Lord! forgets to rove,
But rises gladly free,
On wings of everlasting love,
And finds its home in thee.

3 When evening's silent shades descend,
And nature sinks to rest,
Still, to my Father and my Friend,
My wishes are addressed.

4 Though tears may dim my hours of joy,
And bid my pleasures flee,
Thou reign'st where grief cannot annoy;
I will be glad in thee.

5 And ev'n when midnight's solemn gloom
Above, around is spread,
Sweet dreams of everlasting bloom
Are hovering o'er my head.

6 I dream of that fair land, O Lord!
Where all thy saints shall be;
I wake to lean upon thy word,
And still delight in thee.

132.
"Our Father."

1 Father of mercies! God of love!
My Father and my God!
I'll sing the honors of thy name,
And spread thy praise abroad.

2 In every period of my life
Thy thoughts of love appear;
Thy mercies gild each transient scene,
And crown each passing year.

3 In all thy mercies, may my soul
A Father's bounty see;
Nor let the gifts thy grace bestows
Estrange my heart from thee.

4 Teach me, in times of deep distress,
To own thy hand, O God!
And in submissive silence learn
The lessons of thy rod.

5 Through every period of my life,
Each bright, each clouded scene,
Give me a meek and humble mind,
Still equal and serene.

6 Then may I close my eyes in death,
Redeemed from anxious fear;
For death itself, my God, is life,
If thou art with me there.

133.
Providence.

1 God, in the high and holy place,
Looks down upon the spheres;
Yet in his providence and grace,
To every eye appears.

2 He bows the heavens; the mountains stand
A highway for our God;
He walks amid the desert land;
'T is Eden where he trod.

3 The forests in his strength rejoice;
Hark! on the evening breeze,
As once of old, Jehovah's voice
Is heard among the trees.

4 In every stream his bounty flows,
Diffusing joy and wealth;
In every breeze his Spirit blows,—
The breath of life and health.

5 His blessings fall in plenteous showers
Upon the lap of earth,
That teems with foliage, fruits, and flowers,
And rings with infant mirth.

6 If God hath made this world so fair,
Where sin and death abound;
How beautiful, beyond compare,
Will Paradise be found!

134.
Watchful Care.

1 How are thy servants blest, O Lord!
How sure is their defence!
Eternal wisdom is their guide,
Their help, omnipotence.

2 In foreign realms, and lands remote,
Supported by thy care,
Through burning climes they pass unhurt,
And breathe in tainted air.

3 When by the dreadful tempest borne
High on the broken wave,
They know thou art not slow to hear,
Nor impotent to save.

4 The storm is laid, the winds retire,
Obedient to thy will;
The sea, that roars at thy command,
At thy command is still.

5 In midst of dangers, fears, and deaths,
Thy goodness we'll adore;
We'll praise thee for thy mercies past,
And humbly hope for more.

6 Our life, while thou preserv'st that life,
Thy sacrifice shall be;
And death, when death shall be our lot,
Shall join our souls to thee.

ST. ANN'S. C. M. DR. CROFT.

1. The Lord our God is full of might, The winds o-bey his will:
He speaks, and in his heaven-ly height, The roll-ing sun stands still.

135.
Power.

2 Rebel, ye waves, and o'er the land
With threatening aspect roar:
The Lord uplifts his awful hand,
And chains you to the shore.

3 Howl, winds of night, your force combine;
Without his high behest
Ye shall not, in the mountain-pine,
Disturb the sparrow's nest.

4 His voice sublime is heard afar,
In distant peals it dies;
He yokes the whirlwind to his car,
And sweeps the howling skies.

5 Ye nations, bend—in reverence bend;
Ye monarchs, wait his nod,
And bid the choral song ascend
To celebrate our God.

136.
Majesty.

1 O God! we praise thee, and confess
That thou the only Lord
And everlasting Father art,
By all the earth adored.

2 To thee, all angels cry aloud;
To thee the powers on high,
Both cherubim and seraphim,
Continually do cry:

3 O holy, holy, holy Lord,
Whom heavenly hosts obey,
The world is with the glory filled
Of thy majestic sway!

4 The apostles' glorious company,
And prophets crowned with light,
With all the martyrs' noble host
Thy constant praise recite.

5 The holy church throughout the world,
O Lord, confesses thee,
That thou th' eternal Father art,
Of boundless majesty.

137.
Providence.

1 KEEP silence, all created things!
And wait your Maker's nod;
My soul stands trembling, while she sings
The honors of her God.

2 Life, death, and hell, and worlds unknown,
Hang on his firm decree;
He sits on no precarious throne,
Nor borrows leave to be.

3 His providence unfolds the book,
And makes his counsels shine;
Each opening leaf, and every stroke,
Fulfills some deep design.

4 My God! I would not long to see
My fate, with curious eyes—
What gloomy lines are writ for me,
Or what bright scenes may rise.

5 In thy fair book of life and grace,
Oh! may I find my name
Recorded in some humble place,
Beneath my Lord, the Lamb.

THAXTED. C. M. BEETHOVEN.

1. In all my vast con-cerns with thee, In vain my soul would try,....

To shun thy pres-ence, Lord! or flee The no-tice of thine eye....

138.
Omniscience.

2 Thine all-surrounding sight surveys
  My rising and my rest,
My public walks, my private ways,
  And secrets of my breast.

3 My thoughts lie open to the Lord,
  Before they 're formed within;
And, ere my lips pronounce the word,
  He knows the sense I mean.

4 Oh! wondrous knowledge, deep and high,
  Where can a creature hide?
Within thy circling arms I lie,
  Enclosed on every side.

5 So let thy grace surround me still,
  And like a bulwark prove,
To guard my soul from every ill,
  Secured by sovereign love.

139.
Providence.

1 God moves in a mysterious way
  His wonders to perform;
He plants his footsteps in the sea,
  And rides upon the storm.

2 Deep in unfathomable mines
  Of never-failing skill,
He treasures up his bright designs,
  And works his sovereign will.

3 Ye fearful saints, fresh courage take!
  The clouds ye so much dread
Are big with mercy, and will break
  In blessings on your head.

4 Judge not the Lord by feeble sense,
  But trust him for his grace;
Behind a frowning providence
  He hides a smiling face.

5 His purposes will ripen fast,
  Unfolding every hour;
The bud may have a bitter taste,
  But sweet will be the flower.

6 Blind unbelief is sure to err,
  And scan his work in vain;
God is his own interpreter,
  And he will make it plain.

140.
Lord of all.

1 The Lord our God is Lord of all;
  His station who can find?
I hear him in the waterfall;
  I hear him in the wind.

2 If in the gloom of night I shroud,
  His face I cannot fly;
I see him in the evening cloud,
  And in the morning sky.

3 He smiles, we live! he frowns, we die!
  We hang upon his word;
He rears his mighty arm on high,
  We fall before his sword.

4 He bids his gales the fields deform;
  Then, when his thunders cease,
He paints his rainbow on the storm,
  And lulls the winds to peace.

DUNDEE. C. M.

1. Great God! how in - fi - nite art thou! What worth-less worms are we!

Let the whole race of crea - tures bow, And pay their praise to thee.

141.

Eternity.

2 Thy throne eternal ages stood,
Ere seas or stars were made :
Thou art the ever-living God,
Were all the nations dead.

3 Eternity, with all its years,
Stands present in thy view ;
To thee there's nothing old appears—
Great God! there's nothing new.

4 Our lives thro' various scenes are drawn,
And vexed with trifling cares ;
While thine eternal thought moves on
Thine undisturbed affairs.

5 Great God! how infinite art thou!
What worthless worms are we!
Let the whole race of creatures bow,
And pay their praise to thee.

142.

Perfections.

1 I sing th' almighty power of God,
That made the mountains rise,
That spread the flowing seas abroad,
And built the lofty skies.

2 I sing the wisdom that ordained
The sun to rule the day ;
The moon shines full at his command,
And all the stars obey.

3 I sing the goodness of the Lord,
That filled the earth with food ;
He formed the creatures with his word,
And then pronounced them good.

4 Lord! how thy wonders are displayed
Where'er I turn mine eye!
If I survey the ground I tread,
Or gaze upon the sky!

5 There's not a plant or flower below
But makes thy glories known ;
And clouds arise, and tempests blow,
By order from thy throne.

6 Creatures that borrow life from thee
Are subject to thy care ;
There's not a place where we can flee
But God is present there.

143.

Perfections.

1 Eternal Wisdom! thee we praise,
Thee the creation sings ;
With thy loved name, rocks, hills, and
seas,
And heaven's high palace rings.

2 How wide thy hand hath spread the sky!
How glorious to behold!
Tinged with a blue of heavenly dye,
And starred with sparkling gold.

3 Infinite strength, and equal skill,
Shine through the worlds abroad,
Our souls with vast amazement fill,
And speak the builder, God.

4 But still the wonders of thy grace
Our softer passions move ;
Pity divine in Jesus' face
We see, adore, and love.

CHESTERFIELD. C. M.

Dr. Haweis.

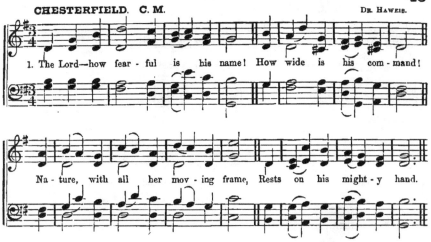

1. The Lord—how fear - ful is his name! How wide is his com - mand!
Na - ture, with all her mov - ing frame, Rests on his might - y hand.

144.
Supremacy.

2 Immortal glory forms his throne,
And light his awful robe;
While with a smile, or with a frown,
He manages the globe.

3 A word of his almighty breath
Can swell or sink the seas;
Build the vast empires of the earth,
Or break them as he please.

4 On angels, with unvailed face
His glory beams above;
On men, he looks with softest grace,
And takes his title, Love.

145.
Holiness.

1 Holy and reverend is the name
Of our eternal King;
Thrice holy Lord! the angels cry;
Thrice holy! let us sing.

2 The deepest reverence of the mind,
Pay, O my soul! to God:
Lift with thy hands a holy heart
To his sublime abode.

3 With sacred awe pronounce his name
Whom words nor thoughts can reach;
A broken heart shall please him more
Than the best forms of speech.

4 Thou holy God! preserve our souls
From all pollution free;
The pure in heart are thy delight,
And they thy face shall see.

146.
In nature.

1 Great Ruler of all nature's frame!
We own thy power divine;
We hear thy breath in every storm,
For all the winds are thine.

2 Wide as they sweep their sounding way,
They work thy sovereign will;
And, awed by thy majestic voice,
Confusion shall be still.

3 Thy mercy tempers every blast
To them that seek thy face,
And mingles with the tempest's roar
The whispers of thy grace.

4 Those gentle whispers let me hear,
Till all the tumult cease;
And gales of paradise shall lull
My weary soul to peace.

147.
Mystery.

1 Thy way, O Lord, is in the sea;
Thy paths I cannot trace,
Nor comprehend the mystery
Of thine unbounded grace.

2 'Tis but in part I know thy will;
I bless thee for the sight:
When will thy love the rest reveal,
In glory's clearer light?

3 With rapture shall I then survey
Thy providence and grace;
And spend an everlasting day
In wonder, love, and praise.

CHRISTMAS. C. M.   HANDEL.

1. While shepherds watched their flocks by night, All seated on the ground, The an-gel of the Lord came down, And glo-ry shone a-round, And glo-ry shone a-round.

148.

2 "Fear not," said he,—for mighty dread
  Had seized their troubled mind,—
"Glad tidings of great joy I bring,
  To you and all mankind.

3 "To you, in David's town, this day,
  Is born of David's line,
The Saviour, who is Christ, the Lord,
  And this shall be the sign ;—

4 "The heavenly babe you there shall find
  To human view displayed,
All meanly wrapped in swathing bands,
  And in a manger laid."

5 Thus spake the seraph—and forthwith
  Appeared a shining throng
Of angels, praising God, who thus
  Addressed their joyful song :—

6 "All glory be to God on high,
  And to the earth be peace ;
Good-will henceforth from heaven to men
  Begin, and never cease !

149.

1 Joy to the world ! the Lord is come !
  Let earth receive her King ;
Let every heart prepare him room,
  And heaven and nature sing.

2 Joy to the world ! the Saviour reigns !
  Let men their songs employ ;
While fields and floods, rocks, hills, and
    plains,
  Repeat the sounding joy.

3 No more let sin and sorrow grow,
  Nor thorns infest the ground :
He comes to make his blessings flow
  Far as the curse is found.

4 He rules the world with truth and grace,
  And makes the nations prove
The glories of his righteousness,
  And wonders of his love.

150.

1 AWAKE, awake the sacred song
  To our incarnate Lord !
Let every heart and every tongue
  Adore th' eternal Word.

2 That awful Word, that sovereign Power,
  By whom the worlds were made—
Oh happy morn ! illustrious hour !—
  Was once in flesh arrayed !

3 Then shone almighty power and love,
  In all their glorious forms,
When Jesus left his throne above,
  To dwell with sinful worms.

4 Adoring angels tuned their songs
  To hail the joyful day ;
With rapture then let mortal tongues
  Their grateful worship pay.

5 What glory, Lord, to thee is due !
  With wonder we adore ;
But could we sing as angels do,
  Our highest praise were poor.

NEWBOLD. C. M. KINGSLEY.

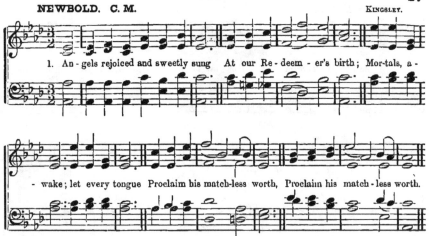

1. An-gels rejoiced and sweetly sung At our Re-deem-er's birth; Mortals, a-
- wake; let every tongue Proclaim his match-less worth, Proclaim his match-less worth.

151.

1 ANGELS rejoiced and sweetly sung
    At our Redeemer's birth;
Mortals! awake; let every tongue
    Proclaim his matchless worth.

2 Glory to God, who dwells on high,
    And sent his only Son
To take a servant's form, and die,
    For evils we had done!

3 Good-will to men; ye fallen race!
    Arise, and shout for joy;
He comes, with rich, abounding grace
    To save, and not destroy.

4 Lord! send the gracious tidings forth,
    And fill the world with light,
That Jew and Gentile, through the earth,
    May know thy saving might.

152.

1 HARK, the glad sound! the Saviour comes,
    The Saviour promised long;
Let every heart prepare a throne,
    And every voice a song.

2 He comes, the prisoner to release,
    In Satan's bondage held;
The gates of brass before him burst,
    The iron fetters yield.

3 He comes, from thickest films of vice
    To clear the mental ray,
And, on the eyes long closed in night,
    To pour celestial day.

4 He comes, the broken heart to bind,
    The bleeding soul to cure,
And, with the treasures of his grace,
    Enrich the humble poor.

5 Our glad hosannas, Prince of Peace,
    Thy welcome shall proclaim,
And heaven's eternal arches ring
    With thy beloved name.

153.

1 CALM on the listening ear of night,
    Come heaven's melodious strains,
Where wild Judea stretches far
    Her silver-mantled plains.

2 Celestial choirs, from courts above,
    Shed sacred glories there,
And angels, with their sparkling lyres,
    Make music on the air.

3 The answering hills of Palestine
    Send back the glad reply;
And greet, from all their holy heights,
    The day-spring from on high.

4 O'er the blue depths of Galilee
    There comes a holier calm,
And Sharon waves, in solemn praise,
    Her silent groves of palm.

5 "Glory to God!" the sounding skies
    Loud with their anthems ring —
"Peace to the earth, good-will to men,
    From heaven's eternal King!"

TRENT. C. M.   GREATOREX COLL.

1. Be - hold! where, in a mor - tal form, Ap-pears each grace di - vine:

The vir - tues, all in Je - sus met, With mild - est ra - diance shine.

154.

2 To spread the rays of heavenly light,
   To give the mourner joy,
To preach glad tidings to the poor,
   Was his divine employ.

3 Mid keen reproach and cruel scorn,
   He, meek and patient stood;
His foes, ungrateful, sought his life,
   Who labored for their good.

4 In the last hour of deep distress,
   Before his Father's throne,
With soul resigned he bowed, and said,—
   "Thy will, not mine, be done!"

5 Be Christ our pattern, and our guide,
   His image may we bear;
Oh! may we tread his holy steps,—
   His joy and glory share.

155.

1 The Saviour! what a noble flame
   Was kindled in his breast,
When hasting to Jerusalem,
   He marched before the rest!

2 Good-will to men, and zeal for God,
   His every thought engross;
He longs to be baptized with blood,
   He pants to reach the cross.

3 With all his sufferings full in view,
   And woes to us unknown,
Forth to the task his spirit flew;
   'T was love that urged him on.

4 Lord, we return thee what we can;
   Our hearts shall sound abroad;
Salvation to the dying man,
   And to the rising God!

5 And while thy bleeding glories here
   Engage our wondering eyes,
We learn our lighter cross to bear,
   And hasten to the skies.

156.

1 WHAT grace, O Lord, and beauty shone
   Around thy steps below;
What patient love was seen in all
   Thy life and death of woe.

2 For, ever on thy burdened heart
   A weight of sorrow hung;
Yet no ungentle, murmuring word
   Escaped thy silent tongue.

3 Thy foes might hate, despise, revile,
   Thy friends unfaithful prove;
Unwearied in forgiveness still,
   Thy heart could only love.

4 Oh, give us hearts to love like thee!
   Like thee, O Lord, to grieve
Far more for others' sins than all
   The wrongs that we receive.

5 One with thyself, may every eye,
   In us, thy brethren, see
The gentleness and grace that spring
   From union, Lord! with thee.

HELENA. C. M.

Wm. B. Bradbury.

1. Je - sus! thy love shall we for - get, And nev - er bring to mind

The grace that paid our hope - less debt, And bade us par - don find?

157.

2 Shall we thy life of grief forget,
    Thy fasting and thy prayer;
Thy locks with mountain vapors wet,
    To save us from despair?

3 Gethsemane can we forget—
    Thy struggling agony;
When night lay dark on Olivet,
    And none to watch with thee?

4 Our sorrows and our sins were laid
    On thee, alone on thee:
Thy precious blood our ransom paid—
    Thine all the glory be!

5 Life's brightest joys we may forget—
    Our kindred cease to love;
But he who paid our hopeless debt,
    Our constancy shall prove.

158.

1 LORD, as to thy dear cross we flee,
    And pray to be forgiven,
So let thy life our pattern be,
    And form our souls for heaven.

2 Help us, through good report and ill,
    Our daily cross to bear;
Like thee, to do our Father's will,
    Our brother's griefs to share.

3 Let grace our selfishness expel,
    Our earthliness refine;
And kindness in our bosoms dwell
    As free and true as thine.

4 If joy shall at thy bidding fly,
    And grief's dark day come on,
We, in our turn, would meekly cry,
    "Father, thy will be done!"

5 Should friends misjudge, or foes defame,
    Or brethren faithless prove,
Then, like thine own, be all our aim
    To conquer them by love.

6 Kept peaceful in the midst of strife,
    Forgiving and forgiven,
Oh, may we lead the pilgrim's life,
    And follow thee to heaven!

159.

1 THOU art the Way: to thee alone
    From sin and death we flee;
And he who would the Father seek,
    Must seek him, Lord, by thee.

2 Thou art the Truth: thy word alone
    True wisdom can impart;
Thou only canst instruct the mind,
    And purify the heart.

3 Thou art the Life: the rending tomb
    Proclaims thy conquering arm;
And those who put their trust in thee
    Nor death nor hell shall harm.

4 Thou art the Way, the Truth, the Life:
    Grant us to know that Way;
That Truth to keep, that Life to win,
    Which leads to endless day.

ROCKINGHAM. L. M.

Dr. L. Mason.

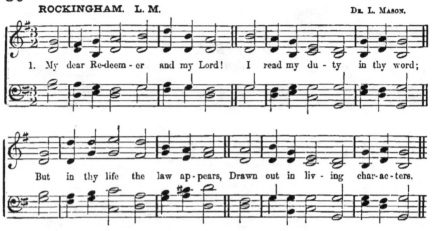

1. My dear Re-deem - er and my Lord! I read my du - ty in thy word;

But in thy life the law ap-pears, Drawn out in liv - ing char-ac-ters.

160.

2 Such was thy truth, and such thy zeal,
Such deference to thy Father's will,
Thy love and meekness so divine,
I would transcribe and make them mine.

3 Cold mountains, and the midnight air,
Witnessed the fervor of thy prayer;
The desert thy temptations knew,
Thy conflict, and thy victory too.

4 Be thou my pattern; make me bear
More of thy gracious image here;
Then God, the Judge, shall own my name
Among the followers of the Lamb.

161.

1 How sweetly flowed the gospel sound
From lips of gentleness and grace,
When listening thousands gathered round,
And joy and gladness filled the place!

2 From heaven he came, of heaven he spoke,
To heaven he led his followers' way;
Dark clouds of gloomy night he broke,
Unvailing an immortal day.

3 "Come, wanderers, to my Father's home,
Come, all ye weary ones, and rest:"
Yes, sacred Teacher, we will come,
Obey thee, love thee, and be blest!

4 Decay, then, tenements of dust;
Pillars of earthly pride, decay:
A nobler mansion waits the just,
And Jesus has prepared the way.

162.

1 How beauteous were the marks divine,
That in thy meekness used to shine;
That lit thy lonely pathway, trod
In wondrous love, O Son of God!

2 Oh! who like Thee—so calm, so bright,
So pure, so made to live in light?
Oh! who like thee did ever go
So patient through a world of woe?

3 Oh! who like thee so humbly bore
The scorn, the scoffs of men, before!
So meek, forgiving, godlike, high,
So glorious in humility!

4 Oh! in thy light be mine to go,
Illuming all my way of woe;
And give me ever on the road
To trace thy footsteps, Son of God!

163.

1 Not to condemn the sons of men,
Did Christ, the Son of God, appear;
No weapons in his hands are seen,
No flaming sword, nor thunder there.

2 Such was the pity of our God,
He loved the race of man so well,
He sent his Son to bear our load
Of sins, and save our souls from hell.

3 Sinners, believe the Saviour's word;
Trust in his mighty name, and live:
A thousand joys his lips afford,
His hands a thousand blessings give.

BEETHOVEN. L. M. HAYDN.

1. O'er the dark wave of Ga - li - lee The gloom of twi - light gath-ers fast,

And on the wa - ters drear - i - ly De-scends the fit - ful evening blast.

164.

2 The weary bird hath left the air,
And sunk into his sheltered nest;
The wandering beast has sought his lair,
And laid him down to welcome rest.

3 Still near the lake, with weary tread,
Lingers a form of human kind;
And on his lone, unsheltered head,
Flows the chill night-damp of the wind.

4 Why seeks he not a home of rest?
Why seeks he not a pillowed bed?
Beasts have their dens, the bird its nest;
He hath not where to lay his head.

5 Such was the lot he freely chose,
To bless, to save the human race;
And through his poverty there flows
A rich, full stream of heavenly grace.

165.

1 THE morning dawns upon the place
Where Jesus spent the night in prayer;
Through yielding glooms behold his face!
Nor form, nor comeliness is there.

2 Brought forth to judgment, now he stands
Arraigned, condemned, at Pilate's bar;
Here, spurned by fierce prætorian bands,
There, mocked by Herod's men of war.

3 He bears their buffeting and scorn—
Mock-homage of the lip, the knee—
The purple robe, the crown of thorn—
The scourge, the nail, th' accursed tree.

4 No guile within his mouth is found;
He neither threatens, nor complains;
Meek as a lamb for slaughter bound,
Dumb, 'mid his murderers he remains.

5 But hark! he prays: 't is for his foes:
And speaks: 't is comfort to his friends;
Answers: and paradise bestows;
He bows his head: the conflict ends.

166.

1 WHEN, like a stranger on our sphere
The lowly Jesus wandered here,
Where'er he went, affliction fled,
And sickness reared her fainting head.

2 The eye that rolled in irksome night,
Beheld his face,—for God is light;
The opening ear, the loosened tongue,
His precepts heard, his praises sung.

3 With bounding steps, the halt and lame,
To hail their great deliverer came;
O'er the cold grave he bowed his head,
He spake the word, and raised the dead.

4 Despairing madness, dark and wild,
In his inspiring presence smiled;
The storm of horror ceased to roll,
And reason lightened through the soul.

5 Through paths of loving-kindness led,
Where Jesus triumphed we would tread;
To all, with willing hands, dispense
The gifts of our benevolence.

HAMBURG. L. M　　　　　　　　　　*Arranged by* Dr. L. Mason.

1. From Cal - va - ry　a　cry was heard— A bit - ter and heart - rend - ing cry:

My Sa - viour! ev - ery mourn - ful word　Bespeaks thy soul's deep ag - o - ny.

167.

2 A horror of great darkness fell
On thee, thou spotless, holy One!
And all the swarming hosts of hell
Conspired to tempt God's only Son.

3 The scourge, the thorns, the deep dis-
　grace—
These thou could'st bear, nor once repine;
But when Jehovah vailed his face,
Unutterable pangs were thine.

4 Let the dumb world its silence break;
Let pealing anthems rend the sky;
Awake, my sluggish soul, awake!
He died, that we might never die.

5 Lord! on thy cross I fix mine eye,
If e'er I lose its strong control,
Oh! let that dying, piercing cry,
Melt and reclaim my wandering soul.

168.

1 Jesus, whom angel hosts adore,
Became a man of griefs for me;
In love, though rich, becoming poor,
That I through him enriched might be.

2 Though Lord of all, above, below,
He went to Olivet for me;
There drank my cup of wrath and woe,
When bleeding in Gethsemane.

3 The ever-blessèd Son of God
Went up to Calvary for me;
There paid my debt, there bore my load,
In his own body on the tree.

4 Jesus, whose dwelling is the skies,
Went down into the grave for me;
There overcame my enemies,
There won the glorious victory.

5 'Tis finished all: the vail is rent,
The welcome sure, the access free;—
Now then, we leave our banishment,
O Father, to return to thee!

169.

1 When I survey the wondrous cross,
On which the Prince of glory died,
My richest gain I count but loss,
And pour contempt on all my pride.

2 Forbid it, Lord! that I should boast,
Save in the death of Christ, my God;
All the vain things that charm me most,
I sacrifice them to his blood.

3 See, from his head, his hands, his feet,
Sorrow and love flow mingled down;
Did e'er such love and sorrow meet,
Or thorns compose so rich a crown?

4 His dying crimson, like a robe,
Spreads o'er his body on the tree;
Then I am dead to all the globe,
And all the globe is dead to me.

5 Were the whole realm of nature mine,
That were a present far too small;
Love so amazing, so divine,
Demands my soul, my life, my all.

SOLITUDE. L. M.

V. C. Taylor.

1. 'Tis mid-night—and on O - live's brow The star is dimmed that lately shone;

'Tis mid-night— in the gar - den now The suf-fering Sa-viour prays a - lone.

170.

2 'T is midnight—and from all removed,
Immanuel wrestles lone with fears;
Ev'n the disciple that he loved,
Heeds not his Master's griefs and tears.

3 'T is midnight—and for others' guilt
The Man of sorrows weeps in blood;
Yet he that hath in anguish knelt,
Is not forsaken by his God.

4 'T is midnight—and from ether-plains
Is borne the song that angels know;
Unheard by mortals are the strains
That sweetly soothe the Saviour's woe.

171.

1 "'T is finished!"—so the Saviour cried,
And meekly bowed his head, and died:
'T is finished!—yes, the race is run,
The battle fought, the victory won.

2 'T is finished!—all that heaven foretold
By prophets in the days of old;
And truths are opened to our view,
That kings and prophets never knew.

3 'T is finished!—Son of God, thy power
Hath triumphed in this awful hour;
And yet, our eyes with sorrow see
That life to us was death to thee.

4 'T is finished!—let the joyful sound
Be heard through all the nations round;
'T is finished!—let the echo fly
Thro' heaven and hell, thro' earth and sky.

172.

1 Deep in our hearts let us record
The deeper sorrows of our Lord;
Behold the rising billows roll,
To overwhelm his holy soul!

2 Yet, gracious God, thy power and love
Have made the curse a blessing prove:
Those dreadful sufferings of thy Son
Atoned for crimes which we had done.

3 Oh, for his sake, our guilt forgive,
And let the mourning sinner live!
The Lord will hear us in his name,
Nor shall our hope be turned to shame.

173.

1 Stretched on the cross the Saviour dies!
Hark! his expiring groans arise:
See—from his hands, his feet, his side;
Fast flows the sacred, crimson tide!

2 But life attends the deathful sound,
And flows from every bleeding wound:
The vital stream,—how free it flows,
To save and cleanse his rebel foes.

3 Can I survey this scene of woe,
Where mingling grief and wonder flow,
And yet my heart unmoved remain,
Insensible to love or pain?

4 Come, dearest Lord! thy grace impart
To warm this cold, this stupid heart;
Till all its powers and passions move
In melting grief, and ardent love.

AVON. C. M.   *Scottish.*

1. A - las! and did my Sa - viour bleed, And did my Sovereign die?

Would he de - vote that sa - cred head For such a worm as I?

174.

1 ALAS! and did my Saviour bleed,
  And did my Sovereign die?
  Would he devote that sacred head
  For such a worm as I?

2 Was it for crimes that I had done
  He groaned upon the tree?
  Amazing pity! grace unknown!
  And love beyond degree!

3 Well might the sun in darkness hide,
  And shut his glories in,
  When Christ, the great Creator, died
  For man, the creature's sin.

4 Thus might I hide my blushing face
  While his dear cross appears;
  Dissolve my heart in thankfulness,
  And melt my eyes to tears.

5 But drops of grief can ne'er repay
  The debt of love I owe;
  Here, Lord, I give myself away,
  'T is all that I can do.

175.

1 BEHOLD the Saviour of mankind,
  Nailed to the shameful tree!
  How vast the love that him inclined
  To bleed and die for me!

2 Hark! how he groans, while nature shakes,
  And earth's strong pillars bend!
  The temple's vail asunder breaks,
  The solid marbles rend.

3 'T is finished! now the ransom's paid,
  "Receive my soul!" he cries:
  See—how he bows his sacred head!
  He bows his head and dies!

4 But soon he 'll break death's iron chain,
  And in full glory shine;
  O Lamb of God! was ever pain—
  Was ever love like thine!

176.

1 OH! if my soul were formed for woe,
  How would I vent my sighs!
  Repentance should like rivers flow
  From both my streaming eyes.

2 'T was for my sins my dearest Lord
  Hung on the cursed tree,
  And groaned away a dying life
  For thee, my soul! for thee.

3 Oh! how I hate these lusts of mine
  That crucified my Lord;
  Those sins that pierced and nailed his flesh
  Fast to the fatal wood!

4 Yes, my Redeemer—they shall die;
  My heart has so decreed;
  Nor will I spare the guilty things
  That made my Saviour bleed.

5 While with a melting, broken heart,
  My murdered Lord I view,
  I 'll raise revenge against my sins,
  And slay the murderers too.

LENOX. H. M.

1. Come, ev-ery pi-ous heart, That loves the Saviour's name! Your noblest powers ex-

-ert To cel-e-brate his fame; Tell all a-bove, And

Tell all a-bove, And all be-low, Tell

all be-low, Tell all a-bove, And all be-low, The debt of love To him you owe.

all a-bove, And all be-low, The debt of love To him you owe.

177.

2 He left his starry crown,
　And laid his robes aside ;
On wings of love came down,
　And wept, and bled, and died :
What he endured, | To save our souls
No tongue can tell, | From death and hell.

3 From the dark grave he rose—
　The mansion of the dead ;
And thence his mighty foes
　In glorious triumph led ;
Up through the sky | And reigns on high,
The conqueror rode, | The Saviour-God.

4 From thence he'll quickly come—
　His chariot will not stay—
And bear our spirits home
　To realms of endless day :
There shall we see | And ever be
His lovely face, | In his embrace.

178.

1 YES, the Redeemer rose ;
　The Saviour left the dead ;
And o'er our hellish foes
　High raised his conquering head,
In wild dismay, | Fall to the ground,
The guards around | And sink away.

2 Lo ! the angelic bands
　In full assembly meet,
To wait his high commands,
　And worship at his feet :
Joyful they come, | From realms of day,
And wing their way, | To Jesus' tomb.

3 Then back to heaven they fly,
　And the glad tidings bear ;
Hark ! as they soar on high,
　What music fills the air !
Their anthems say : | Hath left the dead ;
" Jesus who bled | He rose to-day."

4 Ye mortals, catch the sound,
　Redeemed by him from hell ;
And send the echo round
　The globe on which you dwell :
Transported cry : | Hath left the dead,
" Jesus who bled | No more to die."

5 All hail, triumphant Lord,
　Who sav'st us with thy blood !
Wide be thy name adored,
　Thou rising, reigning God !
With thee we rise, | And empires gain
With thee we reign, | Beyond the skies.

BENNINGTON. L. M. Double.　　　　　　　　*Arranged from* PERCIVAL.

1. Our Lord is ris-en from the dead, Our Je-sus is gone up on high; The powers of hell are cap-tive led, Dragged to the portals of the sky. 2. There his triumphal chariot waits, And angels chant the sol-emn lay: "Lift up your heads, ye heav'nly gates, Ye everlasting doors! give way."

179.

3　Loose all your bars of massy light,
　And wide unfold th' ethereal scene :
　He claims these mansions as his right ;
　Receive the King of glory in.

4　Who is the King of glory—who?
　The Lord who all our foes o'ercame ;
　Who sin, and death, and hell o'erthrew :
　And Jesus is the conqueror's name.

5　Lo! his triumphal chariot waits,
　And angels chant the solemn lay :—
　"Lift up your heads, ye heavenly gates !
　Ye everlasting doors! give way."

6　Who is the King of glory—who?
　The Lord of boundless power possessed ;
　The King of saints and angels, too,
　God over all, forever blessed.

180.

1　THE King of saints,—how fair his face !
　Adorned with majesty and grace,
　He comes, with blessings from above,
　And wins the nations to his love.

2　At his right hand, our eyes behold
　The queen, arrayed in purest gold ;
　The world admires her heavenly dress,
　Her robe of joy and righteousness.

3　Oh ! happy hour, when thou shalt rise
　To his fair palace in the skies ;
　And all thy sons, a numerous train,
　Each, like a prince, in glory reign.

4　Let endless honors crown his head ;
　Let every age his praises spread ;
　While we, with cheerful songs, approve
　The condescension of his love.

181.

1　ETERNAL God, celestial King !
　Exalted be thy glorious name ;
　Let hosts in heaven thy praises sing,
　And saints on earth thy love proclaim.

2　My heart is fixed on thee, my God !
　I rest my hope on thee alone :
　I 'll spread thy sacred truths abroad,
　To all mankind thy love make known.

3　Awake, my tongue ! awake, my lyre !
　With morning's earliest dawn arise ;
　To songs of joy my soul inspire,
　And swell your music to the skies.

4　With those who in thy grace abound,
　To thee I 'll raise my thankful voice ;
　While every land, the earth around,
　Shall hear, and in thy name rejoice.

DUKE STREET. L. M.   J. HATTON.

1. Now to the Lord, who makes us know The won-ders of his dy - ing love,

Be hum-ble hon - ors paid be - low, And strains of no - bler praise a - bove.

182.

2 'T was he who cleansed our foulest sins,
And washed us in his precious blood;
'T is he who makes us priests and kings,
And brings us rebels near to God.

3 To Jesus, our atoning Priest,
To Jesus, our eternal King,
Be everlasting power confessed!
Let every tongue his glory sing.

4 Behold! on flying clouds he comes,
And every eye shall see him move;
Though with our sins we pierced him once,
He now displays his pardoning love.

5 The unbelieving world shall wail,
While we rejoice to see the day;
Come, Lord! nor let thy promise fail,
Nor let thy chariot long delay.

183.

1 COME, let us sing the song of songs—
The saints in heaven began the strain—
The homage which to Christ belongs:
"Worthy the Lamb, for he was slain!"

2 Slain to redeem us by his blood,
To cleanse from every sinful stain,
And make us kings and priests to God—
"Worthy the Lamb, for he was slain!"

3 To him who suffered on the tree,
Our souls, at his soul's price, to gain,
Blessing, and praise, and glory be:
"Worthy the Lamb, for he was slain!"

4 To him, enthroned by filial right,
All power in heaven and earth proclaim,
Honor, and majesty, and might:
"Worthy the Lamb, for he was slain!"

5 Long as we live, and when we die,
And while in heaven with him we reign;
This song, our song of songs shall be:
"Worthy the Lamb, for he was slain;"

184.

1 BRIGHT King of Glory, dreadful God!
Our spirits bow before thy feet:
To thee we lift an humble thought,
And worship at thine awful seat.

2 A thousand seraphs strong and bright
Stand round the glorious Deity;
But who, among the sons of light,
Pretends comparison with thee?

3 Yet there is One of human frame,
Jesus, arrayed in flesh and blood,
Thinks it no robbery to claim
A full equality with God.

4 Their glory shines with equal beams:
Their essence is forever one,
Though they are known by different names,
The Father God, and God the Son.

5 Then let the name of Christ our King
With equal honors be adored;
His praise let every angel sing
And all the nations own the Lord.

HARWELL. 8s & 7s.   Dr. L. Mason.

1. { Hark! ten thousand harps and voices Sound the note of praise above;
      Jesus reigns, and heaven rejoices; Jesus reigns, the God of love: See, he sits on yonder throne;

Je-sus rules   the world alone. Hal-le - lu-jah, hal-le - lu-jah, hal-le - lu-jah, A - men.

185.

2 Jesus! hail! whose glory brightens
   All above, and gives it worth ;
Lord of life! thy smile enlightens,
   Cheers, and charms thy saints on earth:
When we think of love like thine,
Lord! we own it love divine.

3 King of glory! reign for ever—
   Thine an everlasting crown ;
Nothing, from thy love, shall sever
   Those whom thou hast made thine
Happy objects of thy grace, [own ;—
Destined to behold thy face.

4 Saviour! hasten thine appearing;
   Bring—oh, bring the glorious day,
When the awful summons hearing,
   Heaven and earth shall pass away ;—
Then, with golden harps, we 'll sing,—
"Glory, glory to our King."

186.

1 Hail, thou once despised Jesus!
   Crowned in mockery a king !
Thou didst suffer to release us ;
   Thou didst free salvation bring.
Hail, thou agonizing Saviour,
   Bearer of our sin and shame!
By thy merits we find favor;
   Life is given through thy name.

2 Jesus, hail! enthroned in glory,
   There for ever to abide ;

All the heavenly host adore thee,
   Seated at thy Father's side :
There for sinners thou art pleading :
   There thou dost our place prepare :
Ever for us interceding,
   Till in glory we appear.

3 Worship, honor, power, and blessing
   Thou art worthy to receive;
Loudest praises, without ceasing,
   Meet it is for us to give.
Help, ye bright angelic spirits ;
   Bring your sweetest, noblest lays;
Help to sing our Saviour's merits ;
   Help to chant Immanuel's praise.

187.

1 Hail, my ever-blessed Jesus!
   Only thee I wish to sing;
To my soul thy name is precious,
   Thou my Prophet, Priest, and King.
Oh! what mercy flows from heaven!
   Oh! what joy and happiness!
Love I much? I'm much forgiven;
   I'm a miracle of grace.

2 Once, with Adam's race in ruin,
   Unconcerned in sin I lay,
Swift destruction still pursuing,
   Till my Saviour passed that way.
Witness, all ye hosts of heaven,
   My Redeemer's tenderness ;
Love I much? I'm much forgiven;
   I'm a miracle of grace.

CARTHAGE. 8s & 7s.

ROOT & SWEETSER'S COLL.

1. Christ, a - bove all glo - ry seat - ed! King e - ter - nal, strong to save!

To thee, Death by death de - feat - ed, Tri - umph high and glo - ry gave.

188.

2 Thou art gone, where now is given,
What no mortal might could gain :
On the eternal throne of heaven,
In thy Father's power to reign.

3 There thy kingdoms all adore thee,
Heaven above and earth below,
While the depths of hell before thee,
Trembling and defeated bow.

4 We, O Lord! with hearts adoring,
Follow thee above the sky.
Hear our prayers thy grace imploring,
Lift our souls to thee on high.

5 So when thou again in glory
On the clouds of heaven shalt shine,
We thy flock may stand before thee,
Owned forevermore as thine.

189.

1 Lo! Jehovah, we adore thee—
Thee, our Saviour—thee, our God ;
From thy throne let beams of glory
Shine through all the world abroad.

2 Jesus! thee our Saviour hailing,
Thee our God in praise we own ;
Highest honors, never failing,
Rise eternal round thy throne.

3 Now, ye saints, his power confessing,
In your grateful strains adore ;
For his mercy, never ceasing,
Flows, and flows forevermore.

190.

1 ONE there is, above all others,
Well deserves the name of Friend ·
His is love beyond a brother's,
Costly, free, and knows no end.

2 Which of all our friends, to save us,
Could or would have shed his blood?
But our Jesus died to have us
Reconciled in him to God.

3 When he lived on earth abased,
Friend of sinners was his name ;
Now above all glory raised,
He rejoices in the same.

4 Oh ! for grace our hearts to soften!
Teach us, Lord, at length, to love ;
We, alas ! forget too often
What a friend we have above.

191.

1 JESUS comes, his conflict over,
Comes to claim his great reward ;
Angels round the victor hover,
Crowding to behold their Lord.

2 Yonder throne for him erected,
Now becomes the victor's seat ;
Lo, the man on earth rejected !
Angels worship at his feet.

3 Day and night they cry before him,—
" Holy, holy, holy Lord !"
All the powers of heaven adore him;
All obey his sovereign word.

MOZART. 7s.   *Arranged from* MOZART.

1. Christ, the Lord, is risen to-day! Sons of men and an-gels say: Raise your joys and triumphs high; Sing, ye heavens! and earth, reply! Sing, ye heavens! and earth, re-ply!

192.

2 Love's redeeming work is done,
Fought the fight, the battle won:
Lo! our sun's eclipse is o'er;
Lo! he sets in blood no more.

3 Vain the stone, the watch, the seal—
Christ hath burst the gates of hell:
Death in vain forbids his rise,
Christ hath opened paradise.

4 Lives again our glorious King!
Where, O Death, is now thy sting?
Once he died, our souls to save;
Where's thy victory, boasting Grave?

193.
Advent.

1 HARK! the herald angels sing,
"Glory to the new-born King!
Peace on earth, and mercy mild;
God and sinners reconciled."

2 Joyful, all ye nations, rise;
Join the triumphs of the skies;
With the angelic hosts proclaim,
"Christ is born in Bethlehem."

3 Mild he lays his glory by;
Born that man no more may die;
Born to raise the sons of earth;
Born to give them second birth.

4 Hail, the heaven-born Prince of Peace!
Hail, the Sun of Righteousness!
Light and life to all he brings,
Risen with healing in his wings.

5 Let us then with angels sing,
"Glory to the new-born King!—
Peace on earth and mercy mild,
God and sinners reconciled!"

194.

1 ANGELS! roll the rock away;
Death! yield up thy mighty prey;
See! the Saviour leaves the tomb,
Glowing with immortal bloom.

2 Hark! the wondering angels raise
Louder notes of joyful praise:
Let the earth's remotest bound
Echo with the blissful sound.

3 Now, ye saints, lift up your eyes,
See him high in glory rise!
Hosts of angels, on the road,
Hail him—the incarnate God.

4 Heaven unfolds its portals wide,
See the Conqueror through them ride!
King of glory! mount thy throne—
Boundless empire is thine own.

5 Praise him, ye celestial choirs!
Tune, and sweep your golden lyres;
Raise, O earth! your noblest songs,
From ten thousand thousand tongues.

6 Every note with wonder swell,
Sin o'erthrown, and captive hell!
Where, O death, is now thy sting?
Where thy terrors, vanquished king!

CORONATION. C. M.   OLIVER HOLDEN.

1. All hail! the power of Jesus' name! Let angels prostrate fall! Bring forth the royal diadem, And crown him Lord of all, Bring forth the royal di-a - dem, And crown him Lord of all.

195.

2 Ye chosen seed of Israel's race,
    Ye ransomed from the fall;
Hail him, who saves you by his grace,
    And crown him Lord of all.

3 Sinners, whose love can ne'er forget
    The wormwood and the gall;
Go, spread your trophies at his feet,
    And crown him Lord of all.

4 Let every kindred, every tribe,
    On this terrestrial ball,
To him all majesty ascribe,
    And crown him Lord of all.

5 Oh! that with yonder sacred throng,
    We at his feet may fall;
We 'll join the everlasting song,
    And crown him Lord of all.

196.

1 BEHOLD the glories of the Lamb,
    Amid his Father's throne;
Prepare new honors for his name,
    And songs before unknown.

2 Let elders worship at his feet,
    The church adore around,
With vials full of odors sweet,
    And harps of sweeter sound.

3 Those are the prayers of all the saints,
    And these the hymns they raise:
Jesus is kind to our complaints;
    He loves to hear our praise.

4 Now to the Lamb that once was slain,
    Be endless blessings paid!
Salvation, glory, joy remain
    Forever on thy head!

5 Thou hast redeemed our souls with blood,
    Hast set the prisoners free,
Hast made us kings and priests to God,
    And we shall reign with thee.

197.

1 HOSANNA to the Prince of light,
    That clothed himself in clay;
Entered the iron gates of death,
    And tore the bars away.

2 See how the Conqueror mounts aloft,
    And to his Father flies,
With scars of honor in his flesh,
    And triumph in his eyes.

3 There our exalted Saviour reigns,
    And scatters blessings down,
Our Jesus fills the middle seat,
    Of the celestial throne.

4 Raise your devotion, mortal tongues,
    To reach his blessed abode;
Sweet be the accents of your songs
    To our incarnate God.

5 Bright angels! strike your loudest strings
    Your sweetest voices raise;
Let heaven, and all created things,
    Sound our Immanuel's praise.

ORTONVILLE. C. M.

Dr. Hastings.

1. Ma-jes- tic sweetness sits enthroned On my Redeemer's brow; His head with radiant glo-ries crowned, His lips with grace o'er - flow, His lips with grace o'erflow.

198.

2 No mortal can with him compare
Among the sons of men ;
Fairer he is than all the fair
That fill the heavenly train.

3 He saw me plunged in deep distress,
He flew to my relief ;
For me he bore the shameful cross,
And carried all my grief.

4 To him I owe my life, and breath,
And all the joys I have :
He makes me triumph over death,
And saves me from the grave.

5 Since from his bounty I receive
Such proofs of love divine,
Had I a thousand hearts to give,
Lord, they should all be thine !

199.

1 The Saviour ! oh ! what endless charms
Dwell in the blissful sound !
Its influence every fear disarms,
And spreads sweet comfort round.

2 Here pardon, life and joys divine,
In rich effusion flow,
For guilty rebels lost in sin,
And doomed to endless woe.

3 The almighty Former of the skies
Stooped to our vile abode ;
While angels viewed with wondering eyes
And hailed the incarnate God.

4 Oh! the rich depths of love divine !
Of bliss a boundless store !
Dear Saviour, let me call thee mine ;
I cannot wish for more.

5 On thee alone my hope relies,
Beneath thy cross I fall ;
My Lord, my Life, my Sacrifice,
My Saviour, and my All !

200.

1 Oh ! for a thousand tongues to sing
My dear Redeemer's praise !
The glories of my God and King,
The triumphs of his grace !

2 My gracious Master and my God !
Assist me to proclaim,
To spread, through all the earth abroad,
The honors of thy name.

3 Jesus—the name that calms my fears,
That bids my sorrows cease ;
'Tis music to my ravished ears ;
'Tis life, and health, and peace.

4 He breaks the power of reigning sin,
He sets the prisoner free ;
His blood can make the foulest clean ;
His blood availed for me.

5 Let us obey, we then shall know,
Shall feel our sins forgiven ;
Anticipate our heaven below,
And own, that love is heaven.

BRADFORD. C. M.　　　　　　　　　　　　　　　　　HANDEL.

1. I know that my Re - deem - er lives, And ev - er prays for me:

A to - ken of his love he gives, A pledge of lib - er - ty.

201.

2 I find him lifting up my head;
　He brings salvation near:
His presence makes me free indeed,
　And he will soon appear.

3 He wills that I should holy be:
　What can withstand his will?
The counsel of his grace in me
　He surely shall fulfill.

4 Jesus, I hang upon thy word;
　I steadfastly believe
Thou wilt return, and claim me, Lord,
　And to thyself receive.

5 When God is mine, and I am his,
　Of paradise possessed,
I taste unutterable bliss,
　And everlasting rest.

202.

1 He, who on earth as man was known,
　And bore our sins and pains,
Now, seated on th' eternal throne,
　The God of glory reigns.

2 His hands the wheels of nature guide
　With an unerring skill;
And countless worlds, extended wide,
　Obey his sovereign will.

3 While harps unnumbered sound his praise
　In yonder world above,
His saints on earth admire his ways,
　And glory in his love.

4 When troubles, like a burning sun,
　Beat heavy on their head;
To this almighty rock they run,
　And find a pleasing shade.

5 How glorious he—how happy they,
　In such a glorious friend!
Whose love secures them all the way,
　And crowns them at the end.

203.

1 Come, let us join our songs of praise
　To our ascended Priest;
He entered heaven, with all our names
　Engraven on his breast.

2 Below he washed our guilt away,
　By his atoning blood;
Now he appears before the throne,
　And pleads our cause with God.

3 Clothed with our nature still, he knows
　The weakness of our frame,
And how to shield us from the foes
　Whom he himself o'ercame.

4 Nor time, nor distance, e'er shall quench
　The fervor of his love;
For us he died in kindness here,
　For us he lives above.

5 Oh! may we ne'er forget his grace,
　Nor blush to bear his name;
Still may our hearts hold fast his faith—
· 　Our lips his praise proclaim.

WIMBORNE. L. M.

GREATOREX COLL.

1. E - ter - nal Spi - rit, we con - fess, And sing the won - ders of thy grace:

Thy pow'r conveys our blessings down From God the Fa - ther and the Son.

204.

2 Enlightened by thy heavenly ray,
Our shades and darkness turn to day;
Thine inward teachings make us know
Our danger, and our refuge too.

3 Thy power and glory work within,
And break the chains of reigning sin;
All our imperious lusts subdue,
And form our wretched hearts anew.

4 The troubled conscience knows thy voice;
Thy cheering words awake our joys;
Thy words allay the stormy wind,
And calm the surges of the mind.

205.

1 COME, O Creator Spirit blest!
And in our souls take up thy rest;
Come, with thy grace and heavenly aid,
To fill the hearts which thou hast made.

2 Great Comforter! to thee we cry;
O highest gift of God most high!
O fount of life! O fire of love!
Send sweet anointing from above!

3 Kindle our senses from above,
And make our hearts o'erflow with love;
With patience firm, and virtue high,
The weakness of our flesh supply.

4 Far from us drive the foe we dread,
And grant us thy true peace instead;
So shall we not, with thee for guide,
Turn from the path of life aside.

206.

1 COME, blesséd Spirit! source of light!
Whose power and grace are unconfined,
Dispel the gloomy shades of night,—
The thicker darkness of the mind.

2 To mine illumined eyes, display
The glorious truth thy word reveals;
Cause me to run the heavenly way,
Thy book unfold, and loose the seals.

3 Thine inward teachings make me know
The mysteries of redeeming love,
The vanity of things below,
And excellence of things above.

4 While through this dubious maze I stray,
Spread, like the sun, thy beams abroad,
To show the dangers of the way,
And guide my feeble steps to God.

207.

1 COME, Holy Spirit! calm my mind,
And fit me to approach my God;
Remove each vain, each worldly thought,
And lead me to thy blest abode.

2 Hast thou imparted to my soul
A living spark of holy fire?
Oh! kindle now the sacred flame;
Make me to burn with pure desire.

3 A brighter faith and hope impart,
And let me now my Saviour see;
Oh! soothe and cheer my burdened heart,
And bid my spirit rest in thee.

ZEPHYR. L. M.   WM. B. BRADBURY.

1. Sure, the blest Com-fort-er is nigh, 'Tis he sus-tains my faint-ing heart;

Else would my hope for-ev-er die, And ev-ery cheer-ing ray de-part.

208.

2 Whene'er, to call the Saviour mine,
With ardent wish my heart aspires,—
Can it be less than power divine,
That animates these strong desires?

3 And, when my cheerful hope can say,—
I love my God and taste his grace,—
Lord! is it not thy blissful ray,
That brings this dawn of sacred peace?

4 Let thy good Spirit in my heart
Forever dwell, O God of love!
And light and heavenly peace impart,—
Sweet earnest of the joys above.

209.

1 Stay, thou insulted Spirit! stay,
Though I have done thee such despite;
Cast not a sinner quite away,
Nor take thine everlasting flight.

2 Though I have most unfaithful been
Of all who e'er thy grace received;
Ten thousand times thy goodness seen,
Ten thousand times thy goodness
grieved;—

3 Yet, oh! the chief of sinners spare,
In honor of my great High-Priest;
Nor, in thy righteous anger, swear
I shall not see thy people's rest.

4 My weary soul, O God! release,
Uphold me with thy gracious hand;
Guide me into thy perfect peace,
And bring me to the promised land.

210.

1 Come, gracious Spirit, heavenly Dove,
With light and comfort from above:
Be thou our guardian, thou our guide!
O'er every thought and step preside.

2 To us the light of truth display,
And make us know and choose thy way;
Plant holy fear in every heart,
That we from God may ne'er depart.

3 Lead us to holiness—the road
That we must take to dwell with God;
Lead us to Christ, the living way,
Nor let us from his precepts stray.

4 Lead us to God, our final rest,
To be with him forever blessed;
Lead us to heaven, its bliss to share,
And drink our fill of pleasure there.

211.

1 As when in silence, vernal showers
Descend, and cheer the fainting flowers,
So, in the secrecy of love,
Falls the sweet influence from above.

2 That heavenly influence let me find
In holy silence of the mind,
While every grace maintains its bloom,
Diffusing wide its rich perfume.

3 Nor let these blessings be confined
To me, but poured on all mankind,
Till earth's wild wastes in verdure rise,
And a young Eden bless our eyes.

STEPHENS. C. M.   W. JONES.

1. Come, Ho - ly Spi - rit, heaven-ly Dove! With all thy quickening powers,

Kin - dle a flame of sa - cred love In these cold hearts of ours.

212.

2 Look! how we grovel here below,
  Fond of these trifling toys!
Our souls can neither fly nor go
  To reach eternal joys.

3 In vain we tune our formal songs;
  In vain we strive to rise;
Hosannas languish on our tongues,
  And our devotion dies.

4 Dear Lord, and shall we ever live
  At this poor, dying rate—
Our love so faint, so cold to thee,
  And thine to us so great?

5 Come, Holy Spirit, Heavenly Dove,
  With all thy quickening powers,
Come, shed abroad a Saviour's love,
  And that shall kindle ours.

213.

1 Spirit Divine! attend our prayer,
  And make our hearts thy home;
Descend with all thy gracious power:
  Come, Holy Spirit, come!

2 Come as the light: to us reveal
  Our sinfulness and woe;
And lead us in those paths of life
  Where all the righteous go.

3 Come as the fire, and purge our hearts,
  Like sacrificial flame:
Let our whole soul an offering be
  To our Redeemer's name.

4 Come as the dew, and sweetly bless
  This consecrated hour;
May barrenness rejoice to own
  Thy fertilizing power.

5 Come as the wind, with rushing sound,
  With Pentecostal grace;
And make the great salvation known
  Wide as the human race.

6 Spirit Divine, attend our prayer,
  And make our hearts thy home;
Descend with all thy gracious power:
  Come, Holy Spirit, come!

214.

1 Come, Holy Ghost, Creator, come,
  Inspire these souls of thine;
Till every heart which thou hast made
  Be filled with grace divine.

2 Thou art the Comforter, the gift
  Of God, and fire of love;
The everlasting spring of joy,
  And unction from above.

3 Enlighten our dark souls, till they
  Thy sacred love embrace;
Assist our minds, by nature frail,
  With thy celestial grace.

4 Teach us the Father to confess,
  And Son, from death revived,
And thee, with both, O Holy Ghost,
  Who art from both derived.

BOARDMAN. C. M.   Templi Carmina.

1. Why should the chil-dren of a King Go mourn-ing all their days?

Great Com - fort - er! de - scend, and bring Some to - kens of thy grace.

215.

1 Why should the children of a King
  Go mourning all their days?
  Great Comforter! descend, and bring
    Some tokens of thy grace.

2 Dost thou not dwell in all the saints,
  And seal the heirs of heaven?
  When wilt thou banish my complaints,
    And show my sins forgiven?

3 Assure my conscience of her part
  In the Redeemer's blood;
  And bear thy witness with my heart
    That I am born of God.

4 Thou art the earnest of his love,
  The pledge of joys to come;
  And thy soft wings, celestial Dove,
    Will safe convey me home.

216.

1 Enthroned on high, Almighty Lord!
  The Holy Ghost send down;
  Fulfill in us thy faithful word,
    And all thy mercies crown.

2 Though on our heads no tongues of fire
  Their wondrous powers impart,
  Grant, Saviour, what we more desire,
    Thy Spirit in our heart.

3 Spirit of life, and light, and love,
  Thy heavenly influence give;
  Quicken our souls, our guilt remove,
    That we in Christ may live.

4 To our benighted minds reveal
  The glories of his grace,
  And bring us where no clouds conceal
    The brightness of his face.

5 His love within us shed abroad,
  Life's ever-springing well;
  Till God in us, and we in God,
    In love eternal dwell.

217.

1 Spirit of power and might, behold
  A world by sin destroyed!
  Creator Spirit, as of old,
    Move on the formless void.

2 Give thou the word: that healing sound
  Shall quell the deadly strife,
  And earth again, like Eden crowned,
    Produce the tree of life.

3 If sang the morning stars for joy
  When nature rose to view,
  What strains will angel harps employ
    When thou shalt all renew!

4 And if the sons of God rejoice
  To hear a Saviour's name,
  How will the ransomed raise their voice,
    To whom that Saviour came!

5 Lo! every kindred, tongue, and tribe,
  Assembling round the throne,
  The new creation shall ascribe
    To sovereign love alone.

HAYDN. S. M. *Arranged from* HAYDN.

1. Come, Ho - ly Spi - rit, come; Let thy bright beams a - rise;

Dis - pel the sor - row from our minds, The dark - ness from our eyes.

218.

2 Convince us of our sin;
  Then lead to Jesus' blood,
And to our wondering view reveal
  The mercies of our God.

3 Revive our drooping faith,
  Our doubts and fears remove,
And kindle in our breasts the flame
  Of never-dying love.

4 'T is thine to cleanse the heart,
  To sanctify the soul,
To pour fresh life in every part,
  And new-create the whole.

5 Come, Holy Spirit, come;
  Our minds from bondage free;
Then shall we know, and praise, and love,
  The Father, Son, and thee.

219.

1 LORD God, the Holy Ghost!
  In this accepted hour,
As on the day of Pentecost
  Descend in all thy power!

2 We meet with one accord
  In our appointed place,
And wait the promise of our Lord,
  The Spirit of all grace.

3 Like mighty rushing wind
  Upon the waves beneath,
Move with one impulse every mind,
  One soul, one feeling breathe.

4 The young, the old inspire
  With wisdom from above;
And give us hearts and tongues of fire
  To pray, and praise, and love.

5 Spirit of light, explore,
  And chase our gloom away,
With lustre shining more and more
  Unto the perfect day.

6 Spirit of truth, be thou
  In life and death our guide;
O Spirit of adoption, now
  May we be sanctified.

220.

1 BLEST Comforter divine!
  Let rays of heavenly love
Amid our gloom and darkness shine,
  And guide our souls above.

2 Turn us, with gentle voice,
  From every sinful way,
And bid the mourning saint rejoice,
  Though earthly joys decay.

3 By thine inspiring breath
  Make every cloud of care,
And ev'n the gloomy vale of death,
  A smile of glory wear.

4 Oh! fill thou every heart
  With love to all our race;
Great Comforter, to us impart
  These blessings of thy grace.

HORTON. 7s.   *German.*

1. Gra-cious Spi-rit, Love di-vine! Let thy light with-in me shine;

All my guilt-y fears re-move, Fill me full of heaven and love.

221.

1 GRACIOUS Spirit, Love divine!
Let thy light within me shine;
All my guilty fears remove,
Fill me full of heaven and love.

2 Speak thy pardoning grace to me,
Set the burdened sinner free;
Lead me to the Lamb of God,
Wash me in his precious blood.

3 Life and peace to me impart,
Seal salvation on my heart;
Breathe thyself into my breast,—
Earnest of immortal rest.

4 Let me never from thee stray,
Keep me in the narrow way;
Fill my soul with joy divine,
Keep me, Lord! forever thine.

222.

1 HOLY Spirit! Lord of light!
From thy clear celestial height,
Come, thou Light of all that live!
Thy pure beaming radiance give!

2 Come, thou Father of the poor!
Come with treasures which endure;
Thou, of all consolers best,
Visiting the troubled breast.

3 Thou in toil art comfort sweet;
Pleasant coolness in the heat;
Solace in the midst of woe;
Dost refreshing peace bestow.

4 Light immortal! light divine!
Visit thou these hearts of thine;
If thou take thy grace away,
Nothing pure in man will stay.

5 Heal our wounds—our strength renew;
On our dryness pour thy dew;
Wash the stains of guilt away;
Guide the steps that go astray.

6 Give us comfort when we die;
Give us life with thee on high;
In thy sevenfold gifts descend;
Give us joys which never end.

223.

1 HOLY GHOST! with light divine,
Shine upon this heart of mine;
Chase the shades of night away,
Turn my darkness into day.

2 Holy Ghost! with power divine,
Cleanse this guilty heart of mine;
Long hath sin, without control,
Held dominion o'er my soul.

3 Holy Ghost! with joy divine,
Cheer this saddened heart of mine;
Bid my many woes depart,
Heal my wounded, bleeding heart.

4 Holy Spirit! all-divine,
Dwell within this heart of mine;
Cast down every idol-throne,
Reign supreme—and reign alone.

WINDHAM. L. M.   Daniel Read.

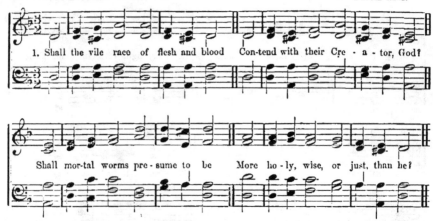

1. Shall the vile race of flesh and blood   Con-tend with their Cre - a - tor, God?

Shall mor-tal worms pre - sume to be   More ho - ly, wise, or just, than he?

224.

2 Behold! he puts his trust in none
Of all the spirits round his throne;
Their natures, when compared with his,
Are neither holy, just, nor wise.

3 But how much meaner things are they
Who spring from dust, and dwell in clay;
Touched by the finger of thy wrath,
We faint and vanish like the moth.

4 From night to day, from day to night,
We die by thousands in thy sight;
Buried in dust whole nations lie,
Like a forgotten vanity.

5 Almighty Power, to thee we bow;
How frail are we! how glorious thou!
No more the sons of earth shall dare
With an eternal God compare.

225.

1 Lord, I am vile, conceived in sin,
And born unholy and unclean;
Sprung from the man, whose guilty fall
Corrupts the race, and taints us all.

2 Soon as we draw our infant breath,
The seeds of sin grow up for death:
Thy law demands a perfect heart—
But we're defiled in every part.

3 Great God! create my heart anew,
And form my spirit pure and true;
No outward rites can make me clean,—
The leprosy lies deep within.

4 No bleeding bird, nor bleeding beast,
Nor hyssop branch, nor sprinkling priest,
Nor running brook, nor flood, nor sea,
Can wash the dismal stain away.

5 Jesus, my God, thy blood alone,
Hath power sufficient to atone:
Thy blood can make me white as snow,
No Jewish types could cleanse me so.

6 While guilt disturbs and breaks my peace,
Nor flesh nor soul hath rest or ease;
Lord, let me hear thy pardoning voice,
And make my broken bones rejoice.

226.

1 Broad is the road that leads to death,
And thousands walk together there;
But wisdom shows a narrow path,
With here and there a traveler.

2 "Deny thyself and take thy cross,"—
Is the Redeemer's great command:
Nature must count her gold but dross,
If she would gain this heavenly land.

3 The fearful soul that tires and faints,
And walks the ways of God no more,
Is but esteemed almost a saint,
And makes his own destruction sure.

4 Lord! let not all my hopes be vain:
Create my heart entirely new:
Which hypocrites could ne'er attain,
Which false apostates never knew.

MALVERN. L. M.

Dr. L. Mason.

1. Je-sus, en-grave it on my heart, That thou the one thing need-ful art;

I could from all things part-ed be, But nev-er, nev-er, Lord, from thee.

227.

2 Needful is thy most precious blood,
To reconcile my soul to God ;
Needful is thy indulgent care ;
Needful thy all-prevailing prayer.

3 Needful thy presence, dearest Lord,
True peace and comfort to afford ;
Needful thy promise, to impart
Fresh life and vigor to my heart.

4 Needful art thou, my guide, my stay,
Through all life's dark and weary way ;
Nor less in death thou 'lt needful be,
To bring my spirit home to thee.

5 Then needful still, my God, my King,
Thy name eternally I 'll sing !
Glory and praise be ever his,
The one thing needful Jesus is !

228.

1 How shall the sons of men appear,
Great God ! before thine awful bar ?
How may the guilty hope to find
Acceptance with th' eternal Mind ?

2 Not vows, nor groans, nor broken cries,
Not the most costly sacrifice,
Not infant blood, profusely spilt,
Will expiate a sinner's guilt.

3 Thy blood, dear Jesus, thine alone,
Hath sovereign virtue to atone :
Here will we rest our only plea,
When we approach, Great God ! to thee.

229.

1 What shall the dying sinner do,
That seeks relief for all his woe ?
Where shall the guilty conscience find
Ease for the torment of the mind ?

2 In vain we search, in vain we try,
Till Jesus brings his gospel nigh !
'T is there the power and glory dwell,
That save rebellious souls from hell.

3 This is the pillar of our hope,
That bears our fainting spirits up ;
We read the grace, we trust the word,
And find salvation in the Lord.

230.

1 Like morning, when her early breeze
Breaks up the surface of the seas,
That, in their furrows, dark with night,
Her hand may sow the seeds of light,—

2 Thy grace can send its breathings o'er
The spirit dark and lost before ;
And, freshening all its depths, prepare
For truth divine to enter there.

3 Till David touched his sacred lyre,
In silence lay the unbreathing wire ;
But when he swept its chords along,
Then angels stooped to hear the song.

4 So sleeps the soul, till thou, O Lord,
Shalt deign to touch its lifeless chord ;
Till, waked by thee, its breath shall rise
In music worthy of the skies.

MONSON. C. M.   BROWN.

1. How help-less guilt-y na-ture lies, Un-con-scious of its load!

The heart, un-changed, can nev-er rise To hap-pi-ness and God.

231.

1 How helpless guilty nature lies,
   Unconscious of its load !
The heart, unchanged, can never rise
   To happiness and God.

2 Can aught, beneath a power divine,
   The stubborn will subdue ?
'T is thine, almighty Spirit ! thine,
   To form the heart anew.

3 'T is thine, the passions to recall,
   And upward bid them rise ;
To make the scales of error fall,
   From reason's darkened eyes ;—

4 To chase the shades of death away,
   And bid the sinner live ;
A beam of heaven, a vital ray,
   'T is thine alone to give.

5 Oh ! change these wretched hearts of ours,
   And give them life divine ;
Then shall our passions and our powers,
   Almighty Lord, be thine.

232.

1 Is vain we seek for peace with God
   By methods of our own :
Nothing, O Saviour ! but thy blood
   Can bring us near the throne.

2 The threatenings of the broken law
   Impress the soul with dread :
If God his sword of vengeance draw,
   It strikes the spirit dead.

3 But thine illustrious sacrifice
   Hath answered these demands ;
And peace and pardon from the skies
   Are offered by thy hands.

4 'T is by thy death we live, O Lord !
   'T is on thy cross we rest :
Forever be thy love adored,
   Thy name forever blessed.

233.

1 LORD, how secure my conscience was,
   And felt no inward dread !
I was alive without the law,
   And thought my sins were dead.

2 My hopes of heaven were firm and bright ;
   But since the precept came
With a convincing power and light,
   I find how vile I am.

3 My guilt appeared but small before,
   Till terribly I saw
How perfect, holy, just, and pure,
   Is thine eternal law.

4 Then felt my soul the heavy load ;
   My sins revived again :
I had provoked a dreadful God,
   And all my hopes were slain.

5 My God, I cry with every breath
   For some kind power to save,
To break the yoke of sin and death,
   And thus redeem the slave.

HUMMEL. C. M. ZEUNER.

1. Not all the out-ward forms on earth, Nor rites that God has given,

Nor will of man, nor blood, nor birth, Can raise a soul to heaven.

234.

2 The sovereign will of God alone
Creates us heirs of grace;
Born in the image of his Son,
A new, peculiar race.

3 The Spirit, like some heavenly wind,
Breathes on the sons of flesh,
New-models all the carnal mind,
And forms the man afresh.

4 Our quickened souls awake and rise
From the long sleep of death;
On heavenly things we fix our eyes,
And praise employs our breath.

235.

1 How sad our state by nature is!
Our sin—how deep it stains!
And Satan holds our captive minds
Fast in his slavish chains.

2 But there's a voice of sovereign grace
Sounds from the sacred word:
"Ho! ye despairing sinners, come,
And trust a pardoning Lord."

3 My soul obeys th' almighty call,
And runs to this relief;
I would believe thy promise, Lord:
Oh, help my unbelief!

4 A guilty, weak, and helpless worm,
On thy kind arms I fall:
Be thou my Strength and Righteousness,
My Saviour and my All.

236.

1 VAIN are the hopes, the sons of men
On their own works have built;—
Their hearts, by nature, all unclean,
And all their actions, guilt.

2 Let Jew and Gentile stop their mouths,
Without a murmuring word;
And the whole race of Adam stand
Guilty before the Lord.

3 In vain we ask God's righteous law
To justify us now;
Since to convince, and to condemn,
Is all the law can do.

4 Jesus! how glorious is thy grace;—
When in thy name we trust,
Our faith receives a righteousness,
That makes the sinner just.

237.

1 STRAIT is the way, the door is strait,
That leads to joys on high;
'T is but a few that find the gate,
While crowds mistake and die.

2 Belovéd self must be denied,
The mind and will renewed,
Passion suppressed, and patience tried,
And vain desires subdued.

3 Lord! can a feeble, helpless worm,
Fulfill a task so hard?
Thy grace must all my work perform,
And give the free reward.

SHAWMUT. S. M.　　　　　　　　　　　　　　　Dr. L. Mason.

1. My form-er hopes are fled, My ter-ror now be-gins;

I feel, a-las! that I am dead In tres-pass-es and sins.

* The small notes are for the Organ.

238.

1 My former hopes are fled,
　My terror now begins;
　I feel, alas! that I am dead
　In trespasses and sins.

2 Ah! whither shall I fly?
　I hear the thunder roar;
　The law proclaims destruction nigh,
　And vengeance at the door.

3 When I review my ways,
　I dread impending doom;
　But sure a friendly whisper says—
　" Flee from the wrath to come."

4 I see, or think I see,
　A glimmering from afar;
　A beam of day that shines for me
　To save me from despair.

5 Forerunner of the sun,
　It marks the pilgrim's way;
　I 'll gaze upon it while I run,
　And watch the rising day.

239.

1 Ah! how shall fallen man
　Be just before his God?
　If he contend in righteousness,
　We fall beneath his rod.

2 If he our ways should mark,
　With strict inquiring eyes,
　Could we, for one of thousand faults,
　A just excuse devise?

3 All-seeing, powerful God!
　Who can with thee contend?
　Or who, that tries th' unequal strife,
　Shall prosper in the end?

4 The mountains, in thy wrath,
　Their ancient seats forsake;
　The trembling earth deserts her place.
　Her rooted pillars shake.

5 Ah! how shall guilty man
　Contend with such a God?
　None—none can meet him, and escape,
　But through the Saviour's blood.

240.

1 Can sinners hope for heaven,
　Who love this world so well?
　Or dream of future happiness,
　While on the road to hell?

2 Shall they hosannas sing,
　With an unhallowed tongue?
　Shall palms adorn the guilty hand
　Which does its neighbor wrong?

3 Can sin's deceitful way
　Conduct to Zion's hill?
　Or those expect with God to reign
　Who disregard his will?

4 Thy grace, O God, alone,
　Good hope can e'er afford!
　The pardoned and the pure shall see
　The glory of the Lord.

CAPELLO. S. M.

CANTICA LAUDIS.

1. Did Christ o'er sin - ners weep, And shall our cheeks be dry?

Let floods of pen - i - ten - tial grief Burst forth from ev - ery eye.

241.

2 The Son of God in tears,
Angels with wonder see!
Be thou astonished, O my soul,
He shed those tears for thee.

3 He wept that we might weep;
Each sin demands a tear;
In heaven alone no sin is found,
And there's no weeping there.

242.

1 How heavy is the night
That hangs upon our eyes,
Till Christ with his reviving light
Over our souls arise!

2 Our guilty spirits dread
To meet the wrath of heaven;
But, in his righteousness arrayed,
We see our sins forgiven.

3 Unholy and impure
Are all our thoughts and ways:
His hands infected nature cure
With sanctifying grace.

4 The powers of hell agree
To hold our souls in vain;
He sets the sons of bondage free,
And breaks the cursed chain.

5 Lord, we adore thy ways
To bring us near to God,
Thy sovereign power, thy healing grace,
And thine atoning blood.

243.

1 Is this the kind return?
Are these the thanks we owe!
Thus to abuse eternal love,
Whence all our blessings flow!

2 To what a stubborn frame
Hath sin reduced our mind!
What strange, rebellious wretches we,—
And God as strangely kind!

3 Turn, turn us, mighty God!
And mould our souls afresh;
Break, sovereign grace! these hearts of
stone,
And give us hearts of flesh.

244.

1 Astonished and distressed,
I turn mine eyes within;
My heart with loads of guilt oppressed,
The seat of every sin.

2 What crowds of evil thoughts,
What vile affections there!
Distrust, presumption, artful guile,
Pride, envy, slavish fear!

3 Almighty King of saints!
These hateful sins subdue;
Dispel the darkness from my mind,
And all my powers renew.

4 This done,—my cheerful voice
Shall loud hosannas raise;
My soul shall glow with gratitude,—
My lips pronounce thy praise.

COWPER. C. M.   Dr. L. Mason.

1. There is a foun-tain filled with blood, Drawn from Immanuel's veins; And sinners, plunged beneath that flood, Lose all their guilt-y stains, Lose all their guilt-y stains.

245.

2 The dying thief rejoiced to see
That fountain in his day;
And there may I, as vile as he,
Wash all my sins away.

3 Dear, dying Lamb, thy precious blood
Shall never lose its power,
Till all the ransomed church of God
Be saved, to sin no more.

4 E'er since, by faith, I saw the stream
Thy flowing wounds supply,
Redeeming love has been my theme,
And shall be, till I die.

5 Then in a nobler, sweeter song,
I'll sing thy power to save,
When this poor, lisping, stammering
tongue
Lies silent in the grave.

246.

1 Come, happy souls, approach your God
With new, melodious songs;
Come, render to almighty Grace
The tribute of your tongues.

2 So strange, so boundless was the love
That pitied dying men,
The Father sent his equal Son
To give them life again.

3 Thy hands, dear Jesus, were not armed
With a revenging rod;
No hard commission to perform
The vengeance of a God.

4 But all was merciful and mild,
And wrath forsook the throne,
When Christ on the kind errand came,
And brought salvation down.

5 Here, sinners, come and heal your wounds;
Come, wipe your sorrows dry:
Come, trust the mighty Saviour's name,
And you shall never die.

6 See, dearest Lord, our willing souls
Accept thine offered grace;
We bless the great Redeemer's love,
And give the Father praise.

247.

1 O Lord, how infinite thy love!
How wondrous are thy ways!
Let earth beneath, and heaven above,
Combine to sing thy praise.

2 Man in immortal beauty shone,
Thy noblest work below;
Too soon by sin made heir alone
To death and endless woe.

3 Then, "Lo! I come," the Saviour said:
Oh, be his name adored,
Who, with his blood, our ransom paid,
And life and bliss restored!

4 O Lord, how infinite thy love!
How wondrous are thy ways!
Let earth beneath, and heaven above,
Combine to sing thy praise.

GLASGOW. C. M.

ROOT & SWEETSER'S COLL.

1. Great God! when I ap-proach thy throne, And all thy glo-ry see,

This is my stay, and this a-lone, That Je-sus died for me.

248.

2 How can a soul condemned to die
Escape the just decree?
Helpless and full of sin am I,
But Jesus died for me.

3 Burdened with sin's oppressive chain,
Oh! how can I get free?
No peace can all my efforts gain,
But Jesus died for me.

4 My anxious heart no joy could cheer,
On life's tempestuous sea;
Did not this truth relieve my fear,
That Jesus died for me.

5 And, Lord, when I behold thy face,
This must be all my plea;
Save me by thine almighty grace,
For Jesus died for me.

249.

1 Oh! what amazing words of grace
Are in the Gospel found,
Suited to every sinner's case
Who hears the joyful sound!

2 Come, then, with all your wants and
wounds,
Your every burden bring;
Here love, unchanging love, abounds—
A deep, celestial spring.

3 This spring with living water flows,
And heavenly joy imparts;
Come, thirsty souls! your wants disclose,
And drink, with thankful hearts.

250.

1 SALVATION!—oh, the joyful sound!
'T is pleasure to our ears;
A sovereign balm for every wound,
A cordial for our fears.

2 Buried in sorrow and in sin,
At hell's dark door we lay;—
But we arise by grace divine,
To see a heavenly day.

3 Salvation!—let the echo fly
The spacious earth around;
While all the armies of the sky
Conspire to raise the sound.

251.

1 JESUS,—and didst thou leave the sky,
To bear our griefs and woes?
And didst thou bleed and groan and die
For thy rebellious foes?

2 Well might the heavens with wonder view
A love so strange as thine!
No thought of angels ever knew
Compassion so divine!

3 Is there a heart that will not bend
To thy divine control?
Descend, O sovereign love, descend,
And melt that stubborn soul.

4 Oh! may our willing hearts confess
Thy sweet, thy gentle sway;
Glad captives of thy matchless grace,
Thy righteous rule obey.

BALERMA. C. M.   *Scottish.*

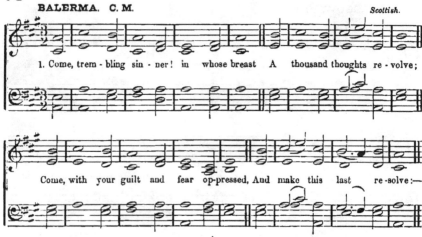

1. Come, trem - bling sin - ner! in whose breast A thousand thoughts re - volve; Come, with your guilt and fear op-pressed, And make this last re - solve:—

252.

2 " I 'll go to Jesus, though my sins
Like mountains round me close ;
I know his courts, I 'll enter in,
Whatever may oppose.

3 " Prostrate I 'll lie before his throne,
And there my guilt confess :
I 'll tell him I 'm a wretch undone,
Without his sovereign grace.

4 " Perhaps he will admit my plea,
Perhaps will hear my prayer ;
But if I perish, I will pray,
And perish only there.

5 " I can but perish if I go ;
I am resolved to try ;
For if I stay away, I know
I must forever die."

253.

1 THERE is a line, by us unseen,
That crosses every path,
The hidden boundary between
God's patience and his wrath.

2 To pass that limit is to die,
To die as if by stealth ;
It does not quench the beaming eye,
Nor pale the glow of health.

3 The conscience may be still at ease,
The spirit light and gay ,
That which is pleasing still may please,
And care be thrust away.

4 Oh ! where is this mysterious bourne
By which our path is crossed ;
Beyond which God himself hath sworn
That he who goes is lost ?

5 How far may we go on to sin ?
How long will God forbear ?
Where does hope end, and where begin
The confines of despair ?

6 An answer from the skies is sent,—
" Ye that from God depart,
While it is called to-day, repent,
And harden not your heart."

254.

1 O SINNER, bring not tears alone,
Or outward form of prayer,
But let it in thy heart be known
That penitence is there.

2 To smite the breast, the clothes to rend,
God asketh not of thee ;
Thy secret soul he bids thee bend
In true humility.

3 Oh ! let us, then, with heartfelt grief,
Draw near unto our God,
And pray to him to grant relief,
And stay the lifted rod.

4 O righteous Judge ! if thou wilt deign
To grant us what we need,
We pray for time to turn again,
And grace to turn indeed.

RETURN. C. M.

DR. HASTINGS.

1. Re-turn, O wan-derer, to thy home, Thy Fa-ther calls for thee:

No long-er now an ex-ile roam, In guilt and mis-e-ry. Re-turn, re-turn!

255.

2 Return, O wanderer, to thy home,
  'T is Jesus calls for thee;
The Spirit and the Bride say—come;
  Oh! now for refuge flee;
    Return, return!

3 Return, O wanderer, to thy home,
  'T is madness to delay;
There are no pardons in the tomb,
  And brief is mercy's day:
    Return, return!

256.

1 RETURN, O wanderer, now return,
  And seek thy Father's face!
Those new desires, which in thee burn,
  Were kindled by his grace.

2 Return, O wanderer, now return!
  He hears thy humble sigh;
He sees thy softened spirit mourn,
  When no one else is nigh.

3 Return, O wanderer, now return!
  Thy Saviour bids thee live:
Go to his bleeding feet, and learn
  How freely he'll forgive.

4 Return, O wanderer, now return,
  And wipe the falling tear!
Thy Father calls—no longer mourn:
  His love invites thee near.

257.

1 COME to the ark, come to the ark;
  To Jesus come away:
The pestilence walks forth by night,
  The arrow flies by day.

2 Come to the ark: the waters rise,
  The seas their billows rear;
While darkness gathers o'er the skies,
  Behold a refuge near!

3 Come to the ark, all, all that weep
  Beneath the sense of sin:
Without, deep calleth unto deep,
  But all is peace within.

4 Come to the ark, ere yet the flood
  Your lingering steps oppose;
Come, for the door which open stood
  Is now about to close.

258.

1 WHEN rising from the bed of death
  O'erwhelmed with guilt and fear,
I see my Maker face to face—
  Oh! how shall I appear!

2 E'en now, while pardon may be found
  And mercy may be sought,
My heart with inward horror shrinks,
  And trembles at the thought.

3 When thou, O Lord! shalt stand disclosed
  In majesty severe,
And sit in judgment on my soul,
  Oh! how shall I appear!

BERA. L. M.　　　　　　　　　　　　　ROOT & SWEETSER'S COLL.

1. Why will ye waste on tri - fling cares That life which God's com-pas- sion spares?

While, in the va - rious range of thought, The one thing need- ful is for - got!

259.

1 Why will ye waste on trifling cares
That life which God's compassion spares?
While, in the various range of thought,
The one thing needful is forgot?

2 Shall God invite you from above?
Shall Jesus urge his dying love?
Shall troubled conscience give you pain?
And all these pleas unite in vain?

3 Not so your eyes will always view
Those objects which you now pursue:
Not so will heaven and hell appear,
When death's decisive hour is near.

4 Almighty God! thy grace impart;
Fix deep conviction on each heart;
Nor let us waste on trifling cares
That life which thy compassion spares.

260.

1 While life prolongs its precious light,
Mercy is found, and peace is given;
But soon, ah! soon, approaching night
Shall blot out every hope of heaven.

2 While God invites, how blest the day!
How sweet the gospel's charming sound!
Come, sinners, haste, oh, haste away,
While yet a pardoning God is found.

3 Soon, borne on time's most rapid wing,
Shall death command you to the grave,
Before his bar your spirits bring,
And none be found to hear or save.

4 In that lone land of deep despair
No Sabbath's heavenly light shall rise;
No God regard your bitter prayer,
Nor Saviour call you to the skies.

5 Now God invites—how blest the day!
How sweet the gospel's charming sound!
Come, sinners, haste, oh, haste away,
While yet a pardoning God is found.

261.

1 Say, sinner! hath a voice within
Oft whispered to thy secret soul,
Urged thee to leave the ways of sin,
And yield thy heart to God's control?

2 Sinner! it was a heavenly voice,—
It was the Spirit's gracious call;
It bade thee make the better choice,
And haste to seek in Christ thine all.

3 Spurn not the call to life and light;
Regard, in time, the warning kind;
That call thou may'st not always slight,
And yet the gate of mercy find.

4 God's Spirit will not always strive
With hardened, self-destroying man;
Ye who persist his love to grieve,
May never hear his voice again.

5 Sinner! perhaps, this very day,
Thy last accepted time may be:
Oh! shouldst thou grieve him now away,
Then hope may never beam on thee.

DESIRE. L. M.

1. Come, wea-ry souls, with sin distressed, Come, and ac-cept the promised rest;

The Saviour's gra-cious call o-bey, And cast your gloom-y fears a-way.

262.

2 Oppressed with guilt,—a painful load,—
Oh, come and bow before your God!
Divine compassion, mighty love
Will all the painful load remove.

3 Here mercy's boundless ocean flows,
To cleanse your guilt and heal your woes;
Pardon, and life, and endless peace—
How rich the gift, how free the grace!

4 Dear Saviour! let thy powerful love
Confirm our faith, our fears remove;
Oh, sweetly reign in every breast,
And guide us to eternal rest.

263.

1 "Come hither, all ye weary souls;
Ye heavy-laden sinners, come!
I 'll give you rest from all your toils,
And raise you to my heavenly home.

2 "They shall find rest who learn of me:
I 'm of a meek and lowly mind;
But passion rages like the sea,
And pride is restless as the wind.

3 "Blest is the man whose shoulders take
My yoke, and bear it with delight:
My yoke is easy to his neck,
My grace shall make the burden light."

4 Jesus, we come at thy command;
With faith, and hope, and humble zeal;
Resign our spirits to thy hand,
To mould and guide us at thy will.

264.

1 Behold a Stranger at the door:
He gently knocks, has knocked before;
Has waited long, is waiting still:
You treat no other friend so ill.

2 Oh, lovely attitude! he stands
With melting heart and open hands:
Oh, matchless kindness!—and he shows
This matchless kindness to his foes!

3 Rise, touched with gratitude divine,
Turn out his enemy and thine;
Turn out thy soul-enslaving sin,
And let the heavenly stranger in.

4 Oh, welcome him, the Prince of Peace!
Now may his gentle reign increase!
Throw wide the door, each willing mind;
And be his empire all mankind.

265.

1 Ho! every one that thirsts! draw nigh;
'T is God invites the fallen race;
Mercy and free salvation buy,
Buy wine, and milk, and gospel grace.

2 Ye nothing in exchange can give,—
Leave all ye have, and are, behind;
Freely the gift of God receive,
Pardon and peace in Jesus find.

3 Come to the living waters, come;
Sinners! obey your Maker's voice;
Return, ye weary wanderers! home,
And in redeeming love rejoice.

OLMUTZ. S. M.

Arranged by Dr. L. Mason.

1. Come to the land of peace; From shadows come a - way;

Where all the sounds of weep-ing cease, And storms no more have sway.

266.

2 Fear hath no dwelling here;
But pure repose and love
Breathe through the bright celestial air
The spirit of the dove.

3 Come to the bright and blest,
Gathered from every land;
For here thy soul shall find its rest,
Amid the shining band.

4 In this divine abode
Change leaves no saddening trace;
Come, trusting spirit, to thy God,
Thy holy resting-place.

267.

1 The Spirit, in our hearts,
Is whispering, " Sinner, come ;"
The bride, the church of Christ, proclaims
To all his children, "Come !"

2 Let him that heareth say
To all about him, "Come !"
Let him that thirsts for righteousness,
To Christ, the fountain, come !

3 Yes, whosoever will,
Oh ! let him freely come,
And freely drink the stream of life ;
'T is Jesus bids him come.

4 Lo ! Jesus, who invites,
Declares, "I quickly come :"
Lord, even so ! we wait thine hour ;
O blest Redeemer, come !

268.

1 My Father bids me come,
Oh ! why do I delay ?
He calls the wandering spirit home,
And yet from him I stay.

2 Father, the hindrance show,
Which I have failed to see ;
And let me now consent to know
What keeps me far from thee.

3 Searcher of hearts ! in mine
Thy trying powers display ;
Into its darkest corners shine—
Take every vail away.

4 In me the hindrance lies ;
The fatal bar remove,
And let me see, in sweet surprise,
Thy full redeeming love.

269.

1 And canst thou, sinner ! slight
The call of love divine ?
Shall God, with tenderness invite,
And gain no thought of thine ?

2 Wilt thou not cease to grieve
The Spirit from thy breast,
Till he thy wretched soul shall leave
With all thy sins oppressed ?

3 To-day, a pardoning God
Will hear the suppliant pray ;
To-day, a Saviour's cleansing blood
Will wash thy guilt away.

WANDERER. S. M.   J. P. HOLBROOK.

1. Oh! where shall rest be found— Rest for the wea-ry soul?....

'T were vain the o - cean depths to sound, Or pierce to ei - ther pole.....

270.

1 Oh! where shall rest be found—
   Rest for the weary soul?
   'T were vain the ocean depths to sound,
   Or pierce to either pole.

2 The world ean never give
   The bliss for which we sigh :
   'T is not the whole of life to live,
   Nor all of death to die.

3 Beyond this vale of tears
   There is a life above,
   Unmeasured by the flight of years ;
   And all that life is love.

4 There is a death whose pang
   Outlasts the fleeting breath :
   Oh, what eternal horrors hang
   Around the second death !

5 Lord God of truth and grace !
   Teach us that death to shun ;
   Lest we be banished from thy face,
   And evermore undone.

271.

1 THOU Judge of quick and dead,
   Before whose bar severe,
   With holy joy, or guilty dread,
   We all shall soon appear :—

2 Our cautioned souls prepare
   For that tremendous day ;
   Oh! fill us now with watchful care,
   And stir us up to pray.

3 To damp our earthly joys,
   To wake our gracious fears,
   Forever let th' archangel's voice
   Be sounding in our ears.

4 The solemn, midnight cry—
   " Ye dead, the Judge is come !
   Arise, and meet him in the sky,
   And meet your instant doom !"

5 Oh! may we thus be found,
   Obedient to thy word ;
   Attentive to the trumpet's sound,
   And looking for our Lord !

272.

1 Now is th' accepted time,
   Now is the day of grace ;
   O'sinners ! come, without delay,
   And seek the Saviour's face.

2 Now is th' accepted time,
   The Saviour calls to-day ;
   To-morrow it may be too late ;—
   Then why should you delay ?

3 Now is th' accepted time,
   The gospel bids you come ;
   And every promise, in his word,
   Declares there yet is room.

4 Lord ! draw reluctant souls,
   And melt them by thy love ;
   Then will the angels speed their way,
   To bear the news above.

MARTYN. 7s. Double.   MARSH.

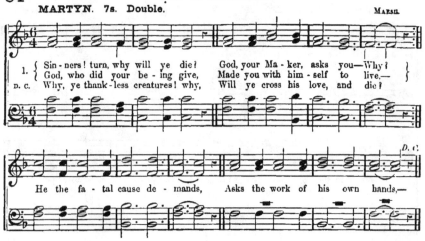

1. { Sin - ners ! turn, why will ye die?   God, your Ma - ker, asks you—Why ?
   { God, who did your be - ing give,   Made you with him - self to live.—
D. C. Why, ye thank - less creatures ! why, Will ye cross his love, and die ?

He the fa - tal cause de - mands, Asks the work of his own hands,—

273.

2 Sinners, turn, why will ye die ?
God, your Saviour, asks you—Why ?
He who did your souls retrieve,
Died himself, that ye might live.
Will ye let him die in vain ?
Crucify your Lord again ?
Why, ye ransomed sinners, why
Will ye slight his grace, and die ?

3 Sinners, turn, why will ye die ?
God, the Spirit, asks you—Why ?
He, who all your lives hath strove,
Urged you to embrace his love :
Will ye not his grace receive ?
Will ye still refuse to live ?
O ye dying sinners ! why,
Why will ye forever die ?

274.

1 Pilgrim, burdened with thy sin,
Come the way to Zion's gate ;
There, till mercy speaks within,
Knock, and weep, and watch, and wait :
Knock—he knows the sinner's cry ;
Weep—he loves the mourner's tears ;
Watch, for saving grace is nigh ;
Wait, till heavenly grace appears.

2 Hark ! it is the Saviour's voice,
" Welcome, pilgrim, to thy rest."
Now within the gate rejoice,
Safe, and owned, and bought, and blest :

Safe, from all the lures of vice ;
Owned, by joys the contrite know ;
Bought by love, and life the price ;
Blest, the mighty debt to owe.

3 Holy pilgrim ! what for thee
In a world like this remains ?
From thy guarded breast shall flee
Fear, and shame, and doubts, and pains :
Fear—the hope of heaven shall fly,
Shame, from glory's view retire ;
Doubt, in full belief, shall die,
Pain, in endless bliss, expire.

275.

1 Sinner, art thou still secure ?
Wilt thou still refuse to pray !
Can thy heart or hands endure
In the Lord's avenging day ?
See his mighty arm made bare !
Awful terrors clothe his brow !
For his judgment now prepare,
Thou must either break or bow.

2 At his presence nature shakes,
Earth affrighted hastes to flee ;
Solid mountains melt like wax,
What will then become of thee ?
Who his coming may abide ?
You that glory in your shame,
Will you find a place to hide
When the world is wrapt in flame ?

HORTON. 7s. *German.*

1. Come! said Je-sus' sa-cred voice; Come and make my paths your choice;

I will guide you to your home, Wea-ry wanderer! hith-er come.

276.

2 Thou, who homeless and forlorn,
Long hast borne the proud world's scorn,
Long hast roamed the barren waste,
Weary wanderer, hither haste.

3 Ye, who tossed on beds of pain
Seek for ease, but seek in vain;
Ye, by fiercer anguish torn,
In remorse for guilt who mourn :—

4 Hither come, for here is found
Balm that flows for every wound!
Peace, that ever shall endure,
Rest eternal, sacred, sure.

277.

1 WEARY sinner! keep thine eyes
On th' atoning Sacrifice;
View him bleeding on the tree,
Pouring out his life for thee.

2 Surely Christ thy griefs hath borne;
Weeping soul, no longer mourn :
Now by faith the Son embrace,
· Plead his promise, trust his grace.

3 Cast thy guilty soul on him;
Find him mighty to redeem :
At his feet thy burden lay;
Look thy doubts and care away.

4 Lord, come thou with power to heal!
Now thy mighty arm reveal :
At thy feet myself I lay;
Take, oh, take my sins away!

278.

1 HASTEN, sinner! to be wise,
Stay not for the morrow's sun :
Wisdom, if you still despise,
Harder is it to be won.

2 Hasten mercy to implore,
Stay not for the morrow's sun,
Lest thy season should be o'er,
Ere this evening's stage be run.

3 Hasten, sinner! to return,
Stay not for the morrow's sun,
Lest thy lamp should cease to burn,
Ere salvation's work is done.

4 Hasten, sinner! to be blest,
Stay not for the morrow's sun,
Lest perdition thee arrest,
Ere the morrow is begun.

279.

1 BROTHER, hast thou wandered far
From thy Father's happy home,
With thyself and God at war?
Turn thee, brother; homeward come.

2 Hast thou wasted all the powers
God for noble uses gave?
Squandered life's most golden hours?
Turn thee, brother; God can save.

3 He can heal thy bitterest wound,
He thy gentlest prayer can hear:
Seek him, for he may be found;
Call upon him; he is near.

AVA. P. M.

DR. HASTINGS.

1. { Child of sin and sor-row, Filled with dismay, }
   { Wait not for to-mor-row, Yield thee to-day ; } Heav'n bids thee come,While yet there's
   D. C. Child of sin and sor-row, Hear, and o-bey.   [room,

280.

2 Child of sin and sorrow,
  Why wilt thou die ?
Come while thou canst borrow
  Help from on high :
  Grieve not that love
  Which from above,
Child of sin and sorrow,
  Would bring thee nigh.

3 Child of sin and sorrow,
  Thy moments glide,
Like the flitting arrow,
  Or the rushing tide ;
  Ere time is o'er,
  Heaven's grace implore ;
Child of sin and sorrow,
  In Christ confide.

EXPOSTULATION. 11s.

1. Oh ! turn ye, oh ! turn ye, for why will ye die,When God in great mercy is com-ing so nigh!

Now Je-sus invites you, the Spirit says, Come, And angels are waiting to welcome you home.

281.

2 How vain the delusion, that while you
  delay,
Your hearts may grow better by staying
  away ;
Come wretched, come starving, come just
  as you are,
While streams of salvation are flowing
  so near.

3 And now Christ is ready your souls to
  receive,
Oh ! how can you question if you will
  believe ?
If sin is your burden, why will you not
  come ?
'T is you he bids welcome ; he bids you
  come home.

GOSHEN. 11s.

1. De - lay not, de - lay not, O sin - ner, draw near, The wa - ters of

D. S. Re - demp - tion is

FINE.

life are now flow - ing for thee; No price is de - mand - ed, the Sa - viour is here,

purchased, sal - va - tion is free!

282.

2 Delay not, delay not, why longer abuse
The love and compassion of Jesus thy God?
A fountain is opened, how canst thou
refuse
To wash and be cleansed in his pardoning
blood?

3 Delay not, delay not, O sinner, to come,
For mercy still lingers, and calls thee
to-day:

Her voice is not heard in the vale of the
tomb;
Her message unheeded will soon pass
away.

4 Delay not, delay not, the Spirit of Grace,
Long grieved and resisted, may take its
sad flight;
And leave thee in darkness to finish thy
race,
To sink in the gloom of eternity's night.

SAY, BROTHERS.

ANNIVERSARY HYMNS, S. S. U.

1. Say, brothers, will you meet us, Say, brothers, will you meet us,

Chorus. Glo - ry, glo - ry, hal - le - lu - jah, Glo - ry, glo - ry, hal - le - lu - jah,

Say, bro - thers, will you meet us, On Ca - naan's hap - py shore?

Glo - ry, glo - ry, hal - le - lu - jah, For ev - er, ev - er - more.

283.

2 By the grace of God we'll meet you,
By the grace of God we'll meet you,
By the grace of God we'll meet you,
Where parting is no more.—*Chorus.*

3 Jesus lives and reigns for ever,
Jesus lives and reigns for ever,
Jesus lives and reigns for ever,
On Canaan's happy shore.—*Chorus.*

COME, YE DISCONSOLATE.   WEBBE.

Choir.

1. Come, ye dis - con - so - late, where'er ye lan - guish; Come to the

Congregation.

mer - cy - seat, fer - vent - ly kneel; Here bring your wound - ed hearts,

here tell your an - guish, Earth has no sor - row that Heaven can - not heal.

284.

2 Joy of the comfortless, light of the straying,
Hope of the penitent, fadeless and pure;
Here speaks the Comforter, tenderly saying—
Earth has no sorrow that Heaven cannot cure.

3 Here see the Bread of Life; see waters flowing
Forth from the throne of God, pure from above;
Come to the feast prepared—come, ever knowing
Earth has no sorrow but Heaven can remove.

TO-DAY. 6s & 4s.   DR. L. MASON.

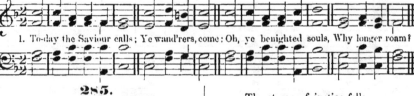

1. To-day the Saviour calls; Ye wand'rers, come: Oh, ye benighted souls, Why longer roam?

285.

2 To-day the Saviour calls;
Oh! hear him now;
Within these sacred walls
To Jesus bow.

3 To-day the Saviour calls;
For refuge fly;

The storm of justice falls,
And death is nigh.

4 The Spirit calls to-day:
Yield to his power;
Oh! grieve him not away:
'T is mercy's hour.

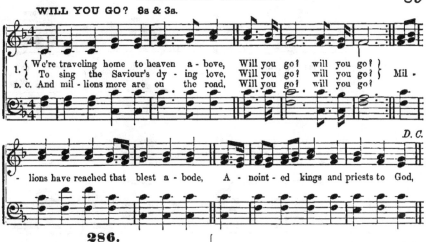

WILL YOU GO? 8s & 3s.

1. We're traveling home to heaven a-bove, Will you go? will you go?
To sing the Saviour's dy-ing love, Will you go? will you go? Mil-
D. C. And mil-lions more are on the road, Will you go? will you go?

-lions have reached that blest a-bode, A-noint-ed kings and priests to God,

286.

2 We 're going to see the bleeding Lamb,
    Will you go?
In rapturous strains to praise his name,
    Will you go?
The crown of life we there shall wear,
The conqueror's palms our hands shall bear,
And all the joys of heaven we 'll share,
    Will you go?

3 We 're going to join the heavenly choir,
    Will you go?
To raise our voice and tune the lyre,
    Will you go?
There saints and angels gladly sing
Hosanna to their God and King,
And make the heavenly arches ring,
    Will you go?

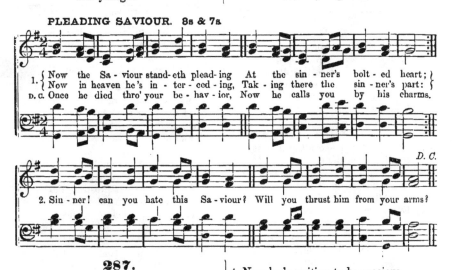

PLEADING SAVIOUR. 8s & 7s.

1. Now the Sa-viour stand-eth plead-ing At the sin-ner's bolt-ed heart;
Now in heaven he's in-ter-ced-ing, Tak-ing there the sin-ner's part:
D. C. Once he died thro' your be-hav-ior, Now he calls you by his charms.

2. Sin-ner! can you hate this Sa-viour? Will you thrust him from your arms?

287.

3 Sinner! hear your God and Saviour,
Hear his gracious voice to-day,
Turn from all your vain behavior,
Oh! repent, return and pray!

4 Now he 's waiting to be gracious,
    Now he stands and looks on thee:
See what kindness, love, and pity,
    Shine around on you and me.

NELSON. 8s, 7s & 4s.   J. P. HOLBROOK.

1. Hear, O sinner! mercy hails you; Now with sweetest voice she calls;

Bids you haste to seek the Saviour, Ere the hand of justice falls:

Hear, O sinner! Hear, O sinner! 'Tis the voice of mercy calls.

288.

2 Haste, O sinner, to the Saviour!
  Seek his mercy while you may;
Soon the day of grace is over;
  Soon your life will pass away :
    Haste, O sinner!
You must perish if you stay.

289.

1 Sinners, will you scorn the message,
  Coming from the courts above?
Mercy beams in every passage;
  Every line is full of love;
    Oh! believe it,
Every line is full of love.

2 Now, the heralds of salvation,
  Joyful news from heaven proclaim :
Sinners freed from condemnation,
  Through the all-atoning Lamb !
    Life receiving
Through the all-atoning Lamb.

3 O ye angels, hovering round us,
  Waiting spirits, speed your way;

Haste ye to the court of heaven,
  Tidings bear without delay :
    Rebel sinners
Glad the message will obey.

290.

1 Come, ye sinners, poor and wretched,
  This is your accepted hour :
Jesus ready stands to save you,
  Full of pity, love, and power :
    He is able,
He is willing; doubt no more.

2 Agonizing in the garden,
  Lo! the Saviour prostrate lies;
On the bloody tree behold him !
  Hear him cry before he dies,
    "It is finished !"
Sinners, will not this suffice ?

3 Lo! th' incarnate God ascended
  Pleads the merit of his blood ;
Venture on him, venture wholly,
  Let no other trust intrude :
    None but Jesus
Can do helpless sinners good.

NETTLETON. 8s & 7s.

FINE.

1. Come to Cal - vary's ho - ly moun - tain, Sin - ners, ru - ined by the fall!
D. C. In a full, per - pet - ual tide,.... O - pened when our Sa - viour died.

Here a pure and heal - ing foun - tain Flows to you, to me, to all—

D. C.

291.

1 COME to Calvary's holy mountain,
Sinners, ruined by the fall!
Here a pure and healing fountain
Flows to you, to me, to all,—
In a full, perpetual tide,
Opened when our Saviour died.

2 Come, in sorrow and contrition,
Wounded, impotent, and blind!
Here the guilty, free remission,
Here the troubled, peace may find;
Health this fountain will restore,
He that drinks shall thirst no more—

3 He that drinks shall live forever;
'T is a soul-renewing flood:
God is faithful ; God will never
Break his covenant in blood,
Signed when our Redeemer died,
Sealed when he was glorified.

292.

1 WHEN I view my Saviour bleeding,
For my sins, upon the tree,
Oh! how wondrous!—how exceeding
Great his love appears to me !
Floods of deep distress and anguish,
To impede his labors, came ;
Yet they all could not extinguish
Love's eternal, burning flame.

2 Now redemption is completed,
Full salvation is procured :
Death and Satan are defeated,
By the sufferings he endured.

Now the gracious Mediator,
Risen to the courts of bliss,
Claims for me, a sinful creature,
Pardon, righteousness, and peace.

3 Sure such infinite affection
Lays the highest claims to mine ;
All my powers, without exception,
Should in fervent praises join.
Jesus, fit me for thy service ;
Form me for thyself alone ;
I am thy most costly purchase ;
Take possession of thine own.

293.

1 COME, ye souls by sin afflicted,
Bowed with fruitless sorrow down,
By the perfect law convicted,
Through the cross behold the crown;
Look to Jesus ;
Mercy flows through him alone.

2 Take his easy yoke, and wear it ;
Love will make obedience sweet ;
Christ will give you strength to bear it,
While his wisdom guides your feet
Safe to glory,
Where his ransomed captives meet.

3 Sweet as home to pilgrims weary,
Light to newly-opened eyes ;
Or full springs in deserts dreary,
Is the rest the cross supplies ;
All who taste it
Shall to rest immortal rise.

WOODWORTH. L. M.   WM. B. BRADBURY.

1. Just as I am, with-out one plea, But that thy blood was shed for me, And that thou bid'st me come to thee, O Lamb of God, I come! I come!

294.

1 JUST as I am, without one plea,
But that thy blood was shed for me,
And that thou bid'st me come to thee,
O Lamb of God, I come! I come!

2 Just as I am, and waiting not
To rid my soul of one dark blot,
To thee whose blood can cleanse each spot,
O Lamb of God, I come! I come!

3 Just as I am, though tossed about
With many a conflict, many a doubt,
Fightings within, and fears without,
O Lamb of God, I come! I come!

4 Just as I am—poor, wretched, blind;
Sight, riches, healing of the mind,
Yea, all I need, in thee to find,
O Lamb of God, I come! I come!

5 Just as I am—thou wilt receive,
Wilt welcome, pardon, cleanse, relieve;
Because thy promise I believe,
O Lamb of God, I come! I come!

6 Just as I am—thy love unknown
Hath broken every barrier down;
Now, to be thine, yea, thine alone,
O Lamb of God, I come! I come!

295.

1 WITH tearful eyes I look around;
Life seems a dark and stormy sea:
Yet, 'mid the gloom, I hear a sound,
A heavenly whisper, "Come to me."

2 It tells me of a place of rest;
It tells me where my soul may flee:
Oh, to the weary, faint, oppressed,
How sweet the bidding, "Come to me!"

3 "Come, for all else must fail and die;
Earth is no resting-place for thee;
To heaven direct thy weeping eye,
I am thy portion; Come to me."

4 O voice of mercy! voice of love!
In conflict, grief, and agony,
Support me, cheer me from above!
And gently whisper, "Come to me."

296.

1 GOD of my life! thy boundless grace,
Chose, pardoned, and adopted me;
My rest, my home, my dwelling-place;
Father! I come, I come to thee.

2 Jesus, my hope, my rock, my shield!
Whose precious blood was shed for me,
Into thy hands my soul I yield;
Saviour! I come, I come to thee.

3 Spirit of glory and of God!
Long hast thou deigned my guide to be;
Now be thy comfort sweet bestowed;
My God! I come, I come to thee.

4 I come to join that countless host
Who praise thy name unceasingly;
Blest Father, Son, and Holy Ghost!
My God! I come, I come to thee.

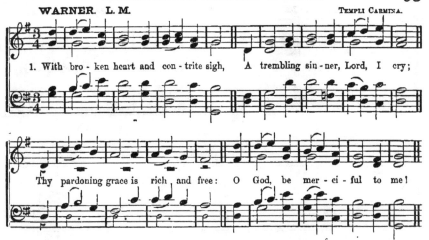

WARNER. L. M.   TEMPLI CARMINA.

1. With bro - ken heart and con - trite sigh, A trembling sin - ner, Lord, I cry;

Thy pardoning grace is rich and free: O God, be mer - ci - ful to me!

297.

2 I smite upon my troubled breast,
With deep and conscious guilt oppressed;
Christ and his cross my only plea:
O God, be merciful to me!

3 Far off I stand with tearful eyes,
Nor dare uplift them to the skies;
But thou dost all my anguish see:
O God, be merciful to me!

4 Nor alms, nor deeds that I have done
Can for a single sin atone;
To Calvary alone I flee:
O God, be merciful to me!

5 And when redeemed from sin and hell,
With all the ransomed throng I dwell,
My raptured song shall ever be,
God has been merciful to me!

298.

1 My sufferings all to thee are known,
Tempted in every point like me;
Regard my grief, regard thine own:
Jesus, remember Calvary!

2 For whom didst thou the cross endure?
Who nailed thy body to the tree?
Did not thy death my life procure?
Oh! let thy mercy answer me.

3 Art thou not touched with human woe?
Hath pity left the Son of Man?
Dost thou not all my sorrows know,
And claim a share in all my pain?

4 Thou wilt not break a bruiséd reed,
Or quench the smallest spark of grace,
Till through the soul thy power is spread,
Thy all-victorious righteousness.

5 The day of small and feeble things,
I know thou never wilt despise;
I know, with healing in his wings,
The Sun of Righteousness shall rise.

299.

1 HERE at thy cross, my dying Lord!
I lay my soul beneath thy love,
Beneath the droppings of thy blood,
Jesus, nor shall it e'er remove.

2 Not all that tyrants think or say,
With rage and lightning in their eyes,
Nor hell shall fright my heart away,
Should hell with all its legions rise.

3 Should worlds conspire to drive me
thence,
Moveless and firm this heart should lie:
Resolved, for that's my last defence,
If I must perish, there to die.

4 But speak, my Lord, and calm my fear;
Am I not safe beneath thy shade?
Thy vengeance will not strike me here,
Nor Satan dare my soul invade.

5 Yes, I'm secure beneath thy blood,
And all my foes shall lose their aim;
Hosanna to my dying Lord,
And my best honors to his name.

HAMBURG. L. M.   *Arranged by* Dr. L. Mason.

1. Oh! for a glance of heaven-ly day, To take this stub-born heart a - way,

And thaw, with beams of love di - vine, This heart, this fro - zen heart of mine.

300.

2 The rocks can rend ; the earth can quake ;
The seas can roar ; the mountains shake :
Of feeling, all things show some sign,
But this unfeeling heart of mine.

3 To hear the sorrows thou hast felt,
O Lord, an adamant would melt ;
But I can read each moving line,
And nothing moves this heart of mine.

4 Thy judgments, too, which devils fear—
Amazing thought—unmoved I hear ;
Goodness and wrath in vain combine
To stir this stupid heart of mine.

5 But Power Divine can do the deed ;
And, Lord, that power I greatly need
Thy Spirit can from dross refine,
And melt and change this heart of mine.

301.

1 Snow pity, Lord! O Lord, forgive ;
Let a repenting rebel live ;
Are not thy mercies large and free ?
May not a sinner trust in thee ?

2 My crimes are great, but ne'er surpass
The power and glory of thy grace :
Great God! thy nature hath no bound,
So let thy pardoning love be found.

3 Oh, wash my soul from every sin,
And make my guilty conscience clean !
Here on my heart the burden lies,
And past offences pain mine eyes.

4 My lips with shame my sins confess,
Against thy law, against thy grace ;
Lord, should thy judgment grow severe,
I am condemned, but thou art clear.

5 Should sudden vengeance seize my breath
I must pronounce thee just in death ;
And if my soul were sent to hell,
Thy righteous law approves it well.

6 Yet save a trembling sinner, Lord !
Whose hope, still hovering round thy word,
Would light on some sweet promise there,
Some sure support against despair.

302.

1 No more, my God! I boast no more,
Of all the duties I have done ;
I quit the hopes I held before,
To trust the merits of thy Son.

2 Now, for the love I bear his name,
What was my gain, I count my loss ;
My former pride I call my shame,
And nail my glory to his cross.

3 Yes,—and I must, and will esteem
All things but loss for Jesus' sake ;
Oh! may my soul be found in him,
And of his righteousness partake.

4 The best obedience of my hands
Dares not appear before thy throne ;
But faith can answer thy demands,
By pleading what my Lord has done.

EASTON. L. M.

MOZART.

1. Oh! that my load of sin were gone! Oh! that I could at last sub-mit

At Je-sus' feet to lay it down— To lay my soul at Je-sus' feet!

303.

1 Oh! that my load of sin were gone!
  Oh! that I could at last submit
  At Jesus' feet to lay it down—
  To lay my soul at Jesus' feet!

2 Rest for my soul I long to find:
  Saviour of all, if mine thou art,
  Give me thy meek and lowly mind,
  And stamp thine image on my heart.

3 Break off the yoke of inbred sin,
  And fully set my spirit free:
  I cannot rest, till pure within—
  Till I am wholly lost in thee.

4 Fain would I learn of thee, my God;
  Thy light and easy burden prove,—
  The cross all stained with hallowed blood,
  The labor of thy dying love.

5 I would—but thou must give the power;
  My heart from every sin release;
  Bring near, bring near the joyful hour,
  And fill me with thy perfect peace!

304.

1 I send the joys of earth away;
  Away, ye tempters of the mind,
  False as the smooth, deceitful sea,
  And empty as the whistling wind.

2 Your streams were floating me along,
  Down to the gulf of dark despair;
  And while I listened to your song,
  Your streams had ev'n conveyed me there.

3 Lord, I adore thy matchless grace,
  Which warned me of that dark abyss,
  Which drew me from those treacherous
        seas,
  And bade me seek superior bliss.

4 Now to the shining realms above,
  I stretch my hands and glance my eyes;
  Oh! for the pinions of a dove,
  To bear me to the upper skies!

5 There, from the bosom of our God,
  Oceans of endless pleasure roll;
  There would I fix my last abode,
  And drown the sorrows of my soul.

305.

1 Jesus, the sinner's Friend, to thee,
  Lost and undone, for aid I flee;
  Weary of earth, myself, and sin,
  Open thine arms and take me in.

2 Pity and save my ruined soul;
  'T is thou alone canst make me whole;
  Dark, till in me thine image shine,
  And lost I am, till thou art mine.

3 At last I own it cannot be
  That I should fit myself for thee:
  Here, then, to thee I all resign;
  Thine is the work, and only thine.

4 What can I say thy grace to move?
  Lord, I am sin,—but thou art love:
  I give up every plea beside,
  Lord, I am lost,—but thou hast died!

MANOAH. C. M.   GREATOREX COLL

1. I saw One hang-ing on a tree, In ag-o-ny and blood,

Who fixed his lan-guid eyes on me, As near the cross I stood.

306.

2 Sure, never, till my latest breath,
  Can I forget that look :
It seemed to charge me with his death,
  Though not a word he spoke.

3 Alas! I knew not what I did,
  But now my tears are vain ;
Where shall my trembling soul be hid,
  For I the Lord have slain !

4 A second look he gave, that said,
  "I freely all forgive:
This blood is for thy ransom paid ;
  I die that thou may'st live."

5 Thus while his death my sin displays
  In all its blackest hue,
Such is the mystery of grace,
  It seals my pardon too !

307.

1 APPROACH, my soul! the mercy-seat,
  Where Jesus answers prayer ;
There humbly fall before his feet,
  For none can perish there.

2 Thy promise is my only plea,
  With this I venture nigh :
Thou callest burdened souls to thee,
  And such, O Lord! am I.

3 Bowed down beneath a load of sin,
  By Satan sorely pressed ;
By wars without, and fears within,
  I come to thee for rest.

4 Be thou my shield and hiding-place,
  That, sheltered near thy side,
I may my fierce accuser face,
  And tell him—thou hast died.

5 Oh ! wondrous Love—to bleed and die,
  To bear the cross and shame,
That guilty sinners, such as I,
  Might plead thy gracious name !

308.

1 LORD ! at thy feet we sinners lie,
  And knock at mercy's door :
With heavy heart and downcast eye,
  Thy favor we implore.

2 On us the vast extent display
  Of thy forgiving love ;
Take all our heinous guilt away ;
  This heavy load remove.

3 'T is mercy—mercy we implore ;
  We would thy pity move :
Thy grace is an exhaustless store,
  And thou thyself art love.

4 Oh, for thine own, for Jesus' sake,
  Our numerous sins forgive !
Thy grace our rocky hearts can break :
  Heal us, and bid us live.

5 Thus melt us down, thus make us bend,
  And thy dominion own ;
Nor let a rival more pretend
  To repossess thy throne.

AVON. C. M.　　　　　　　　　　　　　　　　　　　　　　　　*Scottish.*

1. O Thou, whose ten - der mer - cy hears Con - tri - tion's hum - ble sigh;

Whose hand, in - dul - gent, wipes the tears From sor - row's weep - ing eye,—

309.

2 See, low before thy throne of grace,
   A wretched wanderer mourn ;
   Hast thou not bid me seek thy face !
   Hast thou not said—" Return ?"

3 And shall my guilty fears prevail
   To drive me from thy feet ?
   Oh ! let not this dear refuge fail,
   This only safe retreat !

4 Oh ! shine on this benighted heart,
   With beams of mercy shine !
   And let thy healing voice impart
   A taste of joys divine.

310.

1 O GOD of mercy ! hear my call,
   My load of guilt remove ;
   Break down this separating wall,
   That bars me from thy love.

2 Give me the presence of thy grace ;
   Then my rejoicing tongue
   Shall speak aloud thy righteousness,
   And make thy praise my song.

3 No blood of goats, nor heifer slain,
   For sin could e'er atone :
   The death of Christ shall still remain
   Sufficient and alone.

4 A soul, oppressed with sin's desert,
   My God will ne'er despise ;
   An humble groan, a broken heart,
   Is our best sacrifice.

311.

1 MY God, accept my heart this day,
   And make it always thine ;
   That I from thee no more may stray,
   No more from thee decline.

2 Before the cross of him who died,
   Behold, I prostrate fall ;
   Let every sin be crucified,
   Let Christ be all in all.

3 May the dear blood, once shed for me,
   My blest atonement prove ;
   That I, from first to last, may be
   The purchase of thy love.

4 Let every thought and work and word
   To thee be ever given ;
   Then life shall be thy service, Lord,
   And death the gate of heaven !

312.

1 WELCOME, O Saviour ! to my heart ;
   Possess thine humble throne ;
   Bid every rival hence depart,
   And claim me for thine own.

2 The world and Satan I forsake—
   To thee, I all resign ;
   My longing heart, O Jesus ! take,
   And fill with love divine.

3 Oh ! may I never turn aside,
   Nor from thy bosom flee ;
   Let nothing here my heart divide—
   I give it all to thee.

ADRIAN. S. M.   J. E. GOULD.

1. Oh! cease, my wandering soul, On rest-less wing to roam, All this wide world, to ei-ther pole, Hath not for thee a home.

313.

1 Oh, cease, my wandering soul,
  On restless wing to roam;
All this wide world, to either pole,
  Hath not for thee a home.

2 Behold the ark of God!
  Behold the open door!
Oh, haste to gain that dear abode,
  And rove, my soul, no more.

3 There safe thou shalt abide,
  There sweet shall be thy rest,
And every longing satisfied,
  With full salvation blest.

314.

1 Ah! what avails my strife,
  My wandering to and fro?
Thou hast the words of endless life;
  Ah! whither should I go?

2 Thy condescending grace
  To me did freely move;
It calls me still to seek thy face,
  And stoops to ask my love.

3 My worthless heart to gain,
  The God of all that breathe
Was found in fashion as a man,
  And died a cursèd death.

4 And can I yet delay
  My little all to give?
To tear my soul from earth away,
  For Jesus to receive?

5 Ah! no: I all forsake,
  My all to thee resign:
Gracious Redeemer, take, oh, take,
  And seal me ever thine!

315.

1 Shall we go on to sin,
  Because thy grace abounds?
Or crucify the Lord again,
  And open all his wounds?

2 Forbid it, mighty God!
  Nor let it e'er be said,
That we, whose sins are crucified,
  Should raise them from the dead.

3 We will be slaves no more,
  Since Christ has made us free,
Has nailed our tyrants to the cross,
  And bought our liberty.

316.

1 Unto thine altar, Lord,
  A broken heart I bring;
And wilt thou graciously accept
  Of such a worthless thing?

2 To Christ, the bleeding Lamb,
  My faith directs its eyes;
Thou mayst reject that worthless thing,
  But not his sacrifice.

3 When he gave up the ghost,
  The law was satisfied;
And now to its most rigorous claims
  I answer, "Jesus died."

FERGUSON. S. M.

GEO. KINGSLEY.

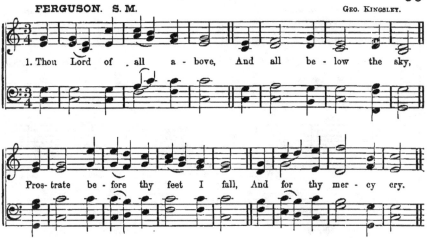

1. Thou Lord of all a - bove, And all be - low the sky,

Pros- trate be - fore thy feet I fall, And for thy mer - cy cry.

317.

2 Forgive my follies past,
  The crimes which I have done ;
  Oh ! bid a contrite sinner live,
  Through thy incarnate Son.

3 Guilt, like a heavy load,
  Upon my conscience lies ;
  To thee I make my sorrows known,
  And lift my weeping eyes.

4 The burden which I feel,
  Thou only canst remove ;
  Display, O Lord ! thy pardoning grace,
  And thy unbounded love.

5 One gracious look of thine
  Will ease my troubled breast ;
  Oh ! let me know my sins forgiven,
  And I shall then be blest.

318.

1 JESUS ! I come to thee,
  A sinner doomed to die ;
  My only refuge is thy cross,—
  Here at thy feet I lie.

2 Can mercy reach my case,
  And all my sins remove ?
  Break, O my God ! this heart of stone,
  And melt it by thy love.

3 Too long my soul has gone,
  Far from my God, astray ;
  I 've sported on the brink of hell,
  In sin's delusive way.

4 But, Lord ! my heart is fixed,—
  I hope in thee alone ;
  Break off the chains of sin and death,
  And bind me to thy throne.

5 Thy blood can cleanse my heart,
  Thy hand can wipe my tears ;—
  Oh ! send thy blessed Spirit down,
  To banish all my fears.

6 Then shall my soul arise,
  From sin and Satan free ;
  Redeemed from hell and every foe,
  I 'll trust alone in thee.

319.

1 THOU seest my feebleness,
  Jesus, be thou my power,—
  My help and refuge in distress,
  My fortress and my tower.

2 Give me to trust in thee ;
  Be thou my sure abode :
  My horn, and rock, and buckler be,
  My Saviour and my God.

3 Myself I cannot save,
  Myself I cannot keep ;
  But strength in thee I surely have,
  Whose eyelids never sleep.

4 My soul to thee alone,
  Now, therefore, I commend :
  Lord Jesus, love me as thine own,
  And love me to the end.

MERIBAH. L. C. M.   DR. L. MASON.

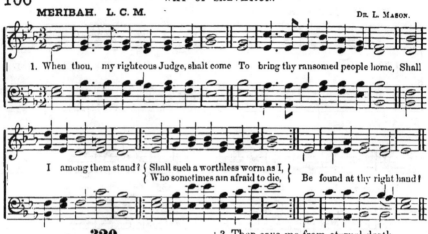

1. When thou, my righteous Judge, shalt come To bring thy ransomed people home, Shall

I among them stand? { Shall such a worthless worm as I, }
                    { Who sometimes am afraid to die, } Be found at thy right hand?

320.

2 I love to meet thy people now,
  Before thy feet with them to bow,
    Though vilest of them all;
  But, can I bear the piercing thought,
  What if my name should be left out,
    When thou for them shalt call?

3 O Lord, prevent it by thy grace,
  Be thou my only hiding-place,
    In this the accepted day;
  Thy pardoning voice, oh, let me hear,
  To still my unbelieving fear,
    Nor let me fall, I pray.

4 Among thy saints let me be found,
  Whene'er the archangel's trump shall
    sound,
    To see thy smiling face;
  Then loudest of the throng I'll sing,
  While heaven's resounding mansions ring
    With shouts of sovereign grace.

321.

1 O thou who hear'st the prayer of faith,
  Wilt thou not save a soul from death,
    That casts itself on thee?
  I have no refuge of my own,
  But fly to what my Lord hath done,
    And suffered once for me.

2 Slain in the guilty sinner's stead,
  His spotless righteousness I plead,
    And his availing blood;
  Thy merit, Lord, my robe shall be;
  Thy merit shall atone for me,
    And bring me near to God.

3 Then save me from eternal death,
  The spirit of adoption breathe,
    His consolations send;
  By him some word of life impart,
  And sweetly whisper to my heart,
    "Thy Maker is thy Friend."

4 The king of terrors then would be
  A welcome messenger to me,
    To bid me come away:
  Unclogged by earth, or earthly things,
  I'd mount, I'd fly with eager wings
    To everlasting day!

322.

1 The mind was formed, to mount sublime,
  Beyond the narrow bounds of time,
    To everlasting things;
  But earthly vapors dim her sight,
  And hang, with cold oppressive weight,
    Upon her drooping wings.

2 Bright scenes of bliss,—unclouded skies,
  Invite my soul;—Oh! could I rise,
    Nor leave a thought below,
  I'd bid farewell to anxious care,
  And say, to every tempting snare,—
    Heaven calls, and I must go:—

3 Heaven calls,—and can I yet delay?
  Can aught on earth engage my stay?
    Ah! wretched lingering heart!
  Come, Lord! with strength, and life, and
    light,
  Assist and guide my upward flight,
    And bid the world depart.

323.

1 Lord, thou hast won—at length I yield;
My heart, by mighty grace compelled,
Surrenders all to thee:
Against thy terrors long I strove,
But who can stand against thy love?—
Love conquers even me.

2 But since thou hast thy love revealed,
And shown my soul a pardon sealed,
I can resist no more;
Couldst thou for such a sinner bleed?
Canst thou for such a rebel plead?
I wonder and adore!

3 If thou hadst bid thy thunders roll,
And lightnings flash to blast my soul,
I still had stubborn been;
But mercy has my heart subdued,
A bleeding Saviour I have viewed,
And now, I hate my sin.

4 Now, Lord, I would be thine alone—
Come, take possession of thine own,
For thou hast set me free;
Released from Satan's hard command,
See all my powers in waiting stand,
To be employed by thee.

324.

1 Awaked by Sinai's awful sound,
My soul in bonds of guilt I found,
And knew not where to go;
One simple truth increased my pain,
The sinner "must be born again,"
Or sink to endless woe.

2 I heard the law its thunders roll,
While guilt lay heavy on my soul—
A vast oppressive load;
All creature-aid I saw was vain;
The sinner "must be born again,"
Or drink the wrath of God.

3 The saints I heard with rapture tell—
How Jesus conquered death and hell
To bring salvation near;
Yet still I found this truth remain—
The sinner "must be born again,"
Or sink in deep despair.

4 But while I thus in anguish lay,
The bleeding Saviour passed that way,
My bondage to remove;
The sinner, once by justice slain,
Now by his grace is born again,
And sings redeeming love.

325.

1 Lo! on a narrow neck of land,
'Twixt two unbounded seas, I stand,
Secure! insensible!
A point of time, a moment's space,
Removes me to that heavenly place,
Or shuts me up in hell.

2 O God! my inmost soul convert,
And deeply on my thoughtful heart
Eternal things impress;
Give me to feel their solemn weight,
And save me ere it be too late;
Wake me to righteousness.

3 Before me place, in bright array,
The pomp of that tremendous day,
When thou with clouds shalt come
To judge the nations at thy bar;
And tell me, Lord! shall I be there
To meet a joyful doom?

4 Be this my one great business here,—
With holy trembling, holy fear,
To make my calling sure!
Thine utmost counsel to fulfill,
And suffer all thy righteous will,
And to the end endure!

5 Then, Saviour, then my soul receive,
Transported from this earth, to live
And reign with thee above;
Where faith is sweetly lost in sight,
And hope, in full, supreme delight,
And everlasting love.

326.

1 No room for mirth or trifling here,
For worldly hope, or worldly fear,
If life so soon is gone;
If now the Judge is at the door,
And all mankind must stand before
The inexorable throne!

2 Nothing is worth a thought beneath,
But how I may escape the death
That never, never dies!
How make mine own election sure;
And when I fail on earth, secure
A mansion in the skies.

3 Jesus, vouchsafe a pitying ray;
Be thou my Guide, be thou my Way
To glorious happiness!
Ah! write the pardon on my heart;
And whensoe'er I hence depart,
Let me depart in peace.

ALETTA. 7s.

WM. B. BRADBURY.

1. Depth of mer - cy! can there be Mer - cy still re - served for me?

Can my God his wrath for - bear? Me, the chief of sin - ners, spare!

327.

2 I have long withstood his grace;
Long provoked him to his face;
Would not hearken to his calls;
Grieved him by a thousand falls.

3 Kindled his relentings are;
Me he now delights to spare;
Cries, How shall I give thee up?—
Lets the lifted thunder drop.

4 There for me the Saviour stands;
Shows his wounds and spreads his hands,
God is love! I know, I feel:
Jesus weeps, and loves me still.

328.

1 WHEN on Sinai's top I see
God descend, in majesty,
To proclaim his holy law,
All my spirit sinks with awe.

2 When, in ecstacy sublime,
Tabor's glorious steep I climb;
At the too transporting light,
Darkness rushes o'er my sight.

3 When on Calvary I rest;
God in flesh made manifest,
Shines in my Redeemer's face,
Full of beauty, truth, and grace.

4 Here I would forever stay,
Weep and gaze my soul away;
Thou art heaven on earth to me,
Lovely, mournful Calvary!

329.

1 JESUS! full of truth and love,
We thy kindest word obey;
Faithful let thy mercies prove;
Take our load of guilt away.

2 Weary of this war within,
Weary of this endless strife,
Weary of ourselves and sin,
Weary of a wretched life;

3 Burdened with a world of grief,
Burdened with our sinful load,
Burdened with this unbelief,
Burdened with the wrath of God:

4 Lo! we come to thee for ease,
True and gracious as thou art:
Now our weary souls release;
Write forgiveness on each heart.

330.

1 LORD of mercy, just and kind!
Wilt thou ne'er my guilt forgive?
Never shall my troubled mind,
In thy kind remembrance, live?

2 Lord! how long shall Satan's art
Tempt my harassed soul to sin,
Triumph o'er my humbled heart,—
Fears without and guilt within?

3 Lord, my God! thine ear incline,
Bending to the prayer of faith;
Cheer my eyes with light divine
Lest I sleep the sleep of death.

ROSEFIELD. 7s.

Dr. Malan.

1. Peo - ple of the liv - ing God, I have sought the world a - round,

Paths of sin and sor - row trod, Peace and com - fort no - where found.

331.

2 Now to you my spirit turns—
Turns, a fugitive unblest;
Brethren, where your altar burns,
Oh, receive me into rest!

3 Lonely I no longer roam,
Like the cloud, the wind, the wave:
Where you dwell shall be my home,
Where you die shall be my grave;

4 Mine the God whom you adore,
Your Redeemer shall be mine;
Earth can fill my soul no more,
Every idol I resign.

332.

1 Sovereign Ruler, Lord of all!
Prostrate at thy feet I fall!
Hear, oh, hear my earnest cry,
Frown not, lest I faint and die.

2 Vilest of the sons of men,—
Chief of sinners I have been;
Oft abused thee to thy face,
Trampled on thy richest grace.

3 Justly might thy righteous dart
Pierce this bleeding, broken heart;
Justly might thine angry breath
Blast me in eternal death.

4 But with thee there's mercy found,
Balm to heal my every wound:
Soothe, oh, soothe the troubled breast,
Give the weary wanderer rest.

333.

1 Jesus, save my dying soul;
Make the broken spirit whole:
Humble in the dust I lie:
Saviour, leave me not to die.

2 Jesus, full of every grace,
Now reveal thy smiling face;
Grant the joys of sin forgiven,
Foretaste of the bliss of heaven.

3 All my guilt to thee is known;
Thou art righteous, thou alone:
All my help is from thy cross;
All beside I count but loss.

4 Lord, in thee I now believe;
Wilt thou, wilt thou not forgive?
Helpless at thy feet I lie;
Saviour, leave me not to die.

334.

1 Jesus, all-atoning Lamb,
Thine, and only thine, I am:
Take my body, spirit, soul;
Only thou possess the whole.

2 Thou my one thing needful be;
Let me ever cleave to thee;
Let me choose the better part;
Let me give thee all my heart.

3 Whom have I on earth below?
Thee, and only Thee, I know:
Whom have I in heaven but thee?
Thou art all in all to me.

DORRNANCE. 8s & 7s.

I. B. WOODBURY.

1. Take my heart, O Fa - ther, take it! Make and keep it all thine own;

Let thy Spi - rit melt and break it— This proud heart of sin and stone.

335.

2 Father, make me pure and lowly,
Fond of peace and far from strife;
Turning from the paths unholy
Of this vain and sinful life.

3 Ever let thy grace surround me;
Strengthen me with power divine;
Till thy cords of love have bound me:
Make me to be wholly thine.

4 May the blood of Jesus heal me,
And my sins be all forgiven;
Holy Spirit, take and seal me,
Guide me in the path to heaven.

336.

1 Sweet the moments, rich in blessing,
Which before the cross I spend;
Life, and health, and peace possessing,
From the sinner's dying Friend.

2 Here I 'll sit, for ever viewing
Mercy streaming in his blood;
Precious drops! my soul bedewing,
Plead and claim my peace with God.

3 Truly blessèd is this station,
Low before his cross to lie;
While I see divine compassion
Beaming in his gracious eye.

4 Here it is I find my heaven,
While upon the cross I gaze;
Love I much? I 've much forgiven,
I 'm a miracle of grace.

5 Love and grief my heart dividing,
With my tears his feet I 'll bathe;
Constant still in faith abiding,
Life deriving from his death.

6 Lord! in ceaseless contemplation,
Fix my heart and eyes on thine,
Till I taste thy whole salvation,
Where, unvailed, thy glories shine.

337.

1 LABORING and heavy laden
With my sins, O Lord, I roam,
While I know thou hast invited
All such wanderers to their home.

2 Make my stubborn spirit willing
To obey thy gracious voice,
At the cross to leave its burden,
And departing to rejoice.

3 Thy sweet yoke I 'd take upon me,
And would learn, O Lord, of thee;
Thou art meek in heart, and lowly,
Teach me like thyself to be.

4 Rest my weary soul is seeking
From its sins and all its woes;
In thy bosom I would place me,
There to find a blest repose.

5 Laboring and heavy laden,
Lord, no longer will I roam:
Here I fix my habitation,
In thy sheltering love at home.

RATHBUN. 8s & 7s. GREATOREX COLL.

1. In the cross of Christ I glo-ry, Towering o'er the wrecks of time;

All the light of sa-cred sto-ry Gath-ers round its head sub-lime.

338.

1 In the cross of Christ I glory,
Towering o'er the wrecks of time;
All the light of sacred story
Gathers round its head sublime.

2 When the woes of life o'ertake me,
Hopes deceive, and fears annoy,
Never shall the cross forsake me:
Lo! it glows with peace and joy.

3 When the sun of bliss is beaming
Light and love upon my way,
From the cross the radiance streaming,
Adds new lustre to the day.

4 Bane and blessing, pain and pleasure,
By the cross are sanctified;
Peace is there, that knows no measure,
Joys that through all time abide.

5 In the cross of Christ I glory,
Towering o'er the wrecks of time;
All the light of sacred story
Gathers round its head sublime.

339.

1 Jesus, who on Calvary's mountain
Poured thy precious blood for me,
Wash me in its flowing fountain,
That my soul may spotless be.

2 I have sinned, but oh, restore me!
For unless thou smile on me,
Dark is all the world before me,
Darker yet eternity.

3 In thy word I hear thee saying,
Come and I will give you rest;
And the gracious call obeying,
See, I hasten to thy breast.

4 Grant, oh, grant thy Spirit's teaching,
That I may not go astray,
Till the gate of heaven reaching,
Earth and sin are passed away.

340.

1 Come, thou Fount of every blessing,
Tune my heart to sing thy grace;
Streams of mercy, never ceasing,
Call for songs of loudest praise.

2 Teach me some melodious measure,
Sung by flaming tongues above;
Oh, the vast, the boundless treasure
Of thy free, unchanging love!

3 Jesus sought me when a stranger,
Wandering from the fold of God;
He, to rescue me from danger,
Interposed his precious blood.

4 Oh, to grace how great a debtor
Daily I'm constrained to be!
Let thy goodness, like a fetter,
Bind my wandering heart to thee.

5 Prone to wander, Lord, I feel it;
Prone to leave the God I love;
Here's my heart; oh, take and seal it,—
Seal it for thy courts above!

ROSE HILL. L. M.

ROOT & SWEETSER'S COLL.

1. O God, thou art my God a-lone: Ear-ly to thee my soul shall cry—

A pil-grim in a land un-known, A thirsty land, whose springs are dry.

341.

2 Oh, that it were as it hath been,
When, praying in the holy place,
Thy power and glory I have seen,
And marked the footsteps of thy grace!

3 Yet, through this rough and thorny maze,
I follow hard on thee, my God:
Thy hand unseen upholds my ways;
I safely tread where thou hast trod.

4 Thee, in the watches of the night,
When I remember on my bed,
Thy presence makes the darkness light;
Thy guardian wings are round my head.

5 Better than life itself thy love,
Dearer than all beside to me;
For whom have I in heaven above,
Or what on earth, compared with thee?

342.

1 See a poor sinner, dearest Lord,
Whose soul, encouraged by thy word,
At mercy's footstool would remain,
And then would look,—and look again.

2 Ah! bring a wretched wanderer home,
Now to thy footstool let me come,
And tell thee all my grief and pain,
And wait and look,—and look again!

3 Take courage, then, my trembling soul;
One look from Christ will make thee
whole:
Trust thou in him, 't is not in vain,
But wait and look,—and look again.

4 Look to the Lord, his word, his throne;
Look to his grace, and not your own;
There wait and look, and look again;
You shall not wait, nor look in vain.

5 Ere long that happy day will come,
When I shall reach my blissful home;
And when to glory I attain,
Oh, then I 'll look,—and look again!

343.

1 I LEFT the God of truth and light;
I left the God who gave me breath,
To wander in the wilds of night,
And perish in the snares of death!

2 Sweet was his service, and his yoke
Was light and easy to be borne:
Through all his bonds of love I broke;
I cast away his gifts with scorn!

3 Heart-broken, friendless, poor, cast down,
Where shall the chief of sinners fly,
Almighty Vengeance! from thy frown,
Eternal Justice! from thine eye?

4 Lo! through the gloom of guilty fears,
My faith discerns a dawn of grace:
The Sun of Righteousness appears
In Jesus' reconciling face!

5 Prostrate before the mercy-seat,
I dare not, if I would, despair;
None ever perished at thy feet,
And I will lie forever there.

BLAKE. L. M.

J. P. HOLBROOK.

1. Thou on-ly Sovereign of my heart, My Refuge, my al-might-y Friend—

And can my soul from thee de-part, On whom a-lone my hopes de-pend!

344.

1 THOU only Sovereign of my heart,
My Refuge, my almighty Friend—
And can my soul from thee depart
On whom alone my hopes depend!

2 Whither, ah! whither shall I go,
A wretched wanderer from my Lord?
Can this dark world of sin and woe
One glimpse of happiness afford?

3 Eternal life thy words impart;
On these my fainting spirit lives;
Here sweeter comforts cheer my heart,
Than all the round of nature gives.

4 Thy name my inmost powers adore;
Thou art my life, my joy, my care;
Depart from thee—'tis death—'tis more—
'T is endless ruin, deep despair!

5 Low at thy feet my soul would lie;
Here safety dwells, and peace divine;
Still let me live beneath thine eye,
For life, eternal life, is thine.

345.

1 O THOU, to whose all-searching sight
The darkness shineth as the light,
Search, prove my heart, it pants for thee;
Oh! burst these bonds, and set it free.

2 Wash out its stains, refine its dross;
Nail my affections to the cross;
Hallow each thought; let all within
Be clean, as thou, my Lord, art clean.

3 If in this darksome wild I stray,
Be thou my light, be thou my way:
No foes, no violence I fear,
No fraud, while thou, my God, art near.

4 When rising floods my soul o'erflow,
When sinks my heart in waves of woe—
Jesus, thy timely aid impart,
And raise my head, and cheer my heart.

5 Saviour, where'er thy steps I see,
Dauntless, untired, I follow thee;
Oh! let thy hand support me still,
And lead me to thy holy hill.

346.

1 OH! where is now that glowing love
That marked our union with the Lord!
Our hearts were fixed on things above,
Nor could the world a joy afford.

2 Where is the zeal that led us then
To make our Saviour's glory known?
That freed us from the fear of men,
And kept our eye on him alone?

3 Where are the happy seasons spent
In fellowship with him we loved?
The sacred joy, the sweet content,
The blessedness that then we proved!

4 Behold, again we turn to thee;
Oh! cast us not away, though vile;
No peace we have, no joy we see,
O Lord our God, but in thy smile.

COOLING. C. M.   ABBEY.

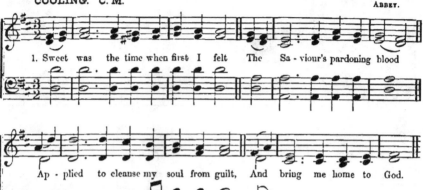

1. Sweet was the time when first I felt The Saviour's pardoning blood

Ap-plied to cleanse my soul from guilt, And bring me home to God.

347.

2 Soon as the morn the light revealed,
   His praises tuned my tongue;
And, when the evening shade prevailed,
   His love was all my song.

3 In prayer, my soul drew near the Lord,
   And saw his glory shine;
And when I read his holy word,
   I called each promise mine.

4 Now, when the evening shade prevails,
   My soul in darkness mourns;
And, when the morn the light reveals,
   No light to me returns.

5 Rise, Saviour! help me to prevail,
   And make my soul thy care;
I know thy mercy cannot fail,
   Let me that mercy share.

348.

1 With tears of anguish I lament,
   Here, at thy feet, my God,
My passion, pride, and discontent,
   And vile ingratitude.

2 Sure there was ne'er a heart so base,
   So false as mine has been;
So faithless to its promises,
   So prone to every sin!

3 My reason tells me thy commands
   Are holy, just, and true;
Tells me whate'er my God demands
   Is his most righteous due.

4 Reason, I hear, her counsels weigh,
   And all her words approve;
But still I find it hard t' obey,
   And harder yet to love.

5 How long, dear Saviour, shall I feel
   These struggles in my breast?
When wilt thou bow my stubborn will,
   And give my conscience rest?

6 Break, sovereign grace, oh, break the
     charm,
   And set the captive free;
Reveal, almighty God, thine arm,
   And haste to rescue me.

349.

1 Oh! for that tenderness of heart,
   That bows before the Lord;
That owns how just and good thou art.
   And trembles at thy word.

2 Oh! for those humble, contrite tears,
   Which from repentance flow;
That sense of guilt, which, trembling, fears
   The long-suspended blow!

3 Saviour! to me, in pity give,
   For sin, the deep distress;
The pledge thou wilt, at last, receive,
   And bid me die in peace.

4 Oh! fill my soul with faith and love,
   And strength to do thy will;
Raise my desires and hopes above,—
   Thyself to me reveal.

EVAN. C. M.   HAVERGAL.

1. How oft, a-las! this wretch-ed heart Has wandered from the Lord!

How oft my rov-ing thoughts de-part, For-get-ful of his word!

350.

2 Yet sovereign mercy calls—" Return !"
   Dear Lord, and may I come ?
My vile ingratitude I mourn :
   Oh, take the wanderer home !

3 And canst thou—wilt thou yet forgive,
   And bid my crimes remove ?
And shall a pardoned rebel live,
   To speak thy wondrous love ?

4 Almighty grace, thy healing power,
   How glorious, how divine !
That can to life and bliss restore
   A heart so vile as mine.

5 Thy pardoning love, so free, so sweet,
   Dear Saviour, I adore ;
Oh, keep me at thy sacred feet,
   And let me rove no more !

351.

1 SEARCHER of Hearts !—from mine erase
   All thoughts that should not be,
And in its deep recesses trace
   My gratitude to thee !

2 Hearer of Prayer !—oh, guide aright
   Each word and deed of mine ;
Life's battle teach me how to fight,
   And be the victory thine.

3 Giver of All !—for every good
   That in the Saviour came—
For raiment, shelter and for food,
   I thank thee in his name.

4 Father and Son and Holy Ghost !
   Thou glorious Three in One !
Thou knowest best what I need most,
   And let thy will be done.

352.

1 OH ! for a closer walk with God,
   A calm and heavenly frame,—
A light to shine upon the road
   That leads me to the Lamb !

2 Where is the blessedness I knew
   When first I saw the Lord ?
Where is the soul-refreshing view
   Of Jesus and his word ?

3 What peaceful hours I once enjoyed !
   How sweet their memory still !
But they have left an aching void
   The world can never fill.

4 Return, O holy Dove, return,
   Sweet messenger of rest !
I hate the sins that made thee mourn,
   And drove thee from my breast.

5 The dearest idol I have known,
   Whate'er that idol be,
Help me to tear it from thy throne,
   And worship only thee.

6 So shall my walk be close with God,
   Calm and serene my frame ;
So purer light shall mark the road
   That leads me to the Lamb.

LITCHFIELD. C. M.   DR. L. MASON.

1. Oh! that I knew the se - cret place Where I might find my God!

I'd spread my wants be - fore his face, And pour my woes a - broad.

353.

2 I 'd tell him how my sins arise,
  What sorrows I sustain ;
How grace decays, and comfort dies,
  And leaves my heart in pain.

3 He knows what arguments I 'd take
  To wrestle with my God :
I 'd plead for his own mercy's sake—
  I 'd plead my Saviour's blood.

4 My God will pity my complaints ;
  And drive my foes away ;
He knows the meaning of his saints
  When they in sorrow pray.

5 Arise, my soul ! from deep distress,
  And banish every fear ;
He calls thee to his throne of grace,
  To spread thy sorrows there.

354.

1 ALAS ! what hourly dangers rise !
  What snares beset my way !
To heaven, oh, let me lift mine eyes,
  And hourly watch and pray.

2 How oft my mournful thoughts complain,
  And melt in flowing tears !
My weak resistance, ah, how vain !
  How strong my foes and fears !

3 O gracious God ! in whom I live,
  My feeble efforts aid ;
Help me to watch, and pray, and strive,
  Though trembling and afraid.

4 Increase my faith, increase my hope,
  When foes and fears prevail ;
And bear my fainting spirit up,
  Or soon my strength will fail.

5 Whene'er temptations fright my heart,
  Or lure my feet aside,
My God, thy powerful aid impart,
  My Guardian and my Guide.

6 Oh, keep me in thy heavenly way,
  And bid the tempter flee !
And let me never, never stray
  From happiness and thee.

355.

1 Oh ! could I find, from day to day,
  A nearness to my God,
Then would my hours glide sweet away
  While leaning on his word.

2 Lord, I desire with thee to live
  Anew from day to day,
In joys the world can never give,
  Nor ever take away.

3 Blest Jesus, come and rule my heart,
  And make me wholly thine,
That I may never more depart,
  Nor grieve thy love divine.

4 Thus, till my last, expiring breath,
  Thy goodness I 'll adore,
And when my frame dissolves in death,
  My soul shall love thee more.

CHESTERFIELD. C. M.

DR. HAWEIS.

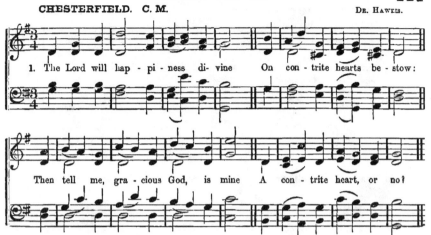

1. The Lord will hap - pi - ness di - vine On con - trite hearts be - stow:

Then tell me, gra - cious God, is mine A con - trite heart, or no?

356.

2 I hear, but seem to hear in vain,
  Insensible as steel ;
If aught is felt, 't is only pain
  To find I cannot feel.

3 My best desires are faint and few :
  Fain would I strive for more ;
But, when I cry, " My strength renew,"
  Seem weaker than before.

4 Thy saints are comforted, I know,
  And love the house of prayer ;
I therefore go where others go,
  But find no comfort there.

5 Oh! make this heart rejoice or ache ;
  Decide this doubt for me ;
And if it be not broken, break—
  And heal it if it be.

357.

1 Why is my heart so far from thee,
  My God! my chief delight ?
Why are my thoughts no more, by day,—
  With thee, no more by night ?

2 Why should my foolish passions rove ?
  Where can such sweetness be,
As I have tasted in thy love,—
  As I have found in thee ?

3 When my forgetful soul renews
  The savor of thy grace,
My heart presumes, I cannot lose
  The relish all my days.

4 But, ere one fleeting hour is past,
  The flattering world employs
Some sensual bait, to seize my taste,
  And to pollute my joys.

5 Wretch that I am, to wander thus,
  In chase of false delight !
Let me be fastened to thy cross,
  Rather than lose thy sight.

6 Make haste, my days ! to reach the goal,
  And bring my heart to rest
On the dear centre of my soul,—
  My God, my Saviour's breast.

358.

1 I WOULD be thine ; Oh ! take my heart,
  And fill it with thy love :
Thy sacred image, Lord, impart,
  And seal it from above.

2 I would be thine ; but while I strive
  To give myself away,
I feel rebellion still alive,
  And wander while I pray.

3 I would be thine ; but, Lord, I feel
  Evil still lurks within ;—
Do thou thy majesty reveal,
  And overcome my sin.

4 I would be thine ; I would embrace
  The Saviour, and adore :
Inspire with faith, infuse thy grace,
  And now my soul restore.

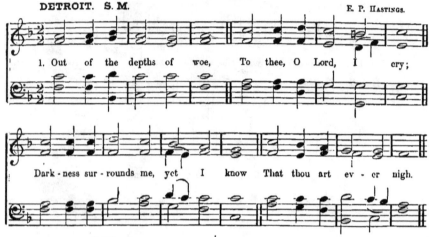

DETROIT. S. M. E. P. HASTINGS.

1. Out of the depths of woe, To thee, O Lord, I cry;
Dark-ness sur-rounds me, yet I know That thou art ev-er nigh.

359.

1 Out of the depths of woe,
  To thee, O Lord! I cry;
Darkness surrounds me, yet I know
That thou art ever nigh.

2 I cast my hopes on thee;
  Thou canst, thou wilt forgive;
If thou shouldst mark iniquity,
Who in thy sight could live?

3 I wait for thee; I wait,
  Confessing all my sin:
Lord! I am knocking at thy gate;
Open, and take me in.

4 Glory to God above!
  The waters soon will cease;
For lo! the swift-returning dove
Brings home the pledge of peace.

5 Though storms his face obscure,
  And dangers threaten loud,
Jehovah's covenant is sure,
His bow is in the cloud.

360.

1 And shall I sit alone,
  Oppressed with grief and fear?
To God, my Father, make my moan,
And he refuse to hear?

2 If he my Father be,
  His pity he will show;
From cruel bondage set me free,
And inward peace bestow.

3 If still he silence keep,
  'T is but my faith to try;
He knows and feels whene'er I weep,
And softens every sigh.

4 Then will I humbly wait,
  Nor once indulge despair:
My sins are great,—but not so great
As his compassions are.

361.

1 I FAINT, my soul doth faint,
  My strength, a broken reed!
Would this so long be my complaint,
Were I a saint indeed?

2 The sins I fancied quelled,
  Again in arms arise;
The promise that I thought I held,
Refuses its supplies.

3 My bosom burns with shame,
  And yet is icy cold;
Even to breathe the Saviour's name
Seems now to be too bold.

4 So oft my soul hath trod
  The same sad path astray,
How can I turn again to God?
What venture now to say?

5 Thou, Saviour, only thou
  Canst meet my utter need,
And shouldst thou save the rebel now,
It will be grace indeed!

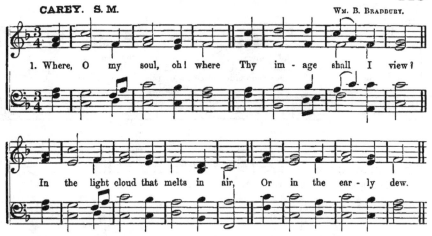

CAREY. S. M.

WM. B. BRADBURY.

1. Where, O my soul, oh! where Thy im-age shall I view?

In the light cloud that melts in air, Or in the ear-ly dew.

362.

1 WHERE, O my soul, oh, where
  Thy image shall I view?
In the light cloud that melts in air
Or in the early dew.

2 This hour, with flowing tears,
  My follies I bewail:
The next, my heart a waste appears,
  Where all the fountains fail.

3 To-day, her glimmering light
  Hope kindles in my breast;
The morrow, with despair's black night,
  Has all my soul oppressed.

4 Oh! my unsteadfast mind,
  Tossed between good and ill!
While brutes, with instinct sure though
    blind,
  Their Maker's law fulfill.

5 Oh! wavering, wretched state,
  Of hope by fear subdued!
On thee, O Lord, for help I wait,—
  Fix, fix my soul in good.

363.

1 A CHARGE to keep I have;
  A God to glorify;
A never-dying soul to save,
  And fit it for the sky;

2 To serve the present age,
  My calling to fulfill;
Oh! may it all my powers engage
  To do my Master's will.

3 Arm me with jealous care,
  As in thy sight to live;
And oh! thy servant, Lord, prepare
  A strict account to give.

4 Help me to watch and pray,
  And on thyself rely;
Assured if I my trust betray,
  I shall forever die.

364.

1 I LIFT my soul to God,
  My trust is in his name;
Let not my foes that seek my blood
  Still triumph in my shame.

2 From the first dawning light
  Till the dark evening rise,
For thy salvation, Lord! I wait
  With ever-longing eyes.

3 Remember all thy grace,
  And lead me in thy truth;
Forgive the sins of riper days,
  And follies of my youth.

4 The Lord is just and kind,
  The meek shall learn his ways;
And every humble sinner find
  The methods of his grace.

5 For his own goodness' sake
  He saves my soul from shame;
He pardons, though my guilt be great,
  Through my Redeemer's name.

MARTYN. 7s.

MARSH.
FINE

1. { Je - sus, lov - er of my soul, Let me to thy bo - som fly,
{ While the bil - lows near me roll, While the tem - pest still is high:
D. C. Safe in - to the ha - ven guide: Oh! re - ceive my soul at last!

Hide me, O my Sa - viour, hide, Till the storm of life is past;

365.

2 Other refuge have I none ;
  Hangs my helpless soul on thee :
Leave, ah ! leave me not alone,
  Still support and comfort me :
All my trust on thee is stayed,
  All my help from thee I bring ;
Cover my defenceless head
  With the shadow of thy wing.

3 Thou, O Christ, art all I want,
  More than all in thee I find :
Raise the fallen, cheer the faint,
  Heal the sick, and lead the blind :
Just and holy is thy name ;
  I am all unrighteousness :
False and full of sin I am ;
  Thou art full of truth and grace.

4 Plenteous grace with thee is found,
  Grace to cover all my sin ;
Let the healing streams abound,
  Make and keep me pure within :
Thou of life the fountain art,
  Freely let me take of thee ;
Spring thou up within my heart ;
  Rise to all eternity.

366.

1 JESUS, merciful and mild,
  Lead me as a helpless child :
On no other arm but thine
  Would my weary soul recline ;

Thou art ready to forgive,
Thou canst bid the sinner live—
Guide the wanderer, day by day,
In the strait and narrow way.

2 I am weakness, thou art might ;
I am darkness, thou art light ;
I am all defiled with sin,
Thou canst make me pure within ;
Foes that threaten to devour,
In thy presence have no power ;
Thou canst bid their rage be still,
And my heart with comfort fill.

3 Thou canst fit me by thy grace
For the heavenly dwelling-place ;
All thy promises are sure,
Ever shall thy love endure ;
Then what more could I desire,
How to greater bliss aspire ?
All I need, in thee I see,
Thou art all in all to me.

4 Jesus, Saviour all divine,
Hast thou made me truly thine ?
Hast thou bought me by thy blood !
Reconciled my heart to God ?
Hearken to my tender prayer,
Let me thy own image bear ;
Let me love thee more and more,
Till I reach heaven's blissful shore.

MESSIAH. 7s. Double.   *Arranged by* GEO. KINGSLEY.

1. Brethren, while we sojourn here, Fight we must, but should not fear; Foes we have, but we've a Friend, One that loves us to the end. Forward, then, with courage go, Long we shall not dwell be-low: Soon the joy-ful news will come, "Child, your Father calls—come home!"

367.

2 In the way a thousand snares
Lie, to take us unawares;
Satan, with malicious art,
Watches each unguarded part:
But, from Satan's malice free,
Saints shall soon victorious be;
Soon the joyful news will come,
"Child, your Father calls—come home!"

3 But of all the foes we meet,
None so oft mislead our feet,
None betray us into sin
Like the foes that dwell within;
Yet let nothing spoil our peace,
Christ shall also conquer these;
Soon the joyful news will come,
"Child, your Father calls—come home!"

368.

1 SAVIOUR, when in dust, to thee
Low we bow th' adoring knee;
When, repentant, to the skies
Scarce we lift our streaming eyes:
Oh! by all thy pains and woe,
Suffered once for man below,
Bending from thy throne on high,
Hear thy people when they cry.

2 By thy birth and early years,
By thy human griefs and fears,
By thy fasting and distress
In the lonely wilderness:
By thy victory in the hour
Of the subtle tempter's power;
Jesus, look with pitying eye;
Hear thy people when they cry.

3 By thine hour of dark despair,
By thine agony of prayer,
By the purple robe of scorn,
By thy wounds—thy crown of thorn;
By thy cross—thy pangs and cries;
By thy perfect sacrifice;
Jesus, look with pitying eye;
Hear thy people when they cry.

4 By thy deep expiring groan,
By the sealed sepulchral stone,
By thy triumph o'er the grave,
By thy power from death to save;
Mighty God, ascended Lord,
To thy throne in heaven restored,
Saviour, Prince, exalted high,
Hear thy people when they cry.

AUTUMN. 8s & 7s. Double.   *Spanish.*

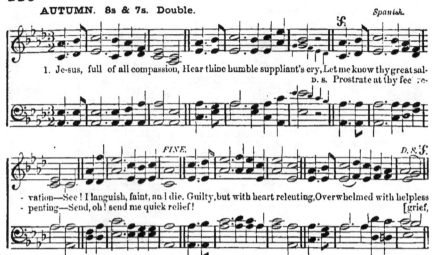

1. Je-sus, full of all compassion, Hear thine humble suppliant's cry, Let me know thy great sal-
D. S. Prostrate at thy feet re-

FINE.   D. S. *f.*

- vation—See! I languish, faint, and die. Guilty, but with heart relenting, Overwhelmed with helpless
- penting—Send, oh! send me quick relief!   [grief,

369.

2 Whither should a wretch be flying,
  But to him who comfort gives?
Whither, from the dread of dying,
  But to him who ever lives?
While I view thee, wounded, grieving,
  Breathless, on the cursèd tree,
Fain I'd feel my heart believing
  Thou didst suffer thus for me.

3 In the world of endless ruin,
  Let it never, Lord, be said,
"Here's a soul that perished, sueing
  For the Saviour's boasted aid!"
Saved!—the deed shall spread new glory
  Through the shining realms above;
Angels sing the pleasing story,
  All enraptured with thy love.

370.

1 Jesus, I my cross have taken,
  All to leave, and follow thee;
Naked, poor, despised, forsaken,
  Thou, from hence, my all shalt be!
Perish, every fond ambition,
  All I've sought, or hoped, or known;
Yet how rich is my condition,
  God and heaven are still my own!

2 Let the world despise and leave me,
  They have left my Saviour, too;
Human hearts and looks deceive me—
  Thou art not, like them, untrue;

Oh! while thou dost smile upon me,
  God of wisdom, love, and might,
Foes may hate, and friends disown me,
  Show thy face, and all is bright.

3 Man may trouble and distress me,
  'T will but drive me to thy breast,
Life with trials hard may press me,
  Heaven will bring me sweeter rest!
Oh! 't is not in grief to harm me,
  While thy love is left to me;
Oh! 't were not in joy to charm me,
  Were that joy unmixed with thee.

371.

1 Lord, I hear of showers of blessing
  Thou art scattering full and free;
Showers the thirsty soul refreshing;
  Let some droppings fall on me!
Pass me not, O gracious Father!
  Lost and sinful though I be;
Thou might'st curse me, but the rather
  Let thy mercy light on me.

2 Have I long in sin been sleeping?
  Long been slighting, grieving thee?
Has the world my heart been keeping?
  Oh! forgive and rescue me!
Pass me not, O mighty Spirit!
  Thou canst make the blind to see;
Testify of Jesus' merit,
  Speak the word of power to me.

GAYLORD. 8s & 7s.   *Arranged by* J. P. HOLBROOK.

1. Full of trem-bling ex-pec-ta-tion, Feel-ing much, and fear-ing more,

FINE.

Might-y God of my sal-va-tion! I thy time-ly aid im-plore;

D. S. By thy sor-er griefs to cheer me, By thy more than mor-tal pain.

D. S.

Suffering Son of Man! be near me, All my sufferings to sus-tain,

372.

1 FULL of trembling expectation,
    Feeling much, and fearing more,
Mighty God of my salvation!
    I thy timely aid implore;
Suffering Son of Man! be near me,
    All my sufferings to sustain,
By thy sorer griefs to cheer me,
    By thy more than mortal pain.

2 Call to mind that unknown anguish,
    In thy days of flesh below ;
When thy troubled soul did languish
    Under a whole world of woe ;
When thou didst our curse inherit,
    Groan beneath our guilty load,
Burdened with a wounded spirit,
    Bruised by all the wrath of God.

3 By thy most severe temptation,
    In that dark, satanic hour ;
By thy last mysterious passion,
    Screen me from the adverse power!
By thy fainting in the garden,
    By thy bloody sweat, I pray,
Write upon my heart the pardon,
    Take my sins and fears away.

373.

1 SAVIOUR, visit thy plantation!
    Grant us, Lord, a gracious rain :
All will come to desolation,
    Unless thou return again.
Keep no longer at a distance,
    Shine upon us from on high,
Lest, for want of thine assistance,
    Every plant should droop and die.

2 Once, O Lord, thy garden flourished ;
    Every part looked gay and green ;
Then thy word our spirits nourished :
    Happy seasons we have seen.
But a drought has since succeeded,
    And a sad decline we see :
Lord, thy help is greatly needed :
    Help can only come from thee.

3 Let our mutual love be fervent :
    Make us prevalent in prayers ;
Let each one esteemed thy servant
    Shun the world's bewitching snares.
Break the tempter's fatal power,
    Turn the stony heart to flesh,
And begin from this good hour
    To revive thy work afresh.

HOLLEY. 7s.

GEO. HEWS.

1. Soft-ly now the light of day Fades up-on my sight a-way;

Free from care, from la-bor free, Lord, I would com-mune with thee!

374.

2 Thou, whose all-pervading eye
  Naught escapes without, within,
Pardon each infirmity
  Open fault, and secret sin.

3 Thou who, sinless, yet hast known
  All of man's infirmity;
Now from thine eternal throne,
  Jesus, look with pitying eye.

4 Soon, for me, the light of day
  Shall forever pass away;
Then, from sin and sorrow free,
  Take me, Lord, to dwell with thee!

375.

1 Prince of Peace, control my will;
  Bid this struggling heart be still;
Bid my fears and doubtings cease;
  Hush my spirit into peace.

2 Thou hast bought me with thy blood,
  Opened wide the gate to God:
Peace I ask—but peace must be,
  Lord, in being one with thee.

3 May thy will, not mine, be done;
  May thy will and mine be one;
Chase these doubtings from my heart;
  Now thy perfect peace impart.

4 Saviour! at thy feet I fall;
  Thou my life, my God, my all!
Let thy happy servant be
  One forevermore with thee!

376.

1 When, my Saviour, shall I be
  Perfectly resigned to thee?
Poor and vile in mine own eyes,
  Only in thy wisdom wise?

2 Only thee content to know,
  Ignorant of all below?
Only guided by thy light,
  Only mighty in thy might?

3 Fully in my life express
  All the heights of holiness?
Sweetly let my spirit prove
  All the depths of humble love.

377.

1 Gently, gently, lay the rod
  On my sinful head, O God!
Stay thy wrath, in mercy stay,
  Lest I sink beneath its sway.

2 Heal me, for my flesh is weak;
  Heal me, for thy grace I seek;
This my only plea I make,—
  Heal me for thy mercy's sake.

3 Who, within the silent grave,
  Shall proclaim thy power to save?
Lord! my sinking soul reprieve;
  Speak, and I shall rise and live.

4 Lo! he comes—he heeds my plea;
  Lo! he comes—the shadows flee;
Glory round me dawns once more;
  Rise, my spirit! and adore.

SEYMOUR. 7s.   *Arranged from* WEBER.

1. God of mer-cy! God of love! Hear our sad, re-pent-ant song;

Sor-row dwells on ev-ery face, Pen-i-tence on ev-ery tongue.

378.

2 Deep regret for follies past,
  Talents wasted, time misspent;
Hearts debased by worldly cares,
  Thankless for the blessings lent;

3 Foolish fears and fond desires,
  Vain regrets for things as vain;
Lips too seldom taught to praise,
  Oft to murmur and complain;

4 These, and every secret fault,
  Filled with grief and shame we own;
Humbled at thy feet we lie,
  Seeking pardon from thy throne.

5 God of mercy! God of grace!
  Hear our sad, repentant songs;
Oh, restore thy suppliant race,
  Thou to whom all praise belongs!

379.

1 Does the Gospel word proclaim
  Rest for those that weary be?
Then, my soul, put in thy claim—
  Sure that promise speaks to thee!

2 Marks of grace I cannot show,
  All polluted is my best;
But I weary am, I know,
  And the weary long for rest.

3 Burdened with a load of sin,
  Harassed with tormenting doubt,
Hourly conflicts from within,
  Hourly crosses from without;—

4 All my little strength is gone,
  Sink I must without supply;
Sure upon the earth is none
  Can more weary be than I.

5 In the ark the weary dove
  Found a welcome resting-place;
Thus my spirit longs to prove
  Rest in Christ, the Ark of grace

6 Tempest-tossed I long have been,
  And the flood increases fast;
Open, Lord, and take me in,
  Till the storm be overpast!

380.

1 WAIT, my soul, upon the Lord,
  To his gracious promise flee,
Laying hold upon his word,
  "As thy days thy strength shall be."

2 If the sorrows of thy case
  Seem peculiar still to thee,
God has promised needful grace,
  "As thy days thy strength shall be."

3 Days of trial, days of grief,
  In succession thou may'st see;
This is still thy sweet relief,
  "As thy days thy strength shall be."

4 Rock of Ages, I'm secure,
  With thy promise full and free;
Faithful, positive, and sure—
  "As thy days thy strength shall be."

MILNER. 7s. 6 lines. HARP OF DAVID.

1. Hearken, Lord, to my com-plaints, For my soul with-in me faints;
Thee, far off, I call to mind, In the land I left be - - - hind,
Where the streams of Jor-dan flow, Where the heights of Her-mon glow.

381.

2 Tempest-tossed, my failing bark
Founders on the ocean dark;
Deep to deep around me calls,
With the rush of waterfalls,
While I plunge to lower caves,
Overwhelmed by all thy waves.

3 Once the morning's earliest light
Brought thy mercy to my sight,
And my wakeful song was heard
Later than the evening bird;
Hast thou all my prayers forgot?
Dost thou scorn, or hear them not?

4 Why, my soul, art thou perplexed?
Why with faithless troubles vexed?
Hope in God, whose saving name
Thou shalt joyfully proclaim,
When his countenance shall shine
Through the clouds that darken thine.

382.

1 Once I thought my mountain strong,
Firmly fixed no more to move;
Then my Saviour was my song,
Then my soul was filled with love;
Those were happy, golden days,
Sweetly spent in prayer and praise.

2 Little then myself I knew,
Little thought of Satan's power;
Now I feel my sins anew;
Now I feel the stormy hour!
Sin has put my joys to flight;
Sin has turned my day to night.

3 Saviour, shine and cheer my soul,
Bid my dying hopes revive;
Make my wounded spirit whole,
Far away the tempter drive;
Speak the word and set me free,
Let me live alone to thee.

383.

1 Lord! I look for all to thee;
Thou hast been a rock to me:
Still thy wonted aid afford:
Still be near, my shield, my sword!
I my soul commit to thee,
Lord! thy blood has ransomed me.

2 Faint and sinking on my road,
Still I cling to thee, my God!
Bending 'neath a weight of woes,
Harassed by a thousand foes,
Hope still chides my rising fears
Joys still mingle with my tears.

3 On thy word I take my stand;
All my times are in thy hand:
Make thy face upon me shine;
Take me 'neath thy wings divine;
Lord! thy grace is all my trust;
Save, oh! save thy trembling dust.

4 Oh! what mercies still attend
Those who make the Lord their friend!
Sweetly, safely shall they 'bide
'Neath his eye, and at his side:
Lord! may this my station be:
Seek it, all ye saints! with me.

OLIVET. 6s & 4s.   DR. L. MASON.

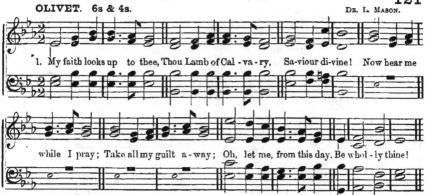

1. My faith looks up to thee, Thou Lamb of Cal-va-ry, Sa-viour di-vine! Now hear me while I pray; Take all my guilt a-way; Oh, let me, from this day, Be whol-ly thine!

384.

2 May thy rich grace impart
Strength to my fainting heart ;
  My zeal inspire ;
As thou hast died for me,
Oh ! may my love to thee
Pure, warm, and changeless be—
  A living fire.

3 While life's dark maze I tread,
And griefs around me spread,
  Be thou my Guide ;
Bid darkness turn to day,
Wipe sorrow's tear away,
Nor let me ever stray
  From thee aside.

4 When ends life's transient dream,
When death's cold sullen stream
  Shall o'er me roll,
Blest Saviour ! then in love,
Fear and distress remove ;
Oh ! bear me safe above,—
  A ransomed soul.

385.

1 SAVIOUR, I look to thee,
Be not thou far from me,
  'Mid storms that lower :
On me thy care bestow,
Thy loving kindness show,
Thine arms around me throw,
  This trying hour.

2 Saviour, I look to thee,
Feeble as infancy,
  Gird up my heart :
Author of life and light,
Thou hast an arm of might,
Thine is the sovereign right,
  Thy strength impart.

3 Saviour, I look to thee,
Let me thy fullness see,
  Save me from fear ;
While at thy cross I kneel,
All my backslidings heal,
And a free pardon seal,
  My soul to cheer.

4 Saviour I look to thee,
Thine shall the glory be,
  Hearer of prayer :
Thou art my only aid,
On thee my soul is stayed,
Naught can my heart invade,
  While thou art near.

386.

1 PEACE, peace, I leave with you,
My peace I give to you,
  Trust to my care !
Thus the Redeemer said,
And bowed his sacred head,
Lone in the garden shade,
  Wrestling in prayer.

2 Peace, peace, I leave with you,
My peace I give to you,
  Perfect and pure ;
Not as the world doth give,
Words that the soul deceive ;
Ye who in me believe
  Shall rest secure.

3 Peace, peace, I leave with you,
My peace I give to you,
  Though foes invade ;
All power is given to me,
I will your refuge be,
Now and eternally,
  Be not dismayed !

PENITENCE. 7s, 6s & 8s.
W. H. OAKLEY.

1. Je - sus, let thy pity - ing eye Call back a wan - dering sheep;

False to thee, like Pe - ter, I Would fain like Pe - ter weep!
D. S. Turn, and look up - on me, Lord! And break my heart of stone.

Let me be by grace re - stored; On me be all long suffering shown;

387.

1 JESUS, let thy pitying eye
   Call back a wandering sheep;
False to thee, like Peter, I
   Would fain like Peter weep!
Let me be by grace restored,
   On me be all long-suffering shown,
Turn, and look upon me, Lord!
   And break my heart of stone.

2 Saviour, Prince, enthroned above,
   Repentance to impart,
Give me, through thy dying love,
   The humble, contrite heart:
Give what I have long implored,
   A portion of thy grief unknown;
Turn, and look upon me, Lord!
   And break my heart of stone.

3 For thine own compassion's sake,
   The gracious wonder show;
Cast my sins behind thy back,
   And wash me white as snow:
If thy mercies now are stirred,
   If now I do myself bemoan,
Turn, and look upon me, Lord!
   And break my heart of stone.

388.

1 VAIN, delusive world, adieu,
   With all of creature good!
Only Jesus I pursue,
   Who bought me with his blood:
All thy pleasures I forego;
   I trample on thy wealth and pride;
Only Jesus will I know,
   And Jesus crucified.

2 Other knowledge I disdain;
   'Tis all but vanity:
Christ, the Lamb of God, was slain,—
   He tasted death for me.
Me to save from endless woe
   The sin-atoning Victim died:
Only Jesus will I know,
   And Jesus crucified.

3 Him to know is life and peace,
   And pleasure without end;
This is all my happiness,
   On Jesus to depend;
Daily in his grace to grow,
   And ever in his faith abide;
Only Jesus will I know,
   And Jesus crucified.

GERHARDT. 7s & 6s.
J. P. HOLBROOK.

1. O sacred Head, now wounded, With grief and shame weighed down, Now scorn-ful-ly sur-

- round - ed With thorns, thy on - ly crown; O sa - cred Head, what glo - ry, What

bliss till now was thine! Yet, tho' de-spised and go - ry, I joy to call thee mine.

389.

2 How art thou pale with anguish,
　With sore abuse and scorn!
How does that visage languish,
　Which once was bright as morn!
Thy grief, and thy compassion,
　Were all for sinners' gain;
Mine, mine was the transgression,
　But thine the deadly pain.

3 What language shall I borrow,
　To praise thee, heavenly Friend:
For this, thy dying sorrow,
　Thy pity without end?
Lord, make me thine forever,
　Nor let me faithless prove:
Oh! let me never, never,
　Abuse such dying love.

4 Forbid that I should leave thee;
　O Jesus, leave not me;
By faith I would receive thee;
　Thy blood can make me free:
When strength and comfort languish,
　And I must hence depart:
Release me then from anguish,
　By thine own wounded heart.

5 Be near when I am dying,
　Oh! show thy cross to me!
And for my succor flying,
　Come, Lord, to set me free:
These eyes new faith receiving,
　From Jesus shall not move;
For he who dies believing,
　Dies safely—through thy love.

390.

1 WHEN human hopes all wither,
　And friends no aid supply,
Then whither, Lord, ah! whither
　Can turn my straining eye?
'Mid storms of grief still rougher,
　'Midst darker, deadlier shade,
That cross where thou didst suffer,
　On Calvary was displayed.

2 On that my gaze I fasten,
　My refuge that I make;
Though sorely thou may'st chasten,
　Thou never canst forsake:
Thou, on that cross didst languish,
　Ere glory crowned thy head!
And I, through death, and anguish,
　Must be to glory led.

PLEYEL'S HYMN. 7s.   PLEYEL.

1. Chil-dren of the heaven-ly King, As ye jour-ney, sweet-ly sing;

Sing your Sa-viour's wor-thy praise, Glo-rious in his works and ways.

391.

1 CHILDREN of the heavenly King,
  As ye journey, sweetly sing;
  Sing your Saviour's worthy praise,
  Glorious in his works and ways.

2 Ye are traveling home to God,
  In the way the fathers trod;
  They are happy now—and ye
  Soon their happiness shall see.

3 Shout, ye little flock, and blest;
  You on Jesus' throne shall rest:
  There your seat is now prepared—
  There your kingdom and reward.

4 Fear not, brethren, joyful stand
  On the borders of your land;
  Jesus Christ, your Father's Son,
  Bids you undismayed go on.

5 Lord! submissive make us go,
  Gladly leaving all below;
  Only thou our leader be,
  And we still will follow thee.

392.

1 To thy pastures fair and large,
  Heavenly Shepherd, lead thy charge,
  And my couch, with tenderest care,
  'Mid the springing grass prepare.

2 When I faint with summer's heat,
  Thou shalt guide my weary feet,
  To the streams that, still and slow,
  Through the verdant meadows flow.

3 Safe the dreary vale I tread,
  By the shades of death o'erspread,
  With thy rod and staff supplied,
  This my guard,—and that my guide.

4 Constant to my latest end,
  Thou my footsteps shalt attend;
  And shalt bid thy hallowed dome
  Yield me an eternal home.

393.

1 FAINT not, Christian! though the road,
  Leading to thy blest abode,
  Darksome be, and dangerous too,
  Christ thy Guide will bring thee through.

2 Faint not, Christian! though in rage
  Satan would thy soul engage,
  Gird on faith's anointed shield,
  Bear it to the battle-field.

3 Faint not, Christian! though the world
  Has its hostile flag unfurled;
  Hold the cross of Jesus fast,
  Thou shalt overcome at last.

4 Faint not, Christian! though within,
  There's a heart so prone to sin;
  Christ the Lord is over all,
  He'll not suffer thee to fall.

5 Faint not, Christian! look on high,
  See the harpers in the sky;
  Patient wait, and thou wilt join—
  Chant with them of love divine.

WILLIS. 7s.

R. STORRS WILLIS.

1. Now be-gin the heavenly theme, Sing a-loud in Je-sus' name! Ye, who his sal- -va-tion prove, Triumph in re-deem-ing love, Tri-umph in re-deeming love.

394.

1 Now begin the heavenly theme,
Sing aloud in Jesus' name!
Ye, who his salvation prove,
Triumph in redeeming love.

2 Ye who see the Father's grace
Beaming in the Saviour's face,
As to Canaan on ye move,
Praise and bless redeeming love.

3 Mourning souls, dry up your tears;
Banish all your guilty fears;
See your guilt and curse remove,
Canceled by redeeming love.

4 Hither, then, your tribute bring,
Strike aloud each joyful string;
Saints below, and saints above,
Join to praise redeeming love.

395.

1 Hark! my soul! it is the Lord;
'T is thy Saviour—hear his word;
Jesus speaks, and speaks to thee,
"Say, poor sinner, lovest thou me?

2 "I delivered thee when bound,
And when bleeding, healed thy wound:
Sought thee wandering, set thee right,
Turned thy darkness into light.

3 "Can a woman's tender care
Cease toward the child she bare?
Yes, she may forgetful be,
Yet will I remember thee.

4 "Mine is an unchanging love,
Higher than the heights above;
Deeper than the depths beneath—
Free and faithful—strong as death.

5 "Thou shalt see my glory soon,
When the work of grace is done;
Partner of my throne shalt be!
Say, poor sinner! lovest thou me?"

6 Lord! it is my chief complaint,
That my love is weak and faint;
Yet I love thee, and adore;—
Oh! for grace to love thee more.

396.

1 Much in sorrow, oft in woe,
Onward, Christians, onward go;
Fight the fight; and worn with strife,
Steep with tears the bread of life.

2 Onward, Christians, onward go;
Join the war, and face the foe;
Faint not: much doth yet remain;
Dreary is the long campaign.

3 Shrink not, Christians—will ye yield?
Will ye quit the battle-field?
Fight till all the conflict 's o'er,
Nor your foes shall rally more.

3 But when loud the trumpet blown,
Speaks their forces overthrown,
Christ, your Captain, shall bestow
Crowns to grace the conqueror's brow.

MISSIONARY CHANT. L. M.   Ch. Zeuner.

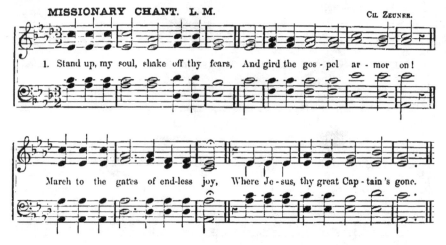

1. Stand up, my soul, shake off thy fears, And gird the gos-pel ar-mor on!

March to the gates of end-less joy, Where Je-sus, thy great Cap-tain's gone.

397.

1 STAND up, my soul, shake off thy fears,
And gird the gospel armor on;
March to the gates of endless joy,
Where Jesus, thy great Captain's gone.

2 Hell and thy sins resist thy course;
But hell and sin are vanquished foes;
Thy Saviour nailed them to the cross,
And sung the triumph when he rose.

3 Then let my soul march boldly on,—
Press forward to the heavenly gate;
There peace and joy eternal reign,
And glittering robes for conquerors wait.

4 There shall I wear a starry crown,
And triumph in almighty grace,
While all the armies of the skies
Join in my glorious Leader's praise.

398.

1 AWAKE, our souls! away, our fears!
Let every trembling thought be gone;
Awake, and run the heavenly race,
And put a cheerful courage on!

2 True, 't is a strait and thorny road,
And mortal spirits tire and faint;
But they forget the mighty God,
Who feeds the strength of every saint—

3 The mighty God, whose matchless power
Is ever new and ever young,
And firm endures, while endless years
Their everlasting circles run.

4 From thee, the overflowing spring,
Our souls shall drink a fresh supply;
While such as trust their native strength,
Shall melt away, and droop, and die.

5 Swift as an eagle cuts the air,
We 'll mount aloft to thine abode;
On wings of love our souls shall fly,
Nor tire amid the heavenly road!

399.

1 AWAKE, my soul! lift up thine eyes;
See where thy foes against thee rise,
In long array, a numerous host;
Awake, my soul! or thou art lost.

2 See where rebellious passions rage,
And fierce desires and lusts engage;
The meanest foe of all the train
Has thousands and ten thousands slain.

3 Thou treadest on enchanted ground;
Perils and snares beset thee round;
Beware of all, guard every part—
But most the traitor in thy heart.

4 The terror and the charm repel,
And powers of earth, and powers of hell;
The Man of Calvary triumphed here:
Why should his faithful followers fear?

5 Come then, my soul! now learn to wield
The weight of thine immortal shield;
Put on the armor, from above,
Of heavenly truth, and heavenly love.

CHRISTMAS. C. M. HANDEL.

1. A-wake, my soul! stretch ev-ery nerve, And press with vigor on: A heaven-ly

race demands thy zeal, A bright im-mor-tal crown, A bright im-mor-tal crown.

400.

2 A cloud of witnesses around
Hold thee in full survey:
Forget the steps already trod,
And onward urge thy way.

3 'T is God's all-animating voice,
That calls thee from on high;
'T is his own hand presents the prize
To thine aspiring eye,—

4 That prize with peerless glories bright,
Which shall new lustre boast,
When victor's wreaths and monarch's gems
Shall blend in common dust.

5 Blest Saviour, introduced by thee,
Have I my race begun;
And, crowned with victory, at thy feet
I'll lay my honors down.

401.

1 Am I a soldier of the cross,
A follower of the Lamb?
And shall I fear to own his cause,
Or blush to speak his name?

2 Must I be carried to the skies
On flowery beds of ease?
While others fought to win the prize,
And sailed through bloody seas?

3 Are there no foes for me to face?
Must I not stem the flood?
Is this vile world a friend to grace,
To help me on to God?

4 Sure I must fight, if I would reign;
Increase my courage, Lord!
I'll bear the toil, endure the pain,
Supported by thy word.

5 Thy saints, in all this glorious war,
Shall conquer, though they die;
They view the triumph from afar,
And seize it with their eye.

6 When that illustrious day shall rise,
And all thy armies shine
In robes of victory through the skies,
The glory shall be thine.

402.

1 I'm not ashamed to own my Lord,
Or to defend his cause;
Maintain the honor of his word,
The glory of his cross.

2 Jesus, my God!—I know his name—
His name is all my trust;
Nor will he put my soul to shame,
Nor let my hope be lost.

3 Firm as his throne his promise stands,
And he can well secure
What I've committed to his hands,
Till the decisive hour.

4 Then will he own my worthless name
Before his Father's face,
And in the New Jerusalem
Appoint my soul a place.

ARLINGTON. C. M.   Dr. Arne.

1. A - maz - ing grace! how sweet the sound That saved a wretch like me!

I once was lost, but now am found,—Was blind, but now I see.

403.

1 Amazing grace! how sweet the sound
  That saved a wretch like me!
  I once was lost, but now am found—
  Was blind, but now I see.

2 'T was grace that taught my heart to fear,
  And grace my fears relieved;
  How precious did that grace appear,
  The hour I first believed!

3 Through many dangers, toils, and snares,
  I have already come;
  'T is grace hath brought me safe thus far,
  And grace will lead me home.

4 Yea—when this flesh and heart shall fail,
  And mortal life shall cease,
  I shall possess, within the vail,
  A life of joy and peace.

5 The earth shall soon dissolve like snow,
  The sun forbear to shine;
  But God, who called me here below,
  Will be forever mine.

404.

1 Whence do our mournful thoughts arise,
  And where's our courage fled?
  Has restless sin, or raging hell,
  Struck all our comforts dead?

2 Have we forgot th' almighty Name
  That formed the earth and sea?
  And can an all-creating arm
  Grow weary or decay?

3 Treasures of everlasting might
  In our Jehovah dwell;
  He gives the conquest to the weak,
  And treads their foes to hell.

4 Mere mortal power shall fade and die,
  And youthful vigor cease;
  But we who wait upon the Lord
  Shall feel our strength increase.

5 The saints shall mount on eagles' wings,
  And taste the promised bliss,
  Till their unwearied feet arrive
  Where perfect pleasure is.

405.

1 How can I sink with such a prop
  As my eternal God,
  Who bears the earth's huge pillars up
  And spreads the heavens abroad?

2 How can I die while Jesus lives,
  Who rose and left the dead?
  Pardon and grace my soul receives
  From my exalted Head.

3 All that I am, and all I have,
  Shall be forever thine;
  Whate'er my duty bids me give,
  My cheerful hands resign.

4 Yet, if I might make some reserve,
  And duty did not call,
  I love my God with zeal so great,
  That I should give him all.

MOUNT AUBURN. C. M.

GEO. KINGSLEY.

1. Chil - dren of God, who, faint and slow, Your pil - grim path pur - sue,

In strength and weak - ness, joy and woe, To God's high call - ing true!—

406.

2 Why move ye thus, with lingering tread,
   A doubting mournful band?
Why faintly hangs the drooping head?
Why fails the feeble hand?

3 Oh! weak to know a Saviour's power,
   To feel a father's care;
A moment's toil, a passing shower,
   Is all the grief ye share.

4 The orb of light, though clouds awhile
   May hide his noon-tide ray,
Shall soon in lovelier beauty smile
   To gild the closing day,—

5 And, bursting through the dusky shroud
   That dared his power invest,
Ride throned in light o'er every cloud,
   Triumphant to his rest.

6 Then, Christian, dry the falling tear,
   The faithless doubt remove;
Redeemed at last from guilt and fear,
   Oh! wake thy heart to love.

407.

1 YE trembling souls! dismiss your fears,
   Be mercy all your theme;—
Mercy,—which, like a river, flows,
   In one perpetual stream.

2 Fear not the powers of earth and hell;—
   Those powers will God restrain;
His arm shall all their rage repel,
   And make their efforts vain.

3 Fear not the want of outward good;
   For his he will provide,
Grant them supplies of daily food,
   And all they need beside.

4 Fear not that he will e'er forsake,
   Or leave his work undone;
He's faithful to his promises,
   And faithful to his Son.

5 Fear not the terrors of the grave,
   Nor death's tremendous sting;
He will, from endless wrath, preserve—
   To endless glory bring.

408.

1 WHEN I can read my title clear
   To mansions in the skies,
I bid farewell to every fear,
   And wipe my weeping eyes.

2 Should earth against my soul engage,
   And fiery darts be hurled,
Then I can smile at Satan's rage,
   And face a frowning world.

3 Let cares like a wild deluge come,
   And storms of sorrow fall;
May I but safely reach my home,
   My God, my heaven, my all!

4 There shall I bathe my weary soul
   In seas of heavenly rest;
And not a wave of trouble roll
   Across my peaceful breast.

OLMUTZ. S. M.   *Arranged by* Dr. L. Mason.

1. Your harps, ye trem - bling saints, Down from the wil - lows take:

Loud to the praise of love di - vine Bid ev - ery string a - wake.

409.

2 Though in a foreign land,
  We are not far from home,
And nearer to our house above
  We every moment come.

3 His grace will to the end
  Stronger and brighter shine,
Nor present things, nor things to come,
  Shall quench the spark divine.

4 When we in darkness walk,
  Nor feel the heavenly flame,
Then is the time to trust our God,
  And rest upon his name.

5 Soon shall our doubts and fears
  Subside at his control;
His loving-kindness shall break through
  The midnight of the soul.

6 Blest is the man, O God,
  That stays himself on thee!
Who waits for thy salvation, Lord,
  Shall thy salvation see.

410.

1 Give to the winds thy fears,
  Hope, and be undismayed;
God hears thy sighs, and counts thy tears,
  God shall lift up thy head.

2 Through waves, and clouds, and storms,
  He gently clears the way;
Wait thou his time; so shall this night
  Soon end in joyous day.

3 Still heavy is thy heart?
  Still sink thy spirits down?
Cast off the weight, let fear depart,
  And every care be gone.

4 What though thou rulest not?
  Yet heaven, and earth, and hell
Proclaim God sitteth on the throne,
  And ruleth all things well.

5 Leave to his sovereign sway,
  To choose and to command;
So shalt thou, wondering, own his way
  How wise, how good his hand!

411.

1 The sun himself shall fade,
  The starry worlds shall fall;
Yet through a vast eternity,
  Shall God be all in all.

2 Though now his ways are dark,
  Concealed from mortal sight,
His counsels are divinely wise,
  And all his judgments right.

3 In God my trust shall stand,
  While waves of sorrow roll;
In life or death his name shall be
  The refuge of my soul.

4 Cease, cease my tears to flow,
  Cease, cease my heart to moan;
Betide what may to me, I'll say,
  His holy will be done!

DENNIS. S. M.

NAGELI.

1. The Lord my Shep-herd is, I shall be well sup-plied:

Since he is mine, and I am his, What can I want be - side?

412.

2 He leads me to the place,
  Where heavenly pasture grows,
  Where living waters gently pass,
  And full salvation flows.

3 If e'er I go astray,
  He doth my soul reclaim;
  And guides me in his own right way,
  For his most holy name.

4 While he affords his aid,
  I cannot yield to fear;
  Tho' I should walk thro' death's dark
      shade,
  My Shepherd's with me there.

5 In spite of all my foes,
  Thou dost my table spread;
  My cup with blessings overflows,
  And joy exalts my head.

6 The bounties of thy love
  Shall crown my future days;
  Nor from thy house will I remove,
  Nor cease to speak thy praise.

413.

1 THE harvest dawn is near,
  The year delays not long;
  And he who sows with many a tear,
  Shall reap with many a song.

2 Sad to his toil he goes,
  His seed with weeping leaves;
  But he shall come, at twilight's close,
  And bring his golden sheaves.

414.

1 How gentle God's commands!
  How kind his precepts are!
  Come, cast your burdens on the Lord,
  And trust his constant care.

2 Beneath his watchful eye
  His saints securely dwell;
  That hand which bears all nature up,
  Shall guard his children well.

3 Why should this anxious load
  Press down your weary mind?
  Haste to your heavenly Father's throne,
  And sweet refreshment find.

4 His goodness stands approved,
  Unchanged from day to day:
  I'll drop my burden at his feet,
  And bear a song away.

415.

1 I STAND on Zion's mount,
  And view my starry crown;
  No power on earth my hope can shake,
  Nor hell can thrust me down.

2 The lofty hills and towers,
  That lift their heads on high,
  Shall all be leveled low in dust—
  Their very names shall die.

3 The vaulted heavens shall fall,
  Built by Jehovah's hands;
  But firmer than the heavens, the Rock
  Of my salvation stands!

BAYLEY. 8s & 7s.   *Arranged.* J. P. H.

1. Love di - vine, all love ex - cel - ling, Joy of heaven, to earth come down!

Fix in us thy hum - ble dwell - ing, All thy faith - ful mer - cies crown;
D. S. Vis - it us with thy sal - va - tion, En - ter ev - ery trem - bling heart.

Je - sus! thou art all com - pas - sion, Pure, un - bound - ed love thou art;

416.

Breathe, oh, breathe thy loving spirit
  Into every troubled breast!
Let us all in thee inherit,
  Let us find, thy promised rest :
Come, Almighty to deliver,
  Let us all thy life receive!
Speedily return, and never,
  Never more thy temples leave !

3 Finish then thy new creation,
  Pure, unspotted may we be:
Let us see our whole salvation
  Perfectly secured by thee !
Changed from glory into glory,
  Till in heaven we take our place;
Till we cast our crowns before thee,
  Lost in wonder, love, and praise.

417.

1 Know, my soul! thy full salvation;
  Rise o'er sin, and fear, and care ;
Joy to find, in every station,
  Something still to do or bear :
Think what Spirit dwells within thee ;
  Think what Father's smiles are thine;
Think that Jesus died to win thee :
  Child of heaven, canst thou repine?

2 Haste thee on from grace to glory,
  Armed by faith, and winged by prayer !
Heaven's eternal day 's before thee,
  God's own hand shall guide thee there :
Soon shall close thy earthly mission,
  Soon shall pass thy pilgrim days,
Hope shall change to glad fruition,
  Faith to sight, and prayer to praise.

418.

1 Hear what God, the Lord, hath spoken :
  O my people, faint and few,
Comfortless, afflicted, broken,
  Fair abodes I build for you ;
Scenes of heartfelt tribulation
  Shall no more perplex your ways ;
You shall name your walls " Salvation,"
  And your gates shall all be " Praise."

2 Ye no more your suns descending,
  Waning moons no more shall see ;
But your griefs forever ending,
  Find eternal noon in me :
God shall rise, and, shining o'er you,
  Change to day the gloom of night,
He, the Lord, shall be your Glory,
  God your everlasting Light.

WESTMINSTER. 8s & 7s. J. P. HOLBROOK.

1. On - ward, Chris-tian, though the re - gion Where thou art be drear and lone;

God has set a guar - dian le - gion Ve - ry near thee; press thou on.

419.

1 ONWARD, Christian, though the region
Where thou art be drear and lone;
God has set a guardian legion
Very near thee; press thou on.

2 Listen, Christian; their hosanna
Rolleth o'er thee: "God is love."
Write upon thy red-cross banner,
"Upward ever; heaven's above."

3 By the thorn-road, and none other,
Is the mount of vision won;
Tread it without shrinking, brother;
Jesus trod it; press thou on.

4 Be this world the wiser, stronger,
For thy life of pain and peace;
While it needs thee, oh! no longer
Pray thou for thy quick release.

5 Pray thou, Christian, daily rather,
That thou be a faithful son;
By the prayer of Jesus, "Father,
Not My will, but Thine, be done."

420.

1 ALWAYS with us, always with us—
Words of cheer and words of love;
Thus the risen Saviour whispers,
From his dwelling-place above.

2 With us when we toil in sadness,
Sowing much and reaping none,
Telling us that in the future
Golden harvests shall be won.

3 With us when the storm is sweeping
O'er our pathway dark and drear,
Waking hope within our bosoms,
Stilling every anxious fear.

4 With us in the lonely valley,
When we cross the chilling stream,
Lighting up the steps to glory
With salvation's radiant beam.

421.

1 CALL Jehovah thy salvation,
Rest beneath th' Almighty's shade;
In his secret habitation
Dwell, and never be dismayed!

2 There no tumult can alarm thee,
Thou shalt dread no hidden snare;
Guile nor violence can harm thee,
In eternal safeguard there.

3 Thee, tho' winds and waves are swelling,
God, thy Hope, shall bear through all;
Plague shall not come nigh thy dwelling,
Thee no evil shall befall.

4 He shall charge his angel legions
Watch and ward o'er thee to keep,
Though thou walk through hostile regions,
Though in desert wilds thou sleep.

5 Since, with firm and pure affection,
Thou on God hast set thy love,
With the wings of his protection
He shall shield thee from above.

PORTUGUESE HYMN. 11s.

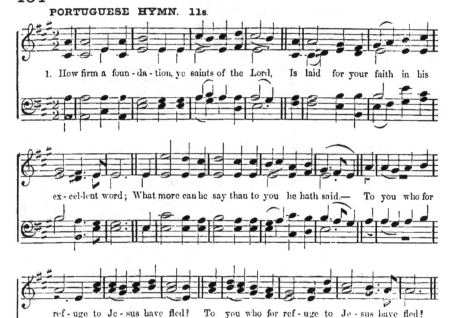

1. How firm a foun-da-tion, ye saints of the Lord, Is laid for your faith in his ex-cel-lent word; What more can he say than to you he hath said,— To you who for ref-uge to Je-sus have fled? To you who for ref-uge to Je-sus have fled?

422.

2 "Fear not, I am with thee, oh, be not dismayed,
For I am thy God, I will still give thee aid:
I 'll strengthen thee, help thee, and cause thee
    to stand,
Upheld by my righteous, omnipotent hand.

3 "When thro' the deep waters I call thee to go,
The rivers of sorrow shall not overflow;
For I will be with thee thy trials to bless,
And sanctify to thee thy deepest distress.

4 "When thro' fiery trials thy pathway shall lie,
My grace, all-sufficient, shall be thy supply,
The flame shall not hurt thee; I only design
Thy dross to consume, and thy gold to refine.

5 "Ev'n down to old age all my people shall prove
My sovereign, eternal, unchangeable love;
And then, when gray hairs shall their temples
    adorn,
Like lambs they shall still in my bosom be borne.

6 "The soul that on Jesus hath leaned for repose,
I will not—I will not desert to his foes;

That soul—though all hell should endeavor to
    shake,
I 'll never—no never—no never forsake!"

423.

1 THE Lord is my shepherd, no want shall I know,
I feed in green pastures, safe-folded I rest;
He leadeth my soul where the still waters flow,
Restores me when wandering, redeems when
    oppressed.

2 Thro' the valley and shadow of death, tho' I stray,
Since thou art my guardian, no evil I fear;
Thy rod shall defend me, thy staff be my stay;
No harm can befall, with my comforter near.

3 In the midst of affliction my table is spread;
With blessings unmeasured my cup runneth o'er;
With perfume and oil thou anointest my head;
Oh! what shall I ask of thy providence more?

4 Let goodness and mercy, my bountiful God!
Still follow my steps till I meet thee above;
I seek—by the path which my forefathers trod,
Thro' the land of their sojourn—thy kingdom
    of love.

424.

1 O ZION, afflicted with wave upon wave!
Whom no man can comfort, whom no man can
save ;
With darkness surrounded, by terrors dismayed,
In toiling and rowing, thy strength is decayed.

2 Loud roaring, the billows now nigh overwhelm,
But skilful 's the Pilot who sits at the helm ;
His wisdom conducts thee, his power defends ;
In safety and quiet thy warfare he ends.

3 "O fearful! O faithless !" in mercy he cries ;
"My promise, my truth, are they light in thine
eyes?
Still, still I am with thee, my promise shall stand ;
Thro' tempest and tossing I 'll bring thee to land.

4 "Forget thee I will not—I cannot ; thy name,
Engraved on my heart doth forever remain ;
The palms of my hands while I look on, I see
The wounds that I suffered, when dying for thee.

5 "Then trust me, and fear not! thy life is secure,
My wisdom is perfect, supreme is my power ;
In love I correct thee, thy soul to refine,
To make thee at length in my likeness to shine."

425.

1 THO' faint, yet pursuing, we go on our way ;
The Lord is our Leader, his word is our stay ;
Tho' suffering, and sorrow, and trial be near,
The Lord is our refuge, and whom can we fear ?

2 He raiseth the fallen, he cheereth the faint ;
The weak, and oppressed—he will hear their
complaint ;
The way may be weary, and thorny the road,
But how can we falter ? our help is in God !

3 And to his green pastures our footsteps he
leads ;
His flock in the desert how kindly he feeds !
The lambs in his bosom he tenderly bears,
And brings back the wanderers all safe from the
snares.

4 Tho' clouds may surround us, our God is our
light ;
Tho' storms rage around us, our God is our
might ;
So faint, yet pursuing, still onward we come ;
The Lord is our Leader, and heaven is our
home !

426.

1 O EYES that are weary, and hearts that are sore !
Look off unto Jesus, now sorrow no more !
The light of his countenance shineth so bright,
That here, as in heaven, there need be no night.

2 While looking to Jesus, my heart cannot fear ;
I tremble no more when I see Jesus near ;
I know that his presence my safeguard will be.
For, "Why are ye troubled ?" he saith unto me.

3 Still looking to Jesus, oh, may I be found,
When Jordan's dark waters encompass me
round :
They bear me away in his presence to be :
I see him still nearer whom always I see.

4 Then, then shall I know the full beauty and
grace
Of Jesus, my Lord, when I stand face to face ;
Shall know how his love went before me each
day,
And wonder that ever my eyes turned away.

427.

1 I ONCE was a stranger to grace and to God ;
I knew not my danger, and felt not my load ;
Tho' friends spoke in rapture of Christ on the
tree,
Jehovah, my Saviour, seemed nothing to me.

2 When free grace awoke me by light from on
high,
Then legal fears shook me : I trembled to die :
No refuge, no safety, in self could I see :
Jehovah, thou only my Saviour must be !

3 My terrors all vanished before his sweet name ;
My guilty fears banished, with boldness I came
To drink at the fountain, so copious and free :
Jehovah, my Saviour, is all things to me.

4 Jehovah, the Lord, is my treasure and boast ;
Jehovah my Saviour, I ne'er can be lost :
In thee I shall conquer, by flood and by field,
Jehovah my anchor, Jehovah my shield !

5 Ev'n treading the valley, the shadow of death,
This watchword shall rally my faltering breath ;
For, while from life 's fever my God sets me free,
Jehovah, my Saviour, my death-song shall be !

WARE. L. M.   KINGSLEY.

1. Oh, that I could for-ev-er dwell De-light-ed at the Sa-viour's feet;
Be-hold the form I love so well, And all his ten-der words re-peat!

428.

1 Oh that I could forever dwell,
Delighted at the Saviour's feet;
Behold the form I love so well,
And all his tender words repeat!

2 The world shut out from all my soul,
And heaven brought in with all its bliss,—
Oh! is there aught, from pole to pole,
One moment to compare with this?

3 This is the hidden life I prize—
A life of penitential love;
When most my follies I despise,
And raise my highest thoughts above;

4 When all I am I clearly see,
And freely own with deepest shame;
When the Redeemer's love to me
Kindles within a deathless flame.

5 Thus would I live till nature fail,
And all my former sins forsake;
Then rise to God within the vail,
And of eternal joys partake.

429.

1 Sun of my soul! thou Saviour dear,
It is not night if thou be near:
Oh, may no earth-born cloud arise
To hide thee from thy servant's eyes!

2 When soft the dews of kindly sleep
My wearied eyelids gently steep,
Be my last thought,—how sweet to rest
Forever on my Saviour's breast!

3 Abide with me from morn till eve,
For without thee I cannot live;
Abide with me when night is nigh,
For without thee I dare not die.

4 Be near to bless me when I wake,
Ere through the world my way I take;
Abide with me till in thy love
I lose myself in heaven above.

430.

1 Oh, sweetly breathe the lyres above,
When angels touch the quivering string,
And wake, to chant Immanuel's love,
Such strains as angel-lips can sing!

2 And sweet, on earth, the choral swell,
From mortal tongues, of gladsome lays;
When pardoned souls their raptures tell,
And, grateful, hymn Immanuel's praise.

3 Jesus, thy name our souls adore;
We own the bond that makes us thine;
And carnal joys, that charmed before,
For thy dear sake we now resign.

4 Our hearts, by dying love subdued,
Accept thine offered grace to-day;
Beneath the cross, with blood bedewed,
We bow, and give ourselves away.

5 In thee we trust,—on thee rely;
Though we are feeble, thou art strong:
Oh, keep us till our spirits fly
To join the bright, immortal throng!

PARK STREET. L. M.   VENUA.

1. Fountain of grace, rich, full, and free, What need I, that is not in thee? Full par-don,

strength to meet the day, And peace which none can take away, And peace which none can take away.

431.

2 Doth sickness fill the heart with fear?
'T is sweet to know that thou art near;
Am I with dread of justice tried?
'T is sweet to feel that Christ hath died.

3 In life, thy promises of aid
Forbid my heart to be afraid;
In death, peace gently vails the eyes;
Christ rose, and I shall surely rise.

4 O all-sufficient Saviour! be
This all-sufficiency to me;
Nor pain, nor sin, nor death can harm
The weakest, shielded by thine arm.

432.

1 Jesus! and shall it ever be,
A mortal man ashamed of thee?
Ashamed of thee, whom angels praise,
Whose glories shine through endless days?

2 Ashamed of Jesus! sooner far
Let evening blush to own a star; ·
He sheds the beams of light divine
O'er this benighted soul of mine.

3 Ashamed of Jesus! that dear Friend
On whom my hopes of heaven depend!
No; when I blush—be this my shame,
That I no more revere his name.

4 Ashamed of Jesus! yes, I may,
When I 've no guilt to wash away;
No tear to wipe, no good to crave,
No fears to quell, no soul to save.

5 Till then—nor is my boasting vain—
Till then I boast a Saviour slain!
And oh, may this my glory be,
That Christ is not ashamed of me!

433.

1 Light of the soul! O Saviour blest!
Soon as thy presence fills the breast,
Darkness and guilt are put to flight,
And all is sweetness and delight.

2 Son of the Father! Lord most high!
How glad is he who feels thee nigh!
Come in thy hidden majesty;
Fill us with love, fill us with thee.

3 Jesus is from the proud concealed,
But evermore to babes revealed,
Through him, unto the Father be
Glory and praise eternally.

434.

1 None loves me, Saviour, with thy love,
None else can meet such needs as mine;
Oh, grant me, as thou shalt approve,
All that befits a child of thine!

2 Give me a faith shall never fail,
One that shall always work by love;
And then, whatever foes assail,
They shall but higher courage move.

3 A heart that, when my days are glad,
May never from thy way decline,
A heart that loves to trust in thee,
A patient heart, create in me!

CHURCH. C. M.   J. P. HOLBROOK.

1. Dear Ref - uge of my wea - ry soul, On thee, when sor-rows rise—

On thee, when waves of trouble roll, My faint-ing heart re - lies.

435.

2 To thee I tell each rising grief,
   For thou alone canst heal;
   Thy word can bring a sweet relief
   For every pain I feel.

3 But oh! when gloomy doubts prevail,
   I fear to call thee mine;
   The springs of comfort seem to fail,
   And all my hopes decline.

4 Yet, gracious God, where shall I flee?
   Thou art my only trust:
   And still my soul would cleave to thee,
   Though prostrate in the dust.

5 Thy mercy-seat is open still,
   Here let my soul retreat,
   With humble hope attend thy will,
   And wait beneath thy feet.

436.

1 SPEAK to me, Lord, thyself reveal,
   While here on earth I rove;
   Speak to my heart, and let me feel
   The kindling of thy love.

2 With thee conversing, I forget
   All time and toil and care;
   Labor is rest, and pain is sweet,
   If thou, my God, art here.

3 Here then, my God, be pleased to stay,
   And make my heart rejoice;
   My bounding heart shall own thy sway,
   And echo to thy voice.

4 Thou callest me to seek thy face;
   Thy face, O God, I seek,—
   Attend the whispers of thy grace,
   And hear thee inly speak.

5 Let this my every hour employ,
   Till I thy glory see,
   Enter into my Master's joy,
   And find my heaven in thee.

437

1 DEAREST of all the names above,
   My Jesus and my God,
   Who can resist thy heavenly love,
   Or trifle with thy blood?

2 'T is by the merits of thy death
   Thy Father smiles again;
   'T is by thine interceding breath
   The Spirit dwells with men.

3 Till God in human flesh I see,
   .My thoughts no comfort find:
   The holy, just, and sacred Three
   Are terror to my mind.

4 But if Immanuel's face appear,
   My hope, my joy, begin:
   His name forbids my slavish fear;
   His grace removes my sin.

5 While Jews on their own law rely,
   And Greeks of wisdom boast,
   I love th' incarnate Mystery,
   And there I fix my trust.

HEBER. C. M.   KINGSLEY.

1. How sweet the name of Je - sus sounds In a be - liev - er's ear!

It soothes his sor - rows, heals his wounds, And drives a - way his fear.

438.

2 It makes the wounded spirit whole,
  And calms the troubled breast;
'T is manna to the hungry soul,
  And to the weary, rest.

3 Jesus! my Shepherd, Guardian, Friend,
  My Prophet, Priest, and King;
My Lord, my Life, my Way, my End,
  Accept the praise I bring!

4 Weak is the effort of my heart,
  And cold my warmest thought;
But when I see thee as thou art,
  I 'll praise thee as I ought.

5 Till then, I would thy love proclaim,
  With every fleeting breath;
And may the music of thy name
  Refresh my soul in death.

439.

1 Jesus! I love thy charming name,
  'T is music to mine ear;
Fain would I sound it out so loud,
  That earth and heaven should hear.

2 Yes!—thou art precious to my soul,
  My transport and my trust;
Jewels, to thee, are gaudy toys,
  And gold is sordid dust.

3 All my capacious powers can wish,
  In thee doth richly meet;
Not to mine eyes is light so dear,
  Nor friendship half so sweet.

4 Thy grace still dwells upon my heart,
  And sheds its fragrance there;—
The noblest balm of all its wounds,
  The cordial of its care.

5 I 'll speak the honors of thy name,
  With my last laboring breath;
Then, speechless, clasp thee in mine arms,
  The antidote of death.

440.

1 Jesus, the very thought of thee,
  With sweetness fills my breast:
But sweeter far thy face to see,
  And in thy presence rest.

2 Nor voice can sing, nor heart can frame,
  Nor can the memory find
A sweeter sound than thy blest name,
  O Saviour of mankind!

3 O Hope of every contrite heart!
  O Joy of all the meek!
To those who fall, how kind thou art!
  How good to those who seek!

4 But what to those who find? Ah! this,
  Nor tongue nor pen can show,
The love of Jesus, what it is,
  None but his loved ones know.

5 Jesus, our only joy be thou,
  As thou our prize wilt be;
Jesus, be thou our glory now,
  And through eternity.

TAPPAN. C. M.   KINGSLEY.

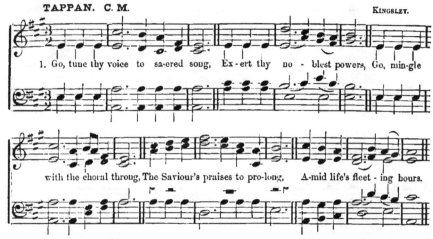

1. Go, tune thy voice to sacred song, Exert thy no - blest powers, Go, min-gle with the choral throng, The Saviour's praises to pro-long, A-mid life's fleet - ing hours.

441.

1 Go, tune thy voice to sacred song,
  Exert thy noblest powers,
Go, mingle with the choral throng,
The Saviour's praises to prolong,
  Amid life's fleeting hours.

2 Oh! hast thou felt a Saviour's love,
  That flame of heavenly birth?
Then let thy strains melodious prove,
With raptures soaring far above
  The trifling toys of earth.

3 Hast found the pearl of price unknown,
  That cost a Saviour's blood?
Heir of a bright celestial crown,
That sparkles near the eternal throne,
  Oh, sing the praise of God!

4 Sing of the Lamb that once was slain
  That man might be forgiven;
Sing how he broke death's bars in twain
Ascending high in bliss to reign,
  The God of earth and heaven!

442.

1 Wouldst thou eternal life obtain!
  Now to the cross repair;
There stand and gaze and weep and pray,
Where Jesus breathes his life away;
  Eternal life is there!

2 Go—'t is the Son of God expires!
  Approach the shameful tree;
See quivering there the mortal dart,
In the Redeemer's loving heart,
  O sinful soul, for thee!

3 Go—there from every streaming wound
  Flows rich atoning blood:
That blood can cleanse thy deepest stain,
Bid frowning justice smile again,
  And seal thy peace with God.

4 Go—at that cross thy heart subdued,
  With thankful love shall glow;
By wondrous grace thy soul set free,
Eternal life from Christ to thee
  A vital stream shall flow!

443.

1 O Saviour, lend a listening ear,
  And answer my request!
Forgive, and wipe the falling tear,
Now with thy love my spirit cheer,
  And set my heart at rest.

2 I mourn the hidings of thy face;
  The absence of that smile,
Which led me to a throne of grace,
And gave my soul a resting-place,
  From earthly care and toil.

3 'T is sin that separates from thee
  This poor benighted soul;
My folly and my guilt I see,
And now upon the bended knee,
  I yield to thy control.

4 Up to the place of thine abode
  I lift my waiting eye;
To thee, O holy Lamb of God!
Whose blood for me so freely flowed,
  I raise my ardent cry.

BRIDGMAN. C. M. *Arranged from* BEETHOVEN.

1. Do not I love thee, O my Lord? Be-hold my heart and see;

And turn the dear-est i - dol out That dares to ri - val thee.

444.

2 Do not I love thee from my soul?
　Then let me nothing love:
Dead be my heart to every joy
　When Jesus cannot move.

3 Is not thy name melodious still
　To mine attentive ear?
Doth not each pulse with pleasure bound,
　My Saviour's voice to hear?

4 Hast thou a lamb in all thy flock
　I would disdain to feed?
Hast thou a foe before whose face
　I fear thy cause to plead?

5 Would not my heart pour forth its blood
　In honor of thy name?
And challenge the cold hand of death
　To damp th' immortal flame?

6 Thou know'st I love thee, dearest Lord;
　But oh! I long to soar
Far from the sphere of mortal joys,
　And learn to love thee more.

445.

1 Oh, see how Jesus trusts himself
　Unto our childish love!
As though by his free ways with us
　Our earnestness to prove.

2 His sacred name a common word
　On earth he loves to hear;
There is no majesty in him
　Which love may not come near.

3 The light of love is round his feet,
　His paths are never dim;
And he comes nigh to us when we
　Dare not come nigh to him.

4 Let us be simple with him, then,
　Not backward, stiff, nor cold,
As though our Bethlehem could be
　What Sinai was of old.

446.

1 JESUS! thou art the sinner's Friend;
　As such I look to thee;
Now, in the fullness of thy love,
　O Lord! remember me.

2 Remember thy pure word of grace,—
　Remember Calvary;
Remember all thy dying groans,
　And then remember me.

3 Thou wondrous Advocate with God!
　I yield myself to thee;
While thou art sitting on thy throne,
　Dear Lord! remember me.

4 Lord! I am guilty—I am vile,
　But thy salvation 's free;
Then, in thine all-abounding grace,
　Dear Lord! remember me.

5 And, when I close my eyes in death,
　When creature-helps all flee,
Then, O my dear Redeemer God!
　I pray, remember me.

DENFIELD. C. M.   *Arranged by* Dr. L. Mason.

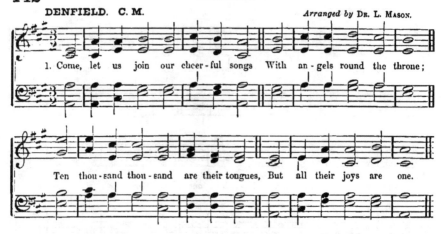

1. Come, let us join our cheer-ful songs With an-gels round the throne;
Ten thou-sand thou-sand are their tongues, But all their joys are one.

447.

2 " Worthy the Lamb that died," they cry,
   " To be exalted thus !"
   " Worthy the Lamb !" our lips reply,
   " For he was slain for us."

3 Jesus is worthy to receive
   Honor and power divine ;
   And blessings, more than we can give,
   Be, Lord, forever thine !

4 Let all that dwell above the sky
   And air, and earth, and seas,
   Conspire to lift thy glories high,
   And speak thine endless praise.

5 The whole creation join in one,
   To bless the sacred name
   Of him who sits upon the throne,
   And to adore the Lamb !

448.

1 My God ! the spring of all my joys,
   The life of my delights,
   The glory of my brightest days,
   And comfort of my nights !

2 In darkest shades if he appear,
   My dawning is begun :
   He is my soul's sweet morning star,
   And he my rising sun.

3 The opening heavens around me shine
   With beams of sacred bliss,
   While Jesus shows his heart is mine,
   And whispers, I am his !

4 My soul would leave this heavy clay,
   At that transporting word ;
   Run up with joy the shining way,
   T'embrace my dearest Lord !

5 Fearless of hell and ghastly death,
   I 'd break through every foe ;
   The wings of love and arms of faith
   Should bear me conqueror through.

449.

1 Blest Jesus ! when my soaring thoughts
   O'er all thy graces rove,
   How is my soul in transport lost,—
   In wonder, joy, and love !

2 Not softest strains can charm my ears,
   Like thy beloved name ;
   Nor aught beneath the skies inspire
   My heart with equal flame.

3 Where'er I look, my wondering eyes
   Unnumbered blessings see ;
   But what is life, with all its bliss,
   If once compared with thee?

4 Hast thou a rival in my breast?
   Search, Lord, for thou canst tell
   If aught can raise my passions thus,
   Or please my soul so well.

5 No : thou art precious to my heart,
   My portion and my joy :
   Forever let thy boundless grace
   My sweetest thoughts employ.

GEER. C. M.

GREATOREX COLL.

1. To our Re-deem-er's glo-rious name, A-wake the sa-cred song!

Oh! may his love—im-mor-tal flame—Tune ev-ery heart and tongue!

450.

1 To our Redeemer's glorious name,
   Awake the sacred song!
Oh! may his love—immortal flame—
   Tune every heart and tongue!

2 His love, what mortal thought can reach?
   What mortal tongue display?
Imagination's utmost stretch,
   In wonder, dies away.

3 Dear Lord! while we adoring pay
   Our humble thanks to thee,
May every heart with rapture say,—
   "The Saviour died for me!"

4 Oh! may the sweet, the blissful theme,
   Fill every heart and tongue,
Till strangers love thy charming name,
   And join the sacred song.

451.

1 THOU, O my Jesus, thou didst me
   Upon the cross embrace!
For me didst bear the nails and spear,
   And manifold disgrace.

2 And griefs and torments numberless,
   And sweat of agony—
Yea, death itself—and all for one
   That was thine enemy.

3 Then why, O blessed Jesus Christ,
   Should I not love thee well?
Not for the hope of winning heaven,
   Nor of escaping hell!

4 Not with the hope of gaining aught,
   Not seeking a reward;
But as thyself hast loved me,
   O everlasting Lord!

5 Ev'n so I love thee, and will love,
   And in thy praise will sing,
Solely because thou art my God,
   And my eternal King!

452.

1 OH, speak that gracious word again,
   And cheer my broken heart!
No voice but thine can soothe my pain,
   Or bid my fears depart.

2 And wilt thou still vouchsafe to own
   A worm so vile as I?
And may I still approach thy throne,
   And "Abba, Father," cry?

3 Oh, then, let saints and angels join,
   And help me to proclaim
The grace that healed a soul like mine,
   And put my foes to shame!

4 My Saviour, by his powerful word,
   Has turned my night to day;
And all those heavenly joys restored,
   Which I had sinned away.

5 Dear Lord, I wonder and adore;
   Thy grace is all divine:
Oh, keep me, that I sin no more
   Against such love as thine!

ARIEL. L. C. M.

DR. L. MASON.

1. Oh, could I speak the match-less worth, Oh, could I sound the glo-ries forth,

Which in my Saviour shine! I'd soar, and touch the heavenly strings, And vie with Gabriel,

while he sings In notes al-most di-vine, In notes al-most di-vine.

453.

1 Oh, could I speak the matchless worth,
Oh, could I sound the glories forth,
  Which in my Saviour shine!
I'd soar, and touch the heavenly strings,
And vie with Gabriel, while he sings
  In notes almost divine.

2 I'd sing the precious blood he spilt,
My ransom from the dreadful guilt
  Of sin and wrath divine!
I'd sing his glorious righteousness,
In which all-perfect, heavenly dress
  My soul shall ever shine.

3 I'd sing the characters he bears,
And all the forms of love he wears,
  Exalted on his throne:
In loftiest songs of sweetest praise,
I would to everlasting days
  Make all his glories known.

4 Well—the delightful day will come,
When my dear Lord will bring me home,
  And I shall see his face:
Then with my Saviour, Brother, Friend,
A blest eternity I'll spend,
  Triumphant in his grace.

454.

1 Come join, ye saints, with heart and voice,
Alone in Jesus to rejoice,
  And worship at his feet;
Come, take his praises on your tongues,
And raise to him your thankful songs,
  "In him ye are complete!"

2 In him, who all our praise excels
The fullness of the Godhead dwells,
  And all perfections meet;
The head of all celestial powers,
Divinely theirs, divinely ours;
  "In him ye are complete."

3 Still onward urge your heavenly way,
Dependent on him day by day,
  His presence still entreat;
His precious name forever bless,
Your glory, strength and righteousness,
  "In him ye are complete!"

4 Nor fear to pass the vale of death;
In his dear arms resign your breath,
  He'll make the passage sweet;
The gloom and fears of death shall flee,
And your departing souls shall see
  "In him ye are complete!"

LOVING-KINDNESS. L. M.

1. A-wake, my soul, to joy-ful lays, And sing thy great Redeemer's praise; He justly claims a song from me, His

lov-ing-kind - ness, O how free! Lov-ing-kindness, Lov-ing-kindness, His lov-ing-kind - ness, O how free!

455.

2 He saw me ruined in the fall,
Yet loved me notwithstanding all;
He saved me from my lost estate;
His loving-kindness, oh! how great!

3 Though numerous hosts of mighty foes,
Though earth and hell my way oppose,
He safely leads my soul along;
His loving-kindness, oh! how strong!

4 When trouble, like a gloomy cloud,
Has gathered thick, and thundered loud,
He near my soul has always stood;
His loving-kindness, oh! how good!

5 Often I feel my sinful heart,
Prone from my Saviour to depart;
But though I oft have him forgot,
His loving-kindness changes not.

6 Soon shall I pass the gloomy vale,
Soon all my mortal powers must fail;
Oh! may my last expiring breath,
His loving-kindness sing in death.

CRUSADER'S HYMN. Hymn **456.** *Arranged by* R. STORRS WILLIS.

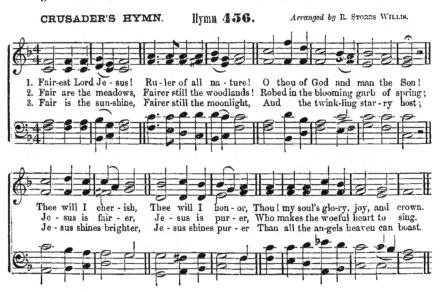

1. Fair-est Lord Je - sus! Ru - ler of all na - ture! O thou of God and man the Son!
2. Fair are the meadows, Fairer still the woodlands! Robed in the blooming garb of spring;
3. Fair is the sun-shine, Fairer still the moonlight, And the twink-ling star-ry host;

Thee will I cher - ish, Thee will I hon - or, Thou! my soul's glo-ry, joy, and crown.
Je - sus is fair - er, Je - sus is pur - er, Who makes the woeful heart to sing.
Je - sus shines brighter, Je - sus shines pur - er Than all the an-gels heaven can boast.

BONAR. S. M. Double.   J. P. HOLBROOK.

1. I was a wandering sheep, I did not love the fold : I did not love my Shepherd's voice, I would not be con-trolled ; I was a way-ward child, I did not love my home, I did not love my Shepherd's voice, I loved a - far to roam.

457.

2 The Shepherd sought his sheep,
    The Father sought his child ;
He followed me o'er vale and hill,
    O'er deserts waste and wild ;
He found me nigh to death,
    Famished, and faint, and lone ;
He bound me with the bands of love,
    He saved the wandering one.

3 He spake in tender love,
    He raised my drooping head ;
He gently closed my bleeding wounds,
    My fainting soul he fed ;
He washed my filth away,
    He made me clean and fair ;
He brought me to my home in peace,
    The long-sought wanderer.

4 Jesus my Shepherd is,
    'T was he that loved my soul,
'T was he that washed me in his blood,
    'T was he that made me whole :
'T was he that sought the lost,
    That found the wandering sheep,
'T was he that brought me to the fold—
    'T was he that still doth keep.

5 No more a wandering sheep,
    I love to be controlled,
I love my tender Shepherd's voice,
    I love the peaceful fold :
No more a wayward child,
    I seek no more to roam,
I love my heavenly Father's voice—
    I love, I love his home.

458.

1 For me to live is Christ,
    To die is endless gain,
For him I gladly bear the cross,
    And welcome grief and pain.
Faithful may I endure,
    And hear my Saviour say,
Thrice welcome home, beloved child,
    Inherit endless day !

2 A pilgrimage my lot,
    My home is in the skies,
I nightly pitch my tent below,
    And daily higher rise :
My journey soon will end,
    My scrip and staff laid down ;
Oh ! tempt me not with earthly toys,
    I go to wear a crown.

SHEPHERD. 11s & 10s.   SPIRITUAL SONGS.

1. The Lord is my Shep-herd, he makes me re - pose Where the pas - tures in beau - ty are grow - ing; He leads me a - far from the world and its woes, Where in peace the still wa - ters are flow - ing.

459.

2 He strengthens my spirit, he shows me the path,
   Where the arms of his love shall en-
fold me;
And when I walk through the dark
   valley of death,
His rod and his staff will uphold me!

460.

1 On, tell me, thou life and delight of my
   soul,
   Where the flock of thy pasture are
feeding;
I seek thy protection, I need thy control,
   I would go where my Shepherd is
leading.

2 Oh, tell me the place where thy flock are
   at rest,
   Where the noontide will find them re-
posing;
The tempest now rages, my soul is distressed,
And the pathway of peace I am losing.

3 And why should I stray with the flocks
   of thy foes,
   In the desert where now they are
roving;
Where hunger and thirst, where contentions and woes,
   And fierce conflicts their ruin are
proving?

4 Ah, when shall my woes and my wandering cease,
   And the follies that fill me with weeping?
O Shepherd of Israel, restore me that
   peace
   Thou dost give to the flock thou art
keeping!

5 A voice from the Shepherd now bids me
   return,
   By the way where the foot-prints are
lying;
No longer to wander, no longer to mourn:
   And homeward my spirit is flying.

MADISON. 8s. Double.

Arranged from S. B. POND.

1. Ye angels! who stand round the throne, And view my Immanuel's face,—In rapturous songs make him known, Oh! tune your soft harps to his praise: He formed you, the spirits you are, So hap-py, so no-ble, so good; When others sunk down in de-spair, Confirmed by his pow-er, ye stood.

461.

2 Ye saints! who stand nearer than they,
And cast your bright crowns at his feet,
His grace and his glory display,
And all his rich mercy repeat;
He snatched you from hell and the grave,
He ransomed from death and despair:
For you he was mighty to save,
Almighty to bring you safe there.

3 Oh! when will the period appear
When I shall unite in your song?
I'm weary of lingering here,
And I to your Saviour belong!
I'm fettered and chained up in clay;
I struggle and pant to be free;
I long to be soaring away,
My God and my Saviour to see!

4 I want to put on my attire,
Washed white in the blood of the Lamb;
I want to be one of your choir,
And tune my sweet harp to his name;
I want oh! I want to be there,
Where sorrow and sin bid adieu—
Your joy and your friendship to share—
To wonder, and worship with you!

462.

1 My Saviour, whom absent I love,
Whom, not having seen, I adore,
Whose name is exalted above
All glory, dominion, and power,—
Dissolve thou those bands that detain
My soul from her portion in thee;
Ah! strike off this adamant chain,
And make me eternally free!

2 When that happy era begins,
When arrayed in thy glories I shine,
Nor grieve any more, by my sins,
The bosom on which I recline,
Oh! then shall the vail be removed,
And round me thy brightness be poured!
I shall meet him, whom absent I loved,
I shall see, whom unseen I adored.

3 And then, nevermore shall the fears,
The trials, temptations, and woes,
Which darken this valley of tears,
Intrude on my blissful repose:
To Jesus, the crown of my hope,
My soul is in haste to be gone;
Oh, bear me, ye cherubim, up,
And waft me away to his throne!

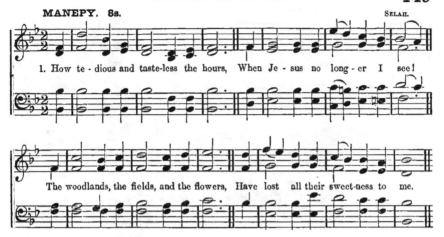

MANEPY. 8s.   SELAH.

1. How te - dious and taste-less the hours, When Je - sus no long - er I see!

The woodlands, the fields, and the flowers, Have lost all their sweet-ness to me.

463.

1 How tedious and tasteless the hours,
    When Jesus no longer I see!
The woodlands, the fields, and the flowers
Have lost all their sweetness to me.

2 His name yields the richest perfume,
    And softer than music his voice;
His presence can banish my gloom,
    And bid all within me rejoice.

3 Dear Lord! if indeed thou art mine,
    And thou art my light and my song;
Say, why do I languish and pine,
    And why are my winters so long?

4 Oh! drive these dark clouds from the sky,
    Thy soul-cheering presence restore;
Or bid me soar upward on high,
    Where winter and storms are no more.

464.

1 INSPIRER and hearer of prayer,
    Thou Shepherd and Guardian of thine,
My all to thy covenant care
    I sleeping or waking resign.

2 If thou art my shield and my sun,
    The night is no darkness to me;
And, fast as my moments roll on,
    They bring me but nearer to thee.

3 Thy ministering spirits descend
    To watch while thy saints are asleep;
By day and by night they attend,
    The heirs of salvation to keep.

4 Bright seraphs, despatched from the
    throne,
    Repair to their stations assigned;
And angels elect are sent down,
    To guard the redeemed of mankind.

5 Thy worship no interval knows;
    Their fervor is still on the wing;
And, while they protect my repose,
    They chant to the praise of my King.

6 I, too, at the season ordained,
    Their chorus forever shall join,
And love and adore, without end,
    Their faithful Creator and mine.

465.

1 MY gracious Redeemer I love,
    His praises aloud I'll proclaim:
And join with the armies above,
    To shout his adorable name.

2 To gaze on his glories divine
    Shall be my eternal employ;
To see them incessantly shine,
    My boundless, ineffable joy.

3 He freely redeemed, with his blood,
    My soul from the confines of hell,
To live on the smiles of my God,
    And in his sweet presence to dwell:—

4 To shine with the angels in light,
    With saints and with seraphs to sing,
To view, with eternal delight,
    My Jesus, my Saviour, my King!

TRUST. 7s. 6 lines.   J. P. HOLBROOK.

1. Hap - py, Sa-viour, shall I be, When I do but trust in thee;

Trust thy wis - dom me to guide; Trust thy good-ness to pro - vide;

Trust thy sav - ing love and power; Trust thee ev - ery day and hour:

466.

2 Trust thee as the only light
  In the darkest hour of night;
  Trust in sickness, trust in health;
  Trust in poverty and wealth;
  Trust in joy and trust in grief;
  Trust thy promise for relief:

3 Trust thy blood to cleanse my soul;
  Trust thy grace to make me whole;
  Trust thee living, dying, too;
  Trust thee all my journey through;
  Trust thee till my feet shall be
  Planted on the crystal sea.

467.

1 Chosen not for good in me,
  Waked from coming wrath to flee,
  Hidden in the Saviour's side,
  By the Spirit sanctified—
  Teach me, Lord, on earth to show,
  By my love, how much I owe.

2 Oft I walk beneath the cloud,
  Dark as midnight's gloomy shroud;
  But, when fear is at the height,
  Jesus comes, and all is light;
  Blessèd Jesus! bid me show
  Doubting saints how much I owe.

3 Oft the nights of sorrow reign—
  Weeping, sickness, sighing, pain;
  But a night thine anger burns—
  Morning comes, and joy returns:
  God of comforts! bid me show
  To thy poor how much I owe.

4 When in flowery paths I tread,
  Oft by sin I 'm captive led;
  Oft I fall, but still arise—
  Jesus comes—the tempter flies:
  Blessèd Jesus! bid me show
  Weary sinners all I owe.

468.

1 As the hart, with eager looks,
  Panteth for the water-brooks,
  So my soul, athirst for thee,
  Pants the living God to see;
  When, oh, when, with filial fear,
  Lord, shall I to thee draw near?

2 Why art thou cast down, my soul?
  God, thy God, shall make thee whole;
  Why art thou disquieted?
  God shall lift thy fallen head,
  And his countenance benign
  Be the saving health of thine.

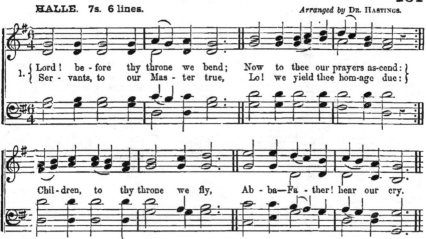

HALLE. 7s. 6 lines. *Arranged by* Dr. Hastings.

1. { Lord! be-fore thy throne we bend; Now to thee our prayers as-cend: }
   { Ser-vants, to our Mas-ter true, Lo! we yield thee hom-age due: }

Chil-dren, to thy throne we fly, Ab-ba—Fa-ther! hear our cry.

469.

2 Low before thee, Lord! we bow,
  We are weak—but mighty thou:
  Sore distressed, yet suppllant still,
  Here we wait thy holy will;
  Bound to earth and rooted here,
  Till our Saviour God appear.

3 Leave us not beneath the power
  Of temptation's darkest hour:
  Swift to seal their captives' doom,
  See our foes exulting come!
  Jesus, Saviour! yet be nigh,
  Lord of life and victory.

470.

1 O thou God who hearest prayer
  Every hour and everywhere!
  For his sake, whose blood I plead,
  Hear me in my hour of need:
  Only hide not now thy face,
  God of all-sufficient grace!

2 Hear and save me, gracious Lord!
  For my trust is in thy word;
  Wash me from the stain of sin,
  That thy peace may rule within:
  May I know myself thy child,
  Ransomed, pardoned, reconciled.

3 Dearest Lord! may I so much
  As thy garment's hem but touch,
  Or but raise my languid eye,
  To the cross where thou didst die,
  It shall make my spirit whole,—
  It shall heal and save my soul.

4 Leave me not, my Strength, my Trust!
  Oh, remember I'm but dust!
  Leave me not again to stray;
  Leave me not the tempter's prey:
  Fix my heart on things above;
  Make me happy in thy love.

471.

1 Weary, Lord, of struggling here
  With this constant doubt and fear,
  Burdened by the pains I bear,
  And the trials I must share—
  Help me, Lord, again to flee
  To the rest that's found in thee.

2 Weakened by the wayward will
  Which controls, yet cheats me still;
  Seeking something undefined
  With an earnest, darkened mind—
  Help me, Lord, again to flee
  To the light that breaks from thee.

3 Fettered by this earthly scope
  In the reach and aim of hope,
  Fixing thought in narrow bound
  Where no living truth is found—
  Help me, Lord, again to flee
  To the hope that's fixed in thee.

4 Fettered, burdened, wearied, weak,
  Lord, once more thy grace I seek;
  Turn, oh, turn me not away,
  Help me, Lord, to watch and pray—
  That I never more may flee
  From the rest that's found in thee.

GREENWOOD. S. M.

Root & Sweetser's Coll.

1. Not with our mor-tal eyes Have we be-held the Lord;

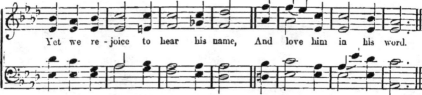

Yet we re-joice to hear his name, And love him in his word.

472.

1 On earth we want the sight
    Of our Redeemer's face ;
Yet, Lord, our inmost thoughts delight
    To dwell upon thy grace.

3 And when we taste thy love,
    Our joys divinely grow
Unspeakable, like those above,
    And heaven begins below.

473.

1 Since Jesus is my friend,
    And I to him belong,
It matters not what foes intend,
    However fierce and strong.

2 He whispers in my breast
    Sweet words of holy cheer,
How they who seek in God their rest
    Shall ever find him near ;

3 How God hath built above
    A city fair and new,
Where eye and heart shall see and prove
    What faith has counted true.

4 My heart for gladness springs ;
    It cannot more be sad ;
For very joy it smiles and sings,—
    Sees naught but sunshine glad.

5 The sun that lights mine eyes,
    Is Christ, the Lord I love ;
I sing for joy of that which lies
    Stored up for me above.

474.

1 While my Redeemer's near,
    My shepherd and my guide,
I bid farewell to anxious fear :
    My wants are all supplied.

2 To ever fragrant meads,
    Where rich abundance grows,
His gracious hand indulgent leads,
    And guards my sweet repose.

3 Dear Shepherd, if I stray,
    My wandering feet restore ;
To thy fair pastures guide my way,
    And let me rove no more.

475.

1 My spirit on thy care,
    Blest Saviour, I recline,
Thou wilt not leave me to despair,
    For thou art love divine.

2 In thee I place my trust,
    On thee I calmly rest ;
I know thee good—I know thee just,
    And count thy choice the best.

3 Whate'er events betide,
    Thy will they all perform ;
Safe in thy breast my head I hide,
    Nor fear the coming storm.

4 Let good or ill befall,
    It must be good for me,—
Secure of having thee in all,
    Of having all in thee.

GOLDEN HILL. S. M.

1. Dear Sa - viour! we are thine, By ev - er - last - ing bands,

Our hearts, our souls, we would re - sign En - tire - ly to thy hands.

476.

2 To thee we still would cleave
With ever-growing zeal;
If millions tempt us Christ to leave,
Oh, let them ne'er prevail!

3 Thy Spirit shall unite
Our souls to thee, our Head;
Shall form in us thine image bright,
And teach thy paths to tread.

4 Death may our souls divide
From these abodes of clay;
But love shall keep us near thy side,
Through all the gloomy way.

5 Since Christ and we are one,
Why should we doubt or fear?
If he in heaven has fixed his throne,
He 'll fix his members there.

477.

1 My God, my Life, my Love,
To thee, to thee I call;
I cannot live, if thou remove,
For thou art all in all.

2 To thee, and thee alone,
The angels owe their bliss:
They sit around thy gracious throne,
And dwell where Jesus is.

3 Not all the harps above
Can make a heavenly place,
If God his residence remove,
Or but conceal his face.

4 Nor earth, nor all the sky,
Can one delight afford—
No, not a drop of real joy
Without thy presence, Lord.

5 Thou art the sea of love,
Where all my pleasures roll;
The circle where my passions move,
And centre of my soul.

478.

1 Not all the blood of beasts,
On Jewish altars slain,
Could give the guilty conscience peace,
Or wash away the stain.

2 But Christ, the heavenly Lamb,
Takes all our sins away—
A sacrifice of nobler name,
And richer blood than they.

3 My faith would lay her hand
On that dear head of thine,
While like a penitent I stand,
And there confess my sin.

4 My soul looks back to see
The burdens thou didst bear
When hanging on the cursèd tree,
And hopes her guilt was there.

5 Believing, we rejoice
To see the curse remove;
We bless the Lamb with cheerful voice,
And sing his bleeding love.

YARMOUTH. 7s & 6s.   Dr. L. Mason.

1. Stand up! stand up for Je-sus! Ye soldiers of the cross; Lift high his roy-al ban-ner, It must not suffer loss: From victory un-to vic-tory His army shall be led, Till every foe is vanquished, Till every foe is vanquished, Till every foe is vanquished, And Christ is Lord indeed.

479.

2 Stand up!—stand up for Jesus!
  The trumpet call obey;
Forth to the mighty conflict,
  In this his glorious day:
"Ye that are men, now serve him,"
  Against unnumbered foes;
Your courage rise with danger,
  And strength to strength oppose.

3 Stand up!—stand up for Jesus!
  Stand in his strength alone;
The arm of flesh will fail you—
  Ye dare not trust your own:
Put on the gospel armor,
  And, watching unto prayer,
Where duty calls or danger,
  Be never wanting there!

4 Stand up!—stand up for Jesus!
  The strife will not be long;
This day the noise of battle,
  The next the victor's song:
To him that overcometh,
  A crown of life shall be:
He with the King of Glory
  Shall reign eternally.

480.

1 In heavenly love abiding,
  No change my heart shall fear,
And safe is such confiding,
  For nothing changes here:
The storm may roar without me,
  My heart may low be laid,
But God is round about me,
  And can I be dismayed?

2 Wherever he may guide me,
  No want shall turn me back;
My Shepherd is beside me,
  And nothing can I lack:
His wisdom ever waketh,
  His sight is never dim:
He knows the way he taketh,
  And I will walk with him.

3 Green pastures are before me,
  Which yet I have not seen;
Bright skies will soon be o'er me,
  Where darkest clouds have been:
My hope I cannot measure;
  My path to life is free;
My Saviour has my treasure,
  And he will walk with me.

TULLY. 7s & 6s.   Dr. L. Mason.

1. I lay my sins on Je - sus, The spot-less Lamb of God;

He bears them all, and frees us From the ac - curs - ed load:
D. s. White in his blood most pre - cious, Till not a stain re - mains.

D. S.

I bring my guilt to Je - sus, To wash my crim - son stains,

481.

2 I lay my wants on Jesus;
    All fullness dwells in him;
He healeth my diseases,
    He doth my soul redeem:
I lay my griefs on Jesus,
    My burdens and my cares;
He from them all releases,
    He all my sorrow shares.

3 I rest my soul on Jesus,
    This weary soul of mine;
His right hand me embraces,
    I on his breast recline:
I love the name of Jesus,
    Immanuel, Christ, the Lord;
Like fragrance on the breezes,
    His name abroad is poured.

4 I long to be like Jesus,
    Meek, loving, lowly, mild;
I long to be like Jesus,
    The Father's holy child:
I long to be with Jesus
    Amid the heavenly throng,
To sing with saints his praises,
    And learn the angels' song.

482.

1 To thee, my God and Saviour!
    My heart exulting sings,
Rejoicing in thy favor,
    Almighty King of kings!
I'll celebrate thy glory,
    With all thy saints above,
And tell the joyful story
    Of thy redeeming love.

2 Soon as the morn, with roses,
    Bedecks the dewy east,
And when the sun reposes
    Upon the ocean's breast,
My voice, in supplication,
    Well-pleased the Lord shall hear:
Oh! grant me thy salvation,
    And to my soul draw near.

3 By thee, through life supported,
    I'll pass the dangerous road,
With heavenly hosts escorted,
    Up to thy bright abode;
Then cast my crown before thee,
    And, all my conflicts o'er,
Unceasingly adore thee :—
    What could an angel more?

ST. PETERSBURGH. L. M. 6 lines. BORTNIANSKY.

1. As, pant-ing in the sul-try beam, The hart de-sires the cool-ing stream,
So to thy pres-ence, Lord, I flee, So longs my soul, O God, for thee;
A-thirst to taste thy liv-ing grace, And see thy glo-ry face to face.

483.

2 High waves of sorrow o'er me roll,
And troubles overwhelm my soul;
For many an evil voice is near,
To chide my woe and mock my fear;
And silent memory weeps alone,
O'er hours of peace and gladness flown.

3 For I have walked the happy round,
That circles Zion's holy ground;
And gladly swelled the choral lays,
That hymned my great Redeemer's
praise,
What time, the hallowed arch along,
Responsive swelled the solemn song.

4 Ah, why by passing clouds oppressed,
Should rising thoughts distract my
breast!
Turn, turn to him in every pain,
Whom never suppliant sought in vain:
Thy strength in joy's ecstatic day,
Thy hope where joy has passed away.

484.

1 As oft with worn and weary feet,
We tread earth's rugged valley o'er,
The thought, how comforting and sweet,
Christ trod this very path before;
Our wants and weaknesses he knows,
From life's first dawning till its close.

2 Does sickness, feebleness, or pain,
Or sorrow in our path appear;
The recollection will remain,
More deeply did he suffer here,
His life how truly sad and brief,
Filled up with suffering and with grief.

3 If Satan tempt our hearts to stray,
And whisper evil things within,
So did he in the desert way,
Assail our Lord with thoughts of sin:
When worn, and in a feeble hour,
The tempter came with all his power.

4 Just such as I, this earth he trod,
With every human ill but sin;
And, though indeed the very God,
As I am now, so he has been:
My God, my Saviour! look on me
With pity, love, and sympathy.

485.

1 Why should I fear the darkest hour,
Or tremble at the tempest's power?
Jesus vouchsafes to be my tower.
Though hot the fight, why quit the field?
Why should I either flee or yield,
Since Jesus is my mighty shield?

2 Though all the flocks and herds were
dead,
My soul a famine need not dread,
For Jesus is my living bread.
I know not what may soon betide,
Or how my wants shall be supplied;
But Jesus knows and will provide.

3 Though sin would fill me with distress,
The throne of grace I dare address,
For Jesus is my righteousness.
Against me earth and hell combine,
But on my side is power divine:
Jesus is all, and he is mine.

BROWNELL. L. M. 6 lines. HAYDN.

1. The Lord my pas-ture shall pre-pare, And feed me with a shepherd's care;

His pres-ence shall my wants sup-ply, And guard me with a watch-ful eye:

My noon-day walks he shall at-tend, And all my mid-night hours de-fend.

486.

2 When in the sultry glebe I faint,
Or on the thirsty mountain pant,
To fertile vales, and dewy meads,
My weary, wandering steps he leads;
Where peaceful rivers, soft and slow,
Amid the verdant landscape flow.

3 Though in the paths of death I tread,
With gloomy horrors overspread,
My steadfast heart shall fear no ill,
For thou, O Lord, art with me still:
Thy friendly rod shall give me aid,
And guide me through the dreadful shade.

4 Though in a bare and rugged way,
Through devious, lonely wilds I stray,
Thy presence shall my pains beguile:
The barren wilderness shall smile,
With sudden greens and herbage crowned;
And streams shall murmur all around.

487.

1 "Perfect in love!"—Lord, can it be,
Amid this state of doubt and sin?
While foes so thick without, I see,
With weakness, pain, disease within;
Can perfect love inhabit here,
And, strong in faith, extinguish fear?

2 O Lord! amid this mental night,
Amid the clouds of dark dismay,
Arise! arise! shed forth thy light,
And kindle love's meridian day:
My Saviour God, to me appear,
So love shall triumph over fear.

488.

1 Jesus, thou source of calm repose,
All fullness dwells in thee divine;
Our strength, to quell the proudest foes;
Our light, in deepest gloom to shine;
Thou art our fortress, strength, and
tower,
Our trust and portion, evermore.

2 Jesus, our Comforter thou art;
Our rest in toil, our ease in pain;
The balm to heal each broken heart,
In storms our peace, in loss our gain;
Our joy, beneath the worldling's frown;
In shame, our glory and our crown;—

3 In want, our plentiful supply;
In weakness, our almighty power;
In bonds, our perfect liberty;
Our refuge in temptation's hour;
Our comfort, amidst grief and thrall;
Our life in death; our all in all.

BETHANY. 6s & 4s.

Dr. L. Mason.

1. Nearer, my God, to thee, Nearer to thee: Ev'n tho' it be a cross That raiseth me,

Still all my song shall be, Nearer, my God, to thee, Nearer, my God, to thee, Near-er to thee.

489.

1 Saviour! I follow on,
   Guided by thee,
   Seeing not yet the hand
   That leadeth me;
   Hushed be my heart and still,
   Fear I no further ill,
   Only to meet thy will
   My will shall be.

2 Riven the rock for me
   Thirst to relieve,
   Manna from heaven falls
   Fresh every eve;
   Never a want severe
   Causeth my eye a tear,
   But thou art whispering near,
   "Only believe!"

3 Often to Marah's brink
   Have I been brought;
   Shrinking the cup to drink,
   Help I have sought;
   And with the prayer's ascent,
   Jesus the branch has rent;—
   Quickly relief he sent,
   Sweetening the draught.

4 Saviour! I long to walk
   Closer with thee;
   Led by thy guiding hand,
   Ever to be;
   Constantly near thy side,
   Quickened and purified,
   Living for him who died
   Freely for me!

490.

1 Fade, fade, each earthly joy;
   Jesus is mine!
   Break, every tender tie;
   Jesus is mine.
   Dark is the wilderness;
   Earth has no resting-place;
   Jesus alone can bless;
   Jesus is mine.

2 Tempt not my soul away;
   Jesus is mine:
   Here would I ever stay;
   Jesus is mine:
   Perishing things of clay
   Born but for one brief day,
   Pass from my heart away;
   Jesus is mine.

3 Farewell, ye dreams of night,
   Jesus is mine:
   Lost in this dawning bright,
   Jesus is mine:
   All that my soul has tried
   Left but a dismal void;
   Jesus has satisfied;
   Jesus is mine.

4 Farewell, mortality;
   Jesus is mine:
   Welcome, eternity;
   Jesus is mine:
   Welcome, O loved and blest!
   Welcome, sweet scenes of rest;
   Welcome, my Saviour's breast;
   Jesus is mine!

ELY. 6s & 4s.   J. P. HOLBROOK.

1. Near-er, my God, to thee, Near-er to thee: Ev'n tho' it be a cross That raiseth me, Still all my song shall be, Near-er, my God, to thee, Near-er to thee.

491.

2 Though like a wanderer,
   Daylight all gone,
Darkness be over me,
   My rest a stone,
Yet in my dreams I'd be
Nearer, my God, to thee,
   Nearer to thee.

3 There let the way appear
   Steps up to heaven;
All that thou sendest me
   In mercy given,
Angels to beckon me
Nearer, my God, to thee,
   Nearer to thee.

4 Then with my waking thoughts,
   Bright with thy praise,
Out of my stony griefs,
   Bethel I 'll raise;
So by my woes to be
Nearer, my God, to thee,
   Nearer to thee.

5 Or if on joyful wing,
   Cleaving the sky,
Sun, moon, and stars forgot,
   Upward I fly,
Still all my song shall be,
Nearer, my God, to thee,
   Nearer to thee.

492.

1 SAVIOUR! thy gentle voice
   Gladly we hear;
Author of all our joys,
   Ever be near;

Our souls would cling to thee,
Let us thy fullness see,
   Our life to cheer.

2 Fountain of life divine!
   Thee we adore;
We would be wholly thine
   Forevermore;
Freely forgive our sin,
Grant heavenly peace within,
   Thy light restore.

3 Though to our faith unseen,
   While darkness reigns,
On thee alone we lean
   While life remains;
By thy free grace restored,
Our souls shall bless the Lord
   In joyful strains!

493.

1 GOD leads me—and I go!
   He takes the care;
I need not wish to know,
   Or question where;
The goal is drawing near,
My way will all be clear,
   When I am there.

2 God leads me—so my heart
   In faith shall rest;
No fear my soul shall part
   From Jesus' breast;
What path my life doth go,
Since he permitteth so,
   That must be best.

DUKE STREET. L. M.   J. Hatton.

1. 'Tis by the faith of joys to come, We walk thro' des-erts dark as night;

Till we ar-rive at heaven, our home, Faith is our guide, and faith our light.

494.
Faith.

2 The want of sight she well supplies,
She makes the pearly gates appear;
Far into distant worlds she pries,
And brings eternal glories near.

3 Cheerful we tread the desert through,
While faith inspires a heavenly ray,
Though lions roar, and tempests blow,
And rocks and dangers fill the way.

4 So Abra'm by divine command,
Left his own house to walk with God;
His faith beheld the promised land,
And fired his zeal along the road.

495.
Self-Denial.

1 If on our daily course our mind
Be set, to hallow all we find,
New treasures still, of countless price,
God will provide for sacrifice.

2 Old friends, old scenes, will lovelier be,
As more of heaven in each we see;
Some softening gleam of love and prayer
Shall dawn on every cross and care.

3 Oh! could we learn that sacrifice,
What light would all around us rise!
How would our hearts with wisdom talk,
Along life's dullest, dreariest walk!

4 The trivial round, the common task,
Will furnish all we ought to ask;—
Room to deny ourselves, a road
To bring us daily nearer God.

496.
Love.

1 Had I the tongues of Greeks and Jews,
And nobler speech than angels use,
If love be absent, I am found
Like tinkling brass, an empty sound.

2 Were I inspired to preach and tell
All that is done in heaven and hell—
Or could my faith the world remove,
Still I am nothing without love.

3 Should I distribute all my store
To feed the hungry, clothe the poor;
Or give my body to the flame,
To gain a martyr's glorious name:

4 If love to God and love to men
Be absent, all my hopes are vain;
Nor tongues, nor gifts, nor fiery zeal,
The work of love can e'er fulfill.

497.
Consistency.

1 So let our lips and lives express
The holy gospel, we profess;
So let our works and virtues shine,
To prove the doctrine all-divine.

2 Thus shall we best proclaim abroad
The honors of our Saviour God;
When his salvation reigns within,
And grace sub1ues the power of sin.

3 Religion bears our spirits up,
While we expect that blessed hope,—
The bright appearance of the Lord:
And faith stands leaning on his word.

GRATITUDE. L. M.

Bost.

1. My God, how end-less is thy love! Thy gifts are ev-ery eve-ning new;

And morn-ing mer-cies from a-bove, Gen-tly dis-till like ear-ly dew.

498.
Gratitude.

2 Thou spread'st the curtains of the night,
Great Guardian of my sleeping hours!
Thy sovereign word restores the light,
And quickens all my drowsy powers.

3 I yield my powers to thy command;
To thee I consecrate my days;
Perpetual blessings, from thy hand,
Demand perpetual songs of praise.

499.
Completeness.

1 COMPLETE in thee, no work of mine
May take, dear Lord, the place of thine;
Thy blood has pardon bought for me,
And I am now complete in thee.

2 Complete in thee—no more shall sin
Thy grace has conquered, reign within;
Thy voice will bid the tempter flee,
And I shall stand complete in thee.

3 Complete in thee—each want supplied,
And no good thing to me denied,
Since thou my portion, Lord, wilt be,
I ask no more—complete in thee.

4 Dear Saviour! when, before thy bar
All tribes and tongues assembled are,
Among thy chosen may I be
At thy right hand—complete in thee.

5 Complete in thee, forever blest,
Of all thy fullness, Lord, possessed,
Thy praise throughout eternity—
Thy love I'll sing, complete in thee.

500.
Contentment.

1 O LORD, how full of sweet content
Our years of pilgrimage are spent!
Where'er we dwell, we dwell with thee,
In heaven, in earth, or on the sea.

2 To us remains nor place nor time;
Our country is in every clime:
We can be calm and free from care
On any shore, since God is there.

3 While place we seek, or place we shun,
The soul finds happiness in none;
But with our God to guide our way,
'T is equal joy to go or stay.

4 Could we be cast where thou art not,
That were indeed a dreadful lot;
But regions none remote we call,
Secure of finding God in all.

501.
Meekness.

1 HAPPY the meek whose gentle breast,
Clear as the summer's evening ray,
Calm as the regions of the blest,
Enjoys on earth celestial day.

2 His heart no broken friendships sting,
No storms his peaceful tent invade;
He rests beneath th' Almighty's wing,
Hostile to none, of none afraid.

3 Spirit of grace, all meek and mild!
Inspire our breasts, our souls possess:
Repel each passion rude and wild,
And bless us as we aim to bless.

VALENTIA. C. M.   EBERWEIN.

1. Oh, gift of gifts! Oh, grace of faith! My God! how can it be

That thou, who hast dis-cern-ing love, Shouldst give that gift to me?

502.
Faith.

2 How many hearts thou mightst have had
  More innocent than mine!
How many souls more worthy far
  Of that sweet touch of thine!

3 Ah, grace! into unlikeliest hearts
  It is thy boast to come,
The glory of thy light to find
  In darkest spots a home.

4 The crowd of cares, the weightiest cross,
  Seem trifles less than light—
Earth looks so little and so low
  When faith shines full and bright.

5 Oh, happy, happy that I am!
  If thou canst be, O faith,
The treasure that thou art in life,
  What wilt thou be in death?

503.
Gentleness.

1 SPEAK gently—it is better far
  To rule by love than fear;
Speak gently—let no harsh word mar
  The good we may do here.

2 Speak gently to the young—for they
  Will have enough to bear;
Pass through this life as best they may,
  'T is full of anxious care.

3 Speak gently to the aged one,
  Grieve not the careworn heart;
The sands of life are nearly run,
  Let them in peace depart.

4 Speak gently to the erring ones—
  They must have toiled in vain;
Perchance unkindness made them so;
  Oh, win them back again!

5 Speak gently—'t is a little thing,
  Dropped in the heart's deep well;
The good, the joy, that it may bring,
  Eternity shall tell.

504.
Godly Sincerity.

1 WALK in the light! so shalt thou know
  That fellowship of love,
His Spirit only can bestow,
  Who reigns in light above.

2 Walk in the light! and thou shalt find
  Thy heart made truly his,
Who dwells in cloudless light enshrined,
  In whom no darkness is.

3 Walk in the light! and sin abhorred
  Shall ne'er defile again;
The blood of Jesus Christ the Lord
  Shall cleanse from every sin.

4 Walk in the light! and ev'n the tomb
  No fearful shade shall wear;
Glory shall chase away its gloom,
  For Christ hath conquered there.

5 Walk in the light! and thou shalt see
  Thy path, though thorny, bright,
For God by grace shall dwell in thee,
  And God himself is light.

NAOMI. C. M.

Dr. L. Mason.

1. Fa - ther! what - e'er of earth - ly bliss Thy sovereign will de - nies,

Ac - cept - ed at thy throne of grace, Let this pe - ti - tion rise:—

505.
Devotion.

2 "Give me a calm, a thankful heart,
From every murmur free;
The blessings of thy grace impart,
And make me live to thee.

3 "Let the sweet hope that thou art mine
My life and death attend;
Thy presence through my journey shine,
And crown my journey's end."

506.
Calmness.

1 Calm me, my God, and keep me calm:
Let thine outstretched wing
Be like the shade of Elim's palm,
Beside her desert spring.

2 Yes, keep me calm, though loud and rude
The sounds my ear that greet,—
Calm in the closet's solitude,
Calm in the bustling street,—

3 Calm in the hour of buoyant health,
Calm in the hour of pain,
Calm in my poverty or wealth,
Calm in my loss or gain,—

4 Calm in the sufferance of wrong,
Like him who bore my shame,
Calm 'mid the threatening, taunting
throng,
Who hate thy holy name.

5 Calm me, my God, and keep me calm,
Soft resting on thy breast;
Soothe me with holy hymn and psalm,
And bid my spirit rest.

507.
Charitableness.

1 Think gently of the erring one!
And let us not forget,
However darkly stained by sin,
He is our brother yet.

2 Heir of the same inheritance,
Child of the self-same God;
He hath but stumbled in the path,
We have in weakness trod.

3 Speak gently to the erring one:
Thou yet may'st lead him back,
With holy words, and tones of love,
From misery's thorny track.

4 Forget not thou hast often sinned,
And sinful yet must be:
Deal gently with the erring one,
As God has dealt with thee.

508.
Humility.

1 Is there ambition in my heart?
Search, gracious God, and see;
Or do I act a haughty part?
Lord, I appeal to thee.

2 I charge my thoughts, be humble still,
And all my carriage mild;
Content, my Father, with thy will,
And quiet as a child.

3 The patient soul, the lowly mind,
Shall have a large reward;
Let saints in sorrow lie resigned,
And trust a faithful Lord.

CAMBRIDGE. C. M.

Dr. Randall.

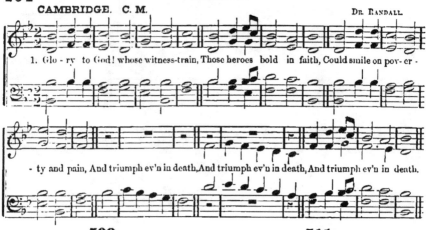

1. Glo - ry to God! whose witness-train, Those heroes bold in faith, Could smile on pov - er -

- ty and pain, And triumph ev'n in death, And triumph ev'n in death, And triumph ev'n in death.

509.
Martyr-Faith.

2 Oh! may that faith our hearts sustain,
Wherein they fearless stood,
When, in the power of cruel men,
They poured their willing blood.

3 God, whom we serve, our God, can save,
Can damp the scorching flame,
Can build an ark, can smooth the wave,
For such as love his name.

4 Lord! if thine arm support us still
With its eternal strength,
We shall o'ercome the mightiest ill,
And conquerors prove at length.

510.
Trust.

1 What though no flowers the fig-tree
clothe,
Though vines their fruit deny,
The labor of the olive fail,
And fields no food supply;—

2 Though from the fold with sad surprise,
My flock cut off I see;
Though famine pine in empty stalls,
Where herds were wont to be:—

3 Yet in the Lord will I be glad,
And glory in his love;
In him rejoice, who will the God
Of my salvation prove.

4 God is the treasure of my soul,
The source of lasting joy;
A joy, which want shall not impair,
Nor death itself destroy.

511.
Submission.

1 O Lord! my best desires fulfill,
And help me to resign
Life, health, and comfort to thy will,
And make thy pleasure mine.

2 Why should I shrink at thy command,
Thy love forbids my fears;
Why tremble at the gracious hand,
That wipes away my tears?

3 No,—let me rather freely yield
What most I prize, to thee;
Thou never hast a good withheld,
Nor wilt withhold from me.

4 Thy favor, all my journey through,
Shall be my rich supply;
What more I want, or think I do,
Let wisdom still deny.

512.
Humility.

1 Thy home is with the humble, Lord!
The simple are the best;
Thy lodging is in child-like hearts;
Thou makest there thy rest.

2 Dear Comforter! eternal Love!
If thou wilt stay with me,
Of lowly thoughts and simple ways
I'll build a house for thee.

3 Who made this breathing heart of mine
But thou, my heavenly Guest?
Let no one have it, then, but thee,
And let it be thy rest!

MOUNT AUBURN. C. M.   KINGSLEY.

1. Hap - py the heart where graces reign, Where love in - spires the breast;

Love is the bright - est of the train, And strengthens all the rest.

513.
Love.

2 Knowledge, alas! 't is all in vain,
  And all in vain our fear;
Our stubborn sins will fight and reign,
  If love be absent there.

3 This is the grace that lives and sings,
  When faith and hope shall cease;
'T is this shall strike our joyful strings,
  In the sweet realms of bliss.

4 Before we quite forsake our clay,
  Or leave this dark abode,
The wings of love bear us away,
  To see our smiling God.

514.
Faith.

1 Lord, I believe; thy power I own;
  Thy word I would obey;
I wander comfortless and lone,
  When from thy truth I stray.

2 Lord, I believe; but gloomy fears
  Sometimes bedim my sight;
I look to thee with prayers and tears,
  And cry for strength and light.

3 Lord, I believe; but oft, I know,
  My faith is cold and weak:
My weakness strengthen, and bestow
  The confidence I seek.

4 Yes! I believe; and only thou
  Canst give my soul relief:
Lord, to thy truth my spirit bow;
  "Help thou mine unbelief!"

515.
Sensibility.

1 And can mine eyes, without a tear,
  A weeping Saviour see?
Shall I not weep his groans to hear
  Who groaned and died for me?

2 Blest Jesus! let those tears of thine
  Subdue each stubborn foe;
Come, fill my heart with love divine,
  And bid my sorrows flow.

516.
Faith.

1 Faith adds new charms to earthly bliss,
  And saves me from its snares;
Its aid, in every duty, brings,
  And softens all my cares.

2 The wounded conscience knows its power
  The healing balm to give;
That balm the saddest heart can cheer,
  And make the dying live.

3 Wide it unvails celestial worlds,
  Where deathless pleasures reign;
And bids me seek my portion there,
  Nor bids me seek in vain.

4 It shows the precious promise sealed
  With the Redeemer's blood;
And helps my feeble hope to rest
  Upon a faithful God.

5 There—there unshaken would I rest,
  Till this vile body dies;
And then, on faith's triumphant wings,
  To endless glory rise.

TUCKER. S. M.   ABBEY.

1. Re - joice in God al - way; When earth looks heaven - ly bright, When joy makes glad the live - long day, And peace shuts in the night.

517.
Joy.

2 Rejoice when care and woe
  The fainting soul oppress;
When tears at wakeful midnight flow,
  And morn brings heaviness.

3 Rejoice in hope and fear;
  Rejoice in life and death;
Rejoice when threatening storms are near,
  And comfort languisheth.

4 When should not they rejoice,
  Whom Christ his brethren calls;
Who hear and know his guiding voice,
  When on their hearts it falls?

5 So, though our path is steep,
  And many a tempest lowers,
Shall his own peace our spirits keep,
  And Christ's dear love be ours.

518.
Self-Renunciation.

1 MAN's wisdom is to seek
  His strength in God alone;
And ev'n an angel would be weak,
  Who trusted in his own.

2 Retreat beneath his wings,
  And in his grace confide;
This more exalts the King of kings,
  Than all your works beside.

3 In Jesus is our store;
  Grace issues from his throne;
Whoever says,—" I want no more,"
  Confesses he has none.

519.
Resignation.

1 Be tranquil, O my soul,
  Be quiet every fear!
Thy Father hath supreme control,
  And he is ever near.

2 Ne'er of thy lot complain,
  Whatever may befall;
Sickness or sorrow, care or pain,
  'T is well appointed all.

3 A Father's chastening hand
  Is leading thee along;
Nor distant is the promised land,
  Where swells th' immortal song.

4 Oh! then, my soul, be still!
  Await heaven's high decree;
Seek but to do thy Father's will,
  It shall be well with thee.

520.
Confidence.

1 IN true and patient hope,
  My soul, on God attend;
And calmly, confidently look
  Till he salvation send.

2 I shall his goodness see,
  While on his name I call;
He will defend and strengthen me,
  And I shall never fall.

3 Jesus, to thee I fly,
  My refuge, and my tower;
Upon thy faithful love rely,
  And find thy saving power.

DENNIS. S. M.   NAGELI.

1. If, through un - ruf - fled seas, Toward heaven we calm - ly sail,
With grate - ful hearts, O God, to thee, We'll own the fa - voring gale.

521.
Faith in Trouble.

1 IF, through unruffled seas,
  Toward heaven we calmly sail,
With grateful hearts, O God, to thee,
  We'll own the favoring gale.

2 But should the surges rise,
  And rest delay to come,
Blest be the sorrow—kind the storm,
  Which drives us nearer home.

3 Soon shall our doubts and fears
  All yield to thy control:
Thy tender mercies shall illume
  The midnight of the soul.

4 Teach us, in every state,
  To make thy will our own;
And when the joys of sense depart,
  To live by faith alone.

522.
Devotion.

1 JESUS, my strength, my hope,
  On thee I cast my care,
With humble confidence look up,
  And know thou hear'st my prayer.

2 Give me on thee to wait,
  Till I can all things do;
On thee, almighty, to create,
  Almighty to renew.

3 I want a sober mind,
  A self-renouncing will,
That tramples down, and casts behind
  The baits of pleasing ill;

4 A soul inured to pain,
  To hardship, grief and loss,
Bold to take up, firm to sustain
  The consecrated cross;

5 I want a godly fear,
  A quick-discerning eye,
That looks to thee when sin is near,
  And sees the tempter fly;

6 A spirit still prepared,
  And armed with jealous care,
Forever standing on its guard,
  And watching unto prayer.

523.
Trust in God.

1 WHERE wilt thou put thy trust?
  In a frail form of clay,
That to its element of dust
  Must soon resolve away?

2 Where wilt thou cast thy care?
  Upon an erring heart,
Which hath its own sore ills to bear,
  And shrinks from sorrow's dart?

3 No,—place thy trust above
  This shadowy realm of night,
In him, whose boundless power and love
  Thy confidence invite.

4 His mercies still endure
  When skies and stars grow dim,
His changeless promise standeth sure,—
  Go,—cast thy care on him.

HENDON. 7s.   Dr. Malan.

1. Christ, of all my hopes the Ground, Christ, the Spring of all my joy, Still in thee let me be found, Still for thee my powers em - ploy, Still for thee my powers employ.

524.
Living to Christ.

1 CHRIST, of all my hopes the Ground,
  Christ, the Spring of all my joy,
  Still in thee let me be found,
  Still for thee my powers employ.

2 Fountain of o'erflowing grace!
  Freely from thy fullness give;
  Till I close my earthly race,
  Be it " Christ for me to live!"

3 Firmly trusting in thy blood,
  Nothing shall my heart confound;
  Safely I shall pass the flood,
  Safely reach Immanuel's ground.

4 When I touch the blessed shore,
  Back the closing waves shall roll!
  Death's dark stream shall nevermore
  Part from thee my ravished soul.

5 Thus,—oh, thus an entrance give
  To the land of cloudless sky;
  Having known it, " Christ to live,"
  Let me know it "gain to die."

525.
Likeness to Christ.

1 FATHER of eternal grace!
  Glorify thyself in me;
  Meekly beaming in my face,
  May the world thine image see.

2 Happy only in thy love,
  Poor, unfriended, or unknown;
  Fix my thoughts on things above,—
  Stay my heart on thee alone.

3 Humble, holy, all-resigned
  To thy will :—thy will be done !
  Give me, Lord ! the perfect mind
  Of thy well-beloved Son.

4 Counting gain and glory loss,
  May I tread the path he trod ;
  Die with Jesus on the cross,—
  Rise with him, to thee, my God !

526.
Rejoicing.

1 JOYFUL be the hours to-day ;
  Joyful let the season be ;
  Let us sing, for well we may :
  Jesus ! we will sing of thee.

2 Should thy people silent be,
  Then the very stones would sing:
  What a debt we owe to thee,
  Thee, our Saviour, thee, our King !

3 Joyful are we now to own,
  Rapture thrills us as we trace
  All the deeds thy love hath done,
  All the riches of thy grace.

4 'T is thy grace alone can save ;
  Every blessing comes from thee—
  All we have and hope to have,
  All we are and hope to be.

5 Thine the name to sinners dear !
  Thine the Name all names before !
  Blessed here and everywhere ;
  Blessed now and evermore !

KARL. 7s, or 8s & 7s. WEBER.

1. Lord, for - ev - er at thy side Let my place and por - tion be;

Strip me of the robe of pride, Clothe me with hu - mil - i - ty.

527.
Humility.

1 Lord, forever at thy side
  Let my place and portion be ;
Strip me of the robe of pride ;
  Clothe me with humility.

2 Meekly may my soul receive
  All thy Spirit hath revealed ;
Thou hast spoken ; I believe,
  Though the oracle be sealed.

3 Humble as a little child,
  Weanèd from the mother's breast,
By no subtleties beguiled,
  On thy faithful word I rest.

4 Israel, now and evermore
  In the Lord Jehovah trust ;
Him in all his ways adore,
  Wise, and powerful, and just.

528.
Consistency.

1 Jesus, Lord, we look to thee ;
  Let us in thy name agree ;
Show thyself the Prince of Peace ;
  Bid our jars forever cease.

2 By thy reconciling love,
  Every stumbling-block remove :
Each to each unite, endear ;
  Come, and spread thy banner here.

3 Make us of one heart and mind—
  Courteous, pitiful, and kind ;
Lowly, meek, in thought and word—
  Altogether like our Lord.

4 Let us for each other care ;
  Each the other's burden bear ;
To thy church the pattern give ;
  Show how true believers live.

5 Free from anger and from pride,
  Let us thus in God abide ;
All the depths of love express—
  All the heights of holiness.

6 Let us then with joy remove
  To the family above ;
On the wings of angels fly ;
  Show how true believers die.

529.
Humility.

1 Lord, if thou thy grace impart,
  Poor in spirit, meek in heart,
I shall as my Master be,
  Rooted in humility ;

2 Simple, teachable, and mild,
  Changed into a little child ;
Pleased with all the Lord provides,
  Weaned from all the world besides.

3 Father, fix my soul on thee ;
  Every evil let me flee ;
Nothing want, beneath, above,
  Happy in thy precious love.

4 Oh, that all may seek and find
  Every good in Jesus joined !
Him let Israel still adore,
  Trust him, praise him evermore.

BLENDON. L. M. GIARDINI.

1. Not all the no - bles of the earth, Who boast the hon - ors of their birth,

So high a dig - ni - ty can claim, As those who bear the Chris - tian name.

530.
Adoption.

1 Not all the nobles of the earth,
Who boast the honors of their birth,
So high a dignity can claim,
As those who bear the Christian name.

2 To them the privilege is given
To be the sons and heirs of heaven ;
Sons of the God who reigns on high,
And heirs of joy beyond the sky.

3 His will he makes them early know,
And teaches their young feet to go ;
Whispers instruction to their minds,
And on their hearts his precepts binds.

4 Their daily wants his hands supply,
Their steps he guards with watchful eye ;
Leads them from earth to heaven above,
And crowns them with eternal love.

531.
Perseverance.

1 Who shall the Lord's elect condemn ?
'T is God that justifies their souls ;
And mercy, like a mighty stream,
O'er all their sins divinely rolls.

2 Who shall adjudge the saints to hell ?
'T is Christ that suffered in their stead :
And their salvation to fulfill,
Behold him rising from the dead !

3 He lives, he lives, and sits above,
Forever interceding there :
Who shall divide us from his love,
Or what shall tempt us to despair ?

4 Shall persecution, or distress,
Famine, or sword, or nakedness ?
He who hath loved us bears us through,
And makes us more than conquerors too !

5 Not all that men on earth can do,
Nor powers on high, nor powers below,
Shall cause his mercy to remove,
Or wean our hearts from Christ, our love.

532.
Security.

1 Lord, how secure and blest are they,
Who feel the joys of pardoned sin !
Should storms of wrath shake earth and
sea,
Their minds have heaven and peace within.

2 The day glides swiftly o'er their heads,
Made up of innocence and love ;
And soft and silent as the shades,
Their nightly minutes gently move.

3 Quick as their thoughts their joys come on,
But fly not half so swift away ;
Their souls are ever bright as noon,
And calm as summer evenings be.

4 How oft they look to heavenly hills,
Where streams of living pleasures flow ;
And longing hopes and cheerful smiles
Sit undisturbed upon their brow !

5 They scorn to seek earth's golden toys,
But spend the day, and share the night,
In numbering o'er the richer joys
That heaven prepares for their delight.

SMITH. L. M.   *Arranged by* KINGSLEY.

1. Now to the power of God su-preme Be ev - er - last - ing hon - ors given;

He saves from hell—we bless his name,— He calls our wandering feet to heaven.

533.
Grace.

2 Not for our duties or deserts,
But of his own abounding grace,
He works salvation in our hearts,
And forms a people for his praise.

3 'T was his own purpose that begun
To rescue rebels doomed to die:
He gave us grace in Christ, his Son,
Before he spread the starry sky.

4 Jesus, the Lord, appears at last,
And makes his Father's counsels known;
Declares the great transactions past,
And brings immortal blessings down.

5 He died; and in that dreadful night
Did all the powers of hell destroy;
Rising he brought our heaven to light,
And took possession of the joy.

534.
Grace sufficient.

1 LET me but hear my Saviour say,
"Strength shall be equal to thy day;"
Then I rejoice in deep distress,
Leaning on all-sufficient grace.

2 I can do all things—or can bear
All suffering, if my Lord be there;
Sweet pleasures mingle with the pains,
While my sinking head sustains.

3 I glory in infirmity,
That Christ's own power can rest on me;
When I am weak, then am I strong;
Grace is my shield, and Christ my song.

535.
Grace.

1 No more, ye wise! your wisdom boast;
No more, ye strong! your valor trust;
No more, ye rich! survey your store,
Elate with heaps of shining ore.

2 Glory, ye saints, in this alone,—
That God, your God, to you is known;
That you have owned his sovereign sway,—
That you have felt his cheering ray.

3 All else, which we our treasure call,
May in one fatal moment fall;
But what their happiness can move,
Whom God, the blessed, deigns to love?

536.
Resort to Christ.

1 AWAY from earth my spirit turns,
Away from every transient good;
With strong desire my bosom burns,
To feast on heaven's immortal food.

2 Thou, Saviour, art the living bread;
Thou wilt my every want supply:
By thee sustained, and cheered, and led,
I'll press through dangers to the sky.

3 What though temptations oft distress,
And sin assails and breaks my peace;
Thou wilt uphold, and save, and bless,
And bid the storms of passion cease.

4 Then let me take thy gracious hand,
And walk beside thee onward still;
Till my glad feet shall safely stand,
Forever firm on Zion's hill.

BROWN. C. M.   Wm. B. Bradbury.

1. Now let our cheer-ful eyes sur-vey Our great High Priest a-bove,

And cel-e-brate his con-stant care, And sym-pa-thet-ic love.

537.
Perseverance.

2 Though raised to a superior throne,
   Where angels bow around,
   And high o'er all the shining train,
   With matchless honors crowned;—

3 The names of all his saints he bears
   Engraven on his heart;
   Nor shall a name once treasured there
   E'er from his care depart.

4 Those characters shall fair abide,
   Our everlasting trust,
   When gems, and monuments, and crowns
   Are mouldered down to dust.

5 So, gracious Saviour! on my breast,
   May thy dear name be worn,
   A sacred ornament and guard,
   To endless ages borne.

538.
God's Peace.

1 We bless thee for thy peace, O God!
   Deep as the soundless sea,
   Which falls like sunshine on the road
   Of those who trust in thee.

2 We ask not, Father, for repose
   Which comes from outward rest,
   If we may have through all life's woes
   Thy peace within our breast;—

3 That peace which suffers and is strong,
   Trusts where it cannot see,
   Deems not the trial way too long,
   But leaves the end with thee;—

4 That peace which, though the billows
     surge,
   And angry tempests roar,
   Rings forth no melancholy dirge,
   But joyeth evermore;—

5 That peace which flows serene and deep—
   A river in the soul,
   Whose banks a living verdure keep:
   God's sunshine o'er the whole!—

6 Such, Father, give our hearts such peace,
   Whate'er the outward be,
   Till all life's discipline shall cease,
   And we go home to thee.

539.
"All things are yours."

1 If God is mine, then present things
   And things to come are mine;
   Yea, Christ, his word, and Spirit too,
   And glory all divine.

2 If he is mine, then from his love
   He every trouble sends;
   All things are working for my good,
   And bliss his rod attends.

3 If he is mine, let friends forsake,
   Let wealth and honor flee;
   Sure he who giveth me himself
   Is more than these to me.

4 Oh! tell me, Lord, that thou art mine;
   What can I wish beside?
   My soul shall at the fountain live,
   When all the streams are dried.

BRIDGMAN. C. M.

Arranged from BEETHOVEN.

1. O God of Beth-el! by whose hand Thy peo-ple still are fed;

Who through this wea-ry pil-grim-age Hast all our fa-thers led;

540.
Divine Guidance.

2 Our vows, our prayers, we now present
Before thy throne of grace;
God of our fathers! be the God
Of their succeeding race.

3 Through each perplexing path of life
Our wandering footsteps guide;
Give us, each day, our daily bread,
And raiment fit provide.

4 Oh, spread thy covering wings around,
Till all our wanderings cease,
And at our Father's loved abode,
Our souls arrive in peace.

5 Such blessings from thy gracious hand
Our humble prayers implore;
And thou shalt be our chosen God,
Our portion evermore.

541.
Adoption.

1 My Father, God! how sweet the sound,
How tender and how dear!
Not all the melody of heaven
Could so delight the ear.

2 Come, sacred Spirit, seal the name
On my expanding heart;
And show, that in Jehovah's grace
I share a filial part.

3 Cheered by a signal so divine,
Unwavering I believe;
My spirit Abba, Father, cries,
Nor can the sign deceive.

542.
Perseverance.

1 FIRM as the earth thy gospel stands,
My Lord, my hope, my trust;
If I am found in Jesus' hands,
My soul can ne'er be lost.

2 His honor is engaged to save
The meanest of his sheep;
All, whom his heavenly Father gave,
His hands securely keep.

3 Nor death nor hell shall e'er remove
His favorites from his breast;
In the dear bosom of his love
They must forever rest.

543.
Adoption.

1 My God, my Father, blissful name!
Oh, may I call thee mine?
May I with sweet assurance claim
A portion so divine?

2 Whate'er thy providence denies
I calmly would resign,
For thou art good and just and wise:
Oh, bend my will to thine!

3 Whate'er thy sacred will ordains,
Oh, give me strength to bear!
And let me know my Father reigns,
And trust his tender care.

4 Thy sovereign ways are all unknown
To my weak, erring sight;
Yet let my soul adoring own
That all thy ways are right.

THATCHER. S. M. HANDEL.

1. Thou ve - ry pres - ent aid In suf - fering and dis - tress,

The mind which still on thee is stayed, Is kept in per - fect peace.

544.
Rest in God.

1 Thou very present aid
  In suffering and distress,
The mind which still on thee is stayed,
  Is kept in perfect peace.

2 The soul by faith reclined
  On the Redeemer's breast;
'Mid raging storms, exults to find
  An everlasting rest.

3 Sorrow and fear are gone,
  Whene'er thy face appears;
It stills the sighing orphan's moan,
  And dries the widow's tears.

4 It hallows every cross;
  It sweetly comforts me;
Makes me forget my every loss,
  And find my all in thee.

5 Jesus, to whom I fly,
  Doth all my wishes fill;
What though created streams are dry?
  I have the fountain still.

6 Stripped of each earthly friend,
  I find them all in one,
And peace and joy which never end,
  And heaven, in Christ, begun.

545.
Love of God.

1 In every trying hour
  My soul to Jesus flies;
I trust in his almighty power,
  When swelling billows rise.

2 His comforts bear me up;
  I trust a faithful God;
The sure foundation of my hope
  Is in my Saviour's blood.

3 Loud hallelujahs sing
  To our Redeemer's name;
In joy or sorrow—life or death—
  His love is still the same.

546.
Kept of God.

1 What cheering words are these;
  Their sweetness who can tell?
In time and to eternal days,
  "'T is with the righteous well."

2 In every state secure,
  Kept as Jehovah's eye,
'T is well with them while life endures,
  And well when called to die.

3 Well when they see his face,
  Or sink amidst the flood;
Well in affliction's thorny maze,
  Or on the mount with God.

4 'T is well when joys arise,
  'T is well when sorrows flow,
'T is well when darkness vails the skies,
  And strong temptations grow.

5 'T is well when Jesus calls,
  "From earth and sin arise,
To join the hosts of ransomed souls,
  Made to salvation wise!"

SILVER STREET. S. M.   L Smith.

1. Here I can firm-ly rest; I dare to boast of this,
That God, the high-est and the best, My Friend and Fa-ther is.

547.
Adoption.

2 Naught have I of my own,
  Naught in the life I lead;
What Christ hath given, that alone
  Is worth all love indeed.

3 I rest upon the ground
  Of Jesus and his blood;
It is through him that I have found
  My soul's eternal good.

4 At cost of all I have,
  At cost of life and limb,
I cling to God who yet shall save;—
  I will not turn from him.

5 His Spirit in me dwells,
  O'er all my mind he reigns;
My care and sadness he dispels,
  And soothes away my pains.

6 He prospers day by day
  His work within my heart,
Till I have strength and faith to say,
  Thou, God, my Father art!

548.
Grace.

1 Grace! 't is a charming sound!
  Harmonious to the ear!
Heaven with the echo shall resound,
  And all the earth shall hear.

2 Grace first contrived a way
  To save rebellious man;
And all the steps that grace display,
  Which drew the wondrous plan.

3 Grace led my roving feet
  To tread the heavenly road;
And new supplies each hour I meet
  While pressing on to God.

4 Grace all the work shall crown,
  Through everlasting days;
It lays in heaven the topmost stone,
  And well deserves the praise.

549.
Adoption.

1 Behold what wondrous grace
  The Father has bestowed
On sinners of a mortal race,
  To call them sons of God!

2 Nor doth it yet appear
  How great we must be made;
But when we see our Saviour here,
  We shall be like our head.

3 A hope so much divine
  May trials well endure,
May purge our souls from sense and sin,
  As Christ the Lord is pure.

4 If in my Father's love
  I share a filial part,
Send down thy Spirit, like a dove,
  To rest upon my heart.

5 We would no longer lie
  Like slaves beneath the throne;
Our faith shall Abba, Father! cry,
  And thou the kindred own.

BISHOP. L. M.   Don José.

1. Go, la-bor on; spend and be spent,—Thy joy to do the Father's will:

It is the way the Mas-ter went; Should not the ser-vant tread it still?

550.
Zeal.

2 Go, labor on; 't is not for naught;
Thine earthly loss is heavenly gain :
Men heed thee, love thee, praise thee not ;
The Master praises,—what are men ?

3 Go, labor on ; enough, while here,
If he shall praise thee, if he deign
Thy willing heart to mark and cheer :
No toil for him shall be in vain.

4 Toil on, and in thy toil rejoice ;
For toil comes rest, for exile home ;
Soon shalt thou hear the Bridegroom's
voice,
The midnight peal : "Behold, I come !"

551.
Liberality.

1 When Jesus dwelt in mortal clay,
What were his works from day to day,
But miracles of power and grace,
That spread salvation through our race?

2 Teach us, O Lord, to keep in view
Thy pattern, and thy steps pursue ;
Let alms bestowed, let kindness done,
Be witnessed by each rolling sun.

3 That man may last, but never lives,
Who much receives, but nothing gives ;
Whom none can love, whom none can
thank,
Creation's blot, creation's blank !

4 But he who marks, from day to day,
In generous acts his radiant way,
Treads the same path his Saviour trod,
The path to glory and to God.

552.
Zeal.

1 Go, labor on, while it is day ;
The world's dark night is hastening on :
Speed, speed thy work,—cast sloth away !
It is not thus that souls are won.

2 Men die in darkness at your side,
Without a hope to cheer the tomb :
Take up the torch and wave it wide—
The torch that lights time's thickest
gloom.

3 Toil on,—faint not ; keep watch and pray !
Be wise the erring soul to win ;
Go forth into the world's highway ;
Compel the wanderer to come in.

4 Go, labor on ; your hands are weak ;
Your knees are faint, your soul cast down ;
Yet falter not ; the prize you seek
Is near,—a kingdom and a crown !

553.
The Poor.

1 Thou God of hope, to thee we bow !
Thou art our refuge in distress ;
The Husband of the widow thou,
The Father of the fatherless.

2 The poor are thy peculiar care ;
To them thy promises are sure :
Thy gifts the poor in spirit share ;
Oh ! may we always thus be poor !

3 May we thy law of love fulfill,
To bear each other's burdens here,
Endure and do thy righteous will,
And walk in all thy faith and fear.

REMSEN. C. M.　　　　　　　　　　　　　　　J. P. HOLBROOK.

1. Fa - ther of mer - cies, send thy grace, All power-ful from a - bove,

To form, in our o - be - dient souls, The im - age of thy love.

554.
Brotherly Kindness.

1 FATHER of mercies ! send thy grace,
　All powerful from above,
　To form, in our obedient souls,
　The image of thy love.

2 Oh, may our sympathizing breasts
　The generous pleasure know,
　Kindly to share in others' joy,
　And weep for others' woe !

3 When the most helpless sons of grief
　In low distress are laid,
　Soft be our hearts their pains to feel,
　And swift our hands to aid.

4 So Jesus looked on dying men,
　When throned above the skies ;
　And mid th' embraces of his God,
　He felt compassion rise.

5 On wings of love the Saviour flew,
　To raise us from the ground,
　And made the richest of his blood,
　A balm for every wound.

555.
Charity.

1 BLEST is the man whose softening heart
　Feels all another's pain ;
　To whom the supplicating eye
　Was never raised in vain:—

2 Whose breast expands with generous
　　　　warmth,
　A stranger's woes to feel ;
　And bleeds in pity o'er the wound
　He wants the power to heal.

3 He spreads his kind, supporting arms,
　To every child of grief ;
　His secret bounty largely flows,
　And brings unasked relief.

4 To gentle offices of love
　His feet are never slow :
　He views, through mercy's melting eye,
　A brother in a foe.

5 Peace from the bosom of his God,
　The Saviour's grace shall give ;
　And when he kneels before the throne,
　His trembling soul shall live.

556.
Trivial Efforts.

1 SCORN not the slightest word or deed,
　Nor deem it void of power ;
　There's fruit in each wind-wafted seed,
　That waits its natal hour.

2 A whispered word may touch the heart
　And call it back to life ;
　A look of love bid sin depart,
　And still unholy strife.

3 No act falls fruitless ; none can tell
　How vast its power may be,
　Nor what results infolded dwell
　Within it silently.

4 Work on, despair not, bring thy mite,
　Nor care how small it be ;
　God is with all that serve the right,
　The holy, true, and free.

LABAN. S. M.

Dr. L. Mason.

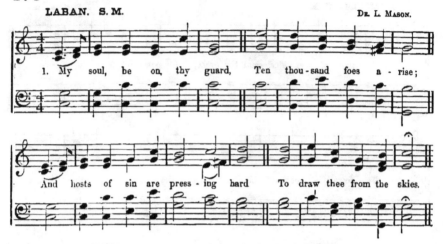

1. My soul, be on, thy guard, Ten thou-sand foes a - rise;

And hosts of sin are press-ing hard To draw thee from the skies.

557.
Watchfulness.

1 My soul, be on thy guard,
    Ten thousand foes arise;
And hosts of sin are pressing hard
    To draw thee from the skies.

2 Oh, watch, and fight, and pray!
    The battle ne'er give o'er;
Renew it boldly every day,
    And help divine implore.

3 Ne'er think the victory won,
    Nor once at ease sit down;
Thy arduous work will not be done
    Till thou obtain thy crown.

4 Fight on, my soul, till death
    Shall bring thee to thy God!
He'll take thee at thy parting breath,
    Up to his blest abode.

558.
Seed-Sowing.

1 Sow in the morn thy seed;
    At eve hold not thy hand;
To doubt and fear give thou no heed;
    Broadcast it o'er the land!

2 Beside all waters sow,
    The highway furrows stock,
Drop it where thorns and thistles grow,
    Scatter it on the rock.

3 The good, the fruitful ground
    Expect not here nor there;
O'er hill and dale by plots 't is found;
    Go forth, then, everywhere.

4 And duly shall appear,
    In verdure, beauty, strength,
The tender blade, the stalk, the ear,
    And the full corn at length.

5 Thou canst not toil in vain;
    Cold, heat and moist, and dry,
Shall foster and mature the grain
    For garners in the sky.

6 Then, when the glorious end,
    The day of God shall come,
The angel-reapers shall descend,
    And heaven cry, " Harvest home!"

559.
Energy of Zeal.

1 Make haste, O man, to live,
    For thou so soon must die;
Time hurries past thee like the breeze;
    How swift its moments fly!

2 To breathe, and wake, and sleep,
    To smile, to sigh, to grieve,
To move in idleness through earth—
    This, this is not to live.

3 Make haste, O man, to do
    Whatever must be done;
Thou hast no time to lose in sloth,
    Thy day will soon be gone.

4 Up, then, with speed, and work;
    Fling ease and self away—
This is no time for thee to sleep—
    Up, watch, and work and pray!

LEIGHTON. S. M.   GREATOREX COLL.

1. La-borers of Christ, a-rise, And gird you for the toil!

The dew of prom-ise from the skies Al-rea-dy cheers the soil.

560.
Active Effort.

1 LABORERS of Christ, arise,
  And gird you for the toil!
The dew of promise from the skies
  Already cheers the soil.

2 Go where the sick recline,
  Where mourning hearts deplore;
And where the sons of sorrow pine,
  Dispense your hallowed lore.

3 Be faith, which looks above,
  With prayer, your constant guest;
And wrap the Saviour's changeless love
  A mantle round your breast.

4 So shall you share the wealth
  That earth may ne'er despoil,
And the blest gospel's saving health
  Repay your arduous toil.

561.
Waiting.

1 MINE eyes and my desire
  Are ever to the Lord;
I love to plead his promises,
  And rest upon his word.

2 Lord, turn thee to my soul;
  Bring thy salvation near:
When will thy hand release my feet
  From sin's destructive snare?

3 When shall the sovereign grace
  Of my forgiving God
Restore me from those dangerous ways
  My wandering feet have trod?

4 Oh, keep my soul from death,
  Nor put my hope to shame!
For I have placed my only trust
  In my Redeemer's name.

5 With humble faith I wait
  To see thy face again;
Of Israel it shall ne'er be said,
  He sought the Lord in vain.

562.
Reform.

1 MOURN for the thousands slain,
  The youthful and the strong;
Mourn for the wine-cup's fearful reign,
  And the deluded throng.

2 Mourn for the tarnished gem—
  For reason's light divine,
Quenched from the soul's bright diadem,
  Where God had bid it shine.

3 Mourn for the ruined soul—
  Eternal life and light
Lost by the fiery, maddening bowl,
  And turned to helpless night.

4 Mourn for the lost—but call,
  Call to the strong, the free;
Rouse them to shun that dreadful fall;
  And to the refuge flee.

5 Mourn for the lost—but pray,
  Pray to our God above,
To break the fell destroyer's sway,
  And show his saving love.

STOCKWELL. 8s & 7s.   D. E. JONES.

1. He that go-eth forth with weep-ing, Bear-ing pre-cious seed in love,

Nev-er tir-ing, nev-er sleep-ing, Find-eth mer-cy from a-bove.

563.
Work Encouraged.

2 Soft descend the dews of heaven,
  Bright the rays celestial shine;
Precious fruits will thus be given,
  Through an influence all divine.

3 Sow thy seed, be never weary,
  Let no fears thy soul annoy;
Be the prospect ne'er so dreary,
  Thou shalt reap the fruits of joy.

4 Lo, the scene of verdure brightening!
  See the rising grain appear;
Look, again! the fields are whitening,
  For the harvest time is near.

564.
Success from God.

1 VAINLY through night's weary hours,
  Keep we watch, lest foes alarm ;—
Vain our bulwarks, and our towers,
  But for God's protecting arm.

2 Vain were all our toil and labor,
  Did not God that labor bless;
Vain, without his grace and favor,
  Every talent we possess.

3 Vainer still the hope of heaven,
  That on human strength relies;
But to him shall help be given,
  Who in humble faith applies.

4 Seek we, then, the Lord's Anointed;
  He shall grant us peace and rest:
Ne'er was suppliant disappointed,
  Who to Christ his prayer addressed.

565.
Self-Denial.

1 PILGRIMS in this vale of sorrow,
  Pressing onward toward the prize,
Strength and comfort here we borrow
  From the Hand that rules the skies.

2 'Mid these scenes of self-denial,
  We are called the race to run;
We must meet full many a trial
  Ere the victor's crown is won.

3 Love shall every conflict lighten,
  Hope shall urge us swifter on,
Faith shall every prospect brighten,
  Till the morn of heaven shall dawn.

4 On th' Eternal arm reclining,
  We at length shall win the day;
All the powers of earth combining,
  Shall not snatch our crown away.

566.
Progress.

1 LIKE the eagle, upward, onward,
  Let my soul in faith be borne ;
Calmly gazing, skyward, sunward,
  Let my eye unshrinking turn!

2 Where the cross, God's love revealing,
  Sets the fettered spirit free,
Where it sheds its wondrous healing,
  There, my soul, thy rest shall be!

3 Oh, may I no longer dreaming,
  Idly waste my golden day,
But, each precious hour redeeming,
  Upward, onward press my way!

SOLNEY. 8s & 7s. SCHULZ.

1. Cast thy bread up-on the wa-ters, Think-ing not 'tis thrown a-way;

God him-self saith, thou shalt gath-er It a-gain some fu-ture day.

567.
Benevolent Efforts.

1 CAST thy bread upon the waters,
  Thinking not 't is thrown away;
  God himself saith, thou shalt gather
  It again some future day.

2 Cast thy bread upon the waters;
  Wildly though the billows roll,
  They but aid thee as thou toilest
  Truth to spread from pole to pole.

3 As the seed, by billows floated,
  To some distant island lone,
  So to human souls benighted,
  That thou flingest may be borne.

4 Cast thy bread upon the waters;
  Why wilt thou still doubting stand?
  Bounteous shall God send the harvest,
  If thou sow'st with liberal hand.

5 Give then freely of thy substance—
  O'er this cause the Lord doth reign;
  Cast thy bread, and toil with patience,
  Thou shalt labor not in vain.

568.
"Brother's Keeper."

1 BLESSÉD angels, high in heaven
  O'er the penitent rejoice;
  Hast thou for thy brother striven
  With an importuning voice?

2 Art thou not thy brother's keeper?
  Canst thou not his soul obtain?
  He that wakes his brother sleeper
  Double light himself shall gain.

3 Ah! how many may be given
  To that during, fiery lake,
  Who had found a place in heaven
  Had'st thou toiled for Jesus' sake.

4 Think how words in season spoken,
  In the sinful heart sink deep,
  And the first link may have broken
  Of the chains that round him creep.

5 Think of *that* day when each brother
  To his brother shall be known:
  If thy prayers have saved another,
  God will then thy service own.

6 Then, when ends this life's short fever,
  They, who many turn to God,
  Like the stars shall shine for ever,
  In th' eternal brotherhood!

569.
Contribution.

1 WITH my substance I will honor
  My Redeemer and my Lord;
  Were ten thousand worlds my manor,
  All were nothing to his word.

2 While the heralds of salvation
  His abounding grace proclaim,
  Let his friends, of every station,
  Gladly join to spread his fame.

3 Be his kingdom now promoted,
  Let the earth her Monarch know;
  Be my all to him devoted;
  To my Lord my all I owe.

WOODWORTH. L. M.

WM. B. BRADBURY.

1. My God, my Fa-ther, while I stray Far from my home on life's rough way,

Oh! teach me from my heart to say, "Thy will be done, thy will be done."

570.

1 My God, my Father, while I stray
Far from my home, on life's rough way,
Oh, teach me from my heart to say,
"Thy will be done, thy will be done!"

2 What though in lonely grief I sigh
For friends beloved no longer nigh;
Submissive still would I reply,
"Thy will be done, thy will be done!"

3 If thou should'st call me to resign
What most I prize,—it ne'er was mine;
I only yield thee what was thine:
"Thy will be done, thy will be done!"

4 If but my fainting heart be blest
With thy sweet Spirit for its guest,
My God, to thee I leave the rest;
"Thy will be done, thy will be done!"

5 Renew my will from day to day;
Blend it with thine, and take away
Whate'er now makes it hard to say,
"Thy will be done, thy will be done!"

6 Then when on earth I breathe no more,
The prayer oft mixed with tears before
I'll sing upon a happier shore:
"Thy will be done, thy will be done!"

571.

1 I bless thee, Lord, for sorrows sent
To break the dream of human power,
For now my shallow cistern 's spent,
I find thy fount and thirst no more.

2 I take thy hand and fears grow still;
Behold thy face, and doubts remove;
Who would not yield his wavering will
To perfect truth and boundless love!

3 That truth gives promise of a dawn,
Beneath whose light I am to see,
When all these blinding vails are drawn,
This was the wisest path for me.

4 That love this restless soul doth teach
The strength of thy eternal calm;
And tune its sad and broken speech,
To sing ev'n now the angels' psalm.

572.

1 I cannot always trace the way
Where thou, Almighty One, dost move;
But I can always, always say,
That God is love, that God is love.

2 When fear her chilling mantle throws
O'er earth, my soul to heaven above,
As to her native home, upsprings,
For God is love, for God is love.

3 When mystery clouds my darkened path,
I'll check my dread, my doubts reprove,
In this my soul sweet comfort hath,
That God is love, that God is love.

4 Yes, God is love;—a thought like this
Can every gloomy thought remove,
And turn all tears, all woes, to bliss,
For God is love, for God is love.

BEETHOVEN. L. M.

HAYDN.

1. Oh, deem not they are blest a-lone, Whose lives a peace-ful ten-or keep;

For God, who pit-ies man, hath shown A bless-ing for the eyes that weep.

573.

1 Oh, deem not they are blest alone,
Whose lives a peaceful tenor keep;
For God, who pities man, hath shown
A blessing for the eyes that weep.

2 The light of smiles shall fill again
The lids that overflow with tears;
And weary hours of woe and pain
Are promises of happier years.

3 There is a day of sunny rest
For every dark and troubled night;
And grief may bide an evening guest,
But joy shall come with early light.

4 Nor let the good man's trust depart,
Though life its common gifts deny;
Though with a pierced and broken heart,
And spurned of men, he goes to die.

5 For God has marked each sorrowing day,
And numbered every secret tear,
And heaven's long age of bliss shall pay
For all his children suffer here.

574.

1 Thy will be done! I will not fear
The fate provided by thy love;
Tho' clouds and darkness shroud me here,
I know that all is bright above.

2 The stars of heaven are shining on,
Tho' these frail eyes are dimmed with tears,
The hopes of earth indeed are gone,
But are not ours the immortal years?

3 Father! forgive the heart that clings,
Thus trembling, to the things of time;
And bid my soul, on angel wings,
Ascend into a purer clime.

4 There shall no doubts disturb its trust,
No sorrows dim celestial love;
But these afflictions of the dust,
Like shadows of the night, remove.

5 Ev'n now, above, there's radiant day,
While clouds and darkness brood below;
Then, Father, joyful on my way
To drink the bitter cup I go.

575.

1 If life in sorrow must be spent,
So be it; I am well content;
And meekly wait my last remove,
Desiring only trustful love.

2 No bliss I'll seek, but to fulfill
In life, in death, thy perfect will;
No succors in my woes I want,
But what my Lord is pleased to grant.

3 Our days are numbered: let us spare
Our anxious hearts a needless care:
'T is thine to number out our days;
'T is ours to give them to thy praise.

4 Faith is our only business here—
Faith simple, constant, and sincere;
Oh, blessèd days thy servants see!
Thus spent, O Lord! in pleasing thee.

SILOAM. C. M.   I. B. Woodbury.

1. When mus-ing sor-row weeps the past, And mourns the pres-ent pain,
'T is sweet to think of peace at last, And feel that death is gain.

576.

2 'T is not that murmuring thoughts arise,
   And dread a Father's will;
'T is not that meek submission flies,
   And would not suffer still.

3 It is that heaven-born faith surveys
   The path that leads to light,
And longs her eagle plumes to raise,
   And lose herself in sight.

4 Oh! let me wing my hallowed flight
   From earth-born woe and care,
And soar above these clouds of night,
   My Saviour's bliss to share.

577.

1 Ir is the Lord—enthroned in light,
   Whose claims are all divine,
Who has an undisputed right
   To govern me and mine.

2 It is the Lord—who gives me all—
   My wealth, my friends, my ease;
And of his bounties may recall
   Whatever part he please.

3 It is the Lord—my covenant God,
   Thrice blessèd be his name;
Whose gracious promise, sealed with blood,
   Must ever be the same.

4 Can I, with hopes so firmly built,
   Be sullen, or repine?
No—gracious God—take what thou wilt,
   To thee I all resign.

578.

1 I cannot call affliction sweet;
   And yet 't was good to bear:
Affliction brought me to thy feet,
   And I found comfort there.

2 My wearied soul was all resigned
   To thy most gracious will:
Oh, had I kept that better mind,
   Or been afflicted still!

3 Where are the vows which then I vowed!
   The joys which then I knew?
Those, vanished like the morning cloud;
   These, like the early dew.

4 Lord, grant me grace for every day,
   Whate'er my state may be
Through life, in death, with truth to say.
   "My God is all to me."

579.

1 My times of sorrow and of joy,
   Great God! are in thy hand;
My choicest comforts come from thee,
   And go at thy command.

2 If thou should'st take them all away,
   Yet would I not repine;
Before they were possessed by me,
   They were entirely thine.

3 Nor would I drop a murmuring word,
   Though the whole world were gone,
But seek enduring happiness,
   In thee, and thee alone.

DOWNS. C. M.   DR. L. MASON.

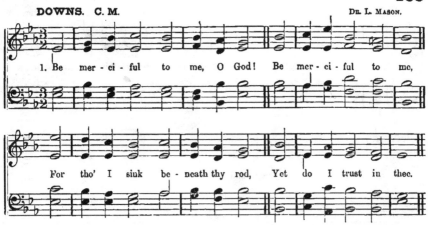

1. Be mer-ci-ful to me, O God! Be mer-ci-ful to me,

For tho' I sink be-neath thy rod, Yet do I trust in thee.

580.

2 Thou art my refuge, and I know
  My burden thou dost bear,
And I would seek, where'er I go,
  To cast on thee my care.

3 Thou knowest, Lord, my flesh how frail,
  Strong though my spirit be;
Oh! then assist when foes assail,
  The soul that clings to thee.

4 And, gracious Lord, whate'er befall,
  A thankful heart be mine—
A heart that answers to thy call,
  One that is wholly thine.

5 And may I ne'er forget that thou
  Wilt soon return again,
And those who love thy coming now
  Shall shine in glory then.

581.

1 WHEN waves of trouble round me swell,
  My soul is not dismayed;
I hear a voice I know full well,—
  "'T is I; be not afraid."

2 When black the threatening skies appear,
  And storms my path invade,
Those accents tranquilize each fear,—
  "'T is I; be not afraid."

3 There is a gulf that must be crossed;
  Saviour, be near to aid!
Whisper, when my frail bark is tossed,—
  "'T is I; be not afraid."

4 There is a dark and fearful vale,
  Death hides within its shade;
Oh, say, when flesh and heart shall fail,—
  "'T is I; be not afraid."

582.

1 I WORSHIP thee, sweet Will of God!
  And all thy ways adore;
And every day I live, I long
  To love thee more and more.

2 Man's weakness, waiting upon God,
  Its end can never miss;
For man on earth no work can do
  More angel-like than this.

3 He always wins who sides with God,
  To him no chance is lost;
God's will is sweetest to him, when
  It triumphs at his cost.

4 Ill, that God blesses, is our good,
  And unblest good is ill;
And all is right that seems most wrong,
  If it be his dear will!

5 When obstacles and trials seem
  Like prison-walls to be,
I do the little I can do,
  And leave the rest to thee.

6 I have no cares, O blessed Will!
  For all my cares are thine;
I live in triumph, Lord! for thou
  Hast made thy triumphs mine.

HELENA. C. M.　　　　　　　　　　　　　　Wm. B. Bradbury.

1. O thou, who driest the mourn-er's tear, How dark this world would be,

If, when by sor-rows wound-ed here, We could not fly to thee!

583.

2 But thou wilt heal the broken heart,
　Which, like the plants that throw
Their fragrance from the wounded part,
Breathes sweetness out of woe.

3 When joy no longer soothes or cheers,
　And ev'n the hope that threw
A moment's sparkle o'er our tears
Is dimmed and vanished too;

4 Oh, who would bear life's stormy doom,
　Did not thy wing of love
Come, brightly wafting through the gloom,
Our peace-branch from above?

5 Then sorrow touched by thee grows
　　　　bright,
With more than rapture's ray;
As darkness shows us worlds of light
We never saw by day.

584.

1 One prayer I have—all prayers in one—
　When I am wholly thine;
Thy will, my God, thy will be done,
And let that will be mine.

2 All-wise, almighty, and all-good,
　In thee I firmly trust;
Thy ways, unknown or understood,
Are merciful and just.

3 May I remember that to thee
　Whate'er I have I owe;
And back, in gratitude, from me
May all thy bounties flow.

4 And though thy wisdom takes away,
　Shall I arraign thy will?
No, let me bless thy name, and say,
"The Lord is gracious still."

5 A pilgrim through the earth I roam,
　Of nothing long possessed;
And all must fail when I go home,
For this is not my rest.

585.

1 O thou whose gently chastening hand
　In mercy deals the blow!
Make but thy servant understand
Wherefore thou layest me low!

2 I ask thee not the rod to spare
　While thus thy love I see;
But oh! let every suffering bear
Some message, Lord, from thee!

3 Perhaps an erring wish I knew
　To read my future fate,
And thou wouldst say: "Thy days are
　　　　few,
And vain thy best estate."

4 Perhaps thy glory seemed my choice,
　While I secured my own,
And thus my kind Reprover's voice
Tells me he works alone!

5 Oh! silence thou this murmuring will,
　Nor bid thy rough wind stay,
Till with a furnace hotter still
My dross is purged away!

CROSS AND CROWN. C. M.

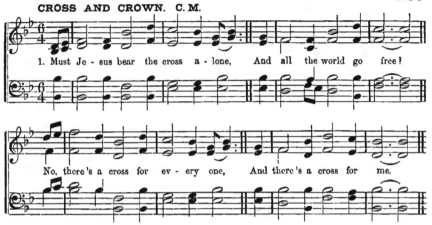

1. Must Je - sus bear the cross a - lone, And all the world go free!

No, there's a cross for ev - ery one, And there's a cross for me.

586.

1 Must Jesus bear the cross alone,
   And all the world go free?
No, there's a cross for every one,
   And there's a cross for me.

2 The consecrated cross I'll bear,
   Till death shall set me free,
And then go home my crown to wear,
   For there's a crown for me.

3 Upon the crystal pavement, down
   At Jesus' pierced feet,
Joyful, I'll cast my golden crown,
   And his dear name repeat.

4 And palms shall wave, and harps shall
      ring,
   Beneath heaven's arches high;
The Lord that lives, the ransomed sing,
   That lives no more to die.

5 Oh, precious cross! Oh, glorious crown!
   Oh, resurrection day!
Ye angels, from the stars come down,
   And bear my soul away.

587.

1 Jesus, in sickness and in pain,
   Be near to succor me;
My sinking spirit still sustain:
   To thee I turn, to thee.

2 When cares and sorrows thicken round,
   And nothing bright I see,
In thee alone can help be found;
   To thee I turn, to thee.

3 Should strong temptations fierce assail,
   And Satan buffet me,
Then in thy strength will I prevail,
   While still I turn to thee.

4 Through all my pilgrimage below,
   Whate'er my lot may be,
In joy or sadness, weal or woe,
   Jesus, I'll turn to thee.

588.

1 When languor and disease invade
   This trembling house of clay,
'Tis sweet to look beyond my pain,
   And long to fly away;

2 Sweet to look inward, and attend
   The whispers of his love;
Sweet to look upward to the place
   Where Jesus pleads above;

3 Sweet on his faithfulness to rest,
   Whose love can never end;
Sweet on his covenant of grace
   For all things to depend;

4 Sweet, in the confidence of faith,
   To trust his firm decrees;
Sweet to lie passive in his hands,
   And know no will but his.

5 If such the sweetness of the streams,
   What must the fountain be,
Where saints and angels draw their bliss
   Immediately from thee!

CAPELLO. S. M.   CANTICA LAUDIS.

1. Oh, throw a - way thy rod!   Oh, throw a - way   thy wrath!

My gra-cious Sa - viour and my God,   Oh, take the gen - tle path!

589.

2 Thou seest my heart's desire
  Still unto thee is bent;
  Still does my longing soul aspire
  To an entire consent.

3 Although I fail, I weep;
  Although I halt in pace,
  Yet still with trembling steps I creep
  Unto the throne of grace.

4 Oh, then let wrath remove;
  For love will do the deed;
  Love will the conquest gain; with love
  Ev'n stony hearts will bleed.

5 Oh, throw away thy rod!
  What though man frailties hath?
  Thou art my Saviour and my God;
  Oh, throw away thy wrath!

590.

1 IT is thy hand, my God;
  My sorrow comes from thee:
  I bow beneath thy chastening rod,
  'Tis love that bruises me.

2 I would not murmur, Lord:
  Before thee I am dumb:
  Lest I should breathe one murmuring
      word,
  To thee for help I come.

3 My God, thy name is Love;
  A Father's hand is thine;
  With tearful eyes I look above,
  And cry, "Thy wil be mine!"

4 I know thy will is right,
  Though it may seem severe;
  Thy path is still unsullied light,
  Though dark it oft appear.

5 Jesus for me hath died;
  Thy Son thou didst not spare:
  His piercéd hands, his bleeding side
  Thy love for me declare.

6 Here my poor heart can rest;
  My God, it cleaves to thee :
  Thy will is love, thine end is blest,
  All work for good to me.

591.

1 THY way, not mine, O Lord,
  However dark it be!
  Lead me by thy own faithful hand,
  Choose out the path for me.

2 Smooth let it be or rough,
  It will be still the best,
  Winding or straight, it matters not,
  It leads me to thy rest.

3 I dare not choose my lot:
  I would not if I might;
  Choose thou for me, my gracious God,
  So shall I walk aright.

4 The kingdom that I seek
  Is thine; so let the way
  That leads to it be truly thine,
  Else I must surely stray.

DENNIS. S. M.

NAGELI.

1. How ten - der is thy hand, O thou be - lov - ed Lord!

Af - flic - tions come at thy com - mand, And leave us at thy word.

592.

1 How tender is thy hand,
   O thou beloved Lord!
Afflictions come at thy command,
   And leave us at thy word.

2 How gentle was the rod
   That chastened us for sin!
How soon we found a smiling God,
   Where deep distress had been!

3 A Father's hand we felt,
   A Father's heart we knew;
With tears of penitence we knelt,
   And found his word was true.

4 We told him all our grief,
   We thought of Jesus' love;
A sense of pardon brought relief,
   And bade our pains remove.

5 Now we will bless the Lord,
   And in his strength confide;
Forever be his name adored;
   For there is none beside.

593.

1 "My times are in thy hand:"
   My God! I wish them there;
My life, my friends, my soul, I leave
   Entirely to thy care.

2 "My times are in thy hand,"
   Whatever they may be;
Pleasing or painful, dark or bright,
   As best may seem to thee.

3 "My times are in thy hand;"—
   Why should I doubt or fear?
My Father's hand will never cause
   His child a needless tear.

4 "My times are in thy hand,"—
   Jesus, the crucified!
The hand my cruel sins had pierced,
   Is now my guard and guide.

5 "My times are in thy hand;"
   I'll always trust in thee;
And, after death, at thy right hand
   I shall forever be.

594.

1 WHEN overwhelmed with grief,
   My heart within me dies;
Helpless, and far from all relief,
   To heaven I lift mine eyes.

2 Oh, lead me to the Rock
   That's high above my head,
And make the covert of thy wings
   My shelter and my shade.

3 Within thy presence, Lord,
   Forever I'll abide;
Thou art the tower of my defense,
   The refuge where I hide.

4 Thou givest me the lot
   Of those that fear thy name;
If endless life be their reward,
   I shall possess the same.

PALESTINE. L. M. 6 lines.   MAZZINGHI.

1. Peace, troubled soul, whose plaintive moan Hath taught each scene the notes of woe;

Cease thy complaint, suppress thy groan, And let thy tears for-get to flow;

Be-hold, the pre-cious balm is found, To lull thy pain, to heal thy wound.

595.

2 Come, freely come, by sin oppressed;
On Jesus cast thy weighty load;
In him thy refuge find, thy rest,
Safe in the mercy of thy God;
Thy God's thy Saviour—glorious word!
Forever love and praise the Lord.

596.

1 WHEN gathering clouds around I view,
And days are dark, and friends are few,
On him I lean, who, not in vain,
Experienced every human pain;
He sees my wants, allays my fears,
And counts and treasures up my tears.

2 If aught should tempt my soul, to stray
From heavenly virtue's narrow way,—
To fly the good I would pursue,
Or do the sin I would not do,—
Still he, who felt temptation's power,
Shall guard me in that dangerous hour.

3 When sorrowing o'er some stone I bend,
Which covers all that was a friend,
And from his voice, his hand, his smile,
Divides me, for a little while,
My Saviour sees the tears I shed,
For Jesus wept o'er Lazarus dead.

4 And oh! when I have safely passed
Through every conflict, but the last,—
Still, still unchanging, watch beside
My painful bed,—for thou hast died;
Then point to realms of cloudless day,
And wipe my latest tear away.

597.

1 WHEN adverse winds and waves arise,
And in my heart despondence sighs;
When life her throng of cares reveals,
And weakness o'er my spirit steals,
Grateful I hear the kind decree,
That "as my day, my strength shall be."

2 When, with sad footsteps, memory roves
'Mid smitten joys and buried loves,
When sleep my tearful pillow flies,
And dewy morning drinks my sighs,
Still to thy promise, Lord! I flee,
That "as my day, my strength shall be."

3 One trial more must yet be past,
One pang—the keenest and the last;
And when, with brow convulsed and pale,
My feeble, quivering heart-strings fail,
Redeemer! grant my soul to see
That "as her day, her strength shall be."

MONTAGUE. 7s & 6s.

J. P. HOLBROOK.

1. Why sinks my soul de - spond - ing, Why fill my eyes with tears,

When na - ture all sur - round - ing The smile of beau - ty wears?
D. S. Each vis - ion that I bor - row With gloom and sad - ness fraught?

Why bur - dened still with sor - row Is ev - ery laboring thought!

598.

2 The pleasures that deceived me
My soul no more can charm;
Of rest they have bereaved me,
And filled me with alarm:
The objects I have cherished
Are empty as the wind;
My earthly joys have perished,—
What comfort shall I find?

3 If inward still inquiring
I turn my searching eye,
Or upward now aspiring,
I raise my feeble cry,
No heavenly light is beaming
To cheer my troubled breast;
No ray of comfort gleaming
To give my spirit rest.

4 Oh! from this dreadful anguish
Is there no refuge nigh?
'T is guilt that makes me languish,
And leaves me thus to die:
I will renounce my folly
Before the throne of grace;
And make the Lord most holy
My strength and righteousness.

599.

1 LORD God of my salvation,
To thee, to thee I cry;
Oh, let my supplication
Arrest thine ear on high!
Distresses round me thicken,
My life draws nigh the grave,
Descend, O Lord, to quicken,
Descend my soul to save.

2 Thy wrath lies hard upon me,
Thy billows o'er me roll;
My friends all seem to shun me,
And foes beset my soul.
Where'er on earth I turn me,
No comforter is near:
Wilt thou, my Father, spurn me,
Wilt thou refuse to hear?

3 No! banished and heart-broken,
My soul still clings to thee;
The promise thou hast spoken,
Still, still my refuge be;
To present ills and terrors,
My future joy increase,
And scourge me from my errors
To duty, hope, and peace.

ALL SAINTS. L. M.   WM. KNAPP.

1. Fa-ther of mer-cies, bow thine ear, At-ten-tive to our ear-nest prayer:

We plead for those who plead for thee; Suc-cess-ful plead-ers may they be.

600.
Ministry.

2 Clothe thou with energy divine
Their words, and let those words be thine;
Teach them immortal souls to gain,
Nor let them labor, Lord, in vain.

3 Let thronging multitudes around
Hear from their lips the joyful sound;
And light thro' distant realms be spread,
Till Zion rears her drooping head.

601.
Dedication.

1 On, bow thine ear, Eternal One!
On thee our heart adoring calls;
To thee the followers of thy Son
Have raised, and now devote these walls.

2 Here let thy holy days be kept;
And be this place to worship given,
Like that bright spot where Jacob slept,
The house of God, the gate of heaven.

3 Here may thine honor dwell; and here,
As incense, let thy children's prayer,
From contrite hearts and lips sincere,
Rise on the still and holy air.

4 Here be thy praise devoutly sung;
Here let thy truth beam forth to save,
As when, of old, thy Spirit hung,
On wings of light, o'er Jordan's wave.

5 And when the lips, that with thy name
Are vocal now, to dust shall turn,
On others may devotion's flame
Be kindled here, and purely burn!

602.
Seeking a Pastor.

1 O LORD, thy pitying eye surveys
Our wandering paths, our trackless ways:
Send forth, in love, thy truth and light,
To guide our doubtful footsteps right.

2 In humble faith, behold we wait:
On thee we call at mercy's gate;
Our drooping hearts, O God! sustain,—
Shall Israel seek thy face in vain?

3 O Lord! in ways of peace return,
Nor let thy flock neglected mourn;
May our blest eyes a shepherd see,
Dear to our souls, and dear to thee.

603.
Welcoming a Pastor.

1 WE bid thee welcome in the name
Of Jesus, our exalted Head;
Come as a servant: so he came,
And we receive thee in his stead.

2 Come as a shepherd; guard and keep
This fold from hell, and earth, and sin;
Nourish the lambs, and feed the sheep,
The wounded heal, the lost bring in.

3 Come as a teacher, sent from God,
Charged his whole counsel to declare;
Lift o'er our ranks the prophet's rod,
While we uphold thy hands with prayer.

4 Come as a messenger of peace,
Filled with the Spirit, fired with love!
Live to behold our large increase,
And die to meet us all above.

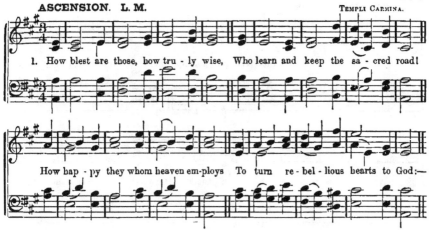

ASCENSION. L. M.   TEMPLI CARMINA.

1. How blest are those, how tru - ly wise, Who learn and keep the sa - cred road!

How hap - py they whom heaven em-ploys To turn re - bel - lious hearts to God:—

604.
Ministry.

2 To win them from the fatal way
Where erring folly thoughtless roves,
And that blest righteousness display
Which Jesus wrought and God approves.

3 The shining firmament shall fade,
And sparkling stars resign their light;
But these shall know nor change nor
shade,
Forever fair, forever bright.

605.
Convocation of Ministers.

1 Pour out thy Spirit from on high;
Lord! thine assembled servants bless;
Graces and gifts to each supply,
And clothe thy priests with righteousness.

2 Within thy temple where we stand,
To teach the truth as taught by thee,
Saviour! like stars in thy right hand,
The angels of the churches be!

3 Wisdom and zeal, and faith impart,
Firmness with meekness from above,
To bear thy people on our hearts,
And love the souls whom thou dost
love :—

4 To watch and pray, and never faint;
By day and night strict guard to keep;
To warn the sinner, cheer the saint,
Nourish thy lambs, and feed thy sheep.

5 Then, when our work is finished here,
In humble hope, our charge resign :
When the chief Shepherd shall appear,
O God! may they and we be thine.

606.
Prayer for Pastor.

1 With heavenly power, O Lord, defend
Him whom we now to thee commend ;
Thy faithful messenger secure,
And make him to the end endure.

2 Gird him with all-sufficient grace ;
Direct his feet in paths of peace ;
Thy truth and faithfulness fulfill,
And arm him to obey thy will.

607.
For Dedication.

1 The perfect world, by Adam trod,
Was the first temple built to God ;
His fiat laid the corner-stone,
And heaved its pillars one by one.

2 He hung its starry roof on high—
The broad, illimitable sky ;
He spread its pavement, green and bright,
And curtained it with morning light.

3 The mountains in their places stood,
The sea—the sky—and " all was good;"
And when its first few praises rang,
The " morning stars together sang."

4 Lord, 't is not ours to make the sea,
And earth, and sky, a house for thee ;
But in thy sight our offering stands—
An humbler temple, " made with hands."

5 We cannot bid the morning star
To sing how bright thy glories are ;
But, Lord, if thou wilt meet us here,
Thy praise shall be the Christian's tear.

ST. ANN'S. C. M.   DR. CROFT.

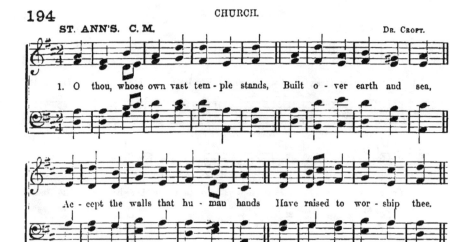

1. O thou, whose own vast tem-ple stands, Built o-ver earth and sea,

Ac-cept the walls that hu-man hands Have raised to wor-ship thee.

608.
For Dedication.

1 O THOU, whose own temple stands,
Built over earth and sea,
Accept the walls that human hands
Have raised to worship thee.

2 Lord, from thine inmost glory send,
Within these courts to bide,
The peace that dwelleth without end,
Serenely by thy side!

3 May erring minds that worship here
Be taught the better way;
And they who mourn, and they who fear,
Be strengthened as they pray.

4 May faith grow firm, and love grow warm,
And pure devotion rise,
While round these hallowed walls the storm
Of earth-born passion dies.

609.
For Organization.

1 CHURCH of the ever-living God,
The Father's gracious choice,
Amid the voices of this earth
How feeble is thy voice!

2 A little flock!—so calls he thee
Who bought thee with his blood;
A little flock, disowned of men,
But owned and loved of God.

3 Not many rich or noble called,
Not many great or wise;
They whom God makes his kings and
priests
Are poor in human eyes.

4 But the chief Shepherd comes at length;
Their feeble days are o'er,
No more a handful in the earth,
A little flock no more.

5 No more a lily among thorns,
Weary and faint and few;
But countless as the stars of heaven,
Or as the early dew.

6 Then entering th' eternal halls,
In robes of victory,
That mighty multitude shall keep
The joyous jubilee.

610.
For Organization.

1 On, where are kings and empires now
Of old that went and came?
But, Lord, thy church is praying yet,
A thousand years the same.

2 We mark her goodly battlements,
And her foundations strong;
We hear within the solemn voice
Of her unending song.

3 For not like kingdoms of the world
Thy holy church, O God!
Though earthquake shocks are threaten-
ing her,
And tempests are abroad;

4 Unshaken as eternal hills,
Immovable she stands,
A mountain that sha'l fill the earth,
A house not made by hands.

SILOAM. C. M.

I. B. WOODBURY.

1. By cool Si - lo - am's sha - dy rill How sweet the li - ly grows!

How sweet the breath, be - neath the hill, Of Sha - ron's dew - y rose!

611.

2 Lo! such the child whose early feet ·
  The paths of peace have trod,
Whose secret heart, with influence sweet,
  Is upward drawn to God.

3 By cool Siloam's shady rill
  The lily must decay;
The rose, that blooms beneath the hill,
  Must shortly fade away.

4 O thou who givest life and breath,
  We seek thy grace alone,
In childhood, manhood, age, and death,
  To keep us still thine own.

612.*

1 Come, Holy Spirit, from on high;
  Baptizer of our spirits thou!
The sacramental seal apply,
  And witness with the water now.

2 Exert thy energy divine,
  And sprinkle the atoning blood;
May Father, Son, and Spirit, join
  To seal this child, a child of God.

613.

1 "Forbid them not," the Saviour cried,
  "But suffer them to come;"
Ah, then maternal tears were dried,
  And unbelief was dumb.

2 Lord, we believe, and we obey;
  We bring them at thy word;
Be thou our children's strength and stay,
  Their portion and reward.

* Sing Hebron, p. 23.

614.

1 See Israel's gentle Shepherd stand,
  With all-engaging charms;
Hark! how he calls the tender lambs,
  And folds them in his arms!

2 "Permit them to approach," he cries,
  "Nor scorn their humble name;
It was to bless such souls as these
  The Lord of angels came."

3 We bring them, Lord, with fervent prayer,
  And yield them up to thee;
Joyful that we ourselves are thine,
  Thine let our offspring be!

615.

1 How large the promise! how divine!
  To Abr'ham and his seed:
"I'll be a God to thee and thine,
  Supplying all their need."

2 The words of his extensive love
  From age to age endure:
The angel of the covenant proves,
  And seals the blessings sure.

3 Jesus the ancient faith confirms
  To our great fathers given;
He takes young children to his arms,
  And calls them heirs of heaven.

4 Our God!—how faithful are his ways!
  His love endures the same;
Nor from the promise of his grace
  Blots out the children's name.

PORTUGAL. L. M.   THORLET.

1. This child we ded - i - cate to thee, O God of grace and pu - ri - ty!

Shield it from sin and threatening wrong, And let thy love its life pro - long.

616.

1 This child we dedicate to thee,
  O God of grace and purity!
  Shield it from sin and threatening wrong,
  And let thy love its life prolong.

2 Oh, may thy Spirit gently draw
  Its willing soul to keep thy law;
  May virtue, piety, and truth,
  Dawn even with its dawning youth.

3 We, too, before thy gracious sight,
  Once shared the blest baptismal rite,
  And would renew its solemn vow
  With love, and thanks, and praises, now.

4 Grant that, with true and faithful heart,
  We still may act the Christian's part,
  Cheered by each promise thou hast given,
  And laboring for the prize in heaven.

617.

1 Obedient to our Zion's King,
  We to his holy laver bring
  These happy converts, who have known
  And trusted in his grace alone.

2 Lord, in thy house they seek thy face;
  Oh, bless them with peculiar grace;
  Refresh their souls with love divine;
  Let beams of glory round them shine.

3 Ye, who your native vileness mourn,
  And to the great Redeemer turn,
  Arise, his gracious call obey,
  And be baptized without delay.

618.

1 O Lord! encouraged by thy grace,
  We bring our infant to thy throne;
  Give it within thy heart a place,
  Let it be thine, and thine alone.

2 Wash it from every stain of guilt,
  And let this child be sanctified;
  Lord! thou canst cleanse it, if thou wilt,
  And all its native evils hide.

3 We ask not, for it, earthly bliss,
  Or earthly honors, wealth or fame:
  The sum of our request is this—
  That it may love and fear thy name.

619.

1 Dear Saviour, if these lambs should stray,
  From thy secure inclosure's bound,
  And, lured by worldly joys away,
  Among the thoughtless crowd be found;

2 Remember still that they are thine,
  That thy dear sacred name they bear;
  Think that the seal of love divine,
  The sign of covenant grace they wear.

3 In all their erring, sinful years,
  Oh! let them ne'er forgotten be;
  Remember all the prayers and tears
  Which made them consecrate to thee.

4 And when these lips no more can pray,
  These eyes can weep for them no more,
  Turn thou their feet from folly's way;
  The wanderers to thy fold restore.

HAMBURG. L. M.

Arranged by DR. L. MASON.

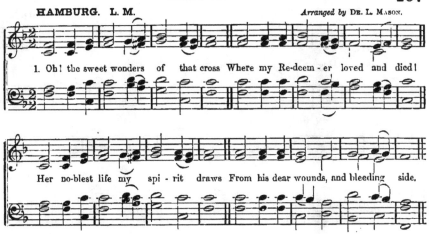

1. Oh! the sweet wonders of that cross Where my Re-deem-er loved and died!

Her no-blest life my spi-rit draws From his dear wounds, and bleeding side.

620.

1 Oh! the sweet wonders of that cross
Where my Redeemer loved and died!
Her noblest life my spirit draws
From his dear wounds, and bleeding side.

2 I would forever speak his name
In sounds to mortal ears unknown;
With angels join to praise the Lamb,
And worship at his Father's throne.

621.

1 Lord, I am thine, entirely thine,
Purchased and saved by blood divine!
With full consent thine I would be,
And own thy sovereign right in me.

2 Grant one poor sinner more a place,
Among the children of thy grace;
A wretched sinner, lost to God,
But ransomed by Immanuel's blood.

3 Thine would I live, thine would I die,
Be thine through all eternity;
The vow is pass'd beyond repeal;
Now will I set the solemn seal.

4 Here at that cross where flows the blood
That bought my guilty soul for God;
Thee, my new Master, now I call,
And consecrate to thee my all.

5 Do thou assist a feeble worm,
The great engagement to perform;
Thy grace can full assistance lend,
And on that grace I dare depend.

622.

1 We pray thee, wounded Lamb of God,
Cleanse us in thy atoning blood;
Grant us by faith to view thy cross,
Then life or death is gain to us.

2 Take our poor hearts and let them be
Forever closed to all but thee;
Seal thou our breasts, and let us wear
That pledge of love forever there.

623.

1 My gracious Lord, I own thy right
To every service I can pay,
And call it my supreme delight
To hear thy dictates and obey.

2 What is my being, but for thee,
Its sure support, its noblest end?
Thine ever smiling face to see,
And serve the cause of such a Friend.

3 I would not breathe for worldly joy,
Or to increase my worldly good;
Nor future days nor powers employ
To spread a sounding name abroad.

4 'Tis to my Saviour I would live,
To him who for my ransom died;
Nor could the bowers of Eden give
Such bliss as blossoms at his side.

5 His work my hoary age shall bless,
When youthful vigor is no more;
And my last hour of life confess
His dying love, his saving power.

DEDHAM. C. M.   GARDNER.

1. Ac-cord-ing to thy gra-cious word, In meek hu-mil-i-ty,

This will I do, my dy-ing Lord! I will re-mem-ber thee.

624.

1 ACCORDING to thy gracious word,
　In meek humility,
This will I do, my dying Lord!
　I will remember thee.

2 Thy body, broken for my sake,
　My bread from heaven shall be;
Thy testamental cup I take,
　And thus remember thee.

3 Gethsemane can I forget?
　Or there thy conflict see,
Thine agony and bloody sweat—
　And not remember thee?

4 When to the cross I turn my eyes,
　And rest on Calvary,
O Lamb of God! my sacrifice,
　I must remember thee!

5 Remember thee and all thy pains,
　And all thy love to me;
Yea, while I breathe, a pulse remains,
　Will I remember thee.

6 And when these failing lips grow dumb,
　And mind and memory flee,
When in thy kingdom thou shalt come,
　Jesus, remember me!

625.

1 JESUS, at whose supreme command,
　We now approach to God,
Before us in thy vesture stand,
　Thy vesture dipped in blood.

2 Now, Saviour, now thyself reveal,
　And make thy nature known;
Affix thy blessed Spirit's seal,
　And stamp us for thine own.

3 Obedient to thy gracious word,
　We break the hallowed bread,
Commemorate our dying Lord,
　And trust on thee to feed.

4 The cup of blessing, blest by thee,
　Let it thy blood impart;
The broken bread thy body be,
　To cheer each languid heart.

626.

1 OPPRESSED with noon-day's scorching
　　heat,
To yonder cross I flee;
Beneath its shelter take my seat:
　No shade like this for me!

2 Beneath that cross clear waters burst—
　A fountain sparkling free;
And there I quench my desert thirst:
　No spring like this for me!

3 A stranger here, I pitch my tent
　Beneath this spreading tree;
Here shall my pilgrim life be spent:
　No home like this for me!

4 For burdened ones a resting-place,
　Beside that cross I see;
I here cast off my weariness:
　No rest like this for me!

DUNDEE. C. M. — Scottish.

1. How sweet and aw - ful is the place, With Christ with - in the doors;

While ev - er - last - ing love dis - plays The choi - cest of her stores!

627.

2 While all our hearts, and all our songs,
    Join to admire the feast,
Each of us cries, with thankful tongue,—
    " Lord, why was I a guest?

3 " Why was I made to hear thy voice,
    And enter while there 's room,
When thousands make a wretched choice,
    And rather starve than come ?"

4 'T was the same love that spread the feast,
    That sweetly drew us in ;
Else we had still refused to taste,
    And perished in our sin.

5 Pity the nations, O our God !
    Constrain the earth to come ;
Send thy victorious word abroad,
    And bring the strangers home.

6 We long to see thy churches full,
    That all the chosen race
May, with one voice and heart and soul,
    Sing thy redeeming grace.

628.

1 Prepare us, Lord, to view thy cross,
    Who all our griefs hast borne ;
To look on thee, whom we have pierced—
    To look on thee, and mourn.

2 While thus we mourn, we would rejoice,
    And, as thy cross we see,
Let each exclaim in faith and hope—
    "The Saviour died for me !"

629.

1 Together with these symbols, Lord,
    Thy blessèd self impart ;
And let thy holy flesh and blood
    Feed the believing heart.

2 Let us from all our sins be washed
    In thy atoning blood ;
And let thy Spirit be the seal
    That we are born of God.

3 Come, Holy Ghost, with Jesus' love,
    Prepare us for this feast ;
Oh ! let us banquet with our Lord,
    And lean upon his breast.

630.

1 If human kindness meets return,
    And owns the grateful tie ;
If tender thoughts within us burn,
    To feel a friend is nigh ;—

2 Oh, shall not warmer accents tell
    The gratitude we owe
To him, who died, our fears to quell—
    Who bore our guilt and woe !

3 While yet in anguish he surveyed
    Those pangs he would not flee,
What love his latest words displayed,—
    "Meet and remember me !"

4 Remember thee—thy death, thy shame,
    Our sinful hearts to share !—
O memory ! leave no other name
    But his recorded there.

SICILIAN HYMN. 8s & 7s.

1. Cross, re-proach, and trib-u-la-tion! Ye to me are wel-come guests, When I have this con-so-la-tion, That my soul in Je-sus rests.

631.

1 Cross, reproach, and tribulation!
  Ye to me are welcome guests,
When I have this consolation,
  That my soul in Jesus rests.

2 The reproach of Christ is glorious!
  Those who here his burden bear,
In the end shall prove victorious,
  And eternal gladness share.

3 Bear, then, the reproach of Jesus,
  Ye who live a life of faith!
Lift triumphant songs and praises
  Ev'n in martyrdom and death.

4 Bonds and stripes, and evil story,
  Are our honorable crowns;
Pain is peace, and shame is glory,
  Gloomy dungeons are as thrones.

632.

1 Jesus spreads his banner o'er us,
  Cheers our famished souls with food;
He the banquet spreads before us,
  Of his mystic flesh and blood.

2 Precious banquet; bread of heaven;
  Wine of gladness, flowing free;
May we taste it, kindly given,
  In remembrance, Lord, of thee!

3 In thy trial and rejection;
  In thy sufferings on the tree;
In thy glorious resurrection;
  May we, Lord, remember thee.

633.

1 From the table now retiring,
  Which for us the Lord hath spread,
May our souls, refreshment finding,
  Grow in all things like our Head!

2 His example by beholding,
  May our lives his image bear;
Him our Lord and Master calling,
  His commands may we revere.

3 Love to God and man displaying,
  Walking steadfast in his way,
Joy attend us in believing,
  Peace from God through endless day.

4 Praise and honor to the Father,
  Praise and honor to the Son,
Praise and honor to the Spirit,
  Ever Three and ever One.

634.

1 While in sweet communion feeding
  On this earthly bread and wine,
Saviour, may we see thee bleeding
  On the cross, to make us thine.

2 Though unseen, now be thou near us,
  With the still small voice of love;
Whispering words of peace to cheer us—
  Every doubt and fear remove.

3 Bring before us all the story,
  Of thy life and death of woe;
And with hopes of endless glory,
  Wean our hearts from all below.

PLEYEL'S HYMN. 7s.　　　　　　　　PLEYEL.

1. Bread of heaven! on thee we feed, For thy flesh is meat in-deed:

Ev - er let our souls be fed With this true and liv - ing bread!

635.

1 BREAD of heaven! on thee we feed,
For thy flesh is meat indeed:
Ever let our souls be fed
With this true and living bread!

2 Vine of heaven! thy blood supplies
This blest cup of sacrifice:
Lord! thy wounds our healing give,
To thy cross we look and live.

3 Day by day with strength supplied,
Through the life of him who died:
Lord of life! oh, let us be
Rooted, grafted, built on thee!

636.

1 JESUS, Master! hear me now,
While I would renew my vow,
And record thy dying love;
Hear, and help me from above.

2 Feed me, Saviour, with this bread,
Broken in thy body's stead;
Cheer my spirit with this wine,
Streaming like that blood of thine.

3 And as now I eat and drink,
Let me truly, sweetly think,
Thou didst hang upon the tree,
Broken, bleeding, there—for me!

637.

1 HOLY Lamb, who thee receive,
Who in thee begin to live,
Day and night they cry to thee,
"As thou art, so let us be!"

2 Gladly would we now be clean;
Cleanse us, Lord, from every sin:
Fix, oh, fix our wavering mind!
To thy cross our spirit bind.

3 Dust and ashes though we be,
Full of sin and misery,
Thine we are, thou Son of God:
Take the purchase of thy blood!

638.

1 AT the Lamb's high feast we sing,
Praise to our victorious King,
Who hath washed us in the tide,
Flowing from his wounded side.

2 Praise we him, whose love divine
Gives his sacred blood for wine,
Gives his body for the feast,
Christ the victim, Christ the Priest.

3 Where the Paschal blood is poured,
Death's dark angel sheaths his sword;
Israel's hosts triumphant go
Through the wave that drowns the foe.

4 Christ, our Paschal Lamb, is slain,
Holy victim, without stain;
Death and hell defeated lie,
Heaven unfolds its gates on high.

5 Hymns of glory and of praise,
Father, unto thee we raise;
Risen Lord, all praise to thee,
With the Spirit ever be.

ROCK OF AGES. 7s.

Dr. Hastings.

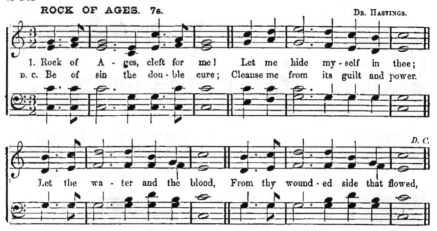

1. Rock of A - ges, cleft for me! Let me hide my - self in thee;
D. C. Be of sin the dou - ble cure; Cleanse me from its guilt and power.

Let the wa - ter and the blood, From thy wound - ed side that flowed,

639.

1 Rock of Ages, cleft for me!
Let me hide myself in thee;
Let the water and the blood,
From thy wounded side that flowed,
Be of sin the double cure;
Cleanse me from its guilt and power.

2 Not the labor of my hands
Can fulfill the law's demands;
Could my zeal no respite know,
Could my tears forever flow,
All for sin could not atone,
Thou must save, and thou alone.

3 Nothing in my hand I bring,
Simply to thy cross I cling;
Naked, come to thee for dress,
Helpless, look to thee for grace,
Vile, I to the fountain fly,
Wash me, Saviour, or I die!

4 While I draw this fleeting breath,
When my eyelids close in death,
When I soar to worlds unknown,
See thee on thy judgment-throne,
Rock of Ages, cleft for me!
Let me hide myself in thee.

640.

1 From the cross uplifted high,
Where the Saviour deigns to die,
What melodious sounds we hear,
Bursting on the ravished ear!—
"Love's redeeming work is done—
Come and welcome, sinner, come!

2 "Sprinkled now with blood the throne—
Why beneath thy burdens groan?
On my piercéd body laid,
Justice owns the ransom paid—
Bow the knee, and kiss the Son—
Come and welcome, sinner, come!

3 "Spread for thee, the festal board
See with richest bounty stored;
To thy Father's bosom pressed,
Thou shalt be a child confessed,
Never from his house to roam;
Come and welcome, sinner, come!

4 "Soon the days of life shall end—
Lo, I come—your Saviour, Friend!
Safe your spirit to convey
To the realms of endless day,
Up to my eternal home—
Come and welcome, sinner, come!"

641.

1 Ye who in these courts are found,
Listening to the joyful sound,—
Lost and helpless, as ye are,
Sons of sorrow, sin, and care,—
Glorify the King of Kings,
Take the peace the gospel brings.

2 Turn to Christ your longing eyes,
View his bleeding sacrifice;
See, in him your sins forgiven,
Pardon, holiness, and heaven:
Glorify the King of kings,
Take the peace the gospel brings.

ZADOC. 7s. 6 lines.   Dr. Hastings.

1. Sa - viour of our ru - ined race, Foun - tain of re - deem - ing grace,
D. C. Heark - en to our ar - dent prayer— Let us all thy bless - ing share.

Let us now thy full - ness see, While we here con - verse with thee;

642.

2 While we thus, with glad accord
  Meet around thy table, Lord,
  Bid us feast with joy divine,
  On th' appointed bread and wine :
  Emblems may they truly prove
  Of the Saviour's bleeding love.

3 Weak, unworthy, sinful, vile,
  Yet we seek thy heavenly smile :
  Canst thou all our sins forgive ?
  Dost thou bid us look and live ?
  Lord, we wonder and adore !
  Oh, for grace to love thee more !

643.

1 Son of God ! to thee I cry :
  By the holy mystery
  Of thy dwelling here on earth,
  By thy pure and holy birth,
  Hear, oh, hear my lowly plea,
  Manifest thyself to me !

2 Lamb of God ! to thee I cry :
  By thy bitter agony,
  By thy pangs to us unknown,
  By thy spirit's parting groan,
  Hear, oh, hear my lowly plea :
  Manifest thyself to me !

3 Prince of Life ! to thee I cry :
  By thy glorious majesty,
  By thy triumph o'er the grave,
  Meek to suffer, strong to save,
  Hear, oh, hear my fervid plea :
  Manifest thyself to me !

4 Lord of glory, God most high !
  Man exalted to the sky,
  With thy love my bosom fill ;
  Prompt me to perform thy will :
  Then thy glory I shall see—
  Thou wilt bring me home to thee.

644.

1 Blessèd Saviour ! thee I love,
  All my other joys above ;
  All my hopes in thee abide,
  Thou my hope, and naught beside :
  Ever let my glory be,
  Only, only, only thee.

2 Once again beside the cross,
  All my gain I count but loss ;
  Earthly pleasures fade away,—
  Clouds they are that hide my day :
  Hence, vain shadows ! let me see
  Jesus crucified for me.

3 From beneath that thorny crown
  Trickle drops of cleansing down ;
  Pardon from thy piercèd hand
  Now I take, while here I stand :
  Only then I live to thee,
  When thy wounded side I see.

4 Blessèd Saviour ! thine am I,
  Thine to live, and thine to die ;
  Height or depth, or earthly power
  Ne'er shall hide my Saviour more :
  Ever shall my glory be,
  Only, only, only thee !

WINDHAM. L. M.   READ.

1. 'Twas on that dark, that dole-ful night, When powers of earth and hell a-rose

A-gainst the Son of God's de-light, And friends be-trayed him to his foes.

645.

2 Before the mournful scene began,
He took the bread, and blessed and brake;
What love through all his actions ran !
What wondrous words of grace he spake !

3 " This is my body broke for sin :
Receive and eat the living food ;"
Then took the cup and blessed the wine ;
" 'T is the new covenant in my blood."

4 " Do this, (he cried,) 'till time shall end,
In memory of your dying Friend ;
Meet at my table, and record
The love of your departed Lord."

5 Jesus, thy feast we celebrate,
We show thy death, we sing thy name,
'Till thou return, and we shall eat
The marriage supper of the Lamb.

646.

1 HERE we have seen thy face, O Lord,
And viewed salvation with our eyes,
Tasted and felt the living Word,
The Bread descending from the skies.

2 Thou hast prepared this dying Lamb,
Hast set his blood before our face,
To teach the terrors of thy name,
And show the wonders of thy grace.

3 He is our Light ; our Morning-star
Shall shine on nations yet unknown ;
The glory of thine Israel here,
And joy of spirits near thy throne.

647.

1 DEAR Lord, amid the throng that pressed
Around thee on the cursèd tree,
Some loyal, loving hearts were there,
Some pitying eyes that wept for thee.

2 Like them may we rejoice to own
Our dying Lord, though crowned with
thorn ;
Like thee, thy blessèd self, endure
The cross with all its joy or scorn.

3 Thy cross, thy lonely path below,
Show what thy brethren all should be ;
Pilgrims on earth, disowned by those
Who see no beauty, Lord, in thee.

648.

1 AT thy command, O Lord, our hope,
We come around thy table here ;
We break the bread, we bless the cup,
That show thy death till thou appear.

2 Our faith adores thy bleeding love,
And trusts for life in One that died ;
We hope for heavenly crowns above,
From a Redeemer crucified.

3 Let the vain world pronounce it shame,
And cast their scandals on thy cause !
We come to boast our Saviour's name,
And make our triumph in his cross.

4 With joy we tell the scoffing age,—
He that was dead hath left his tomb ;
He lives above their utmost rage,
And we are waiting till he come.

FEDERAL STREET. L. M.   H. K. OLIVER.

1. I feed by faith on Christ, my bread, His bo-dy bro-ken on the tree;

I live in him, my liv-ing Head, Who died, and rose a-gain, for me.

649.

2 This be my joy and comfort here,
This pledge of future glory mine;
Jesus, in spirit now appear,
And break the bread and pour the wine.

3 From thy dear hand may I receive
The tokens of thy dying love;
And, while I feast on earth, believe
That I shall feast with thee above.

650.

1 Oh, happy day that fixed my choice
On thee, my Saviour, and my God!
Well may this glowing heart rejoice,
And tell its raptures all abroad.

2 Oh, happy bond, that seals my vows
To him who merits all my love!
Let cheerful anthems fill his house,
While to that sacred shrine I move.

3 'T is done ; the great transaction 's done :
I am my Lord's, and he is mine;
He drew me, and I followed on,
Charmed to confess the voice divine.

4 Now rest, my long-divided heart!
Fixed on this blissful centre, rest;
Here have I found a nobler part,
Here heavenly pleasures fill my breast.

5 High Heaven, that hears the solemn vow,
That vow renewed, shall daily hear;
Till, in life's latest hour, I bow,
And bless in death a bond so dear.

651.

1 DRAW near, O Holy Dove, draw near,
With peace and gladness on thy wing ;
Reveal the Saviour's presence here,
And light, and life, and comfort bring.

2 "Eat, O my friends—drink, O beloved !"
We hear the Master's voice exclaim:
Our hearts with new desire are moved,
And kindled with a heavenly flame.

3 No room for doubt, no room for dread,
Nor tears, nor groans, nor anxious sighs ;
We do not mourn a Saviour dead,
But hail him living in the skies !

4 While this we do, remembering thee.
Dear Saviour, let our graces prove
We have thy blesséd company,
Thy banner over us is love.

652.

1 WHILE to thy table I repair,
And seal the sacred contract there,
Witness, O Lord ! my solemn vow ;
Angels and men ! attest it too.

2 Here at that cross, where flows the blood
That bought my guilty soul for God,
Thee, Lord and Master, now I call,
I consecrate to thee my all.

3 Do thou assist a feeble worm
The great engagement to perform ;
Thy grace can full assistance lend,
And on that grace I dare depend.

MISSIONARY HYMN. 7s & 6s.   Dr. L. Mason.

1. From Greenland's i-cy mountains, From In-dia's co-ral strand, Where Afric's sun-ny foun-tains Roll down their gold-en sand: From many an an-cient riv-er, From many a palm-y plain, They call us to de-liv-er Their land from error's chain.

653.

2 What though the spicy breezes
  Blow soft o'er Ceylon's isle—
Though every prospect pleases,
  And only man is vile?—
In vain with lavish kindness
  The gifts of God are strown;
The heathen, in his blindness,
  Bows down to wood and stone.

3 Shall we, whose souls are lighted
  With wisdom from on high,—
Shall we to men benighted,
  The lamp of life deny?
Salvation! Oh, Salvation!—
  The joyful sound proclaim,
Till earth's remotest nation,
  Has learned Messiah's name.

4 Waft—waft, ye winds! his story,
  And you, ye waters, roll,—
Till, like a sea of glory,
  It spreads from pole to pole!
Till o'er our ransomed nature,
  The Lamb for sinners slain,
Redeemer, King, Creator,
  In bliss returns to reign!

654.

1 Now be the gospel banner,
  In every land, unfurled;
And be the shout,—"Hosanna!"
  Re-echoed through the world;
Till every isle and nation,
  Till every tribe and tongue,
Receive the great salvation,
  And join the happy throng.

2 What, though th' embattled legions
  Of earth and hell combine?
His arm, throughout their regions,
  Shall soon resplendent shine:
Ride on, O Lord! victorious,
  Immanuel, Prince of Peace!
Thy triumph shall be glorious,—
  Thy empire still increase.

3 Yes,—thou shalt reign for ever,
  O Jesus, King of kings!
Thy light, thy love, thy favor,
  Each ransomed captive sings:
The isles for thee are waiting,
  The deserts learn thy praise,
The hills and valleys greeting,
  The song responsive raise.

WEBB. 7s & 6s.

Geo. James Webb.

1. The morn- ing light is break - ing, The darkness dis - ap-pears; The sons of earth are wak - ing To pen - i - ten - tial tears: Each breeze that sweeps the ocean Brings ti-dings from a - far Of na - tions in com - mo - tion, Prepared for Zion's war.

655.

2 See heathen nations bending
  Before the God we love,
And thousand hearts ascending
  In gratitude above ;
While sinners, now confessing,
  The gospel call obey,
And seek the Saviour's blessing,—
  A nation in a day.

3 Blest river of salvation !
  Pursue thine onward way ;
Flow thou to every nation,
  Nor in thy richness stay :
Stay not till all the lowly
  Triumphant reach their home :
Stay not till all the holy
  Proclaim—" The Lord is come !"

656.

1 Hail to the Lord's Anointed,
  Great David's greater Son !
Hail in the time appointed,
  His reign on earth begun !
He comes to break oppression,
  To set the captive free,
To take away transgression,
  And rule in equity.

2 He comes with succor speedy,
  To those who suffer wrong ;
To help the poor and needy,
  And bid the weak be strong ;
To give them songs for sighing,
  Their darkness turn to light,
Whose souls condemned and dying,
  Were precious in his sight.

3 He shall come down, like showers
  Upon the fruitful earth,
And love, and joy, like flowers,
  Spring in his path to birth :
Before him on the mountains,
  Shall peace, the herald, go ;
And righteousness, in fountains,
  From hill to valley flow.

4 For him shall prayer unceasing
  And daily vows ascend ;
His kingdom still increasing,—
  A kingdom without end :
The tide of time shall never
  His covenant remove ;
His name shall stand forever,—
  That name to us is—Love.

ELLICOTT. L. M.

J. N. PATTISON.

1. From day to day, be-fore our eyes, Grows and ex-tends the work be-gun;

When shall the new cre - a - tion rise O'er ev - ery land be-neath the sun?

657.

2 When, in the sabbath of his love,
Shall God from all his labors rest;
And bending from his throne above,
Again pronounce his creatures blest?

3 As sang the morning stars of old,
Shouted the sons of God for joy;
His widening reign while we behold,
Let praise and prayers our tongues employ.

4 Till the redeemed in every clime,
Yea, all that breathe, and move, and live,
To Christ, through every age of time,
The kingdom, power, and glory give.

658.

1 INDULGENT Sovereign of the skies!
And wilt thou bow thy gracious ear?
While feeble mortals raise their cries,
Wilt thou, the great Jehovah, hear?

2 How shall thy servants give thee rest,
Till Zion's mouldering walls thou raise?
Till thine own power shall stand confessed,
And make Jerusalem a praise?

3 Look down, O God! with pitying eye,
And view the desolations round;
See, what wide realms in darkness lie,
What scenes of woe and crime abound!

4 Loud let the gospel trumpet blow,
And call the nations from afar;
Let all the isles their Saviour know,
And earth's remotest ends draw near.

659.

1 O SUN of righteousness, arise,
With gentle beams on Zion shine;
Dispel the darkness from our eyes,
And souls awake to life divine.

2 On all around, let grace descend,
Like heavenly dew, or copious showers;
That we may call our God our friend;
That we may hail salvation ours.

660.

1 GREAT God, whose universal sway
The known and unknown worlds obey,
Now give the kingdom to thy Son,
Extend his power, exalt his throne.

2 Thy sceptre well becomes his hands,
All heaven submits to his commands;
His justice shall avenge the poor,
And pride and rage prevail no more.

3 With power he vindicates the just,
And treads th' oppressor in the dust;
His worship and his fear shall last,
Till hours, and years, and time be past.

4 The heathen lands that lie beneath
The shades of overspreading death,
Revive at his first dawning light,
And deserts blossom at the sight.

5 The saints shall flourish in his days,
Dressed in the robes of joy and praise;
Peace, like a river from his throne,
Shall flow to nations yet unknown.

WARD. L. M.   Dr. L. Mason.

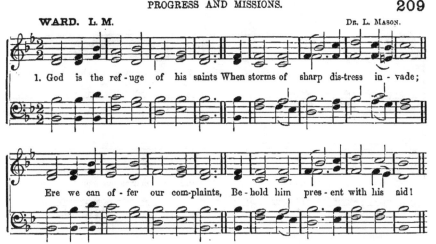

1. God is the ref-uge of his saints When storms of sharp dis-tress in-vade;

Ere we can of-fer our com-plaints, Be-hold him pres-ent with his aid!

661.

2 Let mountains from their seats be hurled
Down to the deep, and buried there,
Convulsions shake the solid world—
Our faith shall never yield to fear.

3 Loud may the troubled ocean roar;
In sacred peace our souls abide;
While every nation, every shore,
Trembles and dreads the swelling tide.

4 There is a stream whose gentle flow
Supplies the city of our God,
Life, love, and joy, still gliding through,
And watering our divine abode.

5 That sacred stream, thine holy word,
Our grief allays, our fear controls;
Sweet peace thy promises afford,
And give new strength to fainting souls.

6 Zion enjoys her Monarch's love,
Secure against a threatening hour;
Nor can her firm foundation move,
Built on his truth and armed with power.

662.

1 Behold th' expected time draw near,
The shades disperse, the dawn appear!
Behold the wilderness assume
The beauteous tints of Eden's bloom!

2 Events with prophecies conspire,
To raise our faith, our zeal to fire:
The ripening fields, already white,
Present a harvest to the sight.

3 The untaught heathen waits to know
The joy the gospel will bestow;
The exiled captive, to receive
The freedom Jesus has to give.

4 Come, let us, with a grateful heart,
In the blest labor share a part;
Our prayers and offerings gladly bring,
To aid the triumphs of our King.

663.

1 O Spirit of the living God,
In all thy plenitude of grace,
Where'er the foot of man hath trod,
Descend on our apostate race.

2 Give tongues of fire, and hearts of love,
To preach the reconciling word;
Give power and unction from above,
Where'er the joyful sound is heard.

3 Be darkness, at thy coming, light;
Confusion—order, in thy path;
Souls without strength, inspire with
might;
Bid mercy triumph over wrath.

4 Baptize the nations, far and nigh
The triumphs of the cross record;
The name of Jesus glorify,
Till every kindred call him Lord.

5 O Spirit of the Lord! prepare
All the round earth her God to meet,
Breathe thou abroad like morning air,
Till hearts of stone begin to beat.

ASHWELL. L. M.   Dr. L. Mason.

1. When we, our wearied limbs to rest, Sat down by proud Eu-phra-tes' stream,

We wept, with doleful thoughts oppressed, And Zi-on was our mourn-ful theme.

664.

1 When we, our wearied limbs to rest,
Sat down by proud Euphrates' stream,
We wept, with doleful thoughts oppressed,
And Zion was our mournful theme.

2 Our harps that, when with joy we sung,
Were wont their tuneful parts to bear,
With silent strings neglected hung
On willow trees that withered there.

3 How shall we tune our voice to sing,
Or touch our harps with skillful hands?
Shall hymns of joy, to God our King,
Be sung by slaves in foreign lands?

4 O Salem! our once happy seat,
When I of thee forgetful prove,
Let then my trembling hand forget
The tuneful strings with art to move.

665.

1 O Zion! when I think on thee,
I wish for pinions like the dove,
And mourn to think that I should be
So distant from the place I love.

2 A captive here, and far from home,
For Zion's sacred walls I sigh;
Thither the ransomed nations come,
And see the Saviour eye to eye.

3 While here I walk on hostile ground;
The few, that I can call my friends,
Are like myself with fetters bound,
And weariness our steps attends.

4 But we shall yet behold the day
When Zion's children shall return;
Our sorrows then shall flee away,
And we again shall never mourn.

5 The hope that such a day will come,
Makes ev'n the captive's portion sweet;
Though now we wander far from home,
In Zion soon we all shall meet.

666.

1 Why, on the bending willows hung,
Israel! still sleeps thy tuneful string?—
Still mute remains thy sullen tongue,
And Zion's song denies to sing?

2 Awake! thy sweetest raptures raise;
Let harp and voice unite their strains:
Thy promised King his sceptre sways;
Jesus, thine own Messiah, reigns!

3 No taunting foes the song require;
No strangers mock thy captive chain;
But friends provoke the silent lyre,
And brethren ask the holy strain.

4 Nor fear thy Salem's hills to wrong,
If other lands thy triumph share:
A heavenly city claims thy song;
A brighter Salem rises there.

5 By foreign streams no longer roam;
Nor, weeping, think of Jordan's flood:
In every clime behold a home,
In every temple see thy God.

PARK STREET.. L. M.

VENUA.

1. Hark! how the choral song of heaven Swells full of peace and joy a - bove; Hark! how they

strike their golden harps, And raise the tuneful notes of love, And raise the tuneful notes of love.

667.

2 No anxious care nor thrilling grief,
No deep despair, nor gloomy woe
They feel, when high their lofty strains
In noblest, sweetest concord flow.

3 When shall we join the heavenly host,
Who sing Immanuel's praise on high,
And leave behind our doubts and fears,
To swell the chorus of the sky?

4 Oh! come, thou rapture-bringing morn,
And usher in the joyful day;
We long to see thy rising sun
Drive all these clouds of grief away.

668.

1 ETERNAL Father! thou hast said,
That Christ all glory shall obtain;
That he who once a sufferer bled,
Shall o'er the world, a conqueror, reign.

2 We wait thy triumph, Saviour King!
Long ages have prepared thy way;
Now all abroad thy banner fling,
Set Time's great battle in array.

3 Thy hosts are mustered to the field;
"The Cross! The Cross!" the battle-call;
The old grim towers of darkness yield,
And soon shall totter to their fall.

4 On mountain tops the watch-fires glow,
Where scattered wide the watchmen
stand;
Voice echoes voice, and onward flow
The joyous shouts, from land to land.

5 Oh, fill thy church with faith and power!
Bid her long night of weeping cease;
To groaning nations haste the hour,
Of life and freedom, light and peace.

6 Come, Spirit, make thy wonders known!
Fulfill the Father's high decree;
Then earth, the might of hell o'erthrown,
Shall keep her last great jubilee.

669.

1 JESUS shall reign where'er the sun
Does his successive journeys run;
His kingdom stretch from shore to shore,
Till moons shall wax and wane no more.

2 For him shall endless prayer be made,
And praises throng to crown his head;
His name, like sweet perfume, shall rise
With every morning sacrifice.

3 People and realms of every tongue
Dwell on his love with sweetest song;
And infant voices shall proclaim
Their early blessings on his name.

4 Blessings abound where'er he reigns,
The prisoner leaps to lose his chains;
The weary find eternal rest,
And all the sons of want are blest.

5 Let every creature rise, and bring
Peculiar honors to their King:
Angels descend with songs again,
And earth repeat the long amen.

ANVERN. L. M.   *Arranged by* DR. L. MASON.

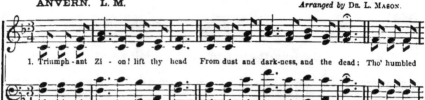

1. Triumph-ant Zi - on! lift thy head From dust and dark-ness, and the dead; Tho' humbled

long, a-wake at length, And gird thee with thy Saviour's strength, And gird thee with thy Saviour's strength.

670.

2 Put all thy beauteous garments on,
And let thy various charms be known ;
Then decked in robes of righteousness,
The world thy glories shall confess.

3 No more shall foes unclean invade,
And fill thy hallowed walls with dread ;
No more shall hell's insulting host
Their victory and thy sorrows boast.

4 God, from on high, thy groans will hear ;
His hands thy ruins shall repair ;
Nor will thy watchful Monarch cease
To guard thee in eternal peace.

671.

1 YE Christian heralds ! go, proclaim
Salvation through Immanuel's name ;
To distant climes the tidings bear,
And plant the rose of Sharon there.

2 He'll shield you with a wall of fire,
With flaming zeal your breast inspire,
Bid raging winds their fury cease,
And hush the tempest into peace.

3 And when our labors all are o'er,
Then we shall meet to part no more,—
Meet with the blood-bought throng, to fall,
And crown our Jesus—Lord of all !

672.

1 SOVEREIGN of worlds ! display thy power ;
Be this thy Zion's favored hour ;
Bid the bright morning Star arise,
And point the nations to the skies.

2 Set up thy throne where Satan reigns,—
On Afric's shore, on India's plains,
On wilds and continents unknown,—
And make the nations all thine own.

3 Speak ! and the world shall hear thy
voice ;
Speak ! and the desert shall rejoice ;
Scatter the gloom of heathen night,
And bid all nations hail the light.

673.

1 ASCEND thy throne, almighty King,
And spread thy glories all abroad ;
Let thine own arm salvation bring,
And be thou known the gracious God.

2 Let millions bow before thy seat,
Let humble mourners seek thy face,
Bring daring rebels to thy feet,
Subdued by thy victorious grace.

3 Oh, let the kingdoms of the world
Become the kingdoms of the Lord !
Let saints and angels praise thy name,
Be thou thro' heaven and earth adored

674.

1 Worthy the Lamb of boundless sway—
In earth and heaven the Lord of all !
Let all the powers of earth obey,
And low before his footstool fall.

2 Higher—still higher, swell the strain,
Creation's voice the note prolong !
Jesus, the Lamb, shall ever reign :—
Let hallelujahs crown the song.

MISSIONARY CHANT. L. M.   Ch. Zeuner.

1. Soon may the last glad song a - rise Thro' all the mil - lions of the skies— That song of tri-umph which re - cords That all the earth is now the Lord's!

675.

1 Soon may the last glad song arise
Through all the millions of the skies—
That song of triumph which records
That all the earth is now the Lord's!

2 Let thrones and powers and kingdoms be
Obedient, mighty God, to thee!
And, over land and stream and main,
Wave thou the sceptre of thy reign!

3 Oh, let that glorious anthem swell,
Let host to host the triumph tell,
That not one rebel heart remains,
But over all the Saviour reigns!

676.

1 Assembled at thy great command,
Before thy face, dread King, we stand;
The voice that marshaled every star,
Has called thy people from afar.

2 We meet, thro' distant lands to spread
The truth for which the martyrs bled;
Along the line, to either pole,
The thunder of thy praise to roll.

3 Our prayers assist, accept our praise,
Our hopes revive, our courage raise;
Our counsels aid, to each impart
The single eye, the faithful heart.

4 Forth with thy chosen heralds come,
Recall the wandering spirits home;
From Zion's mount send forth the sound,
To spread the spacious earth around.

677.

1 Marked as the purpose of the skies,
This promise meets our anxious eyes,
That heathen lands the Lord shall know,
And warm with faith each bosom glow.

2 Ev'n now the hallowed scenes appear;
Ev'n now unfolds the promised year;
Lo! distant shores thy heralds trace,
And bear the tidings of thy grace.

3 'Mid burning climes and frozen plains,
Where pagan darkness brooding reigns,
Lord! mark their steps, their fears subdue,
And nerve their arm, and clear their view.

4 When, worn by toil, their spirits fail,
Bid them the glorious future hail;
Bid them the crown of life survey,
And onward urge their conquering way.

678.

1 Though now the nations sit beneath
The darkness of o'erspreading death,
God will arise with light divine,
On Zion's holy towers to shine.

2 That light shall glance on distant lands,
And heathen tribes, in joyful bands,
Come with exulting haste to prove
The power and greatness of his love.

3 Lord, spread the triumphs of thy grace;
Let truth and righteousness and peace,
In mild and lovely forms, display
The glories of the latter day.

HAIL TO THE BRIGHTNESS. 11s & 10s.

Dr. L. Mason.

1. Hail to the brightness of Zion's glad morning! Joy to the lands that in darkness have lain;

Hushed be the accents of sorrow and mourning, Zi - on in triumph begins her mild reign.

679.

2 Hail to the brightness of Zion's glad
    morning,
Long by the prophets of Israel foretold ;
Hail to the millions from bondage re-
    turning,
Gentiles and Jews the blest vision behold.

3 Lo! in the desert rich flowers are spring-
    ing,
Streams ever copious are gliding along :
Loud from the mountain-tops echoes are
    ringing,
Wastes rise in verdure and mingle in song.

4 See, from all lands—from the isles of the
    ocean,
Praise to Jehovah ascending on high ;
Fallen are the engines of war and com-
    motion,
Shouts of salvation are rending the sky.

680.

1 Daughter of Zion, awake from thy sad-
    ness ;
Awake, for thy foes shall oppress thee no
    more :
Bright o'er thy hills dawns the day-star of
    gladness ;
Arise, for the night of thy sorrow is o'er.

2 Strong were thy foes ; but the arm that
    subdued them,
And scattered their legions, was mightier
    far ;

They fled like the chaff from the scourge
    that pursued them ;
Vain were their steeds and their chariots
    of war.

3 Daughter of Zion, the power that hath
    saved thee
Extolled with the harp and the timbrel
    should be ;
Shout, for the foe is destroyed that en-
    slaved thee ;
Th' oppressor is vanquished, and Zion is
    free.

681.

1 Wake thee, O Zion—thy mourning is
    ended ;
God—thine own God, hath regarded thy
    prayer :
Wake thee—and hail him, in glory de-
    scended,
Thy darkness to scatter—thy wastes to
    repair.

2 Wake thee, O Zion—his Spirit of power
To newness of life is awaking the dead ;
Array thee in beauty, and greet the glad
    hour,
That brings thee salvation, through Jesus
    who bled.

3 Saviour—we gladly with voices resound-
    ing,
Loud as the thunder—our chorus would
    swell ;
Till from rock, wood and mountain its
    echoes rebounding,
To all the wide world of salvation shall tell.

ZION. 8s, 7s & 4s.   Dr. Hastings.

1. { On the moun-tain's top ap-pear-ing, Lo! the sa-cred her-ald stands, }
   { Welcome news to Zi-on bear-ing, Zi-on long in hos-tile lands. } Mourning

capive, God himself shall loose thy bands, Mourning captive, God himself shall loose thy bands.

682.

2 Has thy night been long and mournful?
 Have thy friends unfaithful proved?
 Have thy foes been proud and scornful,
 By thy sighs and tears unmoved?
   Cease thy mourning;
   Zion still is well beloved.

3 God, thy God, will now restore thee;
 He himself appears thy Friend;
 All thy foes shall flee before thee;
 Here their boasts and triumphs end;
   Great deliverance
   Zion's King will surely send.

4 Peace and joy shall now attend thee;
 All thy warfare now is past;
 God thy Saviour will defend thee;
 Victory is thine at last;
   All thy conflicts
   End in everlasting rest.

683.

1 O'er the realms of pagan darkness
 Let the eye of pity gaze;
 See the kindreds of the people,
 Lost in sin's bewildering maze;—
   Darkness brooding
   On the face of all the earth!

2 Light of them who sit in error!
 Rise and shine—thy blessings bring;
 Light—to lighten all the Gentiles!
 Rise with healing in thy wing:
   To thy brightness,
   Let all kings and nations come.

3 Let the heathen, now adoring
 Idol gods of wood and stone,
 Come, and, worshiping before him,
 Serve the living God alone:
   Let thy glory
   Fill the earth, as floods the sea.

4 Thou! to whom all power is given,
 Speak the word; at thy command,
 Let the company of heralds
 Spread thy name from land to land:
   Lord! be with them,
   Always till time's latest end.

684.

1 O'er the gloomy hills of darkness,
 Cheered by no celestial ray,
 Sun of righteousness! arising,
 Bring the bright, the glorious day;
   Send the gospel
   To the earth's remotest bound.

2 Kingdoms wide that sit in darkness,—
 Grant them, Lord! the glorious light;
 And, from eastern coast to western,
 May the morning chase the night;
   And redemption,
   Freely purchased, win the day.

3 Fly abroad, thou mighty gospel!
 Win and conquer, never cease;
 May thy lasting, wide dominions,
 Multiply and still increase;
   Sway thy sceptre,
   Saviour! all the world around.

PERRY. 7s. Double.   *Arranged by* J. P. HOLBROOK.

1. Hark, the song of Ju - bi - lee, Loud as might-y thun-ders roar; Or the full-ness

of the sea, When it breaks up - on the shore! Hal - le - lu - jah, for the Lord

God Om-ni - po-tent shall reign! Hal-le - lu - jah! let the word E-cho thro' the earth and main.

685.

2 Hallelujah! hark, the sound,
　From the depths unto the skies,
Wakes above, beneath, around,
　All creation's harmonies!
See Jehovah's banners furled,
　Sheathed his sword, he speaks—'t is
　　done!
And the kingdoms of this world
　Are the kingdoms of his Son.

3 He shall reign from pole to pole,
　With illimitable sway;
He shall reign, when like a scroll
　Yonder heavens are passed away;
Then the end: beneath his rod
　Man's last enemy shall fall:
Hallelujah! Christ in God,
　God in Christ, is all in all!

686.

1 HASTEN, Lord, the glorious time,
　When, beneath Messiah's sway,
Every nation, every clime,
　Shall the gospel call obey.

2 Mightiest kings his power shall own,
　Heathen tribes his name adore;
Satan and his host, o'erthrown,
　Bound in chains, shall hurt no more.

3 Then shall wars and tumults cease,
　Then be banished grief and pain;
Righteousness, and joy, and peace,
　Undisturbed shall ever reign.

4 Bless we, then, our gracious Lord,
　Ever praise his glorious name;
All his mighty acts record,
　All his wondrous love proclaim.

687.

1 SEE the ransomed millions stand,—
　Palms of conquest in their hands!
This before the throne their strain,—
　"Hell is vanquished—death is slain!—

2 "Blessing, honor, glory, might,
　Are the Conqueror's native right;
Thrones and powers before him fall,—
　Lamb of God, and Lord of all!"

3 Hasten, Lord! the promised hour;
　Come in glory and in power;
Still thy foes are unsubdued—
　Nature sighs to be renewed:

4 Time has nearly reached its sum;
　All things with the bride, say, "Come!"
Jesus! whom all worlds adore,
　Come,—and reign forevermore.

NUREMBURG. 7s. *German.*

1. Sons of men, be-hold from far, Hail the long-ex-pect-ed star!

Star of truth that gilds the night, Guides be-wildered men a-right.

688.

2 Mild it shines on all beneath,
Piercing through the shades of death;
Scattering error's wide-spread night;
Kindling darkness into light.

3 Nations all, remote and near,
Haste to see your Lord appear;
Haste, for him your hearts prepare,
Meet him manifested there!

4 There behold the day-spring rise,
Pouring light on mortal eyes;
See it chase the shades away,
Shining to the perfect day.

689.

1 Come, Desire of nations, come!
Hasten, Lord, the general doom!
Hear the Spirit and the Bride;
Come, and take us to thy side.

2 Thou, who hast our place prepared,
Make us meet for our reward;
Then with all thy saints descend:
Then our earthly trials end.

3 Mindful of thy chosen race,
Shorten these vindictive days;
Hear us now, and save thine own,
Who for full redemption groan.

4 Now destroy the man of sin,
Now thine ancient flock bring in!
Filled with righteousness divine,
Claim a ransomed world for thine.

5 Plant thy heavenly kingdom here;
Glorious in thy saints appear:
Speak the sacred number sealed;
Speak the mystery revealed.

6 Take to thee thy royal power:
Reign! when sin shall be no more;
Reign! when death no more shall be;
Reign to all eternity!

690.

1 Saw ye not the cloud arise,
Little as the human hand?
Now it spreads along the skies,
Hangs o'er all the thirsty land.

2 Lo, the promise of a shower
Drops already from above;
But the Lord will shortly pour
All the blessings of his love.

3 When he first the work begun,
Small and feeble was the day;
Now the word doth swiftly run,
Now it wins its widening way.

4 More and more it spreads and grows,
Ever mighty to prevail;
Sin's strongholds it now o'erthrows,
Shakes the trembling gates of hell.

5 Sons of God! your Saviour praise;
He the door hath opened wide;
He hath given the word of grace;
Jesus' word is glorified.

ORIOLA. C. M. Double.   WM. B. BRADBURY.

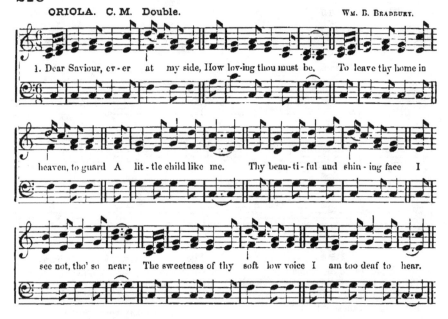

1. Dear Saviour, ev-er at my side, How lov-ing thou must be, To leave thy home in heaven, to guard A lit-tle child like me. Thy beau-ti-ful and shin-ing face I see not, tho' so near; The sweetness of thy soft low voice I am too deaf to hear.

691.

2 I cannot feel thee touch my hand
  With pressure light and mild,
To check me, as my mother did,
  When I was but a child;
But I have felt thee in my thoughts
  Fighting with sin for me;
And when my heart loves God, I know
  The sweetness is from thee.

3 And when, dear Saviour! I kneel down
  Morning and night to prayer,
Something there is within my heart
  Which tells me thou art there;
Yes! when I pray, thou prayest too—
  Thy prayer is all for me;
But when I sleep, thou sleepest not,
  But watchest patiently.

692.

1 REMEMBER thy Creator now,
  In these thy youthful days;
He will accept thine earliest vow,
  And listen to thy praise.

2 Remember thy Creator now,
  Seek him while he is near;
For evil days will come, when thou
  Shalt find no comfort here.

3 Remember thy Creator now;
  His willing servant be:
Then, when thy head in death shall bow,
  He will remember thee.

4 Almighty God! our hearts incline
  Thy heavenly voice to hear;
Let all our future days be thine,
  Devoted to thy fear.

693.

1 DEAR Jesus, let thy pitying eye
  Look kindly down on me:
A sinful, weak, and helpless child,
  I come thy child to be.

2 O blessèd Saviour! take my heart,
  This sinful heart of mine,
And wash it clean in every part;
  Make me a child of thine.

3 My sins, though great, thou canst forgive,
  For thou hast died for me;
Amazing love! Help me, O God,
  Thine own dear child to be.

4 For thou hast said, "Forbid them not:
  Let children come to me:"
I hear thy voice, and now, dear Lord,
  I come thy child to be.

BROWN. C. M.

WM. B. BRADBURY.

1. How glo - rious is our heaven-ly King, Who reigns a - bove the sky!

How shall a child pre - sume to sing His dread - ful maj - es - ty!

694.

2 How great his power, none can tell,
Nor think how large his grace ;
Not men below, nor saints that dwell
On high before his face ;

3 Not angels that stand round the Lord
Can search his secret will ;
But they perform his holy word,
And sing his praises still.

4 Then let me join this heavenly train,
And my first offerings bring;
Th' eternal God will not disdain
To hear an infant sing.

5 My heart resolves, my tongue obeys,
And angels shall rejoice,
To bear their mighty Maker's praise
Sound from a feeble voice.

695.

1 THERE is a fold whence none can stray,
And pastures ever green,
Where sultry sun, or stormy day,
Or night, is never seen.

2 Far up the everlasting hills,
In God's own light it lies ;
His smile its vast dimension fills
With joy that never dies.

3 One narrow vale, one darksome wave,
Divides that land from this ;
I have a Shepherd pledged to save,
And bear me home to bliss.

4 Soon at his feet my soul will lie,
In life's last struggling breath ;
But I shall only seem to die,
I shall not taste of death.

5 Far from this guilty world, to be
Exempt from toil and strife ;
To spend eternity with thee,
My Saviour, this is life !

696.

1 THERE is a glorious world of light,
Above the starry sky,
Where saints departed, clothed in white,
Adore the Lord most high.

2 And hark ! amid the sacred songs
Those heavenly voices raise,
Ten thousand thousand infant tongues
Unite in perfect praise.

3 Those are the hymns that we shall know,
If Jesus we obey :
That is the place where we shall go,
If found in wisdom's way.

4 Soon will our earthly race be run,
Our mortal frame decay ;
Parents and children, one by one,
Must die and pass away.

5 Great God, impress the serious thought,
This day, on every breast,
That both the teachers and the taught,
May enter to thy rest.

DUANE. L. M. Double.   REV. G. COLE.

1. A poor, way-far-ing man of grief Hath often crossed me on my way, Who sued so humbly for re-lief, That I could nev-er an-swer nay. I had not power to ask his name, Whith- - - er he went, or whence he came; Yet there was something in his eye, That won my love, I knew not why.

697.

1 A poor, wayfaring man of grief
 Hath often crossed me on my way,
Who sued so humbly for relief,
 That I could never answer nay.
I had not power to ask his name,
Whither he went, or whence he came;
Yet there was something in his eye,
That won my love, I knew not why.

2 Once when my scanty meal was spread,
 He entered; not a word he spake;
Just perishing for want of bread,
 I gave him all; he blessed it, brake,
And ate, but gave me part again;
Mine was an angel's portion then;
And while I fed wi h eager haste,
The crust was manna to my taste.

3 I spied him where a fountain burst
 Clear from the rock; his strength was
  gone;
The heedless water mocked his thirst;
 He heard it, saw it hurrying on:
I ran and raised the sufferer up:
Thrice from the stream he drained my
  cup;
Dipped, and returned it running o'er—
I drank and never thirsted more.

4 Then, in a moment, to my view
 The stranger started from disguise;
The tokens in his hands I knew;
 My Saviour stood before my eyes!
He spake, and my poor name he named:
"Of me, thou hast not been ashamed:
These deeds shall thy memorial be;
Fear not! thou didst it unto me."

698.

1 What are those soul-reviving strains,
 Which echo thus from Salem's plains!
What anthems loud, and louder still,
 Sweetly resound from Zion's hill?
2 Lo! 't is an infant chorus sings,
 Hosanna to the King of kings:
The Saviour comes! and babes proclaim
Salvation, sent in Jesus' name.

3 Nor these alone their voice shall raise,
 For we will join this song of praise;
Still Israel's children forward press
 To hail the Lord their Righteousness.
4 Proclaim hosannas loud and clear;
 See David's son and Lord appear!
Glory and praise on earth be given;
Hosanna in the highest heaven!

FULTON. 7s.　　WM. B. BRADBURY.

1. Chil - dren! lis - ten to the Lord, And o - bey his gra - cious word;

Seek his face with heart and mind— Ear - ly seek, and you shall find.

699.

2 Sorrowful, your sins confess;
Plead his perfect righteousness ;
See the Saviour's bleeding side ;—
Come—you will not be denied.

3 For his worship now prepare ;
Kneel to him in fervent prayer ;
Serve him with a perfect heart;
Never from his ways depart.

700.

1 Saviour! teach me, day by day,
Love's sweet lesson to obey ;
Sweeter lesson cannot be,
Loving him who first loved me.

2 With a child-like heart of love,
At thy bidding may I move ;
Prompt to serve and follow thee,
Loving him who first loved me.

3 Teach me all thy steps to trace,
Strong to follow in thy grace ;
Learning how to love from thee,
Loving him who first loved me.

4 Love in loving finds employ—
In obedience all her joy ;
Ever new that joy will be,
Loving him who first loved me.

5 Thus may I rejoice to show
That I feel the love I owe;
Singing, till thy face I see,
Of his love who first loved me.

701.

1 Glory to the Father give,
God in whom we move and live ;
Children's prayers he deigns to hear,
Children's songs delight his ear.

2 Glory to the Son we bring,
Christ our Prophet, Priest, and King;
Children, raise your sweetest strain
To the Lamb, for he was slain.

3 Glory to the Holy Ghost ;
Be this day a Pentecost;
Children's minds may he inspire,
Give them tongues of holy fire.

4 Glory in the highest be
To the blessèd Trinity,
For the gospel from above,
For the word, that "God is love."

702.

1 God of mercy! throned on high,
Listen from thy lofty seat;
Hear, oh, hear our feeble cry ;
Guide, oh, guide our wandering feet.

2 Young and erring travelers, we
All our dangers do not know ;
Scarcely fear the stormy sea,
Hardly feel the tempest blow.

3 Jesus, lover of the young,
Cleanse us with thy love divine ;
Ere the tide of sin grow strong,
Save us, keep us, make us thine.

BRIGHT CROWN. C. M.　　　　　　　　　Wm. B. Bradbury.

1. Ye val - iant sol - diers of the cross, Ye hap - py, pray - ing band;
Tho' in this world you suf - fer loss, You'll reach fair Ca - naan's land; Let us

nev - er mind the scoffs nor the frowns of the world, For we've all got the cross to bear;

It will on - ly make the crown the bright-er to shine, When we have the crown to wear.

703.

2 All earthly pleasures we'll forsake,
When heaven appears in view;
In Jesus' strength we'll undertake
To fight our passage through.
Chorus.—Let us never, etc.

3 Oh, what a glorious shout there'll be,
When we arrive at home!
Our friends and Jesus we shall see,
And God shall say, " Well done!"
Chorus.—Let us never, etc.

GOLDEN SHORE. 8s & 7s.　　　　　　　Wm. B. Bradbury.

1. Girls. We are out on the ocean sailing, Homeward bound we sweetly glide;
Boys. We are out on the ocean sailing, To a home be- yond the tide. All the storms will

soon be o-ver, Then we'll an-chor in the har-bor; We are out on the o-cean sail-ing,

GOLDEN SHORE. (Concluded.)

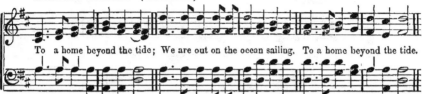

To a home beyond the tide; We are out on the ocean sailing, To a home beyond the tide.

704.

2 Millions now are safely landed
   Over on the golden shore;
   Millions now are on their journey,
   Yet there's room for millions more.—
                                    Chorus.

3 Spread your sails, while heavenly breezes
   Gently waft our vessel on;

All on board are sweetly singing—
   Free salvation is the song.—*Chorus.*

4 When we all are safely anchored,
   We will shout—our trials o'er;
   We will walk about the city,
   And we'll sing forevermore.—*Chorus.*

Hymn **705.**

PRAISE. 8s & 7s.

Sabb. School Pearl.

1. High we raise our hal-le-lu-jahs To our dear Re-deemer's name, Who, to seek the
3. Praise him for the great sal-va-tion He to young and old extends, Bids them strive for

END.

lost and wandering, And to save the sinner, came. 2. Praise him for his blest example, For his life of
heavenly mansions, Calls believing souls his friends. 4. We would better learn to praise him,
                                                                                Love and serve him

Close with First Verse as Chorus.

peace and truth, Fold-ing chil-dren to his bo-som, Gen-tly guid-ing age and youth.
till we die, Till our joy-ful hal-le-lu-jahs Join the an-them of the sky.

SING OF JESUS. 7s & 6s.

SABB. SCHOOL BELL.

1. Come, let us sing of Je - sus, While hearts and accents blend; Come, let us sing of Je - sus, The sinner's on - ly Friend; His ho-ly soul re-joic - es, Amid the choirs a - - - bove, To hear our youth-ful voic - es Ex - ult - ing in his love.

706.

2 We love to sing of Jesus,
  Who wept our path along ;
We love to sing of Jesus,
  The tempted and the strong ;
None who besought his healing,
  He passed unheeded by :
And still retains his feeling
  For us above the sky.

3 We love to sing of Jesus,
  Who died our souls to save ;
We love to sing of Jesus,
  Triumphant o'er the grave ;

And in our hour of danger,
  We'll trust his love alone,
Who once slept in a manger,
  And now sits on the throne.

4 Then let us sing of Jesus,
  While yet on earth we stay,
And hope to sing of Jesus
  Throughout eternal day ;
For those who here confess him,
  He will in heaven confess ;
And faithful hearts that bless him,
  He will forever bless.

GOLDEN CHAIN. 8s & 7s. Double.

WM. B. BRADBURY.

1. Tho' the days are dark with trouble, And thy heart is filled with fear, There is One that

GOLDEN CHAIN. (Concluded.)

sees thee ev - er, And will hold thee near and dear. Cheerful hearts and smiling fa - ces

Oft - en make thee happy here, Yet no one was e'er so hap-py, But sometimes the clouds appear.

REFRAIN.

There's a Friend that's ev-er near, Nev-er fear, He is ev - er near, Nev-er, nev-er fear;

Repeat pp

There's a Friend that's ev - er near, Nev-er fear, He is ev - er near, Nev-er fear!

707.

2 All thy prospects will seem brighter
　　When the shadow leaves the heart,
　And the steps of time beat lighter,
　　When the gloomy clouds depart.
　Many days have dawned serenely,
　　While the birds sang with delight,
　But the skies were dark and gloomy
　　Ere the sun had reached its height.—
　　　　　　　　　　　Ref.

3 Soon will dawn a brighter morning
　　On a blessèd, tranquil shore;
　Sighs will then give place to singing,
　　Tears to bliss forevermore.
　Thou shalt see a world of glory,
　　And eternal joy and bliss;
　Let not then thy soul be moaning
　　O'er the woes and cares of this.—*Ref.*

708.

1 Jesus, on thy throne of glory!
　　Higher than the angels are;
　Stoop to hear the children's story,
　　Deign to grant the children's prayer:
　Thou so great, and we so feeble,
　　Thou so full, and we in need,
　Jesus, listen to our pleading,
　　Be to us a friend indeed.—*Ref.*

2 When temptations spread around us,
　　And in snares our feet are twined,
　In the hour when we forget thee,
　　Jesus, bear us still in mind:
　Through the years thy love may grant us,
　　When we sleep at life's last end,
　In the morning of our waking,
　　Jesus, Saviour, be our friend.—*Ref.*

PARTING HYMN. C. M.

1. { How pleasant thus to dwell below, In fellowship of love; }
   { And tho' we part, 'tis bliss to know The good shall meet above. } The good shall meet above,

D. S. To meet to part no more.

FINE.

The good shall meet a - bove; And tho' we part, 'tis bliss to know The good shall meet a - bove.
On Canaan's happy shore, And sing the ev - er - lasting song, With those who've gone before.

D. S. S.

Oh, that will be joy-ful, joy-ful, joy-ful! Oh, that will be joy-ful, To meet to part no more.

709.

2 Yes, happy thought! when we are free
  From earthly grief and pain,
In heaven we shall each other see,
  And never part again.
     Oh, that will be joyful! &c.

3 Then let us each, in strength divine,
  Still walk in wisdom's ways;
That we, with those we love, may join
  In never ending praise.
     Oh, that will be joyful! &c.

710.

1 On, haste away, my brethren dear!
  And come to Canaan's shore;
We'll meet and sing forever there,
  When all our toils are o'er.
     Oh, that will be joyful! &c.

2 How sweet to hear the hallowed theme
  That saints shall ever sing;
To hear their voices all proclaim
  "Salvation to the King!"
     Oh, that will be joyful! &c.

3 Around his throne, all clothed in white
  Will all his saints appear;
And, shining in his glory bright,
  We'll see our Saviour there.
     Oh, that will be joyful! &c.

4 Thro' heaven the shouts of angels ring,
  When sons to God are born:
Oh, what a company will sing
  On the millennial morn!
     Oh, that will be joyful! &c.

5 Through one eternal day we'll sing,
  And bless his sacred name,
With hallelujah to the King,
  And "Worthy is the Lamb!"
     Oh, that will be joyful! &c.

GRATITUDE. L. M. Bost.

1. How blest the sa-cred tie that binds, In u-nion sweet, ac-cord-ing minds !
How swift the heaven-ly course they run, Whose hearts, whose faith, whose hopes are one.

711.

2. To each, the soul of each how dear!
What watchful love, what holy fear!
How doth the generous flame within
Refine from earth, and cleanse from sin !

3. Their streaming eyes together flow
For human guilt and mortal woe ;
Their ardent prayers together rise,
Like mingling flames in sacrifice.

4. Together oft they seek the place
Where God reveals his awful face ;
How high, how strong their raptures swell,
There 's none but kindred souls can tell.

5. Nor shall the glowing flame expire
'Midst nature's drooping, sickening fire :
Soon shall they meet in realms above,
A heaven of joy, because of love.

712.

1. Kindred in Christ ! for his dear sake
A hearty welcome here receive ;
May we together now partake
The joys which only he can give.

2. May he, by whose kind care we meet,
Send his good Spirit from above ;
Make our communications sweet,
And cause our hearts to burn with love.

3. Forgotten be each worldly theme,
When Christians meet together thus ;
We only wish to speak of him,
Who lived, and died, and reigns, for us.

4. We 'll talk of all he did and said,
And suffered for us here below ;—
The path he marked for us to tread,
And what he 's doing for us now.

5. Thus,—as the moments pass away,—
We 'll love, and wonder, and adore ;
And hasten on the glorious day,
When we shall meet to part no more.

713.

1. Great God ! to thee my evening song
With humble gratitude I raise ;
Oh, let thy mercy tune my tongue,
And fill my heart with lively praise.

2. My days unclouded as they pass,
And every gentle, rolling hour,
Are monuments of wondrous grace,
And witness to thy love and power.

3. And yet this thoughtless, wretched heart,
Too oft regardless of thy love,
Ungrateful, can from thee depart,
And, fond of trifles, vainly rove.

4. Seal my forgiveness in the blood
Of Jesus; his dear name alone
I plead for pardon, gracious God !
And kind acceptance at thy throne.

5. Let this blest hope mine eyelids close,
With sleep refresh my feeble frame ;
Safe in thy care may I repose,
And wake with praises to thy name.

BOARDMAN. C. M.   TEMPLI CARMINA.

1. Oh, it is joy in one to meet Whom one com - mu - nion blends,

Coun - cil to hold in con - verse sweet, And talk as Chris - tian friends.

714.

1 Oh, it is joy in one to meet
  Whom one communion blends,
  Council to hold in converse sweet,
    And talk as Christian friends.

2 'T is joy to think the angel train,
  Who 'mid heaven's temple shine,
  To seek our earthly temples deign,
    And in our anthems join.

3 But chief 't is joy to think that He,
  To whom his church is dear,
  Delights her gathered flock to see,
    Her joint devotions hear.

4 Then who would choose to walk abroad,
  While here such joys are given?
  "This is indeed the house of God,
    And this the gate of heaven!"

715.

1 BLEST be the dear, uniting love,
  That will not let us part:
  Our bodies may far off remove;
    We still are one in heart.

2 Joined in one spirit to our Head,
  Where he appoints we go;
  We still in Jesus' footsteps tread,
    And show his praise below.

3 Oh, may we ever walk in him,
  And nothing know beside!
  Nothing desire, nothing esteem,
    But Jesus crucified!

4 Partakers of the Saviour's grace,
  The same in mind and heart,
  Not joy nor grief nor time nor place
    Nor life nor death can part.

716.

1 LET saints below in concert sing
  With those to glory gone:
  For all the servants of our King,
    In earth and heaven, are one.

2 One family—we dwell in him—
  One church above, beneath,
  Though now divided by the stream,—
    The narrow stream of death;

3 One army of the living God,
  To his command we bow;
  Part of the host have crossed the flood,
    And part are crossing now.

4 Ev'n now to their eternal home
  Some happy spirits fly;
  And we are to the margin come,
    And soon expect to die.

5 Ev'n now, by faith, we join our hands
  With those that went before,
  And greet the ransomed blessèd bands
    Upon th' eternal shore.

6 Lord Jesus! be our constant guide:
  And, when the word is given,
  Bid death's cold flood its waves divide,
    And land us safe in heaven.

HEBER. C. M.

Geo. Kingsley.

1. Hail, sweet - est, dear - est tie that binds Our glow - ing hearts in one;

Hail, sa - cred hope, that tunes our minds To har - mo - ny di - vine.

717.

2 What though the northern wintry blast
   Shall howl around our cot;
   What though beneath an eastern sun
   Be cast our distant lot;—

3 No lingering look, no parting sigh,
   Our future meeting knows;
   There friendship beams from every eye,
   And love immortal glows.

4 Oh, sacred hope! Oh, blissful hope!
   Which Jesus' grace has given—
   The hope, when days and years are past,
   We all shall meet in heaven!

718.

1 Our souls, by love together knit,
   Cemented, mixed in one,
   One hope, one heart, one mind, one voice,
   'T is heaven on earth begun.

2 Our hearts have often burned within,
   And glowed with sacred fire,
   While Jesus spoke, and fed, and blessed,
   And filled the enlarged desire.

3 The little cloud increases still,
   The heavens are big with rain;
   We haste to catch the teeming shower,
   And all its moisture drain.

4 A rill, a stream, a torrent flows!
   But pour a mighty flood;
   Oh, sweep the nations, shake the earth,
   'Till all proclaim thee, God!

5 And when thou mak'st thy jewels up,
   And sett'st thy starry crown;
   When all thy sparkling gems shall shine,
   Proclaimed by thee thine own;—

6 May we, a little band of love,
   We sinners, saved by grace,
   From glory unto glory changed,
   Behold thee face to face.

719.

1 How sweet, how heavenly is the sight,
   When those who love the Lord
   In one another's peace delight,
   And so fulfill his word!

2 When each can feel his brother's sigh,
   And with him bear a part!
   When sorrow flows from eye to eye,
   And joy from heart to heart!

3 When, free from envy, scorn and pride,
   Our wishes all above,
   Each can his brother's failings hide,
   And show a brother's love!

4 Let love, in one delightful stream,
   Through every bosom flow,
   And union sweet, and dear esteem,
   In every action glow.

5 Love is the golden chain that binds
   The happy souls above;
   And he 's an heir of heaven who finds
   His bosom glow with love.

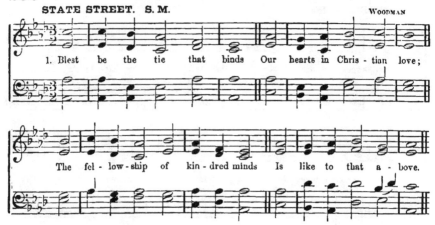

STATE STREET. S. M.   WOODMAN

1. Blest be the tie that binds Our hearts in Chris - tian love;

The fel - low - ship of kin - dred minds Is like to that a - bove.

720.

2 Before our Father's throne
  We pour our ardent prayers;
Our fears, our hopes, our aims are one,
  Our comforts and our cares.

3 We share our mutual woes,
  Our mutual burdens bear;
And often for each other flows
  The sympathizing tear.

4 When we asunder part,
  It gives us inward pain;
But we shall still be joined in heart,
  And hope to meet again.

5 This glorious hope revives
  Our courage by the way;
While each in expectation lives,
  And longs to see the day.

6 From sorrow, toil, and pain,
  And sin, we shall be free,
And perfect love and friendship reign
  Through all eternity.

721.

1 I LOVE thy kingdom, Lord,
  The house of thine abode,
The Church, our blest Redeemer saved
  With his own precious blood.

2 I love thy church, O God!
  Her walls before thee stand,
Dear as the apple of thine eye,
  And graven on thy hand.

3 For her my tears shall fall,
  For her my prayers ascend;
To her my cares and toils be given,
  Till toils and cares shall end.

4 Beyond my highest joy
  I prize her heavenly ways,
Her sweet communion, solemn vows,
  Her hymns of love and praise.

5 Jesus, thou Friend divine,
  Our Saviour, and our King!
Thy hand from every snare and foe,
  Shall great deliverance bring.

6 Sure as thy truth shall last,
  To Zion shall be given
The brightest glories earth can yield,
  And brighter bliss of heaven.

722.

1 LET party names no more
  The Christian world o'erspread;
Gentile and Jew, and bond and free,
  Are one in Christ their head.

2 Among the saints on earth,
  Let mutual love be found;
Heirs of the same inheritance,
  With mutual blessings crowned.

3 Thus will the church below
  Resemble that above;
Where streams of pleasure ever flow,
  And every heart is love.

SHIRLAND. S. M.

STANLEY.

1. Our heaven-ly Fa-ther calls, And Christ in-vites us near;

With both, our friend-ship shall be sweet, And our com-mu-nion dear.

723.

1 OUR heavenly Father calls,
 And Christ invites us near;
 With both, our friendship shall be sweet,
 And our communion dear.

2 God pities all our griefs:
 He pardons every day;
 Almighty to protect our souls,
 And wise to guide our way.

3 How large his bounties are!
 What various stores of good,
 Diffused from our Redeemer's hand,
 And purchased with his blood!

4 Jesus, our living head,
 We bless thy faithful care;
 Our advocate before the throne,
 And our forerunner there.

5 Here fix, my roving heart!
 Here wait, my warmest love!
 Till the communion be complete,
 In nobler scenes above.

724.

1 BEHOLD the throne of grace!
 The promise calls me near;
 There Jesus shows a smiling face,
 And waits to answer prayer.

2 That rich atoning blood,
 Which sprinkled round I see,
 Provides for those who come to God
 An all-prevailing plea.

3 My soul! ask what thou wilt;
 Thou canst not be too bold:
 Since his own blood for thee he spilt,
 What else can he withhold?

4 Thine image, Lord, bestow,
 Thy presence and thy love;
 I ask to serve thee here below,
 And reign with thee above.

5 Teach me to live by faith;
 Conform my will to thine;
 Let me victorious be in death,
 And then in glory shine.

725.

1 JESUS, who knows full well
 The heart of every saint,
 Invites us, all our grief to tell,
 To pray and never faint.

2 He bows his gracious ear,—
 We never plead in vain;
 Then let us wait till he appear,
 And pray, and pray again.

3 Jesus, the Lord, will hear
 His chosen when they cry;
 Yes, though he may a while forbear,
 He'll help them from on high.

4 Then let us earnest cry,
 And never faint in prayer;
 He sees, he hears, and, from on high,
 Will make our cause his care.

RETREAT. L. M.

Dr. HASTINGS.

1. From ev - ery storm - y wind that blows, From ev - ery swell - ing tide of woes,

There is a calm, a sure re - treat, 'Tis found be-neath the mer - cy - seat.

726.

2 There is a place where Jesus sheds
The oil of gladness on our heads,—
A place, than all besides, more sweet;
It is the blood-bought mercy-seat.

3 There is a scene where spirits blend,
Where friend holds fellowship with friend;
Though sundered far, by faith they meet
Around one common mercy-seat!

4 There, there, on eagle wings we soar,
And sense and sin molest no more,
And heaven comes down our souls to greet,
And glory crowns the mercy-seat.

5 Oh! let my hand forget her skill,
My tongue be silent, cold, and still,
This throbbing heart forget to beat,
If I forget the mercy-seat.

727.

1 Where high the heavenly temple stands,
The house of God not made with hands,
A great High Priest our nature wears,—
The Guardian of mankind appears.

2 Though now ascended up on high,
He bends on earth a brother's eye;
Partaker of the human name,
He knows the frailty of our frame.

3 Our Fellow-sufferer yet retains
A fellow-feeling of our pains;
And still remembers, in the skies,
His tears, his agonies, and cries.

4 In every pang that rends the heart,
The Man of Sorrows had a part;
He sympathizes with our grief,
And to the sufferer sends relief.

5 With boldness, therefore, at the throne,
Let us make all our sorrows known;
And ask the aid of heavenly power,
To help us in the evil hour.

728.

1 Forth from the dark and stormy sky,
Lord, to thine altar's shade we fly;
Forth from the world, its hope and fear,
Saviour, we seek thy shelter here.

2 Long have we roamed in want and pain,
Long have we sought thy rest in vain;
Weary and weak, thy grace we pray;
Turn not, O Lord! thy guests away.

729.

1 Where two or three, with sweet accord,
Obedient to their sovereign Lord,
Meet to recount his acts of grace,
And offer solemn prayer and praise;—

2 There will the gracious Saviour be,
To bless the little company;—
There, to unvail his smiling face,
And bid his glories fill the place.

3 We meet at thy command, O Lord!
Relying on thy faithful word;
Now send the Spirit from above,
And fill our hearts with heavenly love.

SOMERVILLE. L. M.

Templi Carmina.

1. Je - sus, where'er thy peo - ple meet, There they be - hold thy mer - cy - seat;

Where'er they seek thee thou art found, And ev - ery place is hallowed ground.

730.

2 For thou, within no walls confined,
Inhabitest the humble mind;
Such ever bring thee where they come,
And going, take thee to their home.

3 Great Shepherd of thy chosen few!
Thy former mercies here renew;
Here to our waiting hearts proclaim
The sweetness of thy saving name.

731.

1 And dost thou say, "Ask what thou wilt?"
Lord, I would seize the golden hour:
I pray to be released from guilt,
And freed from sin and Satan's power.

2 More of thy presence, Lord, impart;
More of thine image let me bear:
Erect thy throne within my heart,
And reign without a rival there.

3 Give me to read my pardon sealed,
And from thy joy to draw my strength;
Oh, be thy boundless love revealed
In all its height and breadth and length!

4 Grant these requests—I ask no more,
But to thy care the rest resign:
Sick, or in health, or rich, or poor,
All shall be well, if thou art mine.

732.

1 How sweet to leave the world awhile,
And seek the presence of our Lord!
Dear Saviour! on thy people smile,
And come, according to thy word.

2 From busy scenes we now retreat,
That we may here converse with thee:
Ah! Lord! behold us at thy feet;—
Let this the "gate of heaven" be.

3 "Chief of ten thousand!" now appear,
That we by faith may see thy face:
Oh! speak, that we thy voice may hear,
And let thy presence fill this place.

733.

1 What various hindrances we meet
In coming to a mercy-seat!
Yet who that knows the worth of prayer
But wishes to be often there?

2 Prayer makes the darkened clouds withdraw;
Prayer climbs the ladder Jacob saw,
Gives exercise to faith and love,
Brings every blessing from above.

3 Restraining prayer, we cease to fight;
Prayer makes the Christian's armor bright;
And Satan trembles when he sees
The weakest saint upon his knees.

4 Have you no words? ah! think again;
Words flow apace when you complain,
And fill a fellow-creature's ear
With the sad tale of all your care.

5 Were half the breath thus vainly spent
To heaven in supplication sent,
Our cheerful song would oftener be,
"Hear what the Lord hath done for me!"

BYEFIELD. C. M.   DR. HASTINGS.

1. Prayer is the soul's sin-cere de-sire, Ut-tered or un-ex-pressed;

The mo-tion of a hid-den fire, That trem-bles in the breast.

734.

2 Prayer is the burden of a sigh,
The falling of a tear,
The upward glancing of an eye,
When none but God is near.

3 Prayer is the simplest form of speech
That infant lips can try;
Prayer the sublimest strains that reach
The Majesty on high.

4 Prayer is the Christian's vital breath,
The Christian's native air:
His watchword at the gates of death,—
He enters heaven with prayer.

5 Prayer is the contrite sinner's voice,
Returning from his ways;
While angels in their songs rejoice,
And cry—" Behold he prays!"

6 O thou, by whom we come to God—
The Life, the Truth, the Way;
The path of prayer thyself hast trod;
Lord! teach us how to pray.

735.

1 THE Saviour bids thee watch and pray
Through life's momentous hour;
And grants the Spirit's quickening ray
To those who seek his power.

2 The Saviour bids thee watch and pray,
Maintain a warrior's strife;
O Christian! hear his voice to-day:
Obedience is thy life.

3 The Saviour bids thee watch and pray,
For soon the hour will come
That calls thee from the earth away
To thy eternal home.

4 The Saviour bids thee watch and pray,
Oh, hearken to his voice,
And follow where he leads the way,
To heaven's eternal joys!

736.

1 HAIL, tranquil hour of closing day!
Begone, disturbing care!
And look, my soul, from earth away,
To him who heareth prayer.

2 How sweet the tear of penitence,
Before his throne of grace,
While, to the contrite spirit's sense,
He shows his smiling face.

3 How sweet, thro' long-remembered years,
His mercies to recall;
And, pressed with wants, and griefs, and fears,
To trust his love for all.

4 How sweet to look, in thoughtful hope,
Beyond this fading sky,
And hear him call his children up
To his fair home on high.

5 Calmly the day forsakes our heaven
To dawn beyond the west;
So let my soul, in life's last even,
Retire to glorious rest.

WOODSTOCK. C. M.   D. DUTTON.

1. I love to steal a-while a-way From ev-ery cum-bering care,

And spend the hours of set-ting day In hum-ble, grate-ful prayer.

737.

1 I LOVE to steal awhile away
From every cumbering care,
And spend the hours of setting day
In humble, grateful prayer.

2 I love in solitude to shed
The penitential tear,
And all his promises to plead,
Where none but God can hear.

3 I love to think on mercies past,
And future good implore,
And all my cares and sorrows cast
On him whom I adore.

4 I love by faith to take a view
Of brighter scenes in heaven ;
The prospect doth my strength renew,
While here by tempests driven.

5 Thus, when life's toilsome day is o'er,
May its departing ray
Be calm as this impressive hour,
And lead to endless day.

738.

1 THERE is an eye that never sleeps
Beneath the wing of night;
There is an ear that never shuts,
When sink the beams of light.

2 There is an arm that never tires,
When human strength gives way ;
There is a love that never fails,
When earthly loves decay.

3 That eye is fixed on seraph throngs;
That arm upholds the sky ;
That ear is filled with angel songs ;
That love is throned on high.

4 But there's a power which man can wield
When mortal aid is vain,
That eye, that arm, that love to reach,
That listening ear to gain.

5 That power is prayer, which soars on high,
Through Jesus, to the throne ;
And moves the hand which moves the
world,
To bring salvation down !

739.

1 DEAR Father, to thy mercy-seat
My soul for shelter flies :
'T is here I find a safe retreat
When storms and tempests rise.

2 My cheerful hope can never die,
If thou, my God, art near;
Thy grace can raise my comforts high,
And banish every fear.

3 My great Protector, and my Lord !
Thy constant aid impart ;
Oh ! let thy kind, thy gracious word
Sustain my trembling heart.

4 Oh ! never let my soul remove
From this divine retreat ;
Still let me trust thy power and love,
And dwell beneath thy feet.

HORTON. 7s.   *German.*

1. Come, my soul, thy suit pre-pare, Je-sus loves to an-swer prayer;

He him-self has bid thee pray, There-fore will not say thee nay.

740.

2 With my burden I begin;—
Lord! remove this load of sin;
Let thy blood, for sinners spilt,
Set my conscience free from guilt.

3 Lord! I come to thee for rest,
Take possession of my breast;
There, thy sovereign right maintain,
And, without a rival, reign.

4 While I am a pilgrim here,
Let thy love my spirit cheer;
Be my guide, my guard, my friend,
Lead me to my journey's end.

5 Show me what I have to do,
Every hour my strength renew;
Let me live a life of faith,
Let me die thy people's death.

741.

1 Lord! I cannot let thee go,
Till a blessing thou bestow;
Do not turn away thy face,
Mine's an urgent, pressing case.

2 Once, a sinner, near despair,
Sought thy mercy-seat by prayer;
Mercy heard and set him free—
Lord! that mercy came to me.

3 Many days have passed since then,
Many changes I have seen;
Yet have been upheld till now;
Who could hold me up but thou?

4 Thou hast helped in every need—
This emboldens me to plead;
After so much mercy past,
Canst thou let me sink at last?

5 No—I must maintain my hold;
'Tis thy goodness makes me bold;
I can no denial take,
Since I plead for Jesus' sake.

742.

1 Lord, we come before thee now,
At thy feet we humbly bow;
Oh, do not our suit disdain!
Shall we seek thee, Lord, in vain!

2 Lord, on thee our souls depend,
In compassion now descend;
Fill our hearts with thy rich grace,
Tune our lips to sing thy praise.

3 In thine own appointed way,
Now we seek thee; here we stay;
Lord, we know not how to go,
Till a blessing thou bestow.

4 Comfort those who weep and mourn;
Let the time of joy return;
Those that are cast down lift up;
Make them strong in faith and hope.

5 Grant that all may seek and find
Thee a God supremely kind;
Heal the sick; the captive free;
Let us all rejoice in thee.

ALETTA. 7s.

Wm. B. Bradbury.

1. Soft and ho - ly is the place, Where the light that beams from heaven

Shows the Sa - viour's smil - ing face, With the joy of sin for - given.

743.

2 There, with one accord we meet,
All the words of life to hear ;
Bending low at Jesus' feet,
Worshiping with godly fear.

3 Let the world and all its cares
Now retire from every breast ;
Let the tempter and his snares
Cease to hinder or molest.

4 Precious Sabbath of the Lord,
Fairest type of heaven above !
Purest joy thy scenes afford
To the heart that's tuned to love.

744.

1 Stealing from the world away,
We are come to seek thy face ;
Kindly meet us, Lord, we pray,
Grant us thy reviving grace.

2 Yonder stars that gild the sky
Shine but with a borrowed light ;
We, unless thy light be nigh,
Wander, wrapt in gloomy night.

3 Sun of Righteousness ! dispel
All our darkness, doubts, and fears ;
May thy light within us dwell,
Till eternal day appears.

4 Warm our hearts in prayer and praise,
Lift our every thought above ;
Hear the grateful songs we raise,
Fill us with thy perfect love.

745.

1 Thou, from whom we never part,
Thou, whose love is everywhere,
Thou, who seest every heart,
Listen to our evening prayer.

2 Father, fill our hearts with love,
Love unfailing, full and free ;
Love no injury can move,
Love that ever rests on thee.

3 Heavenly Father ! through the night
Keep us safe from every ill,
Cheerful as the morning light
May we wake to do thy will.

746.

1 They who seek the throne of grace
Find that throne in every place ;
If we live a life of prayer,
God is present everywhere.

2 In our sickness and our health,
In our want, or in our wealth,
If we look to God in prayer,
God is present everywhere.

3 When our earthly comforts fail,
When the woes of life prevail,
'T is the time for earnest prayer ;
God is present everywhere.

4 Then, my soul, in every strait,
To thy Father come, and wait ;
He will answer every prayer :
God is present everywhere.

FATHERLAND. 6s & 4s.

Geo. Kingsley.

1. I'm but a stranger here, Heaven is my home; Earth is a desert drear, Heaven is my home:
2. What tho' the tempest rage, Heaven is my home; Short is my pilgrim-age, Heaven is my home:

Danger and sorrow stand Round me on every hand; Heaven is my fatherland, Heaven is my home.
Time's cold and wintry blast Soon will be overpast; I shall reach home at last, Heaven is my home.

747.

3 There, at my Saviour's side,
   Heaven is my home;
I shall be glorified—
   Heaven is my home:

There are the good and blest,
Those I loved most and best,
And there I, too, shall rest;—
Heaven is my home!

SHINING SHORE. 8s & 7s. Hymn 748.

G. F. Root.

1. My days are gliding swiftly by, And I, a pilgrim stranger, Would not de-tain them
2. We'll gird our loins, my brethren dear, Our distant home discerning; Our ab-sent Lord has
3. Should coming days be cold and dark, We need not cease our sing-ing; That per-fect rest nought
4. Let sorrow's rudest tempest blow, Each chord on earth to sev-er, Our King says, come, and

as they fly! Those hours of toil and dan-ger, For oh! we stand on Jordan's strand, Our
left us word, Let ev-ery lamp be burning— For oh! &c.
can mo-lest, Where golden harps are ring-ing, For oh! &c.
there's our home, For-ev-er, oh! for-ev-er! For oh! &c.

friends are passing o-ver, And just before, the shining shore We may al-most dis-cov-er.

HEAVENLY HOME. 11s. *English.*

1. My home is in heaven, my rest is not here; Then why should I murmur when trials are near?

Be hushed, my dark spirit, the worst that can come,But shortens my journey, and hastens me home.

749.

2 It is not for me to be seeking my bliss,
And building my hopes in a region like
this;
I look for a city which hands have not
piled,
I pant for a country by sin undefiled.

3 The thorn and the thistle around me
may grow,
I would not recline upon roses below,
I ask not my portion, I seek not my rest,
Till ever with Jesus, I lie on his breast.

750.

1 Oh, had I, my Saviour, the wings of a
dove,
How soon would I soar to thy presence
above;
How soon would I flee where the weary
have rest,
And hide all my cares in thy sheltering
breast.

2 I flutter, I struggle, I long to be free,
I feel me a captive while banished from
thee;
A pilgrim and stranger, the desert I roam;
And look on to heaven, and fain would
be home.

3 Ah, there the wild tempest forever shall
cease,
No billow shall ruffle that haven of
peace;

Temptation and trouble alike shall depart,
All tears from the eye, and all sin from
the heart.

4 Soon, soon may this Eden of promise be
mine;
Rise, bright sun of glory, no more to decline!
Thy light, yet unrisen, the wilderness
cheers—
Oh, what will it be when the fullness
appears!

751.

1 'Mid scenes of confusion, and creature
complaints,
How sweet to my soul is communion
with saints;
To find at the banquet of mercy there's
room,
And feel in the presence of Jesus at home.

2 Sweet bonds that unite all the children
of peace!
And thrice precious Jesus, whose love
cannot cease!
Though oft from thy presence in sadness
I roam,
I long to behold thee in glory at home.

3 I sigh from this body of sin to be free,
Which hinders my joy and communion
with thee;
Though now my temptation like billows
may foam,
All, all will be peace, when I'm with
thee at home.

MT. BLANC. 7s & 6s.   PLYMOUTH COLL.

1. We are on our journey home, Where Christ our Lord is gone; We shall meet around his throne,

When he makes his people one, In the new, In the new Je - ru - sa - lem.

In the new Je-ru-sa-lem.

752

2 We can see that distant home,
  Tho' clouds rise dark between;
Faith views the radiant dome,
  And a lustre flashes keen,
    From the new Jerusalem.

3 Oh, glory shining far
  From the never setting Sun!
Oh, trembling morning star!
  Our journey 's almost done,
    To the new Jerusalem.

4 Oh, holy, heavenly home!
  Oh, rest eternal there!
When shall the exiles come,
  Where they cease from earthly care,
    In the new Jerusalem.

5 Our hearts are breaking now
  Those mansions fair to see;
O Lord! thy heavens bow,
  And raise us up with thee
    To the new Jerusalem.

I'M A PILGRIM.

1. I'm a pil-grim, and I'm a stranger; I can tar-ry, I can tar-ry but a night;

D. C.

Do not de-tain me, for I am go-ing To where the fountains are ev-er flow-ing.

753.

2 There the glory is ever shining!
  Oh, my longing heart, my longing heart
    is there!
Here in this country so dark and dreary,
I long have wandered forlorn and weary.

3 There 's the city to which I journey:
  My Redeemer, my Redeemer is its light!
There is no sorrow, nor any sighing,
Nor any tears there, nor any dying!

REST FOR THE WEARY. 8s & 7s.   Rev. J. W. Dadmun.

1. In the Christian's home in glory There remains a land of rest, There my Saviour's gone before me

CHORUS.

To ful-fill my soul's request; There is rest for the wea-ry, There is rest for the wea-ry,

There is rest for the wea-ry, There is rest for you— On the oth-er side of Jor-dan,

In the sweet fields of E-den, Where the tree of life is blooming, There is rest for you!

754.

2 He is fitting up my mansion,
  Which eternally shall stand,
For my stay shall not be transient
  In that holy, happy land.
    There is rest, etc.

3 Pain nor sickness ne'er shall enter,
  Grief nor woe my lot shall share;
But in that celestial centre
  I a crown of life shall wear.
    There is rest, etc.

4 Death itself shall then be vanquished,
  And his sting shall be withdrawn;
Shout for gladness, O ye ransomed!
  Hail with joy the rising morn.
    There is rest, etc.

5 Sing, oh, sing, ye heirs of glory!
  Shout your triumph as you go;
Zion's gates will open for you,
  You shall find an entrance through.
    There is rest, etc.

BEAUTIFUL ZION. 8s.   WM. B. BRADBURY.

1. Beau-ti-ful Zi-on, built a-bove, Beau-ti-ful cit-y that I love;

Beau-ti-ful gates of pearl-y white, Beau-ti-ful tem-ple—God its light;

He who was slain on Cal-va-ry, Opens those pearl-y gates to me.

755.

2 Beautiful heaven, where all is light,
Beautiful angels, clothed in white,
Beautiful strains, that never tire,
Beautiful harps through all the choir;
There shall I join the chorus sweet,
Worshiping at the Saviour's feet.

3 Beautiful crowns on every brow,
Beautiful palms the conquerors show,

Beautiful robes the ransomed wear,
Beautiful all who enter there;
Thither I press with eager feet,
There shall my rest be long and sweet.

4 Beautiful throne of Christ our King,
Beautiful songs the angels sing,
Beautiful rest, all wanderings cease,
Beautiful home of perfect peace;
There shall my eyes the Saviour see;
Haste to this heavenly home with me!

LOOKING HOME.   WM. B. BRADBURY.

1. Ah! this heart is void and chill, 'Mid earth's noisy throng-ing; For my Father's

REFRAIN.

man - sions still Ear - nest - ly is long - ing, Look-ing home, look - ing home,

Towards the heavenly man-sions Je - sus hath prepared for me In his Father's king-dom.

756.

2 Soon the glorious day will dawn,
  Heavenly pleasures bringing;
  Night will be exchanged for morn,
  Sighs give place to singing.—*Refrain.*

3 Oh! to be at home again,
  All for which we're sighing,
  From all earthly want and pain
  To be swiftly flying.—*Refrain.*

4 With this load of sin and care,
  Then no longer bending,
  But with waiting angels there
  On our soul attending.—

Refrain. Blesséd home, blesséd home,
  All for which we're sighing,
  Soon our Lord will bid us come
  To our Father's kingdom.—

SWEET LAND OF REST. C. M.   WM. B. BRADBURY.

1. Sweet land of rest! for thee I sigh, When will the moment come When I shall lay my ar-mor by,
2. No tranquil joys on earth I know, No peaceful, sheltering dome; This world's a wilderness of woe,

REFRAIN.

And dwell with Christ at home. Home, home, sweet, sweet home, And dwell with Christ at home. home.
This world is not my home. Home, home, &c.

757.

3 To Jesus Christ I sought for rest,
  He bade me cease to roam,
  But fly for succor to his breast,
  And he'd conduct me home.
  Home, home, etc.

4 Weary of wandering round and round,
  This vale of sin and gloom,
  I long to leave the unhallowed ground,
  And dwell with Christ at home.
  Home, home, etc.

ZEPHYR. L. M.   Wm. B. Bradbury.

1. A-sleep in Je - sus! bless-ed sleep! From which none ev - er wake to weep;

A calm and un - dis-turbed re - pose, Un - broken by the last of foes.

758.

1 Asleep in Jesus! blessèd sleep!
From which none ever wake to weep;
A calm and undisturbed repose,
Unbroken by the last of foes.

2 Asleep in Jesus! oh, how sweet
To be for such a slumber meet!
With holy confidence to sing
That death hath lost its venomed sting!

3 Asleep in Jesus! peaceful rest!
Whose waking is supremely blest;
No fear—no woe, shall dim the hour
That manifests the Saviour's power.

4 Asleep in Jesus! oh, for me
May such a blissful refuge be:
Securely shall my ashes lie,
And wait the summons from on high.

5 Asleep in Jesus! far from thee
Thy kindred and their graves may be:
But there is still a blessèd sleep
From which none ever wake to weep.

759.

1 Why should we start, and fear to die!
What timorous worms we mortals are!
Death is the gate of endless joy,
And yet we dread to enter there.

2 The pains, the groans, and dying strife
Fright our approaching souls away;
We still shrink back again to life,
Fond of our prison and our clay.

3 Oh, if my Lord would come and meet,
My soul should stretch her wings in haste,
Fly fearless through death's iron gate,
Nor feel the terrors as she passed!

4 Jesus can make a dying bed
Feel soft as downy pillows are,
While on his breast I lean my head,
And breathe my life out sweetly there!

760.

1 How blest the righteous when he dies!
When sinks a weary soul to rest!
How mildly beam the closing eyes!
How gently heaves th' expiring breast!

2 So fades a summer cloud away;
So sinks the gale when storms are o'er:
So gently shuts the eye of day;
So dies a wave along the shore.

3 A holy quiet reigns around,
A calm which life nor death destroys:
And naught disturbs that peace profound
Which his unfettered soul enjoys.

4 Farewell, conflicting hopes and fears,
Where lights and shades alternate dwell;
How bright th' unchanging morn appears!
Farewell, inconstant world, farewell!

5 Life's labor done, as sinks the clay,
Light from its load the spirit flies,
While heaven and earth combine to say,
"How blest the righteous when he dies!"

DODGE. L. M.   J. P. HOLBROOK.

1. Let me be with thee where thou art, My Saviour, my e-ter-nal Rest;

Then on-ly will this long-ing heart Be ful-ly and for-ev-er blest.

761.

1 LET me be with thee where thou art,
My Saviour, my eternal Rest;
Then only will this longing heart
Be fully and forever blest.

2 Let me be with thee where thou art,
Thine unvailed glory to behold;
Then only will this wandering heart
Cease to be false to thee and cold.

3 Let me be with thee where thou art,
Where spotless saints thy name adore;
Then only will this sinful heart
Be evil and defiled no more.

4 Let me be with thee where thou art,
Where none can die, where none remove;
There neither death nor life will part
Me from thy presence and thy love.

762.

1 THE hour of my departure 's come,
I hear the voice that calls me home;
At last, O Lord! let trouble cease,
And let thy servant die in peace.

2 Not in mine innocence I trust;
I bow before thee in the dust;
And thro' my Saviour's blood alone,
I look for mercy at thy throne.

3 I leave the world without a tear,
Save for the friends I held so dear;
To heal their sorrows, Lord, descend,
And to the friendless prove a friend.

4 I come, I come at thy command,
I give my spirit to thy hand;
Stretch forth thine everlasting arms,
And shield me in the last alarms.

5 The hour of my departure 's come,
I hear the voice that calls me home;
Now, oh! my God, let trouble cease,
Now let thy servant die in peace.

763.

1 GENTLY, my Saviour, let me down,
To slumber in the arms of death;
I rest my soul on thee alone,
Ev'n till my last, expiring breath.

2 Soon will the storm of life be o'er,
And I shall enter endless rest;
There I shall live to sin no more,
And bless thy name, forever blest.

3 Bid me possess sweet peace within;
Let child-like patience keep my heart;
Then shall I feel my heaven begin,
Before my spirit hence depart.

4 Oh, speed thy chariot, God of love,
And take me from this world of woe;
I long to reach those joys above,
And bid farewell to all below.

5 There shall my raptured spirit raise
Still louder notes than angels sing,—
High glories to Immanuel's grace,
My God, my Saviour, and my King!

FEDERAL STREET. L. M.   H. K. OLIVER.

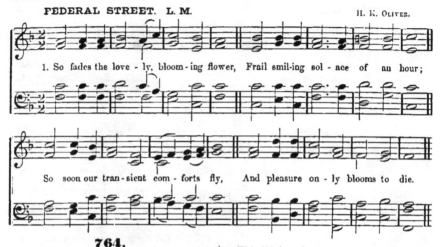

1. So fades the love - ly, bloom - ing flower, Frail smil-ing sol - ace of an hour;

So soon our tran - sient com - forts fly, And pleasure on - ly blooms to die.

764.

2 Is there no kind, no healing art,
To soothe the anguish of the heart?
Divine Redeemer, be thou nigh :
Thy comforts were not made to die.

3 Then gentle patience smiles on pain ;
And dying hope revives again ;
Hope wipes the tear from sorrow's eye,
And faith points upward to the sky.

765.

1 Unvail thy bosom, faithful tomb ;
Take this new treasure to thy trust,
And give these sacred relics room
To slumber in the silent dust.

2 Nor pain, nor grief, nor anxious fear,
Invade thy bounds ; no mortal woes
Can reach the peaceful sleeper here,
While angels watch the soft repose.

3 So Jesus slept ; God's dying Son
Passed thro' the grave, and blessed the bed :
Rest here, blest saint, till from his throne
The morning break, and pierce the shade.

4 Break from his throne, illustrious morn !
Attend, O earth ! his sovereign word :
Restore thy trust : a glorious form
Shall then ascend to meet the Lord !

766.

1 What sinners value I resign ;
Lord ! 't is enough that thou art mine ;
I shall behold thy blissful face,
And stand complete in righteousness.

2 This life 's a dream—an empty show ;
But the bright world, to which I go,
Hath joys substantial and sincere ;
When shall I wake, and find me there ?

3 Oh ! glorious hour !—oh ! blest abode !
I shall be near, and like my God ;
And flesh and sin no more control
The sacred pleasures of the soul.

4 My flesh shall slumber in the ground,
Till the last trumpet's joyful sound ;
Then burst the chains, with sweet surprise,
And in my Saviour's image rise.

767.

1 "We 've no abiding city here :"
Sad truth, were this to be our home ;
But let this thought our spirits cheer,
"We seek a city yet to come."

2 "We 've no abiding city here ;"
We seek a city out of sight :
Zion its name—the Lord is there,
It shines with everlasting light.

3 O sweet abode of peace and love,
Where pilgrims freed from toil are blest !
Had I the pinions of a dove,
I 'd fly to thee, and be at rest.

4 But hush, my soul ! nor dare repine ;
The time my God appoints is best :
While here, to do his will be mine,
And his to fix my time of rest.

JUDGMENT HYMN. L. M. M. LUTHER.

1. { Great God, what do I see and hear! The end of things cre-a - ted! }
{ The Judge of mankind doth appear, On clouds of glo-ry seat - ed: } The trumpet sounds; the

graves re - store The dead which they contained before: Pre-pare, my soul, to meet him.

768.

2 The dead in Christ shall first arise,
At the last trumpet's sounding,
Caught up to meet him in the skies,
With joy their Lord surrounding;
No gloomy fears their souls dismay,
His presence sheds eternal day
On those prepared to meet him.

3 But sinners, filled with guilty fears,
Behold his wrath prevailing;
For they shall rise, and find their tears
And sighs are unavailing:
The day of grace is past and gone;
Trembling they stand before the throne,
All unprepared to meet him.

4 Great God! what do I see and hear!
The end of things created!
The Judge of man I see appear,
On clouds of glory seated:
Beneath his cross I view the day
When heaven and earth shall pass away,
And thus prepare to meet him.

769.

1 THE day of wrath! that dreadful day,
When heaven and earth shall pass away!—
What power shall be the sinner's stay?
How shall he meet that dreadful day?—

2 When, shriveling like a parchéd scroll,
The flaming heavens together roll,

And louder yet, and yet more dread,
Swells the high trump that wakes the dead!

3 Oh, on that day, that wrathful day,
When man to judgment wakes from clay,
Be thou, O Christ, the sinner's stay,
Tho' heaven and earth shall pass away.

770.

1 THE Lord shall come! the earth shall quake;
The mountains to their centre shake;
And withering from the vault of night,
The stars withdraw their feeble light.

2 The Lord shall come! but not the same
As once in lowly form he came,—
A silent Lamb before his foes,
A weary man, and full of woes.

3 The Lord shall come! a dreadful form,
With wreath of flame, and robe of storm,
On cherub-wings, and wings of wind,
Anointed Judge of human kind!

4 Can this be he, who wont to stray
A pilgrim on the world's highway,
By power oppressed, and mocked by pride,—
The Nazarene, the Crucified?

5 While sinners in despair shall call,
"Rocks, hide us! mountains, on us fall!"
The saints, ascending from the tomb,
Shall sing for joy, "The Lord is come!"

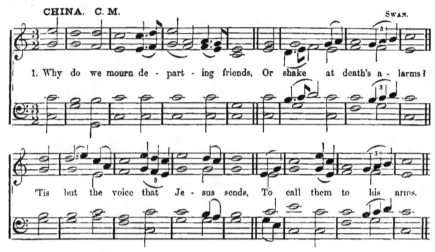

CHINA. C. M.   SWAN.

1. Why do we mourn de - part - ing friends, Or shake at death's a - larms?

'Tis but the voice that Je - sus sends, To call them to his arms.

771.

1 Why do we mourn departing friends,
Or shake at death's alarms?
'Tis but the voice that Jesus sends,
To call them to his arms.

2 Are we not tending upward, too,
As fast as time can move?
Nor would we wish the hours more slow,
To keep us from our love.

3 Why should we tremble to convey
Their bodies to the tomb?
There the dear flesh of Jesus lay,
And scattered all the gloom.

4 The graves of all his saints he blessed,
And softened every bed;
Where should the dying members rest,
But with the dying Head?

5 Thence he arose, ascending high,
And showed our feet the way;
Up to the Lord we, too, shall fly,
At the great rising day.

6 Then let the last loud trumpet sound,
And bid our kindred rise;
Awake! ye nations under ground;
Ye saints! ascend the skies.

772.

1 Why should our tears in sorrow flow,
When God recalls his own;
And bids them leave a world of wo
For an immortal crown?

2 Is not ev'n death a gain to those
Whose life to God was given?
Gladly to earth their eyes they close,
To open them in heaven.

3 Their toils are past, their work is done,
And they are fully blest:
They fought the fight, the victory won,
And entered into rest.

4 Then let our sorrows cease to flow,—
God has recalled his own;
And let our hearts in every woe,
Still say,—"Thy will be done!"

773.

1 How still and peaceful is the grave!
Where, life's vain tumults past,
Th' appointed house, by heaven's decree,
Receives us all at last.

2 The wicked there from troubling cease;
Their passions rage no more;
And there the weary pilgrim rests
From all the toils he bore.

3 There servants, masters, small and great,
Partake the same repose;
And there, in peace, the ashes mix
Of those who once were foes.

4 All, leveled by the hand of death,
Lie sleeping in the tomb,
Till God in judgment calls them forth,
To meet their final doom.

BARBY. C. M.   TANSUR.

1. Oh, for an o - ver - com - ing faith To cheer my dy - ing hours!

To tri - umph o'er the mon - ster, death, And all his fright - ful powers.

774.

1 OH, for an overcoming faith
  To cheer my dying hours!
To triumph o'er the monster, death,
  And all his frightful powers.

2 Joyful, with all the strength I have,
  My quivering lips should sing,
" Where is thy boasted victory, grave?
  And where the monster's sting?"

3 If sin be pardoned, I'm secure ;
  Death has no sting beside :
The law gives sin its damning power,
  But Christ, my ransom, died.

4 Now to the God of victory
  Immortal thanks be paid,
Who makes us conquerors while we die,
  Through Christ our living Head.

775.

1 THRO' sorrow's night, and danger's path,
  Amid the deepening gloom,
We, followers of our suffering Lord,
  Are marching to the tomb.

2 There, when the turmoil is no more,
  And all our powers decay,
Our cold remains in solitude
  Shall sleep the years away.

3 Our labors done, securely laid
  In this our last retreat,
Unheeded o'er our silent dust
  The storms of earth shall beat.

4 Yet not thus buried or extinct,
  The vital spark shall lie ;
For o'er life's wreck that spark shall rise
  To seek its kindred sky.

5 These ashes, too, this little dust,
  Our Father's care shall keep,
Till the last angel rise and break
  The long and dreary sleep.

6 Then love's soft dew o'er every eye
  Shall shed its mildest rays,
And the long-silent voice awake
  With shouts of endless praise.

776.

1 DEAR as thou wert, and justly dear,
  We will not weep for thee :
One thought shall check the starting tear :
  It is, that thou art free.

2 And thus shall faith's consoling power
  The tears of love restrain :
Oh, who that saw thy parting hour,
  Could wish thee back again !

3 Triumphant in thy closing eye
  The hope of glory shone ;
Joy breathed in thy expiring sigh,
  To think the fight was won.

4 Gently the passing spirit fled,
  Sustained by grace divine :
Oh, may such grace on me be shed,
  And make my end like thine !

MORNINGTON. S. M.   Lord Mornington.

1. How swift the tor - rent rolls, That bears us to the sea!

The tide that hur - ries thoughtless souls To vast o - ter - ni - ty.

777.

2 Our fathers, where are they,
   With all they called their own?
Their joys and griefs, and hopes and cares,
   And wealth and honor gone!

3 And where the fathers lie,
   Must all the children dwell;
Nor other heritage possess,
   But such a gloomy cell.

4 God of our fathers hear,
   Thou everlasting Friend!
While we, as on life's utmost verge,
   Our souls to thee commend.

5 Of all the pious dead
   May we the footsteps trace,
Till with them, in the land of light,
   We dwell before thy face.

778.

1 And must this body die?—
   This mortal frame decay?
And must these active limbs of mine
   Lie mouldering in the clay?

2 God, my Redeemer, lives,
   And, often from the skies,
Looks down and watches all my dust,
   Till he shall bid it rise.

3 Arrayed in glorious grace,
   Shall these vile bodies shine;
And every shape, and every face,
   Look heavenly and divine.

4 These lively hopes we owe
   To Jesus' dying love;
We would adore his grace below,
   And sing his power above.

5 Dear Lord! accept the praise
   Of these our humble songs;
Till tunes of nobler sound we raise,
   With our immortal tongues.

779.

1 Come, Lord, and tarry not!
   Bring the long-looked-for day;
Oh, why these years of waiting here,
   These ages of delay?

2 Come, for thy saints still wait;
   Daily ascends their sigh;
The Spirit and the Bride say, Come!
   Dost thou not hear the cry?

3 Come, for creation groans,
   Impatient of thy stay,
Worn out with these long years of ill,
   These ages of delay.

4 Come, and make all things new,
   Build up this ruined earth,
Restore our faded paradise,
   Creation's second birth.

5 Come and begin thy reign
   Of everlasting peace,
Come, take the kingdom to thyself,
   Great King of Righteousness!

GREENWOOD. S. M.

ROOT & SWEETSER'S COLL.

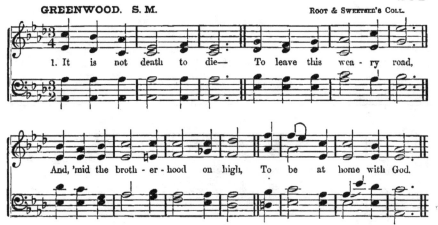

1. It is not death to die— To leave this wea - ry road,

And, 'mid the broth - er - hood on high, To be at home with God.

780.

2 It is not death to close
  The eye long dimmed by tears,
And wake, in glorious repose
  To spend eternal years.

3 It is not death to bear
  The wrench that sets us free
From dungeon chain,—to breathe the air
  Of boundless liberty.

4 It is not death to fling
  Aside this sinful dust,
And rise, on strong exulting wing,
  To live among the just.

5 Jesus, thou Prince of life!
  Thy chosen cannot die;
Like thee, they conquer in the strife,
  To reign with thee on high.

781.

1 " Servant of God, well done,
  Rest from thy loved employ:
The battle fought, the victory won,
  Enter thy Master's joy."

2 The voice at midnight came,
  He started up to hear;
A mortal arrow pierced his frame,
  He fell—but felt no fear.

3 Tranquil amidst alarms,
  It found him on the field,
A veteran slumbering on his arms,
  Beneath his red-cross shield.

4 His spirit, with a bound,
  Left its encumbering clay;
His tent, at sunrise, on the ground,
  A darkened ruin lay.

5 The pains of death are past,
  Labor and sorrow cease;
And, life's long warfare closed at last,
  His soul is found in peace.

6 Soldier of Christ, well done!
  Praise be thy new employ;
And while eternal ages run,
  Rest in thy Saviour's joy.

782.

1 Alas the brittle clay,
  That built our body first!
And, every month, and every day,
  'T is mouldering back to dust.

2 Our moments fly apace,
  Nor will our minutes stay;
Just like a flood, our hasty days
  Are sweeping us away.

3 Well, if our days must fly,
  We 'll keep their end in sight;
We 'll spend them all in wisdom's way,
  And let them speed their flight.

4 They 'll waft us sooner o'er
  This life's tempestuous sea:
Soon we shall reach the peaceful shore
  Of blest eternity.

OLMUTZ. S. M.   *Arranged by* Dr. L. Mason.

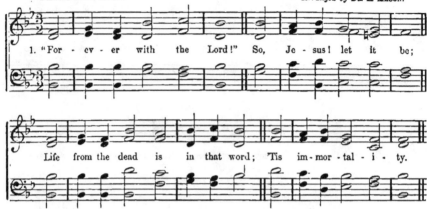

1. "For - ev - er with the Lord!" So, Je - sus! let it be;

Life from the dead is in that word; 'Tis im - mor - tal - i - ty.

783.

1 " Forever with the Lord!"
 So, Jesus! let it be;
 Life from the dead is in that word;
 'T is immortality.

2 Here, in the body pent,
 Absent from thee I roam:
 Yet nightly pitch my moving tent
 A day's march nearer home.

3 My Father's house on high,
 Home of my soul! how near,
 At times, to faith's aspiring eye,
 Thy golden gates appear!

4 " Forever with the Lord!"
 Father, if 't is thy will,
 The promise of thy gracious word,
 Ev'n here to me fulfill.

5 So, when my latest breath
 Shall rend the vail in twain,
 By death I shall escape from death,
 And life eternal gain.

6 Knowing " as I am known,"
 How shall I love that word,
 And oft repeat before the throne,
 " Forever with the Lord!"

784.

1 Oh, for the death of those
 Who slumber in the Lord!
 Oh, be like theirs my last repose,
 Like theirs my last reward!

2 Their bodies in the ground,
 In silent hope may lie,
 Till the last trumpet's joyful sound
 Shall call them to the sky.

3 Their ransomed spirits soar
 On wings of faith and love,
 To meet the Saviour they adore,
 And reign with him above.

4 With us their names shall live
 Through long succeeding years,
 Embalmed with all our hearts can give,
 Our praises and our tears.

5 Oh, for the death of those
 Who slumber in the Lord!
 Oh, be like theirs my last repose,
 Like theirs my last reward!

785.

1 Behold, the day is come;
 The righteous Judge is near;
 And sinners, trembling at their doom,
 Shall soon their sentence hear.

2 How awful is the sight!
 How loud the thunders roar!
 The sun forbears to give his light,
 And stars are seen no more.

3 The whole creation groans;
 But saints arise and sing:
 They are the ransomed of the Lord,
 And he their God and King.

BOYLSTON. S. M. Dr. L. Mason.

1. My soul, re - peat his praise, Whose mer - cies are so great;
Whose an - ger is so slow to rise, So rea - dy to a - bate.

786.

2 The pity of the Lord,
  To those that fear his name,
Is such as tender parents feel;
  He knows our feeble frame.

3 Our days are as the grass,
  Or like the morning flower:
If one sharp blast sweep o'er the field,
  It withers in an hour.

4 But thy compassions, Lord,
  To endless years endure;
And children's children ever find
  Thy words of promise sure.

787.

1 Lord, let me know mine end,
  My days, how brief their date,
That I may timely comprehend
  How frail my best estate.

2 My life is but a span,
  Mine age is nought with thee;
Sure, in his highest honor, man
  Is dust and vanity.

3 Dumb at thy feet I lie,
  For thou hast brought me low;
Remove thy judgments, lest I die;
  I faint beneath thy blow.

4 At thy rebuke, the bloom
  Of man's vain beauty flies;
And grief shall like a moth consume
  All that delights our eyes.

5 Have pity on my fears,
  Hearken to my request;
Turn not in silence from my tears,
  But give the mourner rest.

6 Oh, spare me yet, I pray,
  Awhile my strength restore,
Ere I am summoned hence away,
  And seen on earth no more.

788.

1 Rest for the toiling hand,
  Rest for the anxious brow,
Rest for the weary, way-worn feet,
  Rest from all labor now;—

2 Rest for the fevered brain,
  Rest for the throbbing eye;
Through these parched lips of thine no
    more
  Shall pass the moan or sigh.

3 Soon shall the trump of God
  Give out the welcome sound,
That shakes thy silent chamber-walls,
  And breaks the turf-sealed ground.

4 Ye dwellers in the dust,
  Awake! come forth and sing;
Sharp has your frost of winter been,
  But bright shall be your spring.

5 'T was sown in weakness here;
  'T will then be raised in power:
That which was sown an earthly seed,
  Shall rise a heavenly flower!

FULTON. 7s.   Wm. B. Bradbury.

1. Broth - er, though from yon - der sky Com - eth nei - ther voice nor cry,

Yet we know for thee to - day, Ev - ery pain hath passed a - way.

789.

1 Brother, though from yonder sky
Cometh neither voice nor cry ;
Yet we know for thee to-day,
Every pain hath passed away.

2 Not for thee shall tears be given,
Child of God, and heir of heaven !
For he gave thee sweet release ;
Thine the Christian's death of peace.

3 Well we know thy living faith
Had the power to conquer death ;
As a living rose may bloom
By the border of the tomb.

4 Brother, in that solemn trust
We commend thee, dust to dust !
In that faith we wait, till, risen,
Thou shalt meet us all in heaven.

5 While we weep as Jesus wept,
Thou shalt sleep as Jesus slept :
With thy Saviour thou shalt rest,
Crowned, and glorified, and blest.

790.

1 Hark ! that shout of rapturous joy,
Bursting forth from yonder cloud !
Jesus comes, and through the sky
Angels tell their joy aloud !

2 Hark ! the trumpet's awful voice
Sounds abroad, through sea and land ;
Let his people now rejoice !
Their redemption is at hand.

3 See ! the Lord appears in view ;
Heaven and earth before him fly !
Rise, ye saints, he comes for you—
Rise to meet him in the sky.

4 Go, and dwell with him above,
Where no foe can e'er molest :
Happy in the Saviour's love !
Ever blessing, ever blest.

791.

1 Hark ! a voice divides the sky !
Happy are the faithful dead
In the Lord who sweetly die !
They from all their toils are freed.

2 Ready for their glorious crown,
Sorrows past and sins forgiven,—
Here they lay their burden down,
Hallowed and made meet for heaven.

3 Yes ! the Christian's course is run !
Ended is the glorious strife ;
Fought the fight, the work is done ;
Death is swallowed up in life !

4 Lo ! the prisoner is released—
Lightened of his heavy load ;
Where the weary are at rest,
He is gathered unto God !

5 When from flesh the spirit freed,
Hastens homeward to return,
Mortals cry, " A man is dead !"
Angels sing, " A child is born !"

FREDERICK. 11s.

GEO. KINGSLEY.

1. I would not live alway; I ask not to stay Where storm after storm ris-es dark o'er the way;

The few lurid mornings that dawn on us here, Are enough for life's woes, full enough for its cheer.

792.

2 I would not live alway; no,—welcome the tomb;
Since Jesus hath lain there, I dread not its gloom;
There, sweet be my rest, till he bid me arise,
To hail him in triumph descending the skies.
Who—who would live alway, away from his God;
Away from yon heaven, that blissful abode,
Where the rivers of pleasure flow o'er the bright plains,
And the noontide of glory eternally reigns?

4 There saints of all ages in harmony meet,
Their Saviour and brethren transported to greet;
While anthems of rapture unceasingly roll,
And the smile of the Lord is the feast of the soul.

BAXTER. 10s.

FRANK SLYE.

1. Go to the grave in all thy glorious prime, In full ac-tiv-i-ty of zeal and power;

Thou art not called away before thy time— The Lord's appointment is the servant's hour.

793.

2 Go to the grave: at noon from labor cease;
Rest on thy sheaves, thy harvest task is done;
Come from the heat of battle, and in peace,
Soldier, go home; with thee the fight is won.

3 Go to the grave; for there thy Saviour lay
In death's embraces, ere he rose on high;
And all the ransomed, by that narrow way,
Passed to eternal life beyond the sky.

4 Go to the grave:—no; take thy seat above;
Be thy pure spirit present with the Lord,
Where thou for faith and hope hast perfect love,
And open vision for the written word.

REQUIEM. S. H. M.   Dr. Hastings.

1. This place is ho - ly ground; World, with its cares, a - way!
A ho - ly, sol - emn still - ness round This life - less, mouldering clay;
Nor pain, nor grief, nor anx - ious fear Can reach the peace - ful sleep - er here.

794.

2 Behold the bed of death—
  The pale and mortal clay;
Heard ye the sob of parting breath?
Marked ye the eye's last ray?
No; life so sweetly ceased to be,
It lapsed in immortality.

3 Why mourn the pious dead?
  Why sorrows swell our eyes?
Can sighs recall the spirit fled?
Shall vain regrets arise?
Tho' death has caused this altered mien,
In heaven the ransomed soul is seen.

4 Bury the dead and weep
  In stillness o'er the loss;
Bury the dead! in Christ they sleep,
  Who bore on earth his cross;
And from the grave their dust shall rise,
In his own image to the skies.

795.

1 Friend after friend departs:
  Who hath not lost a friend?

There is no union here of hearts
  That finds not here an end;
Were this frail world our only rest,
Living or dying, none were blest.

2 Beyond the flight of time,
  Beyond this vale of death,
There surely is some blessèd clime
  Where life is not a breath,
Nor life's affections transient fire,
Whose sparks fly upward to expire.

3 There is a world above,
  Where parting is unknown;
A whole eternity of love,
  Formed for the good alone;
And faith beholds the dying here
Translated to that happier sphere.

4 Thus star by star declines,
  Till all are passed away,
As morning high and higher shines,
  To pure and perfect day;
Nor sink those stars in empty night—
They hide themselves in heaven's own
    light.

SCOTLAND. 12s.

DR. CLARKE.

1. The voice of free grace cries, Es-cape to the mountain, For Adam's lost race Christ hath

opened a fountain; { For sin and un-cleanness, and ev-ery trans-gression, His
{ Halle-lu-jah to the Lamb, who hath purchased our pardon, We'll

blood flows most freely in streams of salvation, His blood flows most freely in streams of salvation.
praise him again, when we pass over Jordan, We'll praise him again, when we pass over Jordan.

796.

2 Ye souls that are wounded! oh, flee to the
 Saviour;
He calls you in mercy,—'t is infinite favor;
Your sins are increasing,—escape to the moun-
 tain,—
His blood can remove them,—it flows from the
 fountain.

3 O Jesus! ride onward, triumphantly glorious,
O'er sin, death, and hell, thou art more than
 victorious;
Thy name is the theme of the great congregation,
While angels and men raise the shout of salvation.

4 With joy shall we stand, when escaped to the
 shore;
With harps in our hands, we 'll praise him the
 more;
We 'll range the sweet plains on the bank of the
 river,
And sing of salvation forever and ever!

797.

1 THOU art gone to the grave! but we will not
 deplore thee,
Though sorrow and darkness encompass the
 tomb;

The Saviour hath passed through its portals before thee,
And the lamp of his love is thy guide through
 the gloom.

2 Thou art gone to the grave! we no longer behold thee,
Nor tread the rough paths of the world by thy
 side;
But the wide arms of mercy are spread to en-
 fold thee,
And sinners may hope, for the Sinless hath died.

3 Thou art gone to the grave! and, its mansion
 forsaking,
What though thy weak spirit in fear lingered
 long:
The sunshine of Paradise beamed on thy waking,
And the sound which thou heard'st, was the
 seraphim's song.

4 Thou art gone to the grave! but we will not de-
 plore thee,
For God was thy ransom, thy Guardian, and
 Guide
He gave thee, he took thee, and he will restore
 thee;
And death hath no sting, for the Saviour hath
 died.

DORRNANCE. 8s & 7s.   L. B. WOODBURY.

1. Je-sus, while our hearts are bleed-ing O'er the spoils that death has won,

We would, at this sol-emn meet-ing, Calm-ly say,—thy will be done.

798.

1 JESUS, while our hearts are bleeding
  O'er the spoils that death has won,
  We would at this solemn meeting,
  Calmly say,—thy will be done.

2 Though cast down, we 're not forsaken ;
  Though afflicted, not alone ;
  Thou didst give, and thou hast taken ;
  Blessèd Lord,—thy will be done.

3 Tho' to-day we 're filled with mourning,
  Mercy still is on the throne ;
  With thy smiles of love returning,
  We can sing—thy will be done.

4 By thy hands the boon was given,
  Thou hast taken but thine own :
  Lord of earth, and God of heaven,
  Evermore,—thy will be done !

799.

1 TARRY with me, O my Saviour !
  For the day is passing by ;
  See ! the shades of evening gather,
  And the night is drawing nigh.

2 Deeper, deeper grow the shadows,
  Paler now the glowing west,
  Swift the night of death advances ;
  Shall it be the night of rest ?

3 Lonely seems the vale of shadow ;
  Sinks my heart with troubled fear ;
  Give me faith for clearer vision,
  Speak thou, Lord, in words of cheer.

4 Let me hear thy voice behind me,
  Calming all these wild alarms ;
  Let me, underneath my weakness,
  Feel the everlasting arms.

5 Feeble, trembling, fainting, dying,
  Lord, I cast myself on thee ;
  Tarry with me through the darkness ;
  While I sleep, still watch by me.

6 Tarry with me, O my Saviour !
  Lay my head upon thy breast
  Till the morning ; then awake me—
  Morning of eternal rest !

800.

1 CEASE, ye mourners, cease to languish
  O'er the grave of those you love ;
  Pain and death and night and anguish
  Enter not the world above.

2 While our silent steps are straying
  Lonely thro' night's deepening shade,
  Glory's brightest beams are playing
  Round the happy Christian's head.

3 Light and peace at once deriving
  From the hand of God most high,
  In his glorious presence living,
  They shall never, never die.

4 Now, ye mourners, cease to languish
  O'er the grave of those you love ;
  Far removed from pain and anguish,
  They are chanting hymns above.

MT. VERNON. 8s & 7s.   Dr. L. Mason.

1. Sis - ter, thou wast mild and love - ly, Gen - tle as the sum - mer breeze,

Pleas - ant as the air of eve - ning, When it floats a - mong the trees.

801.

2 Peaceful be thy silent slumber—
  Peaceful in the grave so low :
Thou no more wilt join our number;
  Thou no more our songs shalt know.

3 Dearest sister, thou hast left us,
  Here thy loss we deeply feel ;
But 't is God that hath bereft us,
  He can all our sorrows heal.

4 Yet again we hope to meet thee,
  When the day of life is fled ;
Then in heaven with joy to greet thee,
  Where no farewell tear is shed.

802.

1 See the leaves around us falling,
  Dry and withered to the ground ;
Thus to thoughtless mortals calling,
  In a sad and solemn sound.

2 Sons of Adam, once in Eden,
  When like him, ye blighted fell,
Hear the lesson we are reading,
  'T is alas! the truth we tell.

3 Youth, on length of days presuming,
  Who the paths of pleasure tread,
View us, late in beauty blooming,
  Numbered now among the dead.

4 Though as yet no losses grieve you,
  Gay with health and many a grace,
Let no cloudless skies deceive you ;
  Summer gives to autumn place.

5 Yearly in our course appearing,
  Messengers of shortest stay,
Thus we preach in mortal hearing—
  Ye, like us, shall pass away.

6 On the tree of life eternal,
  Oh, let all our hopes be laid !
This alone, forever vernal,
  Bears a leaf that shall not fade.

803.

1 Great Redeemer, Friend of sinners !
  Thou hast wondrous power to save;
Grant me grace, and still protect me,
  Over life's tempestuous wave.

2 May my soul, with sacred transport,
  View the dawn while yet afar ;
And, until the sun arises,
  Lead me by the Morning Star.

3 See the happy spirits waiting
  On the banks beyond the stream ;
Sweet responses still repeating,
  Jesus, Jesus is their theme.

4 Swiftly roll, ye lingering hours,
  Seraphs lend your glittering wings ;
Love absorbs my ransomed powers,
  Heavenly sounds around me ring.

5 Worlds of light ! and crowns of glory !
  Far above yon azure sky ;
Though by faith I now behold you,
  I 'll enjoy you soon on high.

TAMWORTH. 8s, 7s & 4s.   LOCKHART.

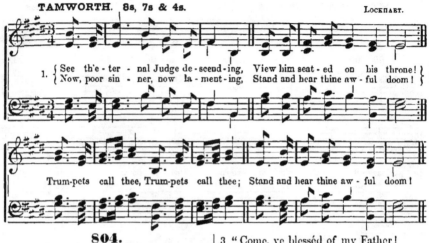

1. { See th'e - ter - nal Judge de - scend - ing, View him seat - ed on his throne! }
{ Now, poor sin - ner, now la - ment - ing, Stand and hear thine aw - ful doom! }

Trum-pets call thee, Trum-pets call thee; Stand and hear thine aw - ful doom!

804.

2 Hear the cries he now is venting,
  Filled with dread of fiercer pain;
While in anguish thus lamenting,
  That he ne'er was born again:
    Greatly mourning,
  That he ne'er was born again.

3 " Yonder sits the slighted Saviour,
  With the marks of dying love;
Oh, that I had sought his favor,
  When I felt his Spirit move!
    Golden moments,
  When I felt his Spirit move."

4 Now, despisers, look and wonder;
  Hope and sinners here must part:
Louder than a peal of thunder,
  Hear the dreadful sound, " Depart!"
    Lost forever,
  Hear the dreadful sound, " Depart!"

805.

1 Lo! he cometh,—countless trumpets
  Wake to life the slumbering dead;
Mid ten thousand saints and angels,
  See their great exalted Head:
    Hallelujah!—
  Welcome, welcome, Son of God!

2 Full of joyful expectation,
  Saints behold the Judge appear:
Truth and justice go before him—
  Now the joyful sentence hear;
    Hallelujah!—
  Welcome, welcome, Judge divine!

3 " Come, ye blessèd of my Father!
  Enter into life and joy;
Banish all your fears and sorrows;
  Endless praise be your employ:"
    Hallelujah!—
  Welcome, welcome to the skies!

806.

1 Lo! he comes with clouds descending,
  Once for favored sinners slain!
Thousand thousand saints attending,
  Swell the triumph of his train!
    Hallelujah!
  Jesus comes, and comes to reign.

2 Every eye shall now behold him,
  Robed in dreadful majesty!
Those who set at naught and sold him,
  Pierced and nailed him to the tree,
    Deeply wailing,
  Shall the true Messiah see!

3 When the solemn trump has sounded,
  Heaven and earth shall flee away;
All who hate him must, confounded,
  Hear the summons of that day—
    Come to judgment!
  Come to judgment! come away!

4 Yea, Amen! let all adore thee,
  High on thine eternal throne!
Saviour, take the power and glory;
  Make thy righteous sentence known!
    Oh, come quickly,
  Claim the kingdom for thine own!

BREST. 8s, 7s & 4s. CARMINA SACRA.

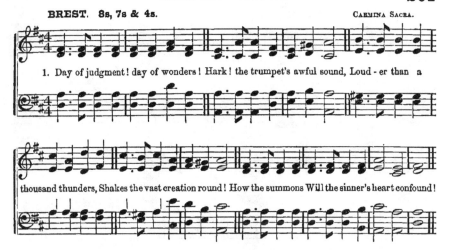

1. Day of judgment! day of wonders! Hark! the trumpet's awful sound, Loud - er than a

thousand thunders, Shakes the vast creation round! How the summons Will the sinner's heart confound!

807.

1 Day of judgment! day of wonders!
Hark!—the trumpet's awful sound,
Louder than a thousand thunders,
Shakes the vast creation round :
How the summons
Will the sinner's heart confound!

2 See the Judge, our nature wearing,
Clothed in majesty divine!
You, who long for his appearing,
Then shall say, " This God is mine!"
Gracious Saviour!
Own me in that day for thine.

3 At his call, the dead awaken,
Rise to life from earth and sea ;
All the powers of nature, shaken
By his looks, prepare to flee :
Careless sinner!
What will then become of thee?

4 But to those who have confessèd,
Loved and served the Lord below,
He will say,—" Come near, ye blessèd!
See the kingdom I bestow :
You forever
Shall my love and glory know."

808.

1 Lo! the mighty God appearing—
From on high Jehovah speaks!

Eastern lands the summons hearing,
O'er the west his thunder breaks :
Earth beholds him :
Universal nature shakes.

2 Zion all its light unfolding,
God in glory shall display :
Lo! he comes,—nor silence holding,
Fire and clouds prepare his way :
Tempests round him
Hasten on the dreadful day.

3 To the heavens his voice ascending,
To the earth beneath he cries—
" Souls immortal now descending,
Let the sleeping dust arise!
Rise to judgment ;
Let my throne adorn the skies.

4 " Gather first my saints around me,
Those who to my covenant stood ;
Those who humbly sought and found me,
Through the dying Saviour's blood :
Blest Redeemer!
Choicest sacrifice to God!"

5 Now the heavens on high adore him,
And his righteousness declare :
Sinners perish from before him,
But his saints his mercies share :
Just his judgment!
God, himself the Judge, is there.

LOWRY. L. M.

Root & Sweetser's Coll.

1. Oh, for a sweet, in-spiring ray, To an-i-mate our fee - ble strains,

From the bright realms of end-less day— The bliss-ful realms where Je - sus reigns.

809.

2 There, low before his glorious throne,
Adoring saints and angels fall ;
And, with delightful worship, own
His smile their bliss, their heaven, their all.

3 Immortal glories crown his head,
While tuneful hallelujahs rise,
And love and joy and triumph spread
Through all th' assemblies of the skies.

4 He smiles,—and seraphs tune their songs
To boundless rapture, while they gaze ;
Ten thousand thousand joyful tongues
Resound his everlasting praise.

5 There all the followers of the Lamb
Shall join at last the heavenly choir :
Oh, may the joy-inspiring theme
Awake our faith and warm desire !

810.

1 Now let our souls, on wings sublime,
Rise from the vanities of time,
Draw back the parting vail, and see
The glories of eternity.

2 Born by a new celestial birth,
Why should we grovel here on earth ?
Why grasp at transitory toys,
So near to heaven's eternal joys ?

3 Should aught beguile us on the road,
When we are walking back to God ?
For strangers into life we come,
And dying is but going home.

4 Welcome, sweet hour of full discharge !
That sets our longing souls at large,
Unbinds our chains, breaks up our cell,
And gives us with our God to dwell.

5 To dwell with God—to feel his love,
Is the full heaven enjoyed above ;
And the sweet expectation now
Is the young dawn of heaven below.

811.

1 Descend from heaven, immortal Dove !
Stoop down and take us on thy wings ;
And mount, and bear us far above
The reach of these inferior things,—

2 Beyond, beyond this lower sky,
Up where eternal ages roll,
Where solid pleasures never die,
And fruits immortal feast the soul.

3 Oh, for a sight, a pleasing sight,
Of our almighty Father's throne !
There sits our Saviour, crowned with
light,
Clothed in a body like our own.

4 Adoring saints around him stand,
And thrones and powers before him fall :
The God shines gracious through the Man,
And sheds sweet glories on them all.

5 Oh ! what amazing joys they feel,
While to their golden harps they sing,
And sit on every heavenly hill,
And spread the triumph of their king !

PALMER. S. M.

J. N. PATTISON.

1. I have a home a - bove, From sin and sor - row free;

A man - sion which e - ter - nal love De - signed and formed for me.

812.

2 My Father's gracious hand
    Has built this sweet abode;
  From everlasting it was planned—
    My dwelling-place with God.

3 My Saviour's precious blood
    Has made my title sure;
  He passed thro' death's dark raging flood
    To make my rest secure.

4 The Comforter is come,
    The earnest has been given;
  He leads me onward to the home
    Reserved for me in heaven.

5 Loved ones are gone before,
    Whose pilgrim days are done;
  I soon shall greet them on that shore
    Where partings are unknown.

813.

1 AND is there, Lord, a rest
    For weary souls designed,
  Where not a care shall stir the breast,
    Or sorrow entrance find?

2 Is there a blissful home,
    Where kindred minds shall meet,
  And live, and love, nor ever roam
    From that serene retreat?

3 Are there bright, happy fields,
    Where nought that blooms shall die;
  Where each new scene fresh pleasure
        yields,
    And healthful breezes sigh?

4 Are there celestial streams,
    Where living waters glide,
  With murmurs sweet as angel dreams,
    And flowery banks beside?

5 Forever blessèd they,
    Whose joyful feet shall stand,
  While endless ages waste away,
    Amid that glorious land!

6 My soul would thither tend,
    While toilsome years are given;
  Then let me, gracious God, ascend
    To sweet repose in heaven!

814.

1 FAR from my heavenly home,
    Far from my Father's breast.
  Fainting, I cry, "Blest Spirit, come,
    And speed me to my rest!"

2 Upon the willows long
    My harp has silent hung;
  How should I sing a cheerful song,
    Till thou inspire my tongue?

3 My spirit homeward turns,
    And fain would thither flee;
  My heart, O Zion, droops and yearns,
    When I remember thee.

4 To thee, to thee I press—
    A dark and toilsome road:
  When shall I pass the wilderness,
    And reach the saints' abode?

VICTORY. 10s.

1. { Joy - ful - ly, joy - ful - ly on - ward I move, Bound to the land of bright
   { An - gel - ic chor - is - ters sing as I come, "Joy - ful - ly, joy - ful - ly

spi - rits a - bove; } { Soon, with my pil - grim - age end - ed be - low, }
haste to thy home!" } { Home to the land of bright spi - rits I go; }

Pilgrim and stranger no more shall I roam, Joy - ful - ly, joy - ful - ly rest - ing at home.

815.

2 Friends, fondly cherished, have passed on
    before;
  Waiting, they watch me approaching the
    shore;
  Singing to cheer me thro' death's chilling
    gloom:
  "Joyfully, joyfully haste to thy home!"
  Sounds of sweet melody fall on my ear;
  Harps of the blessèd, your voices I hear!
  Rings with the harmony heaven's high
    dome—
  "Joyfully, joyfully haste to thy home!"

3 Death, with thy weapons of war lay me
    low,
  Strike, king of terrors! I fear not the
    blow;
  Jesus hath broken the bars of the tomb!
  Joyfully, joyfully will I go home.
  Bright will the morn of eternity dawn,
  Death shall be banished, his sceptre be
    gone;
  Joyfully, then shall I witness his doom,
  Joyfully, joyfully, safely at home.

816.

1 HAPPY the spirit released from its clay;
  Happy the soul that goes bounding
    away;
  Singing, as upward it hastes to the skies,
  Victory! victory! homeward I rise.
  Many the toils it has passed through
    below,
  Many the seasons of trial and woe;
  Many the doubtings it never should sing,
  Victory! victory! thus on the wing.

2 How can we wish them recalled from
    their home,
  Longer in sorrowing exile to roam?
  Safely they passed from their troubles
    beneath,
  Victory! victory! shouting in death.
  Thus let them slumber, till Christ from
    the skies,
  Bids them in glorified body arise;
  Singing, as upward they spring from the
    tomb,
  Victory! victory! Jesus hath come.

BEULAH. 7s. Double.

E. IVES, JR.

1. Who are these in bright ar - ray, This in - nu - mer - a - ble throng,

Round the al - tar, night and day, Hymn - ing one tri - umph - ant song! —
D. s. Wis - dom, rich - es to ob - tain; New do - min - ion ev - cry hour."

"Wor - thy is the Lamb once slain, Bless - ing, hon - or, glo - ry, power,

817.

2 These through fiery trials trod, —
  These from great affliction came:
Now before the throne of God,
  Scaled with his almighty name,
Clad in raiment pure and white,
  Victor-palms in every hand,
Through their dear Redeemer's might
  More than conquerors they stand.

3 Hunger, thirst, disease unknown,
  On immortal fruits they feed:
Them, the Lamb, amidst the throne,
  Shall to living fountains lead:
Joy and gladness banish sighs,
  Perfect love dispel all fears,
And forever from their eyes
  God shall wipe away the tears.

818.

1 HIGH in yonder realms of light,
  Dwell the raptured saints above;
Far beyond our feeble sight,
  Happy in Immanuel's love:
Once they knew, like us below,
  Pilgrims in this vale of tears,
Torturing pain and heavy woe,
  Gloomy doubts, distressing fears.

2 Oft the big, unbidden tear,
  Stealing down the furrowed cheek,
Told, in eloquence sincere,
  Tales of woe they could not speak.
But these days of weeping o'er,
  Passed this scene of toil and pain,
They shall feel distress no more —
  Never, never weep again.

3 'Mid the chorus of the skies,
  'Mid th' angelic lyres above,
Hark, their songs melodious rise,
  Songs of praise to Jesus' love!
Happy spirits, ye are fled
  Where no grief can entrance find;
Lulled to rest the aching head,
  Soothed the anguish of the mind.

4 All is tranquil and serene,
  Calm and undisturbed repose;
There no cloud can intervene,
  There no angry tempest blows;
Every tear is wiped away,
  Sighs no more shall heave the breast,
Night is lost in endless day,
  Sorrow — in eternal rest.

WOODLAND. C. M.   N. D. GOULD.

1. There is an hour of peaceful rest, To mourning wanderers given; There is a joy for souls distressed, A balm for ev-ery wounded breast: 'Tis found a-bove—in heaven.

819.

1 THERE is an hour of peaceful rest,
    To mourning wanderers given ;
There is a joy for souls distressed,
A balm for every wounded breast :
    'T is found above—in heaven.

2 There is a home for weary souls,
    By sin and sorrow driven,—
When tossed on life's tempestuous shoals,
Where storms arise, and ocean rolls,
    And all is drear—but heaven.

3 There faith lifts up her cheerful eye
    To brighter prospects given ;
And views the tempest passing by,
The evening shadows quickly fly,
    And all serene—in heaven.

4 There fragrant flowers immortal bloom,
    And joys supreme are given ;
There rays divine disperse the gloom ;
Beyond the confines of the tomb
    Appears the dawn of heaven !

820.

1 GIVE me the wings of faith, to rise
    Within the vail, and see
The saints above,—how great their joys,—
How bright their glories be.

2 I ask them,—whence their victory came ?
    They, with united breath,
Ascribe their conquest to the Lamb,—
    Their triumph to his death.

3 They marked the footsteps he had trod ;
    His zeal inspired their breast ;
And following their incarnate God,
    Possess the promised rest.

4 Our glorious Leader claims our praise,
    For his own pattern given,—
While the long cloud of witnesses
    Show the same path to heaven.

821.

1 FATHER ! I long, I faint, to see
    The place of thine abode ;
I 'd leave thine earthly courts, and flee
    Up to thy seat, my God !

2 Here I behold thy distant face,
    And 't is a pleasing sight ;
But, to abide in thine embrace
    Is infinite delight !

3 I 'd part with all the joys of sense,
    To gaze upon thy throne ;
Pleasure springs fresh forever thence,
    Unspeakable, unknown.

4 There all the heavenly hosts are seen ;
    In shining ranks they move ;
And drink immortal vigor in,
    With wonder and with love.

5 Father ! I long, I faint to see
    The place of thine abode ;
I 'd leave thine earthly courts to be
    Forever with my God.

TAPPAN. C. M.

Geo. Kingsley.

1. On Jor-dan's rug-ged banks I stand, And cast a wish-ful eye To Canaan's fair and hap-py land, To Canaan's fair and happy land, Where my possess-ions lie.

822.

2 Oh, the transporting, rapturous scene,
   That rises to my sight!
Sweet fields arrayed in living green ;
   And rivers of delight!

3 O'er all those wide extended plains
   Shines one eternal day ;
There God, the Sun, forever reigns,
   And scatters night away.

4 No chilling winds, or poisonous breath,
   Can reach that healthful shore ;
Sickness and sorrow, pain and death,
   Are felt and feared no more.

5 When shall I reach that happy place,
   And be forever blest?
When shall I see my Father's face,
   And in his bosom rest?

6 Filled with delight, my raptured soul
   Can here no longer stay ;
Though Jordan's waves around me roll,
   Fearless I 'd launch away.

823.

1 There is a land of pure delight,
   Where saints immortal reign,
Infinite day excludes the night,
   And pleasures banish pain.

2 There everlasting spring abides,
   And never-withering flowers :
Death, like a narrow sea, divides
   This heavenly land from ours.

3 Sweet fields beyond the swelling flood
   Stand dressed in living green ;
So to the Jews old Canaan stood,
   While Jordan rolled between.

4 But timorous mortals start and shrink
   To cross this narrow sea,
And linger, shivering on the brink,
   And fear to launch away.

5 Oh, could we make our doubts remove,
   These gloomy doubts that rise,
And see the Canaan that we love,
   With unbeclouded eyes :—

6 Could we but climb where Moses stood,
   And view the landscape o'er,—
Not Jordan's stream, nor death's cold
      flood,
   Should fright us from the shore.

824.

1 Seraphs, with elevated strains,
   Circle the throne around,
And move and charm the starry plains
   With an immortal sound.

2 Jesus, the Lord, their harps employs ;
   Jesus, my Love, they sing :
Jesus, the name of both our joys,
   Sounds sweet from every string.

3 I would begin the music here,
   And so my soul should rise ;
Oh, for some heavenly notes to bear
   My spirit to the skies !

RHINE. C. M.　　　　　　　　　　　　　　　*German Melody.*

1. O moth - er dear, Je - ru - sa - lem, When shall I come to thee? When

shall my sor - rows have an end? Thy joys when shall I see? Thy joys when shall I see?

825.

2 O happy harbor of God's saints!
　O sweet and pleasant soil!
　In thee no sorrow can be found,
　　Nor grief, nor care, nor toil.

3 No dimly cloud o'ershadows thee,
　Nor gloom, nor darksome night;
　But every soul shines as the sun,
　　For God himself gives light.

4 Thy walls are made of precious stone,
　Thy bulwarks diamond-square,
　Thy gates are all of orient pearl—
　　O God! if I were there!

826.

1 O my sweet home, Jerusalem!
　Thy joys when shall I see?—
　The King that sitteth on thy throne
　　In his felicity?

2 Thy gardens and thy goodly walks
　Continually are green,
　Where grow such sweet and pleasant
　　flowers
　As nowhere else are seen.

3 Right thro' thy streets with pleasing
　　sound
　The flood of life doth flow;
　And on the banks, on either side,
　The trees of life do grow.

4 Those trees each month yield ripened
　　fruit;
　Forevermore they spring,
　And all the nations of the earth
　To thee their honors bring.

5 O mother dear, Jerusalem!
　When shall I come to thee?
　When shall my sorrows have an end?
　Thy joys when shall I see?

827.

1 ARISE, my soul, fly up and run
　Through every heavenly street;
　And say there's naught below the sun
　That's worthy of thy feet.

2 There, on a high, majestic throne,
　Th' Almighty Father reigns,
　And sheds his glorious goodness down
　On all the blissful plains.

3 Bright, like a sun, the Saviour sits,
　And spreads eternal noon;
　No evenings there, nor gloomy nights,
　To want the feeble moon.

4 Amid those ever-shining skies
　Behold the sacred Dove;
　While banished sin and sorrow flies
　From all the realms of love.

5 But oh, what beams of heavenly grace
　Transport them all the while!
　Ten thousand smiles from Jesus' face,
　And love in every smile!

6 Jesus, and when shall that dear day,
　That joyful hour appear,
　When I shall leave this house of clay,
　To dwell among them there?

MONSON. C. M.

Brown.

1. In vain our fan - cy strives to paint The mo - ment af - ter death,

The glo - ries that sur - round a saint When yield - ing up his breath.

828.

1 In vain our fancy strives to paint
The moment after death,
The glories that surround a saint
When yielding up his breath.

2 One gentle sigh the bondage breaks;
We scarce can say—he's gone!
Before the willing spirit takes
Its mansion near the throne.

3 Faith strives, but all its efforts fail
To trace the spirit's flight;
No eye can pierce within the vail
Which hides the world of light.

4 Thus much, and 't is enough to know,
Saints are completely blest;
Have done with sin, and care, and woe,
And with their Saviour rest.

5 On harps of gold they praise his name,
And see him face to face;
Oh, let us catch the heavenly flame,
And live in his embrace!

829.

1 While thro' this changing world we roam
From infancy to age,
Heaven is the Christian pilgrim's home,
His rest at every stage.

2 Thither, his raptured thought ascends,
Eternal joys to share;
There, his adoring spirit bends,
While here, he kneels in prayer.

3 From earth his freed affections rise,
To fix on things above,
Where all his hope of glory lies—
Where all is perfect love.

4 There, too, may we our treasure place—
There let our hearts be found;
That still, where sin abounded, grace
May more and more abound.

5 Henceforth, our conversation be,
With Christ before the throne;
Ere long we, eye to eye, shall see,
And know as we are known.

830.

1 There is a house not made with hands,
Eternal, and on high;
And here my spirit waiting stands,
Till God shall bid it fly.

2 Shortly this prison of my clay
Must be dissolved and fall;
Then, O my soul, with joy obey
Thy heavenly Father's call.

3 We walk by faith of joys to come;
Faith lives upon his word;
But while the body is our home,
We 're absent from the Lord.

4 'T is pleasant to believe thy grace,
But we had rather see;
We would be absent from the flesh,
And present, Lord, with thee.

AMSTERDAM. 7s & 6s.   DR. NARES.

1. { Rise, my soul, and stretch thy wings, Thy bet-ter por-tion trace; }
   { Rise from tran-si-to-ry things Toward heaven, thy na-tive place: }

Sun, and moon, and stars de-cay, Time shall soon this earth re-move;

Rise, my soul, and haste a-way To seats pre-pared a-bove.

831.

2 Rivers to the ocean run,
  Nor stay in all their course;
Fire ascending, seeks the sun,
  Both speed them to their source:
So a soul that's born of God,
  Pants to view his glorious face,
Upward tends to his abode,
  To rest in his embrace.

3 Cease, ye pilgrims, cease to mourn,
  Press onward to the prize;
Soon our Saviour will return
  Triumphant in the skies:
There we'll join the heavenly train,
  Welcomed to partake the bliss;
Fly from sorrow and from pain
  To realms of endless peace.

832.

1 TELL me not of earthly toys
  The worldling may admire,
Tell me not of transient joys
  That sparkle and expire;
For there is a heavenly store,
  Earthly riches cannot buy,
Bliss supreme forevermore—
  A glorious home on high.

2 Tell me of my sin forgiven,
  Through Christ's atoning blood,
Point me to the rest of heaven,
  And bid me hope in God:
Tell me of the mansions blest
  By the Lord of life prepared,
Where the weary are at rest,
  No more by sin ensnared.

833.

1 TIME is winging us away
  To our eternal home:
Life is but a winter's day,
  A journey to the tomb;
Youth and vigor soon will flee,
  Blooming beauty lose its charms;
All that's mortal soon will be
  Enclosed in death's cold arms.

2 Time is winging us away
  To our eternal home:
Life is but a winter's day,
  A journey to the tomb:
But the Christian shall enjoy
  Health and beauty soon above:
Far beyond the world's alloy,
  Secure in Jesus' love.

FROST. 7s & 6s. J. P. HOLBROOK.

1. There is a ho - ly cit - y, A hap - py world a - bove,

Be - yond the star - ry re - gions, Built by the God of love;
D. S. There serve their great Re - deem - er, And dwell with him in light.

An ev - er - last - ing tem - ple, And saints ar - rayed in white,

834.

2 The meanest child of glory
 Outshines the radiant sun;
But who can speak the splendor
Of that eternal throne
Where Jesus sits exalted,
 In godlike majesty?
The elders fall before him,
The angels bend the knee.

3 The hosts of saints around him
 Proclaim his work of grace;
The patriarchs and prophets,
And all the godly race,
Who speak of fiery trials
And tortures on their way—
They came from tribulation
To everlasting day.

4 And what shall be my journey,
 How long I'll stay below,
Or what shall be my trials,
 Are not for me to know;
In every day of trouble,
 I'll raise my thoughts on high;
I'll think of the bright temple,
And crowns above the sky.

835.

1 THERE is a land immortal,
 The beautiful of lands;
Beside its ancient portal
 A silent sentry stands;
He only can undo it,
 And open wide the door;
And mortals who pass through it,
 Are mortals nevermore.

2 Though dark and drear the passage
 That leadeth to the gate,
Yet grace comes with the message,
 To souls that watch and wait;
And at the time appointed
 A messenger comes down,
And leads the Lord's anointed
 From cross to glory's crown.

3 Their sighs are lost in singing,
 They're blessèd in their tears;
Their journey heavenward winging,
 They leave on earth their fears:
Death like an angel seemeth;
 "We welcome thee," they cry,
Their face with glory beameth—
 'Tis life for them to die!

WINCHESTER. L. M.　　　　　　　　　Dr. Croft.

1. Great God! we sing that might-y hand, By which sup-port-ed still we stand;

The opening year thy mer-cy shows,— Let mer-cy crown it till it close.

836.
New Year.

2 By day, by night—at home, abroad,
Still we are guarded by our God ;
By his incessant bounty fed,
By his unerring counsel led.

3 With grateful hearts the past we own ;
The future—all to us unknown—
We to thy guardian care commit,
And peaceful leave before thy feet.

4 In scenes exalted or depressed,
Be thou our joy, and thou our rest;
Thy goodness all our hopes shall raise,
Adored, through all our changing days.

5 When death shall close our earthly songs,
And seal, in silence, mortal tongues,
Our helper, God, in whom we trust,
Shall keep our souls and guard our dust.

837.
Thanksgiving.

1 Eternal source of every joy,
Well may thy praise our lips employ,
While in thy temple we appear,
To hail thee, Sovereign of the year !

2 Wide as the wheels of nature roll,
Thy hand supports and guides the whole,
The sun is taught by thee to rise,
And darkness when to vail the skies.

3 The flowery spring at thy command,
Perfumes the air, adorns the land ;
The summer rays with vigor shine,
To raise the corn, and cheer the vine.

4 Thy hand, in autumn, richly pours,
Through all our coasts, redundant stores :
And winters, softened by thy care,
No more the face of horror wear.

5 Seasons and months, and weeks, and days,
Demand successive songs of praise ;
And be the grateful homage paid,
With morning light and evening shade.

6 Here in thy house let incense rise,
And circling Sabbaths bless our eyes,
Till to those lofty heights we soar,
Where days and years revolve no more.

838.
New Year.

1 Our Helper, God ! we bless thy name,
Whose love forever is the same ;
The tokens of thy gracious care
Open, and crown, and close the year.

2 Amid ten thousand snares we stand,
Supported by thy guardian hand ;
And see, when we review our ways,
Ten thousand monuments of praise.

3 Thus far thine arm has led us on ;
Thus far we make thy mercy known ;
And, while we tread this desert land,
New mercies shall new songs demand.

4 Our grateful souls, on Jordan's shore,
Shall raise one sacred pillar more ;
Then bear, in thy bright courts above,
Inscriptions of immortal love.

YOAKLEY. L. M.

Yoakley.

1. While o'er the deep thy ser-vants sail, Send thou, O Lord, the prosperous gale;

And on their hearts, where'er they go, Oh, let thy heavenly breez - es blow!

839.
Seamen.

2 When tempests rock the groaning bark,
Oh, hide them safe in Jesus' ark!
When in the tempting port they ride,
Oh, keep them safe at Jesus' side!

3 If life's wide ocean smile or roar,
Still guide them to the heavenly shore;
And grant their dust in Christ may sleep,
Abroad, at home, or in the deep.

840.
National.

1 O GOD, beneath thy guiding hand,
Our exiled fathers crossed the sea;
And when they trod the wintry strand,
With prayer and psalm they worshiped
thee.

2 Thou heard'st, well pleased, the song, the
prayer:
Thy blessing came; and still its power
Shall onward through all ages bear
The memory of that holy hour.

3 Laws, freedom, truth, and faith in God
Came with those exiles o'er the waves;
And where their pilgrim feet have trod,
The God they trusted guards their graves.

4 And here thy name, O God of love,
Their children's children shall adore,
Till these eternal hills remove,
And spring adorns the earth no more.

841.
Fast.

1 WHILE o'er our guilty land, O Lord,
We view the terrors of thy sword;
Oh, whither shall the hopeless fly?
To whom but thee direct their cry?

2 On thee, our guardian God, we call,
Before thy throne of grace we fall?
And is there no deliverance there?
And must we perish in despair?

3 See, we repent, we weep, we mourn,
To our forsaken God we turn;
Oh, spare our guilty country, spare
The church, which thou hast planted here!

842.
Cemetery.

1 DEAR is the spot where Christians sleep,
And sweet the strains their spirits pour;
Oh, why should we in anguish weep?—
They are not lost, but gone before.

2 Secure from every mortal care,
By sin and sorrow vexed no more,
Eternal happiness they share
Who are not lost, but gone before.

3 To Zion's peaceful courts above
In faith triumphant may we soar,
Embracing in the arms of love,
The friends not lost, but gone before.

4 To Jordan's bank whene'er we come,
And hear the swelling waters roar;
Jesus! convey us safely home,
To friends not lost, but gone before.

GLASGOW. C. M.   ROOT & SWEETSER'S COLL.

1. Lord, while for all man-kind we pray, Of ev-ery clime and coast,

Oh, hear us for our na-tive land— The land we love the most.

843.
National.

2 Oh, guard our shore from every foe,
With peace our borders bless,
With prosperous times our cities crown,
Our fields with plenteousness.

3 Unite us in the sacred love
Of knowledge, truth, and thee;
And let our hills and valleys shout
The songs of liberty.

4 Here may religion, pure and mild,
Smile on our Sabbath hours;
And piety and virtue bless
The home of us and ours.

5 Lord of the nations, thus to thee
Our country we commend;
Be thou her refuge and her trust,
Her everlasting friend.

844.
Seamen.

1 WE come, O Lord, before thy throne,
And, with united plea,
We meet and pray for those who roam
Far off upon the sea.

2 Oh, may the Holy Spirit bow
The sailor's heart to thee,
Till tears of deep repentance flow,
Like rain-drops in the sea!

3 Then may a Saviour's dying love
Pour peace into his breast,
And waft him to the port above
Of everlasting rest.

845.
Fast.

1 SEE, gracious God, before thy throne,
Thy mourning people bend!
'Tis on thy sovereign grace alone,
Our humble hopes depend.

2 Alarming judgments from thy hand,
Thy dreadful power display;
Yet mercy spares this guilty land,
And yet we live to pray.

3 Oh, bid us turn, Almighty Lord,
By thy resistless grace;
Then shall our hearts obey thy word,
And humbly seek thy face.

846.
A Marriage Hymn.

1 SINCE Jesus freely did appear
To grace a marriage feast,
Dear Lord, we ask thy presence here,
To make a wedding guest.

2 Upon the bridal pair look down,
Who now have plighted hands;
Their union with thy favor crown,
And bless the nuptial bands.

3 In purest love their souls unite,
That they, with Christian care,
May make domestic burdens light,
By taking mutual share.

4 Oh, may each soul assembled here,
Be married, Lord, to thee!
Clad in thy robes, made white and fair,
To spend eternity.

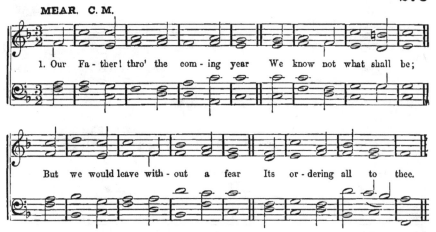

MEAR. C. M.

1. Our Fa - ther! thro' the com - ing year We know not what shall be;

But we would leave with - out a fear Its or - dering all to thee.

847.
New Year.

2 It may be we shall toil in vain
For what the world holds fair;
And all the good we thought to gain,
Deceive and prove but care.

3 It may be it shall darkly blend
Our love with anxious fears,
And snatch away the valued friend,
The tried of many years.

4 It may be it shall bring us days
And nights of lingering pain;
And bid us take a farewell gaze
Of these loved haunts of men.

5 But calmly, Lord, on thee we rest;
No fears our trust shall move;
Thou knowest what for each is best,
And thou art Perfect Love.

848.
Close of Year.

1 THEE we adore, eternal Name!
And humbly own to thee
How feeble is our mortal frame,
What dying worms are we!

2 The year rolls round, and steals away
The breath that first it gave;
Whate'er we do, whate'er we be,
We 're traveling to the grave.

3 Great God! on what a slender thread
Hang everlasting things!
Th' eternal state of all the dead
Upon life's feeble strings!

4 Infinite joy, or endless woe,
Attends on every breath;
And yet, how unconcerned we go
Upon the brink of death!

5 Waken, O Lord, our drowsy sense,
To walk this dangerous road!
And if our souls are hurried hence,
May they be found with God.

849.
Those in Bonds.

1 FOR those in bonds as bound with them
To thee, O God! we pray,
That some celestial, radiant beam
May bring a brighter day.

2 Pity, O Lord! that injured race,
And thy deliverance send;
Grant them the treasures of thy grace,
And bid their bondage end.

3 They sit in darkness, slow to learn
The blessings that they need;
Nor can our anxious thought discern,
How best their cause to plead.

4 All helpless, and without a plan,
We come before thy throne;
We put no confidence in man,
But trust in thee alone.

5 The means of rescue, and the hour,
Thy mercy will reveal:
Thine is the wisdom, thine the power;
Teach us to do thy will.

CASEY. 7s.   HARP OF DAVID.

1. Fount of ev - er - last - ing love! Rich thy streams of mer - cy are—

Flow - ing pure - ly from a - bove, Beau - ty marks their course a - far.

850.
Revival.

2 Lo! thy church, thy garden now
    Blooms beneath the heavenly shower;
Sinners feel, and melt, and bow :
    Mild, yet mighty, is thy power.

3 God of grace, before thy throne
    Here our warmest thanks we bring;
Thine the glory, thine alone :
    Loudest praise to thee we sing.

4 Hear, oh, hear, our grateful song ;
    Let thy Spirit still descend ;
Roll the tide of grace along,
    Widening, deepening, to the end.

851.
Thanksgiving.

1 THANK and praise Jehovah's name,
    For his mercies, firm and sure,
From eternity the same,
    To eternity endure.

2 Let the ransomed thus rejoice,
    Gathered out of every land,
As the people of his choice,
    Plucked from the destroyer's hand.

3 To a pleasant land he brings,
    Where the vine and olive grow,
Where, from flowery hills, the springs
    Through luxuriant valleys flow.

4 Oh, that men would praise the Lord
    For his goodness to their race ;
For the wonders of his word,
    And the riches of his grace.

852.
Thanksgiving.

1 PRAISE to God, immortal praise,
    For the love that crowns our days ;
Bounteous source of every joy !
    Let thy praise our tongues employ.

2 Flocks that whiten all the plain,
    Yellow sheaves of ripened grain ;
Clouds that drop their fattening dews,
    Suns that temperate warmth diffuse : —

3 All that spring with bounteous hand
    Scatters o'er the smiling land ;
All that liberal autumn pours
    From her rich o'erflowing stores ;—

4 Lord, for these our souls shall raise
    Grateful vows, and solemn praise :
And when every blessing 's flown,
    Love thee for thyself alone.

853.
Rain.

1 PRAISE on thee, in Zion's gates,
    Daily, O Jehovah, waits ;
Unto thee, O God, belong
    Grateful words and holy song.

2 Thou dost visit earth, and rain
    Blessings on the thirsty plain,
From the copious founts on high,
    From the rivers of the sky.

3 Thus the clouds thy power confess,
    And thy paths drop fruitfulness,
And the voice of song and mirth
    Rises from the tribes of earth !

WESTMINSTER. 8s & 7s.   J. P. HOLBROOK.

1. Zi-on, drear-y, and in an-guish, In the des-ert hast thou strayed?
O thou wea-ry, cease to lan-guish, Je-sus shall lift up thy head!

854.
Fast.

1 ZION, dreary, and in anguish,
  In the desert hast thou strayed?
  O thou weary, cease to languish,
  Jesus shall lift up thy head!

2 Still lamenting and bemoaning,
  'Mid thy follies and thy woes?
  Soon repenting and returning,
  All thy solitude shall close.

3 Though benighted and forsaken,
  Though afflicted and oppressed,
  His Almighty arm shall waken,
  Zion's King shall give thee rest.

4 Cease thy sadness, unbelieving,
  Soon his glory shalt thou see,
  Joy, and gladness, and thanksgiving,
  And the voice of melody.

855.
Seamen.

1 TOSSED upon life's raging billow,
  Sweet it is, O Lord, to know,
  Thou did'st press a sailor's pillow,
  And canst feel a sailor's woe.

2 Never slumbering, never sleeping,
  Though the night be dark and drear,
  Thou the faithful watch art keeping,
  "All, all 's well," thy constant cheer.

3 And though loud the wind is howling,
  Fierce though flash the lightnings red;
  Darkly though the storm-cloud's scowling
  O'er the sailor's anxious head;—

4 Thou canst calm the raging ocean,
  All its noise and tumult still,
  Hush the tempest's wild commotion,
  At the bidding of thy will.

5 Thus my heart the hope will cherish,
  While to thee I lift mine eye;
  Thou wilt save me ere I perish,
  Thou wilt hear the sailor's cry.

6 And though mast and sail be riven,
  Life's rough course will soon be o'er;
  Safely moored in heaven's wide haven,
  Storm and tempest vex no more.

856.
National Humiliation.

1 DREAD Jehovah! God of nations!
  From thy temple in the skies,
  Hear thy people's supplications,
  Now for their deliverance rise.

2 Lo! with deep contrition turning,
  In thy holy place we bend;
  Hear us, fasting, praying, mourning,
  Hear us, spare us, and defend.

3 Though our sins, our hearts confounding,
  Long and loud for vengeance call,
  Thou hast mercy more abounding,
  Jesus' blood can cleanse them all.

4 Let that mercy vail transgression;
  Let that blood our guilt efface:
  Save thy people from oppression,
  Save from spoil thy holy place.

AMERICA. 6s & 4s.

1. My country, 'tis of thee, Sweet land of lib - er-ty, Of thee I sing: Land where my
fathers died, Land of the pilgrim's pride, From every mountain side Let freedom ring!

857.
National.

2 My native country, thee—
Land of the noble free—
Thy name—I love;
I love thy rocks and rills,
Thy woods and templed hills:
My heart with rapture thrills
Like that above.

3 Let music swell the breeze,
And ring from all the trees
Sweet freedom's song:
Let mortal tongues awake;
Let all that breathe partake;
Let rocks their silence break,—
The sound prolong.

4 Our father's God! to thee,
Author of liberty,
To thee we sing:
Long may our land be bright
With freedom's holy light;
Protect us by thy might,
Great God, our King!

858.
Harvest.

1 THE God of harvest praise;
In loud thanksgiving raise
Hand, heart, and voice!
The valleys laugh and sing;
Forests and mountains ring;
The plains their tribute bring;
The streams rejoice.

2 Yea, bless his holy name,
And joyous thanks proclaim
Through all the earth;

To glory in your lot
Is comely; but be not
God's benefits forgot
Amid your mirth.

3 The God of harvest praise,
Hands, hearts, and voices raise
With sweet accord;
From field to garner throng,
Bearing your sheaves along,
And in your harvest song
Bless ye the Lord.

859.
The Poor.

1 LORD, from thy blessèd throne
Sorrow look down upon!
God save the poor!
Teach them true liberty,
Make them from tyrants free,
Let their homes happy be!
God save the poor!

2 The arms of wicked men
Do thou with might restrain—
God save the poor!
Raise thou their lowliness,
Succor thou their distress,
Thou whom the meanest bless!
God save the poor!

3 Give them stanch honesty,
Let their pride manly be—
God save the poor!
Help them to hold the right,
Give them both truth and might,
Lord of all life and light!
God save the poor!

PART SECOND.

FOR THE CHOIR.

860.
10s.

1 AGAIN returns the day of holy rest,
Which, when he made the world, Jehovah
blessed;
When, like his own, he bade our labors
cease,
And all be piety, and all be peace.

2 Let us devote this consecrated day
To learn his will, and all we learn obey;
So shall he hear, when fervently we raise
Our supplications and our songs of praise.

3 Father of heaven! in whom our hopes
confide,
Whose power defends us, and whose
precepts guide,
In life our Guardian, and in death our
Friend,
Glory supreme be thine, till time shall end.

861.
C. M.

1 AGAIN the Lord of life and light
Awakes the kindling ray,
Dispels the darkness of the night,
And pours increasing day.

2 Oh, what a night was that which wrapt
A guilty world in gloom!
Oh, what a sun which broke this day
Triumphant from the tomb!

3 This day be grateful homage paid,
And loud hosannas sung;
Let gladness dwell in every heart,
And praise on every tongue.

4 Ten thousand thousand voices join
To hail this happy morn,
Which scatters blessings from its wings
On nations yet unborn.

862.
H. M.

1 LORD of the worlds above,
How pleasant and how fair
The dwellings of thy love,
Thine earthly temples are!
To thine abode | With warm desires
My heart aspires, | To see my God.

2 The sparrow for her young
With pleasure seeks a nest;
And wandering swallows long
To find their wonted rest;
My spirit faints | To rise and dwell
With equal zeal, | Among thy saints.

3 Oh, happy souls that pray
Where God appoints to hear!
Oh, happy men, that pay
Their constant service there!
They praise thee still; | That love the way
And happy they | To Zion's hill.

4 They go from strength to strength,
Through this dark vale of tears,
Till each arrives at length,
Till each in heaven appears.
Oh, glorious seat, | Shall thither bring
When God our King | Our willing feet!

863.
S. P. M.

1 How pleased and blessed was I,
To hear the people cry,—
"Come let us seek our God to-day!"
Yes, with a cheerful zeal,
We haste to Zion's hill,
And there our vows and honors pay.

2 Zion, thrice happy place,
Adorned with wondrous grace,
And walls of strength embrace thee round!
In thee our tribes appear
To pray, and praise, and hear
The sacred gospel's joyful sound.

3 Here David's greater Son
 Has fixed his royal throne;
He sits for grace and judgment here:
 He bids the saint be glad;
 He makes the sinner sad;
And humble souls rejoice with fear.

4 May peace attend thy gate,
 And joy within thee wait
To bless the soul of every guest:
 The man that seeks thy peace,
 And wishes thine increase,
A thousand blessings on him rest!

864.
L. C. M.

1 The festal morn, my God! is come,
That calls me to thy sacred dome,
 Thy presence to adore:
My feet the summons shall attend,
With willing steps thy courts ascend,
 And tread the hallowed floor.

2 Ev'n now, to my expecting eyes,
The heaven-built towers of Salem rise;
 Ev'n now, with glad survey,
I view her mansions, that contain
Th' angelic forms,—a glorious train,—
 And shine with cloudless day.

3 Hither, from earth's remotest end,
Lo! the redeemed of God ascend,
 Their tribute hither bring;
Here, crowned with everlasting joy,
In hymns of praise their tongues employ,
 And hail th' immortal King.

865.
C. M.

1 Sing we the song of those who stand
 Around the eternal throne,
Of every kindred, clime, and land,
 A multitude unknown.

2 Life's poor distinctions vanish here;
 To-day the young, the old,
Our Saviour and his flock appear
 One Shepherd and one fold.

3 Toil, trial, suffering, still await
 On earth the pilgrim's throng,
Yet learn we in our low estate
 The Church Triumphant's song.

4 Worthy the Lamb for sinners slain,
 Cry the redeemed above,
Blessing and honor to obtain,
 And everlasting love!

5 Worthy the Lamb, on earth we sing,
 Who died our souls to save!
Henceforth, O Death! where is thy sting!
 Thy victory, O Grave!

866.
S. M.

1 See what a living stone
 The builders did refuse!
Yet God hath built his church thereon,
 In spite of envious Jews.

2 The scribe and angry priest
 Reject thine only Son;
Yet on this rock shall Zion rest
 As the chief corner-stone.

3 The work, O Lord, is thine,
 And wondrous in our eyes;
This day declares it all divine,
 This day did Jesus rise.

4 This is the glorious day,
 That our Redeemer made;
Let us rejoice, and sing, and pray,
 Let all the church be glad.

5 Hosanna to the King
 Of David's royal blood;
Bless him, ye saints; he comes to bring
 Salvation from your God.

6 We bless thy holy word,
 Which all this grace displays;
And offer on thine altar, Lord,
 Our sacrifice of praise.

867.
C. M.

1 And now another week begins,
 This day we call the Lord's;
This day he rose, who bore our sins—
 For so his word records.

2 Hark, how the angels sweetly sing!
 Their voices fill the sky;
They hail their great victorious King,
 And welcome him on high.

3 We'll catch the note of lofty praise;
 May we their rapture feel;
Our thankful songs with theirs we'll raise,
 And emulate their zeal.

4 Come, then, ye saints! and grateful sing
 Of Christ, our risen Lord—
Of Christ, the everlasting King—
 Of Christ, th' incarnate Word.

868.
8s, 7s & 4s.

1 In thy name, O Lord! assembling,
  We thy people now draw near:
  Teach us to rejoice with trembling;
  Speak, and let thy servants hear;
  Hear with meekness—
  Hear thy word with godly fear.

2 While our days on earth are lengthened,
  May we give them, Lord, to thee;
  Cheered by hope, and daily strengthened,
  May we run, nor weary be;
  Till thy glory
  Without cloud in heaven we see.

3 There, in worship purer, sweeter,
  All thy people shall adore;
  Tasting of enjoyment greater
  Than they could conceive before;
  Full enjoyment,—
  Full, and pure, forevermore.

869.
C. M.

1 The Lord of glory is my light,
  And my salvation too;
  God is my strength,—nor will I fear
  What all my foes can do.

2 One privilege my heart desires,—
  Oh! grant me an abode,
  Among the churches of thy saints,—
  The temples of my God.

3 There shall I offer my bequests,
  And see thy beauty still;
  Shall hear thy messages of love,
  And there inquire thy will.

4 When troubles rise, and storms appear,
  There may his children hide;
  God has a strong pavilion, where
  He makes my soul abide.

5 Now shall my head be lifted high
  Above my foes around;
  And songs of joy and victory
  Within thy temple sound.

870.
L. M.

1 When, as returns this solemn day,
  Man comes to meet his Maker God,
  What rites, what honor shall he pay?
  How spread his sovereign name abroad?

2 From marble domes and gilded spires
  Shall curling clouds of incense rise,
  And gems, and gold, and garlands deck
  The costly pomp of sacrifice!

3 Vain, sinful man! creation's Lord
  Thy golden offerings well may spare;
  But give thy heart, and thou shalt find
  Here dwells a God who heareth prayer.

4 Oh, grant us, in this solemn hour,
  From earth and sin's allurements free,
  To feel thy love, to own thy power,
  And raise each raptured thought to thee!

871.
L. M.

1 Blest hour! when mortal man retires
  To hold communion with his God,
  To send to heaven his warm desires,
  And listen to the sacred word.

2 Blest hour! when earthly cares resign
  Their empire o'er his anxious breast,
  While all around the calm divine
  Proclaims the holy day of rest.

3 Blest hour! when God himself draws
      nigh,
  Well pleased his people's voice to hear,
  To hush the penitential sigh,
  And wipe away the mourner's tear.

4 Blest hour! for where the Lord resorts—
  Foretastes of future bliss are given;
  And mortals find his earthly courts
  The house of God, the gate of Heaven!

872.
C. M.

1 Again our earthly cares we leave,
  And to thy courts repair:
  Again with joyful feet we come:
  To meet our Saviour here.

2 Great Shepherd of thy people, hear!
  Thy presence now display;
  We bow within thy house of prayer;
  Oh! give us hearts to pray.

3 The clouds which vail thee from our
      sight,
  In pity, Lord, remove;
  Dispose our minds to hear aright
  The message of thy love.

4 The feeling heart, the melting eye,
  The humble mind bestow;
  And shine upon us from above,
  To make our graces grow.

5 Show us some token of thy love,
  Our fainting hopes to raise;
  And pour thy blessing from above,
  To aid our feeble praise.

873.
L. M.

1 Lo, God is here!—let us adore!
  And own how dreadful is this place!
  Let all within us feel his power,
  And, silent, bow before his face.

2 Lo, God is here!—him day and night
  United choirs of angels sing:
  To him, enthroned above all height,
  Let saints their humble worship bring.

3 Lord God of hosts! oh, may our praise
  Thy courts with grateful incense fill!
  Still may we stand before thy face,
  Still hear and do thy sovereign will.

874.
C. M.

1 Thrice happy souls, who, born from
        heaven,
  While yet they sojourn here,
  Do all their days with God begin,
  And spend them in his fear.

2 'Midst hourly cares, may love present
  Its incense to thy throne;
  And, while the world our hands employs,
  Our hearts be thine alone.

3 As different scenes of life arise,
  Our grateful hearts would be
  With thee, amidst the social band,
  In solitude with thee.

4 In solid, pure delights like these,
  Let all our days be passed;
  Nor shall we then impatient wish,
  Nor shall we fear the last.

875.
7s. Double.

1 Light of life, seraphic fire;
  Love divine, thyself impart;
  Every fainting soul inspire;
  Enter every drooping heart;

Every mournful sinner cheer,
  Scatter all our guilty gloom;
  Father! in thy grace appear,
  To thy human temples come.

2 Come, in this accepted hour,
  Bring thy heavenly kingdom in;
  Fill us with thy glorious power,
  Rooting out the seeds of sin:
  Nothing more can we require,
  We will covet nothing less;
  Be thou all our heart's desire,
  All our joy, and all our peace.

876.
S. M.

1 My God! permit my tongue
  This joy, to call thee mine;
  And let my early cries prevail
  To taste thy love divine.

2 My thirsty, fainting soul
  Thy mercy doth implore;
  Not travelers in desert lands
  Can pant for water more.

3 Within thy churches, Lord!
  I long to find a place,
  Thy power and glory to behold,
  And feel thy quickening grace.

4 Since thou hast been my help,
  To thee my spirit flies;
  And on thy watchful providence
  My cheerful hope relies.

5 The shadow of thy wings
  My soul in safety keeps;
  I follow where my Father leads,
  And he supports my steps.

877.
S. M.

1 Oh, bless the Lord, my soul!
  Let all within me join,
  And aid my tongue to bless his name,
  Whose favors are divine.

2 Oh, bless the Lord, my soul!
  Nor let his mercies lie
  Forgotten in unthankfulness,
  And without praises die.

3 'Tis he forgives thy sins;
  'Tis he relieves thy pain;
  'Tis he that heals thy sicknesses,
  And makes thee young again.

4 He crowns thy life with love,
  When ransomed from the grave;
  He, who redeemed my soul from hell,
  Hath sovereign power to save.

5 His wondrous works and ways
  He made by Moses known;
  But sent the world his truth and grace
  By his beloved Son.

878.
8s & 7s.

1 PRAISE to thee, thou great Creator!
  Praise to thee from every tongue;
  Join, my soul, with every creature,
  Join the universal song.

2 Father! source of all compassion!
  Pure, unbounded grace is thine:
  Hail the God of our salvation,
  Praise him for his love divine!

3 For ten thousand blessings given,
  For the hope of future joy,
  Sound his praise thro' earth and heaven,
  Sound Jehovah's praise on high!

4 Praise to God, the great Creator,
  Father, Son, and Holy Ghost;
  Praise him, every living creature,
  Earth and heaven's united host.

5 Joyfully on earth adore him,
  Till in heaven our song we raise;
  Then enraptured fall before him,
  Lost in wonder, love, and praise!

879.
7s.

1 SONGS of praise the angels sang,
  Heaven with hallelujahs rang,
  When Jehovah's work begun,
  When he spake, and it was done.

2 Songs of praise awoke the morn,
  When the Prince of Peace was born;
  Songs of praise arose, when he,
  Captive led captivity.

3 Heaven and earth must pass away—
  Songs of praise shall crown that day;
  God will make new heavens and earth—
  Songs of praise shall hail their birth.

4 And shall man alone be dumb,
  Till that glorious kingdom come?
  No; the Church delights to raise
  Psalms and hymns and songs of praise.

5 Saints below, with heart and voice,
  Still in songs of praise rejoice;
  Learning here, by faith and love,
  Songs of praise to sing above.

6 Borne upon their latest breath,
  Songs of praise shall conquer death;
  Then, amidst eternal joy,
  Songs of praise their powers employ.

880.
7s.

1 PRAISE the Lord—his power confess;
  Praise him in his holiness;
  Praise him as the theme inspires,—
  Praise him as his fame requires.

2 Let the trumpet's lofty sound
  Spread its loudest notes around;
  Let the harp unite, in praise,
  With the sacred minstrel's lays.

3 Let the organ join to bless
  God, the Lord of righteousness;
  Tune your voice to spread the fame
  Of the great Jehovah's name.

4 All who dwell beneath his light,
  In his praise your hearts unite;
  While the stream of song is poured,
  Praise and magnify the Lord.

881.
7s.

1 THOU who art enthroned above,
  Thou by whom we live and move!
  Oh, how sweet, with joyful tongue,
  To resound thy praise in song!

2 Sweet the day of sacred rest,
  When devotion fills the breast,
  When we dwell within thy house,
  Hear thy word, and pay our vows;

3 Notes to heaven's high mansions raise
  Fill its courts with joyful praise;
  With repeated hymns proclaim
  Great Jehovah's awful name.

4 From thy works our joys arise,
  O thou only good and wise!
  Who thy wonders can declare?
  How profound thy counsels are!

5 Warm our hearts with sacred fire;
  Grateful fervors still inspire;
  All our powers, with all their might,
  Ever in thy praise unite.

882.
C. M.

1 PRAISE ye the Lord, immortal choirs,
　That fill the worlds above;
　Praise him who formed you of his fires,
　And feeds you with his love.

2 Shine to his praise, ye crystal skies,
　The floor of his abode;
　Or vail in shade your thousand eyes,
　Before your brighter God.

3 Shout to the Lord, ye surging seas,
　In your eternal roar;
　Let wave to wave resound his praise,
　And shore reply to shore.

4 Wave your tall heads, ye lofty pines,
　To him that bids you grow;
　Sweet clusters, bend the fruitful vines
　On every thankful bough.

5 Thus while the meaner creatures sing,
　Ye mortals, take the sound;
　Echo the glories of your King
　Through all the earth around.

883.
8s & 7s. Double.

1 LORD, with glowing heart I'd praise thee
　For the bliss thy love bestows;
　For the pardoning grace that saves me,
　And the peace that from it flows:
　Help, O God, my weak endeavor;
　This dull soul to rapture raise;
　Thou must light the flame, or never
　Can my love be warmed to praise.

2 Praise, my soul, the God that sought thee,
　Wretched wanderer, far astray;
　Found thee lost, and kindly brought thee
　From the paths of death away;
　Praise, with love's devoutest feeling,
　Him who saw thy guilt-born fear,
　And, the light of hope revealing,
　Bade the blood-stained cross appear.

3 Lord, this bosom's ardent feeling
　Vainly would my lips express:
　Low before thy footstool kneeling,
　Deign thy suppliant's prayer to bless;
　Let thy grace, my soul's chief treasure,
　Love's pure flame within me raise;
　And, since words can never measure,
　Let my life show forth thy praise.

884.
L. M.

1 OH, render thanks to God above,
　The fountain of eternal love;
　Whose mercy firm, through ages past,
　Hath stood, and shall forever last.

2 Who can his mighty deeds express,
　Not only vast—but numberless?
　What mortal eloquence can raise
　His tribute of immortal praise?

3 Extend to me that favor, Lord,
　Thou to thy chosen dost afford;
　When thou return'st to set them free,
　Let thy salvation visit me.

4 Oh, render thanks to God above,
　The fountain of eternal love:
　His mercy firm, through ages past,
　Hath stood, and shall forever last.

885.
L. M.

1 GIVE to our God immortal praise;
　Mercy and truth are all his ways:
　Wonders of grace to God belong;
　Repeat his mercies in your song.

2 Give to the Lord of lords renown,
　The King of kings with glory crown,
　His mercies ever shall endure,
　When lords and kings are known no
　　more.

3 He built the earth, he spread the sky,
　And fixed the starry lights on high:
　Wonders of grace to God belong;
　Repeat his mercies in your song.

4 He fills the sun with morning light,
　He bids the moon direct the night:
　His mercies ever shall endure,
　When suns and moons shall shine no more.

5 He sent his Son with power to save
　From guilt, and darkness, and the grave;
　Wonders of grace to God belong;
　Repeat his mercies in your song.

6 Through this vain world he guides our
　　feet,
　And leads us to his heavenly seat:
　His mercies ever shall endure,
　When this vain world shall be no more.

886.

L. M.

1 GREAT God ! attend, while Zion sings
The joy that from thy presence springs ;
To spend one day with thee on earth
Exceeds a thousand days of mirth.

2 Might I enjoy the meanest place
Within thy house, O God of grace !
Not tents of ease, nor thrones of power,
Should tempt my feet to leave thy door.

3 God is our sun, he makes our day ;
God is our shield, he guards our way
From all th' assaults of hell and sin,
From foes without, and foes within.

4 All needful grace will God bestow,
And crown that grace with glory, too ;
He gives us all things, and withholds
No real good from upright souls.

887.

L. M.

1 My God ! my King ! thy various praise
Shall fill the remnant of my days ;
Thy grace employ my humble tongue,
Till death and glory raise the song.

2 The wings of every hour shall bear
Some thankful tribute to thine ear ;
And every setting sun shall see
New works of duty, done for thee.

3 Thy works with sovereign glory shine,
And speak thy majesty divine ;
Let every realm, with joy, proclaim
The sound and honor of thy name.

4 Let distant times and nations raise
The long succession of thy praise ;
And unborn ages make my song
The joy and labor of their tongue.

5 But who can speak thy wondrous deeds ?
Thy greatness all our thoughts exceeds :
Vast and unsearchable thy ways,—
Vast and immortal be thy praise.

888.

C. M.

1 WITH songs and honors, sounding loud,
Address the Lord on high ;
Over the heavens he spreads his cloud,
And waters vail the sky.

2 He sends his showers of blessings down,
To cheer the plains below ;
He makes the grass the mountains crown,
And corn in valleys grow.

3 His steady counsels change the face
Of the declining year ;
He bids the sun cut short his race,
And wintry days appear.

4 His hoary frost, his fleecy snow,
Descend and clothe the ground ;
The liquid streams forbear to flow,
In icy fetters bound.

5 He sends his word, and melts the snow,
The fields no longer mourn ;
He calls the warmer gales to blow,
And bids the spring return.

6 The changing wind, the flying cloud,
Obey his mighty word :
With songs and honors, sounding loud,
Praise ye the sovereign Lord.

889.

7s & 6s.

1 PRAISE the Lord, who reigns above,
And keeps his courts below ;
Praise him for his boundless love,
And all his greatness show :
Praise him for his noble deeds ;
Praise him for his matchless power ;
Him, from whom all good proceeds,
Let earth and heaven adore.

2 Publish, spread to all around
The great Immanuel's name ;
Let the gospel trumpet sound,
The Prince of peace proclaim !
Praise him, every tuneful string :
All the reach of heavenly art,
All the power of music bring,
The music of the heart.

3 Him, in whom they move and live,
Let every creature sing ;
Glory to our Saviour give,
And homage to our King :
Hallowed be his name beneath,
As in heaven, on earth adored ;
Praise the Lord in every breath,
Let all things praise the Lord.

890.
C. M.

1 Come, let us lift our joyful eyes
Up to the courts above,
And smile to see our Father there,
Upon a throne of love.

2 Now we may bow before his feet,
And venture near the Lord;
No fiery cherubs guard his seat,
Nor double-flaming sword.

3 The peaceful gates of heavenly bliss
Are opened by the Son;
High let us raise our notes of praise,
And reach the almighty throne.

4 To thee, ten thousand thanks we bring,
Great Advocate on high,
And glory to the eternal King,
Who lays his anger by.

891.
S. M.

1 Our heavenly Father! hear
The prayer we offer now;—
Thy name be hallowed far and near;
To thee all nations bow!

2 Thy kingdom come, thy will
On earth be done in love,
As saints and seraphim fulfill
Thy perfect law above.

3 Our daily bread supply,
While by thy word we live;
The guilt of our iniquity
Forgive, as we forgive.

4 From dark temptation's power,
From Satan's wiles defend;
Deliver in the evil hour,
And guide us to the end!

5 Thine, then, forever be
Glory and power divine;
The sceptre, throne, and majesty
Of heaven and earth are thine!

892.
C. M.

1 Father! how wide thy glory shines!
How high thy wonders rise!
Known through the earth by thousand
signs,—
By thousand through the skies.

2 Those mighty orbs proclaim thy power,
Their motions speak thy skill;
And, on the wings of every hour,
We read thy patience still.

3 But, when we view thy strange design
To save rebellious worms,
Where vengeance and compassion join
In their divinest forms,—

4 Here the whole Deity is known;
Nor dares a creature guess,—
Which of the glories brightest shone,
The justice, or the grace.

5 Now the full glories of the Lamb
Adorn the heavenly plains;
Bright seraphs learn Immanuel's name,
And try their choicest strains.

6 Oh! may I bear some humble part,
In that immortal song;
Wonder and joy shall tune my heart,
And love command my tongue.

893.
8s & 7s.

1 Lord, thy glory fills the heaven;
Earth is with its fullness stored;
Unto thee be glory given,
Holy, holy, holy Lord!
Heaven is still with anthems ringing;
Earth takes up the angels' cry,
Holy, holy, holy, singing,
Lord of hosts, thou Lord most high.

2 Ever thus in God's high praises,
Brethren, let our tongues unite,
While our thoughts his greatness raises,
And our love his gifts excite:
With his seraph train before him,
With his holy church below,
Thus unite we to adore him,
Bid we thus our anthem flow.

3 Lord, thy glory fills the heaven;
Earth is with its fullness stored;
Unto thee be glory given,
Holy, holy, holy Lord!
Thus thy glorious name confessing,
We adopt the angels' cry,
Holy, holy, holy, blessing
Thee, the Lord our God most high!

894.
H. M.

1 The Lord Jehovah reigns,
His throne is built on high ;
The garments he assumes,
Are light and majesty ;
His glories shine with beams so bright,
No mortal eye can bear the sight.

2 The thunders of his hand
Keep the wide world in awe ;
His wrath and justice stand,
To guard his holy law ;
And where his love resolves to bless,
His truth confirms and seals the grace.

3 Through all his perfect work,
Surprising wisdom shines ;
Confounds the powers of hell,
And breaks their cursed designs :
Strong is his arm—and shall fulfill
His great decrees, his sovereign will.

4 And can this mighty King
Of glory condescend—
And will he write his name,
My Father and my Friend !
I love his name, I love his word ;
Join, all my powers, and praise the Lord !

895.
L. M.

1 Millions within thy courts have met,
Millions, this day, before thee bowed ;
Their faces Zion-ward were set,
Vows with their lips to thee they vowed.

2 Soon as the light of morning broke
O'er island, continent, or deep,
Thy far-spread family awoke,
Sabbath, all round the world to keep.

3 From east to west, the sun surveyed,
From north to south, adoring throngs ;
And still, when evening stretched her
shade,
The stars came out to hear their songs.

4 And not a prayer, a tear, a sigh,
Hath failed this day some suit to gain ;
To those in trouble thou wert nigh :
Not one hath sought thy face in vain.

5 Yet one prayer more !—and be it one,
In which both heaven and earth accord :
Fulfill thy promise to thy Son ;
Let all that breathe call Jesus Lord !

896.
H. M.

1 Mark the soft-falling snow,
And the descending rain !
To heaven, from whence it fell,
It turns not back again ;
But waters earth through every pore,
And calls forth all her secret store.

2 Arrayed in beauteous green
The hills and valleys shine,
And man and beast are fed
By providence divine :
The harvest bows its golden ears,
The copious seed of future years.

3 "So," saith the God of grace,
"My Gospel shall descend,
Almighty to effect
The purpose I intend ;
Millions of souls shall feel its power,
And bear it down to millions more."

897.
C. M.

1 Author of good ! to thee we turn :
Thine ever-wakeful eye
Alone can all our wants discern—
Thy hand alone supply.

2 Oh, let thy love within us dwell,
Thy fear our footsteps guide ;
That love shall vainer loves expel,
That fear all fears beside.

3 And since by passion's force subdued,
Too oft with stubborn will,
We blindly shun the latent good,
And grasp the specious ill ;—

4 Not what we wish, but what we want,
Let mercy still supply :
The good we ask not, Father, grant ;
The ill we ask, deny.

898.
8s, 7s & 4s.

1 Guide me, O thou great Jehovah,
Pilgrim through this barren land :
I am weak, but thou art mighty,
Hold me with thy powerful hand ;
Bread of heaven !
Feed me till I want no more.

2 Open thou the crystal fountain,
　Whence the healing waters flow;
Let the fiery, cloudy pillar
　Lead me all my journey through :
　　Strong Deliverer!
　Be thou still my strength and shield.

3 When I tread the verge of Jordan,
　Bid the swelling stream divide :
Death of death, and hell's destruction!
　Land me safe on Canaan's side :
　　Songs of praises
　I will ever give to thee.

899.
S. M.

1 Lord, at this closing hour,
　Establish every heart
Upon thy word of truth and power,
　To keep us when we part.

2 Peace to our brethren give ;
　Fill all our hearts with love ;
In faith and patience may we live,
　And seek our rest above.

3 Through changes, bright or drear,
　We would thy will pursue ;
And toil to spread thy kingdom here,
　Till we its glory view.

4 To God, the Only Wise,
　In every age adored,
Let glory from the church arise
　Through Jesus Christ our Lord!

900.
8s & 7s.

1 Saviour! breathe an evening blessing,
　Ere repose our eyelids seal :
Sin and want we come confessing :
　Thou canst save, and thou canst heal.

2 Though destruction walk around us,
　Though the arrows past us fly,
Angel-guards from thee surround us ;
　We are safe, if thou art nigh.

3 Though the night be dark and dreary,
　Darkness cannot hide from thee :
Thou art he who, never weary,
　Watcheth where thy people be.

4 Should swift death this night o'ertake us,
　And our couch become our tomb,
May the morn in heaven awake us,
　Clad in bright and deathless bloom.

901.
7s.

1 Holy Bible! book divine!
　Precious treasure! thou art mine :
Mine to tell me whence I came ;
　Mine to tell me what I am ;

2 Mine to chide me when I rove ;
　Mine to show a Saviour's love ;
Mine thou art to guide and guard ;
　Mine to punish or reward ;

3 Mine to comfort in distress,
　If the Holy Spirit bless ;
Mine to show, by living faith,
　Man can triumph over death ;

4 Mine to tell of joys to come,
　And the rebel sinner's doom ;
Oh, thou holy book divine!
　Precious treasure, thou art mine!

902.
L. P. M.

1 I love the volume of thy word ;
　What light and joy those leaves afford
　　To souls benighted and distressed!
　Thy precepts guide my doubtful way,
　Thy fear forbids my feet to stray,
　　Thy promise leads my heart to rest.

2 From the discoveries of thy law,
　The perfect rules of life I draw :
　　These are my study and delight ;
　Not honey so invites the taste,
　Nor gold, that has the furnace passed,
　　Appears so pleasing to the sight.

3 Thy threatenings wake my slumbering
　　　eyes,
　And warn me where my danger lies ;
　　But 'tis thy blessèd gospel, Lord!
　That makes my guilty conscience clean,
　Converts my soul, subdues my sin,
　　And gives a free, but large reward.

4 Who knows the errors of his thoughts?
　My God! forgive my secret faults,
　　And from presumptuous sins restrain ;
　Accept my poor attempts of praise,
　That I have read thy book of grace,
　　And book of nature not in vain.

903.
C. M.

1 LADEN with guilt, and full of fears,
  I fly to thee, my Lord,
And not a glimpse of hope appears,
  But in thy written word.

2 The volume of my Father's grace
  Does all my grief assuage;
Here I behold my Saviour's face
  Almost in every page.

3 This is the field where hidden lies,
  The pearl of price unknown;
That merchant is divinely wise,
  Who makes the pearl his own.

4 Here consecrated water flows,
  To quench my thirst of sin;
Here the fair tree of knowledge grows,
  Nor danger dwells therein.

5 This is the judge that ends the strife,
  Where wit and reason fail;
My guide to everlasting life,
  Through all this gloomy vale.

6 Oh, may thy counsels, mighty God!
  My roving feet command;
Nor I forsake the happy road,
  That leads to thy right hand.

904.
C. P. M. *In Nature.*

1 SINCE o'er thy footstool here below
  Such radiant gems are strown,
Oh, what magnificence must glow,
  Great God, about thy throne!
So brilliant here these drops of light!
There the full ocean rolls, how bright!

2 If night's blue curtain of the sky,
  With thousand stars inwrought,
Hung, like a royal canopy,
  With glittering diamonds fraught,
Be, Lord, thy temple's outer vail,
What splendor at the shrine must dwell!

3 The dazzling sun, at noonday hour,
  Forth from his flaming vase,
Flinging o'er earth the golden shower,
  Till vale and mountain blaze,
But shows, O Lord, one beam of thine:
What, then, the Day where thou dost
    shine!

4 Oh, how shall these dim eyes endure
  That noon of living rays?
Or how our spirits, so impure,
  Upon thy glory gaze?
Anoint, O Lord, anoint our sight,
And fit us for that world of light.

905.
L. M., 6 lines. *In Nature.*

1 THOU art, O God, the life and light
  Of all this wondrous world we see;
Its glow by day, its smile by night,
  Are but reflections caught from thee;
Where'er we turn, thy glories shine,
And all things fair and bright are thine.

2 When day, with farewell beam, delays
  Among the opening clouds of even,
And we can almost think we gaze,
  Through opening vistas into heaven,—
Those hues that mark the sun's decline,
So soft, so radiant, Lord, are thine.

3 When night, with wings of starry gloom,
  O'ershadows all the earth and skies,
Like some dark, beauteous bird, whose
    plume
  Is sparkling with unnumbered eyes,—
That sacred gloom, those fires divine,
So grand, so countless, Lord, are thine.

4 When youthful spring around us breathes,
  Thy spirit warms her fragrant sigh;
And every flower that summer wreathes
  Is born beneath thy kindling eye:
Where'er we turn, thy glories shine,
And all things fair and bright are thine.

906.
C. M. *In Nature.*

1 THERE is a book that all may read,
  Which heavenly truth imparts,
And all the lore its scholars need,
  Pure eyes and Christian hearts.

2 The works of God above, below,
  Within us and around,
Are pages in that book, to show
  How God himself is found.

3 The glorious sky, embracing all,
  Is like the Maker's love,
Wherewith encompassed, great and small
  In peace and order move.

4 The dew of heaven is like thy grace,
 It steals in silence down;
 But where it lights, the favored place
 By richest fruits is known.

5 Thou, who hast given me eyes to see,
 And love this sight so fair,
 Give me a heart to find out thee,
 And read thee everywhere.

907.
C. M. *In Nature.*

1 LORD, when my raptured thought surveys
 Creation's beauties o'er,
 All nature joins to teach thy praise,
 And bid my soul adore.

2 Where'er I turn my gazing eyes,
 Thy radiant footsteps shine;
 Ten thousand pleasing wonders rise,
 And speak their source divine.

3 On me thy providence has shone
 With gentle smiling rays;
 Oh, let my lips and life make known
 Thy goodness and thy praise.

4 All-bounteous Lord, thy grace impart,
 Oh, teach me to improve
 Thy gifts with humble, grateful heart,
 And crown them with thy love.

908.
L. M. *In Nature.*

1 THE spacious firmament on high,
 With all the blue, ethereal sky,
 And spangled heavens, a shining frame,
 Their great Original proclaim:
 Th' unwearied sun, from day to day,
 Does his creator's power display;
 And publishes to every land
 The work of an almighty hand.

2 Soon as the evening shades prevail,
 The moon takes up the wondrous tale,
 And nightly, to the listening earth,
 Repeats the story of her birth;
 While all the stars that round her burn,
 And all the planets in their turn,
 Confirm the tidings as they roll,
 And spread the truth from pole to pole.

3 What though in solemn silence all
 Move round the dark terrestrial ball,—
 What though no real voice nor sound
 Amid their radiant orbs be found,—

In reason's ear they all rejoice,
 And utter forth a glorious voice,
 Forever singing as they shine,—
 "The hand that made us is divine."

909.
S. P. M. *Majesty.*

1 THE Lord Jehovah reigns,
 And royal state maintains,
 His head with awful glories crowned;
 Arrayed in robes of light,
 Begirt with sovereign might,
 And rays of majesty around.

2 Upheld by thy commands,
 The world securely stands,
 And skies and stars obey thy word;
 Thy throne was fixed on high
 Before the starry sky;
 Eternal is thy kingdom, Lord!

3 Let floods and nations rage,
 And all their powers engage;
 Let swelling tides assault the sky;
 The terrors of thy frown
 Shall beat their madness down;
 Thy throne forever stands on high.

4 Thy promises are true,
 Thy grace is ever new;
 There fixed, thy church shall ne'er
 remove:
 Thy saints with holy fear
 Shall in their courts appear,
 And sing thine everlasting love.

910.
C. M. *Majesty.*

1 THE Lord descended from above,
 And bowed the heavens most high;
 And underneath his feet he cast
 The darkness of the sky.

2 On cherub and on cherubim,
 Full royally, he rode;
 And on the wings of mighty winds
 Came flying all abroad.

3 He sat serene upon the floods,
 Their fury to restrain;
 And he, as Sovereign, Lord, and King,
 Forevermore shall reign.

911.

11s & 8s. *"King of kings."*

1 THE Lord is great! ye hosts of heaven,
  adore him,
  And ye who tread this earthly ball;
  In holy songs rejoice aloud before him,
  And shout his praise who made you all.

2 The Lord is great; his majesty how
  glorious!
  Resound his praise from shore to shore;
  O'er sin, and death, and hell, now made
  victorious,
  He rules and reigns forevermore.

3 The Lord is great; his mercy how
  abounding!
  Ye angels, strike your golden chords;
  Oh, praise our God, with voice and harp
  resounding,
  The King of kings and Lord of lords!

912.

8s & 7s. *Perfections.*

1 GOD is love; his mercy brightens
  All the path in which we rove;
  Bliss he wakes, and woe he lightens;
  God is wisdom, God is love.

2 Chance and change are busy ever;
  Man decays, and ages move;
  But his mercy waneth never;
  God is wisdom, God is love.

3 Ev'n the hour that darkest seemeth,
  Will his changeless goodness prove;
  From the gloom his brightness streameth,
  God is wisdom, God is love.

4 He with earthly cares entwineth
  Hope and comfort from above:
  Everywhere his glory shineth;
  God is wisdom, God is love.

913.

L. C. M. *Love.*

1 MY God, thy boundless love I praise:
  How bright on high its glories blaze!
  How sweetly bloom below!
  It streams from thy eternal throne;
  Through heaven its joys forever run,
  And o'er the earth they flow.

2 'Tis love that paints the purple morn,
  And bids the clouds, in air upborne,
  Their genial drops distill;

In every vernal beam it glows,
It breathes in every gale that blows,
  And glides in every rill.

3 It robes in cheerful green the ground,
  And pours its flowery beauties round,
  Whose sweets perfume the gale;
  Its bounties richly spread the plain,
  The blushing fruit, the golden grain,
  And smile in every vale.

4 But in thy word I see it shine
  With grace and glories more divine,
  Proclaiming sins forgiven;
  There Faith, bright cherub, points the way
  To realms of everlasting day,
  And opens all her heaven.

5 Then let the love that makes me blest
  With cheerful praise inspire my breast,
  And ardent gratitude,
  And all my thoughts and passions tend
  To thee, my Father and my Friend,
  My soul's eternal good!

914.

L. M. *All in All.*

1 ETERNAL God! eternal King!
  Ruler of heaven and earth beneath!
  From thee our hopes, our comforts spring;
  In thee we live, and move, and breathe.

2 Thy word brought forth the flaming sun,
  The changeful moon, the starry host:
  In thine appointed course they run,
  Till in the final ruin lost.

3 At thy command the storm is dumb;
  And to the sea thy power hath said,
  "No further shalt thou dare to come,
  And here shall thy proud waves be
  stayed."

4 Thy sway is known below, above,
  And full of majesty thy voice:
  And, as it speaks, in wrath or love,
  The nations tremble or rejoice.

5 The final, awful hour is near,
  Time paces on with ceaseless tread,
  When opening graves that voice shall
  hear,
  And render up the sleeping dead.

6 Oh, in that great decisive day,
  May we be found in Christ, and stand,
  While flaming worlds shall melt away,
  Accepted, owned, at thy right hand!

915.
C. M. *Eternity.*

1 O God, our help in ages past,
  Our hope for years to come,
  Our shelter from the stormy blast,
  And our eternal home !

2 Under the shadow of thy throne,
  Thy saints have dwelt secure ;
  Sufficient is thine arm alone,
  And our defence is sure.

3 Before the hills in order stood,
  Or earth received her frame,
  From everlasting thou art God,
  To endless years the same.

4 Thy word commands our flesh to dust :
  " Return, ye sons of men ;"
  All nations rose from earth at first,
  And turn to earth again.

5 Time, like an ever-rolling stream,
  Bears all its sons away ;
  They fly, forgotten, as a dream
  Dies at the opening day.

6 O God, our help in ages past,
  Our hope for years to come,
  Be thou our guard while troubles last,
  And our eternal home !

916.
C. M. 6 lines. *Omnipresence.*

1 Beyond, beyond the boundless sea,
  Above that dome of sky,
  Further than thought itself can flee,
  Thy dwelling is on high :
  Yet dear the awful thought to me,
  That thou, my God ! art nigh :—

2 Art nigh, and yet my laboring mind
  Feels after thee in vain—
  Thee in these works of power to find,
  Or to thy seat attain ;
  Thy messenger—the stormy wind ;
  Thy path—the trackless main.

3 These speak of thee with loud acclaim ;
  They thunder forth thy praise—
  The glorious honor of thy name,
  The wonders of thy ways :
  But thou art not in tempest-flame,
  Nor in the noon-day blaze.

4 We hear thy voice, when thunders roll
  Through the wide fields of air :
  The waves obey thy dread control ;
  Yet still thou art not there :

Where shall I find him, O my soul !
  Who yet is everywhere ?

5 Oh, not in circling depth or height,
  But in the conscious breast,
  Present to faith, though vailed from sight,
  There does his Spirit rest :
  O come, thou Presence infinite !
  And make thy creature blest.

917.
L. M. *Faithfulness.*

1 Praise, everlasting praise, be paid
  To him who earth's foundations laid :
  Praise to the God whose strong decrees
  Sway the creation as he please.

2 Praise to the goodness of the Lord,
  Who rules his people by his word ;
  And there, as strong as his decrees,
  Reveals his kindest promises.

3 Oh, for a strong, a lasting faith,
  To credit what th' Almighty saith !
  T' embrace the message of his Son,
  And call the joys of heaven our own.

4 Then, should the earth's foundations
    shake,
  And all the wheels of nature break,
  Our steady souls shall fear no more
  Than solid rocks when billows roar.

918.
C. M. *Omnipresence.*

1 Lord ! where shall guilty souls retire,
  Forgotten and unknown !
  In hell they meet thy dreadful fire,
  In heaven thy glorious throne.

2 Should I suppress my vital breath
  To shun the wrath divine,
  Thy voice would break the bars of death,
  And make the grave resign.

3 If winged with beams of morning light,
  I fly beyond the west,
  Thy hand, which must support my flight,
  Would soon betray my rest.

4 If o'er my sins I think to draw
  The curtains of the night,
  Those flaming eyes that guard thy law
  Would turn the shades to light.

5 The beams of noon, the midnight hour,
  Are both alike to thee :
  Oh, may I ne'er provoke that power
  From which I cannot flee !

919.
H. M. *Trinity.*

1 WE give immortal praise
For God the Father's love,
For all our comforts here,
And better hopes above :
He sent his own eternal Son
To die for sins that we had done.

2 To God the Son belongs
Immortal glory too,
Who bought us with his blood
From everlasting woe :
And now he lives, and now he reigns,
And sees the fruit of all his pains.

3 To God the Spirit's name
Immortal worship give,
Whose new-creating power
Makes the dead sinner live :
His work completes the great design,
And fills the soul with joy divine.

4 Almighty God! to thee
Be endless honors done,
The undivided Three,
The great and glorious One :
Where reason fails, with all her powers,
There faith prevails and love adores.

920.
7s. *Trinity.*

1 HOLY Father, hear my cry ;
Holy Saviour, bend thine ear ;
Holy Spirit, come thou nigh :
Father, Saviour, Spirit, hear !

2 Father, save me from my sin ;
Saviour, I thy mercy crave ;
Gracious Spirit, make me clean :
Father, Son, and Spirit, save !

3 Father, let me taste thy love ;
Saviour, fill my soul with peace ;
Spirit, come my heart to move :
Father, Son, and Spirit, bless !

4 Father, Son, and Spirit—thou
One Jehovah, shed abroad
All thy grace within me now ;
Be my Father and my God !

921.
C. M. *Trinity.*

1 FATHER of glory ! to thy name
Immortal praise we give,
Who dost an act of grace proclaim,
And bid us rebels live.

2 Immortal honor to the Son,
Who makes thine anger cease ;
Our lives he ransomed with his own,
And died to make our peace.

3 To thine almighty Spirit be
Immortal glory given,
Whose influence brings us near to thee,
And trains us up for heaven.

4 Let men, with their united voice,
Adore th' eternal God ;
And spread his honors and their joys
Through nations far abroad.

5 Let faith, and love, and duty join,
One general song to raise ;
Let saints in earth and heaven combine
In harmony and praise.

922.
8s & 7s. *Trinity.*

1 CEASELESS praise be to the Father,
By whose power and grace we live ;
Who, our wayward souls to gather
Did his well-belovéd give.

2 To the Son be praise unending,
Who, our ruined souls to save,
From his heavenly throne descending,
Hasted to the cross and grave.

3 To the Holy Spirit render
Grateful, everlasting praise ;
Who, long-striving, patient, tender,
Waits our souls from death to raise.

4 Father, Son, and Holy Spirit,
One Jehovah, we adore !
May we all thy peace inherit,
Saved by thee forevermore.

923.
Incarnation. **L. M.**

1 ERE the blue heavens were stretched
abroad,
From everlasting was the Word :
With God he was ; the Word was God,
And must divinely be adored.

2 By his own power were all things made ;
By him supported, all things stand :
He is the whole creation's head,
And angels fly at his command.

3 But, lo ! he leaves those heavenly forms :
The Word descends and dwells in clay,
That he may hold converse with worms,
Dressed in such feeble flesh as they.

4 Mortals with joy behold his face,
Th' eternal Father's only Son;
How full of truth, how full of grace,
When through his eyes the Godhead
 shone!

5 Archangels leave their high abode
To learn new myst'ries here, and tell
The love of our descending God,
The glories of Immanuel.

924.
7s. *Incarnation.*

1 God with us! Oh, glorious name!
Let it shine in endless fame:
God and man in Christ unite;
Oh, mysterious depth and height!

2 God with us! the eternal Son
Took our soul, our flesh, and bone;
Now, ye saints, his grace admire,
Swell the song with holy fire.

3 God with us! but tainted not
With the first transgressor's blot;
Yet did he our sins sustain,
Bear the guilt, the curse, the pain.

4 God with us! Oh, wondrous grace!
Let us see him face to face;
That we may Immanuel sing,
As we ought, our God and King!

925.
11s & 10s.

1 Brightest and best of the sons of the
 morning!
Dawn on our darkness, and lend us
 thine aid;
Star of the east, the horizon adorning,
Guide where our infant-Redeemer is
 laid.

2 Cold on his cradle, the dew-drops are
 shining;
Low lies his head, with the beasts of
 the stall;
Angels adore him in slumber reclining—
Maker, and Monarch, and Saviour
 of all.

3 Say, shall we yield him, in costly devotion,
Odors of Edom, and offerings divine?
Gems of the mountain, and pearls of the
 ocean,
Myrrh from the forest, or gold from
 the mine?

4 Vainly we offer each ample oblation,
Vainly with gold, would his favor
 secure;
Richer, by far, is the heart's adoration,—
Dearer to God are the prayers of the
 poor.

5 Brightest and best of the sons of the
 morning!
Dawn on our darkness, and lend us
 thine aid;
Star of the east, the horizon adorning,
Guide where our infant Redeemer is
 laid.

926.
8s & 7s.

1 Hark! what mean those holy voices,
Sweetly sounding through the skies?
Lo! th' angelic host rejoices;
Heavenly hallelujahs rise.

2 Hear them tell the wondrous story,
Hear them chant in hymns of joy;—
"Glory in the highest, glory!
Glory be to God most high!

3 "Peace on earth, good-will from heaven,
Reaching far as man is found;
Souls redeemed, and sins forgiven!
Loud our golden harps shall sound.

4 "Christ is born, the great Anointed;
Heaven and earth his praises sing!
Oh, receive whom God appointed,
For your Prophet, Priest, and King!

5 "Haste, ye mortals, to adore him;
Learn his name, and taste his joy;
Till in heaven ye sing before him—
"Glory be to God most high!'"

927.
H. M.

1 Hark! what celestial sounds,
What music fills the air!
Soft warbling to the morn,
It strikes the ravished ear;
Now all is still; | In tuneful notes,
Now wild it floats | Loud, sweet, and shrill.

2 The angelic hosts descend,
With harmony divine;
See how from heaven they bend,
And in full chorus join:
"Fear not," say they; | Jesus, your King,
"Great joy we bring: | Is born to-day."

3 He comes, your souls to save
From death's eternal gloom;
To realms of bliss and light
He lifts you from the tomb.
Your voices raise, | Your songs unite
With sons of light; | Of endless praise.

4 Glory to God on high;
Ye mortals, spread the sound,
And let your raptures fly
To earth's remotest bound;
For peace on earth, | To man is given,
From God in heaven, | At Jesus' birth.

928.
C. M.

1 The race that long in darkness pined
Have seen a glorious light;
The people dwell in day, who dwelt
In death's surrounding night.

2 To hail thy rise, thou better Sun,
The gathering nations come,
Joyous as when the reapers bear
The harvest treasures home.

3 To us a child of hope is born,
To us a Son is given;
Him shall the tribes of earth obey,
Him, all the hosts of heaven.

4 His name shall be the Prince of Peace,
Whose rule shall stretch abroad,
The Wonderful, the Counselor,
The great and mighty Lord.

5 His power, increasing, still shall spread;
His reign no end shall know;
Justice shall guard his throne above,
And peace abound below.

929.
H. M.

1 Hark! hark!—the notes of joy
Roll o'er the heavenly plains,
And seraphs find employ
For their sublimest strains;
Some new delight in heaven is known;
Loud sound the harps around the throne.

2 Hark! hark!—the sounds draw nigh,
The joyful hosts descend;
Jesus forsakes the sky,
To earth his footsteps bend;
He comes to bless our fallen race;
He comes with messages of grace.

3 Bear—bear the tidings round;
Let every mortal know
What love in God is found,
What pity he can show;
Ye winds that blow! ye waves that roll!
Bear the glad news from pole to pole.

4 Strike—strike the harps again,
To great Immanuel's name;
Arise, ye sons of men!
And all his grace proclaim;
Angels and men! wake every string,
'Tis God the Saviour's praise we sing.

930.
L. M.

1 When, marshaled on the nightly plain,
The glittering host bestud the sky,
One star alone, of all the train,
Can fix the sinner's wandering eye.

2 Hark! hark!—to God the chorus breaks,
From every host, from every gem;
But one alone the Saviour speaks,—
It is the Star of Bethlehem.

3 Once on the raging seas I rode,
The storm was loud, the night was dark,—
The ocean yawned—and rudely blowed
The wind, that tossed my foundering bark.

4 Deep horror then my vitals froze,
Death-struck, I ceased the tide to stem;—
When suddenly a star arose,—
It was the Star of Bethlehem.

5 It was my guide, my light, my all;
It bade my dark forebodings cease;
And, through the storm, and danger's
thrall,
It led me to the port of peace.

6 Now safely moored—my perils o'er,
I'll sing, first in night's diadem,
Forever and forevermore,
The Star—the Star of Bethlehem!

931.
C. M.

1 A pilgrim through this lonely world,
The blesséd Saviour passed;
A mourner all his life was he,
A dying Lamb at last.

2 That tender heart that felt for all,
For all its life-blood gave;
It found on earth no resting-place,
Save only in the grave.

3 Such was our Lord ; and shall we fear
  The cross, with all its scorn ?
  Or love a faithless evil world,
  That wreathed his brow with thorn ?

4 No, facing all its frowns or smiles,
  Like him, obedient still,
  We homeward press thro' storm or calm,
  To Zion's blessèd hill.

932.
11s.

1 Thou sweet gliding Kedron, by thy silver
    stream,
  Our Saviour, at midnight, when moon-
    light's pale beam
  Shone bright on thy waters, would fre-
    quently stray,
  And lose, in thy murmurs, the toils of the
    day.

2 How damp were the vapors that fell on
    his head !
  How hard was his pillow, how humble
    his bed !
  The angels, astonished, grew sad at the
    sight,
  And followed their master with solemn
    delight.

3 O garden of Olives, thou dear honored spot,
  The fame of thy wonders shall ne'er be
    forgot ;
  The theme most transporting to seraphs
    above ;
  The triumph of sorrow,—the triumph of
    love !

4 Come, saints, and adore him ; come, bow
    at his feet :
  Oh, give him the glory, the praise that is
    meet ;
  Let joyful hosannas unceasing arise,
  And join the full chorus that gladdens
    the skies !

933.
L. M.

1 When power divine, in mortal form,
  Hushed with a word the raging storm,
  In soothing accents Jesus said—
  "Lo ! it is I ; be not afraid."

2 Blest be the voice that breathes from
    heaven,
  To every heart in sunder riven,
  When love, and joy, and hope are fled—
  "Lo ! it is I ; be not afraid."

3 And when the last dread hour is come,
  While shuddering nature waits her doom,
  This voice shall call the pious dead—
  "Lo ! it is I ; be not afraid."

934.
L. M.

1 Ride on, ride on in majesty ;
  Hark ! all the tribes hosanna cry ;
  Thy humble beast pursues his road,
  With palms and scattered garments
    strewed.

2 Ride on, ride on in majesty ;
  In lowly pomp ride on to die ;
  O Christ, thy triumphs now begin
  O'er captive death and conquered sin.

3 Ride on, ride on in majesty ;
  The wingèd squadrons of the sky
  Look down with sad and wondering eyes,
  To see the approaching sacrifice.

4 Ride on, ride on in majesty ;
  Thy last and fiercest strife is nigh ;
  The Father, on his sapphire throne,
  Expects his own anointed Son.

5 Ride on, ride on in majesty ;
  In lowly pomp ride on to die ;
  Bow thy meek head to mortal pain ;
  Then take, O God, thy power, and reign.

935.
7s. 6 lines.

1 Go to dark Gethsemane,
    Ye that feel the tempter's power ;
  Your Redeemer's conflict see,
    Watch with him one bitter hour ;
  Turn not from his griefs away,
  Learn of Jesus Christ to pray.

2 Follow to the judgment-hall ;
    View the Lord of life arraigned ;
  Oh, the wormwood and the gall !
    Oh, the pangs his soul sustained !
  Shun not suffering, shame, or loss ;
  Learn of him to bear the cross.

3 Calvary's mournful mountain climb ;
  There, adoring at his feet,
  Mark that miracle of time,
  God's own sacrifice complete :
  " It is finished," hear him cry ;—
  Learn of Jesus Christ to die.

4 Early hasten to the tomb,
  Where they laid his breathless clay ;
  All is solitude and gloom,
  —Who hath taken him away ?
  Christ is risen ;—he meets our eyes ;
  Saviour, teach us so to rise !

936.

C. L. M.

1 He knelt, the Saviour knelt and prayed,
  When but his Father's eye
  Looked thro' the lonely garden's shade,
  On that dread agony ;
  The Lord of all above, beneath,
  Was bowed with sorrow unto death.

The sun set in a fearful hour,
  The skies might well grow dim,
  When this mortality had power
  So to o'ershadow him !
  That he who gave man's breath, might
    know
  The very depths of human woe.

3 He knew them all ; the doubt, the strife,
  The faint, perplexing dread,
  The mists that hang o'er parting life,
  All darkened round his head ;
  And the Deliverer knelt to pray ;—
  Yet passed it not, that cup, away.

4 It passed not, though the stormy wave
  Had sunk beneath his tread ;
  It passed not, tho' to him the grave
  Had yielded up its dead :
  But there was sent him from on high
  A gift of strength for man to die.

5 And was his mortal hour beset
  With anguish and dismay ?
  How may we meet our conflict yet
  In the dark, narrow way ?
  How but thro' him, that path who trod ?
  Save or we perish, Son of God !

937.

8s, 7s & 4s.

1 Hark ! the voice of love and mercy
  Sounds aloud from Calvary ;
  See !—it rends the rocks asunder—
  Shakes the earth—and vails the sky :
  " It is finished !"—
  Hear the dying Saviour cry.

2 " It is finished !"—Oh ! what pleasure
  Do these charming words afford !
  Heavenly blessings, without measure,
  Flow to us through Christ, the Lord :
  " It is finished !"—
  Saints ! the dying words record.

3 Tune your harps anew, ye seraphs !
  Join to sing the pleasing theme :
  All in earth and heaven, uniting,
  Join to praise Immanuel's name :
  Hallelujah !—
  Glory to the bleeding Lamb !

938.

P. M.

1 'T was the day when God's Anointed
  Died for us the death appointed,
  Bleeding on the dreadful cross ;
  Day of darkness, day of terror,
  Deadly fruit of ancient error,
  Nature's fall, and Eden's loss !

2 Haste, prepare the bitter chalice !
  Gentile hate and Jewish malice
  Lift the royal Victim high ;
  Like the serpent, wonder-gifted,
  Which the prophet once uplifted,
  For a sinful world to die.

3 Conscious of the deed unholy,
  Nature's pulses beat more slowly,
  And the sun his light denied ;
  Darkness wrapped the sacred city,
  And the earth with fear and pity
  Trembled, when the Just One died.

4 It is finished, Man of sorrows !
  From thy cross our nature borrows
  Strength to bear and conquer thus :
  While exalted there we view thee,
  Mighty Sufferer, draw us to thee,
  Sufferer victorious !

5 Not in vain for us uplifted,
Man of sorrows, wonder-gifted,
May that sacred symbol be;
Eminent amid the ages,
Guide of heroes and of sages,
May it guide us still to thee.

939.
L. M.

1 HE dies!—the friend of sinners dies;
Lo! Salem's daughters weep around;
A solemn darkness vails the skies;
A sudden trembling shakes the ground.

2 Here's love and grief beyond degree:
The Lord of glory dies for men;
But lo! what sudden joys we see,
Jesus, the dead, revives again.

3 The rising God forsakes the tomb;
Up to his Father's court he flies;
Cherubic legions guard him home,
And shout him welcome to the skies.

4 Break off your tears, ye saints, and tell
How high our great Deliverer reigns;
Sing how he spoiled the hosts of hell,
And led the tyrant Death in chains.

5 Say—live forever, glorious King,
Born to redeem, and strong to save!
Where now, O Death, where is thy sting!
And where thy victory, boasting Grave?

940.
7s.

1 CHRIST, the Lord, is risen to-day,
Our triumphant holy-day:
He endured the cross and grave,
Sinners to redeem and save.

2 Lo! he rises, mighty King!
Where, O Death! is now thy sting?
Lo! he claims his native sky!
Grave! where is thy victory?

3 Sinners, see your ransom paid,
Peace with God forever made:
With your risen Saviour rise;
Claim with him the purchased skies.

4 Christ, the Lord, is risen to-day,
Our triumphant holy-day;
Loud the song of victory raise;
Shout the great Redeemer's praise.

941.
C. L. M.

1 How calm and beautiful the morn,
That gilds the sacred tomb,
Where Christ the crucified was borne,
And vailed in midnight gloom!
Oh, weep no more the Saviour slain,
The Lord is risen, he lives again.

2 Ye mourning saints, dry every tear
For your departed Lord,
"Behold the place, he is not here!"
The tomb is all unbarred:
The gates of death were closed in vain,
The Lord is risen, he lives again.

3 Now cheerful to the house of prayer,
Your early footsteps bend;
The Saviour will himself be there,
Your Advocate and Friend:
Once by the law, your hopes were slain,
But now in Christ, ye live again.

4 How tranquil now the rising day!
'T is Jesus still appears,
A risen Lord, to chase away
Your unbelieving fears:
Oh, weep no more your comforts slain,
The Lord is risen, he lives again.

5 And when the shades of evening fall,
When life's last hour draws nigh,
If Jesus shines upon the soul,
How blissful then to die!
Since he hath risen that once was slain,
Ye die in Christ to live again.

942.
L. M. An Ancient Hymn.

1 THE morning kindles all the sky,
The heavens resound with anthems high,
The shining angels as they speed,
Proclaim, The Lord is risen indeed!

2 Vainly with rocks his tomb was barred,
While Roman guards kept watch and
ward;
Majestic from the spoiled tomb,
In pomp of triumph, he has come!

3 When the amazed disciples heard,
Their hearts with speechless joy were
stirred;
Their Lord's beloved face to see,
Eager they haste to Galilee.

4 His piercéd hands to them he shows,
His face with love's own radiance glows;
They with the angels' message speed,
And shout, The Lord is risen indeed!

5 O Christ, thou King compassionate!
Our hearts possess, on thee we wait;
Help us to render praises due,
To thee the endless ages through!

943.
C. M.

1 Oh! for a shout of sacred joy
To God, the sovereign King;
Let every land their tongues employ,
And hymns of triumph sing.

2 Jesus, our God, ascends on high;
His heavenly guards around
Attend him rising through the sky,
With trumpets' joyful sound.

3 While angels shout and praise their King,
Let mortals learn their strains;
Let all the earth his honor sing;—
O'er all the earth he reigns.

4 Rehearse his praise, with awe profound;
Let knowledge lead the song;
Nor mock him with a solemn sound
Upon a thoughtless tongue.

944.
L. M.

1 Jesus, my all, to heaven is gone,
He whom I fix my hopes upon;
His track I see, and I'll pursue
The narrow way till him I view.

2 The way the holy prophets went,
The way that leads from banishment;
The King's highway of holiness,
I'll go, for all his paths are peace.

3 This is the way I long had sought,
And mourned because I found it not;
My grief a burden long had been,
Oppressed with unbelief and sin.

4 The more I strove against their power,
I sinned and stumbled but the more;
Till late I heard my Saviour say,
"Come hither, soul, I am the way!"

5 Lo! glad I come, and thou, blest Lamb,
Shalt take me to thee, as I am:
Nothing but sin I thee can give;
Nothing but love shall I receive.

6 Then will I tell to sinners round,
What a dear Saviour I have found;
I'll point to thy redeeming blood,
And say, "Behold the way to God!"

945.
L. M. *An Ancient Hymn.*

1 A hymn of glory let us sing,
New hymns throughout the world shall
ring;
By a new way none ever trod,
Christ mounteth to the throne of God.

2 The angels say to the eleven,
"Why stand ye gazing into heaven?
This is the Saviour—this is He!
Jesus hath triumphed gloriously."

3 They said the Lord should come again,
As these beheld him rising then,
Calm soaring through the radiant sky,
Mounting its dazzling summits high.

4 May our affections thither tend,
And thither constantly ascend,
Where seated on the Father's throne,
Thee, reigning in the heavens, we own!

5 Be thou our present joy, O Lord,
Who wilt be ever our reward;
And as the countless ages flee,
May all our glory be in thee!

946.
C. M.

1 Arise, ye people, and adore,
Exulting strike the chord;
Let all the earth—from shore to shore,
Confess th' Almighty Lord.

2 Glad shouts aloud—wide echoing round,
Th' ascending God proclaim:
The angelic choir respond the sound,
And shake creation's frame.

3 They sing of death and hell o'erthrown
In that triumphant hour:
And God exalts his conquering Son
To his right hand of power.

4 Oh, shout, ye people, and adore,
Exulting strike the chord;
Let all the earth—from shore to shore,
Confess th' Almighty Lord.

947.

8s & 7s. Double.

1 MIGHTY God! while angels bless thee,
  May a mortal lisp thy name?
Lord of men, as well as angels!
  Thou art every creature's theme:
Lord of every land and nation!
  Ancient of eternal days!
Sounded through the wide creation,
  Be thy just and awful praise.

2 For the grandeur of thy nature,—
  Grand, beyond a seraph's thought;
For the wonders of creation,
  Works with skill and kindness wrought;
For thy providence, that governs
  Through thine empire's wide domain,
Wings an angel, guides a sparrow;—
  Blessèd be thy gentle reign.

3 For thy rich, thy free redemption,
  Bright, though vailed in darkness long;
Thought is poor, and poor expression;
  Who can sing that wondrous song?
Brightness of the Father's glory!
  Shall thy praise unuttered lie?
Break, my tongue! such guilty silence,
  Sing the Lord who came to die:—

4 From the highest throne of glory,
  To the cross of deepest woe,
Came to ransom guilty captives!—
  Flow, my praise! forever flow:
Re-ascend, immortal Saviour!
  Leave thy footstool, take thy throne;
Thence return and reign forever;—
  Be the kingdom all thine own!

948.

L. M.

1 Now be my heart inspired to sing
The glories of my Saviour King,—
Jesus the Lord; how heavenly fair
His form! how bright his beauties are!

2 O'er all the sons of human race,
He shines with a superior grace:
Love from his lips divinely flows,
And blessings all his state compose.

3 Thy throne, O God! forever stands;
Grace is the sceptre in thy hands;
Thy laws and works are just and right;
Justice and grace are thy delight.

4 God, thine own God, has richly shed
His oil of gladness on thy head;
And with his sacred Spirit, blessed
His first-born Son above the rest.

949.

6s & 4s.

1 COME, all ye saints of God!
Wide through the earth abroad,
  Spread Jesus' name;
Tell what his love has done,
Trust in his grace alone;
Shout to his lofty throne,—
  "Worthy the Lamb!"

2 Hence, gloomy doubts and fears!
Dry all your mournful tears;
  Swell the glad theme;
Praise ye our gracious King,
Strike each melodious string,
Join heart and voice to sing,—
  "Worthy the Lamb!"

3 Hark! how the choirs above,
Filled with the Saviour's love,
  Dwell on his name!
There, too, may we be found,
With light and glory crowned,
While all the heavens resound,—
  "Worthy the Lamb!"

950.

L. M.

1 Go, worship at Immanuel's feet;
See in his face what wonders meet:
Earth is too narrow to express
His worth, his glory, or his grace.

2 Nor earth, nor seas, nor sun, nor stars,
Nor heaven, his full resemblance bears:
His beauties we can never trace,
Till we behold him face to face.

3 Oh, let me climb those higher skies,
Where storms and darkness never rise:
There he displays his power abroad,
And shines, and reigns, th' incarnate God!

951.

C. M.

1 THE head that once was crowned with
    thorns,
  Is crowned with glory now:
A royal diadem adorns
  The mighty Victor's brow.

2 The highest place that heaven affords
  Is his by sovereign right;
  The King of kings, and Lord of lords,
  He reigns in glory bright;—

3 The joy of all who dwell above,
  The joy of all below,
  To whom he manifests his love,
  And grants his name to know.

4 To them the cross, with all its shame,
  With all its grace, is given;
  Their name, an everlasting name,
  Their joy, the joy of heaven.

5 They suffer with their Lord below,
  They reign with him above;
  Their profit and their joy to know
  The mystery of his love.

6 The cross he bore is life and health,
  Though shame and death to him;
  His people's hope, his people's wealth;
  Their everlasting theme.

952.
C. M.

1 COME, Holy Ghost, my soul inspire—
  This one great gift impart—
  What most I need—and most desire,
  An humble, holy heart.

2 Bear witness I am born again,
  My many sins forgiven:
  Nor let a gloomy doubt remain
  To cloud my hope of heaven.

3 More of myself grant I may know,
  From sin's deceit be free,
  In all the Christian graces grow,
  And live alone to thee.

953.
7s & 5s.

1 HOLY GHOST, the Infinite!
  Shine upon our nature's night
  With thy blessèd inward light,
  Comforter Divine!

2 We are sinful: cleanse us, Lord;
  We are faint: thy strength afford;
  Lost,—until by thee restored,
  Comforter Divine!

3 Like the dew, thy peace distill;
  Guide, subdue our wayward will,
  Things of Christ unfolding still,
  Comforter Divine!

4 In us, for us, intercede,
  And, with voiceless groanings, plead
  Our unutterable need,
  Comforter Divine!

5 In us "Abba, Father," cry—
  Earnest of our bliss on high,
  Seal of immortality,—
  Comforter Divine!

6 Search for us the depths of God;
  Bear us up the starry road,
  To the height of thine abode,
  Comforter Divine!

954.
C. M.

1 OUR blest Redeemer, ere he breathed
  His tender, last farewell,
  A Guide, a Comforter bequeathed,
  With us on earth to dwell.

2 He came in tongues of living flame,
  To teach, convince, subdue;
  All-powerful as the wind he came,
  And all as viewless, too.

3 He came, sweet influence to impart,
  A gracious, willing guest,
  While he can find one humble heart
  Wherein to fix his rest.

4 And his that gentle voice we hear,
  Soft as the breath of even,
  That checks each fault, that calms each fear,
  And whispers us of heaven.

5 And every virtue we possess,
  And every virtue won,
  And every thought of holiness
  Are his and his alone.

6 Spirit of purity and grace!
  Our weakness pitying see;
  Oh, make our hearts thy dwelling-place,
  Purer and worthier thee!

955.
C. M.

1 No track is on the sunny sky,
  No footprints on the air:
  Jesus hath gone; the face of earth
  Is desolate and bare.

2 That Upper Room is heaven on earth;
  Within its precincts lie
  All that earth has of faith, or hope,
  Or heaven-born charity.

3 One moment—and the silentness
    Was breathless as the grave ;
The fluttered earth forgot to quake,
    The troubled trees to wave.

4 He comes! he comes! that mighty Breath
    From heaven's eternal shores ;
His uncreated freshness fills
    His Bride, as she adores.

5 Earth quakes before that rushing blast,
    Heaven echoes back the sound,
And mightily the tempest wheels
    That Upper Room around.

6 One moment—and the Spirit hung
    O'er all with dread desire ;
Then broke upon the heads of all
    In cloven tongues of fire.

956.
H. M.

1 O THOU that hearest prayer!
    Attend our humble cry ;
And let thy servants share
    Thy blessing from on high :
We plead the promise of thy word,
Grant us thy Holy Spirit, Lord !

2 If earthly parents hear
    Their children when they cry ;
If they, with love sincere,
    Their children's wants supply ;
Much more wilt thou thy love display,
And answer when thy children pray.

3 Our heavenly Father thou,—
    We—children of thy grace,—
Oh, let thy Spirit now
    Descend and fill the place ;
That all may feel the heavenly flame,
And all unite to praise thy name.

957.
C. M.

1 PLUNGED in a gulf of dark despair,
    We wretched sinners lay,
Without one cheerful beam of hope,
    Or spark of glimmering day.

2 With pitying eyes the Prince of grace
    Beheld our helpless grief ;
He saw, and—oh, amazing love !—
    He ran to our relief.

3 Down from the shining seats above,
    With joyful haste he fled,
Entered the grave in mortal flesh,
    And dwelt among the dead.

4 Oh! for this love let rocks and hills
    Their lasting silence break ;
And all harmonious human tongues
    The Saviour's praises speak.

5 Angels ! assist our mighty joys ;
    Strike all your harps of gold ;
But, when you raise your highest notes,
    His love can ne'er be told.

958.
C. M.

1 WHEN God, of old, came down from
      heaven,
    In power and wrath he came ;
Before his feet the clouds were riven,
    Half darkness and half flame.

2 But when he came the second time,
    He came in power and love ;
Softer than gales at morning prime,
    Hovered his holy Dove.

3 The fires that rushed on Sinai down
    In sudden torrents dread,
Now gently light a glorious crown
    On every sainted head.

4 Like arrows went those lightnings forth,
    Winged with the sinner's doom ;
But these, like tongues, o'er all the earth
    Proclaiming life to come.

959.
H. M.

1 BLOW ye the trumpet, blow !
    The gladly solemn sound ;
Let all the nations know,
    To earth's remotest bound,
The year of jubilee is come ;
Return, ye ransomed sinners, home.

2 Exalt the Lamb of God,
    The sin-atoning Lamb !
Redemption by his blood,
    Through every land, proclaim ;
The year of jubilee is come ;
Return, ye ransomed sinners, home.

3 Ye slaves of sin and hell !
    Your liberty receive,
And safe in Jesus dwell,
    And blest in Jesus live :
The year of jubilee is come ;
Return, ye ransomed sinners, home.

4 The gospel trumpet hear,
The news of pardoning grace :
Ye happy souls, draw near;
Behold your Saviour's face :
The year of jubilee is come ;
Return, ye ransomed sinners, home.

5 Jesus, our great High Priest,
Has full atonement made ;
Ye weary spirits, rest;
Ye mourning souls, be glad :
The year of jubilee is come ;
Return, ye ransomed sinners, home.

960.
S. M.

1 God's holy law, transgressed,
Speaks nothing but despair ;
Burdened with guilt, with grief oppressed,
We find no comfort there.

2 Not all our groans and tears,
Nor works which we have done,
Nor vows, nor promises, nor prayers,
Can e'er for sin atone.

3 Relief alone is found
In Jesus' precious blood :
'Tis this that heals the mortal wound,
And reconciles to God.

4 High lifted on the cross,
The spotless victim dies ;
This is salvation's only source,
Hence all our hopes arise.

961.
L. M.

1 Hail, sovereign love, that formed the plan
To save rebellious, ruined man !
Hail, matchless, free, eternal grace,
That gave my soul a hiding-place.

2 Against the God that rules the sky
I fought, with weapons lifted high,
I madly ran the sinful race,
Regardless of a hiding-place.

3 Yet when God's justice rose in view,
To Sinai's burning mount I flew ;
Keen were the pangs of my distress—
The mountain was no hiding-place.

4 But a celestial voice I heard,
A bleeding Saviour then appeared,
Led by the Spirit of his grace—
I found in him a hiding-place.

5 On him the weight of vengeance fell,
That else had sunk a world to hell ;
Then, O my soul, forever praise
Thy Saviour God, thy hiding-place !

962.
C. M.

1 Mortals, awake, with angels join
And chant the solemn lay ;
Joy, love, and gratitude, combine
To hail th' auspicious day.

2 In heaven the rapturous song began,
And sweet seraphic fire
Through all the shining legions ran,
And strung and tuned the lyre.

3 Swift through the vast expanse it flew,
And loud the echo rolled ;
The theme, the song, the joy, was new,
'Twas more than heaven could hold.

4 Down through the portals of the sky
Th' impetuous torrent ran ;
And angels flew, with eager joy,
To bear the news to man.

5 Hark ! the cherubic armies shout,
And glory leads the song ;
" Good-will and peace" are heard
throughout
Th' harmonious angel throng.

6 With joy the chorus we'll repeat,—
"Glory to God on high !
Good-will and peace are now complete;
Jesus was born to die!"

7 Hail, Prince of life ! forever hail,
Redeemer, brother, friend !
Though earth, and time, and life, should
fail,
Thy praise shall never end.

963.
L. M. 6 lines.

1 Saviour of all, what hast thou done ?
What hast thou suffered on the tree ?
Why didst thou groan thy mortal groan,
Obedient unto death for me ?
The mystery of thy passion show—
The end of all thy griefs below.

2 Pardon, and grace, and heaven to buy,
My bleeding sacrifice expired ;
But didst thou not my pattern die,
That, by thy glorious Spirit fired,
Faithful to death I might endure,
And make the crown by suffering sure ?

3 Thou didst the meek example leave,
That I might in thy footsteps tread ;
Might like the Man of Sorrows grieve,
And groan, and bow with thee my head :
Thy dying in my body bear,
And all thy state of suffering share.

964.
S. M.

1 LIKE sheep we went astray,
And broke the fold of God ;
Each wandering in a different way,
But all the downward road.

2 How dreadful was the hour,
When God our wanderings laid,
And did at once his vengeance pour
Upon the Shepherd's head !

3 How glorious was the grace,
When Christ sustained the stroke !
His life and blood the Shepherd pays,
A ransom for the flock.

4 But God shall raise his head
O'er all the sons of men,
And make him see a numerous seed,
To recompense his pain.

965.
8s, 7s & 4s.

1 SEE, from Zion's sacred mountain,
Streams of living water flow ;
God has opened there a fountain
That supplies the world below ;
They are blessèd
Who its sovereign virtues know.

2 Through ten thousand channels flowing,
Streams of mercy find their way :
Life, and health, and joy bestowing,
Waking beauty from decay,
O ye nations !
Hail the long-expected day.

3 Gladdened by the flowing treasure,
All-enriching as it goes,
Lo ! the desert smiles with pleasure,
Buds and blossoms as the rose ;
Lo ! the desert
Sings for joy where'er it flows.

966.
C. M.

1 OH, how divine, how sweet the joy,
When but one sinner turns,
And, with an humble, broken heart,
His sins and errors mourns.

2 Pleased with the news, the saints below
In songs their tongues employ ;
Beyond the skies the tidings go,
And heaven is filled with joy.

3 Well pleased, the Father sees and hears
The conscious sinner's moan ;
Jesus receives him in his arms,
And claims him for his own.

4 Nor angels can their joys contain,
But kindle with new fire ;—
" The sinner lost is found," they sing,
And strike the sounding lyre.

967.
C. M.

1 How condescending and how kind
Was God's eternal Son !
Our misery reached his heavenly mind,
And pity brought him down.

2 He sunk beneath our heavy woes,
To raise us to his throne ;
There's ne'er a gift his hand bestows,
But cost his heart a groan.

3 This was compassion, like a God,
That when the Saviour knew
The price of pardon was his blood,
His pity ne'er withdrew.

4 Now, though he reigns exalted high,
His love is still as great ;
Well he remembers Calvary,
Nor let his saints forget.

968.
7s.

1 WOULD you win a soul to God ?
Tell him of a Saviour's blood,
Once for dying sinners spilt,
To atone for all their guilt,

2 Tell him,—it was sovereign grace
Led thee first to seek his face ;
Made thee choose the better part,
Wrought salvation in thy heart.

3 Tell him of that liberty,
  Wherewith Jesus makes us free!
  Sweetly speak of sins forgiven,
  Earnest of the joys of heaven.

969.
C. M.

1 Let every mortal ear attend,
  And every heart rejoice;
  The trumpet of the gospel sounds,
  With an inviting voice.

2 Ho! all ye hungry, starving souls,
  That feed upon the wind,
  And vainly strive with earthly toys
  To fill th' immortal mind,—

3 Eternal wisdom has prepared
  A soul-reviving feast,
  And bids your longing appetites
  The rich provision taste.

4 Ho! ye that pant for living streams,
  And pine away and die—
  Here you may quench your raging thirst
  With springs that never dry.

5 Rivers of love and mercy here
  In a rich ocean join;
  Salvation in abundance flows,
  Like floods of milk and wine.

6 The happy gates of gospel grace
  Stand open night and day;—
  Lord—we are come to seek supplies,
  And drive our wants away.

970.
7s & 6s.

1 Drooping souls, no longer mourn,
  Jesus still is precious;
  If to him you now return,
  Heaven will be propitious:
  Jesus now is passing by,
  Calling wanderers near him;
  Drooping souls, you need not die,
  Go to him and hear him!

2 He has pardons, full and free,
  Drooping souls to gladden;
  Still he cries—" Come unto me,
  Weary, heavy laden!"
  Though your sins like mountains high,
  Rise, and reach to heaven,
  Soon as you on him rely,
  All shall be forgiven.

3 Precious is the Saviour's name,
  Dear to all that love him;
  He to save the dying came;—
  Go to him and prove him!
  Wandering sinners, now return;
  Contrite souls, believe him!
  Jesus calls you, cease to mourn;
  Worship him; receive him.

971.
L. M.

1 Haste, traveler, haste! the night comes on,
  And many a shining hour is gone;
  The storm is gathering in the west,
  And thou far off from home and rest.

2 The rising tempest sweeps the sky;
  The rains descend, the winds are high;
  The waters swell, and death and fear
  Beset thy path, nor refuge near.

3 Oh, yet a shelter you may gain,
  A covert from the wind and rain;
  A hiding-place, a rest, a home,
  A refuge from the wrath to come!

4 Then linger not in all the plain;
  Flee for thy life; the mountain gain;
  Look not behind; make no delay;
  Oh, speed thee, speed thee on thy way!

972.
L. M.

1 Would you see Jesus? come with prayer,
  And heart repentant to his feet;
  None who will rightly seek him there,
  Shall fail his face of love to greet.

2 Would you see Jesus? come with faith,
  And search the Word his grace hath given,
  For help and guidance in the path
  That leads to his abode in heaven.

3 Would you see Jesus? day by day
  Let thought and converse be on high,
  And hastening on the heavenward way,
  With Jesus live, with Jesus die.

973.
C. M.

1 Inquire, ye pilgrims! for the way
  That leads to Zion's hill,
  And thither set your steady face,
  With a determined will.

2 Oh! come, and to his temple haste,
And seek his favor there;
Before his footstool, humbly bow,
And pour your fervent prayer.

3 Oh! come, and join your souls to God
In everlasting bands;
Accept the blessings he bestows,
With thankful hearts and hands.

974.
C. M.

1 Lord, we adore thy boundless grace,
The heights and depths unknown,
Of pardon, life, and joy, and peace,
In thy beloved Son.

2 Come, all ye pining, hungry poor,
The Saviour's bounty taste;
Behold a never-failing store
For every willing guest.

3 Here shall your numerous wants receive
A free, a full supply;
He has unmeasured bliss to give,
And joys that never die.

4 Lord, bring unwilling souls to thee
With sweet, resistless power;
Thy boundless grace let rebels see,
And at thy feet adore.

975.
C. M.

1 The Saviour calls! let every ear
Attend the heavenly sound:
Ye doubting souls, dismiss your fear;
Hope smiles reviving round.

2 For every thirsty, longing heart
Here streams of bounty flow;
And life, and health, and bliss impart
To banish mortal wo.

3 Here springs of sacred pleasure rise
To ease your every pain—
Immortal fountain! full supplies!—
Nor shall you thirst in vain.

4 Dear Saviour, draw reluctant hearts!
To thee let sinners fly,
And take the bliss thy love imparts,
And drink and never die.

976.
L. M.

1 Life is the time to serve the Lord,
The time t' insure the great reward;
And while the lamp holds out to burn,
The vilest sinner may return.

2 The living know that they must die;
But all the dead forgotten lie;
Their memory and their sense are gone,
Alike unknowing and unknown.

3 Their hatred, and their love, is lost,
Their envy buried in the dust;
They have no share in all that's done
Beneath the circuit of the sun.

4 Then what my thoughts design to do,
My hands, with all your might pursue,
Since no device, nor work, is found,
Nor faith, nor hope, beneath the ground.

5 There are no acts of pardon passed
In the cold grave to which we haste;
But darkness, death, and long despair
Reign in eternal silence there.

977.
C. M.

1 Repent! the voice celestial cries,
No longer dare delay:
The soul that scorns the mandate dies,
And meets a fiery day.

2 No more the sovereign eye of God
O'erlooks the crimes of men;
His heralds now are sent abroad
To warn the world of sin.

3 O sinners! in his presence bow,
And all your guilt confess;
Accept the offered Saviour now,
Nor trifle with his grace.

4 Soon, will the awful trumpet sound,
And call you to his bar;
His mercy knows th' appointed bound,
And yields to justice there.

5 Amazing love—that yet will call,
And yet prolong our days!
Our hearts, subdued by goodness, fall,
And weep, and love, and praise.

978.

S. M.

1 AND will the Judge descend,
And must the dead arise,
And not a single soul escape
His all-discerning eyes?

2 How will my heart endure
The terrors of that day,
When earth and heaven before his face
Astonished shrink away?

3 But, ere the trumpet shakes
The mansions of the dead,
Hark, from the Gospel's cheering sound
What joyful tidings spread!

4 Ye sinners! seek his grace
Whose wrath ye cannot bear;
Fly to the shelter of his cross,
And find salvation there.

979.

L. M. 6 lines.

1 O SAVIOUR of a world undone!
Whose dying sorrows blot the sun,
Whose painful groans and bowing head
Could rend the vail and wake the dead,
Say, from that execrated tree
Descends the ruddy tide for me?

2 For me did he who reigns above,
The object of paternal love,
Consent a servant's form to bear
That I a kingly crown might wear?
Is his deep loss my boundless gain,
And comes my victory from his pain?

3 Oh, let me own the deep decree
That wounded him and rescued me!
His death, his cross, his funeral sleep,
Instruct repentance how to weep;
He poured for me the vital flood;
My tears shall mingle with his blood.

4 His cross disarms temptation's power;
His cross can cheer the dying hour,
Make every holy doctrine clear,
And each connected precept dear;
And not a duty, or a loss,
But love can nail it to his cross.

980.

L. M.

1 WHEREWITH, O God, shall I draw near,
And bow myself before thy face?
How, in thy purer eyes, appear?
What shall I bring to gain thy grace?

2 Can gifts avert the wrath of God?
Can these wash out my guilty stain?
Rivers of oil, and seas of blood,
Alas! they all must flow in vain.

3 Ev'n though my life henceforth be thine,
Present for past can ne'er atone:
Though I to thee the whole resign,
I only give thee back thine own.

4 Guilty I stand before thy face;
On me I feel thy wrath abide;
'T is just the sentence should take place;
'T is just,—but oh, thy Son hath died!

981.

10s.

1 I THOUGHT upon my sins, and I was sad;
My soul was troubled sore and filled with
pain;
But then I thought on Jesus, and was
glad—
My heavy grief was turned to joy again.

2 I thought upon the law, the fiery law,
Holy and just, and good in its decree:
I looked to Jesus, and in him I saw
That law fulfilled, its curse endured for me.

3 I thought I saw an angry, frowning God,
Sitting as Judge upon the great white
throne:
My soul was overwhelmed; then Jesus
showed
His gracious face, and all my dread was
gone.

4 I saw my sad estate,—condemned to die:
Then terror seized my heart, and dark
despair;
But when to Calvary I turned my eye,
I saw the cross, and read forgiveness there.

5 I saw that I was lost, far gone astray;
No hope of safe return there seemed to be;
But then I heard that Jesus was the way,
A new and living way prepared for me.

6 Then, in that way, so free, so safe, so sure,
All sprinkled o'er with reconciling blood,
Will I abide, and never wander more,
But walk secure, in fellowship with God.

982.
L. M.

1 TREMBLING before thine awful throne,
O Lord! in dust my sins I own:
Justice and mercy for my life
Contend!—Oh, smile and heal the strife!

2 The Saviour smiles! upon my soul
New tides of hope tumultuous roll—
His voice proclaims my pardon found—
Seraphic transport wings the sound.

3 Earth has a joy unknown in heaven,
The new-born peace of sin forgiven!
Tears of such pure and deep delight,
Ye angels! never dimmed your sight.

4 Ye saw of old, on chaos rise
The beauteous pillars of the skies:
Ye know where morn, exulting springs,
And evening folds her drooping wings.

5 Bright heralds of th' eternal Will,
Abroad his errands ye fulfill;
Or, throned in floods of beamy day,
Symphonious, in his presence play.

6 But I amid your choirs shall shine,
And all your knowledge will be mine:
Ye on your harps must lean to hear
A secret chord that mine will bear.

983.
L. M. 6 lines.

1 WEARY of wandering from my God,
And now made willing to return,
I hear, and bow me to the rod:
Yet not in hopeless grief I mourn;
I have an advocate above,
A friend before the throne of love.

2 O Jesus, full of truth and grace,—
More full of grace than I of sin;
Yet once again I seek thy face,
Open thine arms, and take me in!
And freely my backslidings heal,
And love thy faithless servant still.

3 Thou know'st the way to bring me back,
My fallen spirit to restore;

Oh, for thy truth and mercy's sake,
Forgive, and bid me sin no more:
The ruins of my soul repair,
And make my heart a house of prayer.

984.
L. M.

1 FORGIVE us, Lord! to thee we cry,
Forgive us through thy matchless grace,
On thee alone our souls rely,
Be thou our strength and righteousness.

2 Forgive thou us, as we forgive
The ills we suffer from our foes;
Restore us, Lord! and bid us live;
Oh! let us in thine arms repose.

3 Forgive us, for our guilt is great,
Our wretched souls no merit claim;
For sovereign mercy still we wait,
And ask but in the Saviour's name.

4 Forgive us,—O thou bleeding Lamb!
Thou risen—thou exalted Lord!
Thou great High-Priest! our souls redeem,
And speak the pardon-sealing word.

985.
8s, 7s & 4s.

1 WELCOME, welcome, dear Redeemer!
Welcome to this heart of mine:
Lord, I make a full surrender,
Every power and thought be thine,
Thine entirely,
Through eternal ages thine.

2 Known to all to be thy mansion,
Earth and hell will disappear;
Or in vain attempt possession,
When they find the Lord is near—
Shout, O Zion!
Shout, ye saints, the Lord is here!

986.
C. M.

1 PROSTRATE, dear Jesus, at thy feet
A guilty rebel lies;
And upward to thy mercy-seat
Presumes to lift his eyes.

2 If tears of sorrow would suffice
To pay the debt I owe,
Tears should from both my weeping eyes
In ceaseless torrents flow.

3 But no such sacrifice I plead
  To expiate my guilt;
  No tears, but those which thou hast shed,
  No blood, but thou hast spilt.

4 Think of thy sorrows, dearest Lord!
  And all my sins forgive:
  Justice will well approve the word
  That bids the sinner live.

987.
L. M.

1 A BROKEN heart, my God, my King,
  Is all the sacrifice I bring:
  The God of grace will ne'er despise
  A broken heart for sacrifice.

2 My soul lies humbled in the dust,
  And owns thy dreadful sentence just:
  Look down, O Lord, with pitying eye,
  And save the soul condemned to die.

3 Then will I teach the world thy ways;
  Sinners shall learn thy sovereign grace:
  I'll lead them to my Saviour's blood,
  And they shall praise a pardoning God.

4 Oh, may thy love inspire my tongue!
  Salvation shall be all my song;
  And all my powers shall join to bless
  The Lord, my Strength and Righteous-
  ness.

988.
S. M.

1 OH, that I could repent,
  With all my idols part,
  And to thy gracious eye present
  An humble, contrite heart!

2 A heart with grief oppressed
  For having grieved my God;
  A troubled heart, that cannot rest
  Till sprinkled with thy blood.

3 Jesus, on me bestow
  The penitent desire;
  With true sincerity of woe
  My aching breast inspire.

4 With softening pity look,
  And melt my hardness down:
  Strike with thy love's resistless stroke,
  And break this heart of stone.

989.
7s & 6s.

1 WE stand in deep repentance,
  Before thy throne of love;
  O God of grace, forgive us;
  The stain of guilt remove;
  Behold us while with weeping
  We lift our eyes to thee;
  And all our sins subduing,
  Our Father, set us free!

2 Oh! shouldst thou from us fallen
  Withhold thy grace to guide,
  Forever we should wander,
  From thee, and peace, aside;
  But thou to spirits contrite
  Dost light and life impart,
  That man may learn to serve thee
  With thankful, joyous heart.

3 Our souls—on thee we cast them,
  Our only refuge thou!
  Thy cheering words revive us,
  When pressed with grief we bow:
  Thou bear'st the trusting spirit
  Upon thy loving breast,
  And givest all thy ransomed
  A sweet, unending rest.

990.
L. M.

1 FROM deep distress and troubled thoughts,
  To thee, my God, I raise my cries;
  If thou severely mark our faults,
  No flesh can stand before thine eyes.

2 But thou hast built thy throne of grace,
  Free to dispense thy pardons there;
  That sinners may approach thy face,
  And hope and love, as well as fear.

3 As the benighted pilgrims wait,
  And long and wish for breaking day,
  So waits my soul before thy gate:
  When will my God his face display?

4 My trust is fixed upon thy word,
  Nor shall I trust thy word in vain;
  Let mourning souls address the Lord,
  And find relief from all their pain.

5 Great is his love, and large his grace,
  Through the redemption of his Son;
  He turns our feet from sinful ways,
  And pardons what our hands have done.

991.
C. M.

1 The promise of my Father's love
Shall stand forever good :—
He said, and gave his soul to death,
And sealed the grace with blood.

2 To this dear covenant of thy word,
I set my worthless name ;
I seal th' engagement of my Lord,
And make my humble claim.

3 The light, and strength, and pardoning
grace,
And glory, shall be mine ;
My life and soul, my heart and flesh,
And all my powers are thine.

4 I call that legacy my own,
Which Jesus did bequeath ;
'Twas purchased with a dying groan,
And ratified in death.

5 Sweet is the memory of his name,
Who blessed us in his will,
And to his testament of love,
Made his own life the seal.

992.
C. M.

1 Witness, ye men and angels now,
Before the Lord we speak ;
To him we make our solemn vow,
A vow we dare not break :

2 That long as life itself shall last,
Ourselves to Christ we yield,
Nor from his cause will we depart,
Or ever quit the field.

3 We trust not in our native strength,
But on his grace rely,
That, with returning wants, the Lord
Will all our need supply.

993.
L. M.

1 Oh, turn, great Ruler of the skies ?
Turn from my sin thy searching eyes ;
Nor let th' offences of my hand
Within thy book recorded stand.

2 Give me a will to thine subdued,—
A conscience pure, a soul renewed ;
Nor let me, wrapt in endless gloom,
An outcast from thy presence roam.

3 Oh, let thy Spirit to my heart
Once more its quickening aid impart ;
My mind from every fear release,
And soothe my troubled thoughts to
peace.

994.
L. M.

1 O thou that hear'st when sinners cry,
Though all my crimes before thee lie,
Behold me not with angry look,
But blot their memory from thy book.

2 Create my nature pure within,
And form my soul averse to sin ;
Let thy good Spirit ne'er depart,
Nor hide thy presence from my heart.

3 I cannot live without thy light,
Cast out and banished from thy sight ;
Thy holy joys, my God, restore,
And guard me that I fall no more.

4 Though I have grieved thy Spirit, Lord,
His help and comfort still afford ;
And let a sinner seek thy throne,
To plead the merits of thy Son.

995
7s.

1 'Tis a point I long to know,
Oft it causes anxious thought ;
Do I love the Lord, or no ?
Am I his, or am I not ?

2 Could my heart so hard remain,
Prayer a task and burden prove,
Every trifle give me pain,
If I knew a Saviour's love ?

3 When I turn my eyes within,
All is dark, and vain, and wild,
Filled with unbelief and sin,
Can I deem myself a child ?

4 If I pray, or hear, or read,
Sin is mixed with all I do ;
You who love the Lord indeed,
Tell me—is it thus with you ?

5 Yet I mourn my stubborn will,
Find my sin a grief and thrall ;
Should I grieve for what I feel,
If I did not love at all ?

6 Could I joy with saints to meet,
Choose the ways I once abhorred,
Find at times the promise sweet,
If I did not love the Lord ?

7 Lord, decide the doubtful case,
   Thou who art thy people's Sun ;
   Shine upon thy work of grace,
   If it be indeed begun.

996.
P. M.

1 WILT thou not visit me?
   The plant beside me feels thy gentle
      dew ;
   Each blade of grass I see,
   From thy deep earth its quickening
      moisture drew.

2 Wilt thou not visit me?
   Thy morning calls on me with cheer-
      ing tone ;
   And every hill and tree
   Lend but one voice, the voice of thee
      alone.

3 Come! for I need thy love,
   More than the flower the dew, or grass
      the rain ;
   Come, like thy holy dove,
   And let me in thy sight rejoice to live
      again.

4 Yes! thou wilt visit me;
   Nor plant, nor tree, thine eye delights
      so well
   As when from sin set free,
   Man's spirit comes with thine in peace
      to dwell.

997.
8s & 4s.

1 MY heart lies dead ; and no increase
   Doth my dull husbandry improve ;
   Oh, let thy graces, without cease,
      Drop from above!

2 Thy dew doth every morning fall ;
   And shall the dew outstrip thy Dove?—
   The dew for which earth cannot call,
      "Drop from above!"

3 The world is tempting still my heart
   Unto a hardness void of love ;
   Let heavenly grace, to cross its art,
      Drop from above!

4 Oh, come ; for thou dost know the way!
   Or if to me thou wilt not move,
   Remove me where I need not say,
      "Drop from above!"

998.
8s & 7s.

1 LONE, amidst the dead and dying,
   Lord, my spirit faints for thee;
   Longing, thirsting, drooping, sighing,—
   When shall I thy presence see?

2 Oh, how altered my condition!
   Late I led the joyous throng ;
   Beat my heart with full fruition,
   Flowed my lips with grateful song.

3 Now the storm goes wildly o'er me,
   Waves on waves my soul confound ;
   Nought but boding fears before me,
   Nought but threatening foes around.

4 Save me, save me, O my Father!
   To thy faithful word I cling ;
   Thence, my soul! thy comfort gather ;
   Hope! and thou again shalt sing.

999.
7s.

1 HASTEN, Lord! to my release,
   Haste to help me, O my God!
   Foes, like arméd bands, increase ;
   Turn them back the way they trod.

2 Dark temptations round me press,
   Evil thoughts my soul assail ;
   Doubts and fears, in my distress,
   Rise, till flesh and spirit fail.

3 Those that seek thee shall rejoice ;
   I am bound with misery ;
   Yet I make thy law my choice ;
   Turn, my God! and look on me.

4 Thou mine only helper art,
   My redeemer from the grave ;
   Strength of my desiring heart!
   Do not tarry, haste to save.

1000.
C. M.

1 O THOU, from whom all goodness flows,
   I lift my soul to thee ;
   In all my sorrows, conflicts, woes,
   O Lord, remember me!

2 When on my aching, burdened heart
   My sins lie heavily,
   Thy pardon grant, new peace impart ;
   Then, Lord, remember me!

3 When trials sore obstruct my way,
 And ills I cannot flee,
Oh, let my strength be as my day—
 Dear Lord, remember me!

4 When in the solemn hour of death
 I wait thy just decree;
Be this the prayer of my last breath:
 Now, Lord, remember me!

1001.

L. M.

1 My God, permit me not to be
A stranger to myself and thee;
Amid a thousand thoughts I rove,
Forgetful of my highest love.

2 Why should my passions mix with earth,
And thus debase my heavenly birth?
Why should I cleave to things below,
And let my God, my Saviour go?

3 Call me away from flesh and sense;
One sovereign word can draw me thence;
I would obey the voice divine,
And all inferior joys resign.

4 Be earth, with all her scenes withdrawn;
Let noise and vanity be gone:
In secret silence of the mind
My heaven, and there my God, I find.

1002.

L. M.

1 An! wretched, vile, ungrateful heart!
That can from Jesus thus depart;
Thus, fond of trifles, vainly rove,
Forgetful of a Saviour's love.

2 In vain I charge my thoughts to stay,
And chide earth's vanities away;
There's naught beneath a power divine,
That can this roving heart confine.

3 Jesus! to thee I would return,
And, at thy feet repenting, mourn;
There let me view thy pardoning love,
And never from thy sight remove.

4 Oh! let thy love, with sweet control,
Bind all the passions of my soul;
Bid every earthly charm depart,
And dwell forever in my heart.

1003.

C. M.

1 On! could our thoughts and wishes fly,
Above these gloomy shades,
To those bright worlds, beyond the sky,
Which sorrow ne'er invades!—

2 There, joys, unseen by mortal eyes,
Or reason's feeble ray,
In ever-blooming prospects rise,
Unconscious of decay.

3 Lord! send a beam of light divine,
To guide our upward aim;
With one reviving touch of thine,
Our languid hearts inflame.

4 Oh! then, on faith's sublimest wing,
Our ardent hope shall rise
To those bright scenes, where pleasures
 spring
Immortal in the skies.

1004.

C. M.

1 As pants the hart for cooling streams,
When heated in the chase,
So longs my soul, O God, for thee,
And thy refreshing grace.

2 For thee, my God—the living God,
My thirsty soul doth pine;
Oh, when shall I behold thy face,
Thou Majesty divine!

3 Why restless, why cast down, my soul?
Trust God; who will employ
His aid for thee, and change these sighs
To thankful hymns of joy.

4 God of my strength, how long shall I,
Like one forgotten mourn;
Forlorn, forsaken, and exposed
To my oppressor's scorn?

5 I sigh to think of happier days,
When thou, O Lord! wast nigh;
When every heart was tuned to praise,
And none more blest than I.

6 Why restless, why cast down, my soul?
Hope still; and thou shalt sing
The praise of him who is thy God,
Thy health's eternal spring.

1005.
S. M. Double.

1 I WANT a heart to pray—
　To pray, and never cease;
Never to murmur at thy stay,
　Or wish my sufferings less.
This blessing, above all—
　Always to pray—I want;
Out of the deep on thee to call,
　And never, never faint.

2 I want a true regard,
　A single, steady aim—
Unmoved by threatening or reward,
　To thee and thy great name;
A jealous, just concern,
　For thine immortal praise;
A pure desire that all may learn
　And glorify thy grace.

3 I rest upon thy word—
　The promise is for me;
My succor and salvation, Lord,
　Shall surely come from thee;
But let me still abide,
　Nor from my hope remove,
Till thou my patient spirit guide
　Into thy perfect love.

1006.
7s & 6s.

1 In time of tribulation,
　Hear, Lord! my feeble cries;
With humble supplication
　To thee my spirit flies:
My heart with grief is breaking;
　Scarce can my voice complain:
Mine eyes, with tears kept waking,
　Still watch and weep in vain.

2 Hath God cast off forever?
　Can time his truth impair?
His tender mercy, never
　Shall I presume to share?
Hath he his loving kindness
　Shut up in endless wrath?
No; this is mine own blindness,
　That cannot see his path.

3 I call to recollection
　The years of his right hand;
And, strong in his protection,
　Again through faith I stand:

Thy deeds, O Lord, are wonder,
　Holy are all thy ways;
The secret place of thunder,
　Shall utter forth thy praise.

4 Thee, with the tribes assembled,
　O God, the billows saw;
They saw thee and they trembled,
　Turned, and stood still with awe:
The clouds shot hail,—they lightened,
　The earth reeled to and fro;
The fiery pillar brightened
　The gulf of gloom below.

5 Thy way is in great waters:
　Thy footsteps are not known:
Let Adam's sons and daughters
　Confide in thee alone:
Through the wild sea thou leddest
　Thy chosen flock of yore:
Still on the waves thou treadest,
　And thy redeemed pass o'er.

1007.
C. M.

1 Oh, for a heart to praise my God,
　A heart from sin set free;
A heart that's sprinkled with the blood
　So freely shed for me!

2 A heart resigned, submissive, meek,
　My dear Redeemer's throne;
Where only Christ is heard to speak,
　Where Jesus reigns alone:—

3 An humble, lowly, contrite heart,
　Believing, true, and clean,
Which neither death nor life can part
　From him that dwells within:—

4 A heart in every thought renewed,
　And filled with love divine;
Perfect, and right, and pure, and good;
　An image, Lord! of thine.

1008.
L. M.

1 How long, O Lord, shall I complain,
　Like one that seeks his God in vain?
How long my soul thine absence mourn,
　And still despair of thy return?

2 How long shall my poor troubled breast
　Be with these anxious thoughts oppressed?
If thou withhold thy heavenly light,
　I sleep in everlasting night.

3 Hear, Lord, and grant me quick relief,
Thy mercy now shall end my grief;
For I have trusted in thy grace,
And shall again behold thy face.

1009.
L. M.

1 RETURN, my roving heart! return, .
And chase those shadowy forms no more;
Now seek, in solitude, to mourn,
And thy forsaken God implore.

2 O thou great God! whose piercing eye
Distinctly marks its deep recess;—
In these sequestered hours draw nigh,
And with thy presence fill the place!

3 Through all the windings of my heart,
My search let heavenly wisdom guide,
And still its radiant beams impart,
Till all be cleansed and purified.

4 Oh! with the visits of thy love,
Vouchsafe my inmost soul to cheer;
Till every grace shall join to prove
That God has fixed his dwelling here.

1010.
L. M.

1 JESUS demands this heart of mine,
Demands my love, my joy, my care;
But ah! how dead to things divine,
How cold my best affections are!

2 'T is sin, alas! with dreadful power,
Divides my Saviour from my sight;
Oh, for one happy, cloudless hour
Of sacred freedom, sweet delight!

3 Come, gracious Lord! thy love can raise
My captive powers from sin and death,
And fill my heart and life with praise,
And tune my last expiring breath.

1011.
10s & 4s.

1 LORD, many times I am aweary quite
Of my own self, my sin, and vanity;
Yet be not thou, or I am lost outright,
Weary of me.

2 And hate against myself I often bear,
And enter with myself in fierce debate;
Take thou my part, against myself, nor share
In that just hate.

3 Best friends might loathe us, if what
things perverse
We know of our own selves, they also
knew;
Lord, Holy One! if thou, who knowest
worse,
Shouldst loathe us too!

1012.
7s.

1 SON of God, thy blessing grant,
Still supply my every want;
Tree of life, thine influence shed;
With thy sap my spirit feed.

2 Tenderest branch, alas! I lie,
Withered, without thee, and die;
Weak as helpless infancy;
Oh, confirm my soul in thee!

3 Unsustained by thee, I fall;
Send the strength for which I call:
Weaker than a bruisèd reed,
Help I every moment need.

4 All my hopes on thee depend;
Love me, save me to the end!
Give me the continuing grace,
Take the everlasting praise.

1013.
C. M.

1 LONG have I sat beneath the sound
Of thy salvation, Lord!
But still how weak my faith is found,
And knowledge of thy word!

2 Oft I frequent thy holy place,
And hear almost in vain;
How small a portion of thy grace
My memory can retain!

3 How cold and feeble is my love!
How negligent my fear!
How low my hope of joys above!
How few affections there!

4 Great God! thy sovereign power impart,
To give thy word success:
Write thy salvation in my heart,
And make me learn thy grace.

5 Show my forgetful feet the way
That leads to joys on high:
There knowledge grows without decay,
And love shall never die.

1014.

C. M.

1 DEAR Saviour, when my thoughts recall
The wonders of thy grace,
Low at thy feet ashamed, I fall,
And hide this wretched face.

2 Shall love like thine be thus repaid?
Ah, vile, ungrateful heart!
By earth's low cares so oft betrayed,
From Jesus to depart.

3 But he for his own mercy's sake,
My wandering soul restores;
He bids the mourning heart partake
The pardon it implores.

4 Oh, while I breathe to thee, my Lord,
The deep, repentant sigh,
Confirm the kind, forgiving word,
With pity in thine eye.

5 Then shall the mourner at thy feet
Rejoice to seek thy face;
And grateful, own how kind, how sweet,
Thy condescending grace.

1015.

L. M.

1 WHEN, gracious Lord, when shall it be
That I shall find my all in thee—
The fullness of thy promise prove,
The seal of thine eternal love?

2 Ah! wherefore did I ever doubt?
Thou wilt in no wise cast me out—
A helpless soul that comes to thee
With only sin and misery.

3 Lord, I am blind—be thou my sight;
Lord, I am weak—be thou my might;
A helper of the helpless be;
And let me find my all in thee.

1016.

7s.

1 THOU who didst on Calvary bleed,
Thou who dost for sinners plead,
Help me in my time of need,
Jesus, Saviour, hear my cry!

2 In my darkness and my grief,
With my heart of unbelief,
I, who am of sinners chief,
Jesus, lift to thee mine eye!

3 Foes without and fears within,
With no plea thy grace to win,
But that thou canst save from sin,
Jesus, to thy cross I fly!

4 There on thee I cast my care,
There to thee I raise my prayer,
Jesus, save me from despair,
Save me, save me, or I die!

5 When the storms of trial lower,
When I feel temptation's power,
In the last and darkest hour,
Jesus, Saviour, be thou nigh!

1017.

11s & 5s.

1 FROM the recesses of a lowly spirit,
Our humble prayer ascends; O Father!
hear it,
Upsoaring on the wings of awe and meek-
ness;
Forgive its weakness!

2 We see thy hand; it leads us, it supports us:
We hear thy voice; it counsels and it
courts us:
And then we turn away; and still thy
kindness
Forgives our blindness.

3 Oh, how long-suffering, Lord! but thou
delightest
To win with love the wandering; thou
invitest,
By smiles of mercy, not by frowns or
terrors,
Man from his errors.

4 Father and Saviour! plant within each
bosom
The seeds of holiness, and bid them blossom
In fragrance and in beauty bright and
vernal,
And spring eternal.

5 Then place them in thine everlasting
gardens,
Where angels walk, and seraphs are the
wardens;
Where every flower escaped through
death's dark portal,
Becomes immortal.

1018.

7s & 6s.

1 O Lamb of God! still keep me
　　Near to thy wounded side;
　'T is only then in safety
　　And peace I can abide!
　What foes and snares surround me!
　　What doubts and fears within!
　The grace that sought and found me,
　　Alone can keep me clean.

2 'T is only in thee hiding,
　　I feel my life secure—
　Only in thee abiding,
　　The conflict can endure:
　Thine arm the victory gaineth
　　O'er every hateful foe;
　Thy love my heart sustaineth
　　In all its cares and woe.

3 Soon shall my eyes behold thee
　　With rapture, face to face;
　One half hath not been told me
　　Of all thy power and grace:
　Thy beauty, Lord, and glory,
　　The wonders of thy love,
　Shall be the endless story
　　Of all thy saints above.

1019.

C. M.

1 Love me, O Lord, forgivingly!
　　Oh! ever be my friend;
　And still, when thou reprovest me,
　　Reproof with pity blend.

2 Oh, pity me, when weak I fall!
　　And as with saddened eyes
　I upward look, oh, let thy call
　　Come strengthening me to rise.

3 My sins dispersed by mercy bright,
　　Like clouds again grow black;
　Oh! change the winds that bring such
　　　night,
　　And drive the darkness back.

4 This fearful striving—let it cease!
　　Then fervent, fruitful days
　Shall yield both promise and increase,
　　And make my growth thy praise.

1020.

H. M.

1 The promises I sing,
　　Which sovereign love hath spoke
　Nor will th' eternal King
　　His words of grace revoke;
They stand secure　│　Not Zion's hill
And steadfast still;　│　Abides so sure.

2 The mountains melt away
　　When once the Judge appears,
　And sun and moon decay,
　　That measure mortal years;
But still the same,　│　The promise shines
In radiant lines　│　Through all the flame.

3 Their harmony shall sound
　　Through my attentive ears,
　When thunders cleave the ground
　　And dissipate the spheres;
Midst all the shock　│　I stand serene,
Of that dread scene,　│　Thy word my rock.

1021.

P. M.

1 Jesus lives! no longer now
　Can thy terrors, Death, appall me;
　Jesus lives! and well I know,
　From the dead he will recall me;
　Better life will then commence,
　This shall be my confidence.

2 Jesus lives! to him the throne
　Over all the world is given;
　I shall go where he is gone,
　Live and reign with him in heaven;
　God is pledged, weak doubtings, hence!
　This shall be my confidence.

3 Jesus lives! I know full well,
　Naught from him my heart can sever,
　Life nor death, nor powers of hell,
　Joy nor grief, henceforth, forever.
　God will power and grace dispense,
　This shall be my confidence.

4 Jesus lives! henceforth is death
　Entrance into life immortal;
　Calmly I can yield my breath,
　Fearless tread the frowning portal;
　Lord, when faileth flesh and sense,
　Thou wilt be my confidence!

1022.
C. M.

1 THE earth shall waste, the sun shall fade,
  The stars shall pass away;
  But who the Lord his trust hath made,
  Though suns and stars in dust be laid,
  Shall never know decay.

2 The soul that finds in God delight,
  Unshaken aye shall be,
  When ruined nature sinks in night,
  And years beyond still urge their flight
  'Mid vast Eternity.

3 On eagles' wings it shall ascend
  Along its tireless way,
  To worlds unseen, where sorrows end,
  And love and knowledge sweetly blend
  In everlasting day.

4 Secure in Jesus, there no sin
  Shall ever reach it more;
  For all that world is pure within,
  And naught may e'er admittance win,
  To cloud its radiant shore.

5 O Soul of mine! wilt thou arise
  And stretch an upward wing;
  And thither turn thine ardent eyes
  Where, far beyond these fading skies,
  Eternal pleasures spring?

1023.
H. M.

1 ARISE, my soul, arise,
  Shake off thy guilty fears;
  The bleeding Sacrifice
  In my behalf appears:
  Before the throne my Surety stands;
  My name is written on his hands.

2 He ever lives above,
  For me to intercede,
  His all-redeeming love,
  His precious blood to plead;
  His blood atoned for all our race,
  And sprinkles now the throne of grace.

3 My God is reconciled;
  His pardoning voice I hear:
  He owns me for his child—
  I can no longer fear;
  With confidence I now draw nigh,
  And "Father, Abba, Father," cry.

1024.
L. M.

1 O LOVE divine, that stooped to share
  Our sharpest pang, our bitterest tear,
  On thee we cast each earth-born care,
  We smile at pain while thou art near.

2 Though long the weary way we tread,
  And sorrow crown each lingering year,
  No path we shun, no darkness dread,
  Our hearts still whispering, thou art near.

3 When drooping pleasure turns to grief,
  And trembling faith is changed to fear,
  The murmuring wind, the quivering leaf,
  Shall softly tell us thou art near.

4 On thee we fling our burdening woe,
  O Love divine, forever dear;
  Content to suffer while we know,
  Living or dying, thou art near!

1025.
C. M.

1 GOD'S glory is a wondrous thing,
  Most strange in all its ways,
  And, of all things on earth, least like
  What men agree to praise.

2 Oh, blest is he to whom is given
  The instinct that can tell
  That God is on the field, when he
  Is most invisible!

3 Workman of God! oh, lose not heart,
  But learn what God is like;
  And in the darkest battle-field
  Thou shalt know where to strike.

4 And blest is he who can divine
  Where real right doth lie,
  And dares to take the side that seems
  Wrong to man's blindfold eye!

5 Oh, learn to scorn the praise of men!
  Oh, learn to lose with God!
  For Jesus won the world through shame,
  And beckons thee his road.

1026.
S. M.

1 AND are we yet alive,
  And see each other's face?
  Glory and praise to Jesus give,
  For his redeeming grace.

2 What troubles have we seen!
    What conflicts have we past!
    Fightings without, and fears within,
    Since we assembled last!

3 But out of all, the Lord
    Hath brought us by his love;
    And still he doth his help afford,
    And hides our life above.

4 Then let us make our boast
    Of his redeeming power,
    Which saves us to the uttermost,
    Till we can sin no more.

5 Let us take up the cross,
    Till we the crown obtain;
    And gladly reckon all things loss,
    So we may Jesus gain.

1027.
7s.

1 Cast thy burden on the Lord,
    Only lean upon his word;
    Thou wilt soon have cause to bless
    His unchanging faithfulness.

2 He sustains thee by his hand,
    He enables thee to stand;
    Those, whom Jesus once hath loved,
    From his grace are never moved.

3 Heaven and earth may pass away,
    God's free grace shall not decay;
    He hath promised to fulfill
    All the pleasure of his will.

4 Jesus! guardian of thy flock,
    Be thyself our constant rock;
    Make us, by thy powerful hand,
    Firm as Zion's mountain stand.

1028.
L. C. M.

1 The songs of Zion oft impart,
    To this poor, laboring, care-worn heart,
    The balm of heavenly peace;
    They chase away each boding fear,
    They turn to joy each sorrowing tear,
    And bid the tumult cease.

2 O Thou, who fillest the heavenly throne,
    'Tis not in melody alone
    To set the spirit free;
    Without the breathings of thy love
    The sweetest strains will powerless prove,
    Nor comfort bring to me.

3 But if the Spirit of the Lord
    His hallowed influence will afford,
    The soul will upward rise
    On wings of song with love divine,
    Till heavenly light around me shine,
    Beneath the bending skies.

4 If thou the gracious influence lend,
    The charms of song will sweetly blend
    With pure devotion's flame;
    Will melt the heart, the mind employ,
    And fill the soul with holy joy,
    At mention of thy name.

5 Give me that music of the lyre
    That bids each earthly wish expire,
    And lifts the thoughts on high:
    That fills the soul with heavenly love,
    And bids her a rich foretaste prove
    Of treasures in the sky.

1029.
7s. Double.

1 Lord, thou art my rock of strength,
    And my home is in thine arms;
    Thou wilt send me help at length,
    And I feel no wild alarms:
    Sin nor death can pierce the shield
    Thy defence has o'er me thrown,
    Up to thee myself I yield,
    And my sorrows are thine own.

2 When my trials tarry long
    Unto thee I look and wait;
    Knowing none, though keen and strong,
    Can my trust in thee abate;
    And this faith, I long have nursed,
    Comes alone, O God, from thee;
    Thou my heart didst open first,
    Thou didst set this hope in me.

3 On thee, O my God, I rest,
    Letting life float calmly on;
    For I know the last is best,
    When the crown of joy is won:
    In thy might all things I bear,
    In thy love find bitter, sweet,
    And with all my grief and care,
    Sit in patience at thy feet.

4 Let thy mercy's wings be spread
    O'er me, keep me close to thee;
    In the peace thy love doth shed,
    Let me dwell eternally!

Be my all : in all I do,
Let me only seek thy will;
When the heart to thee is true
All is peaceful, calm, and still.

1030.
7s. Double.

1 WHEN along life's thorny road,
Faints the soul beneath the load,
By its cares and sins oppressed,
Finds on earth no peace or rest;
When the wily tempter's near,
Filling us with doubts and fear :
Jesus, to thy feet we flee,
Jesus, we will look to thee.

2 Thou, our Saviour, from the throne
List'nest to thy people's moan;
Thou, the living Head, dost share
Every pang thy members bear:
Full of tenderness thou art,
Thou wilt heal the broken heart;
Full of power, thine arm shall quell
All the rage and might of hell.

3 Mighty to redeem and save,
Thou hast overcome the grave ;
Thou the bars of death hast riven,
Opened wide the gates of heaven ;
Soon in glory thou shalt come,
Taking thy poor pilgrims home ;
Jesus, then we all shall be,
Ever—ever—Lord, with thee.

1031.
7s.

1 FEEBLE, helpless, how shall I
Learn to live and learn to die ?
Who, O God ! my guide shall be ?
Who shall lead thy child to thee ?

2 Blesséd Father, gracious One !
Thou hast sent thy holy Son ;
He will give the light I need,
He my trembling steps will lead.

3 Thus in deed, and thought, and word,
Led by Jesus Christ the Lord,
In my weakness, thus shall I
Learn to live and learn to die.

4 Learn to live in peace and love,
Like the perfect ones above ;
Learn to die without a fear,
Feeling thee, my Father near.

1032.
C. M.

1 UNSHAKEN as the sacred hill,
And firm as mountains stand,
Firm as a rock the soul shall rest,
That trusts th' almighty hand.

2 Not walls, nor hills, could guard so well
Old Salem's happy ground,
As those eternal arms of love,
That every saint surround.

3 Deal gently, Lord, with souls sincere,
And lead them safely on
To the bright gates of paradise,
Where Christ, the Lord, is gone.

1033.
7s.

1 STRIVE, when thou art called of God,
When he draws thee by his grace,
Strive to cast away the load
That would clog thee in the race.

2 Fight, though it may cost thy life,
Storm the kingdom, but prevail ;
Let not Satan's fiercest strife
Make thee, warrior, faint or quail.

3 Wrestle, till through every vein
Love and strength are glowing warm ;
Love, that can the world disdain—
Half-love will not bide the storm.

4 Art thou faithful ? wake and watch !
Love with all thy heart Christ's ways ;
Seek not transient ease to snatch,
Look not for reward or praise.

5 Soldiers of the Cross ! be strong ;
Watch and war through fear and pain,
Daily conquering woe and wrong,
Till our King shall come to reign !

1034.
C. M. Double.

1 THOU art my hiding-place, O Lord !
In thee I put my trust ;
Encouraged by thy holy word,
A feeble child of dust :
I have no argument beside,
I urge no other plea,
And 'tis enough my Saviour died,
My Saviour died for me !

2 When storms of fierce temptation beat,
  And furious foes assail,
My refuge is the mercy-seat,
  My hope within the vail:
From strife of tongues, and bitter words,
  My spirit flies to thee;
Joy to my heart the thought affords,
  My Saviour died for me!

3 And when thine awful voice commands
  This body to decay,
And life, in its last lingering sands,
  Is ebbing fast away;—
Then, though it be in accents weak,
  My voice shall call on thee,
And ask for strength in death to speak,
  " My Saviour died for me."

1035.
7s.

1 EARTH has nothing sweet or fair,
Lovely forms or beauties rare,
But before my eyes they bring
Christ, of beauty Source and Spring.

2 When the morning paints the skies,
When the golden sunbeams rise,
Then my Saviour's form I find
Brightly imaged on my mind.

3 When the day-beams pierce the night,
Oft I think on Jesus' light,
Think how bright that light will be,
Shining through eternity.

4 Come, Lord Jesus! and dispel
This dark cloud in which I dwell,
And to me the power impart
To behold thee as thou art.

1036.
C. M.

1 O LORD! I would delight in thee,
  And on thy care depend ;
To thee in every trouble flee,
  My best, my only Friend.

2 When all created streams are dried,
  Thy fullness is the same ;
May I with this be satisfied,
  And glory in thy name!

3 No good in creatures can be found,
  But may be found in thee ;
I must have all things, and abound,
  While God is God to me.

4 O Lord! I cast my care on thee ;
  I triumph and adore;
Henceforth my great concern shall be
  To love and please thee more.

1037.
L. M. 6 lines.

1 MY Saviour, thou thy love to me,
In want, in pain, in shame, hast shown,
For me upon the accursèd tree,
Didst by thy precious death atone;
Thy death upon my heart impress,
That nothing may it thence erase.

2 Oh, that I, like a little child,
May follow thee ; nor ever rest
Till sweetly thou hast poured thy mild
And lowly mind into my breast!
Oh, may I now and ever be,
One spirit, dearest Lord, with thee !

3 What in thy love possess I not ?
My Star by night, my Sun by day,
My spring of life when parched with
  drought,
My wine to cheer, my bread to stay ;
My strength, my shield, my safe abode,
My robe before the throne of God.

4 From all eternity with love
Unchangeable thou hast me viewed ;
Ere knew this beating heart to move,
Thy tender mercies me pursued :
Ever with me may they abide,
And close me in on every side.

1038.
L. M. Double.

1 THOUGH sorrows rise, and dangers roll,
In waves of darkness o'er my soul;
Though friends are false, and love decays,
And few and evil are my days ;
Though conscience, fiercest of my foes,
Swells with remembered guilt my woes ;
Yet even in nature's utmost ill,
I love thee, Lord! I love thee still !

2 Though Sinai's curse, in thunder dread,
Peals o'er mine unprotected head,
And memory points, with busy pain,
To grace and mercy given in vain ;
Till nature, shrinking in the strife,
Would fly to hell to 'scape from life ;
Though every thought has power to kill,
I love thee, Lord ! I love thee still !

3 Oh, by the pangs thyself hast borne,
The ruffian's blow, the tyrant's scorn;
By Sinai's curse, whose dreadful doom
Was buried in thy guiltless tomb;
By these my pangs, whose healing smart
Thy grace hath planted in my heart—
I know, I feel thy bounteous will,
Thou lov'st me, Lord! thou lov'st me still!

1039.
C. M.

1 LET worldly minds the world pursue;
It has no charms for me;
Once I admired its trifles too,
But grace has set me free.

2 Its pleasures now no longer please,
No more content afford;
Far from my heart be joys like these,
Now I have seen the Lord.

3 As by the light of opening day
The stars are all concealed;
So earthly pleasures fade away,
When Jesus is revealed.

4 Creatures no more divide my choice;
I bid them all depart;
His name, and love, and gracious voice
Have fixed my roving heart.

1040.
C. M.

1 To whom, my Saviour, shall I go,
If I depart from thee?
My guide through all this vale of woe,
And more than all to me.

2 The world reject thy gentle reign,
And pay thy death with scorn;
Oh! they could plat thy crown again,
And sharpen every thorn.

3 But I have felt thy dying love
Breathe gently through my heart,
To whisper hope of joys above—
And can we ever part?

4 Ah! no, with thee I'll walk below,
My journey to the grave:
To whom, my Saviour, shall I go,
When only thou canst save?

1041.
C. M.

1 FOREVER here my rest shall be,
Close to thy bleeding side;
This all my hope, and all my plea,—
For me the Saviour died.

2 My dying Saviour, and my God,
Fountain for guilt and sin,
Sprinkle me ever with thy blood,
And cleanse and keep me clean.

3 The atonement of thy blood apply,
Till faith to sight improve;
Till hope in full fruition die,
And all my soul be love.

1042.
7s. 6 lines.

1 CHRIST, whose glory fills the skies,
Christ, the true, the only light,
Sun of Righteousness, arise,
Triumph o'er the shades of night;
Day-spring from on high, be near,
Day-star in my heart appear.

2 Dark and cheerless is the morn,
If thy light is hid from me;
Joyless is the day's return,
Till thy mercy's beams I see;
Till they inward light impart,
Warmth and gladness to my heart.

3 Visit, then, this soul of mine;
Pierce the gloom of sin and grief;
Fill me, radiant Sun divine!
Scatter all my unbelief;
More and more thyself display,
Shining to the perfect day.

1043.
L. M.

1 SAVIOUR, when night involves the skies,
My soul, adoring turns to thee;
Thee, self-abased in mortal guise,
And wrapped in shades of death for me.

2 On thee my waking raptures dwell,
When crimson gleams the east adorn;
Thee, Victor of the grave and hell;
Thee, Source of life's eternal morn.

3 When noon her throne in light arrays,
To thee my soul triumphant springs;
Thee, throned in glory's endless blaze;
Thee, Lord of lords, and King of kings.

4 O'er earth when shades of evening steal,
To death and thee my thoughts I give;
To death, whose power I soon must feel;
To thee, with whom I trust to live.

1044.
7s. 6 lines.

1 When this passing world is done,—
When has sunk yon glorious sun;
When I stand with Christ in glory,
Looking o'er life's finished story;
Then, Lord, shall I fully know—
Not till then—how much I owe!

2 When I hear the wicked call
On the rocks and hills to fall;
When I see them start and shrink,
On the fiery deluge brink;
Then, Lord, shall I fully know—
Not till then—how much I owe!

3 When I stand before the throne,
Clothed in beauty not my own;
When I see thee as thou art,
Love thee with unsinning heart;
Then, Lord, shall I fully know—
Not till then—how much I owe!

4 When the praise of heaven I hear,
Loud as thunders to the ear,
Loud as many waters' noise,
Sweet as harp's melodious voice,
Then, Lord, shall I fully know—
Not till then—how much I owe!

1045.
C. M.

1 All that I was—my sin and guilt,
My death was all my own,—
All that I am, I owe to thee,
My gracious God, alone.

2 The evil of my former state
Was mine, and only mine;
The good in which I now rejoice,
Is thine, and only thine.

3 The darkness of my former state,
The bondage, all was mine;
The light of life, in which I walk,
The liberty, is thine.

4 Thy grace first made me feel my sin,
It taught me to believe;
Then, in believing, peace I found,
And now I live—I live!

5 All that I am, ev'n here on earth,
All that I hope to be;
When Jesus comes, and glory dawns,
I owe it, Lord, to thee.

1046.
C. M.

1 If thou impart thyself to me,
No other good I need:
If thou, the Son, shalt make me free,
I shall be free indeed.

2 I cannot rest till in thy blood
I full redemption have;
But thou, through whom I come to God,
Canst to the utmost save.

3 From sin—the guilt, the power, the pain—
Thou wilt redeem my soul:
Lord, I believe—and not in vain;
My faith shall make me whole.

4 I, too, with thee, shall walk in white;
With all thy saints shall prove
What is the length and breadth and height
And depth of perfect love.

1047.
8s & 6s.

1 O Holy Saviour! Friend unseen,
Since on thine arm thou bid'st me lean,
Help me, throughout life's changing scene,
By faith to cling to thee!

2 Blest with this fellowship divine,
Take what thou wilt, I'll not repine;
For, as the branches to the vine,
My soul would cling to thee.

3 Tho' far from home, fatigued, oppressed,
Here have I found a place of rest;
An exile still, yet not unblest,
Because I cling to thee.

4 What though the world deceitful prove,
And earthly friends and hopes remove;
With patient uncomplaining love
Still would I cling to thee.

5 Though oft I seem to tread alone
Life's dreary waste, with thorns o'ergrown,
Thy voice of love, in gentlest tone,
Still whispers, "Cling to me!"

6 Though faith and hope are often tried,
I ask not, need not, aught beside;
So safe, so calm, so satisfied,
The soul that clings to thee!

1048.
C. M. Double.

1 I HEARD the voice of Jesus say,
"Come unto me and rest;
Lay down, thou weary one, lay down
Thy head upon my breast!"
I came to Jesus as I was,
Weary, and worn, and sad,
I found in him a resting-place,
And he has made me glad.

2 I heard the voice of Jesus say,—
"Behold, I freely give
The living water; thirsty one,
Stoop down and drink, and live!"
I came to Jesus, and I drank
Of that life-giving stream;
My thirst was quenched, my soul revived,
And now I live in him.

3 I heard the voice of Jesus say,—
"I am this dark world's light;
Look unto me, thy morn shall rise
And all thy day be bright!"
I looked to Jesus, and I found
In him my Star, my Sun;
And in that light of life I'll walk,
Till all my journey's done.

1049.
L. M. 6 lines.

1 WHEN, streaming from the eastern skies,
The morning light salutes my eyes,
O Sun of Righteousness divine:
On me with beams of mercy shine;
Chase the dark clouds of guilt away,
And turn my darkness into day.

2 When to heaven's great and glorious
King
My morning sacrifice I bring,
And, mourning o'er my guilt and shame,
Ask mercy in my Saviour's name,
Then Jesus, sprinkle with thy blood,
And be my Advocate with God.

3 When each day's scenes and labors close,
And wearied nature seeks repose,
With pardoning mercy richly blessed,
Guard me, my Saviour, while I rest;
And as each morning sun shall rise,
Oh, lead me onward to the skies!

4 And at my life's last setting sun,
My conflicts o'er, my labors done,

Jesus, thine heavenly radiance shed,
To cheer and bless my dying bed,
And from death's gloom my spirit raise,
To see thy face and sing thy praise.

1050.
C. M.

1 To thee, my Shepherd, and my Lord,
A grateful song I'll raise;
Oh, let the humblest of thy flock
Attempt to speak thy praise.

2 My life, my joy, my hope, I owe
To thine amazing love;
Ten thousand thousand comforts here,
And nobler bliss above.

3 To thee my trembling spirit flies,
With sin and grief oppressed;
Thy gentle voice dispels my fears,
And lulls my cares to rest.

4 Lead on, dear Shepherd!—led by thee,
No evil shall I fear;
Soon shall I reach thy fold above,
And praise thee better there.

1051.
C. M.

1 LORD, it belongs not to my care
Whether I die or live;
To love and serve thee is my share,
And this thy grace must give.

2 If life be long, I will be glad
That I may long obey;
If short, yet why should I be sad
To soar to endless day?

3 Christ leads me through no darker rooms
Than he went through before;
No one into his kingdom comes,
But through his opened door.

4 Come, Lord, when grace has made me
meet
Thy blessèd face to see;
For if thy work on earth be sweet,
What will thy glory be!

5 Then shall I end my sad complaints,
And weary, sinful days,
And join with all triumphant saints
Who sing Jehovah's praise.

6 My knowledge of that life is small;
The eye of faith is dim;
But 'tis enough that Christ knows all,
And I shall be with him.

1052.
10s.

1 ABIDE with me! Fast falls the eventide,
The darkness deepens—Lord, with me
abide!
When other helpers fail, and comforts
flee,
Help of the helpless, oh, abide with me!

2 Swift to its close ebbs out life's little day;
Earth's joys grow dim, its glories pass
away;
Change and decay in all around I see;
O thou, who changest not, abide with me!

3 I need thy presence every passing hour:
What but thy grace can foil the tempter's power?
Who, like thyself, my guide and stay
can be?
Through cloud and sunshine, oh, abide
with me!

4 Not a brief glance I long, a passing word,
But as thou dwell'st with thy disciples,
Lord,
Familiar, condescending, patient, free,
Come, not to sojourn, but abide, with me!

1053.
6s & 4s.

1 JESUS, thy name I love,
All other names above,
Jesus, my Lord!
Oh! thou art all to me,
Nothing to please I see,
Nothing apart from thee,
Jesus, my Lord!

2 Thou, blessèd Son of God,
Hast bought me with thy blood,
Jesus, my Lord!
Oh! how great is thy love,
All other loves above,
Love that I daily prove,
Jesus, my Lord!

3 When unto thee I flee,
Thou wilt my refuge be,
Jesus, my Lord!
What need I now to fear?
What earthly grief or care,
Since thou art ever near?
Jesus, my Lord!

4 Soon thou wilt come again!
I shall be happy then,
Jesus, my Lord!
Then thine own face I'll see,
Then I shall like thee be,
Then evermore with thee,
Jesus, my Lord!

1054.
7s.

1 BLESSÈD fountain, full of grace!
Grace for sinners, grace for me,
To this source alone I trace
What I am and hope to be.

2 What I am, as one redeemed,
Saved and rescued by the Lord;
Hating what I once esteemed,
Loving what I once abhorred.

3 What I hope to be ere long,
When I take my place above:
When I join the heavenly throng;
When I see the God of love.

4 Then I hope like him to be,
Who redeemed his saints from sin,
Whom I now obscurely see,
Through a vail that stands between.

5 Blessèd fountain, full of grace!
Grace for sinners, grace for me;
To this source alone I trace
What I am, and hope to be.

1055.
L. M.

1 FAR from my thoughts, vain world!
begone,
Let my religious hours alone:
Fain would mine eyes my Saviour see—
I wait a visit, Lord! from thee.

2 My heart grows warm with holy fire,
And kindles with a pure desire:
Come, my dear Jesus! from above,
And feed my soul with heavenly love.

3 Blest Saviour! what delicious fare—
How sweet thine entertainments are!
Never did angels taste above
Redeeming grace and dying love.

1056.

7s. 6 lines. *Docility.*

1 QUIET, Lord, my froward heart,
Make me teachable and mild,
Upright, simple, free from art,
Make me as a weaned child :
From distrust and envy free,
Pleased with all that pleases thee.

2 What thou shalt to-day provide,
Let me as a child receive ;
What to-morrow may betide,
Calmly to thy wisdom leave :
'T is enough that thou wilt care,—
Why should I the burden bear ?

3 As a little child relies
On a care beyond his own ;
Knows he 's neither strong nor wise,
Fears to stir a step alone ;
Let me thus with thee abide,
As my Father, Guard, and Guide.

1057.

C. M. *Love.*

1 SPIRIT of peace, celestial Dove,
How excellent thy praise !
How rich the gift of Christian love
Thy gracious power displays !

2 Sweet as the dew on hill and flower,
That silently distills,
At evening's soft and balmy hour,
On Zion's fruitful hills.

3 So, with mild influence from above,
Shall promised grace descend ;
Till universal peace and love
O'er all the earth extend.

1058.

C. M. *Devotion.*

1 UNITE, my roving thoughts, unite
In silence soft and sweet :
And thou, my soul, sit gently down
At thy great Sovereign's feet.

2 Jehovah's awful voice is heard,
Yet gladly I attend ;
For lo ! the everlasting God
Proclaims himself my friend.

3 Harmonious accents to my soul
The sounds of peace convey ;
The tempest at his word subsides,
And winds and seas obey.

4 By all its joys, I charge my heart,
To grieve his love no more ;
But charmed by melody divine,
To give its follies o'er.

1059.

C. L. M. *"Beauty of Holiness."*

1 SAY, dost thou mark that beaming eye,
That countenance serene ;
That smile of hope, and love, and joy,
Where gloom so late has been ?
More beautiful that sight appears
Than all the charms that nature wears.

2 And dost thou mark that temper mild,
That image pure of heaven ?
That soul subdued and reconciled,
Which once with hate was riven ?
Sure nothing earthly can impart
Such meltings to a stubborn heart.

3 Oh, glorious change ! 't is all of grace,
By bleeding love bestowed
On outcasts of a fallen race,
To bring them home to God ;
Infinite grace to vileness given,
The sons of earth made heirs of heaven.

1060.

H. M. *Exultant Joy.*

1 REJOICE ! the Lord is King !—
Your God and King adore ;
Mortals ! give thanks, and sing,
And triumph evermore :
Lift up the heart,—lift up the voice,—
Rejoice aloud, ye saints ! rejoice.

2 His kingdom cannot fail ;
He rules o'er earth and heaven ;
The keys of death and hell
Are to our Jesus given :
Lift up the heart,—lift up the voice,—
Rejoice aloud, ye saints ! rejoice.

3 He all his foes shall quell,—
Shall all our sins destroy ;
And every bosom swell
With pure seraphic joy :
Lift up the heart,—lift up the voice,—
Rejoice aloud, ye saints ! rejoice.

4 Rejoice in glorious hope ;
Jesus, the judge, shall come,
And take his servants up
To their eternal home :
We soon shall hear th' archangel's voice,
The trump of God shall sound,—Rejoice.

1061.

S. P. M. *Unity of Spirit.*

1 How pleasant 't is to see
Kindred and friends agree,
Each in his proper station move,
And each fulfill his part,
With sympathizing heart,
In all the cares of life and love.

2 Like fruitful showers of rain,
That water all the plain,
Descending from the neighboring hills,
Such streams of pleasure roll
Through every friendly soul,
Where love, like heavenly dew distills.

3 How pleasant 't is to see
Kindred and friends agree,
Each in his proper station move;
And each fulfill his part,
With sympathizing heart,
In all the cares of life and love!

1062.

H. M. *Faith.*

1 Faith is the polar star
That guides the Christian's way,
Directs his wanderings from afar
To realms of endless day;
It points the course | And safely leads
Where'er he roam | The pilgrim home.

2 Faith is the rainbow's form
Hung on the brow of heaven,
The glory of the passing storm,
The pledge of mercy given;
It is the bright | Thro' which the saints
Triumphal arch | To glory march.

3 The faith that works by love,
And purifies the heart,
A foretaste of the joys above
To mortals can impart;
It bears us through | And triumphs in
This earthly strife | Immortal life.

1063.

C. M. *Likeness to Christ.*

1 Eternal Sun of righteousness!
Display thy beams divine,
And cause the glory of thy face
Upon my heart to shine.

2 Light, in thy light, oh, may I see,
Thy grace and mercy prove,
Revived, and cheered, and blessed by thee,
The God of pardoning love.

3 Lift up thy countenance serene,
And let thy happy child
Behold, without a cloud between,
The Father reconciled.

4 On me thy promised peace bestow,
The peace by Jesus given;—
The joys of holiness below,
And then the joys of heaven.

1064.

L. M. *Devotion.*

1 Be with me, Lord, where'er I go;
Teach me what thou wouldst have me do;
Suggest whate'er I think or say;
Direct me in thy narrow way.

2 Prevent me lest I harbor pride,
Lest I in mine own strength confide;
Show me my weakness, let me see
I have my power, my all from thee.

3 Enrich me always with thy love;
My kind protection ever prove;
Thy signet put upon my breast,
And let thy Spirit on me rest.

4 Oh, may I never do my will,
But thine and only thine fulfill;
Let all my time and all my ways
Be spent and ended to thy praise.

1065.

L. M. *Fidelity.*

1 Jesus, our best-beloved friend,
Draw out our souls in sweet desire;
Jesus, in love to us descend,
Baptize us with thy Spirit's fire.

2 Our souls and bodies we resign,
To fear and follow thy commands;
Oh! take our hearts, our hearts are thine,
Accept the service of our hands.

3 Firm, faithful, watching unto prayer,
Our Master's voice will we obey,
Toil in the vineyard here, and bear
The heat and burden of the day.

4 Yet, Lord, for us a resting-place,
In heaven, at thy right hand, prepare;
And till we see thee face to face,
Be all our conversation there.

1066.

7s. *Submission.*

1 SOVEREIGN Ruler of the skies,
Ever gracious, ever wise,
All my times are in thy hand,
All events at thy command.

2 Times of sickness, times of health;
Times of penury and wealth;
Times of trial and of grief;
Times of triumph and relief;—

3 Times the tempter's power to prove;
Times to taste a Saviour's love;
All must come, and last, and end,
As shall please my heavenly Friend.

4 O thou Gracious, Wise, and Just,
In thy hands my life I trust;
Have I somewhat dearer still?
I resign it to thy will.

1067.

8s & 4s. *Submission.*

1 "THY will be done!" In devious way
The hurrying stream of life may run;
Yet still our grateful hearts shall say,
"Thy will be done."

2 "Thy will be done!" If o'er us shine
A gladdening and a prosperous sun,
This prayer will make it more divine:
"Thy will be done."

3 "Thy will be done!" Tho' shrouded o'er
Our path with gloom, one comfort, one
Is ours: to breathe, while we adore,
"Thy will be done."

1068.

7s. 6 lines. *Adoption.*

1 ABBA, Father, hear thy child,
Late in Jesus reconciled;
Hear, and all the graces shower,
All the joy, and peace, and power;
All my Saviour asks above,
All the life and heaven of love.

2 Heavenly Father, Life divine,
Change my nature into thine;
Move and spread throughout my soul,
Actuate and fill the whole;
Lord, I will not let thee go
Till the blessing thou bestow.

3 Holy Ghost, no more delay;
Come, and in thy temple stay:
Now thine inward witness bear,
Strong, and permanent, and clear:
Spring of life, thyself impart;
Rise eternal in my heart.

1069.

C. M. *Adoption.*

1 LORD, I address thy heavenly throne;
Call me a child of thine;
Send down the Spirit of thy Son,
To form my heart divine.

2 There shed thy choicest love abroad,
And make my comforts strong:
Then shall I say—"My Father, God,"
With an unwavering tongue.

1070.

7s. 6 lines. *God's Chosen.*

1 BLESSÈD are the sons of God,
They are bought with Jesus' blood;
They are ransomed from the grave;
Life eternal they shall have:
With them numbered may we be,
Here, and in eternity.

2 They are justified by grace,
They enjoy the Saviour's peace;
All their sins are washed away;
They shall stand in God's great day:
With them numbered may we be,
Here, and in eternity.

3 They are lights upon the earth,—
Children of a heavenly birth,—
One with God, with Jesus one:
Glory is in them begun:
With them numbered may we be,
Here, and in eternity.

1071.

7s, 6s & 8s. *Saved by Grace.*

1 LET the world their virtue boast,—
Their works of righteousness;
I, a wretch undone and lost,
Am freely saved by grace;
Other title I disclaim;
This, only this, is all my plea:—
I the chief of sinners am,
But Jesus died for me.

2 Happy they whose joys abound
  Like Jordan's swelling stream;
Who their heaven in Christ have found,
  And give the praise to him!
Meanest follower of the Lamb,
  His steps I at a distance see :—
I the chief of sinners am,
  But Jesus died for me.

3 Jesus, thou for me hast died,
  And thou in me wilt live;
I shall feel thy death applied;
  I shall thy life receive :
Yet, when melted in the flame
  Of love, this shall be all my plea,—
I the chief of sinners am,
  But Jesus died for me.

1072.
L. M. *Robe of Righteousness.*

1 Jesus! thy robe of righteousness
  My beauty is,—my glorious dress:
Mid flaming worlds, in this arrayed,
  With joy shall I lift up my head.

2 When, from the dust of death, I rise
  To claim my mansion in the skies,
Ev'n then shall this be all my plea,—
  "Jesus hath lived and died for me."

3 This spotless robe the same appears,
  When ruined nature sinks in years;
No age can change its glorious hue;—
  The robe of Christ is ever new.

4 Oh! let the dead now hear thy voice;
  Now bid thy banished ones rejoice;
Their beauty this—their glorious dress—
  Jesus, the Lord, our righteousness.

1073.
C. M. *Beloved of God.*

1 A mother may forgetful be,
  For human love is frail;
But thy Creator's love to thee,
  O Zion, cannot fail.

2 No, thy dear name engraven stands,
  In characters of love,
On thy almighty Father's hands;
  And never shall remove.

3 Before his ever-watchful eye
  Thy mournful state appears,
And every groan, and every sigh,
  Divine compassion hears.

4 O Zion, learn to doubt no more,
  Be every fear suppressed;
Unchanging truth, and love, and power,
  Dwell in thy Saviour's breast.

1074.
7s, 6s & 8s. *Kept of God.*

1 Thou, O Lord, in tender love,
  Dost all my burdens bear;
Lift my heart to things above,
  And fix it ever there:
Calm on tumult's wheel I sit,
  'Midst busy multitudes alone;
Sweetly waiting at thy feet,
  Till all thy will be done.

2 Careful without care I am,
  Nor feel my happy toil;
Kept in peace by Jesus' name,
  Supported by his smile:
Joyful thus my faith to show,
  I find his service my reward;
Every work I do below,
  I do it to the Lord.

3 To the desert or the cell,
  Let others blindly fly,
In this evil world I dwell,
  Unhurt, unspotted I :
Here I find a house of prayer,
  To which I inwardly retire;
Walking unconcerned in care,
  And unconsumed in fire.

1075.
7s & 6s. *Disclosure of God's Love.*

1 Sometimes a light surprises
  The Christian while he sings;
It is the Lord who rises,
  With healing in his wings;
When comforts are declining,
  He grants the soul again
A season of clear shining,
  To cheer it after rain.

2 In holy contemplation,
  We sweetly then pursue
The theme of God's salvation,
  And find it ever new :
Set free from present sorrow,
  We cheerfully can say,
Let the unknown to-morrow
  Bring with it what it may.

3 It can bring with it nothing,
   But he will bear us through ;
   Who gives the lilies clothing,
    Will clothe his people too :
   Beneath the spreading heavens,
    No creature but is fed ;
   And he who feeds the ravens,
    Will give his children bread.

4 Though vine nor fig-tree neither,
   Their wonted fruit should bear,
   Though all the fields should wither,
    Nor flocks nor herds be there ;
   Yet God the same abiding,
    His praise shall tune my voice,
   For while in him confiding,
    I cannot but rejoice.

1076.
C. M. *Folded and Fed.*

1 My shepherd will supply my need,
   Jehovah is his name ;
   In pastures fresh he makes me feed,
   Beside the living stream.

2 He brings my wandering spirit back,
   When I forsake his ways ;
   And leads me, for his mercy's sake,
   In paths of truth and grace.

3 When I walk through the shades of death,
   Thy presence is my stay ;
   A word of thy supporting breath
   Drives all my fears away.

4 The sure provisions of my God
   Attend me, all my days ;
   Oh ! may thy house be mine abode,
   And all my work be praise.

5 There would I find a settled rest,—
   While others go and come,—
   No more a stranger or a guest,
   But like a child at home.

1077.
L. M. *Union to Christ.*

1 When sins and fears, prevailing rise,
   And fainting hope almost expires,
   To thee, O Lord, I lift my eyes ;
   To thee I breathe my soul's desires.

2 Art thou not mine, my living Lord ?
   And can my hope, my comfort die ?
   'T is fixed on thine almighty word—
   That word which built the earth and sky.

3 If my immortal Saviour lives,
   Then my immortal life is sure ;
   His word a firm foundation gives ;
   Here may I build, and rest secure.

4 Here let my faith unshaken dwell ;
   Forever sure the promise stands ;
   Not all the powers of earth or hell
   Can e'er dissolve the sacred bands.

5 Here, O my soul, thy trust repose ;
   If Jesus is forever mine,
   Not death itself—that last of foes—
   Shall break a union so divine.

1078.
L. M. *Security in Christ.*

1 He lives,—the great Redeemer lives :
   What joy the blest assurance gives !
   And now, before his Father, God,
   Pleads the full merit of his blood.

2 Repeated crimes awake our fears,
   And justice armed with frowns appears ;
   But in the Saviour's lovely face,
   Sweet mercy smiles, and all is peace.

3 Hence, then, ye black, despairing
    thoughts ;
   Above our fears, above our faults,
   His powerful intercessions rise,
   And guilt recedes, and terror dies.

4 In every dark, distressful hour,
   When sin and Satan join their power,
   Let this dear hope repel the dart,
   That Jesus bears us on his heart.

5 Great Advocate ! almighty Friend !
   On thee our humble hopes depend :
   Our cause can never, never fail,
   For thou dost plead, and must prevail.

1079.
C. M. *Safety under the Covenant.*

1 My God ! the covenant of thy love
   Abides forever sure ;
   And in its matchless grace I feel
   My happiness secure.

2 Since thou, the everlasting God,
   My Father art become,
   Jesus my guardian and my friend,
   And heaven my final home ;—

3 I welcome all thy sovereign will,
  For all that will is love;
  And when I know not what thou dost,
  I wait the light above.

4 Thy covenant in the darkest gloom
  Shall heavenly rays impart,
  And when my eyelids close in death,
  Sustain my fainting heart.

1080.
C. M. *Union to Christ.*

1 LORD Jesus, are we one with thee?
  Oh! height, oh! depth of love!
  With thee we died upon the tree,
  In thee we live above.

2 Such was thy grace that for our sake
  Thou didst from heaven come down,
  Our mortal flesh and blood partake,
  In all our misery one.

3 Our sins, our guilt, in love divine,
  Were borne on earth by thee;
  The gall, the curse, the wrath were thine,
  To set thy members free.

4 Ascended now in glory bright,
  Still one with us thou art;
  Nor life, nor death, nor depth, nor height
  Thy saints and thee can part.

5 Soon, soon shall come that glorious day
  When, seated on thy throne,
  Thou shalt to wondering worlds display
  That thou with us art one.

1081.
S. M. *Watchfulness.*

1 YE servants of the Lord!
  Each in his office wait,
  Observant of his heavenly word,
  And watchful at his gate.

2 Let all your lamps be bright,
  And trim the golden flame;
  Gird up your loins as in his sight,
  For awful is his name.

3 Watch,—'t is your Lord's command;
  And while we speak he's near;
  Mark the first signal of his hand,
  And ready all appear.

4 Oh, happy servant he,
  In such a posture found!
  He shall his Lord with rapture see,
  And be with honor crowned.

1082.
C. M. *Consecration.*

1 AND must I part with all I have,
  My dearest Lord, for thee?
  It is but right! since thou hast done
  Much more than this for me.

2 Yes, let it go!—one look from thee
  Will more than make amends
  For all the losses I sustain
  Of credit, riches, friends.

3 Ten thousand worlds, ten thousand lives,
  How worthless they appear,
  Compared with thee, supremely good!
  Divinely bright and fair.

4 Thy favor, Lord, is endless life,—
  Let me that life obtain,
  Then I renounce all earthly joys,
  And glory in my gain.

1083.
C. M. *Beneficence.*

1 JESUS, our Lord, how rich thy grace!
  Thy bounties how complete!
  How shall we count the matchless sum!
  How pay the mighty debt!

2 High on a throne of radiant light
  Dost thou exalted shine;
  What can our poverty bestow,
  When all the worlds are thine?

3 But thou hast brethren here below,
  The partners of thy grace;
  And wilt confess their humble names,
  Before thy Father's face.

4 In them thou may'st be clothed and fed,
  And visited and cheered;
  And in their accents of distress,
  Our Saviour's voice is heard.

1084.
L. M. *Helping the Needy.*

1 OH, what stupendous mercy shines
  Around the Majesty of heaven!
  Rebels he deigns to call his sons—
  Their souls renewed, their sins forgiven.

2 Go, imitate the grace divine—
  The grace that blazes like a sun;
  Hold forth your fair, though feeble light,
  Through all your lives let mercy run.

3 Upon your bounty's willing wings
Swift let the great salvation fly ;
The hungry feed, the naked clothe ;
To pain and sickness help apply.

4 Pity the weeping widow's woe,
And be her counselor and stay;
Adopt the fatherless, and smooth
To useful, happy life, his way.

5 When all is done, renounce your deeds,
Renounce self-righteousness with scorn :
Thus will you glorify your God,
And thus the Christian name adorn.

1085.
C. M. *Prayer.*

1 PRAYER is the breath of God in man,
Returning whence it came ;
Love is the sacred fire within,
And prayer the rising flame.

2 It gives the burdened spirit ease,
And soothes the troubled breast ;
Yields comfort to the mourning soul,
And to the weary rest.

3 When God inclines the heart to pray,
He hath an ear to hear;
To him there's music in a groan,
And beauty in a tear.

4 The humble suppliant cannot fail
To have his wants supplied,
Since he for sinners intercedes,
Who once for sinners died.

1086.
7s. 6 lines. *Prayer.*

1 WHEN the heart, oppressed with grief,
Feels its light and strength decay,
When the night is vexed with sighs,
When sad tears obscure the day,
Turn, oh, turn thy soul to prayer,
Trust thee in thy Saviour's care.

2 Pray not as the heathen pray,
Speaking many a heartless word,
God, thy Father, sees each tear,
Every sigh by him is heard ;
Pray with heart, and soul, and thought,
As the Lord, our Saviour, taught.

3 "Father, hallowed be thy name,
Let thy glorious kingdom come—
Rule in heaven and earth the same,
Let thy holy will be done ;

Daily bread to us impart,
Give an humble, grateful heart.

4 "Pardon all our trespasses,
As we injuries forgive ;
Lead us from temptation's paths,
Far from evil may we live ;
Thine the kingdom, thine the power,
Thine the glory, evermore !"

1087.
8s & 7s. *Constant Effort.*

1 ONE by one the sands are flowing,
One by one the moments fall ;
Some are coming, some are going;
Do not strive to grasp them all.

2 One by one thy duties wait thee,
Let thy whole strength go to each ;
Let no future dreams elate thee,
Learn thou first what these can teach.

3 Hours are golden links, God's token,
Reaching heaven ; but one by one
Take them, lest the chain be broken,
Ere thy pilgrimage be done.

1088.
C. M.

1 AFFLICTION is a stormy deep,
Where wave resounds to wave ;
Though o'er my head the billows roll,
I know the Lord can save.

2 The hand that now withholds my joys
Can soon restore my peace ;
And he who bade the tempest rise
Can bid that tempest cease.

3 In darkest scenes when sorrows rose
And pressed on every side,
The Lord has still sustained my steps,
And still has been my guide.

4 Here will I rest, and build my hope,
Nor murmur at his rod ;
He's more than all the world to me—
My Health, my Life, my God !

1089.
C. L. M.

1 WHEN I can trust my all with God,
In trial's fearful hour,—
Bow all resigned beneath his rod,
And bless his sparing power ;
A joy springs up amid distress,
A fountain in the wilderness.

2 Oh! to be brought to Jesus' feet,
  Though trials fix me there,
Is still a privilege most sweet;
  For he will hear my prayer;
Though sighs and tears its language be,
  The Lord is nigh to answer me.

3 Then, blessèd be the hand that gave,
  Still blessèd when it takes;
Blessèd be he who smites to save,
  Who heals the heart he breaks:
Perfect and true are all his ways,
Whom heaven adores and death obeys.

1090.
C. M.

1 And can my heart aspire so high,
  To say—' My Father God!'
Lord, at thy feet I long to lie,
  And learn to kiss the rod.

2 I would submit to all thy will,
  For thou art good and wise;
Let every anxious thought be still,
  Nor one faint murmur rise.

3 Thy love can cheer the darksome gloom,
  And bid me wait serene;
Till hopes and joys immortal bloom,
  And brighten all the scene.

4 My Father!—oh, permit my heart
  To plead her humble claim;
And ask the bliss those words impart.
  In my Redeemer's name.

1091.
10s & 4s.

1 Send kindly light amid the encircling
    gloom,
  And lead me on!
The night is dark, and I am far from home;
  Lead thou me on!
Keep thou my feet; I do not ask to see
The distant scene; one step 's enough for
    me.

2 I was not ever thus, nor prayed that thou
    Shouldst lead me on!
I loved to choose and see my path; but now
  Lead thou me on!
I loved day's dazzling light, and spite of
    fears,
Pride ruled my will: remember not past
    years!

3 So long thy power hath blessed me,
    surely still
'T will lead me on
Through dreary doubt, through pain and
    sorrow, till
  The night is gone,
And with the morn those angel faces smile
Which I have loved long since, and lost
    awhile.

1092.
7s & 5s.

1 In the dark and cloudy day,
  When earth's riches flee away,
  And the last hope will not stay,
    Saviour, comfort me!

2 When the secret idol 's gone
  That my poor heart yearned upon,—
  Desolate, bereft, alone,
    Saviour, comfort me!

3 Thou, who wast so sorely tried,
  In the darkness crucified,
  Bid me in thy love confide;
    Saviour, comfort me!

4 Comfort me; I am cast down:
  'T is my heavenly Father's frown;
  I deserve it all, I own:
    Saviour, comfort me!

5 So it shall be good for me
  Much afflicted now to be,
  If thou wilt but tenderly,
    Saviour, comfort me!

1093.
11s.

1 For what shall I praise thee, my God
    and my King,
For what blessings the tribute of grati-
    tude bring?
Shall I praise thee for pleasure, for health,
    or for ease,
For the sunshine of youth, for the garden
    of peace?

2 Shall I praise thee for flowers that bloom
    on my breast,
For joys in prospective, for pleasures pos-
    sessed?
For the spirits that heightened my days
    of delight,
And the slumbers that fell on my pillow
    by night?

3 For this I should praise; but if only for
  this,
I should leave half untold the donation
  of bliss!
I thank thee for sickness, for sorrow and
  care,
For the thorns I have gathered, the anguish I bear;—

4 For nights of anxiety, watching and tears,
A present of pain, a prospective of fears;
I praise thee, I bless thee, my Lord and
  my God,
For the good and the evil thy hand hath
  bestowed!

5 The flowers were sweet, but their fragrance is flown,
They yielded no fruit, they are withered
  and gone;
The thorn it was poignant; but precious
  to me
Was the message of mercy—it led me
  to thee.

1094.
L. M.

1 God of my life, to thee I call!
Afflicted. at thy feet I fall;
When the great water-floods prevail,
Leave not my trembling heart to fail.

2 Friend of the friendless and the faint,
Where should I lodge my deep complaint?
Where, but with thee, whose open door
Invites the helpless and the poor?

3 Did ever mourner plead with thee,
And thou refuse that mourner's plea?
Does not the word still fixed remain,
That none shall seek thy face in vain?

4 That were a grief I could not bear,
Didst thou not hear and answer prayer;
But a prayer-hearing, answering God
Supports me under every load.

5 Poor though 1 am—despised, forgot,
Yet God, my God, forgets me not;
And he is safe, and must succeed,
For whom the Saviour deigns to plead.

1095.
6s & 4s.

1 Lowly and solemn be
Thy children's cry to thee,
  Father Divine!
A hymn of suppliant breath,

Owning that life and death
  Alike are thine!

2 O Father, in that hour,
When earth all helping power
  Shall disavow,—
When spear, and shield, and crown,
In faintness are cast down,—
  Sustain us, thou!

3 By him who bowed to take
The death-cup for our sake,
  The thorn, the rod,—
From whom the last dismay
Was not to pass away,
  Aid us, O God!

1096.
C. M.

1 When grief and anguish press me down,
  And hope and comfort flee,
I cling, O Father, to thy throne,
  And stay my heart on thee.

2 When death invades my peaceful home,
  The sundered ties shall be
A closer bond, in time to come,
  To bind my heart to thee.

3 Lord, not my will, but thine be done!
  My soul, from fear set free,
Her faith shall anchor at thy throne,
  And trust alone in thee.

1097.
7s.

1 'T is my happiness below,
  Not to live without the cross,
But the Saviour's power to know,
  Sanctifying every loss.

2 Trials must and will befall;
  But, with humble faith to see
Love inscribed upon them all,—
  This is happiness to me.

3 Trials make the promise sweet;
  Trials give new life to prayer;
Trials bring me to his feet,
  Lay me low, and keep me there.

1098.
8s & 6s.

1 I ask not now for gold to gild,
  With mocking shine, an aching frame;
The yearning of the mind is stilled—
  I ask not now for fame.

2 But, bowed in lowliness of mind,
　　I make my humble wishes known;
　　I only ask a will resigned,
　　O Father, to thine own.

3 In vain I task my aching brain,
　　In vain the sage's thoughts I scan;
　　I only feel how weak I am,
　　How poor and blind is man.

4 And now my spirit sighs for home,
　　And longs for light whereby to see;
　　And, like a weary child, would come,
　　O Father, unto thee.

1099.
L. C. M.

1 SELF-LOVE no grace in sorrow sees,
　　Consults her own peculiar case,—
　　'T is all the bliss she knows;
　　But nobler aims true Love employ,—
　　In self-denial is her joy,
　　In suffering her repose.

2 Sorrow and Love go side by side;
　　Nor height nor depth can e'er divide
　　Their heaven-appointed bands;
　　Those dear associates still are one,
　　Nor, till the race of life is run,
　　Disjoin their wedded hands.

3 Thy choice and mine shall be the same,
　　Inspirer of that holy flame,
　　Which must forever blaze!
　　To take the cross and follow thee,
　　Where love and duty lead, shall be
　　My portion and my praise.

1100.
C. M.

1 O THOU whose mercy guides my way,
　　Though now it seem severe,
　　Forbid my unbelief to say
　　There is no mercy here!

2 Oh! may I, Lord, desire the pain
　　That comes in kindness down,
　　Far more than sweetest earthly gain,
　　Succeeded by a frown.

3 Then though thou bend my spirit low,
　　Love only shall I see;
　　The gracious hand that strikes the blow
　　Was wounded once for me.

1101.
C. M.

1 JESUS, my sorrow lies too deep
　　For human ministry;
　　It knows not how to tell itself
　　To any but to thee.

2 Thou dost remember still amid
　　The glories of God's throne
　　The sorrows of mortality,
　　For they were once thine own.

3 Jesus! my fainting spirit brings
　　Its fearfulness to thee;
　　Thine eye, at least, can penetrate
　　The clouded mystery.

4 It is enough, my precious Lord,
　　Thy tender sympathy!
　　My every sin and sorrow can
　　Devolve itself on thee.

5 Jesus! thou hast availed to search
　　My deepest malady;
　　It freely flows—more freely finds
　　The gracious remedy.

1102.
6s.

1 My Jesus, as thou wilt!
　　Oh! may thy will be mine;
　　Into thy hand of love
　　I would my all resign.
　　Through sorrow, or through joy,
　　Conduct me as thine own,
　　And help me still to say,
　　My Lord, thy will be done!

2 My Jesus, as thou wilt!
　　Though seen through many a tear,
　　Let not my star of hope
　　Grow dim or disappear:
　　Since thou on earth hast wept,
　　And sorrowed oft alone,
　　If I must weep with thee,
　　My Lord, thy will be done!

3 My Jesus, as thou wilt!
　　All shall be well for me;
　　Each changing future scene
　　I gladly trust with thee.
　　Straight to my home above
　　I travel calmly on,
　　And sing, in life or death,
　　My Lord, thy will be done!

1103.
C. M.

1 O Father! compass me about
    With love, for I am weak ;
Forgive, forgive my sinful doubt,
    Thy pitying glance I seek.

2 I know thy thoughts are peace towards
      me,
Safe am I in thy hands ;
Could I but firmly build on thee,
    For sure thy counsel stands !

3 Though mountains crumble into dust,
    Thy covenant standeth fast ;
Who follows thee in pious trust,
    Shall reach the goal at last.

4 Though strange and winding seems the
      way
While yet on earth I dwell ;
In heaven my heart shall gladly say,
    Thou, God, dost all things well !

1104.
L. M.   *Great Commission.*

1 "Go, preach my Gospel," saith the Lord ;
    "Bid the whole earth my grace receive ;
He shall be saved who trusts my word ;
    And they condemned who disbelieve.

2 "I'll make your great commission known,
    And ye shall prove my gospel true
By all the works that I have done,
    By all the wonders ye shall do.

3 "Teach all the nations my commands ;
    I'm with you till the world shall end ;
All power is trusted in my hands ;
    I can destroy and I defend."

4 He spake, and light shone round his head ;
    On a bright cloud to heaven he rode ;
They to the farthest nations spread
    The grace of their ascended God.

1105.
S. M.   *Ministry.*

1 How beauteous are their feet
    Who stand on Zion's hill !
Who bring salvation on their tongues,
    And words of peace reveal.

2 How charming is their voice !
    How sweet their tidings are !
"Zion, behold thy Saviour King ;
    He reigns and triumphs here."

3 How happy are our ears,
    That hear this joyful sound !
Which kings and prophets waited for,
    And sought, but never found.

4 How blessèd are our eyes,
    That see this heavenly light !
Prophets and kings desired it long,
    But died without the sight.

5 The watchmen join their voice,
    And tuneful notes employ ;
Jerusalem breaks forth in songs,
    And deserts learn the joy.

6 The Lord makes bare his arm
    Through all the earth abroad ;
Let every nation now behold
    Their Saviour and their God.

1106.
C. M.   *Ministry.*

1 'T is not a cause of small import,
    The pastor's care demands ;
But what might fill an angel's heart,
    And filled a Saviour's hands.

2 They watch for those for whom the Lord
    Did heavenly bliss forego ;
For souls, that must forever live
    In rapture, or in woe.

3 All to the great tribunal haste,
    Th' account to render there ;
And shouldst thou strictly mark our faults,
    Lord, how should we appear !

4 May they that Jesus, whom they preach,
    Their own Redeemer see ;
And watch thou daily o'er their souls,
    That they may watch for thee.

1107.
C. M.   *Church Organization.*

1 Not to the terrors of the Lord,
    The tempest, fire, and smoke ;
Not to the thunder of that word
    Which God on Sinai spoke ;—

2 But we are come to Zion's hill,
    The city of our God ;
Where milder words declare his will,
    And spread his love abroad.

3 Behold th' innumerable host
    Of angels clothed in light ;
Behold the spirits of the just,
    Whose faith is turned to sight !

4 Behold the blest assembly there,
    Whose names are writ in heaven!
  And God, the Judge of all, declare
    Their vilest sins forgiven.

5 The saints on earth, and all the dead
    But one communion make;
  All join in Christ, their living head,
    And of his grace partake.

6 In such society as this
    My weary soul would rest:
  The man that dwells where Jesus is,
    Must be forever blest.

1108.

6s & 4s. *Installation.*

1 O HOLY Lord, our God,
  By heavenly hosts adored,
    Hear us, we pray :
  To thee the cherubim,
  Angels and seraphim,
  Unceasing praises bring—
    Their homage pay.

2 Here give thy word success ;
  And this thy servant bless;
    His labors own ;
  And while the sinner's Friend
  His life and words commend,
  Thy Holy Spirit send,
    And make him known.

3 May every passing year
  More happy still appear
    Than this glad day ;
  With numbers fill the place,
  Adorn thy saints with grace ;
  Thy truth may all embrace,
    O Lord, we pray.

1109.

H. M. *Church Unity.*

1 ONE sole baptismal sign,
    One Lord, below, above—
  Zion, one faith is thine,
    Only one watchword—love.
  From different temples though it rise,
  One song ascendeth to the skies.

2 Our sacrifice is one ;
    One Priest before the throne—
  The slain, the risen Son,
    Redeemer, Lord alone !
  And sighs from contrite hearts that spring,
  Our chief, our choicest offering.

3 Head of thy church beneath !
    The catholic, the true,
  On all her members breathe,
    Her broken frame renew !
  Then shall thy perfect will be done,
  When Christians love and live as one.

1110.

L. M. *Christ the Corner-Stone.*

1 Lo ! what a glorious corner-stone
  The Jewish builders did refuse ;
  But God hath built his church thereon,
  In spite of envy and the Jews.

2 Great God ! the work is all divine,
  The joy and wonder of our eyes ;
  This is the day that proves it thine,
  The day that saw our Saviour rise.

3 Sinners, rejoice, and saints, be glad ;
  Hosanna, let his name be blest ;
  A thousand honors on his head,
  With peace, and light, and glory rest !

4 In God's own name he comes to bring
  Salvation to our dying race ;
  Let the whole church address their King
  With hearts of joy, and songs of praise.

1111.

8s & 7s. *Baptism.*

1 SAVIOUR ! who thy flock art feeding
    With the shepherd's kindest care,
  All the feeble gently leading,
    While the lambs thy bosom share ;

2 Now these little ones receiving,
    Fold them in thy gracious arm—
  There, we know—thy word believing—
    Only there, secure from harm.

3 Never, from thy pasture roving,
    Let them be the Lion's prey ;
  Let thy tenderness, so loving,
    Keep them all life's dangerous way.

4 Then within thy fold eternal,
    Let them find a resting place ;
  Feed in pastures ever vernal,
    Drink the rivers of thy grace.

1112.

S. M.

1 GREAT God ! now condescend
    To bless our rising race ;
  Soon may their willing spirits bend,
    The subjects of thy grace.

2 Oh, what a pure delight
  Their happiness to see!
  Our warmest wishes all unite
  To lead their souls to thee.

3 Now bless, thou God of love!
  This ordinance divine;
  Send thy good Spirit from above,
  And make these children thine.

1113.
C. M.

1 O LORD, thy covenant is sure
  To all who fear thy name;
  Thy mercies age on age endure,
  Eternally the same.

2 In thee our fathers put their trust;
  Thy ways they humbly trod;
  Honored and sacred is their dust,
  And still they live to God.

3 Heirs to their faith, their hope, their
      prayers,
  We the same path pursue:
  Entail the blessing to our heirs;
  Lord! show thy promise true.

1114.
S. M. *Baptism*

1 OUR children thou dost claim,
  O Lord our God as thine:
  Ten thousand blessings to thy name,
  For goodness so divine.

2 Thee let the fathers own,
    Thee let the sons adore;
  Joined to the Lord in solemn vows,
    To be forgot no more.

3 How great thy mercies, Lord!
    How plenteous is thy grace,
  Which, in the promise of thy love,
    Includes our rising race.

4 Our offspring, still thy care,
    Shall own their father's God;
  To latest times thy blessings share,
    And sound thy praise abroad.

1115.
11s.

1 O THOU who hast died to redeem us from
      hell!
  These signs hast thou left, of thy kind-
      ness to tell;

The bread we have broken, the cup we
    have blessed,
Still speak of thy death, our atonement
    and priest.

2 While thus, in remembrance, thine an-
      guish we see,
  One tie binds our spirits, dear Saviour,
      to thee;
  Thy body was broken to make us thine
      own,—
  All saved from one ruin,—in thee we
      are one.

3 We drink of the wine, remembering thy
      blood
  Once shed to redeem all the chosen of
      God,—
  Oh, come the blest day, when to us 't will
      be given,
  To drink of it new in the kingdom of
      heaven!

1116.
10s.

1 HERE, O my Lord, I see thee face to face;
  Here would I touch and handle things
      unseen;
  Here grasp with firmer hand th' eternal
      grace,
  And all my weariness upon thee lean.

2 Here would I feed upon the bread of God;
  Here drink with thee the royal wine
      of heaven;
  Here would I lay aside each earthly load,
  Here taste afresh the calm of sin for-
      given.

3 Too soon we rise; the symbols disappear;
  The feast tho' not the love, is passed
      and gone;
  The bread and wine remove, but thou
      art here—
  Nearer than ever—still my Shield and
      Sun.

4 Feast after feast thus comes and passes by;
  Yet, passing, points to the glad feast
      above,
  Giving sweet foretaste of the festal joy,
  The Lamb's great bridal feast of bliss
      and love.

1117.
C. L. M.

1 FORGET thyself, Christ bade thee come
To think upon his love,
Which could reverse the sinner's doom,
And write his name above;
Bid the returning rebel live,
And freely all his sins forgive.

2 Forget thyself, and think what pain,
What agony he bore,
To wash away each guilty stain,
To bless thee evermore:
To fit thee for his high abode,
The temple of the living God.

3 Forget thyself, but let thy soul
With memories o'erflow,
Rejoice in his supreme control,
And seek his will to know:
With thankful heart approach the feast,
And thou wilt be a welcome guest.

1118.
C. M.

1 LORD, may the spirit of this feast—
The earnest of thy love—
Maintain a dwelling in our breast,
Until we meet above.

2 The healing sense of pardoned sin,
The hope that never tires,
The strength a pilgrim's race to win,
The joy that heaven inspires.

3 Still may their light our duties trace
In lines of hallowed flame,
Like that upon the prophet's face,
When from the mount he came.

4 But if no more with kindred dear
The broken bread we share,
Nor at the banquet-board appear
To breathe the grateful prayer;

5 Forget us not,—when on the bed
Of dire disease we waste,
Or to the chambers of the dead,
And bar of judgment haste.

6 Forget not,—thou who bore the woe
Of Calvary's fatal tree,—
Those who within these courts below
Have thus remembered thee.

1119.
7s & 6s.

1 LAMB of God! whose bleeding love
We now recall to mind,
Send the answer from above,
And let us mercy find:
Think on us, who think on thee,
Every burdened soul release;
Oh, remember Calvary,
And bid us go in peace!

2 By thine agonizing pain,
And bloody sweat, we pray—
By thy dying love to man,
Take all our sins away:
Burst our bonds, and set us free,
From all sin do thou release;
Oh, remember Calvary,
And bid us go in peace!

3 Let thy blood, by faith applied,
The sinner's pardon seal;
Own us freely justified,
And all our sickness heal:
By thy passion on the tree,
Let our griefs and troubles cease;
Oh, remember Calvary,
And bid us go in peace!

1120.
C. M.

1 LORD! at thy table I behold
The wonders of thy grace;
But most of all admire that I
Should find a welcome place.

2 What strange surprising grace is this,
That such a soul has room!
My Saviour takes me by the hand,
My Jesus bids me come.

3 Ye saints below, and hosts of heaven,
Join all your praising powers;
No theme is like redeeming love,
No Saviour is like ours.

4 Had I ten thousand hearts, dear Lord!
I'd give them all to thee;
Had I ten thousand tongues, they all
Should join the harmony.

1121.
S. M.

1 A PARTING hymn we sing,
Around thy table, Lord,
Again our grateful tribute bring,
Our solemn vows record.

2 Here have we seen thy face,
  And felt thy presence here,
So may the savor of thy grace
  In word and life appear.

3 The purchase of thy blood—
  By sin no longer led—
The path our dear Redeemer trod
  May we rejoicing tread.

4 In self-forgetting love
  Be Christian union shown,
Until we join the church above,
  And know as we are known.

1122.
P. M.

1 BEHOLD the temple of the Lord,
The work of God, by man abhorred,
  Appearing fair and splendid ;
It lifts its head in spite of foes,
And tho' a hostile world oppose,
  The work will yet be ended !

2 A building this, not made with hands ;
On firm foundations, lo ! it stands,
  For God himself has laid them !
The workmanship of God alone—
The rich materials all his own—
  'T was he himself who made them.

3 He builds it for his glory's sake,
Its solid frame no force can shake,
  However men despise it ;
And Time, that other work destroys,
'Gainst this in vain its power employs ;
  The work of God defies it !

1123.
L. M.

1 GREAT Shepherd of thine Israel,
Who didst between the cherubs dwell,
And lead the tribes, thy chosen sheep,
Safe through the desert and the deep :—

2 Thy church is in the desert now ;
Shine from on high and guide us through ;
Turn us to thee, thy love restore,—
We shall be saved and sigh no more.

3 Great God, whom heavenly hosts obey,
How long shall we lament and pray,
And wait in vain thy kind return ?
How long shall thy fierce anger burn ?

4 Instead of wine and cheerful bread,
Thy saints with their own tears are fed ;
Turn us to thee, thy love restore,—
We shall be saved and sigh no more.

1124.
8s & 7s. Double.

1 LIGHT of those whose dreary dwelling
  Borders on the shades of death !
Come, and, by thy love revealing,
  Dissipate the clouds beneath :
The new heaven and earth's Creator,
  In our deepest darkness rise,—
Scattering all the night of nature,
  Pouring eye-sight on our eyes.

2 Still we wait for thine appearing ;
  Life and joy thy beams impart,
Chasing all our fears, and cheering
  Every poor benighted heart :
Come and manifest thy favor
  To the ransomed, helpless race ;
Come, thou glorious God and Saviour !
  Come, and bring the gospel grace.

3 Save us, in thy great compassion,
  O thou mild, pacific Prince !
Give the knowledge of salvation,
  Give the pardon of our sins ;
By thine all-sufficient merit,
  Every burdened soul release ;
Every weary, wandering spirit,
  Guide into thy perfect peace.

1125.
C. M.

1 DAUGHTER of Zion ! from the dust
  Exalt thy fallen head ;
Again in thy Redeemer trust,—
  He calls thee from the dead.

2 Awake, awake, put on thy strength,—
  Thy beautiful array ;
Thy day of freedom dawns at length,—
  The Lord's appointed day.

3 Rebuild thy walls, thy bounds enlarge,
  And send thy heralds forth ;
Say to the south,—" Give up thy charge,
  And keep not back, O north !"

4 They come, they come ;—thine exiled
    bands,
  Where'er they rest or roam,
Have heard thy voice in distant lands,
  And hasten to their home.

5 Thus, though the universe shall burn,
　And God his works destroy,
With songs, thy ransomed shall return,
　And everlasting joy.

1126.
L. M.

1 Arm of the Lord, awake, awake ;
Put on thy strength, the nations shake ;
Now let the world, adoring, see
Triumphs of mercy wrought by thee.

2 Say to the heathen, from thy throne,
" I am Jehovah, God alone :"
Thy voice their idols shall confound,
And cast their altars to the ground.

3 Almighty God, thy grace proclaim
Through every clime, of every name ;
Let adverse powers before thee fall,
And crown the Saviour Lord of all !

1127.
P. M.

1 Wake ! the welcome day appeareth,
Every heart with joy it cheereth !
Wake ! the Lord's great year behold !
That which holy men of old,
Those who throng the sacred pages,
Waited for through countless ages :
　Hallelujah ! Hallelujah !

2 Patriarchs erst and priests aspiring,
Kings and prophets long desiring,
Saw not this before they died :—
Lo, the Light to them denied !
See its beams to earth directed !
Welcome, O thou long-expected !
　Hallelujah ! Hallelujah !

3 In our stead himself he offers,
On the accursed tree he suffers,
That his death's sweet savor may
Take our curse for aye away,
Cross and curse for us enduring,
Hope and heaven to us securing :
　Hallelujah ! Hallelujah !

4 Rent the temple curtain's centre ;
Come, ye nations, freely enter
Through the vail the holy place !
Freely stand before his face,
Here your grateful tributes bringing :
Come thou Bride, forever singing,
　Hallelujah ! Hallelujah !

1128.
7s.　Double.

1 Watchman ! tell us of the night,
　What its signs of promise are.—
Traveler ! o'er yon mountain's height,
　See that glory-beaming star !
Watchman ! does its beauteous ray
　Aught of joy or hope foretell ?—
Traveler ! yes ; it brings the day—
　Promised day of Israel.

2 Watchman ! tell us of the night,
　Higher yet that star ascends.—
Traveler ! blessedness and light,
　Peace and truth its course portends !—
Watchman ! will its beams alone
　Gild the spot that gave them birth ?
Traveler ! ages are its own,
　See, it bursts o'er all the earth.

3 Watchman ! tell us of the night,
　For the morning seems to dawn.—
Traveler ! darkness takes its flight,
　Doubt and terror are withdrawn.—
Watchman ! let thy wanderings cease :
　Hie thee to thy quiet home.—
Traveler ! lo ! the Prince of Peace,
　Lo ! the Son of God is come !

1129.
8s & 7s.　Double.

1 Glorious things of thee are spoken,
　Zion, city of our God !
He whose word cannot be broken,
　Formed thee for his own abode :
On the Rock of Ages founded—
　What can shake thy sure repose ?
With salvation's walls surrounded,
　Thou may'st smile at all thy foes.

2 See, the streams of living waters,
　Springing from eternal love,
Well supply thy sons and daughters,
　And all fear of want remove :
Who can faint, while such a river
　Ever flows their thirst t' assuage ?
Grace, which, like the Lord, the giver,
　Never fails from age to age.

3 Round each habitation hovering,
　See the cloud and fire appear !
For a glory and a covering,
　Showing that the Lord is near :

Thus deriving from their banner,
Light by night, and shade by day;
Safe they feed upon the manna,
Which he gives them when they pray.

1129.
C. M.

1 LET Zion and her sons rejoice—
Behold the promised hour!
Her God hath heard her mourning voice,
And comes t' exalt his power.

2 Her dust and ruins that remain
Are precious in our eyes;
Those ruins shall be built again,
And all that dust shall rise.

3 The Lord will raise Jerusalem,
And stand in glory there;
Nations shall bow before his name,
And kings attend with fear.

4 He sits a sovereign on his throne,
With pity in his eyes;
He hears the dying prisoner's groan,
And sees their sighs arise.

5 He frees the soul condemned to death,
Nor, when his saints complain,
Shall it be said that praying breath
Was ever spent in vain.

6 This shall be known when we are dead,
And left on long record,
That nations yet unborn may read,
And trust and praise the Lord.

1130.
8s, 7s & 4s.

1 ZION stands with hills surrounded—
Zion, kept by power divine;
All her foes shall be confounded,
Though the world in arms combine;
Happy Zion,
What a favored lot is thine!

2 Every human tie may perish;
Friend to friend unfaithful prove;
Mothers cease their own to cherish;
Heaven and earth at last remove;
But no changes
Can attend Jehovah's love.

3 In the furnace God may prove thee,
Thence to bring thee forth more bright,
But can never cease to love thee;
Thou art precious in his sight;
God is with thee—
God, thine everlasting light.

1131.
8s, 7s & 4s.

1 LOOK, ye saints! the day is breaking;
Joyful times are near at hand;
God, the mighty God, is speaking
By his word in every land;
Day advances,—
Darkness flies, at his command.

2 While the foe becomes more daring,
While he enters like a flood,
God, the Saviour, is preparing
Means to spread his truth abroad:
Every language
Soon shall tell the love of God.

3 God of Jacob, high and glorious!
Let thy people see thy power;
Let the gospel be victorious,
Through the world forevermore;
Then shall idols
Perish, while thy saints adore.

1132.
8s & 7s. Double.

1 COME, thou long-expected Jesus,
Born to set thy people free;
From our fears and sins release us,
Let us find our rest in thee:
Israel's Strength and Consolation,
Hope of all the saints thou art;
Dear Desire of every nation,
Joy of every longing heart.

2 Born, thy people to deliver;
Born a child, and yet a King;
Born to reign in us forever,
Now thy precious kingdom bring:
By thine own eternal Spirit,
Rule in all our hearts alone;
By thine all-sufficient merit,
Raise us to thy glorious throne.

1133.
7s & 6s.

1 WHEN shall the voice of singing
Flow joyfully along?
When hill and valley, ringing
With one triumphant song,
Proclaim the contest ended,
And him who once was slain,
Again to earth descended,
In righteousness to reign?

2 Then from the craggy mountains
    The sacred shout shall fly;
And shady vales and fountains
    Shall echo the reply:
High tower and lowly dwelling
    Shall send the chorus round,
All hallelujah swelling
    In one eternal sound.

1134.

7s & 6s.

1 Oh, that the Lord's salvation
    Were out of Zion come,
To heal his ancient nation,
    To lead his outcasts home!
How long the holy city
    Shall heathen feet profane?
Return, O Lord! in pity;
    Rebuild her walls again.

2 Let fall thy rod of terror,
    Thy saving grace impart;
Roll back the vail of error,
    Release the fettered heart;
Let Israel, home returning,
    Their lost Messiah see;
Give oil of joy for mourning,
    And bind thy church to thee.

1135.

7s & 6s.

1 Roll on, thou mighty ocean;
    And, as thy billows flow,
Bear messengers of mercy
    To every land below.
Arise, ye gales, and waft them
    Safe to the destined shore;
That man may sit in darkness,
    And death's black shade no more.

2 O thou eternal Ruler,
    Who holdest in thine arm
The tempests of the ocean,
    Protect them from all harm!
Thy presence, Lord, be with them,
    Wherever they may be;
Though far from us, who love them,
    Still let them be with thee.

1136.

S. M.

1 Ye messengers of Christ!
    His sovereign voice obey;
Arise, and follow where he leads,
    And peace attend your way.

2 The Master, whom you serve,
    Will needful strength bestow;
Depending on his promised aid,
    With sacred courage go.

3 Go, spread the Saviour's name;
    Go, tell his matchless grace;
Proclaim salvation, full and free,
    To Adam's guilty race.

4 Mountains shall sink to plains,
    And hell in vain oppose;
The cause is God's—and will prevail,
    In spite of all his foes.

1137.

7s.

1 Wake the song of jubilee,
    Let it echo o'er the sea!
Now is come the promised hour;
    Jesus reigns with glorious power!

2 All ye nations, join and sing,
    Praise your Saviour, praise your King;
Let it sound from shore to shore—
    "Jesus reigns forevermore!"

3 Hark! the desert lands rejoice;
    And the islands join their voice;
Joy! the whole creation sings,—
    "Jesus is the King of kings!"

1138.

L. C. M.   *Gustavus Adolphus's Battle-Song.*

1 Fear not, O little flock, the foe
    Who madly seeks your overthrow;
    Dread not his rage and power;
What tho' your courage sometimes faints,
His seeming triumphs o'er God's saints
    Lasts but a little hour.

2 Be of good cheer; your cause belongs
To him who can avenge your wrongs;
    Leave it to him, our Lord!
Though hidden yet from all our eyes,
He sees the Gideon that shall rise
    To save us, and his word.

3 As true as God's own word is true,
Not earth nor hell with all their crew
    Against us shall prevail;
A jest and by-word are they grown;
God is with us, we are his own,
    Our victory cannot fail!

4 Amen, Lord Jesus, grant our prayer!
　Great Captain, now thine arm make bare,
　Fight for us once again!
　So shall thy saints and martyrs raise
　A mighty chorus to thy praise,
　World without end : Amen!

1139.
L. M.

1 THROUGH every age, eternal God!
　Thou art our rest, our safe abode ;
　High was thy throne, ere heaven was
　　　made,
　Or earth thy humble footstool laid.

2 Long hadst thou reigned, ere time began,
　Or dust was fashioned to a man ;
　And long thy kingdom shall endure,
　When earth and time shall be no more.

3 But man, weak man, is born to die,
　Made up of guilt and vanity ;
　Thy dreadful sentence, Lord! was just,—
　"Return, ye sinners! to your dust."

4 Death, like an overflowing stream,
　Sweeps us away ; our life 's a dream ;
　An empty tale; a morning flower,
　Cut down and withered in an hour.

1140.
L. M.

1 BEHOLD the path that mortals tread
　Down to the regions of the dead !
　Nor will the fleeting moments stay,
　Nor can we measure back our way.

2 Our kindred and our friends are gone ;
　Know, O my soul, this doom thine own :
　Feeble as theirs, my mortal frame,
　The same my way, my house the same.

3 And must I, from the cheerful light,
　Pass to the grave's perpetual night,—
　From scenes of duty, means of grace,
　Must I to God's tribunal pass ?

4 Awake, my soul, thy way prepare,
　And lose, in this, each mortal care ;
　With steady feet that path be trod,
　Which thro' the grave conducts to God.

1141.
L. M.

1 OH! let me, gracious Lord! extend
　My view, to life's approaching end :
　What are my days?—a span, their line ;
　And what my age, compared with thine?

2 Our life advancing to its close,
　While scarce its earliest dawn it knows,
　Swift, through an empty shade we run,
　And vanity and man are one.

3 God of my fathers! here, as they,
　I walk, the pilgrim of a day ;
　A transient guest, thy works admire,
　And instant to my home retire.

4 Oh! spare me, Lord! in mercy, spare,
　And nature's failing strength repair ;
　Ere, life's short circuit wandered o'er,
　I perish, and am seen no more.

1142.
L. P. M.

1 OF all the thoughts of God, that are
　Borne inward into souls afar,
　　Along the Psalmist's music deep,
　Now tell me if that any is,
　For gift or grace, surpassing this—
　　"He giveth his belovéd sleep."

2 His dews drop mutely on the hill,
　His cloud above it saileth still,
　　Though on its slope men toil and reap ;
　More softly than the dew is shed,
　Or cloud is floated overhead,
　　"He giveth his belovéd sleep."

3 And, friends, dear friends, when it shall be
　That this low breath is gone from me,
　　When round my bier ye come to weep,
　Let one, most loving of you all,
　Say, "Not a tear must o'er her fall ;
　　'He giveth his belovéd sleep.' "

1143.
L. M.

1 HOW vain is all beneath the skies !
　How transient every earthly bliss !
　How slender all the fondest ties,
　That bind us to a world like this !

2 The evening cloud, the morning dew,
　The withering grass, the fading flower,
　Of earthly hopes are emblems true—
　The glory of a passing hour !

3 But though earth's fairest blossoms die,
　And all beneath the skies is vain,
　There is a land, whose confines lie
　Beyond the reach of care and pain.

4 Then let the hope of joys to come
　Dispel our cares, and chase our fears :
　If God be ours, we 're traveling home,
　Though passing through a vale of tears.

1144.
8s & 4s.

1 THERE is a calm for those who weep,
 A rest for weary pilgrims found :
 They softly lie, and sweetly sleep,
  Low in the ground.

2 The storm that racks the wintry sky
 No more disturbs their deep repose
 Than summer evening's latest sigh,
  That shuts the rose.

3 I long to lay this painful head
 And aching heart beneath the soil;
 To slumber, in that dreamless bed,
  From all my toil.

4 The soul, of origin divine,
 God's glorious image, freed from clay,
 In heaven's eternal sphere shall shine,
  A star of day.

5 The sun is but a spark of fire,
 A transient meteor in the sky :
 The soul, immortal as its Sire,
  Shall never die.

1145.
C. M.

1 BEHOLD the western evening light !
 It melts in deepening gloom :
 So calmly Christians sink away,
 Descending to the tomb.

2 The winds breathe low, the withering leaf
 Scarce whispers from the tree :
 So gently flows the parting breath,
 When good men cease to be.

3 How beautiful on all the hills
 The crimson light is shed !
 'T is like the peace the Christian gives
 To mourners round his bed.

4 How mildly on the wandering cloud
 The sunset beam is cast !
 'T is like the memory left behind
 When loved ones breathe their last.

5 And now above the dews of night
 The rising star appears :
 So faith springs in the heart of those
 Whose eyes are bathed in tears.

6 But soon the morning's happier light
 Its glory shall restore,
 And eyelids that are sealed in death
 Shall wake to close no more.

1146.
L. M. 6 lines.

1 AT evening time let there be light ;
 Life's little day draws near its close ;
 Around me fall the shades of night,
 The night of death, the grave's repose ;
 To crown my joys, to end my woes,
 At evening time let there be light.

2 At evening time, let there be light ;
 Stormy and dark hath been my day ;
 Yet rose the morn divinely bright ;
 Dews, birds, and blossoms cheered the
  way ;
 Oh, for one sweet, one parting ray !
 At evening time let there be light.

3 At evening time there shall be light,
 For God hath spoken ; it must be ;
 Fear, doubt, and anguish take their flight ;
 His glory now is risen on me ;
 Mine eyes shall his salvation see ;
 'T is evening time, and there is light.

1147.
C. M.

1 WHEN downward to the darksome tomb
 I thoughtful turn my eyes,
 Frail nature trembles at the gloom,
 And anxious fears arise.

2 Why shrinks my soul ?—in death's em-
  brace
 Once Jesus captive slept ;
 And angels, hovering o'er the place,
 His lowly pillow kept.

3 Thus shall they guard my sleeping dust,
 And, as the Saviour rose,
 The grave again shall yield her trust,
 And end my deep repose.

4 My Lord, before to glory gone,
 Shall bid me come away ;
 And calm and bright shall break the dawn
 Of heaven's eternal day.

5 Then let my faith each fear dispel,
 And gild with light the grave ;
 To him my loftiest praises swell,
 Who died from death to save.

1148.
7s. 6 lines.

1 VITAL spark of heavenly flame !
 Quit, oh, quit this mortal frame ;

Trembling, hoping, lingering, flying—
Oh, the pain!—the bliss of dying!
Cease, fond nature, cease thy strife,
And let me languish into life!

2 Hark! they whisper; angels say,
"Sister spirit, come away:"
What is this absorbs me quite?—
Steals my senses, shuts my sight,
Drowns my spirits, draws my breath?—
Tell me, my soul, can this be death?

3 The world recedes—it disappears!
Heaven opens on my eyes!—my ears
With sounds seraphic ring!
Lend, lend your wings! I mount! I fly!
"O Grave! where is thy victory?
O Death! where is thy sting?"

1149.
7s & 8s.

1 LIFT not thou the wailing voice;
Weep not—'t is a Christian dieth:
Up, where blessèd saints rejoice,
Ransomed now, the spirit flieth:
Freed from earth and earthly failing,
Lift for her no voice of wailing;
High in heaven's own light she dwelleth;
Full the song of triumph swelleth.

2 Pour not thou the bitter tear;
Heaven its book of comfort opeth;
Bids thee sorrow not, nor fear,
But as one who always hopeth;
Humbly here in faith relying,
Peacefully in Jesus dying,
Heavenly joy her eye is flushing,
Why should thine with tears be gushing?

3 They who die in Christ are blest;
Ours then be no thought of grieving;
Sweetly with their God they rest,
All their toils and troubles leaving;
So be ours the faith that saveth,
Hope, that every trial braveth,
Love, that to the end endureth,
And, through Christ, the crown secureth.

1150.
7s & 6s.

1 No, no, it is not dying
To go unto our God;
This gloomy earth forsaking,
Our journey homeward taking
Along the starry road.

2 No, no, it is not dying
Heaven's citizen to be;
A crown immortal wearing,
And rest unbroken sharing,
From care and conflict free.

3 No, no, it is not dying
The Shepherd's voice to know;
His sheep he ever leadeth,
His peaceful flock he feedeth,
Where living pastures grow.

4 No, no, it is not dying
To wear a heavenly crown;
Among God's people dwelling,
The glorious triumph swelling,
Of him whose sway we own.

5 Oh, no! this is not dying,
Thou Saviour of mankind!
There, streams of love are flowing,
No hindrance ever knowing;
Here, only drops we find.

1151.
L. M.

1 EARTH's transitory things decay;
Its pomps, its pleasures, pass away;
But the sweet memory of the good
Survives in the vicissitude.

2 As, 'mid the ever-rolling sea,
The eternal isles established be,
'Gainst which the surges of the main
Fret, dash, and break themselves in
vain;—

3 As, in the heavens, the urns divine
Of golden light forever shine;
Tho' clouds may darken, storms may rage,
They still shine on from age to age;—

4 So, through the ocean tide of years,
The memory of the just appears;
So, through the tempest and the gloom,
The good man's virtues light the tomb.

1152.
9s & 8s.

1 CHRISTIAN, the morn breaks sweetly o'er
thee,
And all the midnight shadows flee,
Tinged are the distant skies with glory,
A beacon light hung out for thee;

Arise, arise! the light breaks o'er thee;
Thy name is graven on the throne;
Thy home is in the world of glory,
Where thy Redeemer reigns alone.

2 Tossed on time's rude, relentless surges,
Calmly, composed, and dauntless stand,
For lo! beyond those scenes emerges
The height that bounds the promised
    land:
Behold! behold! the land is nearing,
Where the wild sea-storm's rage is o'er;
Hark! how the heavenly hosts are
    cheering,
See in what throngs they range the
    shore!

3 Cheer up! cheer up! the day breaks o'er
    thee,
Bright as the summer's noon-tide ray,
The star-gemmed crowns and realms of
    glory
Invite thy happy soul away;
Away! away! leave all for glory,
Thy name is graven on the throne;
Thy home is in that world of glory,
Where thy Redeemer reigns alone.

1153.
C. M.

1 BENEATH our feet and o'er our head
Is equal warning given;
Beneath us lie the countless dead,
Above us is the heaven!

2 Death rides on every passing breeze,
And lurks in every flower;
Each season hath its own disease,
Its peril every hour!

3 Our eyes have seen the rosy light
Of youth's soft cheek decay;
And fate descend in sudden night
On manhood's middle day.

4 Our eyes have seen the steps of age
Halt feebly to the tomb;
And yet shall earth our hearts engage,
And dreams of days to come?

5 Then, mortal, turn! thy danger know;
Where'er thy foot can tread,
The earth rings hollow from below,
And warns thee of her dead!

6 Turn, mortal, turn! thy soul apply
To truths divinely given:
The dead, who underneath thee lie,
Shall live for hell or heaven!

1154.
L. M.

1 TIME grows not old with length of years;
Changes he brings but changes not;
New-born each moment he appears;—
We run our race and are forgot.

2 Stars in perennial rounds return;
As from eternity they came,
And to eternity might burn;—
We are not for one hour the same.

3 Spring-flowers renew their wild perfume,
But ere a second spring they fly;
Our life is longer than their bloom,
Our bloom is sweeter,—yet we die.

4 Yet stars like flowers have but their day,
And Time, like stars, shall cease to roll;
We have what never can decay,—
A living and immortal soul.

5 Lord God! when Time shall end his flight,
Stars set and flowers revive no more;
May we behold thy face in light,
Thy love in Christ may we adore.

1155.
8s & 7s.

1 READY now to spread my pinions,
Glad to wing my flight away
From the gloom that hovers round me,
To the realms of endless day.

2 Ready to be freed from sorrow,
Tears and partings, toil and pain;
Ready for the heavenly mansion;
Life is dear, but death is gain.

3 Ready with the just made perfect,
Clothed in robes of light to be;
Swelling the enraptured chorus,
Singing joy and victory.

4 As the bird with warbling music
Soars above our feeble sight,
Singing still, and still ascending,
Melting in the glorious light,—

5 So the dying saint, departing,
Joyful takes his heavenward way;
Life, and time, and gladness blending
In the light of perfect day.

1156.
C. M.

1 Bright glories rush upon my sight,
　And charm my wondering eyes—
The regions of immortal light,
　The beauties of the skies.

2 All hail, ye fair, celestial shores,
　Ye lands of endless day;
A rich delight your prospect pours,
　And drives my griefs away.

3 There's a delightful clearness now;
　My clouds of doubt are gone;
Fled is my former darkness, too;
　My fears are all withdrawn.

4 Short is the passage, short the space,
　Between my home and me;
There, there, behold the radiant place;
　How near the mansions be!

5 Immortal wonders, boundless things,
　In those dear worlds appear;
Prepare me, Lord, to stretch my wings,
　And in those glories share.

1157.
11s & 10s.

1 We would see Jesus—for the shadows
　　lengthen
Across this little landscape of our life;
We would see Jesus our weak faith to
　　strengthen,
For the last weariness—the final strife.

2 We would see Jesus—the great Rock
　　Foundation,
Whereon our feet were set by sovereign
　　grace;
Not life, nor death, with all their agitation,
Can thence remove us, if we see his face.

3 We would see Jesus—other lights are
　　fading,
Which for long years we have rejoiced
　　to see;
The blessings of our pilgrimage are failing,
We would not mourn them, for we go to
　　thee.

4 We would see Jesus—this is all we're
　　needing,
Strength, joy and willingness come with
　　the sight;
We would see Jesus, dying, risen, pleading,
Then welcome day, and farewell mortal
　　night.

1158.
8s & 7s. Peculiar.

1 What is life? 't is but a vapor,
　Soon it vanishes away.
Life is but a dying taper—
　O my soul, why wish to stay!
Why not spread thy wings and fly
Straight to yonder world of joy?

2 See that glory, how resplendent!
　Brighter far than fancy paints;
There, in majesty transcendent,
　Jesus reigns the King of saints.
Why not spread, etc.

3 Joyful crowds, his throne surrounding,
　Sing with rapture of his love;
Through the heavens his praise re-
　　sounding,
　Filling all the courts above.
Why not spread, etc.

4 Go, and share his people's glory,
　'Midst the ransomed crowd appear;
Thine a joyful, wondrous story,
　One that angels love to hear.
Why not spread, etc.

1159.
C. M.

1 There is an hour when I must part
　With all I hold most dear;
And life, with its best hopes, will then
　As nothingness appear.

2 There is an hour when I must sink
　Beneath the stroke of death;
And yield to him who gave it first,
　My struggling vital breath.

3 There is an hour when I must stand
　Before the judgment-seat;
And all my sins, and all my foes,
　In awful vision meet.

4 There is an hour when I must look
　On one eternity;
And nameless woe, or blissful life,
　My endless portion be.

5 O Saviour, then, in all my need
　Be near, be near to me:
And let my soul, by steadfast faith,
　Find life and heaven in thee.

1160.

S. M.   Irregular.

1 ONE sweetly solemn thought,
   Comes to me o'er and o'er—
   I am nearer home to-day
   Than I ever have been before.

2 Nearer my Father's house,
   Where the many mansions be ;
   Nearer the great white throne ;
   Nearer the crystal sea ;

3 Nearer the bound of life,
   Where we lay our burdens down ;
   Nearer leaving the cross ;
   Nearer gaining the crown.

4 But lying darkly between,
   Winding down through the night,
   Is the deep and unknown stream,
   That leads at last to the light.

5 Father, perfect my trust !
   Strengthen the might of my faith ;
   Let me feel as I would when I stand
   On the rock of the shore of death !

6 Feel as I would when my feet
   Are slipping over the brink ;—
   For it may be, I'm nearer home—
   Nearer now than I think.

1161.

7s.

1 MORNING breaks upon the tomb,
   Jesus scatters all its gloom ;
   Day of triumph through the skies,—
   See the glorious Saviour rise !

2 Ye, who are of death afraid,
   Triumph in the scattered shade ;
   Drive your anxious cares away ;
   See the place where Jesus lay !

3 Christian ! dry your flowing tears,
   Chase your unbelieving fears ;
   Look on his deserted grave ;
   Doubt no more his power to save.

1162.

12s.

1 THE chariot ! the chariot ! its wheels roll
      on fire,
   As the Lord cometh down in the pomp
      of his ire ;

Self-moving, it drives on its pathway of
      cloud,
And the heavens with the burden of God-
      head are bowed.

2 The glory ! the glory ! by myriads are
      poured
   All the hosts of the angels to wait on
      the Lord ;
   And the glorified saints and the martyrs
      are there,
   And there all who the palm wreath of
      victory wear.

3 The trumpet ! the trumpet ! the dead
      have all heard ;
   Lo, the depths of the stone-covered char-
      nels are stirred !
   From the sea, from the land, from the
      south, from the north,
   All the vast generations of man are come
      forth.

4 The judgment ! the judgment ! the thrones
      are all set,
   Where the Lamb and the white-vested
      elders are met ;
   All flesh is at once in the sight of the
      Lord,
   And the doom of eternity hangs on his
      word.

5 Oh, mercy ! oh, mercy ! Look down from
      above,
   Creator, on us, thy sad children, with love ;
   When beneath, to their darkness, the
      wicked are driven,
   May our sanctified souls find a mansion
      in heaven.

1163.

7s.

1 IN the sun, and moon, and stars,
   Signs and wonders there shall be ;
   Earth shall quake with inward wars,
   Nations with perplexity.

2 Soon shall ocean's hoary deep,
   Tossed with stronger tempests, rise ,
   Wilder storms the mountains sweep,
   Louder thunder rock the skies.

3 Dread alarms shall shake the proud,
   Pale amazement, restless fear ;
   And amid the thunder cloud
   Wilt thou, Judge of man ! appear.

4 But, though from thine awful face,
    Heaven shall fade, and earth shall fly;
  Fear not we, thy chosen race,
    Our redemption draweth nigh.

1164.
C. M.

1 That awful day will surely come,
    Th' appointed hour makes haste,
  When I must stand before my Judge,
    And pass the solemn test.

2 Thou lovely Chief of all my joys,
    Thou Sovereign of my heart!
  How could I bear to hear thy voice
    Pronounce the sound, "Depart!"

3 Oh, wretched state of deep despair!
    To see my God remove,—
  And fix my doleful station where
    I must not taste his love!

4 Jesus, I throw my arms around,
    And hang upon thy breast:
  Without a gracious smile from thee,
    My spirit cannot rest.

5 Oh, tell me that my worthless name
    Is graven on thy hands!
  Show me some promise in thy book,
    Where my salvation stands.

6 Give me one kind, assuring word,
    To sink my fears again;
  And cheerfully my soul shall wait
    Her threescore years and ten.

1165.
7s.

1 Earth is past away and gone,
  All her glories, every one,
  All her pomp is broken down;
  God is reigning, God alone!

2 All her high ones lowly lie,
  All her mirth hath passéd by,
  All her merry-hearted sigh;
  God is reigning, God on high!

3 No more sorrow, no more night;
  Perfect joy and purest light!
  With his spotless saints and bright,
  God is reigning in the height!

4 Blessing, praise, and glory bring,
  Offer every holy thing;
  Everlasting praises sing;
  God is reigning, God our King!

1166.
L. M.   7 lines.

1 Eternity! eternity!
  How long art thou, eternity!
  And yet to thee time hastes away,
  Like as the war horse to the fray,
  Or swift as couriers homeward go,
  Or ships to port, or shaft from bow;
  Ponder, O man, eternity.

2 Eternity! eternity!
  How long art thou, eternity!
  As long as God is God, so long
  Endure the pains of hell and wrong,
  So long the joys of heaven remain;
  Oh, lasting joy! Oh, lasting pain!
  Ponder, O man, eternity!

3 Eternity! eternity!
  How long art thou, eternity!
  O man, full oft thy thoughts should dwell
  Upon the pains of sin and hell,
  And on the glories of the pure,
  That do beyond all time endure;
  Ponder, O man, eternity!

1167.
8s & 7s.

1 This is not my place of resting,—
    Mine's a city yet to come;
  Onward to it I am hasting—
    On to my eternal home.

2 In it all is light and glory;
    O'er it shines a nightless day:
  Every trace of sin's sad story,
    All the curse, hath passed away.

3 There the Lamb, our Shepherd, leads us
    By the streams of life along,—
  On the freshest pastures feeds us,
    Turns our sighing into song.

4 Soon we pass this desert dreary,
    Soon we bid farewell to pain;
  Never more are sad or weary,
    Never, never sin again!

1168.
8s & 7s.

1 Time, thou speedest on but slowly,
    Hours, how tardy is your pace!
  Ere with Him, the high and holy,
    I hold converse face to face.

2 Here is nought but care and mourning;
　　Comes a joy, it will not stay ;
　Fairly shines the sun at dawning,
　　Night will soon o'ercloud the day.

3 Onward then ! not long I wander
　　Ere my Saviour comes for me,
　And with him abiding yonder,
　　All his glory I shall see.

4 Oh ! the music and the singing
　　Of the host redeemed by love !
　Oh ! the hallelujahs ringing
　　Through the halls of light above.

1169.

7s.

1 " COME up hither ; come away ;"
　　Thus the ransomed spirits sing ;
　Here is cloudless, endless day ;
　　Here is everlasting spring.

2 Come up hither ; come and dwell
　　With the living hosts above ;
　Come, and let your bosoms swell
　　With their burning songs of love.

3 Come up hither ; come and share
　　In the sacred joys that rise,
　Like an ocean, everywhere
　　Through the myriads of the skies.

4 Come up hither ; come and shine
　　In the robes of spotless white ;
　Palms, and harps, and crowns are thine ;
　　Hither, hither wing your flight.

5 Come up hither ; hither speed ;
　　Rest is found in heaven alone ;
　Here is all the wealth you need ;
　　Come and make this wealth your own.

1170.

L. M.

1 As when the weary traveler gains
　　The height of some o'erlooking hill,
　His heart revives, if, 'cross the plains,
　　He eyes his home though distant still ;—

2 So when the Christian pilgrim views,
　　By faith his mansion in the skies ;
　The sight his fainting strength renews,
　　And wings his speed to reach the prize.

3 'Tis there, he says, I am to dwell,
　　With Jesus in the realms of day :
　Then I shall bid my cares farewell,
　　And he will wipe my tears away.

1171.

7s & 6s.

1 FROM every earthly pleasure,
　　From every transient joy,
　From every mortal treasure,
　　That soon will fade and die ;
　No longer these desiring,
　　Upward our wishes tend,
　To nobler bliss aspiring,
　　And joys that never end.

2 From every piercing sorrow
　　That heaves our breast to-day,
　Or threatens us to-morrow,
　　Hope turns our eyes away :
　On wings of faith ascending,
　　We see the land of light,
　And feel our sorrows ending
　　In infinite delight.

3 What though we are but strangers
　　And sojourners below ;
　And countless snares and dangers
　　Surround the path we go ;
　Though painful and distressing,
　　Yet there's a rest above ;
　And onward still we're pressing,
　　To reach that land of love.

1172.

C. M.

1 Lo ! what a glorious sight appears,
　　To our believing eyes !
　The earth and seas are passed away,
　　And the old rolling skies.

2 From the third heaven, where God
　　　　resides—
　That holy, happy place,—
　The New Jerusalem comes down,
　　Adorned with shining grace.

3 Attending angels shout for joy,
　　And the bright armies sing,—
　" Mortals ! behold the sacred seat
　　Of your descending King :—

4 " The God of glory, down to men,
　　Removes his blest abode ;—
　Men, the dear objects of his grace,
　　And he their loving God :—

5 " His own soft hand shall wipe the tears
　　From every weeping eye ;
　And pains, and groans, and griefs, and
　　　　fears,
　And death itself shall die."

6 How long, dear Saviour! oh, how long
  Shall this bright hour delay?
Fly swifter round, ye wheels of time!
  And bring the welcome day.

1173.
C. M.

1 JERUSALEM! my happy home!
  Name ever dear to me!
When shall my labors have an end,
  In joy, and peace, in thee?

2 Oh, when, thou city of my God,
  Shall I thy courts ascend,
Where congregations ne'er break up,
  And Sabbaths have no end?

3 There happier bowers than Eden's bloom,
  Nor sin nor sorrow know:
Blest seats! thro' rude and stormy scenes,
  I onward press to you.

4 Why should I shrink at pain and woe?
  Or feel, at death, dismay?
I've Canaan's goodly land in view,
  And realms of endless day.

5 Apostles, martyrs, prophets there,
  Around my Saviour stand;
And soon my friends in Christ below,
  Will join the glorious band.

6 Jerusalem! my happy home!
  My soul still pants for thee;
Then shall my labors have an end,
  When I thy joys shall see.

1174.
8s.

1 WE speak of the realms of the blessed,
  That country so bright and so fair,
And oft are its glories confessed;
  But what must it be to be there!

2 We speak of its pathways of gold,
  Its walls decked with jewels so rare,
Its wonders and pleasures untold;
  But what must it be to be there!

3 We speak of its freedom from sin,
  From sorrow, temptation and care,
From trials without and within;
  But what must it be to be there!

4 We speak of its service of love,
  The robes which the glorified wear,
The church of the first-born above;
  But what must it be to be there!

5 Do thou, Lord, 'mid sorrow and woe,
  Still for heaven my spirit prepare,
And shortly I also shall know,
  And feel, what it is to be there.

1175.
C. M.

1 THERE is an hour of hallowed peace,
  For those with cares oppressed,
When sighs and sorrowing tears shall
    cease,
  And all be hushed to rest.

2 'Tis then the soul is freed from fears
  And doubts, which here annoy;
Then they, who oft have sown in tears,
  Shall reap again in joy.

3 There is a home of sweet repose,
  Where storms assail no more;
The stream of endless pleasure flows,
  On that celestial shore.

4 There, purity with love appears,
  And bliss without alloy;
There, they, who oft had sown in tears,
  Shall reap again in joy.

1176.
8s & 7s. Double.

1 JESUS, blessèd Mediator!
  Thou the airy path hast trod;
Thou the Judge, the Consummator!
  Shepherd of the fold of God!
Can I trust a fellow-being?
  Can I trust an angel's care?
O thou merciful All-seeing!
  Beam around my spirit there.

2 Blessèd fold! no foe can enter;
  And no friend departeth thence;
Jesus is their sun, their centre,
  And their shield Omnipotence!
Blessèd! for the Lamb shall feed them,
  All their tears shall wipe away,
To the living fountains lead them,
  Till fruition's perfect day.

3 Lo! it comes, that day of wonder!
  Louder chorals shake the skies:
Hades' gates are burst asunder;
  See! the new-clothed myriads rise!
Thought! repress thy weak endeavor;
  Here must reason prostrate fall;
Oh, th' ineffable Forever!
  And th' eternal All in All!

1177.
8s & 7s. Peculiar.

1 Lo, the seal of death is breaking;
Those who slept its sleep are waking;
  Heaven opes its portals fair.
Hark! the harps of God are ringing,
Hark! the seraph's hymn is flinging
  Music on immortal air.

2 There, no more at eve declining,
Suns without a cloud are shining
  O'er the land of life and love;
There the founts of life are flowing,
Flowers unknown to time are blowing,
  In that radiant scene above.

3 There no sigh of memory swelleth;
There no tear of misery welleth;
  Hearts will bleed or break no more;
Past is all the cold world's scorning,
Gone the night and broke the morning
  Over all the golden shore.

1178.
7s. Double.

1 Who are these arrayed in white,
  Brighter than the noon-day sun?
Foremost of the sons of light;
  Nearest the eternal throne?
These are they that bore the cross;
  Nobly for their Master stood;
Sufferers in his righteous cause;
  Followers of the dying God.

2 Out of great distress they came;
  Washed their robes, by faith below,
In thy blood, O glorious Lamb!
  Blood that washes white as snow;
Therefore are they next the throne;
  Serve their Maker day and night;
God resides among his own,
  God doth in his saints delight.

1179.
7s.

1 Palms of glory, raiment bright,
  Crowns that never fade away,
Gird and deck the saints in light;
  Priests, and kings, and conquerors, they.

2 Yet the conquerors bring their palms
  To the Lamb amid the throne,
And proclaim, in joyful psalms,
  Victory through his cross alone.

3 Kings for harps their crowns resign,
  Crying, as they strike the chords,—
"Take the kingdom; it is thine,
  King of kings, and Lord of lords."

4 Round the altar priests confess,
  If their robes are white as snow,
'T was their Saviour's righteousness,
  And his blood, that made them so.

5 Who are these? On earth they dwelt,
  Sinners once of Adam's race;
Guilt, and fear, and suffering felt,
  But were saved by sovereign grace.

6 They were mortal, too, like us:
  Ah! when we, like them, shall die,
May our souls, translated thus,
  Triumph, reign, and shine, on high!

1180.
7s & 6s.

1 For thee, O dear, dear Country!
  Mine eyes their vigils keep:
For very love, beholding
  Thy happy name, they weep;—
O one, O only, mansion!
  O Paradise of joy!
Where tears are ever banished,
  And bliss hath no alloy.

2 Thy ageless walls are bonded
  With amethyst unpriced;
The saints build up the fabric,
  The corner-stone is Christ!
Upon the Rock of Ages
  They raise thy holy tower;
Thine is the victor's laurel,
  And thine the golden dower.

3 They stand, those halls of Zion,
  Conjubilant with song;
And bright with many an angel,
  With many a martyr-throng;

The Prince is ever in them,
The light is aye serene,
The pastures of the blesséd
Are decked in glorious sheen.

4 There is the throne of David,
And there, from toil released,
The shout of them that triumph,
The song of them that feast ;
And they, beneath their Leader,
Who conquered in the fight,
Forever and forever
Are clad in robes of white !

1181.

7s & 6s.

1 JERUSALEM, the glorious !
The glory of the elect,
O dear and future vision
That eager hearts expect !
Ev'n now by faith I see thee,
Ev'n here thy walls discern ;
To thee my thoughts are kindled,
And strive, and pant, and yearn !

2 The Cross is all thy splendor,
The Crucified, thy praise ;
His laud and benediction
Thy ransomed people raise ;—
Jerusalem ! exulting
On that securest shore,
I hope thee, wish thee, sing thee,
And love thee evermore !

3 O sweet and blesséd Country !
Shall I e'er see thy face ?
O sweet and blesséd Country !
Shall I e'er win thy grace ?
Exult, O dust and ashes !
The Lord shall be thy part;
His only, his forever,
Thou shalt be, and thou art!

1182.

10s & 5s. *New Year.*

1 COME, let us anew our journey pursue—
Roll round with the year,
And never stand still till the Master ap-
pear ;
His adorable will let us gladly fulfill,
And our talents improve
By the patience of hope, and the labor
of love.

2 Our life is a dream ; our time, as a stream,
Glides swiftly away,
And the fugitive moment refuses to stay :
The arrow is flown : the moment is gone ;
The millennial year
Rushes on to our view, and eternity's near.

3 Oh, that each, in the day of his coming,
may say,
" I have fought my way through ;
I have finished the work thou didst give
me to do ;"
Oh, that each from his Lord may receive
the glad word,
" Well and faithfully done !
Enter into my joy, and sit down on my
throne !"

1183.

C. M. *Close of the Year.*

1 AWAKE ye saints ! and raise your eyes,
And raise your voices high :
Awake, and praise that sovereign love,
That shows salvation nigh.

2 On all the wings of time it flies,
Each moment brings it near ;
Then welcome each declining day,
Welcome each closing year.

3 Not many years their rounds shall run,
Nor many mornings rise,
Ere all its glories stand revealed
To our admiring eyes.

4 Ye wheels of nature ! speed your course,
Ye mortal powers ! decay ;
Fast as ye bring the night of death,
Ye bring eternal day.

1184.

L. M. *National.*

1 GREAT God of nations ! now to thee
Our hymn of gratitude we raise ;
With humble heart, and bending knee,
We offer thee our song of praise.

2 Thy name we bless, Almighty God !
For all the kindness thou hast shown,
To this fair land the pilgrims trod,—
This land we fondly call our own.

3 Here, Freedom spreads her banner wide,
And casts her soft and hallowed ray ;—
Here, thou our fathers' steps didst guide
In safety, through their dangerous way.

4 We praise thee, that the gospel's light,
Through all our land, its radiance sheds;
Dispels the shades of error's night,
And heavenly blessings round us spreads.

1185.
6s & 4s. *National.*

1 God bless our native land;
Firm may she ever stand
Through storm and night;
When the wild tempests rave,
Ruler of winds and wave!
Do thou our country save,
By thy great might.

2 For her our prayer shall rise
To God above the skies;
On him we wait;
Thou who hast heard each sigh,
Watching each weeping eye,
Be thou forever nigh;
God save the State!

1186.
S. M. *The Church the Nation's Safety.*

1 Great is the Lord our God,
And let his praise be great;
He makes his churches his abode,
His most delightful seat.

2 These temples of his grace,
How beautiful they stand!
The honors of our native place,
And bulwarks of our land.

3 In Zion, God is known,
A refuge in distress:
How bright hath his salvation shone
Through all her palaces!

4 Oft have our fathers told,—
Our eyes have often seen,—
How well our God secures the fold
Where his own sheep have been.

5 In every new distress,
We'll to his house repair;
We'll think upon his wondrous grace,
And seek deliverance there.

1187.
7s. *Fast.*

1 Why, O God! thy people spurn?
Why permit thy wrath to burn?
God of mercy! turn once more,
All our broken hearts restore.

2 Thou hast made our land to quake,
Heal the sorrows thou dost make
Bitter is the cup we drink,
Suffer not our souls to sink.

3 Be thy banner now unfurled,
Show thy truth to all the world;
Save us, Lord! we cry to thee,
Lift thine arm—thy chosen free.

1188.
7s. *Thanksgiving.*

1 Swell the anthem, raise the song;
Praises to our God belong;
Saints and angels join to sing
Praises to the heavenly King.

2 Blessings from his liberal hand
Flow around this happy land:
Kept by him, no foes annoy;
Peace and freedom we enjoy.

3 Here, beneath a virtuous sway,
May we cheerfully obey;
Never feel oppression's rod,
Ever own and worship God.

4 Hark! the voice of nature sings
Praises to the King of kings;
Let us join the choral song,
And the grateful notes prolong.

1189.
P. M. *Seamen.*

1 Star of peace! to wanderers weary,
Bright the beams that smile on me,
Cheer the pilot's vision dreary,
Far, far at sea.

2 Star of hope! gleam on the billow,
Bless the soul that sighs for thee;
Bless the sailor's lonely pillow,
Far, far at sea.

3 Star of faith! when winds are mocking
All his toil, he flies to thee;
Save him on the billows rocking,
Far, far at sea.

4 Star divine! oh, safely guide him,—
Bring the wanderer home to thee!
Sore temptations long have tried him,
Far, far at sea.

1190.

L. M. *Prayer for Peace.*

1 Great God, whom heaven, and earth,
and sea,
With all their countless hosts obey,
Upheld by thee the nations stand,
And empires fall at thy command.

2 Oh, show thyself the Prince of peace,
Command the din of war to cease ;
With sacred love the world inspire,
And burn its chariots in the fire.

3 In sunder break each warlike spear,
Let all the Saviour's ensigns wear ;
The universal Sabbath prove,
The perfect rest of Christian love !

1191.

C. M. *Winter.*

1 Stern winter throws his icy chains,
Encircling nature round ;
How bleak, how comfortless the plains,
Of late with verdure crowned !

2 The sun withdraws his vital beams,
And light and warmth depart ;
And drooping, lifeless nature seems
An emblem of my heart,—

3 My heart, where mental winter reigns,
In night's dark mantle clad,
Confined in cold, inactive chains ;
How desolate and sad !

4 Return, O blissful sun, and bring
Thy soul-reviving ray ;
This mental winter shall be spring,
This darkness cheerful day.

5 Oh, happy state, divine abode !
Where spring eternal reigns,
And perfect day, the smile of God,
Fills all the heavenly plains.

6 Great Source of light ! thy beams display,
My drooping joys restore,
And guide me to the seats of day,
Where winter frowns no more.

1192.

C. M. *Spring.*

1 While verdant hill and blooming vale
Put on their fresh array,
And fragrance breathes in every gale,
How sweet the vernal day.

2 Oh, let my wondering heart confess,
With gratitude and love,
The bounteous hand that deigns to bless
The garden, field, and grove !

3 The bounteous hand my thoughts adore,
Beyond expression kind,
Hath sweeter, nobler gifts in store,
To bless the craving mind.

4 That hand, in this hard heart of mine
Can make each virtue live ;
And kindly showers of grace divine,
Life, beauty, fragrance give.

1193.

6s & 5s. *Parting Hymn.*

1 When shall we meet again ?
Meet ne'er to sever ?
When will peace wreathe her chain
Round us forever ?
Our hearts will ne'er repose,
Safe from each blast that blows,
In this dark vale of woes,
Never—no, never !

2 When shall love freely flow
Pure as life's river ?
When shall sweet friendship glow
Changeless forever ?
Where joys celestial thrill,
Where bliss each heart shall fill,
And fears of parting chill
Never—no, never !

3 Up to that world of light
Take us, dear Saviour !
May we all there unite,
Happy forever ;
Where kindred spirits dwell,
There may our music swell,
And time our joys dispel
Never—no, never !

4 Soon shall we meet again,
Meet ne'er to sever ;
Soon shall peace wreathe her chain
Round us forever ;
Our hearts will then repose
Secure from worldly woes ;
Our songs of praise shall close
Never—no, never !

1.
L. M.

PRAISE God, from whom all blessings flow!
Praise him, all creatures here below!
Praise him above, ye heavenly host!
Praise Father, Son, and Holy Ghost!

2.
L. M.

To God the Father, God the Son,
And God the Spirit, three in one,
Be honor, praise, and glory given,
By all on earth, and all in heaven.

3.
L. M. Double.

ETERNAL Father! throned above,
Thou fountain of redeeming love!
Eternal Word! who left thy throne
For man's rebellion to atone;
Eternal Spirit, who dost give
That grace whereby our spirits live:
Thou God of our salvation, be
Eternal praises paid to thee!

4.
C. M.

To Father, Son, and Holy Ghost,
One God, whom we adore,
Be glory as it was, is now,
And shall be evermore.

5.
C. M.

LET God the Father, and the Son,
And Spirit, be adored,
Where there are works to make him known,
Or saints to love the Lord.

6.
C. M. Double.

THE God of mercy be adored,
Who calls our souls from death,
Who saves by his redeeming word
And new-creating breath;
To praise the Father and the Son
And Spirit all-divine,—
The one in three, and three in one,—
Let saints and angels join.

7.
S. M.

YE angels round the throne,
And saints that dwell below,
Worship the Father, praise the Son,
And bless the Spirit, too.

8.
S. M.

THE Father and the Son
And Spirit we adore;
We praise, we bless, we worship thee,
Both now and evermore!

9.
H. M.

To God the Father's throne
Your highest honors raise;
Glory to God the Son;
To God, the Spirit, praise;
With all our powers, Eternal King,
Thy name we sing, while faith adores.

10.
7s.

SING we to our God above
Praise eternal as his love;
Praise him, all ye heavenly host—
Father, Son, and holy Ghost.

11.
7s. 6 lines.

PRAISE the name of God most high,
Praise him, all below the sky,
Praise him, all ye heavenly host,
Father, Son, and Holy Ghost;
As through countless ages past,
Evermore his praise shall last.

12.
L. P. M. & L. M. 6 lines.

Now to the great and sacred Three,
The Father, Son, and Spirit, be
Eternal praise and glory given—
Thro' all the worlds where God is know
By all the angels near the throne,
And all the saints in earth and heaven

13.
L. C. M.

To Father, Son, and Holy Ghost,
Be praise amid the heavenly host,
And in the church below ;
From whom all creatures draw their breath,
By whom redemption blessed the earth,
From whom all comforts flow.

14.
8s & 7s.

PRAISE the Father, earth and heaven,
Praise the Son, the Spirit praise,
As it was, and is, be given,
Glory through eternal days.

15.
8s & 7s. Double.

PRAISE the God of all creation ;
Praise the Father's boundless love :
Praise the Lamb, our expiation,
Priest and King enthroned above :
Praise the Fountain of salvation,
Him by whom our Spirits live :
Undivided adoration
To the one Jehovah give.

16.
8s, 7s & 4s.

GREAT Jehovah ! we adore thee,
God, the Father, God, the Son,
God, the Spirit, joined in glory
On the same eternal throne ;
Endless praises
To Jehovah, Three in One.

17.
7s & 6s. Iambic.

To thee be praise forever,
Thou glorious King of kings !
Thy wondrous love and favor
Each ransomed spirit sings :
We 'll celebrate thy glory
With all thy saints above,
And shout the joyful story
Of thy redeeming love.

18.
7s & 6s. Trochaic.

FATHER, Son, and Holy Ghost,
One God whom we adore,
Join we with the heavenly host
To praise thee evermore :
Live, by heaven and earth adored,
Three in One, and One in Three,
Holy, holy, holy Lord,
All glory be to thee !

19.
10s.

To Father, Son, and Spirit, ever blest,
Eternal praise and worship be addressed ;
From age to age, ye saints, his name adore,
And spread his fame, till time shall be no
more.

20.
5s & 6s.

BY angels in heaven
Of every degree,
And saints upon earth,
All praise be addressed
To God in three persons—
One God ever-blest :
As hath been, and now is,
And always shall be.

21.
11s.

O FATHER Almighty, to thee be addressed,
With Christ and the Spirit, one God ever
blest,
All glory and worship, from earth and from
heaven,
As was, and is now, and shall ever be given.

22.
6s & 4s.

To God—the Father, Son,
And Spirit—Three in One,
All praise be given !
Crown him in every song ;
To him your hearts belong ;
Let all his praise prolong—
On earth, in heaven.

SELECTIONS FOR CHANTING.

No. 1.

TALLIS.

1. Psalm VIII.

1 O Lord, our Lord, how excellent is thy name in | all the | earth!
Who hast set thy | glory a- | bove the | heavens.

2 Out of the mouth of babes and sucklings hast thou ordained strength be- | cause of · thine
enemies,
That thou mightest still the | ene - my | and · the a- | venger.

3 When I consider thy heavens, the | work of · thy | fingers,
The moon and the stars | which thou | hast or- | dained ;

4 What is man, that thou art | mindful · of | him ?
And the son of man | that thou | visi - test | him ?

5 For thou hast made him a little lower | than the | angels,
And hast crowned him with | glory | and — | honor.

6 Thou madest him to have dominion over the | works of · thy | hands ;
· Thou hast put | all things | under · his | feet :

7 All | sheep and | oxen,
Yea, and the | beasts — | of the | field ;

8 The fowl of the air, and the | fish · of the | sea,
And whatsoever passeth through the | paths — | of the | seas.

9 O | Lord our | Lord,
How excellent is thy | name in | all the | earth !

2. Psalm XXIII.

1 The Lord | is my | shepherd ;
I | shall — | not — | want.

2 He maketh me to lie down in | green — | pastures :
He leadeth me be- | side the | still — | waters.

3 He re- | storeth · my | soul :
He leadeth me in the path of righteousness | for his | name's — | sake.

4 Yea, though I walk through the valley of the shadow of death, I will | fear no | evil:
For thou art with me ; thy rod and thy | staff they | comfort | me.

5 Thou preparest a table before me in the presence | of mine | enemies:
Thou anointest my head with oil ; my | cup — | runneth | over.

6 Surely goodness and mercy shall follow me all the | days of · my | life ;
And I will dwell in the | house · of the | Lord for- | ever.

No. 2.   GREATOREX COLL.

3. PSALM LXVII.

1 GOD be merciful unto | us, and | bless us ;
  And cause his | face to | shine up- | on us.

2 That thy way may be | known up - on | earth,
  Thy saving | health a- | mong all | nations.

3 Let the people praise | thee, O | God;
  Let | all the | people | praise thee.

4 Oh, let the nations be glad and | sing for | joy :
  For thou shalt judge the people righteously, and govern the | nations | upon | earth.

5 Let the people praise | thee, O | God;
  Let | all the | people | praise thee.

6 Then shall the earth | yield her | increase ;
  And God, even | our own | God, shall | bless us.

7 God | shall — | bless us ;
  And all the ends of the | earth shall | fear — | him.

4. PSALM XIX.

1 THE heavens declare the | glory • of | God ;
  And the firmament | showeth • his | handi- | work.

2 Day unto day uttereth speech, and night unto | night showeth | knowledge.
  There is no speech nor language, where their | voice — | is not | heard.

3 Their line is gone out through | all the | earth,
  And their words to the | end — | of the | world.

4 In them hath he set a tabernacle | for the | sun,
  Which is as a bridegroom coming out of his chamber, and rejoiceth as a strong | man to | run
  a | race.

5 His going forth is from the end of the heaven, and his circuit unto the | ends — | of it :
  And there is nothing | hid • from the | heat there- | of.

6 The law of the Lord is perfect, con- | verting • the | soul :
  The testimony of the Lord is sure, | making | wise the | simple.

7 The statutes of the Lord are right, re- | joicing • the | heart :
  The commandment of the Lord is | pure, en- | lightening • the | eyes.

8 The fear of the Lord is clean, en- | during • for | ever :
  The judgments of the Lord are true and | righteous | alto- | gether.

9 More to be desired are they than gold, yea, than | much fine | gold :
  Sweeter also than honey | and the | honey- | comb.

10 Moreover by them is thy | servant | warned :
   And in keeping of them | there is | great re- | ward.

11 Who can under- | stand his | errors?
   Cleanse thou | me from | secret | faults.

12 Keep back thy servant also from presumptuous sins; let them not have do- | minion | over me :
   Then shall I be upright, and I shall be innocent | from the | great trans- | gression.

13 Let the words of my mouth, and the meditation of my heart, be acceptable | in thy | sight,
   O Lord, my | Strength, and | my Re- | deemer.

No. 3.

Chard.

5. Psalm LXXXIV.

1 How amiable are thy | taber - na- | cles,
   O | Lord — | of — | hosts !
2 My soul longeth, yea, even fainteth for the | courts • of the | Lord :
   My heart and my flesh crieth | out • for the | living | God.
3 Yea, the sparrow hath found an house, and the swallow a nest for herself, where she may | lay her | young,
   Even thine altars, O Lord of hosts, my | King, • and | my — | God.
4 Blessed are they that | dwell in • thy | house :
   They will be | still — | praising | thee.
5 Blessed is the man whose | strength • is in | thee ;
   In whose | heart • are the | ways of | them,
6 Who passing through the valley of Baca | make • it a | well ;
   The rain | also | filleth • the | pools.
7 They go from | strength to | strength,
   Every one of them in Zion ap- | peareth • be- | fore — | God.
8 O Lord God of hosts, | hear my | prayer :
   Give | ear, O | God of | Jacob.
9 Behold, O | God our | shield,
   And look upon the | face of | thine A- | nointed.
10 For a day in thy courts is better | than a | thousand.
   I had rather be a doorkeeper in the house of my God, than to dwell in the | tents of | wicked- | ness.
11 For the Lord God is a | sun and | shield :
   The Lord will give grace and glory: no good thing will he withhold from | them that | walk up- | rightly.
12 O | Lord of | hosts,
   Blessed is the | man that | trusteth • in | thee.

6. Psalm LXIII.

1 O God, | thou art | my God :
   Early | will I | seek — | thee.
2 My soul thirsteth for thee, my flesh | longeth • for | thee,
   In a dry and thirsty land, | where no | water | is ;
3 To see thy power | and thy | glory,
   So as I have seen thee | in the | sanctu- | ary.
4 Because thy loving-kindness is | better • than | life,
   My | lips shall | praise — | thee.
5 Thus will I bless thee | while I | live :
   I will lift up my | hands in | thy — | name.
6 My soul shall be satisfied as with | marrow • and | fatness ;
   And my mouth shall praise | thee with | joyful | lips :
7 When I remember thee up- | on my | bed,
   And meditate on thee | in the | night — | watches.
8 Because thou hast | been my | help,
   Therefore in the shadow of thy | wings will | I re- | joice.

No. 4.

7. Psalms XLII & XLIII.

1 As the hart panteth after the | water | brooks,
   So panteth my soul after | thee — | O — | God.
2 My soul thirsteth for God, for the | living | God!
   When shall I come and ap- | pear be- | fore — | God!
3 My tears have been my meat | day and | night,
   While they continually say unto me, | where is | thy — | God?
4 When I re- | member · these | things,
   I pour | out my | soul — | in me;
5 For I had gone with the multitude, I went with them to the | house of | God,
   With the voice of joy and praise, with a multitude that | kept — | holy- | day.
6 Why art thou cast down, | O my | soul?
   And why art thou dis- | quiet- | ed in | me?
7 Hope | thou in | God:
   For I shall yet praise him for the | help of | his — | countenance.
8 Oh, send out thy light and thy truth : | let them | lead me;
   Let them bring me unto thy holy hill, and | to thy | taber - na- | cles.
9 Then will I go unto the altar of God, unto God my ex- | ceeding | joy :
   Yea, upon the harp will I praise | thee, O | God, my | God.
10 Why art thou cast down, | O my | soul?
   And why art thou dis- | quiet- | ed with- | in me?
11 Hope | in — | God:
   For I shall yet praise him, who is the health of my | counte - nance | and my | God.

8. Psalm LXXXV.

1 LORD, thou hast been favorable | unto · thy | land :
   Thou hast brought back the cap- | tivi- | ty of | Jacob.
2 Thou hast forgiven the iniquity | of thy | people,
   Thou hast | covered | all their | sin.
3 Thou hast taken away | all thy | wrath :
   Thou hast turned thyself from the | fierceness | of thine | anger.
4 Turn us, O God of | our sal- | vation,
   And cause thine | anger · toward | us to | cease.
5 Wilt thou be angry with | us for- | ever?
   Wilt thou draw out thine anger to | all — | gener- | ations !
6 Wilt thou not re- | vive us · a- | gain :
   That thy people | may re- | joice in | thee?
7 Shew us thy | mercy, · O | Lord,
   And | grant us | thy sal- | vation.
8 I will hear what God the | Lord will | speak :
   For he will speak peace unto his people, and to his saints : but let them not | turn a- | gain to | folly.
9 Surely his salvation is nigh | them that | fear him;
   That glory may | dwell — | in our | land.
10 Mercy and truth are | met to- | gether;
   Righteousness and | peace have | kissed · each | other.
11 Truth shall spring | out · of the | earth ;
   And righteousness shall | look — | down from | heaven.
12 Yea, the Lord shall give | that · which is | good ;
   And our | land shall | yield her | increase.
13 Righteousness shall | go be- | fore him ;
   And shall set us in the | way of | his — | steps.

No. 5.   FARRANT.

9. Psalm CXXXIX.

1 O Lord, thou hast searched me, and | known — | me.
     Thou knowest my downsitting and mine uprising, thou understandest my | thoughts a- |
     far — | off.

2 Thou compassest my path and my | lying | down,
     And art acquainted with | all — | my — | ways.

3 For there is not a | word · in my | tongue,
     But lo, O Lord, thou | knowest · it | alto- | gether.

4 Thou hast beset me be- | hind · and be- | fore,
     And | laid thine | hand up- | on me.

5 Such knowledge is too | wonder - ful | for me ;
     It is high, I cannot at- | tain — | unto | it.

6 Whither shall I go from | thy — | Spirit ?
     Or whither shall I | flee from | thy — | presence ?

7 If I ascend up into heaven, | thou art | there :
     If I make my bed in hell, be- | hold, — | thou art | there.

8 If I take the wings of the morning, and dwell in the uttermost | parts · of the | sea ;
     Even there shall thy hand lead me, and thy | right hand | shall — | hold me.

9 If I say, Surely the | darkness · shall | cover me ;
     Even the | night · shall be | light a- | bout me.

10 Yea, the darkness hideth not from thee ; but the night shineth | as the | day :
     The darkness and the light are | both a- | like to | thee.

11 Search me, O God, and | know my | heart :
     Try me, and | know — | my — | thoughts :

12 And see if there be any | wicked · way | in me,
     And lead me in the | way — | ever- | lasting.

10. Psalm LI.

1 Have mercy upon me, O God, according to thy | loving- | kindness :
     According unto the multitude of thy tender mercies | blot out | my trans- | gressions.

2 Wash me thoroughly from | mine in- | iquity,
     And | cleanse me | from my | sin.

3 For I acknowledge | my trans- | gressions :
     And my | sin is | ever · be- | fore me.

4 Hide thy face | from my | sins,
     And blot out | all — | mine in- | iquities.

5 Create in me a clean | heart, O | God ;
     And renew a right | spirit · with- | in me.

6 Cast me not away | from thy | presence ;
     And take not thy | Holy | Spirit | from me.

7 Restore unto me the joy of | thy sal- | vation ;
     And uphold me | with thy | free — | Spirit.

8 Then will I teach trans- | gressors · thy | ways :
     And sinners shall be con- | verted | unto | thee.

9 Deliver me from blood-guiltiness, O God, thou God of | my sal- | vation :
     And my tongue shall sing aloud | of thy | righteous- | ness.

10 O Lord, open | thou my | lips ;
     And my mouth shall | shew forth | thy — | praise.

11 For thou desirest not sacrifice ; | else · would I | give it :
     Thou delightest | not in | burnt- — | offering.

12 The sacrifices of God are a | broken | spirit :
     A broken and a contrite heart, O God, | thou wilt | not de- | spise.

No. 6. KING.

11. PSALM CXXVI.

1 WHEN the Lord turned again the cap- | tivity · of | Zion,
We were | like — | them that | dream.

2 Then was our mouth | filled · with | laughter,
And our | tongue — | with — | singing :

3 Then said they·a- | mong the | heathen,
The Lord hath done | great — | things — | for them.

4 The Lord hath done great | things for | us ;
Where- | of — | we are | glad.

5 Turn again our captivity, | O — | Lord,
As the | streams — | in the | south.

6 They that | sow in | tears
Shall | reap — | in — | joy.

7 He that goeth forth and weepeth, bearing | precious | seed,
Shall doubtless come again with rejoicing, | bringing · his | sheaves — | with him.

12. PSALM CII.

1 WHEN the Lord shall | build up | Zion,
He shall ap- | pear in | his — | glory.

2 He will regard the prayer | of the | destitute,
And | not de- | spise their | prayer.

3 This shall be written for the gener- | ation · to | come :
And the people which shall be cre- | ated · shall | praise the | Lord.

4 For he hath looked down from the height | of his | sanctuary ;
From heaven did the | Lord be- | hold the | earth ;

5 To hear the groaning | of the | prisoner ;
To loose those that are ap- | point- — | ed to | death ;

6 To declare the name of the | Lord in | Zion,
And his praise in | Je- — | rusa- | lem ;

7 When the people are | gathered · to- | gether,
And the | kingdoms, · to | serve the | Lord.

8 He weakened my | strength · in the | way ;
He | shortened | my — | days.

9 I said, O my God, take me not away in the | midst of · my | days :
Thy years are throughout | all — | gener- | ations.

10 Of old hast thou laid the foundation | of the | earth :
And the heavens are the | work of | thy — | hands.

11 They shall perish, but | thou · shalt en- | dure :
Yea, all of them shall wax | old — | like a | garment ;

12 As a vesture | shalt thou | change them,
And they | shall be | chang- — | ed :

13 But thou | art the | same,
And thy | years shall | have no | end.

14 The children of thy servants | shall con- | tinue,
And their seed shall be es- | tablish- | ed be- | fore thee.

No. 7   FELTON.

13. ISAIAH LIII.

1 HE is despised and re- | jected • of | men ;
    A man of sorrows, | and ac- | quainted • with | grief :

2 And we hid as it were our | faces | from him ;
    He was despised, and | we es- | teemed • him | not.

3 Surely he hath borne our griefs, and | carried • our | sorrows :
    Yet we did esteem him strickeu, | smitten • of | God, • and af- | flicted.

4 But he was wounded for | our trans- | gressious,
    He was | bruised • for | our in- | iquities ;

5 The chastisement of our peace | was up- | on him ;
    And with | his stripes | we are | healed.

6 All we like sheep have | gone a- | stray ;
    We have turned every | one to | his own | way ;

7 And the Lord hath | laid on | him
    The in- | iqui - ty | of us | all.

8 When thou shalt make his soul an | offering • for | sin,
    He shall see his seed, he | shall pro- | long his | days.

9 And the pleasure of the Lord shall prosper | in his | hand.
    He shall see of the travail of his soul, and | shall be ¦ satis- | fied.

14. PSALM CXXX.

1 OUT of the | depths
    Have I cried unto thee, O | Lord.

2 Lord, hear my | voice :
    Let thine ears be attentive to the voice of my suppli- | cations.

3 If thou, Lord, shouldst mark in- | iquities,
    O Lord, who shall | stand ?

4 But there is forgiveness with | thee,
    That thou mayest be | feared.

5 I wait for the Lord, my soul doth | wait,
    And in his word do I | hope.

6 My soul waiteth for the Lord more than they that watch for the | morning :
    I say, more than they that watch for the | morning.

7 Let Israel hope in the | Lord :
    For with the Lord there is mercy, and with him is plenteous re- | demption.

8 And he shall redeem | Israel
    From all his in- | iquities.

No. 8.

No. 9.

15. Te Deum Laudamus.

1 WE praise | thee, O | God;
  We acknowledge | thee to | be the | Lord.

2 All the earth doth | worship | thee,
  The | Father | ever- | lasting.

3 To thee all angels | cry a- | loud,
  The heavens, and | all the | powers there- | in.

4 To thee | cherubim • and | seraphim,
  Con- | tinu - al- | ly do | cry.

5 Holy, | holy, | holy,
  Lord | God of | Saba- | oth;

6 Heaven and | earth are | full
  Of the | majes - ty | of thy | glory.

7 The glorious company of the apostles | praise — | thee.
  The goodly fellowship of the | prophets | praise — | thee.

8 The noble army of martyrs | praise — | thee,
  The holy church throughout all the world | doth ac- | knowledge | thee,

9 The Father of an | infi - nite | majesty;
  Thine adorable, | true and | only | Son;

10 Also the | Holy | Ghost,
   The | Com- — | fort- — | er.

11 Thou art the King of | glory, • O | Christ,
   Thou art the everlasting | Son • of the | Father.

12 When thou tookest upon thee to de- | liver | man,
   Thou didst humble thyself to be | born — | of a | virgin.

13 When thou hadst overcome the | sharpness • of | death,
   Thou didst open the kingdom of | heaven to | all be- | lievers.

14 Thou sittest at the right hand of God, in the glory | of the | Father.
   We believe that thou shalt | come to | be our | judge.

15 We therefore pray thee, | help thy | servants,
   Whom thou hast redeemed | with thy | precious | blood.

16 Make them to be numbered | with thy | saints,
   In | glory | ever- | lasting.

17 O Lord, save thy people, and | bless thine | heritage;
   Govern them, and | lift them | up for- | ever.

18 Day by day we | magni - fy | thee;
   And we worship thy name ever, | world with- | out — | end.

19 Vouchsafe, O Lord, to keep us this day | without | sin ;
   O Lord, have mercy upon us, have | mer - cy up- | on us.

20 O Lord, let thy mercy be up- | on — | us,
   As our | trust — | is in | thee.

21 O Lord, in thee | have I | trusted;
   Let me | never | be con- | founded.

No. 10.

CHARD.

16. PSALM CIII.

1 Bless the Lord, | O my | soul :
   And all that is within me, | bless his | holy | name.
2 Bless the Lord, | O my | soul,
   And for- | get not | all his | benefits :
3 Who forgiveth all | thine in- | iquities ;
   Who | healeth · all | thy dis- | eases ;
4 Who redeemeth thy life | from de- | struction ;
   Who crowneth thee with loving | kindness · and | tender | mercies ;
5 Who satisfieth thy mouth with | good — | things :
   So that thy youth is re- | new - ed | like the | eagle's.
6 The Lord executeth | righteousness   and | judgment
   For | all that | are op- | pressed ;
7 He made known his ways | unto | Moses,
   His acts unto the | children · of | Isra- | el.
8 The Lord is | merciful · and | gracious,
   Slow to anger, and | plenteous | in — | mercy.
9 He will not | always | chide :
   Neither will he | keep his | anger · for- | ever.
10 He hath not dealt with us | after · our | sins ;
   Nor rewarded us ac- | cording · to | our in- | iquities.
11 For as the heaven is high a- | bove the | earth,
   So great is his mercy toward | them that | fear — | him.
12 As far as the east is | from the | west,
   So far hath he removed | our trans- | gressions | from us.
13 Like as a father | pitieth · his | children,
   So the Lord | pitieth | them that | fear him.
14 For he | knoweth · our | frame ;
   He remembereth that | we — | are — | dust.
15 As for man, | days · are as | grass :
   As a flower of the field | so he | flourish- | eth.
16 For the wind passeth over it, | and · it is | gone ;
   And the place there- | of shall | know it · no | more.
17 But the mercy of the Lord is from everlasting to everlasting upon | them that | fear him,
   And his righteousness | unto | children's | children ;
18 To such as | keep his | covenant,
   And to those that remember his com- | mand - ments to | do — | them.
19 The Lord hath prepared his | throne · in the | heavens :
   And his kingdom | ruleth | over | all.
20 Bless the Lord, ye his angels, that ex- | cel in | strength,
   That do his commandments, hearkening unto the | voice of | his — | word.
21 Bless ye the Lord, all | ye his | hosts ;
   Ye ministers of | his, that | do his | pleasure.
22 Bless the Lord, all his works, in all places of | his do- | minion :
   Bless the Lord, ' O — | my — | soul.

No. 11.

17. Psalm XLVI.

1 God is our | refuge • and | strength,
   A very | present | help in | trouble,
2 Therefore, will not we fear, though the | earth • be re- | moved,
   And though the mountains be carried into the | midst — | of the | sea;
3 Though the waters thereof | roar • and be | troubled,
   Though the mountains | shake • with the | swelling • there- | of.
4 There is a river, the streams whereof shall make glad the | city • of | God,
   The holy place of the tabernacles | of the | Most — | high.
5 God is in the midst of her; she shall | not be | moved:
   God shall | help her, • and | that right | early.
6 The heathen raged, the | kingdoms • were | moved:
   He uttered his | voice, the | earth — | melted.
7 The Lord of | hosts is | with us;
   The God of | Jacob | is our | refuge.
8 Come, behold the | works • of the | Lord,
   What desolations he hath | made — | in the | earth.
9 He maketh wars to cease unto the | end • of the | earth;
   He breaketh the bow, and cutteth the spear in sunder; he burneth the | chariot | in the | fire
10 Be still, and know that | I am | God:
   I will be exalted among the heathen, I will be ex- | alted | in the | earth.
11 The Lord of | hosts is | with us;
   The God of | Jacob | is our | refuge.

18. Psalm XLVIII.

1 Great is the Lord, and greatly to be praised in the city | of our | God,
   In the mountain | of his | holi- | ness.
2 Beautiful for | situ- | ation,
   The joy of the whole | earth is | Mount — | Zion,
3 On the sides of the north, the city of the | great — | King,
   God is known in her | pala - ces | for a | refuge.
4 We have thought of thy loving- | kindness, • O | God,
   In the | midst of | thy — | temple.
5 According to thy name, O God, so is thy praise unto the | ends • of the | earth;
   Thy right hand is | full of | righteous- | ness.
6 Let Mount Zion rejoice, let the daughters of | Judah • be | glad,
   Be- | cause of | thy — | judgments.
7 Walk about Zion, and go | round a - bout | her;
   Tell the | towers — | there- — | of.
8 Mark ye well her bulwarks, con- | sider • her | palaces;
   That ye may tell it to the gener- | ation | follow- | ing.
9 For this God is our God for- | ever • and | ever:
   He will be our guide | even | unto | death.

No. 12.   GANZBACH.

19. GLORIA IN EXCELSIS.

1 GLORY be to | God on | high,
And on earth | peace, good | will · towards | men.

2 We praise thee, we bless thee, we | worship | thee.
We glorify thee, we give thanks to | thee, for | thy great | glory,

3 O Lord God, | heavenly | King,
God the | Father | Al- — | mighty.

4 O Lord, the only begotten Son. | Jesus | Christ,
O Lord God, Lamb of God, | Son — | of the | Father,

5 That takest away the | sins · of the | world,
Have | mer - cy up- | on — | us.

6 Thou that takest away the | sins · of the | world,
Have | mer - cy up- | on — | us.

7 Thou that takest away the | sins · of the | world,
Re- | ceive — | our — | prayer.

8 Thou that sittest at the right hand of | God the | Father,
Have | mer - cy up- | on — | us.

9 For thou | only · art | holy;
Thou | only | art the | Lord ;

10 Thou only, O Christ, with the | Holy | Ghost,
Art most high in the glory of God the | Father. | A- — | men.

20. ISAIAH LII.

1 How beautiful up- | on the | mountains
Are the feet of him that bringeth good | tidings, · that | publish - eth | peace;

2 That bringeth good tidings of good, that publisheth | sal- — | vation ;
That saith unto Zion, | Thy God | reign- — | eth !

3 Thy watchmen shall lift | up the | voice ;
With the voice to- | gether | shall they | sing:

4 For they shall see | eye to | eye,
When the Lord shall | bring a- | gain — | Zion.

5 Break | forth · into | joy,
Sing together, ye waste places | of Je- | rusa- | lem :

6 For the Lord hath | comforted · his | people,
He hath re- | deemed · Je- | rusa- | lem.

7 The Lord hath made bare his holy arm in the eyes of | all the | nations ;
And all the ends of the earth shall see the sal- | vation | of our | God.

No. 13.

PURCELL.

21. SELECTION FOR BAPTISM.

1 Thus saith the Lord that made thee, and formed thee, | who will | help thee,
Fear not, O Jacob my servant, and | Israel • whom | I have | chosen.

2 The mercy of the Lord is from everlasting to everlasting upon | them that | fear him.
And his righteousness | unto | children's | children,

3 To such as | keep his | covenant:
And to those that remember his com- | mand - ments to | do — | them.

4 One shall say, I am the Lord's; and another shall call himself by the | name of | Jacob;
And another shall subscribe with his hand to the Lord, and surname himself | by the | name of | Israel.

5 Doubtless thou art our Father, though Abraham be ignorant of us, and Israel ac- | knowledge • us | not.
Thou, O Lord, art our Father, our Redeemer; from ever- | lasting | is thy | name.

22. SELECTION FOR BAPTISM.

1 And Jesus said, Suffer little children, and forbid them not to | come • unto | me;
For of | such • is the | kingdom • of | heaven.

2 He shall feed his | flock • like a | shepherd:
He shall gather the lambs with his arm and | carry • them | in his | bosom.

3 I will pour my Spirit upon thy seed, and my blessing up- | on thine | offspring;
And they shall spring up as among the grass, as | willows • by the | water | courses

4 Then will I sprinkle clean | water • up- | on you,
And | ye shall | be — | clean:

5 A new heart also | will I | give you,
And a new spirit | will I | put with- | in you,

6 And I will take away the stony heart | out of • your | flesh,
And I will | give • you a | heart of | flesh.

7 For the promise is unto you, and | to your | children;
And to all that are afar off, even as many as the | Lord our | God shall | call.

8 Go ye, therefore, and teach all nations, baptizing them in the name of the Father, and of the Son, and of the | Holy | Ghost;
Teaching them to observe all things whatsoever I have commanded you, and lo! I am with you always | even • unto the | end • of the | world.

9 Glory be to the Father, and to the Son, and to the | Holy | Ghost;
As it was in the beginning, is now, and ever | shall be, | world • without | end. | Amen.

No. 14.   FELTON.

23. Psalm XC.

1 Lord, thou hast been our | dwelling- | place
In | all — | gener- | ations.

2 Before the mountains were brought forth, or ever thou hadst formed the | earth • and the | world,
Even from everlasting to ever- | lasting, | thou art | God.

3 Thou turnest man | to de- | struction;
And sayest, Re- } turn, ye | children • of | men.

4 For a thousand years in thy sight are but as yesterday | when • it is | past,
And as a | watch — | in the | night.

5 Thou carriest them away as with a flood; they are | as a | sleep:
In the morning they are like | grass which [groweth | up;

6 In the morning it flourisheth, and | groweth | up;
In the evening it is cut | down and | wither- | eth.

7 For we are consumed | by thine | anger,
And by thy | wrath — | are we | troubled,

8 Thou hast set our iniquities be- | fore — | thee,
Our secret sins in the | light of | thy — | countenance.

9 For all our days are passed away | in thy | wrath:
We spend our years as a | tale — | that is | told.

10 The days of our years are threescore | years and | ten:
And if by reason of | strength • they be | fourscore | years,

11 Yet is their strength | labor • and | sorrow;
For it is soon cut off, | and we | fly a- | way.

12 Who knoweth the power | of thine | anger?
Even according to thy | fear, so | is thy | wrath.

13 So teach us to | number • our | days,
That we may apply our | hearts — | unto | wisdom.

24. Funeral.

1 Blessed are the dead, who die in the | Lord f om | henceforth.
Yea, saith the Spirit, that they may rest from their labors, | and their | works do | follow them.

2 Our days on earth are as a shadow, and there is | none a- | biding:
We are but of yesterday; there is but a | step • between | us and | death.

3 Man's days are as grass: as a flower of the field | so he | flourisheth;
He appeareth for a little time, then | vanish - eth | a- — | way.

4 Watch! for ye know not what hour your | Lord doth | come;
Be ye also ready; for in such an hour as ye think not, the | Son of | Man — | cometh.

5 It is the Lord; let him do what | seemeth • him | good;
The Lord gave, and the Lord hath taken away, and blessed be the | name — | of the | Lord.

6 Blessed are the dead, who die in the | Lord from | henceforth;
Yea, saith the Spirit, that they may rest from their labors, | and their | works do | follow them.

BRAYTON. L. M. *Arranged.* METUFESSEL.

1. Sweet is the work, my God! my King! To praise thy name, give thanks and sing;

2. Sweet is the day of sa - cred rest, No mor - tal care shall seize my breast;

To show thy love by morn-ing light, And talk of all thy truth at night.

Oh! may my heart in tune be found, Like Da - vid's harp of sol - emn sound.

KOORBLOH. L. M. *Arranged.* MINK.

Bless, O my soul! the liv - ing God, Call home thy thoughts that rove a - broad:

Let all the powers with-in me, join In work and wor - ship so di - vine.

STAIR. L. M. *Arranged.* MINK.

De-scend from heaven, im-mor - tal Dove, Stoop down, and take us on thy wings:

And mount, and bear us far a - bove The reach of these in - fe - rior things.

HUNTINGTON. L. M.   *Arranged.* HERZ.

1. Come, dear-est Lord! de - scend and dwell By faith and love in ev - ery breast;

2. Come, fill our hearts with in - ward strength, Make our en - larg - ed souls pos - sess,

Then shall we know, and taste, and feel, The joys that can - not be ex-pressed.

And learn the height, and breadth, and length, Of thine e - ter - nal love and grace.

CRAWFORD. L. M.   *Arranged.* HAYDN.

1. 'Tis by the faith of joys to come We walk thro' deserts dark as night; Till we ar-rive at

2. The want of sight she well supplies : She makes the pearly gates appear ; Far in - to distant

heaven, our home, Faith is our guide, and faith our light, Faith is our guide, and faith our light.

worlds she pries, And brings e-ter - nal glo - ries near, And brings e-ter - nal glo - ries near.

BEHRENS. C. M.   *Arranged.* BEHRENS.

Thou love - ly Source of true de - light, Whom I un - seen a - dore !

BEHRENS. (Concluded.)

Un-veil thy beau-ties to my sight, That I may love thee more.

MARIAN. C. M.

GANZBACH.

1. To thee, my Shep-herd and my Lord, A grate-ful song I'll raise;
2. But how shall mor-tal tongue ex-press A sub-ject so di-vine,

Oh, let the fee-blest of thy flock At-tempt to speak thy praise!
Do jus-tice to so vast a theme, Or praise a love like thine?

EDWARDS. S. M.

BEETHOVEN.

UNISON.

Ah! how shall fall-en man Be just be-fore his God,

ORGAN.

If he con-tend in right-eous-ness, We fall be-neath his rod.

BENJAMIN. S. M.   *Arranged by* Wm. B. Bradbury.

"The Lord is risen in - deed!" Then is his work per-formed; The Might-y Cap - tive

now is freed, And death, our foe, dis - armed, And death, our foe, dis - armed.

LEONARD. S. M.   *Arranged from* Spohr.

Blest be the tie, that binds Our hearts in Chris - tian love;

The fel - low - ship of kin - dred minds Is like to that a - bove.

KEITH. S. M.   Ganzbach.

1. My spi - rit on thy care,..... Blest Sa - viour, I re - cline;

2. In thee I place my trust;.... On thee I calm - ly rest;

Thou wilt not leave me to de - spair, For thou art Love di - vine.

I know thee good, I know thee just, And count thy choice the best.

TIPSTANLEY. S. M. *Arranged.* ROSSINI.

Come, Ho - ly Spi - rit, come; Let thy bright beams a - rise;

Dis - pel the sor - row from our minds, The dark - ness from our eyes.

SEVERANCE. S. M. Double. *Arranged from* HESSE.

How beauteous are their feet Who stand on Zi - on's hill! Who bring sal - va - tion

on their tongues, And words of peace re - veal. How charming is their voice! How

sweet their ti - dings are! "Zi - on, behold thy Saviour King, He reigns and triumphs here."

MARTH. 7s & 5s. Peculiar. GANZBACH.

In the dark and cloud - y day, When earth's rich - es flee a - - way,

And the last hope will not stay. Sa - viour, com - fort me!....

JEWETT. 6s.

Arranged from WEBER.

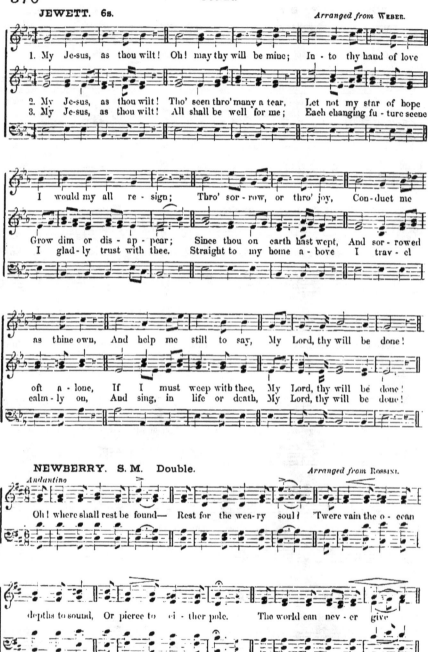

1. My Je-sus, as thou wilt! Oh! may thy will be mine; In - to thy hand of love

2. My Je-sus, as thou wilt! Tho' seen thro' many a tear,   Let not my star of hope
3. My Je-sus, as thou wilt! All shall be well for me;   Each changing fu - ture scene

I would my all re - sign;   Thro' sor - row, or thro' joy,   Con - duct me

Grow dim or dis - ap - pear;   Since thou on earth hast wept, And sor - rowed
I glad - ly trust with thee.   Straight to my home a - bove   I trav - el

as thine own, And help me still to say, My Lord, thy will be done!

oft a - lone, If I must weep with thee, My Lord, thy will be done!
calm - ly on, And sing, in life or death, My Lord, thy will be done!

NEWBERRY. S. M. Double.

Arranged from ROSSINI.

Andantino

Oh! where shall rest be found— Rest for the wea - ry soul! 'Twere vain the o - cean

depths to sound, Or pierce to ei - ther pole. The world can nev - er give

NEWBERRY. (CONCLUDED.)

The bliss for which we sigh: 'Tis not the whole of life to live, Nor

all of death to die, Nor all of death to die, Nor all of death to die.

HANDY. L. M. 6 lines. J. P. HOLBROOK.

1. At eve-ning time let there be light; Life's lit-tle day draws near its close:
2. At eve-ning time let there be light; Storm-y and dark hath been my day;

A-round me fall the shades of night, The night of death, the grave's re-pose;
Yet rose the morn di-vine-ly bright; Dews, buds, and blos-soms cheered the way;

To crown my joys, to end my woes, At eve-ning time let there be light.
Oh, for one sweet, one part-ing ray! At eve-ning time let there be light.

GRISWOLD. 7s. *Arranged from* GOTTSCHALK.

1. Ho-ly Ghost! with light di-vine, Shine up-on this heart of mine;

Chase the shades of night a-way, Turn my dark-ness in-to day.

REFUGE. 7s, or 8s & 7s. Double.   J. P. HOLBROOK.

1. Je-sus, lov-er of my soul, Let me to thy bo-som fly, While the bil - lows near me roll, While the tem - pest still is high; Hide me, O my Sa - viour, hide, Till the storm of life is past; Safe in-to the ha - ven guide, Oh, re-ceive my soul at last.

2. Oth-er ref - uge have I none; Hangs my helpless soul on thee; Leave, oh! leave me not a-lone, Still sup-port and com-fort me; All my trust on thee is stayed, All my help from thee I bring, Cov-er my de-fence-less head With the shad-ow of thy wing.

3. Plenteous grace with thee is found, Grace to cov-er all my sin; Let the heal - ing streams a-bound, Make and keep me pure with-in; Thou of life the fountain art, Free-ly let me take of thee; Spring thou up within my heart, Rise to all e-ter-ni-ty.

STANLEY. 8s & 7s.   Arranged from BAYLEY.

Sa - viour! breathe an evening blessing, Ere re - pose our spi - rits seal;
Sin.... and want we come con - fess - ing: Thou canst save, and thou canst heal.

STANLEY. (Concluded.)

Though de - struc - tion walk a - round us, Though the ar - rows past us fly,

Angel guards, Angel guards from thee surround us, We are safe, if thou art

Angel guards from thee surround us, We are safe, if thou art

An - - - gel guards from thee sur - round us, We are safe, if thou art

nigh........ *p* *Ritard. pp*

nigh, We are safe, if thou art nigh, We are safe, if thou art nigh.

nigh,..........................

SEGUR. 8s, 7s & 4s.

J. P. Holbrook.

1. Guide me, O thou great Je - ho - vah, Pil - grim through this bar - ren land;

I am weak, but thou art might - y; Hold me with thy powerful hand;

Ritard.

Bread of heav - en! Bread of heav - en! Feed me till I want no more.

POMEROY. 7s & 6s.   Ganzbach.

1. No, no, it is not dy-ing To go un-to our God; This gloomy earth for-sak-ing,

2. No, no, it is not dy-ing Heaven's cit-i-zen to be; A crown im-mor-tal wear-ing,

Our jour-ney homeward tak-ing A-long the star-ry road, A-long the star-ry road.

And rest un-brok-en shar-ing. From care and con-flict free, From care and con-flict free.

WILLKEITH. 7s.   *Arranged from* Spindler.

Christ, of all my hopes the ground! Christ, the spring of all my joy!

Still in thee let me be found, Still for thee my powers em-ploy.

CYRUS. 7s.   S. H. Merlin.

SOLO.

Lord! we come be-fore thee now; At thy feet we hum-bly bow;

Oh! do not our suit dis-dain;— Shall we seek thee, Lord, in vain?

GENERAL INDEX OF TUNES.

It is to be understood that most of the Music, included in this Collection, is introduced "by permission," purchased or given. It must, therefore, not be used in any other without the consent of the authors, or of those who hold the copyright of the Tunes.

A.

	PAGE
Adrian	98
Aletta	102, 237
All Saints	192
America	278
Amsterdam	270
Anvern	212
Ariel	114
Arlington	128
Ascension	193
Ashwell	210
Autumn	116
Ava	86
Avon	54, 97

B.

	PAGE
Balerma	73
Barby	249
Baxter	255
Bayley	132
Beautiful Zion	242
Beethoven	51, 183
Behrens	373
Bemerton	9
Benevento	23
Benjamin	374
Bennington	56
Bera	80
Bethany	158
Beulah	265
Bishop	176
Blake	107
Blendon	170
Boardman	67, 228
Bonar	146
Boylston	253
Bradford	63
Brattle Street	40
Brayton	371
Brest	261
Bridgman	141, 173
Bright Crown	222
Brown	172, 219
Brownell	157
Byefield	284

C.

	PAGE
Cambridge	164
Capello	75, 188
Carey	113
Carthage	59
Casey	276
Chesterfield	45, 111
China	248
Christmas	46, 127

	PAGE
Church	5, 138
Colman	7
Come, ye disconsolate	88
Cooling	108
Coronation	61
Cowper	76
Crawford	372
Cross and Crown	187
Crusaders' Hymn	145
Cyrus	380

D.

	PAGE
Dedham	198
Denfield	142
Dennis	131, 167, 189
Desire	81
Detroit	112
Dodge	245
Dorrnance	104, 258
Downs	18, 185
Duane	220
Duke Street	57, 160
Dundee	44, 199

E.

	PAGE
Easton	95
Edwards	373
Ellicott	208
Ely	159
Evan	109
Evening Hymn	16
Expostulation	86

F.

	PAGE
Fatherland	283
Federal Street	205, 246
Ferguson	99
Frederick	255
Frost	271
Fulton	221, 254

G.

	PAGE
Gaylord	117
Geer	148
Gerhardt	128
Glasgow	77, 274
Golden Chain	224
Golden Hill	153
Golden Shore	222
Goshen	87
Gratitude	161, 227
Greenville	86
Greenwood	152, 251
Griswold	377

H.

	PAGE
Hail to the Brightness	214
Halle	151
Hamburg	52, 94, 197
Handy	377
Harwell	58
Haydn	68
Heavenly Home	239
Heber	139, 229
Hebron	28
Helena	49, 186
Hendon	168
Holley	118
Horton	69, 85, 236
Hummel	73
Huntington	372
Hymn	8

I.

	PAGE
I'm a Pilgrim	240
Italian Hymn	27

J.

	PAGE
Jewett	376
Judgment	36
Judgment Hymn	247

K.

	PAGE
Karl	169
Keith	374
Knox	34
Koorbloh	371

L.

	PAGE
Laban	178
Last Beam	31
Leighton	179
Lenox	55
Leonard	374
Lischer	12
Litchfield	110
Long	15
Looking Home	242
Louvan	39
Loving Kindness	145
Lowry	262
Lyons	24

M.

	PAGE
Madison	148
Malvern	71
Manepy	149
Manoah	19, 96
Marian	373
Marlow	4

	PAGE
Marth	375
Martyn	54, 114
Mear	275
Meribah	100
Messiah	115
Migdol	3
Milner	120
Missionary Chant	126, 213
Missionary Hymn	206
Monson	72, 269
Montague	191
Mornington	250
Mozart	60
Mt. Auburn	129, 163
Mt. Blanc	240
Mt. Vernon	259

N.

	PAGE
Naomi	163
Nelson	90
Nettleton	91
Newberry	376
Newbold	47
Nuremburg	217

O.

	PAGE
Octavius	17
Old Hundred	14
Olivet	121
Olmutz	82, 130, 252
Onido	23
Oriola	218
Ortonville	62

P.

	PAGE
Palestine	190
Palmer	263
Park Street	157, 211
Parting Hymn	226
Penitence	122
Perry	216
Pleading Saviour	89
Pleyel's Hymn	124, 201
Pomeroy	350
Portugal	196
Portuguese Hymn	134
Praise	223

R.

	PAGE
Rathbun	105
Refuge	375
Remsen	177
Rest for the Weary	241
Retreat	232
Return	79
Requiem	256
Rhine	268
Righini	26
Rockingham	88, 50
Rock of Ages	202
Rosefield	103
Rose Hill	106

S.

	PAGE
Sabbath	1
Say, Brothers	87
Scotland	257
Seasons	87
Segur	379
Severance	375
Seymour	119
Shawmut	74
Shepherd	147
Shining Shore	238
Shirland	231
Sicilian Hymn	200
Siloam	184, 195
Silver Street	20, 175
Sing of Jesus	224
Smith	171
Solitude	53
Solney	181
Somerville	233
Spohr	2
St. Ann's	42, 194
St. Petersburgh	156
St. Thomas	10
Stair	371
Stanley	378
State Street	21, 230
Stephens	66
Stockwell	180
Sweet Land of Rest	243

T.

	PAGE
Tamworth	260
Tappan	110, 267
Thatcher	174
Thaxted	43
Tipstanley	375
To-day	88
Trent	48
Trust	150
Tucker	166
Tully	155

U.

	PAGE
Uxbridge	52

V.

	PAGE
Valentia	162
Victory	264

W.

	PAGE
Wanderer	83
Ward	209
Ware	13, 136
Warner	94
Warwick	6
Webb	207
Weber	99
Westminster	133, 277
Willington	33
Willis	125
Willkeith	380
Will you go	89
Wilmot	25
Wimborne	64
Winchester	272
Windham	70, 204
Woodland	206
Woodstock	285
Woodworth	92, 182
Wright	11

Y.

	PAGE
Yarmouth	151
Yoakley	273
York	35

Z.

	PAGE
Zadoc	263
Zephyr	65, 244
Zion	215

METRICAL INDEX.

L. M.

	PAGE
All Saints	192
Anvern	212
Ascension	193
Ashwell	210
Beethoven	51, 183
Bennington	56
Bera	80
Bishop	176
Blake	107
Blendon	170
Brayton	371
Crawford	372
Desire	81
Dodge	245
Duane	229
Duke Street	57, 160
Easton	95
Ellicott	208
Evening Hymn	16
Federal Street	205, 246
Gratitude	161, 227
Hamburg	52, 94, 197
Hebron	28
Huntington	372
Judgment	36
Judgment Hymn	247
Koorbloh	371
Long	15
Louvan	39
Loving Kindness	145
Lowry	262
Malvern	71
Migdol	3
Missionary Chant	126, 213
Octavius	17
Old Hundred	14
Park Street	107, 211
Portugal	196
Retreat	232
Rockingham	38, 50
Rose Hill	106
Seasons	37
Smith	171
Solitude	53
Somerville	233
Spohr	2
Stair	371
Uxbridge	32
Ward	209
Ware	13, 136
Warner	93
Willington	33
Wimborne	64
Winchester	272
Windham	70, 204
Woodworth	92, 182
Yoakley	273
Zephyr	65, 244

C. M.

	PAGE
Arlington	128
Avon	54, 97
Balerma	78
Barby	249
Behrens	372
Beinerton	9
Boardman	67, 228
Bradford	63
Brattle Street	40
Bridgman	141, 173
Brown	172, 219
Byefield	234
Cambridge	164
Chesterfield	45, 111
China	248
Christmas	46, 127
Church	5, 138
Colman	7
Cooling	108
Coronation	61
Cowper	76
Cross and Crown	187
Dedham	198
Denfield	142
Downs	18, 185
Dundee	44, 199
Evan	109
Geer	149
Glasgow	77, 274
Heber	189, 229
Helena	49, 186
Hummel	73
Hymn	8
Knox	34
Litchfield	110
Manoah	19, 96
Marian	373
Marlow	4
Mear	275
Monson	72, 269
Mt. Auburn	129, 165
Naomi	163
Newbold	47
Oriola	218
Ortonville	62
Parting Hymn	226
Remsen	177
Return	79
Rhine	268
Siloam	184, 195
St. Ann's	42, 194
Stephens	66
Tappan	140, 267
Thaxted	43
Trent	48
Valentia	162
Warwick	6
Woodland	266

	PAGE
Woodstock	285
York	35

S. M.

	PAGE
Adrian	98
Benjamin	374
Bonar	146
Boylston	253
Capello	75, 188
Carey	276
Dennis	131, 167, 189
Detroit	112
Edwards	373
Ferguson	99
Golden Hill	153
Greenwood	152, 251
Haydn	68
Keith	374
Laban	178
Leighton	179
Leonard	374
Mornington	250
Newberry	376
Olmutz	82, 130, 252
Palmer	263
Severance	375
Shawmut	74
Shirland	231
Silver Street	20, 175
St. Thomas	10
State Street	21, 230
Thatcher	174
Tipstanley	375
Tucker	160
Wanderer	83
Wright	11

L. M. 6 lines.

	PAGE
Beautiful Zion	242
Brownell	187
Handy	377
Palestine	190
St. Petersburgh	156

7s.

	PAGE
Aletta	102, 237
Benevento	22
Beulah	265
Casey	276
Cyrus	380
Fulton	221, 254
Griswold	377
Hendon	168
Holley	118
Horton	69, 85, 236
Karl	169
Martyn	84, 114

	PAGE
Messiah	115
Mozart	60
Nuremburg	217
Onido	28
Perry	216
Pleyel's Hymn	124, 201
Refuge	378
Rosefield	108
Seymour	119
Weber	29
Willis	125
Willkeith	382

7s. 6 lines.

Halle	151
Milner	120
Rock of Ages	202
Sabbath	1
Trust	150
Zadoc	208

L. C. M.

Ariel	144
Meribah	100

8s.

Madison	148
Manepy	149

8s & 7s.

Autumn	116
Bayley	132
Carthage	59
Dorrnance	104, 258
Gaylord	117
Greenville	30
Harwell	58
Mt. Vernon	259
Nettleton	91
Pleading Saviour	59
Praise	223
Rathbun	105
Refuge	378
Sicilian Hymn	200

	PAGE
Solney	181
Stanley	378
Stockwell	180
Westminster	138, 277
Wilmot	25

8s, 7s & 4s.

Brest	261
Nelson	90
Segur	379
Tamworth	260
Zion	215

6s & 4s.

America	278
Bethany	158
Ely	159
Fatherland	288
Italian Hymn	27
Olivet	121
Righini	26

7s, 6s & 8.

Penitence	122

7s & 6s.

Amsterdam	270
Frost	271
Gerhardt	123
Missionary Hymn	206
Montague	191
Pomeroy	380
Sing of Jesus	224
Tully	155
Webb	207
Yarmouth	154

7s & 5s.

Marth	375

10s.

Baxter	255
Victory	264

11s & 10s.

	PAGE
Come, ye Disconsolate	88
Hail to the Brightness	214

1s.

Expostulation	86
Frederick	255
Goshen	87
Heavenly Home	239
Portuguese Hymn	134

12s.

Scotland	257

H. M.

Lenox	55
Lischer	12

S. H. M.

Requiem	256

10s & 11s.

Lyons	21

6s.

Jewett	376

Peculiar.

Ava	86
Bright Crown	223
Crusaders' Hymn	145
Golden Chain	224
Golden Shore	222
I'm a Pilgrim	240
Last Beam	81
Looking Home	242
Mt. Blanc	240
Rest for the Weary	241
Say, Brothers	87
Shepherd	147
Shining Shore	238
To-day	88
Will you go	89

INDEX OF FIRST LINES.

	PAGE
Abba, Father, hear thy child....................	327
Abide with me, fast falls the eventide......... *Lyte.*	324
A broken heart, my God, my King.......... *Watts.*	309
A charge to keep I have................. *C. Wesley.*	113
According to thy gracious word........ *Montgomery.*	198
Affliction is a stormy deep.................... *Cotton.*	381
Again our earthly cares we leave....................	281
Again returns the day of holy rest.......... *Mason.*	279
Again the Lord of life and light..... *Mrs. Barbauld.*	279
A glory gilds the sacred page................ *Cowper.*	35
Ah! how shall fallen man.................... *Watts.*	74
Ah! this heart is void and chill....................	242
Ah! what avails my strife................ *C. Wesley.*	98
Ah! wretched, vile, ungrateful heart...... *Mrs. Steele.*	312
A hymn of glory let us sing.................... *Bede.*	299
Alas! and did my Saviour bleed.............. *Watts.*	54
Alas! the brittle clay....................... *Watts.*	251
Alas! what hourly dangers rise.......... *Mrs. Steele.*	110
All hail the power of Jesus' name.......... *Duncan.*	61
All people that on earth do.....*Sternhold—Hopkins.*	14
All that I was, my sin and guilt............ *Bonar.*	322
Almighty God! thy word is cast....................	35
Always with us, always with us.............. *Nevin.*	183
Amazing grace! how sweet the sound....... *Newton.*	128
Am I a soldier of the cross.................... *Watts.*	127
A mother may forgetful be.............. *Mrs. Steele.*	328
And are we yet alive.................... *C. Wesley.*	317
And can mine eyes without a tear.....*Heginbotham.*	165
And can my heart aspire so high.......... *Mrs. Steele.*	332
And canst thou, sinner, slight.................. *Hyde.*	82
And dost thou say, "Ask what thou wilt"..........	233
And is there, Lord, a rest................... *Palmer.*	263
And must I part with all I have.......... *Beddome.*	330
And must this body die....................... *Watts.*	250
And now another week begins.............. *Kelly.*	280
And shall I sit alone.................... *Beddome.*	112
And will the Judge descend............ *Doddridge.*	307
Angels rejoiced and sweetly sung............. *Hurn.*	47
Angels, roll the rock away................. *Gibbons.*	60
Another day has passed along.......... *Edmeston.*	2
Another six days' work is done.......... *Stennett.*	3
A parting hymn we sing................... *A. R. W.*	338
A pilgrim through this lonely world....................	295
A poor wayfaring man of grief........ *Montgomery.*	220
Approach my soul, the mercy-seat........ *Newton.*	96
Arise, O King of grace, arise.................... *Watts.*	6
Arise, my soul, arise................... *C. Wesley.*	317
Arise, my soul, fly up and run.............. *Watts.*	268
Arise, ye people, and adore.................... *Lyte.*	299
Arm of the Lord, awake, awake........ *Shrubsole.*	340
Ascend thy throne, almighty King.......... *Beddome.*	212
Asleep in Jesus, blessed sleep........ *Mrs. Mackay.*	244
As oft with worn and weary feet.... *Wilberforce.*	156
As panting in the sultry beam....................	156
As pants the hart for cooling streams.. *Tate—Brady.*	312
Assembled at thy great command.......... *Collyer.*	213
As the hart, with eager looks.......... *Montgomery.*	150
Astonished and distressed.................... *Toplady.*	75
As when in silence vernal showers.......... *Rippon.*	65
As when the weary traveler gains.......... *Newton.*	350
At evening time let there be light....................	344
At the Lamb's high feast we sing....................	201
At thy command, O Lord, our hope.......... *Watts.*	204
Author of good! to thee we turn.......... *Merrick.*	287

	PAGE
Awake, and sing the song.............. *Hammond.*	10
Awake, awake, the sacred song.......... *Mrs. Steele.*	46
Awaked by Sinai's awful sound.............. *Ockum.*	101
Awake, my heart, arise, my tongue... .... *Watts.*	19
Awake, my soul, lift up thine eyes... *Mrs. Barbauld.*	126
Awake, my soul, stretch every nerve.... *Doddridge.*	127
Awake, my soul, to joyful lays.............. *Medley.*	145
Awake, my tongue, thy tribute bring...... *Needham.*	17
Awake, our souls! away, our fears............ *Watts.*	126
Awake, ye saints! and raise your eyes... *Doddridge.*	353
Awake, ye saints! awake.................. *Cotterill.*	12
Away from earth my spirit turns....................	171
Beautiful Zion! built above....................	242
Before Jehovah's awful throne.............. *Watts.*	14
Begin, my tongue, some heavenly theme...... *Watts.*	19
Behold a stranger at the door.................. *Gregg.*	81
Behold, the day is come.................... *Beddome.*	252
Behold, th' expected time draws near.......... *Toke.*	209
Behold the glories of the Lamb.............. *Watts.*	61
Behold the morning sun.................... *Watts.*	11
Behold the path that mortals tread....................	343
Behold the Saviour of mankind.......... *Wesley.*	54
Behold the temple of the Lord....................	339
Behold the throne of grace.................... *Newton.*	231
Behold the western evening light.......... *Peabody.*	344
Behold, what wondrous grace.................... *Watts.*	175
Behold, where in a mortal form.............. *Enfield.*	48
Be merciful to me, O God....................	185
Beneath our feet and o'er our head .... *Heber.*	346
Be tranquil, O my soul!.................... *Hastings.*	163
Be with me, Lord, where'er I go....................	326
Beyond, beyond the boundless sea.......... *Conder.*	293
Blessèd angels! high in heaven	161
Blessèd be the sons of God .... *Humphreys.*	327
Blessèd fountain, full of grace.................... *Kelly.*	324
Blessèd Saviour! thee I love.............. *Duffield.*	203
Bless, O my soul! the living God.............. *Watts.*	17
Blest are the souls that hear and know........ *Watts.*	85
Blest be the dear uniting love.......... *C. Wesley.*	228
Blest be the tie that binds.................... *Fawcett.*	230
Blest be thou, O God of Israel....................	25
Blest Comforter divine....................	68
Blest day of God, most calm, most bright..........	8
Blest hour, when mortal man retires......... *Raffles.*	281
Blest is the man, whose softening.... *Mrs. Barbauld.*	177
Blest Jesus! when my journey......... *Heginbotham.*	142
Blest morning, whose young dawning rays.... *Watts.*	4
Blow ye the trumpet, blow....................	302
Bread of heaven, on thee I feed.......... *Conder.*	201
Brethren, while we sojourn here....................	115
Brightest and best of the sons of the.......... *Heber.*	294
Bright glories rush upon my sight....................	347
Bright King of glory! dreadful God......... *Watts.*	57
Broad is the road that leads to death.......... *Watts.*	70
Brother, hast thou wandered far.......... *Clarke.*	85
Brother, though from yonder sky.......... *Bancroft.*	254
By cool Siloam's shady rill.................... *Heber.*	195
Call Jehovah thy salvation.......... *Montgomery.*	138
Calm me, my God, and keep me calm...... *Bonar.*	163
Calm on the listening ear of night.......... *Sears.*	47
Can sinners hope for heaven....................	74
Cast thy bread upon the waters....................	181

	PAGE
Cast thy burden on the Lord	318
Ceaseless praise be to the Father...........*R. W. P.*	293
Cease, ye mourners, cease to languish......*Collyer.*	258
Child of sin and sorrow...............*Hastings.*	86
Children, listen to the Lord...........*Hastings.*	221
Children of God, who faint and slow.......*Bowdler.*	129
Children of the heavenly King.............*Cennick.*	124
Christ, above all glory seated	59
Christian, the morn breaks sweetly o'er thee	345
Christ, of all my hopes the ground.......*Windham.*	168
Christ the Lord is risen to-day, Our	298
Christ the Lord is risen to-day, Sons.....*Cudworth.*	60
Christ, whose glory fills the skies ....*Toplady.*	321
Chosen not for good in me...........*McCheyne.*	150
Church of the ever-living God..............*Bonar.*	194
Come, all ye saints of God	300
Come, blessed Spirit, source of light.......*Beddome.*	64
Come, Desire of nations, come	217
Come, every pious heart.................*Stennett.*	55
Come, gracious Lord, descend and dwell .....*Watts.*	2
Come, gracious Spirit, heavenly Dove.......*Browne.*	65
Come, happy souls, approach your God ......*Watts.*	76
Come hither, all ye weary souls.............*Watts.*	81
Come, Holy Ghost, Creator, come	66
Come, Holy Ghost, my soul inspire	301
Come, Holy Spirit, calm my mind..........*Burder.*	64
Come, Holy Spirit, come.................*Hart.*	68
Come, Holy Spirit, from on high	195
Come, Holy Spirit, heavenly Dove..........*Watts.*	66
Come join, ye saints, with heart and voice	144
Come, let us join our journey pursue......*C. Wesley.*	353
Come, let us join our cheerful songs.........*Watts.*	142
Come, let us join our songs of praise	63
Come, let us lift our joyful eyes.............*Watts.*	286
Come, let us sing of Jesus.................*Bethune.*	224
Come, let us sing the song of songs.....*Montgomery.*	57
Come, Lord, and tarry not.................*Bonar.*	250
Come, my soul, thy suit prepare...........*Newton.*	236
Come, O Creator! Spirit blest...........*Lyra Cath.*	64
Come, O my soul, in sacred lays.........*Blacklock.*	38
Come, said Jesus' sacred voice.........*Barbauld.*	85
Come, shout aloud the Father's grace...*Heginbotham.*	19
Come, sound his praise abroad.............*Watts.*	20
Come, thou almighty King.................*Madan.*	26
Come, thou Desire of all thy saints......*Mrs. Steele.*	8
Come, thou Fount of every blessing......*Robinson.*	165
Come, thou long-expected Jesus	341
Come, thou soul-transforming Spirit	30
Come to Calvary's holy mountain......*Montgomery.*	91
Come to the ark, come to the ark	79
Come to the land of peace	82
Come, trembling sinner, in whose...........*Jones.*	78
Come up hither; come away...............*Nevin.*	350
Come, weary souls, with sins distressed......*Steele.*	81
Come, we who love the Lord...............*Watts.*	10
Come, ye disconsolate, where'er...........*Moore.*	88
Come, ye sinners, poor and wretched.........*Hart.*	90
Come, ye souls, by sin afflicted...........*Swain.*	94
Come, ye that know and fear the Lord......*Burder.*	18
Come, ye that love the Saviour's name.......*Steele.*	7
Complete in thee—no work of mine.......*A. R. W.*	161
Cross, reproach, and tribulation...........*Moravian.*	200
Daughter of Zion! awake from thy sadness	214
Daughter of Zion! from the dust......*Montgomery.*	329
Day of judgment! day of wonders.........*Newton.*	261
Dear as thou wert, and justly dear.........*Dale.*	249
Dearest of all the names above.............*Watts.*	138
Dear Father! to thy mercy-seat.......*Mrs. Steele.*	235
Dear is the spot where Christians sleep	273
Dear Jesus! let thy pitying eye	218
Dear Lord, amid the throng that pressed	204
Dear Refuge of my weary soul.............*Steele.*	138
Dear Saviour! ever at my side.............*Faber.*	218
Dear Saviour! if these lambs should stray .....*Hyde.*	196
Dear Saviour! we are thine ....*Doddridge.*	153
Dear Saviour! when my thoughts recall..*Mrs. Steele.*	315
Deep in our hearts let us record.........*Hastings.*	87
Delay not, delay not, O sinner.............*Hastings.*	87
Depth of mercy! Can there be........*C. Wesley.*	102
Descend from heaven, immortal Dove ....*Watts.*	262
Did Christ o'er sinners weep... ....*Beddome.*	75

	PAGE
Dismiss us with thy blessing, Lord ....*Hart.*	28
Does the gospel word proclaim.............*Newton.*	119
Do not I love thee, O my Lord...........*Doddridge.*	141
Draw near, O holy Dove, draw near ....*A. R. W.*	205
Dread Jehovah, God of nations	277
Drooping souls, no longer mourn	305
Early, my God, without delay.............*Watts.*	4
Earth has nothing sweet or fair	320
Earth is passed away and gone.............*Alford.*	349
Earth's transitory things decay...........*Bowring.*	345
Enthroned on high, almighty Lord.......*Humphries.*	67
Ere the blue heavens were stretched abroad...*Watts.*	293
Ere to the world again we go	28
Eternal Father, thou hast said.............*Palmer.*	211
Eternal God, celestial King............*Wrangham.*	56
Eternal God, eternal King.................*March.*	291
Eternal Source of every joy...........*Doddridge.*	272
Eternal Spirit, we confess.................*Watts.*	64
Eternal Son of Righteousness.............*C. Wesley.*	326
Eternal Wisdom! thee we praise...........*Watts.*	44
Eternity! eternity	349
Fade, fade each earthly joy.................*Bonar.*	158
Fading, still fading	31
Faint not, Christian, though the road	124
Fairest Lord Jesus	145
Faith adds new charms to earthly...........*Watts.*	165
Faith is the polar star	326
Far from my heavenly home...............*Lyte.*	263
Far from my thoughts, vain world.........*Watts.*	324
Far from the world, O Lord, I flee.........*Cowper.*	5
Father, how wide thy glory shines...........*Watts.*	286
Father, I long, I faint to see.............*Watts.*	266
Father of eternal grace.............*Montgomery.*	168
Father of glory, to thy name.............*Watts.*	298
Father of heaven! whose love profound	36
Father of mercies! bow thine ear.........*Beddome.*	192
Father of mercies! God of love.......*Heginbotham.*	41
Father of mercies! in thy word.......*Mrs. Steele.*	85
Father of mercies! send thy grace.......*Doddridge.*	177
Father! whate'er of earthly bliss.......*Mrs. Steele.*	163
Fear not, O little flock! the foe	342
Feeble, helpless, how shall I.............*Furness.*	319
Firm as the earth thy gospel stands.........*Watts.*	173
For a season called to part.............*Newton.*	29
Forbid them not, the Saviour cried.........*Hastings.*	195
Forever here my rest shall be...........*C. Wesley.*	321
Forever with the Lord.................*Montgomery.*	252
Forget thyself, Christ bade thee come.....*Hastings.*	338
Forgive us, Lord, to thee we cry.........*Hastings.*	309
For me to live is Christ	146
For thee, O dear, dear country	352
For the mercies of the day...........*Montgomery.*	29
For what shall I praise thee, my God.......*C. Fry.*	332
Forth from the dark and stormy sky.........*Heber.*	232
For those in bonds, as bound with them...*Hastings.*	275
Fountain of grace! rich, full, and free	187
Fount of everlasting love.................*Palmer.*	276
Frequent the day of God returns...........*Browne.*	5
Friend after friend departs...........*Montgomery.*	256
From all that dwell below the skies...........*Watts.*	14
From Calvary a cry was heard........*Cunningham.*	52
From day to day before our eyes.......*Montgomery.*	208
From deep distress and troubled thoughts.....*Watts.*	300
From every earthly pleasure.............*Davis.*	350
From every stormy wind that blows.........*Stowell.*	232
From Greenland's icy mountains...........*Heber.*	206
From the cross uplifted high.............*Haweis.*	203
From the recesses of a lowly Spirit.......*Bowring.*	315
From the table now retiring	200
Full of trembling expectation...........*C. Wesley.*	117
Gently, gently lay thy rod.................*Lyte.*	118
Gently, Lord, oh, gently lead us.........*Hastings.*	30
Gently, my Saviour, let me down.............*Hill.*	245
Give me the wings of faith to rise ....*Watts.*	266
Give to our God immortal praise ....*Watts.*	284
Give to the Lord, ye sons of fame ....*Watts.*	15
Give to the winds thy fears.............*Gerhardt.*	180
Glorious things of thee are spoken.........*Newton.*	840
Glory to God on high	27

	PAGE
Glory to God the Father be......	18
Glory to God, whose witness-train....	164
Glory to thee, my God, this night.....*Kenn.*	16
Glory to the Father give.....*Montgomery.*	221
Go, labor on; spend and be spent.....*Bonar.*	176
Go, labor on; while it is day.....*Bonar.*	176
Go, preach my gospel, saith the Lord......*Watts.*	385
Go to dark Gethsemane.....*Montgomery.*	296
Go to the grave in all thy glorious.....*Montgomery.*	255
Go, tune thy voice to sacred song......	140
Go, worship at Immanuel's feet.....*Watts.*	300
God bless our native land.....*J. S. Dwight.*	354
God in the gospel of his Son.....	351
God in the high and holy place.....*Montgomery.*	41
God is love, his mercy brightens.....*Bowring.*	291
God is the refuge of his saints.....*Watts.*	209
God leads me—and I go......	159
God moves in a mysterious way.....*Cowper.*	43
God of mercy, God of love.....*J. Taylor.*	119
God of mercy, throned on high.....	221
God of my life, thro' all my days.....*Doddridge.*	13
God of my life, thy boundless grace......	92
God of my life, to thee belong......	37
God of my life, to thee I call.....*Cowper.*	383
God of our salvation, hear us......	30
God of the sun-light hours, how sad.....	9
God's glory is a wondrous thing.....*Lyra Cath.*	317
God's holy law transgressed.....*Beddome.*	303
God with us, oh, glorious name.....	294
Grace! 'tis a charming sound.....*Doddridge.*	175
Gracious Spirit! Love divine.....*Stocker.*	69
Great God, attend while Zion sings.....*Watts.*	285
Great God, how infinite art thou.....*Watts.*	44
Great God, now condescend.....*Fellows.*	336
Great God of nations! now to thee.....	353
Great God, to thee my evening song.....*Mrs. Steele.*	227
Great God, we sing that mighty hand....*Doddridge.*	272
Great God, what do I see and hear.....*Luther.*	247
Great God, when I approach thy throne.....	77
Great God, whom heaven, and earth, and sea.....	355
Great God, whose universal sway.....*Watts.*	208
Great is the Lord our God.....*Watts.*	354
Great Redeemer, Friend of sinners.....	259
Great Ruler of all nature's frame.....*Doddridge.*	45
Great Shepherd of thine Israel.....*Watts.*	339
Guide me, O thou great Jehovah.....*Oliver.*	287
Had I the tongue of Greeks and Jews.....*Watts.*	160
Hail, my ever-blessed Jesus.....*Wingrove.*	58
Hail, sovereign love that formed the.....*Brewer.*	338
Hail, sweetest, dearest tie that binds.....*Sutton.*	223
Hail, thou once despised Jesus.....*Bakewell.*	58
Hail to the brightness of Zion's.....*Hastings.*	214
Hail to the Lord's Anointed.....*Montgomery.*	207
Hail, tranquil hour of closing day.....*Bacon.*	234
Happy, Saviour! shall I be.....	155
Happy the heart where graces reign.....*Watts.*	165
Happy the meek, whose gentle breast.....*J. Scott.*	161
Happy the spirit released from its clay.....	264
Hark! a voice divides the sky.....*C. Wesley.*	254
Hark, hark, the notes of joy.....	205
Hark, how the choral song of heaven.....	211
Hark, my soul, it is the Lord.....*Cowper.*	125
Hark, ten thousand harps and voices.....*Kelly.*	132
Hark! that shout of rapturous joy.....*Kelly.*	254
Hark, the glad sound! the Saviour comes..*Doddridge.*	47
Hark, the herald angels sing.....*C. Wesley.*	60
Hark, the song of jubilee.....*Montgomery.*	216
Hark, the voice of love and mercy.....*Francis.*	297
Hark, what celestial sounds......	294
Hark, what mean those holy voices.....*Cawood.*	294
Hasten, Lord, the glorious time.....*Lyte.*	216
Hasten, Lord, to my release.....*Montgomery.*	311
Hasten, sinner, to be wise.....*T. Scott.*	85
Haste, traveler, haste, the night comes on.....*Collyer.*	315
Hearken, Lord, to my complaints.....*Montgomery.*	120
Hear, O sinner! mercy calls you.....*Reed.*	90
Hear what God the Lord hath spoken.....*Cowper.*	132
He dies! the Friend of sinners dies.....*Watts.*	298
He knelt, the Saviour knelt and prayed.....*Hemans.*	291
He lives, the great Redeemer lives.....*Mrs. Steele.*	329
Here at thy cross, my dying Lord.....*Watts.*	98
	PAGE
Here I can firmly rest.....*Gerhardt.*	175
Here, O my Lord, I see thee face to face.....*Bonar.*	337
Here we have seen thy face, O Lord.....	204
He that goeth forth with weeping.....*Hastings.*	180
He who on earth as man was known.....*Newton.*	63
High in the heavens, eternal God.....*Watts.*	13
High in yonder realms of light.....*Raffles.*	265
High we raise our hallelujahs.....*Sigourney.*	223
Ho! every one that thirsts, draw nigh.....*C. Wesley.*	81
Holy and reverend is the name.....*Needham.*	45
Holy Bible, book divine.....	288
Holy Father, hear my cry.....*Bonar.*	293
Holy Ghost, the Infinite.....	301
Holy Ghost, with light divine.....*Reed.*	69
Holy, holy, holy Lord.....*Montgomery.*	22
Holy Lamb, who thee receive.....*J. Wesley.*	201
Holy Spirit, Lord of light.....*Lyra Cath.*	69
Hosanna to the Prince of light.....*Watts.*	61
How are thy servants blest, O Lord.....*Addison.*	41
How beauteous are their feet.....*Watts.*	385
How beauteous were the marks divine.....*A. C. Coxe.*	50
How blest are those, how truly wise.....*Mrs. Steele.*	193
How blest the righteous when he....*Mrs. Barbauld.*	244
How blest the sacred tie that binds...*Mrs. Barbauld.*	227
How calm and beautiful the morn.....*Hastings.*	298
How can I sink with such a prop.....*Watts.*	128
How charming is the place.....*Stennett.*	11
How condescending and how kind.....*Watts.*	304
How did my heart rejoice to hear.....	7
How firm a foundation, ye saints.....*Kirkham.*	134
How gentle God's commands.....*Doddridge.*	131
How glorious is our heavenly King.....*Watts.*	219
How heavy is the night.....*Watts.*	75
How helpless guilty nature lies.....*Mrs. Steele.*	72
How large the promise, how divine.....*Watts.*	195
How long, O Lord, shall I complain.....*Watts.*	313
How oft, alas! this wretched heart.....*Mrs. Steele.*	109
How pleasant, how divinely fair.....	8
How pleasant 'tis to see.....*Watts.*	326
How pleasant thus to dwell below.....	226
How pleased and blessed was I.....*Watts.*	279
How precious is the book divine.....*Fawcett.*	34
How sad our state by nature is.....*Watts.*	78
How shall the sons of men appear.....*Stennett.*	71
How shall the young secure their hearts.....*Watts.*	34
How still and peaceful is the grave.....	248
How sweet and awful is the place.....*Watts.*	199
How sweet, how heavenly is the sight.....*Swain.*	229
How sweetly flowed the gospel sound....*Bowring.*	50
How sweet the name of Jesus sounds.....*Newton.*	139
How sweet to leave the world awhile.....*Kelly.*	233
How swift the torrent rolls.....*Doddridge.*	250
How tedious and tasteless the hours.....*Newton.*	149
How tender is thy hand.....*Hastings.*	189
How vain is all beneath the skies.....	343
I ask not now for gold to gild.....*Whittier.*	333
I bless thee, Lord, for sorrows sent.....	182
I cannot always trace thy way.....	182
I cannot call affliction sweet.....*Montgomery.*	184
I faint, my soul doth faint.....*Mrs. Gilbert.*	112
I feed my faith on Christ; my bread...*Montgomery.*	205
If God is mine, then present things.....*Beddome.*	172
If human kindness meets return.....*Noel.*	199
If life in sorrow must be spent.....*Guion.*	183
If on our daily course, our mind.....	160
If thou impart thyself to me.....*C. Wesley.*	322
If through unruffled seas.....	167
I have a home above.....	263
I heard the voice of Jesus say.....*Bonar.*	323
I know that my Redeemer lives.....*C. Wesley.*	68
I lay my sins on Jesus.....*Bonar.*	155
I left the God of truth and light.....*Montgomery.*	106
I lift my soul to God.....*Watts.*	113
I love the sacred Book of God.....*Kelly.*	83
I love the volume of thy word.....*Watts.*	283
I love thy kingdom, Lord.....*Dwight.*	280
I love to steal awhile away.....*Mrs. Brown.*	235
I'm a pilgrim, and I'm a stranger.....	240
I'm but a stranger here.....*T. R. Taylor.*	238
I'm not ashamed to own my Lord.....*Watts.*	127
In all my vast concerns with thee.....*Watts.*	43

PAGE

Indulgent Sovereign of the skies ....*Doddridge.* 208
In every trying hour 174
In heavenly love abiding 154
Inspirer and Hearer of prayer ....*Toplady.* 149
Inquire, ye pilgrims, for the way ....*Doddridge.* 305
In the Christian's home in glory 241
In the cross of Christ I glory............*Bowring.* 105
In the dark and cloudy day...................... 332
In the sun and moon and stars ....*Heber.* 345
In thy name, O Lord, assembling ....*Kelly.* 251
In time of tribulation.................*Montgomery.* 313
In true and patient hope...................*C. Wesley.* 166
In vain our fancy strives to paint............*Newton.* 269
In vain we seek for peace with God............*Watts.* 72
I once was a stranger to grace and........*McCheyne.* 135
I saw One hanging on a tree...............*Newton.* 96
I send the joys of earth away.................. *Watts.* 95
I sing th'almighty power of God ....*Watts.* 44
I stand on Zion's mount ....*Swain.* 131
Is there ambition in my heart ....*Watts.* 163
Is this the kind return ....*Watts.* 75
It is not death to die.....................*Bethune.* 251
It is the Lord, enthroned in light............*Green.* 184
It is thy hand, my God....................*Darby.* 188
I thought upon my sins, and I was sad......*Bonar.* 307
I want a heart to pray....................*C. Wesley.* 313
I was a wandering sheep ....*Bonar.* 146
I worship thee, sweet Will of God......*Lyra Cath.* 185
I would be thine, oh, take my heart.................. 111
I would love thee, God and Father.................. 25
I would not live alway, I ask...........*Muhlenberg.* 255

Jehovah reigns, his throne is high ....*Watts.* 14
Jerusalem! my happy home..................... 351
Jerusalem! the glorious...................... 353
Jesus, all-atoning Lamb.................*Wesley.* 103
Jesus, and didst thou leave the sky ....*Steele.* 77
Jesus, and shall it ever be................*Gregg.* 137
Jesus, at whose supreme command...... *C. Wesley.* 198
Jesus, blessèd Mediator..................*Cowper.* 351
Jesus comes, his conflict over.............*Kelly.* 59
Jesus demands this heart of mine ....*Mrs. Steele.* 314
Jesus, engrave it on my heart............*Medley.* 71
Jesus, full of all compassion ....*Turner.* 116
Jesus, full of truth and love 102
I come to thee.......................*Beman.* 99
Jesus, I love thy charming name ....*Doddridge.* 139
Jesus, I my cross have taken ....*Miss Grant.* 116
Jesus, in sickness and in pain ....*Gallaudet.* 187
Jesus, let thy pitying eye.................... 122
Jesus lives, no longer now.................... 316
Jesus, Lord, we look to thee...........*C. Wesley.* 169
Jesus, lover of my soul.................*C. Wesley.* 114
Jesus, Master, hear me now 201
Jesus, merciful and mild...............*Hastings.* 114
Jesus, my all, to heaven is gone............*Cennick.* 299
Jesus, my sorrow lies too deep............*Bonar.* 331
Jesus, my strength, my hope ....*C. Wesley.* 167
Jesus, on thy throne of glory.................... 225
Jesus, our best beloved Friend.................... 326
Jesus, our Lord, how rich thy grace .....*Doddridge.* 330
Jesus, save my dying soul.................*Hastings.* 103
Jesus shall reign where'er the sun............*Watts.* 211
Jesus spreads his banner o'er us.................... 200
Jesus, the sinner's friend, to thee........*C. Wesley.* 95
Jesus, the very thought of thee............*Bernard.* 139
Jesus, thou art the sinner's friend. 141
Jesus, thou source of calm repose.................. 157
Jesus, thy love shall we forget 49
Jesus, thy name I love 324
Jesus, thy robe of righteousness ....*C. Wesley.* 328
Jesus, where'er thy people meet...........*Cowper.* 233
Jesus, while our hearts are bleeding.......*Hastings.* 258
Jesus, who knows full well ....*Newton.* 231
Jesus, whom angel hosts adore............*Bonar.* 52
Jesus, who on Calvary's mountain 105
Joyful be the hours to-day................*Kelly.* 168
Joyfully, joyfully, onward I move.................... 264
Joy to the world! the Lord is come........*Watts.* 46
Just as I am, without one plea ....*C. Elliott.* 92

Keep silence, all created things..............*Watts.* 42

PAGE

Kindred in Christ, for his dear sake.........*Newton.* 227
Kingdoms and crowns to God belong.........*Watts.* 38
Know, my soul, thy full salvation.......*Miss Grant.* 132

Laborers of Christ, arise.................*Sigourney.* 179
Laboring and heavy-laden................*Rankin.* 104
Laden with guilt and full of fears.............*Watts.* 289
Lamb of God, whose bleeding love........*C. Wesley.* 338
Let every mortal ear attend....................*Watts.* 305
Let me be with thee where thou art.................. 245
Let me hut hear my Saviour say.............*Watts.* 171
Let party names no more...................*Beddome.* 230
Let saints below in concert sing...........*C. Wesley.* 228
Let the world their virtue boast.............*Wesley.* 327
Let us awake our joys.................*Kingsbury.* 26
Let us with a joyful mind.................*Milton.* 22
Let worldly minds the world pursue.......*Newton.* 321
Let Zion and her sons rejoice.............*Watts.* 341
Life is the time to serve the Lord.............*Watts.* 366
Lift not thou the wailing voice.............*D. ane.* 345
Light of life, seraphic fire................*C. Wesley.* 282
Light of the soul, O Saviour blest.................. 187
Light of those whose dreary dwelling....*C. Wesley.* 339
Like morning, when her early breeze......*Moore.* 71
Like sheep we went astray...................*Watts.* 304
Like the eagle, upward, onward..........*Bonar.* 180
Lo! God is here—let us adore..........*J. Wesley.* 202
Lo! he comes, with clouds descending......*Brydges.* 260
Lo! he cometh! countless trumpets.................. 260
Lo! Jehovah, we adore thee.................... 59
Lone amidst the dead and dying.................. 311
Long have I sat beneath the sound.............*Watts.* 314
Lo! on a narrow neck of land............*C. Wesley.* 101
Look, ye saints! the day is breaking.........*Kelly.* 341
Lord, as to thy dear cross we flee.................. 49
Lord, at this closing hour...............*E. T. Fitch.* 288
Lord, at thy feet we sinners lie...........*Browne.* 96
Lord, at thy table I beheld...............*Stennett.* 338
Lord, before thy throne we bend.........*Batteller.* 151
Lord, dismiss us with thy blessing.........*Burder.* 30
Lord, forever at thy side...............*Montgomery.* 169
Lord, from thy blessed throne.............*Nicoll.* 278
Lord God of Hosts! by all adored.................. 123
Lord God of my salvation.................*Lyte.* 191
Lord God, the Holy Ghost...........*Montgomery.* 68
Lord, how mysterious are thy ways.....*Mrs. Steele.* 39
Lord, how secure and blest are they ....*Watts.* 170
Lord, how secure my conscience was ....*Watts.* 72
Lord, I address thy heavenly throne...........*Watts.* 327
Lord, I am thine, entirely thine...........*Davies.* 197
Lord, I am vile, conceived in sin.............*Watts.* 70
Lord, I believe, thy power I own ....*Wreford.* 165
Lord, I cannot let thee go...............*Newton.* 236
Lord, if thou thy grace impart.................. 169
Lord, I hear of showers of blessing.................. 116
Lord, I look for all to thee.................*Lyte.* 120
Lord, in the morning thou shalt hear.........*Watts.* 6
Lord, in this sacred hour.................... 21
Lord, it belongs not to my care..........*Baxter.* 323
Lord Jesus! are we one with thee.................. 330
Lord, let me know mine end............*Montgomery.* 253
Lord, many times I am aweary quite......*Trench.* 314
Lord, may the spirit of this feast.......*Sigourney.* 338
Lord, may thy truth upon the heart.................. 28
Lord, now we part in thy blest name.........*Heber.* 28
Lord of all being! throned afar.......*O. W. Holmes.* 39
Lord of earth! thy forming hand ....*Grant.* 23
Lord of mercy, just and kind ....*Goode.* 112
Lord of the worlds above.................*Watts.* 1
Lord, thou art my rock of strength.........*Francke.* 318
Lord, thou hast searched and seen me ....*Watts.* 35
Lord, thou hast won, at length I yield.......*Newton.* 101
Lord, thy glory fills the heavens.................. 286
Lord, we adore thy boundless grace...........*Watts.* 306
Lord, we come before thee now.........*Hammond.* 236
Lord, when my raptured thought surveys......*Steele.* 290
Lord, when we bend before thee.................. 9
Lord, where shall guilty souls retire.............*Watts.* 292
Lord, while for all mankind we pray.........*Welford.* 274
Lord, with glowing heart I'd praise......*S. F. Key.* 284
Lo! the mighty God appearing ....*Goode.* 261
Lo! the seal of death is breaking.................. 352

	PAGE
Lo! what a glorious corner-stone............ *Watts.*	336
Lo! what a glorious sight appears............ *Watts.*	350
Loud hallelujahs to the Lord................ *Watts.*	15
Love divine, all love excelling............ *C. Wesley.*	132
Love me, O Lord, forgivingly................ *Lynch.*	316
Lowly and solemn be...................... *Hemans.*	333
Majestic sweetness sits enthroned.......... *Stennett.*	62
Make haste, O man, to live................	178
Man's wisdom is to seek................ *Cowper.*	166
Marked as the purpose of the skies........... *Noel.*	213
Mark the soft-falling snow................	287
May not the sovereign Lord on high.......... *Watts.*	37
May the grace of God, our Saviour.......... *Newton.*	25
'Mid scenes of confusion and creature..........	239
Mighty God, while angels bless thee........ *Robinson.*	300
Millions within thy courts have met..... *Montgomery.*	287
Mine eyes and my desire................ *Watts.*	179
Morning breaks upon the tomb............ *Collyer.*	348
Mortals, awake! with angels join........... *Medley.*	303
Mourn for the thousands slain................	179
Much in sorrow, oft in woe............ *H. K. White.*	125
Must Jesus bear the cross alone............ *Allen.*	187
My country! 'tis of thee............ *S. F. Smith.*	278
My days are gliding swiftly by................	233
My dear Redeemer and my Lord............ *Watts.*	50
My faith looks up to thee................ *Palmer.*	121
My Father bids me come................ *Wesley.*	82
My Father God! how sweet the sound... *Doddridge.*	173
My former hopes are fled................ *Cowper.*	74
My God, accept my heart this day........ *Lyra Cath.*	97
My God, how endless is thy love............ *Watts.*	161
My God, my Father! blissful name........ *Mrs. Steele.*	173
My God, my Father, while I stray.......... *C. Elliott.*	182
My God, my King, thy various praise.......... *Watts.*	285
My God, my Life, my Love................ *Watts.*	153
My God, permit me not to be................ *Watts.*	312
My God, permit my tongue................ *Watts.*	282
My God, the covenant of thy love........ *Doddridge.*	329
My God, the spring of all my joys........... *Watts.*	142
My God, thy boundless love I praise................	291
My gracious Lord! I own thy right........ *Doddridge.*	197
My gracious Redeemer I love............ *Francis.*	149
My heart lies dead, and no increase........ *Herbert.*	311
My home is in heaven, my rest is not here...... *Lyte.*	239
My Jesus, as thou wilt................ *Schmolk.*	334
My opening eyes with rapture see................	2
My Saviour, thou thy love to me........ *C. Wesley.*	320
My Saviour, whom absent I love............ *Cowper.*	148
My Shepherd will supply my need................	329
My soul, be on thy guard................ *Heath.*	173
My soul, how lovely is the place.......... *Watts.*	5
My soul, repeat his praise................ *Watts.*	253
My spirit on thy care................ *Lyte.*	152
My sufferings all to thee are known........ *C. Wesley.*	93
My times are in thy hand................	189
My times of sorrow and of joy .... *Beddome.*	184
Nearer, my God, to thee................ *S. F. Adams.*	159
No more, my God, I boast no more............ *Watts.*	94
No more, ye wise, your wisdom boast... *Doddridge.*	171
None loves me, Saviour, with thy love............	187
No, no, it is not dying................ *Malan.*	345
No room for mirth or trifling here........ *C. Wesley.*	101
Not all the blood of beasts................ *Watts.*	153
Not all the nobles of the earth............ *Stennett.*	170
Not all the outward forms on earth............ *Watts.*	73
Not to condemn the sons of men............ *Watts.*	50
Not to the terrors of the Lord............ *Watts.*	335
No track is on the sunny sky............ *Faber.*	301
Not with our mortal eyes................ *Watts.*	153
Now begin the heavenly theme............ *Langford.*	125
Now be my heart inspired to sing................	300
Now be the gospel banner................ *Hastings.*	206
Now is th' accepted time................ *Dobell.*	83
Now let my soul, eternal King........ *Heginbotham.*	33
Now let our cheerful eyes survey........ *Doddridge.*	172
Now let our souls on wings sublime........ *Gibbons.*	262
Now let our voices join................ *Doddridge.*	21
Now may He, who from the dead............ *Newton.*	29
Now the Saviour standeth pleading................	89
Now to the Lord a noble song................ *Watts.*	16
Now to the Lord, who makes us know........ *Watts.*	57
Now to the power of God supreme............ *Watts.*	171
Obedient to our Zion's King................	196
O bless the Lord, my soul, His grace... *Montgomery.*	21
O bless the Lord, my soul, Let all............ *Watts.*	282
O bow thine ear, eternal One................	192
O cease, my wandering soul............ *Muhlenberg.*	98
O could I find from day to day................	110
O could I speak the matchless worth........ *Medley.*	144
O could our thoughts and wishes fly....... *Mrs. Steele.*	312
O deem not they are blest alone............ *Bryant.*	183
O'er the dark wave of Galilee............ *Russell.*	51
O'er the gloomy hills of darkness........ *Williams.*	215
O'er the realms of pagan darkness.......... *Cotterell.*	215
O eyes that are weary, and hearts................	135
Of all the thoughts of God that are.. *Mrs. Browning.*	343
O Father! compass me about................	335
O for a closer walk with God............ *Cowper.*	109
O for a glance of heavenly day................ *Hart.*	94
O for a heart to praise my God............ *C. Wesley.*	318
O for an overcoming faith................ *Watts.*	249
O for a shout of sacred joy................ *Watts.*	209
O for a sweet, inspiring ray............ *Mrs. Steele.*	262
O for a thousand tongues to sing............ *C. Wesley.*	62
O for that tenderness of heart............ *C. Wesley.*	108
O for the death of those................	252
O gift of gifts! oh, grace of faith........ *Lyra Cath.*	162
O God, beneath thy guiding hand........ *L. Bacon.*	273
O God, by whom the seed is given............ *Heber.*	9
O God of Bethel, by whose hand........ *Doddridge.*	173
O God of mercy, hear my call................ *Watts.*	97
O God, our help in ages past................ *Watts.*	292
O God, thou art my God alone........ *Montgomery.*	106
O God, we praise thee and confess.......... *Patrick.*	42
O had I, my Saviour, the wings of a dove........ *Lyte.*	239
O happy day, that fixed my choice........ *Doddridge.*	205
O haste away, my brethren dear................	226
O holy, holy, holy Lord................	36
O holy Lord, our God................	336
O holy Saviour, Friend unseen................	322
O how divine, how sweet the joy............ *Needham.*	304
O, if my soul was formed for woe............ *Watts.*	51
O, it is joy in one to meet................	228
O Lamb of God! still keep me................	316
O let me, gracious Lord, extend............ *Merrick.*	343
O Lord, encouraged by thy grace............ *Mrs. Steele.*	193
O Lord, how full of sweet content............ *Guion.*	161
O Lord, how infinite thy love................ *Lyte.*	76
O Lord, I would delight in thee............ *Ryland.*	320
O Lord, my best desires fulfill............ *Cowper.*	164
O Lord, thy covenant is sure............ *Conder.*	337
O Lord, thy pitying eye surveys........ *Doddridge.*	192
O Love divine! that stooped to share... *O. W. Holmes.*	317
O mother dear, Jerusalem................ *Quarles.*	268
O my sweet home, Jerusalem................ *Quarles.*	268
Once I thought my mountain strong........ *Newton.*	121
Once more, my soul, the rising day............ *Watts.*	7
One by one the sands are flowing........ *Dickens.*	331
One prayer I have, all prayers in one... *Montgomery.*	186
One sole baptismal sign................ *Robinson.*	386
One sweetly solemn thought................ *Carey.*	348
One there is above all others................ *Newton.*	59
On Jordan's rugged banks I stand........ *Stennett.*	267
On the mountain's top appearing............ *Kelly.*	215
Onward, Christian! though the region............	133
Oppressed with noonday's scorching heat..... *Bonar.*	193
O praise ye the Lord! prepare your.... *Tate—Brady.*	24
O render thanks to God above........ *Tate—Brady.*	284
O sacred Head! now wounded............ *Gerhardt.*	123
O Saviour! lend a listening ear............ *Hastings.*	140
O Saviour of a world undone................	307
O see how Jesus trusts himself................	141
O sinner, bring not tears alone................	78
O speak that gracious word again........ *Newton.*	143
O spirit of the living God............ *Montgomery.*	219
O Sun of Righteousness, arise................	208
O sweetly breathe the lyres above............ *Palmer.*	136
O tell me, thou Life and Delight............ *Hastings.*	147
O that I could forever dwell................ *Reed.*	136
O that I could repent................ *C. Wesley.*	309
O that I knew the secret place................ *Watts.*	110

PAGE

O that my load of sin were gone..........C. Wesley. 95
O that the Lord's salvation...................Lyte. 342
O the sweet wonders of that cross.............Watts. 197
O thou, above all praise..........Montgomery. 11
O thou, from whom all goodness flows............ 311
O thou God, who hearest prayer............Conder. 151
O thou that hearest prayer................... 302
O thou that hear'st when sinners cry........Watts. 310
O thou, to whose all-searching sight........C. Wesley. 107
O thou, who driest the mourner's tear........Moore. 186
O thou, who hast died to redeem us........L. Bacon. 337
O thou, who hear'st the prayer of faith ....Toplady. 100
O thou, whose gently chastening hand............ 186
O thou, whose mercy guides my way.....Edmeston. 334
O thou, whose own vast temple stands..... ..Bryant. 194
O thou, whose tender mercy hears.......Mrs. Steele. 97
O throw away thy rod........................... 188
O turn, great Ruler of the skies...........Merrick. 319
O turn ye, oh, turn ye, for why will............ 86
Our blest Redeemer, ere he breathed............ 301
Our children thou dost claim................ 387
Our Father! through the coming year. 275
Our heavenly Father calls..............Doddridge. 231
Our heavenly Father, hear............Montgomery. 285
Our Helper, God, we bless thy name.....Doddridge. 272
Our Lord is risen from the dead..........C. Wesley. 56
Our souls by love together knit..................... 229
Out of the depths of woe............Montgomery. 112
O what amazing words of grace........Medley. 77
O what stupendous mercy shines........Rippon. 330
O where are kings and empires now.......t. C. Coxe. 194
O where is now that glowing love........Kelly. 107
O where shall rest be found..........Montgomery. 194
O worship the King, all-glorious above......Grant. 24
O Zion, afflicted with wave upon wave........ 135
O Zion, when I think of thee...............Kelly. 210

Palms of glory, raiment bright.........Montgomery. 252
Peace, peace I leave with you...........Hastings. 121
Peace, troubled soul! whose plaintive........ 190
People of the living God...........Montgomery. 103
"Perfect in love!' Lord, can it be............ 157
Pilgrim, burdened with thy sin............ 84
Pilgrims in this vale of sorrow.........Hastings. 180
Plunged in a gulf of dark despair...... Watts. 302
Pour out thy spirit from on high ......Montgomery. 193
Praise, everlasting praise, be paid........... 85
Praise on thee in Zion's gates.............Conder. 216
Praise the Lord, his power confess... .. Wrangham. 283
Praise the Lord, who reigns above............ 285
Praise the Lord, ye heavens, adore him......... 25
Praise to God, immortal praise......Mrs. Barbauld. 276
Praise to thee, thou great Creator..........Fawcett. 283
Praise ye Jehovah's name..............Goode. 27
Praise ye the Lord, immortal choir..........Watts. 284
Praise ye the Lord, let praise employ.....Mrs. Steele. 17
Prayer is the breath of God in man............ 331
Prayer is the soul's sincere desire......Montgomery. 234
Prepare, us, Lord, to view thy cross............ 199
Prince of Peace! control my will............ 118
Prostrate, dear Jesus, at thy feet..........Sennett. 308

Quiet, Lord, my froward heart............Newton. 325

Raise your triumphant songs............Watts. 20
Ready now to spread my pinions 346
Rejoice in God alway...................Moultrie. 166
Rejoice! the Lord is King............C. Wesley. 325
Remember thy Creator now................. 218
Repent! the voice celestial cries........Doddridge. 306
Rest for the toiling hand................Bonar. 253
Return, my roving heart, return ......Doddridge. 314
Return, O wanderer, now return.........Collyer. 79
Return, O wanderer, to thy home........Hastings. 79
Ride on, ride on, in majesty..............Milman. 296
Rise, my soul, and stretch thy wings......Seagrave. 104
Rock of Ages! cleft for me................Toplady. 202
Roll on, thou mighty ocean.................. 342

Safely through another week............Newton. 1
Salvation, oh, the joyful sound ....Watts. 77
Saviour, breathe an evening blessing......Edmeston. 288

PAGE

Saviour, I follow on..................C. S. R. 138
Saviour, I look to thee...................Hastings. 121
Saviour of all, what hast thou done........C. Wesley. 303
Saviour of our ruined race ....Hastings. 203
Saviour, teach me day by day................. 221
Saviour! thy gentle voice..............Hastings. 159
Saviour! visit thy plantation ....Newton. 117
Saviour, when in dust to thee............Grant. 115
Saviour, when night involves the skies....Gisborne. 321
Saviour, who thy flock art feeding.......... 336
Saw ye not the cloud arise.............C. Wesley. 217
Say, brothers, will you meet us............ 67
Say, dost thou mark that beaming eye....Hastings. 325
Say, sinner, hath a voice within.........Mrs. Hyde. 80
Scorn not the slightest word or deed............ 177
Searcher of hearts! from mine erase...G. P. Morris. 109
See a poor sinner, dearest Lord........Medley. 106
See from Zion's sacred mountain............Kelly. 304
See, gracious God, before thy throne.....Mrs. Steele. 274
See Israel's gentle Shepherd stand......Doddridge. 195
See the eternal Judge descending.......... 260
See the leaves around us falling........Horne. 289
See the ransomed millions stand.........Conder. 216
See what a living stone.................Watts. 280
Self-love no grace in sorrow sees............Guion. 334
Send kindly light amid the encircling........... 332
Seraphs, with elevated strains............Watts. 267
Servant of God, well done...........Montgomery. 251
Shall the vile race of flesh and blood......Watts. 76
Shall we go on in sin.......................Watts. 98
Show pity, Lord, O Lord, forgive..........Watts. 94
Since Jesus freely did appear............Berridge. 274
Since Jesus is my friend...............Gerhardt. 172
Since o'er thy footstool here below........... 289
Sing, sing his lofty praise.................. 26
Sing we the song of those who stand...Montgomery. 280
Sinner, art thou still secure............Newton. 81
Sinners, turn, why will ye die...........C. Wesley. 84
Sinners, will you scorn the message........Allen. 90
Sister, thou wast mild and lovely......S. F. Smith. 279
So fades the lovely, blooming flower....Mrs. Steele. 246
So let our lips and lives express............Watts. 163
Sometimes a light surprises............Cowper. 328
Songs of praise the angels sang.......Montgomery. 283
Son of God, thy blessing grant............ 314
Son of God, to thee I cry................. 203
Sons of men, behold from far...........Wesley. 217
Soon may the last glad song arise............ 218
Sovereign of worlds, display thy power....... 219
Sovereign Ruler, Lord of all..............Raffles. 103
Sovereign Ruler of the skies............Ryland. 327
Sow in the morn thy seed............Montgomery. 178
Speak gently; it is better far..............Bates. 162
Speak to me, Lord, thyself reveal.........Wesley. 138
Spirit divine! attend our prayer............Reed. 66
Spirit of peace! celestial Dove............Lyte. 325
Spirit of power and might, behold....Montgomery. 67
Spirit of truth, on this thy day............Heber. 9
Stand up, my soul, shake off thy fears........Watts. 126
Stand up, stand up for Jesus..............Duffield. 154
Star of peace! to wanderers weary............ 354
Stay, thou insulted Spirit, stay..........C. Wesley. 65
Stealing from the world away............Palmer. 287
Stern winter throws his icy chains ......Mrs. Steele. 355
Strait is the way, the door is strait......Watts. 73
Stretched on the cross, the Saviour dies..Mrs. Steele. 53
Strive, when thou art called of God......... 319
Sun of my soul! thou Saviour dear......Keble. 136
Sure the blest Comforter is nigh......Mrs. Steele. 65
Sweet is the work, my God, my King....Watts. 3
Sweet is the work, O Lord.................Lyte. 11
Sweet land of rest! for thee I sigh......... 243
Sweet the moments, rich in blessing........ 104
Sweet was the time when first I felt....Newton. 108
Swell the anthem, raise the song........... 354

Take my heart, O Father, take it........... 104
Tarry with me, O my Saviour............. 358
Tell me not of earthly toys............Hastings. 270

	PAGE
Thank and praise Jehovah's name...... *Montgomery.*	276
That awful day will surely come.............. *Watts.*	349
The bird, let loose in eastern skies,............ *Moore.*	8
The chariot, the chariot ! its wheels........ *Milman.*	348
The day of wrath, that dreadful day .... *W. Scott.*	247
The earth shall waste, the sun.....................	317
Thee we adore, eternal Name................ *Watts.*	275
The festal morn, my God, is come.......... *Merrick.*	250
The floods, O Lord, lift up their voice....... *Burgess.*	17
The God of harvest praise.............. *Montgomery.*	278
The harvest dawn is near.................. *Burgess.*	181
The head that once was crowned with thorns.. *Kelly.*	300
The heavens declare thy glory, Lord .... *Watts.*	82
The hour of my departure's come............ *Logan.*	245
The King of saints, how fair his face.......... *Watts.*	56
The Lord descended from above.......... *Sternhold.*	290
The Lord, how fearful is his name.............. *Watts.*	45
The Lord, how wondrous are his ways........ *Watts.*	39
The Lord is great, ye hosts of heaven.............	291
The Lord is King, lift up thy voice.......... *Conder.*	16
The Lord is my Shepherd, he makes me ...... *Knox.*	147
The Lord is my Shepherd, no want..... *Montgomery.*	134
The Lord Jehovah reigns, And royal.......... *Watts.*	290
The Lord Jehovah reigns, His throne........ *Watts.*	287
The Lord my pasture shall prepare........ *Addison.*	157
The Lord my Shepherd is.................... *Watts.*	131
The Lord of glory is my light.............. *Watts.*	281
The Lord our God is full of might....... *H. K. White.*	43
The Lord our God is Lord of all........ *H. K. White.*	43
The Lord shall come, the earth shall quake.... *Heber.*	247
The Lord will happiness divine............ *Cowper.*	111
The mind was formed to mount sublime.. *Mrs. Steele.*	100
The morning dawns upon the place.... *Montgomery.*	51
The morning kindles all the sky.....................	298
The morning light is breaking.......... *S. F. Smith.*	207
The perfect world, by Adam trod............ *Willis.*	193
The promise of my Father's love............ *Watts.*	310
The promises I sing.................... *Doddridge.*	316
The race that long in darkness pined...... *C. Wesley.*	295
There is a book that all may read............ *Keble.*	259
There is a calm for those who weep.... *Montgomery.*	344
There is a fold whence none can stray.......... *Enst.*	219
There is a fountain, filled with blood........ *Cowper.*	76
There is a God, all nature speaks........ *Mrs. Steele.*	36
There is a glorious world of light.......... *J. Taylor.*	219
There is a holy city........................	271
There is a house, not made with hands........ *Watts.*	269
There is a land immortal......................	271
There is a land of pure delight.............. *Watts.*	267
There is a line by us unseen.............. *Alexander.*	78
There is an eye that never sleeps....................	235
There is an hour of hallowed peace......... *Tappan.*	351
There is an hour of peaceful rest.......... *Tappan.*	266
There is an hour when I must part..................	347
The Saviour bids thee watch and pray.... *Hastings.*	234
The Saviour calls! let every car........ *Mrs. Steele.*	306
The Saviour! oh! what endless charms.. *Mrs. Steele.*	62
The Saviour! what a noble flame.......... *Cowper.*	48
The songs of Zion oft impart.......... *Hastings.*	318
The sparkling firmament on high......... *Addison.*	291
The Spirit in our hearts......................	82
The starry firmament on high.............. *Grant.*	32
The sun himself shall fade.............. *Gallaher.*	130
The voice of free grace cries, Escape ...... *Thornby.*	257
They who seek the throne of grace	237
Thine earthly Sabbaths, Lord, we love.. *Doddridge.*	2
Think gently of the erring one.......... *Miss Fletcher.*	163
This child we dedicate to thee....................	196
This is not my place of resting............ *Bonar.*	349
This is the day the Lord hath made.......... *Watts.*	4
This place is holy ground............. *Montgomery.*	256
Thou art gone to the grave, but we will...... *Heber.*	257
Thou art my hiding place, O Lord.......... *Raffles.*	319
Thou art, O God, the life and light......... *Moore.*	289
Thou art the Way ; to thee alone............ *Doane.*	49
Thou from whom we never part..................	227
Though faint yet pursuing, we go on.............	145
Though now the nations sit beneath..............	213
Though sorrow rise and dangers roll..............	320
Though the days are dark with trouble.............	224
Thou God of hope, to thee we bow............	176
Thou Judge of quick and dead........... *C. Wesley.*	83

	PA E
Thou, Lord, who rear'st the mountain's..... *Sterling.*	38
Thou lovely Source of true delight....... *Mrs. Steele.*	84
Thou Lord of all above.................... *Beddome.*	90
Thou, O Lord, in tender love.............. *C. Wesley.*	328
Thou, O my Jesus, thou didst me.......... *Xavier.*	143
Thou only Sovereign of my heart........ *Mrs. Steele.*	107
Thou seest my feeblenes................... *C. Wesley.*	99
Thou sweet gliding Kedron, by.... *Marie de Fleury.*	296
Thou very-present aid. .... *C. Wesley.*	174
Thou, who art enthroned above............ *Sandys.*	283
Thou, who didst on Calvary bleed.............	315
Thou, whose almighty word	27
Thrice happy souls, who born of heaven.. *Doddridge.*	282
Through every age, eternal God............ *Watts.*	348
Through sorrow's night, and danger's.... *H. K. White.*	249
Thy home is with the humble, Lord	164
Thy name, almighty Lord.................... *Watts.*	21
Thy way, not mine, O Lord.................. *Bonar.*	188
Thy way, O Lord, is in the sea............ *Fawcett.*	45
Thy will be done ; in devious way........ *Bowring.*	327
Thy will be done, I will not fear.......... *J. Roscoe.*	188
Time grows not old with change of.... *Montgomery.*	346
Time is winging us away................... *J. Burton.*	270
Time, thou speedest on but slowly..... *Lyra Germ.*	349
'Tis a point I long to know................ *Newton.*	310
'Tis by the faith of joys to come.............. *Watts.*	160
" 'Tis finished !" so the Saviour cried....... *Stennett.*	53
'Tis midnight—and on Olive's brow........ *Tappan.*	53
'Tis my happiness below .... *Cowper.*	333
'Tis not a cause of small import....... *Doddridge.*	335
To-day the Saviour calls.....................	88
Together with these symbols, Lord.............	199
To God, the only wise .... *Watts.*	20
To our Redeemer's glorious name........ *Mrs. Steele.*	143
Tossed upon life's raging billow.............	277
To thee, my God and Saviour........... *Haweis.*	165
To thee, my Shepherd and my Lord... *Heginbotham.*	323
To thy pastures, fair and large........... *Merrick.*	124
To whom, my Saviour, shall I go..............	321
Trembling before thine awful throne...... *Hillhouse.*	308
Triumphant Zion! lift thy head........ *Doddridge.*	212
'Twas on that dark, that doleful night........ *Watts.*	204
'Twas the day when God's Anointed..............	297
Unite, my roving thoughts, unite........ *Doddridge.*	325
Unshaken as the sacred hill................ *Watts.*	319
Unto thine altar, Lord......................	98
Unvail thy bosom, faithful tomb........... *Watts.*	246
Upon the Gospel's sacred page........... *Bowring.*	83
Upward I lift mine eyes.................... *Watts.*	12
Vain are the hopes, the sons of men........ *Watts.*	73
Vain, delusive world, adieu................ *C. Wesley.*	122
Vainly through night's weary hours.......... *Lyte.*	180
Vital spark of heavenly flame................. *Pope.*	844
Wait, my soul, upon the Lord.....................	119
Wait, O my soul, thy Maker's will....... *Beddome.*	83
Wake thee, O Zion, thy mourning is.............	214
Wake the song of jubilee............. *L. Bacon.*	342
Wake! the welcome day appeareth.............	340
Walk in the light—so shalt thou know...... *Barton.*	162
Watchman! tell us of the night.......... *Bowring.*	340
We are on our journey home........... *C. Beecher.*	240
We are out on the ocean sailing...............	222
Wearied with earthly toils and cares... *Mrs. Gilbert.*	8
Weary, Lord, of struggling here.............	151
Weary of wandering from my God........ *C. Wesley.*	308
Weary sinner, keep thine eyes..........	85
We bid thee welcome in the name..... *Montgomery.*	192
We bless thee for thy peace, O God.............	172
We come, O Lord, before thy throne.............	274
We give immortal praise.................... *Watts.*	293
Welcome, delightful morn............. *Hayward.*	12
Welcome, O Saviour, to my heart..............	97
Welcome, sweet day of rest.................. *Watts.*	10
Welcome, welcome, dear Redeemer.............	309
We pray thee, wounded Lamb of God.............	197
We're traveling home to heaven above.............	89
We speak of the realms of the blest.............	351
We stand in deep repentance.............. *Palmer.*	309
We've no abiding city here .... *Kelly.*	246

	PAGE
We would see Jesus, for the shadows	347
What are those soul-reviving strains	220
What cheering words are these....Kent.	174
What equal honors shall we bring....Watts.	15
What finite power with ceaseless toil. ...E. Scott.	37
What grace, O Lord, and beauty shone	48
What is life? 'tis but a vapor....Kelly.	347
What shall I render to my God....Watts.	18
What shall the dying sinner do....Watts.	71
What sinners value I resign....Watts.	246
What though no flowers the fig-tree clothe.. Logan.	164
What various hindrances we meet....Cowper.	233
When adverse winds and waves arise....Sigourney.	190
When all thy mercies, O my God....Addison.	40
When along life's thorny road	319
When, as returns this solemn day....Mrs. Barbauld.	281
Whence do our mournful thoughts arise....Watts.	128
When downward to the darksome tomb ....Palmer.	344
When gathering clouds around I view..Sir R. Grant.	190
When God of old came down....Keble.	302
When, gracious Lord, when shall it be.....C. Wesley.	315
When grief and anguish press me down	333
When human hopes all wither	123
When I can read my title clear....Watts.	129
When I can trust my all with God....Conder.	331
When I survey the wondrous cross....Watts.	52
When I view my Saviour bleeding	91
When Jesus dwelt in mortal clay....Gibbons.	176
When languor and disease invade ....Toplady.	187
When like a stranger on our sphere....Montgomery.	51
When marshaled on the nightly plain... H. K. White.	295
When morning's first and hallowed ray	41
When musing sorrow weeps the past....Noel.	184
When, my Saviour, shall I be....C. Wesley.	118
When on Sinai's top I see....Montgomery.	102
When overwhelmed with grief....Watts.	189
When power divine, in mortal form....J. E. Smith.	295
When, rising from the bed of death....Addison.	79
When shall the voice of singing	341
When shall we meet again	355
When sins and fears prevailing rise....Mrs. Steele.	329
When streaming from the eastern....Sir R. Grant.	323
When the heart, oppressed with grief	331
When this passing world is done....McCheyne.	322
When thou, my righteous Judge, shalt come	100
When waves of trouble round me swell	185
When we, our wearied limbs to rest... Tate—Brady.	210
Where high the heavenly temple stands....Logan.	232
Where, O my soul, oh, where ....T. Scott.	113
Where two or three with sweet accord....Stennett.	232
Where wilt thou put thy trust....Sigourney.	167
Wherewith, O God, shall I draw near.....C. Wesley.	307
While in sweet communion feeding	200
While life prolongs its precious light....Dwight.	89
While my Redeemer's near....Mrs. Steele.	152
While now upon this Sabbath eve	28
While o'er our guilty land, O Lord ....Dwight.	273
While o'er the deep thy servants sail.....G. Burgess.	273
While shepherds watched their flocks by....Tate.	46
While thee I seek, protecting...Miss H. M. Williams.	40
While through this changing world we roam	269
While to thy table I repair....Dwight.	205
While verdant hill and blooming vale....Mrs. Steele.	355
While with ceaseless course the sun....Newton.	22
Who are these arrayed in white....C. Wesley.	352
Who are these in bright array....Montgomery.	265
Who shall the Lord's elect condemn....Watts.	170
Why do we mourn departing friends....Watts.	248
Why is my heart so far from thee....Watts.	111
Why, O God, thy people spurn....Hatfield.	354
Why on the bending willows hung	210
Why should I fear the darkest hour....Newton.	156
Why should our tears in sorrow flow	248
Why should the children of a King....Watts.	67
Why should we start and fear to die....Watts.	244
Why sinks my soul desponding....Hastings.	191
Why will ye waste on trifling cares....Doddridge.	60
Wilt thou not visit me	311
With broken heart and contrite sigh	93
With deepest reverence at thy throne	86
With glory clad, with strength arrayed. Tate—Brady.	15
With heavenly power, O Lord, defend	193
With joy we hail the sacred day....Lyte.	6
With my substance I will honor....Francis.	181
With songs and honors sounding loud....Watts.	285
With tearful eyes I look around	92
With tears of anguish I lament ....Stennett.	105
Witness, ye men and angels, now....Beddome.	310
Worthy the Lamb of boundless sway....Shirley.	212
Would'st thou eternal life obtain....Palmer.	140
Would you see Jesus? Come	305
Would you win a soul to God....Hammond.	304
Ye angels, who stand round the throne....De Fleury.	148
Ye Christian heralds! go, proclaim	212
Ye messengers of Christ....Voke.	342
Ye servants of God, your Master ....C. Wesley.	24
Ye servants of the Lord....Doddridge.	330
Yes, the Redeemer rose....Doddridge.	55
Ye trembling souls, dismiss your fears ....Beddome.	129
Ye valiant soldiers of the cross	222
Ye, who in these courts are found	202
Your harps, ye trembling saints....Toplady.	130
Zion dreary, and in anguish....Hastings.	277
Zion stands, with hills surrounded....Kelly.	341

INDEX OF SUBJECTS.

[The figures refer to the numbers of the Hymns.]

ABBA FATHER, 541, 549, 1023, 1068.
Abiding, Christ with Believers, 429, 799, 1052.
Abrahamic Covenant, 615, 619, 1113.
Absence from God, 72, 344, 352, 387, 998, 1008.
Accepted Time, 272, 285, 976.
Access to God, 723—725, 746, 890, 1023.
Activity, 391—427, 550—569, 1025, 1033, 1081—1087.
Adoption, 580, 541, 543, 547, 549, 1023, 1068—1070.
Advent of Christ ;—
  At Birth, 148—153, 923—930.
  To Judgment, 770, 779, 790, 1162—1164.
Advocate, Christ our, 65, 203, 537, 446, 983, 1023, 1078.
Afflictions, 284, 570—599, 1024, 1067, 1089—1103.
Almost Christian, 226, 1033.
Angels ;—
  Attendants of Christ, 151, 178, 193, 194, 926—929, 945.
  Ministering Spirits, 419, 421, 464, 714.
  Sympathy in Redemption, 447, 934, 966.
Anniversaries ;—
  Church, 70, 711—720, 836—838, 847, 848, 1026, 1182, 1183.
  National, 840, 843, 857, 1184—1186.
  Sabbath School, 707, 709, 710, 1193.
Ascension of Christ, 177, 179, 191, 939, 943—945.
Ashamed of Christ, 401, 402, 432, 586, 631.
Asleep in Jesus, 758, 1142, 1144.
Assurance ;—
  Expressed, 402, 403, 415, 417, 547, 1021, 1023, 1071, 1078.
  Prayed for, 215, 358, 384, 385, 995, 1018.
  Urged, 397, 398, 406, 407, 410, 1027, 1033.
Atonement ;—
  Necessary, 224—244, 478, 957, 958, 960.
  Completed, 245—251, 478, 167—176, 292, 639—641, 937—939, 957—968.
  Sufficient, 245—293, 639—641, 796, 957—981.
Autumn, 802, 858.

Backsliding, 341—390, 457, 460, 470, 471, 993—1019.
Baptism, 611—619, 1111—1114.
Benevolence, 550—556, 567—569, 1082—1084.
Bible, 33, 101—113, 896, 901—903.
Brotherly Love, 496, 513, 554, 568, 709—722, 1057, 1061.
Burial of the Dead—See *Death, Heaven.*
  A Brother, 789, 793, 797.
  A Child, 764, 775, 802.
  A Sister, 776, 801, 1149.
  A Pastor, 781, 793.
  A Friend, 765, 795, 842, 1151.

Calmness, 475, 505, 506, 519, 1047, 1074.
Calvary, 167, 328, 937, 1119.
Care—See *Conflict with Sin.*
  Experienced, 383, 385, 598, 599, 999.
  Cast on Jesus, 414, 426, 471, 475, 481, 485, 488, 493, 595, 1027, 1029, 1051, 1074.
Charity—See *Brotherly Love* and *Liberality.*
Cheerfulness, 130, 473, 480, 482, 502, 517, 526, 1051, 1074, 1075.
Children ;—
  Baptism, 611—619, 1111—1114.
  Sabbath School, 691—709.
Child-like Spirit, 508, 512, 527, 529, 1037, 1056, 1069.
Christ ;—
  Adoration as God, 47, 177—203, 430, 441, 451, 456, 461, 432. 942—951, 1053.

Advent, 193, 148—153, 923—931.
Advocate, 65, 203, 537, 446, 983, 1023, 1078.
Ascension, 177, 179, 191, 939, 943—945.
Captain of Salvation, 396, 397, 479, 1138.
Character, 154—166, 931, 1037.
Corner-stone, 610, 866, 1110.
Death, 167—176, 640, 647, 937—939.
Desire of Nations, 689, 1132.
Divinity, 47, 184, 189, 202, 947, 948, 923, 924.
Example, 154—166, 484, 524, 525, 963, 1031, 1037.
Friend of Sinners, 190, 305, 336, 446. See *Friend.*
Hiding Place, 365, 961, 1018, 1034.
Immanuel, 245, 430, 437, 924, 950.
King, 81, 82, 185, 186, 188, 195, 927, 943, 948, 951.
Lamb of God, 47, 85, 183, 196, 384, 949, 959, 984, 1119.
Life, incidents, 154—166, 484, 932—936, 1048.
Lord our Righteousness, 61, 1072.
Love, 157, 169, 190, 199, 247, 292, 323, 340, 395, 426, 434, 440, 455, 1040, 1074.
Mediator, 65, 203, 292, 537, 446, 983, 1023, 1078.
Priest, 163, 182, 186, 203, 959, 1023.
Prince of Glory, 47, 169, 179.
Prince of Peace, 152, 375, 1128.
Prophet, 161, 187, 438, 926.
Refuge, 365, 379, 425, 435, 488, 961, 1018, 1034.
Resurrection, 177, 178, 192, 194, 939—942.
Rock of Ages, 639, 1129.
Shepherd, 392, 412, 423, 457, 459, 460, 474, 480, 486, 964, 1050, 1076.
Sufferings, 167—176, 620, 621, 934—939, 963, 967.
Sun of Righteousness, 102, 128, 193, 429, 928, 1042, 1068.
Way, Truth, and Life, 159, 944.
Word, 150, 923.
Christians, 341—599, 995—1103.
  Afflictions. 570—599, 1088—1103.
  Conflicts, 340—390, 995—1019.
  Duties, 550—569, 1081—1087.
  Encouragements, 391—427, 1020—1034.
  Fellowship, 709—722, 1057, 1061.
  Graces, 493—529, 1056—1067.
  Love for the Saviour, 428—492, 1035—1055.
  Privileges, 530—549, 1068—1080.
Church, 600—757, 1104—1138.
  Afflicted, 664—666, 1123.
  Beloved of God, 681, 682, 721, 1073, 1129, 1130.
  Institutions of, 600—610, 1104—1110.
  Ordinances of, 611—652, 1111—1121.
  Progress and Missions, 653—690, 1122—1133.
  Revival of, 373, 658, 659, 690, 1124, 1129.
  Sabbath School, 691—710.
  Social Meetings, 709—757.
  Triumphant, 670, 679—682, 865, 1122, 1125, 1127, 1138.
  Unity of, 716, 720—722, 865, 1109, 1127.
  Uniting with, 189, 321, 621, 623, 650, 652, 991, 992.
  Close of Worship, 79, 87—100, 895—900.
Comforter—See *Holy Spirit.*
Communion of Christians ;—
  With each other, 709—722, 865, 1061.
  With Christ at the Lord's Supper, 620—652, 1115—1121.
  With God in devotion, 436, 473, 491, 561, 723—746, 1055, 1058, 1064.
Communion of Saints, 716, 865, 1107. See *Heaven.*
Completeness in Christ, 454, 499.
Confession—See *Repentance* and *Conflict with Sin.*

Confidence, 480, 485, 493. 510, 520, 1021, 1023, 1032.
Conflict with Sin, 341—396, 469—471, 995—1019.
Conformity to Christ, 154—160, 162, 458, 524, 525, 981, 1007, 1031, 1037, 1063.
Conscience, 215, 233, 478, 960.
Consecration ;—
  Of Possessions, 169, 569, 1082, 1084.
  Of Self to God, 58, 169, 174, 199, 296, 812, 620—623, 644, 985. 991, 992.
Consistency, 458. 497, 524, 528, 1059.
Consolation—See *Afflictions.*
Constancy, 544, 547. 561. 1005, 1029, 1032.
Contentment, 475, 480, 500, 505, 575, 582, 1074, 1076.
Conversion—See *Repentance.*
Conviction of Sin, 324, 308, 314, 323. See *Repentance.*
Corner-stone ;—
  Christ, 866, 1110.
  Laying, of Sanctuary, 610, 866, 1110, 1122, 1129.
Courage, 391—427, 479, 1020—1084, 1078.
Covenant, 58. 291, 422, 425, 577, 991, 992, 1079, 1113.
Creation, 63, 71, 73, 86, 123, 142, 143, 885, 907, 908, 914.
Cross ;—
  Bearing, 158, 293, 370, 390, 586, 938, 963, 1026.
  Glorying in, 336, 338, 389, 620, 626, 631, 644, 951.
  Salvation by. 169, 174, 277, 298, 299, 302, 306, 311, 442, 621, 640, 644, 937, 979, 981.
Crucifixion of Christ, 173—176, 937—939, 967.

Death, 758—803, 842, 1139—1161. See *Burial.*
Decrees of God, 121, 124, 917. See *Sovereignty.*
Dedication of Sanctuary, 15, 601, 607, 608, 875, 1107, 1122, 1129, 1138.
Dedication of Self to God—See *Consecration.*
Delay of Repentance, 253, 255, 268, 272, 278, 281, 282, 971, 976, 977.
Dependence ;—
  On God's Providence, 123, 128, 129, 130, 134, 140, 564, 836, 876, 897.
  On the Saviour's Grace. 294. 305, 319, 344, 365, 366, 383, 385, 431, 489, 639, 954, 996, 999, 1012, 1044, 1045, 1054.
Depravity, 224—244, 957, 960.
Despondency—See *Conflict with Sin* and *Encouragements.*
Devotion, 436, 473, 491. 561, 728—746, 1055, 1058, 1064.
Diligence—See *Activity.*
Doubt—See *Conflict with Sin* and *Encouragements.*
Doxologies, 34, 44. 68, 79, 620, 674 ; pages 356, 357.

Early Piety, 691—702, 802.
Earnestness—See *Activity.*
Election—See *Decrees* and *Sovereignty.*
Encouragements, 391—427, 1020—1084.
Energy—See *Activity.*
Eternity, 782, 783, 783, 885, 1165, 1166.
Evening, 14, 27, 50, 90, 92, 100, 713, 736, 737, 744, 745, 900, 908.
Exaltation of Christ, 177—203, 939—951.
Example ;—
  Of Christ, 154—166, 484, 524, 525, 551, 935, 963, 1031, 1037.
  Of Christians, 497, 528, 568, 1059, 1070.

Faint-heartedness, 354, 361, 381, 383—386, 393, 425, 1021, 1030.
Faith—See *Confidence* and *Trust.*
  Gift of God, 502, 514. 968, 1029, 1045, 1054.
  Instrument in Justification, 235, 302, 478, 516, 972, 990, 1046.
  Power of, 494, 509, 516, 521, 1027, 1029, 1047, 1062.
  Prayer for, 14, 509, 514, 1003, 1047.
Faithfulness of God—See *God.*
Fall of Man, 236, 239. See *Lost State of Man.*
Family, 611, 615, 691—709, 717—719, 726, 734—739, 745—757.
Fasting, 841, 845, 854, 856, 1187. See *Repentance.*
Father, God our—See *God.*
Fearfulness—See *Conflict with Sin* and *Encouragements.*
Fellowship of Christians, 709—722, 529, 865, 1057, 1061, 1070.
Fidelity, Christian, 311, 863, 458, 495, 497, 504, 509, 524, 992, 1065.

Forbearance ;—
  Divine, 66, 120, 243, 259, 315, 328, 350, 452, 457, 877, 883, 1011, 1017.
  Christian, 154, 156, 158, 162, 507, 528, 931, 1059.
Forgiveness ;—
  Of Sin, 55, 301, 317, 984, 1117. See *Atonement,* and *Repentance.*
  Of Injury, 156, 158, 162, 507, 528, 1057, 1059.
Formality, 25, 212, 232, 234, 254, 351, 358, 504, 952, 1033, 1056.
Funeral—See *Burial.*
Friend, Christ our, 190, 321, 367, 389, 453, 473, 706—708, 1086, 1047.
Friends in heaven—See *Heaven.*
Future Punishment, 253, 260, 270, 275, 804, 1164, 1166.

Gentleness, 156, 508, 507, 1056, 1059.
Gethsemane, 157, 168, 170, 932, 935, 936.
Glory of God. 40, 41, 43, 59, 75, 83, 102, 122, 128, 144, 892—894.
Glorying in Cross—See *Cross.*
God ;—
  All in All, 72, 102, 115, 123, 128. 140, 885, 914.
  Attributes, 39—86, 114—147, 878—894, 904—922.
  Being, 40, 41, 102, 117, 137, 892, 906, 908.
  Benevolence, 40, 52, 55, 57, 58, 62, 66, 122, 127, 131, 887, 892, 907.
  Compassion, 66, 168, 251, 786, 957, 907.
  Condescension, 48, 62, 549, 894.
  Eternity, 41, 44, 141, 884, 885, 914, 915, 1139.
  Faithfulness, 60, 71, 395, 402, 405, 411, 415, 422, 424, 884, 917, 1027.
  Father, 62, 80, 132, 136, 519, 541, 543, 547, 549, 756, 890, 894, 1068, 1069, 1079.
  Forbearance, 66, 120, 243, 259, 315, 328, 350, 452, 457, 877, 883, 1011.
  Goodness, 71. See *Benevolence of God.*
  Holiness, 34, 73, 145, 893.
  Immensity, 115, 118, 128, 884, 914, 916.
  Incomprehensibleness, 124, 126, 147, 916.
  Infinity, 115, 118, 123, 884, 914, 916.
  Jehovah, 46, 114, 115, 894, 909.
  Justice, 40, 43, 124, 224, 232, 236, 239, 892, 894.
  King of Kings, 50, 482, 885, 911, 1043. See *Majesty of God.*
  Love, 34, 52, 57, 62, 144, 572, 884, 890, 912, 913.
  Majesty, 48, 51, 75, 76, 83, 125, 186, 887, 889, 894, 909—911.
  Mercy, 64, 127, 146, 163, 260, 262, 289, 295, 327, 407, 884.
  Omnipotence, 122, 134, 135, 142, 144, 888, 894, 914.
  Omnipresence, 115, 123, 128, 140, 916, 918.
  Omniscience, 54, 119, 138, 894, 916, 918.
  Patience—See *Forbearance of God.*
  Pity—See *Compassion of God.*
  Providence, 124, 126, 129—134, 137, 139, 891, 909, 1025.
  Saviour, 13, 20, 65, 189, 482. 961.
  Shepherd—See *Christ, a Shepherd.*
  Sovereignty, 43, 121, 124, 137, 139, 147, 502, 627, 917.
  Supremacy, 38. 41, 42, 51, 56, 75, 83, 136, 144, 893, 911.
  Trinity, 83, 114, 116, 919—922.
  Truth, 33, 44, 60, 68, 77, 103, 124, 127, 909, 917.
  Unchangeableness, 42, 68, 77, 127, 144, 884, 885, 909, 915, 1139.
  Wisdom, 40, 43, 122, 124, 139, 143, 912.
Gospel—See *Atonement* and *Way of Salvation.*
Grace, 52, 187, 249, 250, 403, 526, 583, 548, 796, 959, 961, 968, 974.
Graces, Christian, 494—529, 1056—1067.
Gratitude, 58, 66, 493, 851, 852, 577, 883—887.
Grave, 765, 771, 778, 794, 842, 1144, 1147, 1161.
Grieving the Holy Spirit—See *Holy Spirit.*
Growth in Grace, 156, 158, 160, 206, 210, 216, 218, 419, 454, 491, 497, 504, 525, 529, 549, 566, 952, 1005, 1014, 1063.
Guidance, Divine, 98, 109, 210, 345, 354, 366, 884, 892, 412, 425, 480, 489, 493, 500, 540, 898, 972, 1031, 1062.

Happiness, 72, 322, 414, 426, 440, 465, 466, 473, 502, 526, 1074, 1075.
Harvest, 413, 887, 852, 858.
Hearing the Word, 84, 88, 97, 112, 113, 896, 899, 1013.
Heart ;—
  Change of—See *Regeneration.*
  Deceitfulness of, 340, 348, 350, 356, 882, 997, 1002.
  Searching of, 254, 268, 345, 351, 358, 953, 995, 1007.
  Surrender of, 311, 316, 335, 358, 387, 985, 987, 988, 1010.

Heaven, 809—835, 1167—1181.
  Christ there, 72, 761, 766, 783, 830, 1167, 1168, 1172, 1176, 1181.
  Friends there, 771, 789, 795, 800, 812, 815, 842, 1173, 1193.
  Home there, 747—757, 812—816, 819, 1160, 1167, 1170.
  Rest there, 754, 757, 788, 791, 793, 1167, 1171.
Hell, 253, 260, 270, 282, 326, 804, 1166.
Heirship with Christ, 215. See *Adoption.*
Hiding-place, Christ, 365, 961, 1018, 1034.
Holiness ;—
  Of Saints—See *Conformity to Christ* and *Purity.*
  Of God—See *God.*
Holy Scriptures—See *Bible.*
Holy Spirit, 204—223, 952—956.
  Divine, 213, 219, 220, 223, 953.
  Grieved, 209, 261, 280, 282, 285, 994.
  Striving, 209, 261, 273, 285.
  Witnessing, 208, 215, 216, 221, 547, 952, 1068.
Home—See *Family* and *Heaven.*
Hope ;—
  Under Affliction—See *Afflictions.*
  Under Conviction, 228, 229, 235, 238, 240, 248, 252, 295, 359, 982, 990.
  Under Despondency, 393, 402, 409, 417, 421, 1004, 1018, 1021.
  In Death—See *Death.*
Humiliation—See *Fasting.*
Humility, 508, 512, 527, 529, 1056.

Immanuel—See *Christ.*
Immortality, 747, 766, 778, 783, 792, 794, 795, 1144, 1150, 1154, 1161, 1177.
Imputation, 61, 168, 169, 174, 302, 306, 478, 639, 964, 967, 979.
Incarnation—See *Advent.*
Importunity, 725, 741, 742, 1085, 1086.
Infants—See *Baptism,* and *Death.*
Ingratitude, 243, 300, 315, 332, 348, 1014.
Inspiration, 104, 107, 111.
Installation, 600, 603, 604, 606, 1104, 1106, 1108.
Intercession—See *Christ a Priest,* and *Prayer.*
Introduction to Worship, 1—38, 860—875.
Invitations, 252—293, 442, 640, 641, 796, 965—978.

Jehovah—See *God.*
Jews, 666, 1125, 1128, 1129, 1184.
Joining the Church, 169, 331, 621, 623, 650, 652, 991, 992.
Joy, 473, 480, 482, 502, 517, 526, 1075.
Jubilee, 668, 685, 959, 1137.
Judgment-Day, 320, 325, 326, 768—770, 804—808, 978, 1162—1164.
Justice—See *God.*
Justification—See *Atonement* and *Faith.*

Kindness—See *Brotherly Love.*
Kingdom of Christ ;—
  Prayer for, 185, 195, 654, 660, 663, 668, 672, 673, 686, 1132.
  Progress of, 655, 657, 669, 678, 680, 685, 690, 1137, 1138.
Knowledge, 104, 106, 111, 206, 513, 902, 903, 906.

Labor—See *Activity.*
Lamb of God—See *Christ.*
Law ;—
  And Gospel, 163, 225, 232, 233, 235, 328, 958, 960, 961.
  Conviction under, 225, 229, 233, 238, 239, 324, 960, 961, 981.
Liberality, 551, 553, 555, 567, 569, 1082—1084.
Life ;—
  Brevity, 141, 280, 325, 766, 777, 782, 915, 1182.
  Object, 260, 270, 295, 322, 326, 388, 458, 559, 976.
  Solemnity, 259, 260, 270, 326, 400, 401, 419, 559, 1081, 1082.
  Uncertainty, 278, 325, 767, 766, 795, 971, 1143, 1153, 1158.
Little Things, 495, 556, 558, 1087.
Likeness to Christ—See *Conformity.*
Longing ;—
  For God, 7, 11, 72, 303, 341, 352, 353, 383, 468, 483, 491, 876, 996, 1004.
  For Christ, 108, 343, 358, 365, 371, 384, 416, 761, 1012. See *Love.*
  For Heaven, 747—757, 761, 779, 783, 792, 814, 821, 829, 1155—1158, 1167—1181.
Long-suffering—See *Forbearance.*

Looking to Jesus, 277, 342, 383, 384, 385, 426.
Lord's Day—See *Sabbath.*
Lord's Prayer, 724, 725, 891, 1086.
Lord's Supper, 620—652, 1115—1121.
Lord our Righteousness, 61, 1072.
Lost State of Man, 224—244, 957, 958, 960.
Love ;—
  Of God—See *God.*
  Of Christ—See *Christ.*
  For God, 72, 83, 311, 341, 491, 493, 541, 547, 549, 1029, 1069.
  For the Saviour, 428—492, 1035—1055.
  For the Saints, 528, 709—722, 865, 1057, 1061, 1070.
  For Souls, 241, 515, 552, 563, 568, 1087.
  For the Church, 313, 331, 665, 716, 721, 1109, 1122.
Loving-Kindness, 455.
Lukewarmness—See *Formality.*

Majesty of God—See *God.*
Man, Fallen—See *Lost State.*
Marriage, 846.
Martyr-faith, 393, 396, 401, 405, 425, 509, 520, 1021, 1025.
Mediator—See *Christ.*
Mediatorial Reign—See *Kingdom.*
Meditation, 104, 108, 110, 732, 787, 996, 1001.
Meekness, 501, 527, 529, 1056. See *Humility.*
Mercifulness, 503, 507, 528, 555, 568, 1084.
Mercy—See *God.*
Mercy-seat, 726, 733, 739. See *Prayer.*
Millennium, 610, 654, 656, 668, 669, 673, 678, 680, 685, 1127, 1128, 1137, 1165, 1172.
Ministry—See *Pastor.*
  Commission, 600, 603, 604, 1104, 1105.
  Convocation, 605, 676, 1105, 1106.
  Installation, 603, 606, 1108, 1104—1106.
  Prayer for, 600, 602, 605, 606, 1108.
Miracles, 166, 551, 933, 1084.
Missions, 653—690, 1122—1138.
Missionaries, 600, 606, 671, 677, 1135, 1136.
Morning, 18, 33, 861, 913. See *Sabbath.*
Mortality—See *Death* and *Life.*
Mystery of Providence, 40, 115, 124, 126, 139, 147, 916.

National, 840, 843, 856, 857, 1184, 1185, 1186.
Nature, Light of, 102, 117, 904—908.
Nature, the Material Universe ;—
  Beauties of, 3, 133, 904, 905, 913.
  God seen in, 40, 48, 49, 54, 102, 117, 122, 128, 133, 140, 142, 143, 146, 904—908.
Nearness to God, 352, 468, 491, 1024. See *Longing.*
Nearness to Heaven, 783, 810, 815, 833, 1155, 1160.
Needful, One Thing, 227, 259.
New Song in Heaven, 31, 183, 447, 667, 824, 865, 1168, 1177.
New Year, 70, 836, 838, 847, 1182.
Night—See *Evening.*

Old Age, 422, 458, 792, 799, 1051, 1052.
Omnipotence—See *God.*
Omnipresence—See *God.*
Omniscience—See *God.*
Opening of Service, 1—38, 860—876.
Oppressed, 849, 859.
Ordinances—See *Church.*
Ordination—See *Ministry.*
Orphans, 553, 1084.

Pardon—See *Forgiveness.*
Parting, 93, 98, 709, 899, 1121, 1193.
Pastor ;—
  Prayed for, 600, 606, 1106, 1108.
  Sought, 602.
  Welcomed, 603, 1105.
  Death of—See *Burial.*
Patience, 121, 124, 139, 390, 508, 509, 528, 534, 561, 1056.
Peace ;—
  Christian, 375, 386, 528, 538, 641, 1018, 1029, 1057, 1070.
  National, 686, 841, 843, 1190.
Peace-makers, 501, 528, 555, 719, 722, 1057, 1061.
Penitence. See *Repentance.*
Pentecost, 213, 219, 955.
Perseverance, 65, 395, 397, 402, 403, 405, 408, 424, 531, 537, 542, 1021, 1022, 1027, 1077.
Pestilence, 845, 856, 1187.

"Pilgrim Fathers," 640.
Pilgrim-Spirit, 341, 367, 391, 409, 458, 747—753, 898, 1091.
Pity of God—See *God's Compassion*.
Pleasures of Worldliness, 259, 271, 304, 313, 331, 388. 1001, 1035, 1089.
Poor, 551, 553, 554, 555, 697, 1083, 1084.
Praise ;—
  Calls to, 20, 29, 31, 37, 57, 63, 74—76, 865, 873, 880, 882.
  Singing, 29, 31, 391, 441, 879, 880.
  To Trinity, 59, 73, 83, 114, 116, 919—922.
  To Father, 84, 114—147, 873, 904—918.
  To Son, 47, 82, 85, 177—203, 924, 939—951.
  To Holy Spirit. 86, 204, 222, 953.
Prayer, 723—746, 1085, 1086.
Preaching—See *Ministry*.
Predestination—See *Decrees*.
Pride—See *Humility*.
Procrastination—See *Delay*.
Prodigal Son, 252, 255, 256, 279, 294, 457, 966.
Profession of Religion—See *Joining the Church*.
Progress—See *Growth in Grace*.
Promises, 60, 422, 424, 917, 1020, 1027.
Providence—See *God*.
Purity, 61, 225, 245, 335, 504, 549. 639, 980, 1007, 1070, 1072.
Punishment of Wicked—See *Future Punishment*.

Race, Christian, 398, 400, 1033.
Rain, 49, 853, 888.
Receiving Christ, 294—340, 979—994.
Redemption—See *Atonement*.
Refuge—See *Christ*.
Regeneration ;—
  Necessary, 224—244, 324, 958, 1010.
  Prayed for, 311, 835, 845, 856, 859, 897, 952, 1007.
  Wrought by God, 204, 218, 223, 230, 231, 234, 952, 953.
Renunciation of the World, 304, 313, 351, 888, 1001, 1039.
Repentance, 174, 176, 294—339, 980—994.
Resignation, 511, 519, 534, 1066, 1067. See *Affliction*.
Rest, 270, 276, 313, 544, 754, 757, 768, 791, 793, 1076, 1167, 1171.
Resurrection ;—
  Of Saints, 765, 766, 775, 779, 784, 1161.
  Of Christ—See *Christ*.
Retirement—See *Meditation*, and *Devotion*.
Return to God, 255, 256, 273, 279, 281, 966, 970.
Revival, 212, 216, 217, 219, 371, 873, 416, 418, 463, 850, 956, 1124.
Riches, 169, 569, 1082, 1084.
Righteousness, 61, 1072. See *Imputation*.
Rock of Ages, 639, 1129.

Sabbath, 1—37, 69, 90, 92, 95, 860—871, 940, 941, 1110.
Sabbath-School, 691—709.
Sacraments, 611—652, 1111—1121.
Sailors, 839, 844, 855, 1189.
Salvation—See *Grace*.
Sanctification—See *Growth in Grace*.
Sanctuary ;—
  Attendance upon—See *Sabbath*, and *Worship*.
  Dedication, Corner-stone, 15, 601, 607, 608, 610, 666, 875, 1107, 1110, 1122, 1129, 1188.
  Love for, 7, 12, 16, 19, 30, 35, 721, 562, 863, 869, 876.
Saviour—See *Christ*, and *God*.
Science and Revelation, 106. See *Knowledge*.
Scriptures—See *Bible*.
Seamen—See *Sailors*.
Seasons, 837, 852, 888.
  Spring, 837, 905, 913, 1192.
  Summer, 858.
  Autumn, 802, 837, 858.
  Winter, 849, 1183, 1191.
Self-deception, 340, 348, 350, 856, 882, 997, 1002.
Self-dedication—See *Consecration* and *Heart*.
Self-denial, 226, 237, 401, 495, 586, 951, 1083.
Self-examination, 254, 268, 845, 851, 858, 952, 995, 1007.
Self-renunciation, 174, 176, 518, 1011. See *Consecration* and *Heart*.

Self-righteousness, 169, 228, 236, 302, 305, 518, 960, 980.
Sensibility—See *Weeping*.
Shepherd—See *Christ*.
Sickness, 66, 467. 498, 575, 587, 588, 599, 877, 1024, 1021 1051, 1093.
Sin ;—
  Indwelling—See *Heart* and *Conflict*.
  Original—See *Lost State of Man*.
  Conviction—See *Repentance*.
Sincerity, 25, 254, 351, 358, 504, 952, 1083.
Sinners ;—
  Warned—See *Invitation*.
  Penitent—See *Repentance*.
Slavery, 849.
Soldier, Christian, 29, 393, 396, 397, 401, 557, 1083.
Songs of Zion, 29, 31, 32, 391, 441, 879, 1028.
Soul of Man—See *Immortality* and *Happiness*.
Souls, Love for—See *Love* and *Weeping*.
Sovereignty—See *God*.
Spirit—See *Holy Spirit*.
Spring, 456, 637, 905, 913, 1192.
Star of Bethlehem, 148, 925, 930.
Steadfastness—See *Constancy*.
Storm, 48, 49, 56, 146, 888.
Strength, As our Day, 880, 534, 597, 1000.
Submission—See *Resignation*.
Summer, 858. See *Seasons*.
Sun of Righteousness—See *Christ*.
Sympathy—See *Brotherly Love*.

Temperance, 562, 563.
Temptation—See *Conflict with Sin*.
Thanksgiving, 837, 851, 852, 858, 1189. See *Praise*.
Time—See *Life*.
To-day, 261, 269, 272, 280, 282, 285.
To-morrow, 278, 280.
Trials—See *Conflict*, and *Afflictions*, and *Care*.
Trinity—See *God*.
Trust ;—
  In Christ, 252, 277, 302, 383, 402, 466, 475, 489, 990, 1021.
  In Providence, 124, 126, 139, 405, 407, 410, 424. 480, 485, 493, 510, 523, 917, 1020, 1027.

Unbelief—See *Faith*, and *Conflict*.
Union of Saints ;—
  To Christ, 454, 458, 476, 489, 499, 539, 542, 547, 639, 715, 1077, 1079, 1080.
  To each other—See *Fellowship*.
  In Heaven and on Earth, 709, 714, 716, 865, 1107.
Unity—See *Church*.

Vows, 58, 992. See *Consecration*, and *Joining the Church*.

Waiting—See *Patience*.
Wandering—See *Conflict with Sin*, and *Backsliding*.
War—See *Peace*.
Warfare, Christian—See *Soldier*.
Warnings—See *Invitations*.
Watchfulness, 271, 497, 557, 735, 1065, 1081.
Way of Salvation. 224—340, 957—994.
Way, Truth, and Life, 150, 944.
Wealth—See *Riches*.
Weeping for Souls, 241, 418, 515, 563.
Winter, 637, 848, 1183, 1191.
Wisdom—See *God*.
Witness—See *Holy Spirit*.
Word of God—See *Bible*.
Worship—See *Opening* and *Close*.
  Family—See *Family*.
  Social, 709—757.
Wrath of God—See *Hell* and *Future Punishment*.

Zeal—See *Activity*.
Zion—See *Church*.

THE

FORM OF GOVERNMENT

OF

THE PRESBYTERIAN CHURCH IN THE UNITED STATES OF AMERICA;

AS AMENDED AND RATIFIED BY THE GENERAL ASSEMBLY OF 1821, AND FURTHER
AMENDED BY THE ASSEMBLIES OF 1826, AND 1833.

BOOK I.

OF GOVERNMENT.

CHAPTER I.

PRELIMINARY PRINCIPLES.*

THE Presbyterian Church in the United States of America, in presenting to the Christian public the system of union, and the form of government and discipline which they have adopted, have thought proper to state, by way of introduction, a few of the general principles by which they have been governed in the formation of the plan. This, it is hoped, will, in some measure, prevent those rash misconstructions, and uncandid reflections, which usually proceed from an imperfect view of any subject; as well as make the several parts of the system plain, and the whole perspicuous and fully understood.

They are unanimously of opinion:

I. That "God alone is Lord of the conscience; and hath left it free from the doctrines and commandments of men, which are in anything contrary to his word, or beside it, in matters of faith or worship:" Therefore, they consider the rights of private judgment, in all matters that respect religion, as universal, and unalienable: they do not even wish to see any religious constitution aided by the civil power, further than may be necessary for protection and security, and, at the same time, equal and common to all others.

II. That, in perfect consistency with the above principle of common right, every Christian church, or union or association of particular churches, is entitled to declare the terms of admission into *its* communion, and the qualifications of its ministers and members, as well as the whole system of its internal government which Christ hath appointed: that, in the exercise of this right, they may, notwithstanding, err, in making the terms of communion either too lax or too narrow: yet, even in this case, they do not infringe upon the liberty, or the rights, of others, but only make an improper use of their own.

III. That our blessed Saviour, for the edification of the visible Church, which is his body, hath appointed officers, not only to preach the Gospel *and administer the sacraments;* but also to exercise discipline, for the preservation both of truth and duty; and, that it is incumbent upon these *officers,* and upon the whole church, in whose

---

* NOTE.—This introductory chapter, with the exception of the first sentence, was first drawn up by the Synod of New York and Philadelphia, and prefixed to the Form of Government, etc., as published by that body in 1788. In that year, after arranging the plan on which the Presbyterian Church is now governed, the Synod was divided into four Synods, and gave place to the General Assembly, which met for the first time in 1789.

---

name they act, to censure, or cast out, the erroneous and scandalous; observing, in *all* cases, the rules contained in the word of God.

IV. That truth is in order to goodness; and the great touchstone of truth, its tendency to promote holiness; according to our Saviour's rule, "by their fruits ye shall know them:" And that no opinion can be either more pernicious or absurd, than that which brings truth and falsehood upon a level, and represents it as of no consequence what a man's opinions are. On the contrary, they are persuaded, that there is an inseparable connection between faith and practice, truth and duty. Otherwise, it would be of no consequence either to discover truth, or to embrace it.

V. That while under the conviction of the above principle, they think it necessary to make effectual provision, that all who are admitted as teachers, be sound in the faith; they also believe that there are truths and forms, with respect to which men of good characters and principles may differ. And in all these they think it the duty, both of private Christians and societies, to exercise mutual forbearance towards each other.

VI. That though the character, qualifications, and authority of church officers, are laid down in the Holy Scriptures, as well as the proper method of their investiture and institution; yet the election of the persons to the exercise of this authority, in any particular society, is in that society.

VII. That all church power, whether exercised by the body in general, or in the way of representation by delegated authority, is only ministerial and declarative; *That is to say,* that the Holy Scriptures are the only rule of faith and manners; that no church judicatory ought to pretend to make laws, to bind the conscience in virtue of their own authority; and that all their decisions should be founded upon the revealed will of God. Now though it will easily be admitted, that all synods and councils may err, through the frailty inseparable from humanity; yet there is much greater danger from the usurped claim of making laws, than from the right of judging upon laws already made, and common to all who profess the gospel; although this right, as necessity requires in the present state, be lodged with fallible men.

VIII. *Lastly.* That, if the preceding scriptural and rational principles be steadfastly adhered to, the vigor and strictness of its discipline will contribute to the glory and happiness of any church. Since ecclesiastical discipline must be purely moral or spiritual in its object, and not attended with any civil effects, it can derive no force whatever, but from its own justice, the approbation of an impartial public, and the countenance and blessing of the great Head of the church universal.

CHAPTER II.

OF THE CHURCH.

I. Jesus Christ, who is now exalted far above all principality and power, hath erected, in this world, a kingdom, which is his church.

II. The universal church consists of all those persons in every nation, together with their children, who make profession of the holy religion of *Christ*, and of submission to his laws.

III. As this immense multitude cannot meet together in one place, to hold communion, or to worship God, it is reasonable, and *warranted by Scripture example*, that they should be divided into many particular churches.

IV. A particular church consists of a number of professing Christians, with their offspring voluntarily associated together, for divine worship and godly living, agreeably to the Holy Scriptures; and submitting to a certain form of government.

CHAPTER III.

OF THE OFFICERS OF THE CHURCH.

I. Our blessed Lord at first collected his church out of different nations, and formed it into one body, by the mission of men endued with miraculous gifts, which have long since ceased.

II. The ordinary and perpetual officers in the church are, *Bishops*, or *Pastors*; the representatives of the people, usually styled *Ruling Elders*, and *Deacons*.

CHAPTER IV.

OF BISHOPS OR PASTORS.

The *pastoral* office is the first in the church, both for dignity and usefulness. *The person who fills this office*, hath, in the Scripture, obtained different names expressive of his various duties. As he has the oversight of the flock of Christ, he is termed Bishop.* As he feeds them with spiritual food he is termed Pastor. As he serves Christ in his church, he is termed Minister. As it is his duty to be grave and prudent, and an example of the flock, and to govern well in the house and kingdom of Christ, he is termed Presbyter or Elder. As he is the messenger of God, he is termed the Angel of the church. As he is sent to declare the will of God to sinners, and to beseech them to be reconciled to God through Christ, he is termed Ambassador. And as he dispenses the manifold grace of God, and the ordinances instituted by Christ, he is termed Steward of the mysteries of God.

CHAPTER V.

OF RULING ELDERS.

Ruling elders are properly the representatives of the people, chosen by them for the purpose of exercising government and discipline, in conjunction with pastors or ministers. This office has been understood, by a great part of the Protestant Reformed Churches, to be designated, in the Holy Scriptures, by the title of government; and of those who rule well, but do not labor in the word and doctrine.

CHAPTER VI.

OF DEACONS.

The Scriptures clearly point out deacons as distinct officers in the church, whose business it is to take care of the poor, and to distribute among them the collections which may be raised for their use. To them also may be properly committed the management of the temporal affairs of the church.

---

* As the office and character of the gospel minister is particularly and fully described in the Holy Scriptures under the title of Bishop; and as this term is peculiarly expressive of his duty as an overseer of the flock, it ought not to be rejected.

CHAPTER VII.

OF ORDINANCES IN A PARTICULAR CHURCH.

The ordinances, established by Christ, the head, in a particular church, which is regularly constituted with its proper officers, are, prayer; singing praises; reading, expounding, and preaching the word of God; administering baptism and the Lord's supper; public solemn fasting and thanksgiving; catechising; making collections for the poor, and other pious purposes; exercising discipline; and blessing the people.

CHAPTER VIII.

OF CHURCH-GOVERNMENT, AND THE SEVERAL KINDS OF JUDICATORIES.

I. It is absolutely necessary that the government of the church be exercised under some certain and definite form. And we hold it to be expedient and agreeable to Scripture and the practice of the primitive Christians, that the church be governed by congregational, presbyterial, and synodical assemblies. In full consistency with this belief, we embrace, in the spirit of charity, those Christians who differ from us, in opinion or in practice, on these subjects.

II. These assemblies ought not to possess any civil jurisdiction, nor to inflict any civil penalties. Their power is wholly moral or spiritual, and that only ministerial and declarative. They possess the right of requiring obedience to the laws of Christ; and of excluding the disobedient and disorderly, from the privileges of the church. To give efficiency, however, to this necessary and Scriptural authority, they possess the powers requisite for obtaining evidence and inflicting censure: They can call before them any offender against the order and government of the church; they can require members of their own society, to appear and give testimony in the cause; but the highest punishment, to which their authority extends, is to exclude the contumacious and impenitent from the congregation of believers.

CHAPTER IX.

OF THE CHURCH-SESSION.

I. The church-session consists of the pastor or pastors, and ruling elders, of a particular congregation.

II. Of this judicatory, two elders, if there be as many in the congregation, with the pastor, shall be necessary to constitute a quorum.

III. The pastor of the congregation shall always be the moderator of the session; except when, for prudential reasons, it may appear advisable that some other minister should be invited to preside; in which case the pastor may, with the concurrence of the session, invite such other minister as they may see meet, belonging to the same Presbytery, to preside in that case. The same expedient may be adopted in case of the sickness or absence of the pastor.

IV. It is expedient, at every meeting of the session, more especially when constituted for judicial business, that there be a presiding minister. When, therefore, a church is without a pastor, the moderator of the session shall be, either the minister appointed for that purpose by the Presbytery, or one invited by the session to preside on a particular occasion. But where it is impracticable, without great inconvenience, to procure the attendance of such a moderator, the session may proceed without it.

V. In congregations where there are two or more pastors, they shall, when present, alternately preside in the session.

VI. The church session is charged with maintaining the spiritual government of the congregation; for which purpose, they have power to inquire into the knowledge and Christian conduct of the members of the church; to call before them offenders and witnesses, being members of their own congregation, and to introduce other witnesses, where it may be necessary to bring the process to issue, and when they can be procured to attend; to receive members into the church, to admonish, to rebuke, to suspend, or exclude from the sacraments, those who are found to deserve censure; to concert the best measures for promoting the spiritual interests of the congregation; and to appoint delegates to the higher judicatories of the church.

VII. The pastor has power to convene the session when he may judge it requisite; and he shall always convene them when requested to do so by any two of the elders. The session shall also convene when directed so to do by the Presbytery.

VIII. Every session shall keep a fair record of its proceedings; which record shall be, at least once in every year, submitted to the inspection of the Presbytery.

IX. It is important that every church session keep a fair register of marriages; of baptisms, with the times of the birth of the individuals baptized; of persons admitted to the Lord's table, and of the deaths, and other removals of church members.

CHAPTER X.

OF THE PRESBYTERY.

I. The Church being divided into many separate congregations, these need mutual counsel and assistance, in order to preserve soundness of doctrine, and regularity of discipline, and to enter into common measures for promoting knowledge and religion, and for preventing infidelity, error, and immorality. Hence arise the importance and usefulness of Presbyterial and Synodical assemblies.

II. A Presbytery consists of all ministers, and one ruling elder from each congregation, within a certain district.

III. Every congregation, which has a stated pastor, has a right to be represented by one elder; and every collegiate church by two or more elders, in proportion to the number of its pastors.

IV. Where two or more congregations are united under one pastor, all such congregations shall have but one elder to represent them.

V. Every vacant congregation, which is regularly organized, shall be entitled to be represented by a ruling elder in Presbytery.

VI. Every elder not known to the Presbytery shall produce a certificate of his regular appointment from the church which he represents.

VII. Any three ministers, and as many elders as may be present, belonging to the Presbytery, being met at the time and place appointed, shall be a quorum competent to proceed to business.

VIII. The Presbytery has power to receive and issue appeals from church-sessions, and references brought before them in an orderly manner; to examine and license candidates for the holy ministry; to ordain, install, remove, and judge ministers; to examine and approve or censure the records of church-sessions; to resolve questions of doctrine or discipline seriously and reasonably proposed; to condemn erroneous opinions which injure the purity or peace of the church; to visit particular churches, for the purpose of inquiring into their state, and redressing the evils that may have arisen in them; to unite or divide congregations, at the request of the people; or to form and receive new congregations; and, in general, to order whatever pertains to the spiritual welfare of the churches under their care.

IX. It shall be the duty of the Presbytery to keep a full and fair record of their proceedings, and to report to the Synod, every year, licensures, ordinations, the receiving or dismissing of members, the removal of members by death, the union or division of congregations, or the formation of new ones, and, in general, all the important changes which may have taken place within their bounds in the course of the year.

X. The Presbytery shall meet on its own adjournment; and when any emergency shall require a meeting sooner than the time to which it stands adjourned, the moderator, or, in case of his absence, death, or inability to act, the stated clerk, shall, with the concurrence, or at the request of two ministers and two elders, the elders being of different congregations, call a special meeting. For this purpose, he shall send a circular letter, specifying the particular business of the intended meeting, to every minister belonging to the Presbytery, and to the session of every vacant congregation, in due time previous to the meeting; which shall not be less than ten days. And nothing shall be transacted, at such special meeting, besides the particular business for which the judicatory has been thus convened.

XI. At every meeting of Presbytery, a sermon shall be delivered, if convenient; and every particular session shall be opened and closed with prayer.

XII. Ministers in good standing in other Presbyteries, or in any sister churches, who may happen to be present, may be invited to sit with the Presbytery, as corresponding members. Such members shall be entitled to deliberate and advise, but not to vote in any decisions of the Presbytery.

CHAPTER XI.

OF THE SYNOD.

I. As a Presbytery is a convention of the Bishops and Elders within a certain district: so a Synod is a convention of the Bishops and Elders within a larger district, including at least three Presbyteries. The ratio of the representation of elders in the Synod is the same as in the Presbytery.

II. Any seven ministers, belonging to the Synod, who shall convene at the time and place of meeting, with as many elders as may be present, shall be a quorum to transact synodical business; provided not more than three of the said ministers belong to one Presbytery.

III. The same rule, as to corresponding members, which was laid down with respect to the Presbytery, shall apply to the Synod.

IV. The Synod has power to receive and issue all appeals regularly brought up from the Presbyteries; to decide on all references made to them; to review the records of Presbyteries, and approve or censure them; to redress whatever has been done by Presbyteries contrary to order; to take effectual care that Presbyteries observe the Constitution of the church; to erect new Presbyteries, and unite or divide those which were before erected; generally to take such order with respect to the Presbyteries, sessions, and people under their care, as may be in conformity with the word of God and the established rules, and which tend to promote the edification of the church; and, finally, to propose to the General Assembly, for their adoption, such measures as may be of common advantage to the whole church.

V. The Synod shall convene at least once in each year; at the opening of which a sermon shall be delivered by the moderator, or, in case of his absence, by some other member; and every particular session shall be opened and closed with prayer.

VI. It shall be the duty of the Synod to keep full and fair records of its proceedings, to submit them annually to the inspection of the General Assembly, and to report to the Assembly the number of its Presbyteries, and of the members and alterations of the Presbyteries.

CHAPTER XII.

OF THE GENERAL ASSEMBLY.*

I. The General Assembly is the highest judicatory of the Presbyterian Church. It shall represent, in one body, all the particular churches of this denomination; and shall bear the title of THE GENERAL ASSEMBLY OF

---

* The radical principles of Presbyterian church government and discipline are:—That the several different congregations of believers, taken collectively, constitute one church of Christ, called emphatically *the church;*—that a larger part of *the church*, or a representation of it, should govern a smaller, or determine matters of controversy which arise therein:—that, in like manner, a representation of the whole should govern and determine in regard to every part, and to all the parts united; that is, that *a majority shall govern:* and consequently that appeals may be carried from lower to higher judicatories, till they be finally decided by the collected wisdom and united voice of *the whole church.* For these principles and this procedure, the example of the apostles, and the practice of the primitive church, is considered as authority.

THE PRESBYTERIAN CHURCH IN THE UNITED STATES OF AMERICA.

II. The General Assembly shall consist of an equal delegation of Bishops and Elders from each Presbytery, in the following proportion: viz., each Presbytery consisting of not more than twenty-four ministers, shall send one minister and one elder; and each Presbytery consisting of more than twenty-four ministers shall send two ministers and two elders; and in the like proportion for every twenty-four ministers in any Presbytery; and these delegates, so appointed, shall be styled *Commissioners to the General Assembly.*

III. Any fourteen or more of these commissioners, one half of whom shall be ministers, being met on the day, and at the place appointed, shall be a quorum for the transaction of business.

IV. The General Assembly shall receive and issue all appeals and references which may be regularly brought before them from the inferior judicatories. They shall review the records of every Synod, and approve or censure them; they shall give their advice and instruction in all cases submitted to them in conformity with the constitution of the church; and they shall constitute the bond of union, peace, correspondence, and mutual confidence among all our churches.

V. To the General Assembly also belongs the power of deciding in all controversies respecting doctrine and discipline; of reproving, warning, or bearing testimony against error in doctrine, or immorality in practice, in any church, Presbytery, or Synod; of erecting new Synods when it may be judged necessary; of superintending the concerns of the whole church; of corresponding with foreign churches, on such terms as may be agreed upon by the Assembly and the corresponding body; of suppressing schismatical contentions and disputations; and, in general, of recommending and attempting reformation of manners, and the promotion of charity, truth, and holiness, through all the churches under their care.

VI. Before any overtures or regulations proposed by the Assembly to be established as constitutional rules, shall be obligatory on the churches, it shall be necessary to transmit them to all the Presbyteries, and to receive the returns of at least a majority of them, in writing, approving thereof.

VII. The General Assembly shall meet at least once in every year. On the day appointed for that purpose the moderator of the last Assembly, if present, or in case of his absence, some other minister, shall open the meeting with a sermon, and preside until a new moderator be chosen. No commissioner shall have a right to deliberate or vote in the Assembly, until his name shall have been enrolled by the clerk, and his commission examined, and filed among the papers of the Assembly.

VIII. Each session of the Assembly shall be opened and closed with prayer. And the whole business of the Assembly being finished, and the vote taken for dissolving the present Assembly, the moderator shall say from the chair,—"By virtue of the authority delegated to me, by the church, let this General Assembly be dissolved, and I do hereby dissolve it, and require another General Assembly, chosen in the same manner, to meet at   on the   day of   A. D.   "—after which he shall pray and return thanks, and pronounce on those present the apostolic benediction.

of these offices, and shall have declared his willingness to accept thereof, he shall. be set apart in the following manner:

IV. After sermon, the minister shall state, in a concise manner, the warrant and nature of the office of Ruling Elder or Deacon, together with the character proper to be sustained, and the duties to be fulfilled by the officer elect: having done this, he shall propose to the candidate, in the presence of the congregation, the following questions: viz.—

1. Do you believe the Scriptures of the Old and New Testaments to be the word of God, the only infallible rule of faith and practice?

2. Do you sincerely receive and adopt the Confession of Faith of this church, as containing the system of doctrine taught in the Holy Scriptures?

3. Do you approve of the government and discipline of the Presbyterian Church in these United States?

4. Do you accept the office of Ruling Elder (or Deacon, as the case may be) in this congregation, and promise faithfully to perform all the duties thereof?

5. Do you promise to study the peace, unity, and purity of the church?

The Elder, or Deacon elect, having answered these questions in the affirmative, the minister shall address to the members of the church the following questions:—viz.

Do you, the members of this church, acknowledge and receive this brother as a Ruling Elder (or Deacon), and do you promise to yield him all that honor, encouragement, and obedience, in the Lord, to which his office, according to the word of God, and the Constitution of this church, entitles him?

The members of the church having answered this question in the affirmative, by holding up their right hands, the minister shall proceed to set apart the candidate, by prayer, to the office of Ruling Elder (or Deacon, as the case may be), and shall give to him, and to the congregation, an exhortation suited to the occasion.

V. Where there is an existing session it is proper that the members of that body, at the close of the service, and in the face of the congregation, take the newly ordained Elder by the hand, saying in words to this purpose,—" We give you the right hand of fellowship, to take part of this office with us."

VI. The offices of Ruling Elder and Deacon are both perpetual, and can not be laid aside at pleasure. No person can be divested of either office but by deposition. Yet an Elder or Deacon may become, by age or infirmity, incapable of performing the duties of his office: or he may, though chargeable with neither heresy nor immorality, become unacceptable, in his official character, to a majority of the congregation to which he belongs. In either of these cases he may, as often happens with respect to a minister, cease to be an acting Elder or Deacon.

VII. Whenever a Ruling Elder or Deacon, from either of these causes, or from any other, not inferring crime, shall be incapable of serving the church to edification, the session shall take order on the subject, and state the fact, together with the reasons of it, on their records. *Provided always,* that nothing of this kind shall be done without the concurrence of the individual in question, unless by the advice of Presbytery.

CHAPTER XIII.

OF ELECTING AND ORDAINING RULING ELDERS AND DEACONS.

I. HAVING defined the officers of the church, and the judicatories by which it shall be governed, it is proper here to prescribe the mode in which ecclesiastical rulers should be ordained to their respective offices, as well as some of the principles by which they shall be regulated in discharging their several duties.

II. Every congregation shall elect persons to the office of Ruling Elder, and to the office of Deacon, or either of them, in the mode most approved and in use in that congregation. But in all cases the persons elected must be male members in full communion in the church in which they are to exercise their office.

III. When any person shall have been elected to either

CHAPTER XIV.

OF LICENSING CANDIDATES OR PROBATIONERS TO PREACH THE GOSPEL.

I. THE Holy Scriptures require that some trial be previously had of those who are to be ordained to the ministry of the gospel, that this sacred office may not be degraded, by being committed to weak or unworthy men; and that the churches may have an opportunity to form a better judgment respecting the talents of those by whom they are to be instructed and governed. For this purpose Presbyteries shall license probationers to preach the gospel, that after a competent trial of their talents, and receiving from the churches a good report, they may, in due time, ordain them to the sacred office.

II. Every candidate for licensure shall be taken on trials by that Presbytery to which he most naturally belongs: and he shall be considered as most naturally belonging to that Presbytery within the bounds of which he has ordinarily resided. But in case any candidate should find it more convenient to put himself under the care of a Presbytery at a distance from that to which he most naturally belongs, he may be received by the said Presbytery, on his producing testimonials either from the Presbytery within the bounds of which he has commonly resided, or from any two ministers of that Presbytery in good standing, of his exemplary piety, and other requisite qualifications.

III. It is proper and requisite that candidates applying to the Presbytery to be licensed to preach the gospel, produce satisfactory testimonials of their good moral character, and of their being regular members of some particular church. And it is the duty of the Presbytery, for their satisfaction with regard to the real piety of such candidates, to examine them respecting their experimental acquaintance with religion, and the motives which influence them to desire the sacred office. This examination shall be close and particular, and, in most cases, may best be conducted in the presence of the Presbytery only. And it is recommended that the candidate be also required to produce a diploma of bachelor or master of arts, from some college or university: or, at least, authentic testimonials of his having gone through a regular course of learning.

IV. Because it is highly reproachful to religion, and dangerous to the church, to intrust the holy ministry to weak and ignorant men, the Presbytery shall try each candidate, as to his knowledge of the Latin language, and of the original languages in which the Holy Scriptures were written. They shall also examine him on the arts and sciences; on theology, natural and revealed; and on ecclesiastical history, the sacraments, and church government. And in order to make trial of his talents to explain and vindicate, and practically to enforce, the doctrines of the gospel, the Presbytery shall require of him,

1. A Latin *exegesis* on some common head in divinity.
2 A *critical exercise;* in which the candidate shall give a specimen of his taste and judgment in sacred criticism; presenting an explication of the original text, stating its connection, illustrating its force and beauties, removing its difficulties, and solving any important questions which it may present.
3. A *lecture*, or exposition of several verses of Scripture; and,
4. A *popular* sermon.

V. These, or other similar exercises, at the discretion of the Presbytery, shall be exhibited until they shall have obtained satisfaction as to the candidate's piety, literature, and aptness to teach in the churches. The lecture and popular sermon, if the Presbytery think proper, may be delivered in the presence of a congregation.

VI. That the most effectual measures may be taken to guard against the admission of insufficient men into the sacred office, it is recommended, that no candidate, except in extraordinary cases, be licensed, unless, after his having completed the usual course of academical studies, he shall have studied divinity at least two years, under some approved divine or professor of theology.

VII. If the Presbytery be satisfied with his trials, they shall then proceed to license him in the following manner: The moderator shall propose to him the following questions: viz.

1. Do you believe the Scriptures of the Old and New Testaments to be the word of God, the only infallible rule of faith and practice?
2. Do you sincerely receive and adopt the Confession of Faith of this church, as containing the system of doctrine taught in the Holy Scriptures?
3. Do you promise to study the peace, unity, and purity of the church?
4. Do you promise to submit yourself, in the Lord, to the government of this Presbytery, or of any other Presbytery in the bounds of which you may be called?

VIII. The candidate having answered these questions in the affirmative, and the moderator having offered up a prayer suitable to the occasion, he shall address himself to the candidate to the following purpose:—"In the name of the Lord Jesus Christ, and by that authority which he hath given to the church for its edification, we do license you to preach the gospel, wherever God in his providence

may call you: and for this purpose, may the blessing of God rest upon you, and the Spirit of Christ fill your heart —*Amen!*" And record shall be made of the licensure in the following or like form: viz.

At ———— the — day of ———— the Presbytery of ———— having received testimonials in favor of——— of his having gone through a regular course of literature; of his good moral character; and of his being in the communion of the church; proceeded to take the usual parts of trial for his licensure: and he having given satisfaction as to his accomplishments in literature; as to his experimental acquaintance with religion; and as to his proficiency in divinity and other studies; the Presbytery did, and hereby do, express their approbation of all these parts of trial: and he having adopted the Confession of Faith of this church, and satisfactorily answered the questions appointed to be put to candidates to be licensed; the Presbytery did, and hereby do license him, the said ———— to preach the Gospel of Christ, as a probationer for the holy ministry, within the bounds of this Presbytery, or wherever else he shall be orderly called.

IX. When any candidate for licensure shall have occasion while his trials are going on, to remove from the bounds of his own Presbytery into those of another, it shall be considered as regular for the latter Presbytery, on his producing proper testimonials from the former, to take up his trials at the point at which they were left, and conduct them to a conclusion, in the same manner as if they had been commenced by themselves.

X. In like manner, when any candidate, after licensure, shall, by the permission of his Presbytery, remove without its limits, an extract of the record of his licensure, accompanied with a Presbyterial recommendation, signed by the clerk, shall be his testimonials to the Presbytery under whose care he shall come.

XI. When a licentiate shall have been preaching for a considerable time, and his services do not appear to be edifying to the churches, the Presbytery may, if they think proper, recall his license.

CHAPTER XV.

OF THE ELECTION AND ORDINATION OF BISHOPS OR PASTORS, AND EVANGELISTS.

I. WHEN any probationer shall have preached so much to the satisfaction of any congregation, as that the people appear prepared to elect a pastor, the session shall take measures to convene them for this purpose: and it shall always be the duty of the session to convene them, when a majority of the persons entitled to vote in the case, shall, by a petition, request that a meeting may be called.

II. When such a meeting is intended, the session shall solicit the presence and counsel of some neighboring minister to assist them in conducting the election contemplated, unless highly inconvenient on account of distance; in which case they may proceed without such assistance.

III. On a Lord's day, immediately after public worship, it shall be intimated from the pulpit, that all the members of that congregation are requested to meet on ———— ensuing, at the church, or usual place for holding public worship; then and there, if it be agreeable to them, to proceed to the election of a pastor for that congregation.

IV. On the day appointed, the minister invited to preside, if he be present, shall, if it be deemed expedient, preach a sermon; and after sermon he shall announce to the people, that he will immediately proceed to take the votes of the electors of that congregation for a pastor, if such be their desire: and when this desire shall be expressed by a majority of voices, he shall then proceed to take votes accordingly. In this election, no person shall be entitled to vote who refuses to submit to the censures of the church, regularly administered; or who does not contribute his just proportion, according to his own engagements, or the rules of that congregation, to all its necessary expenses.

V. When the votes are taken, if it appear that a large minority of the people are averse from the candidate who has a majority of votes, and can not be induced to concur in the call, the presiding minister shall endeavor to dissuade the congregation from prosecuting it further. But if the people be nearly or entirely unanimous; or if the majority shall insist upon their right to call a pastor, the presiding minister, in that case, after using his utmost endeavors to persuade the congregation to unanimity, shall proceed to draw a call, in due form, and to have it subscribed by the electors ; certifying at the same time, in writing, the number and circumstances of those who do not concur in the call: all which proceedings shall be laid before the Presbytery, together with the call.

VI. The call shall be in the following or like form: viz.

The congregation of —— being, on sufficient grounds, well satisfied with the ministerial qualifications of you —— ——, and having good hopes, from our past experience of your labors, that your ministrations in the Gospel will be profitable to our spiritual interests, do earnestly call and desire you to undertake the pastoral office in said congregation ; promising you, in the discharge of your duty, all proper support, encouragement, and obedience in the Lord. And that you may be free from worldly cares and avocations, we hereby promise and oblige ourselves to pay to you the sum of —— in regular quarterly (or half yearly, or yearly) payments, during the time of your being and continuing the regular pastor of this church. In testimony whereof, we have respectively subscribed our names, this — day of —, A. D. —
Attested by A. B., Moderator of the meeting.

VII. But if any congregation choose to subscribe their call by their elders and deacons, or by their trustees, or by a select committee, they shall be at liberty to do so. But it shall, in such cases, be fully certified to the Presbytery, by the minister, or other person who presided, that the persons signing have been appointed for this purpose, by a public vote of the congregation ; and that the call has been, in all other respects, prepared as above directed.

VIII. When a call shall be presented to any minister or candidate, it shall always be viewed as a sufficient petition from the people for his installment. The acceptance of a call, by a minister or candidate, shall always be considered as a request, on his part, to be installed at the same time. And, when a candidate shall be ordained, in consequence of a call from any congregation, the Presbytery shall, at the same time, if practicable, install him pastor of that congregation.

IX. The call, thus prepared, shall be presented to the Presbytery, under whose care the person called shall be; that, if the Presbytery think it expedient to present the call to him, it may be accordingly presented: and no minister or candidate shall receive a call but through the hands of the Presbytery.

X. If the call be to the licentiate of another Presbytery, in that case the commissioners, deputed from the congregation to prosecute the call, shall produce to that judicatory a certificate from their own Presbytery, regularly attested by the moderator and clerk, that the call has been laid before them, and that it is in order. If that Presbytery present the call to their licentiate, and he be disposed to accept it, they shall then dismiss him from their jurisdiction, and require him to repair to that Presbytery, into the bounds of which he is called, and there to submit himself to the usual trials preparatory to ordination.

XI. Trials for ordination, especially in a different Presbytery from that in which the candidate was licensed, shall consist of a careful examination as to his acquaintance with experimental religion ; as to his knowledge of philosophy, theology, ecclesiastical history, the Greek and Hebrew languages, and such other branches of learning as to the Presbytery may appear requisite; and as to his knowledge of the constitution, the rules and principles of the government, and discipline of the church ; together with such written discourse, or discourses, founded on the word of God, as the Presbytery shall seem proper. The Presbytery, being fully satisfied with his qualifications for the sacred office, shall appoint a day for his ordination, which ought to be, if convenient, in that church of which he is to be the minister. It is also recommended that a fast-day be observed in the congregation previous to the day of ordination.

XII. The day appointed for ordination being come, and the Presbytery convened, a member of the Presbytery, previously appointed to that duty, shall preach a sermon adapted to the occasion. The same, or another member

appointed to preside, shall afterward briefly recite from the pulpit, in the audience of the people, the proceedings of the Presbytery preparatory to this transaction: he shall point out the nature and importance of the ordinance ; and endeavor to impress the audience with a proper sense of the solemnity of the transaction.

Then, addressing himself to the candidate, he shall propose to him the following questions: viz.

1. "Do you believe the Scriptures of the Old and New Testaments to be the word of God, the only infallible rule of faith and practice ?

2. "Do you sincerely receive and adopt the confession of faith of this church, as containing the system of doctrine taught in the Holy Scriptures ?

3. "Do you approve of the government and discipline of the Presbyterian Church in these United States?

4. "Do you promise subjection to your brethren in the Lord ?

5. "Have you been induced, as far as you know your own heart, to seek the office of the holy ministry, from love to God, and a sincere desire to promote his glory in the gospel of his Son ?

6. "Do you promise to be zealous and faithful in maintaining the truths of the Gospel and the purity and peace of the church; whatever persecution, or opposition, may arise unto you on that account?

7. "Do you engage to be faithful and diligent in the exercise of all private and personal duties, which become you as a Christian and a minister of the Gospel; as well as in all relative duties, and the public duties of your office ; endeavoring to adorn the profession of the Gospel by your conversation ; and walking with exemplary piety before the flock over which God shall make you overseer ?

8. "Are you now willing to take the charge of this congregation, agreeably to your declaration at accepting their call? And do you promise to discharge the duties of a pastor to them, as God shall give you strength ?"

XIII. The candidate having answered these questions in the affirmative, the presiding minister shall propose to the people the following questions :—

1. "Do you, the people of this congregation, continue to profess your readiness to receive —— ——, whom you have called to be your minister ?

2. "Do you promise to receive the word of truth from his mouth, with meekness and love; and to submit to him in the due exercise of discipline ?

3. "Do you promise to encourage him in his arduous labor, and to assist his endeavors for your instruction and spiritual edification ?

4. "And do you engage to continue to him, while he is your pastor, that competent worldly maintenance which you have promised; and whatever else you may see needful for the honour of religion, and his comfort among you ?"

XIV. The people having answered these questions in the affirmative, by holding up their right hands, the candidate shall kneel down in the most convenient part of the church. Then the presiding minister shall, by prayer, and with the laying on of the hands of the Presbytery, according to the apostolic example, solemnly ordain him to the holy office of the gospel ministry. Prayer being ended, he shall rise from his knees, and the minister who presides shall first, and afterwards all the members of the Presbytery in their order, take him by the right hand, saying, in words to this purpose, "We give you the right hand of fellowship, to take part of this ministry with us." After which the minister presiding, or some other appointed for the purpose, shall give a solemn charge in the name of God, to the newly ordained bishop, and to the people, to persevere in the discharge of their mutual duties ; and shall then, by prayer, recommend them both to the grace of God, and his holy keeping, and finally, after singing a psalm, shall dismiss the congregation with the usual blessing. And the Presbytery shall duly record the transaction.

XV. As it is sometimes desirable and important that a candidate who has not received a call to be the pastor of a particular congregation, should, nevertheless, be ordained to the work of the gospel ministry, as an evangelist to preach the gospel, administer sealing ordinances, and organize churches, in frontier or destitute settlements;

m this case, the last of the preceding questions shall be omitted, and the following used as a substitute: viz.

"Are you now willing to undertake the work of an evangelist; and do you promise to discharge the duties which may be incumbent on you in this character, as God shall give you strength?"

CHAPTER XVI.

OF TRANSLATION, OR REMOVING A MINISTER FROM ONE CHARGE TO ANOTHER.

I. No bishop shall be translated from one church to another, nor shall he receive any call for that purpose, but by the permission of the Presbytery.

II. Any church, desiring to have a settled minister from his present charge, shall, by commissioners properly authorized, represent to the Presbytery the ground on which they plead his removal. The Presbytery, having maturely considered their plea, may, according as it appears more or less reasonable, either recommend to them to desist from prosecuting the call, or may order it to be delivered to the minister to whom it is directed. If the parties be not prepared to have the matter issued at that Presbytery, a written citation shall be given to the minister and his congregation, to appear before the Presbytery at their next meeting. This citation shall be read from the pulpit in that church, by a member of the Presbytery appointed for that purpose, immediately after public worship; so that at least two Sabbaths shall intervene betwixt the citation and the meeting of the Presbytery at which the cause of translation is to be considered. The Presbytery being met, and having heard the parties, shall, upon the whole view of the case, either continue him in his former charge, or translate him, as they shall deem to be most for the peace and edification of the church; or refer the whole affair to the Synod at their next meeting, for their advice and direction.

III. When the congregation calling any settled minister is within the limits of another Presbytery, that congregation shall obtain leave from the Presbytery to which they belong, to apply to the Presbytery of which he is a member: and that Presbytery, having cited him and his congregation as before directed, shall proceed to hear and issue the cause. If they agree to the translation, they shall release him from his present charge; and having given him proper testimonials, shall require him to repair to that Presbytery, within the bounds of which the congregation calling him lies, that the proper steps may be taken for his regular settlement in that congregation; and the Presbytery to which the congregation belongs, having received an authenticated certificate of his release, under the hand of the clerk of that Presbytery, shall proceed to install him in the congregation, as soon as convenient. Provided always, that no bishop or pastor shall be translated, without his own consent previously obtained.

IV. When any minister is to be settled in a congregation, the installment, which consists in constituting a pastoral relation between him and the people of that particular church, may be performed either by the Presbytery, or by a committee appointed, for that purpose, as may appear most expedient: and the following order shall be observed therein:

V. A day shall be appointed for the installment, at such time as may appear most convenient, and due notice thereof given to the congregation.

VI. When the Presbytery, or committee, shall be convened and constituted, on the day appointed, a sermon shall be delivered, by some one of the members previously appointed thereto; immediately after which, the bishop who is to preside shall state to the congregation the design of their meeting, and briefly recite the proceedings of the Presbytery relative thereto. And then, addressing himself to the minister to be installed, shall propose to him the following or similar questions:

1. "Are you now willing to take the charge of this congregation, as their pastor, agreeably to your declaration at accepting their call?

2. "Do you conscientiously believe and declare, as far as you know your own heart, that, in taking upon you this charge, you are influenced by a sincere desire to promote the glory of God, and the good of his church?

3. "Do you solemnly promise, that, by the assistance of the grace of God, you will endeavor faithfully to discharge all the duties of a pastor of this congregation: and will be careful to maintain a deportment, in all respects becoming a minister of the Gospel of Christ, agreeably to your ordination engagements?"

To all these having received satisfactory answers, he shall propose to the people the same, or like, questions as those directed under the head of ordination; which having been also satisfactorily answered, by holding up the right hand in testimony of assent, he shall solemnly pronounce and declare the said minister to be regularly constituted the pastor of that congregation. A charge shall then be given to both parties, as directed in the case of ordination; and, after prayer, and singing a psalm adapted to the transaction, the congregation shall be dismissed with the usual benediction.

VII. It is highly becoming, that, after the solemnity of the installment, the heads of families of that congregation who are then present, or at least the elders and those appointed to take care of the temporal concerns of that church, should come forward to their pastor, and give him their right hand, in token of cordial reception and affectionate regard.

CHAPTER XVII.

OF RESIGNING A PASTORAL CHARGE.

When any minister shall labor under such grievances in his congregation, as that he shall desire leave to resign his pastoral charge, the Presbytery shall cite the congregation to appear, by their commissioners, at their next meeting, to show cause, if any they have, why the Presbytery should not accept the resignation. If the congregation fail to appear, or if their reasons for retaining their pastor be deemed by the Presbytery insufficient, he shall have leave granted to resign his pastoral charge; of which due record shall be made: and that church shall be held to be vacant, till supplied again, in an orderly manner, with another minister: and if any congregation shall desire to be released from their pastor, a similar process, *mutatis mutandis*, shall be observed.

CHAPTER XVIII.

OF MISSIONS.

When vacancies become so numerous in any Presbytery that they cannot be supplied with the frequent administration of the word and ordinances, it shall be proper for such Presbytery, or any vacant congregation within their bounds, with the leave of the Presbytery, to apply to any other Presbytery, or to any Synod, or to the General Assembly, for such assistance as they can afford. And, when any Presbytery shall send any of their ministers or probationers to distant vacancies, the missionary shall be ready to produce his credentials to the Presbytery or Presbyteries, through the bounds of which he may pass, or at least to a committee thereof, and obtain their approbation. And the General Assembly may, of their own knowledge, send missions to any part to plant churches, or to supply vacancies: and, for this purpose, may direct any Presbytery to ordain evangelists, or ministers, without relation to particular churches: *provided always*, that such missions be made with the consent of the parties appointed; and that the judicatory sending them, make the necessary provision for their support and reward in the performance of this service.

CHAPTER XIX.

OF MODERATORS.

I. It is equally necessary in the judicatories of the church, as in other assemblies, that there should be a moderator or president; that the business may be conducted with order and dispatch.

II. The moderator is to be considered as possessing, by delegation from the whole body, all authority necessary for the preservation of order; for convening and adjourning the judicatory; and directing its operations according to the rules of the church. He is to propose to the judicatory every subject of deliberation that comes before them. He may propose what appears to him the most regular and speedy way of bringing any business to issue. He shall prevent the members from interrupting each other; and require them, in speaking, always to address the chair. He shall prevent a speaker from deviating from the subject, and from using personal reflections. He shall silence those who refuse to obey order. He shall prevent members who attempt to leave the judicatory without leave obtained from him. He shall, at a proper season, when the deliberations are ended, put the question and call the votes. If the judicatory be equally divided, he shall possess the casting vote. If he be not willing to decide, he shall put the question a second time; and if the judicatory be again equally divided, and he decline to give his vote, the question shall be lost. In all questions he shall give a concise and clear state of the object of the vote; and the vote being taken, shall then declare how the question is decided. And he shall likewise be empowered, on any extraordinary emergency, to convene the judicatory, by his circular letter, before the ordinary time of meeting.

III. The moderator of the Presbytery shall be chosen from year to year, or at every meeting of the Presbytery, as the Presbytery may think best. The moderator of the Synod, and of the General Assembly, shall be chosen at each meeting, of those judicatories: and the moderator, or, in case of his absence, another member appointed for the purpose, shall open the next meeting with a sermon, and shall hold the chair till a new moderator be chosen.

CHAPTER XX.

OF CLERKS.

EVERY judicatory shall choose a clerk, to record their transactions, whose continuance shall be during pleasure. It shall be the duty of the clerk, besides recording the transactions, to preserve the records carefully; and to grant extracts from them, whenever properly required; and such extracts, under the hand of the clerk, shall be considered as authentic vouchers of the fact which they declare, in any ecclesiastical judicatory, and to every part of the church.

CHAPTER XXI.

OF VACANT CONGREGATIONS ASSEMBLING FOR PUBLIC WORSHIP.

CONSIDERING the great importance of weekly assembling the people, for the public worship of God; in order thereby to improve their knowledge; to confirm their habits of worship, and their desire of the public ordinances; to augment their reverence for the most high God; and to promote the charitable affections which unite men most firmly in society: it is recommended that every vacant congregation meet together, on the Lord's day, at one or more places, for the purpose of

prayer, singing praises, and reading the Holy Scriptures, together with the works of such approved divines, as the Presbytery, within whose bounds they are, may recommend, and they may be able to procure; and that the elders or deacons be the persons who shall preside, and select the portions of Scripture, and of the other books to be read; and to see that the whole be conducted in a becoming and orderly manner.

CHAPTER XXII.

OF COMMISSIONERS TO THE GENERAL ASSEMBLY.

I. THE commissioners to the General Assembly shall always be appointed by the Presbytery from which they come, at its last stated meeting, immediately preceding the meeting of the General Assembly; provided, that there be a sufficient interval between that time and the meeting of the Assembly, for the commissioners to attend to their duty in due season; otherwise, the Presbytery may make the appointment at any stated meeting, not more than seven months preceding the meeting of the Assembly. And as much as possible to prevent all failure in the representation of the Presbyteries, arising from unforeseen accidents to those first appointed, it may be expedient for each Presbytery, in the room of each commissioner, to appoint also an alternate commissioner to supply his place, in case of necessary absence.

II. Each commissioner, before his name shall be enrolled as a member of the Assembly, shall produce from his Presbytery, a commission under the hand of the moderator and clerk, in the following or like form: viz.

"The Presbytery of ——— being met at ——— on the ——— day of ——— do hereby appoint ——— bishop of the congregation of ——— [or ——— ruling elder in the congregation of ——— as the case may be;] (to which the Presbytery may, if they think proper, make a substitution in the following form:) or, in case of his absence, then ——— bishop of the congregation of ——— [or ——— ruling elder in the congregation of ——— as the case may be:] to be a commissioner, on behalf of this Presbytery, to the next General Assembly of the Presbyterian Church in the United States of America, to meet at ——— on the ——— day of ——— A. D. ——— or wherever, and whenever the said Assembly may happen to sit; to consult, vote, and determine, on all things that may come before that body, according to the principles and constitution of this church, and the word of God. And of his diligence herein, he is to render an account at his return.

"*Signed by order of the Presbytery,*

"——— ——— *Moderator.*
"——— ——— *Clerk.*"

And the Presbytery shall make record of the appointment.

III. In order, as far as possible, to procure a respectable and full delegation to all our judicatories, it is proper that the expenses of ministers and elders in their attendance on these judicatories, be defrayed by the bodies which they respectively represent.

BOOK II.

OF DISCIPLINE.

CHAPTER I.

GENERAL PRINCIPLES OF DISCIPLINE.

I. DISCIPLINE is the exercise of that authority, and the application of that system of laws, which the Lord Jesus Christ hath appointed in his church.

II. The exercise of discipline is highly important and necessary. Its ends are, the removal of offences; the

vindication of the honor of Christ; the promotion of the purity and general edification of the church; and also the benefit of the offender himself.

III. An offence is anything in the principles or practice of a church-member, which is contrary to the word of God; or which, if it be not in its own nature sinful, may tempt others to sin, or mar their spiritual edification.

IV. Nothing, therefore, ought to be considered by any judicatory as an offence, or admitted as matter of accusation, which cannot be proved to be such from Scripture, or from the regulations and practice of the church, founded on Scripture; and which does not involve those evils which discipline is intended to prevent.

V. The exercise of discipline, in such a manner as to edify the church, requires not only much of the spirit of piety, but also much prudence and discretion. It becomes the rulers of the church, therefore, to take into view all the circumstances which may give a different character to conduct, and render it more or less offensive; and which may, of course, require a very different mode of proceeding in similar cases, at different times, for the attainment of the same end.

VI. All baptized persons are members of the church, are under its care, and subject to its government and discipline; and, when they have arrived at the years of discretion, they are bound to perform all the duties of church-members.

VI. Offences are either *private* or *public;* to each of which appropriate modes of proceeding belong.

CHAPTER II.

OF PRIVATE OFFENCES.

I. PRIVATE offences are such as are known only to an individual, or, at most, to a very few.

II. Private offences ought not to be immediately prosecuted before a church judicatory, because the objects of discipline may be quite as well, and, in many cases, much better, attained, by a different course; and because a public prosecution, in such circumstances, would tend unnecessarily to spread the knowledge of offences, to exasperate and harden offenders, to extend angry and vexatious litigation, and thus to render the discipline of the church more injurious than the original offence.

III. No complaint, or information, on the subject of personal and private injuries, shall be admitted, unless those means of reconciliation, and of privately reclaiming the offender, have been used, which are required by Christ, Mat. xviii. 15, 16. And, in case of offences, which, though not personal, are private, that is, known only to one, or a very few, it is proper to take the same steps, as far as circumstances admit.

IV. Those who bring information of private and personal injuries before judicatories, without having taken these previous steps, shall themselves be censured, as guilty of an offence against the peace and order of the church.

V. If any person shall spread the knowledge of an offence, unless so far as shall be unavoidable, in prosecuting it before the proper judicatory, or in the due performance of some other indispensable duty, he shall be liable to censure as a slanderer of his brethren.

CHAPTER III.

OF PUBLIC OFFENCES.

I. A PUBLIC offence is that which is attended with such circumstances as to require the cognizance of a church-judicatory.

II. This is always the case, when an offence is either so notorious and scandalous, as that no private steps would obviate its injurious effects; or when, though originally known to one, or a few, the private steps have been ineffectual, and there is, obviously, no way of removing the offence, but by means of a judicial process.

III. An offence, gross in itself, and known to several, may be so circumstanced, that it plainly cannot be prosecuted to conviction. In such cases, however grievous it may be to the pious, to see an unworthy member in the church, it is proper to wait until God, in his righteous providence, shall give further light; as few things tend more to weaken the authority of discipline, and to multiply offences, than to commence process without sufficient proof.

IV. When any person is charged with a crime, not by an individual, or individuals, coming forward as accusers, but by *general rumor*, the previous steps prescribed by our Lord in case of private offences, are not necessary;

but the proper judicatory is bound to take immediate cognizance of the affair.

V. In order to render an offence proper for the cognizance of a judicatory on this ground, the rumor must specify some particular sin or sins; it must be general, or widely spread; it must not be transient, but permanent, and rather gaining strength than declining; and it must be accompanied with strong presumption of truth. Taking up charges on this ground, of course, requires great caution, and the exercise of much Christian prudence.

VI. It may happen, however, that in consequence of a report, which does not fully amount to a *general rumor*, as just described, a slandered individual may request a judicial investigation, which it may be the duty of the judicatory to institute.

CHAPTER IV.

OF ACTUAL PROCESS.

I. WHEN all other means of removing an offence have failed, the judicatory, to which cognizance of it properly belongs, shall judicially take it into consideration.

II. There are two modes in which an offence may be brought before a judicatory: either by an individual or individuals, who appear as accusers, and undertake to substantiate the charge; or by common fame.

III. In the former case, process must be pursued in the name of the accuser or accusers. In the latter, there is no need of naming any person as the accuser. *Common fame* is the accuser. Yet a *general rumor* may be raised by the rashness, censoriousness, or malice, of one or more individuals. When this appears to have been the case, such individuals ought to be censured, in proportion to the degree of criminality which appears attached to their conduct.

IV. Great caution ought to be exercised in receiving accusations from any person who is known to indulge a malignant spirit toward the accused; who is not of good character; who is himself under censure or process; who is deeply interested, in any respect, in the conviction of the accused; or who is known to be litigious, rash, or highly imprudent.

V. When a judicatory enters on the consideration of a crime or crimes alleged, no more shall be done, at the first meeting, unless by consent of parties, than to give the accused a copy of each charge, with the names of the witnesses to support it; and to cite all concerned, to appear at the next meeting of the judicatory, to have the matter fully heard and decided. Notice shall be given to the parties concerned, at least ten days previously to the meeting of the judicatory.

VI. The citations shall be issued, and signed, by the moderator or clerk, by order, and in the name of the judicatory. He shall also furnish citations for such witnesses as the accused shall nominate, to appear on his behalf.

VII. Although it is required that the accused be informed of the names of all the witnesses who are to be adduced against him, at least ten days before the time of trial, (unless he consent to waive the right and proceed immediately,) it is not necessary that he, on his part, give a similar notice to the judicatory of all the witnesses intended to be adduced by him for his exculpation.

VIII. In exhibiting charges, the times, places, and circumstances should, if possible, be ascertained and stated, that the accused may have an opportunity to prove an *alibi*, or to extenuate, or alleviate, his offence.

IX. The judicatory, in many cases, may find it more for edification, to send some members to converse, in a private manner, with the accused person; and, if he confesses guilt, to endeavor to bring him to repentance, than to proceed immediately to citation.

X. When an accused person, or a witness, refuses to obey the citation, he shall be cited a second time: and, if he still continue to refuse, he shall be excluded from the communion of the church, for his contumacy, until he repent.

XI. Although, on the first citation, the person cited shall declare in writing, or otherwise, his fixed determination not to obey it; this declaration shall, in no case, induce the judicatory to deviate from the regular course prescribed for citations. They shall proceed as if no such declaration had been made. The person cited may afterward alter his mind.

XII. The time which must elapse between the *first* citation of an accused person, or a witness, and the meeting of the Judicatory at which he is to appear, is at least ten days. But the time allotted for his appearance, in the *subsequent* citation, is left to the discretion of the judicatory; provided always, however, that it be not *less* than is quite sufficient for a seasonable and convenient compliance with the citation.

XIII. The second citation ought always to be accompanied with a notice, that, if the person cited do not appear at the time appointed, the judicatory, besides censuring him for his contumacy, will, after assigning some person to manage his defence, proceed to take the testimony in his case, as if he were present.

XIV. Judicatories, before proceeding to trial, ought to ascertain that their citations have been duly served on the persons for whom they were intended, and especially before they proceed to ultimate measures for contumacy.

XV. The trial shall be fair and impartial. The witnesses shall be examined in the presence of the accused; or, at least, after he shall have received due citation to attend; and he shall be permitted to ask any questions tending to his own exculpation.

XVI. The judgment shall be regularly entered on the records of the judicatory; and the parties shall be allowed copies of the whole proceedings, at their own expense, if they demand them. And, in case of references, or appeals, the judicatory referring, or appealed from, shall send authentic copies of the whole process to the higher judicatory.

XVII. The person found guilty shall be admonished, or rebuked, or excluded from church-privileges, as the case shall appear to deserve, until he give satisfactory evidence of repentance.

XVIII. As cases may arise in which many days, or even weeks, may intervene before it is practicable to commence process against an accused church-member, the session may, in such cases, and ought, if they think the edification of the church requires it, to prevent the accused person from approaching the Lord's table, until the charge against him can be examined.

XIX. The sentence shall be published only in the church or churches which have been offended. Or, if the offence be of small importance, and such as it shall appear most for edification not to publish, the sentence may pass only in the judicatory.

XX. Such gross offenders, as will not be reclaimed by the private or public admonitions of the church, are to be cut off from its communion, agreeably to our Lord's direction, Matt. xviii. 17, and the apostolic injunction respecting the incestuous person, 1 Cor. v. 1—5.

XXI. No professional counsel shall be permitted to appear and plead in cases of process in any of our ecclesiastical courts. But, if any accused person feels unable to represent and plead his own cause to advantage, he may request any minister, or elder, belonging to the judicatory before which he appears, to prepare and exhibit his cause as he may judge proper. But the minister, or elder, so engaged, shall not be allowed, after pleading the cause of the accused, to sit in judgment as a member of the judicatory.

XXII. Questions of order, which arise in the course of process, shall be decided by the moderator. If an appeal is made from the chair, the question on the appeal shall be taken without debate.

XXIII. In recording the proceedings, in cases of judicial process, the reasons for all decisions, except on questions of order, shall be recorded at length; that the record may exhibit every thing which had an influence on the judgment of the court. And nothing, but what is contained in the record, may be taken into consideration in reviewing the proceedings in a superior court.

CHAPTER V.

OF PROCESS AGAINST A BISHOP, OR MINISTER.

I. As the honor and success of the Gospel depend, in a great measure, on the character of its ministers, each Presbytery ought, with the greatest care and impartial-

ity, to watch over the personal and professional conduct of all its members. But as, on the one hand, no minister ought, on account of his office, to be screened from the hand of justice, nor his offences to be slightly censured; so neither ought scandalous charges to be received against him, by any judicatory, on slight grounds.

II. Process against a Gospel minister shall always be entered before the Presbytery of which he is a member. And the same candor, caution, and general method, substituting only the Presbytery for the session, are to be observed in investigating charges against him, as are prescribed in the case of private members.

III. If it be found, that the facts, with which a minister stands charged, happened without the bounds of his own Presbytery that Presbytery shall send notice to the Presbytery within whose bounds they did happen; and desire them, either (if within convenient distance) to cite the witnesses to appear at the place of trial; or (if the distance be so great as to render that inconvenient), to take the examination themselves, and transmit an authentic record of their testimony; always giving due notice to the accused person of the time and place of such examination.

IV. Nevertheless, in case of a minister being supposed to be guilty of a crime, or crimes, at such a distance from his usual place of residence, as that the offence is not likely to become otherwise known to the Presbytery to which he belongs; it shall, in such case, be the duty of the Presbytery within whose bounds the facts shall have happened, after satisfying themselves that there is probable ground of accusation, to send notice to the Presbytery of which he is a member, who are to proceed against him, and either send and take the testimony themselves, by a commission of their own body, or request the other Presbytery to take it for them, and transmit the same, properly authenticated.

V. Process against a Gospel minister shall not be commenced, unless some person or persons undertake to make out the charge; or unless common fame be so loudly proclaims the scandal, that the Presbytery find it necessary, for the honor of religion, to investigate the charge.

VI. As the success of the Gospel greatly depends upon the exemplary character of its ministers, their soundness in the faith, and holy conversation; and as it is the duty of all Christians to be very cautious in taking up an ill report of any man, but especially of a minister of the Gospel: therefore, if any man knows a minister to be guilty of a private, censurable fault, he should warn him in private. But, if the guilty person persist in his fault, or it become public, he who knows it should apply to some other bishop of the Presbytery for his advice in the case.

VII. The prosecutor of a minister shall be previously warned, that, if he fail to prove the charges, he must himself be censured as a slanderer of the Gospel-ministry, in proportion to the malignancy, or rashness, that shall appear in the prosecution.

VIII. When complaint is laid before the Presbytery, it must be reduced to writing; and nothing further is to be done at the first meeting (unless by consent of parties), than giving the minister a full copy of the charges, with the names of the witnesses annexed; and citing all parties and their witnesses, to appear and be heard at the next meeting; which meeting shall not be sooner than ten days after such citation.

IX. When a member of a church-judicatory is under process, it shall be discretionary with the judicatory, whether his privileges of deliberating and voting, as a member, in other matters, shall be suspended until the process is finally issued, or not.

X. At the next meeting of the Presbytery, the charges shall be read to him, and he shall be called upon to say whether he is guilty or not. If he confess, and the matter be base and flagitious; such as drunkenness, uncleanness, or crimes of a higher nature, however penitent he may appear, to the satisfaction of all, the Presbytery must, without delay, suspend him from the exercise of his office, or depose him from the ministry; and, if the way be clear for the purpose, appoint him a due time to confess publicly before the congregation offended, and to profess his penitence.

XI. If a minister accused of atrocious crimes, being twice duly cited, shall refuse to attend the Presbytery, he shall be immediately suspended. And if, after another citation, he still refuse to attend, he shall be deposed as contumacious.

XII. If the minister, when he appears, will not confess, but denies the facts alleged against him; if, on hearing the witnesses, the charges appear important, and well supported, the Presbytery must, nevertheless, censure him; and admonish, suspend, or depose him, according to the nature of the offence.

XIII. Heresy and schism may be of such a nature as to infer deposition; but errors ought to be carefully considered; whether they strike at the vitals of religion, and are industriously spread; or, whether they arise from the weakness of the human understanding, and are not likely to do much injury.

XIV. A minister, under process for heresy or schism, should be treated with Christian and brotherly tenderness. Frequent conferences ought to be held with him, and proper admonitions administered. For some more dangerous errors, however, suspension may become necessary.

XV. If the Presbytery find, on trial, that the matter complained of amounts to no more than such acts of infirmity as may be amended, and the people satisfied; so that little or nothing remains to hinder his usefulness, they shall take all prudent measures to remove the offence.

XVI. A minister, deposed for scandalous conduct. shall not be restored, even on the deepest sorrow for his sin, until after some time of eminent and exemplary, humble and edifying conversation, to heal the wound made by his scandal. And he ought in no case to be restored, until it shall appear, that the sentiments of the religious public are strongly in his favor, and demand his restoration.

XVII. As soon as a minister is deposed, his congregation shall be declared vacant.

CHAPTER VI.

OF WITNESSES.

I. JUDICATORIES ought to be very careful and impartial in receiving testimony. All persons are not *competent* as witnesses; and all who are competent are not *credible*.

II. A *competent* witness is one who ought to be admitted and heard. The competency of a witness may be affected by his want of the proper age; by a want of any of the senses essential to a knowledge of the matter which he is called to establish; by weakness of understanding; by infamy of character; by being under church-censure for falsehood or perjury; by nearness of relationship to any of the parties; and by a variety of considerations which can not be specified in detail.

III. Where there is room for doubt with regard to any of these points, either party has a right to challenge witnesses; and the judicatory shall candidly attend to the exceptions, and decide upon them.

IV. The *credibility* of a witness, or the degree of credit due to his testimony, may be affected by relationship to any of the parties; by deep interest in the result of the trial; by general rashness, indiscretion, or malignity of character; and by various other circumstances; to which judicatories shall carefully attend, and for which they shall make all proper allowance in their decision.

V. A husband or wife shall not be compelled to bear testimony against each other in any judicatory.

VI. The testimony of more than one witness is necessary in order to establish any charge; yet, if several credible witnesses bear testimony to different *similar* acts, belonging to the same general charge, the crime shall be considered as proved.

VII. No witness, afterward to be examined, except a member of the judicatory, shall be present during the examination of another witness on the same case, unless by consent of parties.

VIII. To prevent confusion, witnesses shall be examined first by the party introducing them: then cross-examined by the opposite party: after which any member of the judicatory, or either party, may put additional interrogatories. But no question shall be put, or answered, except by permission of the moderator.

IX. The oath or affirmation to a witness, shall be administered by the moderator, in the following or like terms: "You solemnly promise, in the presence of the omniscient and heart-searching God, that you will declare the truth, the whole truth, and nothing but the truth, according to the best of your knowledge, in the matter in which you are called to witness, as you shall answer it to the great Judge of quick and dead."

X. Every question put to a witness shall, if required, be reduced to writing. When answered, it shall, together with the answer, be recorded, if deemed by either party of sufficient importance.

XI. The records of a judicatory, or any part of them, whether original or transcribed, if regularly authenticated by the moderator and clerk, or either of them, shall be deemed good and sufficient evidence in every other judicatory.

XII. In like manner, testimony taken by one judicatory, and regularly certified, shall be received by every other judicatory, as no less valid than if it had been taken by themselves.

XIII. Cases may arise, in which it is not convenient for a judicatory to have the whole, or, perhaps, any part, of the testimony in a particular cause, taken in their presence. In this case, a commission of the judicatory, consisting of two or three members, may be appointed, and authorized to proceed to the place where the witness or witnesses reside, and take the testimony in question, which shall be considered as if taken in the presence of the judicatory: of which commission, and of the time and place of their meeting, due notice shall be given to the opposite party, that he may have an opportunity of attending. And, if the accused shall desire on his part, to take testimony at a distance for his own exculpation, he shall give notice to the judicatory of the time and place when it is proposed to take it, that a commission, as in the former case, may be appointed for the purpose.

XIV. When the witnesses have all been examined, the accused and the prosecutor shall have the privilege of commenting on their testimony to any reasonable extent.

XV. A member of the judicatory may be called upon to bear testimony in a case which comes before it. He shall be qualified as other witnesses are; and, after having given his testimony, he may immediately resume his seat as a member of the judicatory.

XVI. A member of the church, summoned as a witness, and refusing to appear, or, having appeared, refusing to give testimony, may be censured for contumacy, according to the circumstances of the case..

XVII. The testimony given by witnesses must be faithfully recorded, and read to them, for their approbation, or subscription.

CHAPTER VII.

OF THE VARIOUS WAYS IN WHICH A CAUSE MAY BE CARRIED FROM A LOWER JUDICATORY TO A HIGHER.

I. IN all governments conducted by men, wrong may be done, from ignorance, from prejudice, from malice, or from other causes. To prevent the continued existence of this wrong, is one great design of superior judicatories. And, although there must be a last resort, beyond which there is no appeal; yet the security against permanent wrong will be as great as the nature of the case admits, when those who had no concern in the origin of the proceedings are brought to review them, and to *annul* or *confirm* them, as they see cause; when a greater number of counsellors are made to sanction the judgments, or to correct the errors, of a smaller; and finally, when the whole Church is called to sit in judgment on the acts of a part.

II. Every kind of decision which is formed in any church-judicatory, except the highest, is subject to the review of a superior judicatory, and may be carried before it in one or the other of the four following ways:

SECTION I.

GENERAL REVIEW AND CONTROL.

I. It is the duty of every judicatory above a church-session, at least once a year, to review the records of the proceedings of the judicatory next below. And, if any lower judicatory shall omit to send up its records for this purpose, the higher may issue an order to produce them, either immediately, or at a particular time, as circumstances may require.

II. In reviewing the records of an inferior judicatory, it is proper to examine, First, Whether the proceedings have been constitutional and regular: Secondly, Whether they have been wise, equitable, and for the edification of the church: Thirdly, Whether they have been correctly recorded.

III. In most cases, the superior judicatory may be considered as fulfilling its duty, by simply recording, on its own minutes, the animadversion, or censure, which it may think proper to pass on records under review; and, also, by making an entry of the same in the book reviewed. But it may be, that, in the course of review, cases of irregular proceedings may be found, so disreputable and injurious as to demand the interference of the superior judicatory. In cases of this kind, the inferior judicatory may be required to review and correct its proceedings.

IV. No judicial decision, however, of a judicatory, shall be reversed, unless it be regularly brought up by appeal or complaint.

V. Judicatories may sometimes entirely neglect to perform their duty; by which neglect, heretical opinions, or corrupt practices, may be allowed to gain ground; or offenders of a very gross character may be suffered to escape; or some circumstances in their proceedings, of very great irregularity, may not be distinctly recorded by them. In any of which cases, their records will by no means exhibit to the superior judicatory a full view of their proceedings. If, therefore, the superior judicatory be well advised by *common fame*, that such neglects or irregularities have occurred on the part of the inferior judicatory, it is incumbent on them to take cognizance of the same; and to examine, deliberate, and judge in the whole matter, as completely as if it had been recorded, and thus brought up by the review of the records.

VI. When any important delinquency, or grossly unconstitutional proceedings, appear in the records of any judicatory, or are charged against them by *common fame*, the first step to be taken by the judicatory next above, is to cite the judicatory alleged to have offended, to appear at a specified time and place, and to show what it has done, or failed to do, in the case in question: after which, the judicatory thus issuing the citation, shall remit the whole matter to the delinquent judicatory, with a direction to take it up, and dispose of it in a constitutional manner, or stay all further proceedings in the case, as circumstances may require.

SECTION II.

OF REFERENCES.

I. A reference is a judicial representation, made by an inferior judicatory to a superior, of a case not yet decided; which representation ought always to be in writing.

II. Cases which are new, important, difficult, of peculiar delicacy, the decision of which may establish principles, or precedents, of extensive influence, on which the sentiments of the inferior judicatory are greatly divided, or on which, for any reason, it is highly desirable that a larger body should first decide, are proper subjects of reference.

III. References are, either for mere advice, preparatory to a decision by the inferior judicatory; or for ultimate trial and decision by the superior.

IV. In the former case, the reference only *suspends* the decision of the judicatory from which it comes; in the latter case, it totally relinquishes the decision, and submits the whole cause to the final judgment of the superior judicatory.

V. Although references may, in some cases, as before stated, be highly proper; yet it is, generally speaking, more conducive to the public good, that each judicatory should fulfil its duty by exercising its judgment.

VI. Although a reference ought, generally, to procure advice from the superior judicatory; yet that judicatory is not necessarily bound to give a final judgment in the case, even if requested to do so; but may remit the whole

cause, either with or without advice, back to the judicatory by which it was referred.

VII. In cases of reference, the members of the inferior judicatory making it retain all the privileges of deliberating and voting, in the course of trial and judgment before the superior judicatory, which they would have had, if no reference had been made.

VIII. References are, generally, to be carried to the judicatory immediately superior.

IX. In cases of reference, the judicatory referring ought to have all the testimony, and other documents, duly prepared, produced, and in perfect readiness; so that the superior judicatory may be able to consider and issue the case with as little difficulty or delay as possible.

SECTION III.

OF APPEALS.

I. An appeal is the removal of a cause already decided, from an inferior to a superior judicatory, by a party aggrieved.

II. All persons who have submitted to a regular trial in an inferior, may appeal to a higher judicatory.

III. Any irregularity in the proceedings of the inferior judicatory; a refusal of reasonable indulgence to a party on trial; declining to receive important testimony; hurrying to a decision before the testimony is fully taken; a manifestation of prejudice in the case; and mistake, or injustice, in the decision—are all proper grounds of appeal.

IV. Appeals may be, either from a part of the proceedings of a judicatory, or from a definitive sentence.

V. Every appellant is bound to give notice of his intention to appeal, and also to lay the reasons thereof, in writing, before the judicatory appealed from, either before its rising, or within ten days thereafter. If this notice, or these reasons, be not given to the judicatory while in session, they shall be lodged with the moderator.

VI. Appeals are generally to be carried in regular gradation, from an inferior judicatory to the one immediately superior.

VII. The appellant shall lodge his appeal, and the reasons of it, with the clerk of the higher judicatory, before the close of the second day of their session.

VIII. In taking up an appeal, after ascertaining that the appellant, on his part, has conducted it regularly, the *first* step shall be to read the sentence appealed from; *secondly*, to read the reasons which were assigned by the appellant for his appeal, and which are on record: *thirdly*, to read the whole record of the proceedings of the inferior judicatory in the case, including all the testimony, and the reasons of their decision: *fourthly*, to hear the original parties: *fifthly*, to hear any of the members of the inferior judicatory, in explanation of the grounds of their decision, or of their dissent from it.

IX. After all the parties shall have been fully heard, and all the information gained by the members of the superior judicatory, from those of the inferior, which shall be deemed requisite, the original parties, and all the members of the inferior judicatory, shall withdraw; when the clerk shall call the roll, that every member may have an opportunity to express his opinion on the case; after which, the final vote shall be taken.

X. The decision may be, either to confirm, or reverse, in whole, or in part, the decision of the inferior judicatory; or to remit the cause, for the purpose of amending the record, should it appear to be incorrect, or defective; or for a new trial.

XI. If an appellant, after entering his appeal to a superior judicatory, fail to prosecute it, it shall be considered as abandoned, and the sentence appealed from shall be final. And an appellant shall be considered as abandoning his appeal, if he do not appear before the judicatory appealed to, on the first or second day of its meeting, next ensuing the date of his notice of appeal: except in cases in which the appellant can make it appear, that he was prevented from seasonably prosecuting his appeal by the providence of God.

XII. Members of judicatories appealed from cannot be allowed to vote in the superior judicatory, on any question connected with the appeal.

XIII. If the members of the inferior judicatory, in case of a sentence appealed from, appear to have acted according to the best of their judgment, and with good intention, they incur no censure, although their sentence be reversed. Yet, if they appear to have acted irregularly, or corruptly, they shall be censured as the case may require.

XIV. If an appellant is found to manifest a litigious, or other unchristian, spirit, in the prosecution of his appeal, he shall be censured according to the degree of his offence.

XV. The necessary operation of an appeal is, to suspend all further proceedings on the ground of the sentence appealed from. But, if a sentence of suspension, or excommunication from church-privileges, or of deposition from office, be the sentence appealed from, it shall be considered as in force until the appeal shall be issued.

XVI. It shall always be deemed the duty of the judicatory, whose judgment is appealed from, to send authentic copies of all their records, and of the whole testimony relating to the matter of the appeal. And, if any judicatory shall neglect its duty in this respect, especially, if thereby an appellant, who has conducted with regularity on his part, is deprived of the privilege of having his appeal seasonably issued; such judicatory shall be censured according to the circumstances of the case.

XVII. An appeal shall in no case be entered, except by one of the original parties.

SECTION IV.

OF COMPLAINTS.

I. Another method by which a cause, which has been decided by an inferior judicatory, may be carried before a superior, is by complaint.

II. A complaint is a representation made to a superior, by any member, or members, of a minority of an inferior judicatory, or by any other person or persons, respecting a decision by an inferior judicatory, which, in the opinion of the complainants, has been irregularly or unjustly made.

III. The cases, in which complaint is proper and advisable, are such as the following: viz. The judgment of an inferior judicatory may be favorable to the only party who has been placed at their bar; or the judgment in question may do no wrong to any individual: or the party who is aggrieved by it may decline the trouble of conducting an appeal. In any of these cases no appeal is to be expected. And yet the judgment may appear to some of the members of the judicatory, to be contrary to the Constitution of the Church, injurious to the interests of religion, and calculated to degrade the character of those who have pronounced it. In this case, the minority have not only a right to record, in the minutes of the judicatory, their dissent from this judgment, or their protest against it, but they have also a right to complain to the superior judicatory.

IV. Notice of a complaint shall always be given before the rising of the judicatory, or within ten days thereafter, as in the case of an appeal.

V. This complaint brings the whole proceedings in the case under the review of the superior judicatory; and, if the complaint appears to be well founded, it may have the effect, not only of drawing down censure upon those who concurred in the judgment complained of; but also of reversing that judgment, and placing matters in the same situation in which they were before the judgment was pronounced.

VI. In cases of complaint, however, as in those of appeal, the reversal of a judgment of an inferior judicatory is not necessarily connected with censure on that judicatory.

VII. None of the members of the judicatory whose act is complained of can vote in the superior judicatory, on any question connected with the complaint.

CHAPTER VIII.

OF DISSENTS AND PROTESTS.

I. A DISSENT is a declaration on the part of one or more members of a minority in a judicatory, expressing a different opinion from that of the majority in a particular case. A dissent, unaccompanied with reasons, is always entered on the records of the judicatory.

II. A protest is a more solemn and formal declaration, made by members of a minority as before mentioned, bearing their testimony against what they deem a mischievous, or erroneous, judgment; and is generally accompanied with a detail of the reasons on which it is founded.

III. If a protest, or dissent, be couched in decent and respectful language, and contain no offensive reflections, or insinuations, against the majority of the judicatory, those who offer it have a right to have it recorded on the minutes.

IV. A dissent, or protest, may be accompanied with a complaint to a superior judicatory, or not, at the pleasure of those who offer it. If not thus accompanied, it is simply left to speak for itself, when the records containing it come to be reviewed by the superior judicatory.

V. It may sometimes happen that a protest, though not infringing the rules of decorum, either in its language, or matter, may impute to the judicatory whose judgment it opposes, some principles, or reasonings, which it never adopted. In this case, the majority of the judicatory may with propriety appoint a committee to draw up an answer to the protest, which, after being adopted as the act of the judicatory, ought to be inserted on the records.

VI. When, in such a case, the answer of the majority is brought in, those who entered their protest may be of the opinion, that fidelity to their cause calls upon them to make a reply to the answer. This, however, ought by no means to be admitted; as the majority might, of course, rejoin, and litigation might be perpetuated, to the great inconvenience and disgrace of the judicatory.

VII. When, however, those, who have protested, consider the answer of the majority as imputing to them opinions, or conduct, which they disavow; the proper course is, to ask leave to take back their protest, and modify it in such manner as to render it more agreeable to their views. This alteration may lead to a corresponding alteration in the answer of the majority; with which the whole affair ought to terminate.

VIII. None can join in a protest against a decision of any judicatory, excepting those who had a right to vote in said decision.

CHAPTER IX.

NEW TESTIMONY.

I. IF, after a trial before any judicatory, new testimony be discovered, which is supposed to be highly to the exculpation of the accused, it is proper for him to ask, and for the judicatory to grant, a new trial.

II. It sometimes happens, in the prosecution of appeals, that testimony, which had not been exhibited before the inferior judicatory, is represented to exist, and to be of considerable importance in the case.

III. Representations of this kind ought not to be lightly, or of course, sustained. But the superior judicatory ought to be well satisfied, that the alleged testimony is of real importance, before they determine to put the inferior judicatory to the trouble of a new trial.

IV. When such testimony, therefore, is alleged to exist, either by the appellant, or the judicatory appealed from, it will be proper for the superior judicatory to inquire into the nature and import of the testimony; what is intended to be proved by it; and, whether there is any probability that it will really establish the point intended to be established.

V. If it appear that the fact proposed to be established by the new testimony is important; that is, if it appear to be such a fact as, if proved, would materially alter the aspect of the cause; and if there be any probability that the testimony in question will be sufficient to establish the alleged fact, then the superior judicatory ought to send the cause back to the inferior for a new trial.

VI. Cases may arise, however, in which the judicatory appealed from, and the appellant, may concur in requesting the superior judicatory to take up and issue the appeal, with the additional light which the new evidence may afford. In this case, and especially, if very serious injury is likely to happen, either to the appellant, or to the church, by the delay which a new trial would occasion, the superior judicatory may proceed to hear the new testimony, and to issue the appeal, with the aid of the additional light which that testimony may afford.

VII. When, however, the judgment of the inferior judicatory is reversed; and it is apparent that the new testimony had considerable influence in procuring the reversal; it ought to be so stated in the decision of the superior judicatory; inasmuch as it would be injustice to the inferior judicatory to reverse their decision, upon grounds which were never before them, without explaining the fact.

CHAPTER X.

JURISDICTION.

I. When a member shall be dismissed from one church, with a view to his joining another, if he commit an offence, previous to his joining the latter, he shall be considered as under the jurisdiction of the church which dismissed him, and amenable to it, up to the time when he actually becomes connected with that to which he was dismissed and recommended.

II. The same principle applies to a minister; who is always to be considered as remaining under the jurisdiction of the presbytery which dismissed him, until he actually becomes a member of another.

III. If, however, either a minister, or a private member, shall be charged with a crime, which appears to have been committed during the interval between the date of his dismission and his actually joining the new body, but which did not come to light until after he had joined the new body, that body shall be empowered and bound to conduct the process against him.

IV. No presbytery shall dismiss a minister, or licentiate, or candidate for licensure, without specifying the particular presbytery, or other ecclesiastical body, with which he is to be connected.

CHAPTER XI.

LIMITATION OF TIME.

I. When any member shall remove from one congregation to another, he shall produce satisfactory testimonials of his church-membership and dismission, before he be admitted as a regular member of that church; unless the church, to which he removes, has other satisfactory means of information.

II. No certificate of church-membership shall be considered as valid testimony of the good standing of the bearer, if it be more than one year old, except where there has been no opportunity of presenting it to a church.

III. When persons remove to a distance, and neglect, for a considerable time, to apply for testimonials of dismission and good standing, the testimonials given them shall testify to their character only up to the time of their removal, unless the judicatory have good information of a more recent date.

IV. If a church-member have been more than two years absent from the place of his ordinary residence and ecclesiastical connections, if he apply for a certificate of membership, his absence, and the ignorance of the church respecting his demeanor for that time, shall be distinctly stated in the certificate.

V. Process, in case of scandal, shall commence within the space of one year after the crime shall have been committed; unless it shall have recently become flagrant. It may happen, however, that a church-member, after removing to a place far distant from his former residence, and where his connection with the church is unknown, may commit a crime, on account of which process cannot be instituted within the time above specified. In all such cases, the recent discovery of the church-membership of the individual shall be considered as equivalent to the crime itself having recently become flagrant. The same principle also applies to ministers, if similar circumstances should occur.

THE DIRECTORY

FOR

THE WORSHIP OF GOD IN THE PRESBYTERIAN CHURCH IN THE UNITED STATES OF AMERICA;

AS AMENDED AND RATIFIED BY THE GENERAL ASSEMBLY IN MAY, 1821.

CHAPTER I.

OF THE SANCTIFICATION OF THE LORD'S DAY.

I. It is the duty of every person to remember the Lord's day; and to prepare for it, before its approach. All worldly business should be so ordered, and seasonably laid aside, as that we may not be hindered thereby from sanctifying the Sabbath, as the Holy Scriptures require.

II. The whole day is to be kept holy to the Lord; and to be employed in the public and private exercises of religion. Therefore, it is requisite, that there be a holy resting, all the day, from unnecessary labors; and an abstaining from those recreations, which may be lawful on other days; and also, as much as possible, from worldly thoughts and conversation.

III. Let the provisions, for the support of the family

on that day, be so ordered, that servants, or others, be not improperly detained from the public worship of God; nor hindered from sanctifying the Sabbath.

IV. Let every person, and family, in the morning, by secret and private prayer, for themselves and others, especially for the assistance of God to their minister, and for a blessing upon his ministry, by reading the Scriptures, and by holy meditation, prepare for communion with God in his public ordinances.

V. Let the people be careful to assemble at the appointed time; that, being all present at the beginning, they may unite, with one heart, in all the parts of public worship; and let none unnecessarily depart, till after the blessing be pronounced.

VI. Let the time, after the solemn services of the congregation in public are over, be spent in reading; meditation ; repeating of sermons ; catechising ; religious conversation ; prayer for a blessing upon the public ordinances ; the singing of psalms, hymns, or spiritual songs ; visiting the sick ; relieving the poor, and in performing such like duties of piety, charity, and mercy.

CHAPTER II.

OF THE ASSEMBLING OF THE CONGREGATION, AND THEIR BEHAVIOR DURING DIVINE SERVICE.

I. WHEN the time appointed for public worship is come, let the people enter the church, and take their seats in a decent, grave, and reverent manner.

II. In time of public worship, let all the people attend with gravity and reverence ; forbearing to read any thing, except what the minister is then reading or citing ; abstaining from all whisperings, from salutations of persons present or coming in, and from gazing about, sleeping, smiling, and all other indecent behavior.

CHAPTER III.

OF THE PUBLIC READING OF THE HOLY SCRIPTURES.

I. THE reading of the Holy Scriptures, in the congregation, is a part of the public worship of God, and ought to be performed by the ministers and teachers.

II. The Holy Scriptures of the Old and New Testament shall be publicly read, from the most approved translation, in the vulgar tongue, that all may hear and understand.

III. How large a portion shall be read at once, is left to the discretion of every minister: however, in each service, he ought to read, at least, one chapter ; and more, when the chapters are short, or the connection requires it. He may, when he thinks it expedient, expound any part of what is read: always having regard to the time, that neither reading, singing, praying, preaching, or any other ordinance, be disproportionate the one to the other ; nor the whole rendered too short, or too tedious.

CHAPTER IV.

OF THE SINGING OF PSALMS.

I. IT is the duty of Christians to praise God, by singing psalms, or hymns, publicly in the church, as also privately in the family.

II. In singing the praises of God, we are to sing with the spirit, and with the understanding also ; making melody in our hearts unto the Lord. It is also proper, that we cultivate some knowledge of the rules of music ; that we may praise God in a becoming manner with our voices, as well as with our hearts.

III. The whole congregation should be furnished with books, and ought to join in this part of worship. It is proper to sing without parceling out the psalm, line by line. The practice of reading the psalm, line by line, was introduced in times of ignorance, when many in the congregation could not read : therefore, it is recommended, that it be laid aside, as far as convenient.

IV. The proportion of the time of public worship to be spent in singing is left to the prudence of every minister; but it is recommended, that more time be allowed for this excellent part of divine service, than has been usual in most of our churches.

CHAPTER V.

OF PUBLIC PRAYER.

I. IT seems very proper to begin the public worship of the sanctuary by a short prayer; humbly adoring the infinite majesty of the living God; expressing a sense of our distance from him as creatures, and unworthiness as sinners ; and humbly imploring his gracious presence, the assistance of his Holy Spirit in the duties of his worship, and his acceptance of us through the merits of our Lord and Saviour Jesus Christ.

II. Then, after singing a psalm, or hymn, it is proper

that, before sermon, there should be a full and comprehensive prayer. *First,* Adoring the glory and perfections of God, as they are made known to us in the works of creation, in the conduct of providence, and in the clear and full revelation he hath made of himself in his written word. *Second,* Giving thanks to him for all his mercies of every kind, general and particular, spiritual and temporal, common and special ; above all, for Christ Jesus, his unspeakable gift ; and the hope of eternal life through him. *Third,* Making humble confession of sin, both original and actual ; acknowledging, and endeavoring to impress the mind of every worshiper with, a deep sense of the evil of all sin, as such ; as being a departure from the living God ; and also taking a particular and affecting view of the various fruits which proceed from this root of bitterness :—as, sins against God, our neighbor, and ourselves ; sins in thought, in word, and in deed ; sins secret and presumptuous ; sins accidental and habitual. Also, the aggravations of sin, arising from knowledge, or the means of it ; from distinguishing mercies ; from valuable privileges ; from breach of vows, etc. *Fourth,* Making earnest supplication for the pardon of sin, and peace with God, through the blood of the atonement, with all its important and happy fruits ; for the spirit of sanctification, and abundant supplies of the grace that is necessary to the discharge of our duty ; for support and comfort, under all the trials to which we are liable, as we are sinful and mortal ; and for all temporal mercies that may be necessary, in our passage through this valley of tears. Always remembering to view them as flowing in the channel of covenant-love, and intended to be subservient to the preservation and progress of the spiritual life. *Fifth,* Pleading from every principle warranted in Scripture; from our own necessity ; the all-sufficiency of God ; the merit and intercession of our Saviour ; and the glory of God in the comfort and happiness of his people. *Sixth,* Intercession for others, including the whole world of mankind ; the kingdom of Christ, or his Church universal ; the church or churches with which we are more particularly connected ; the interest of human society in general, and in that community to which we immediately belong ; all that are invested with civil authority; the ministers of the everlasting Gospel; and the rising generation: with whatever else, more particular, may seem necessary, or suitable, to the interest of that congregation where divine worship is celebrated.

III. Prayer after sermon ought generally to have a relation to the subject that has been treated of in the discourse ; and all other public prayers, to the circumstances that gave occasion for them.

IV. It is easy to perceive that in all the preceding directions there is a very great compass and variety; and it is committed to the judgment and fidelity of the officiating pastor, to insist chiefly on such parts, or to take in more or less of the several parts, as he shall be led to by the aspect of providence, the particular state of the congregation in which he officiates, or the disposition and exercise of his own heart at the time. But we think it necessary to observe, that, although we do not approve, as is well known, of confining ministers to set or fixed forms of prayer for public worship ; yet it is the indispensable duty of every minister, previously to his entering on his office, to prepare and qualify himself for this part of his duty, as well as for preaching. He ought, by a thorough acquaintance with the Holy Scriptures, by reading the best writers on the subject, by meditation, and by a life of communion with God in secret, to endeavor to acquire both the spirit and the gift of prayer. Not only so ; but, when he is to enter on particular acts of worship, he should endeavor to compose his spirit, and to digest his thoughts for prayer, that it may be performed with dignity and propriety, as well as to the profit of those who join in it; and that he may not disgrace that important service by mean, irregular, or extravagant effusions.

CHAPTER VI.

OF THE PREACHING OF THE WORD.

I. THE preaching of the word being an institution of God for the salvation of men, great attention should be paid to the manner of performing it. Every minister ought to give diligent application to it; and endeavor to prove himself a workman that needeth not to be ashamed; rightly dividing the word of truth.

II. The subject of a sermon should be some verse, or verses, of Scripture; and its object, to explain, defend, and apply some part of the system of divine truth; or, to point out the nature, and state the bounds and obligation, of some duty. A text should not be merely a motto, but should fairly contain the doctrine proposed to be handled. It is proper, also, that large portions of Scripture be sometimes expounded, and particularly improved, for the instruction of the people in the meaning and use of the Sacred Oracles.

III. The method of preaching requires much study, meditation, and prayer. Ministers ought, in general, to prepare their sermons with care; and not to indulge themselves in loose, extemporary harangues; nor to serve God with that which cost them nought. They ought, however, to keep to the simplicity of the Gospel; expressing themselves in language agreeable to Scripture, and level to the understanding of the meanest of their hearers; carefully avoiding ostentation, either of parts or learning. They ought also to adorn, by their lives, the doctrine which they teach; and to be examples of the believers, in word, in conversation, in charity, in spirit, in faith, in purity.

IV. As one primary design of public ordinances is to pay social acts of homage to the *Most High God*, ministers ought to be careful, not to make their sermons so long as to interfere with, or exclude, the more important duties of prayer and praise; but preserve a just proportion between the several parts of public worship.

V. The sermon being ended, the minister is to pray, and return thanks to Almighty God: then let a psalm be sung; a collection raised for the poor, or other purposes of the church; and the assembly dismissed with the apostolic benediction.

VI. It is expedient, that no person be introduced to preach in any of the churches under our care, unless by the consent of the pastor, or church-session.

CHAPTER VII.

OF THE ADMINISTRATION OF BAPTISM.

I. BAPTISM is not to be unnecessarily delayed; nor to be administered, in any case, by any private person; but by a minister of Christ, called to be the steward of the mysteries of God.

II. It is usually to be administered in the church, in the presence of the congregation; and it is convenient that it be performed immediately after sermon.

III. After previous notice is given to the minister, the child to be baptized is to be presented, by one or both the parents; signifying their desire that the child may be baptized.

IV. Before baptism, let the minister use some words of instruction, respecting the institution, nature, use, and ends of this ordinance; showing,

"That it is instituted by Christ; that it is a seal of the righteousness of faith; that the seed of the faithful have no less a right to this ordinance, under the Gospel, than the seed of Abraham to circumcision, under the Old Testament; that Christ commanded all nations to be baptized; that he blessed little children, declaring that of such is the kingdom of heaven; that children are federally holy, and therefore ought to be baptized; that we are, by nature, sinful, guilty, and polluted, and have need of cleansing by the blood of Christ, and by the sanctifying influences of the Spirit of God."

The minister is also to exhort the parents to the careful performance of their duty: requiring,

"That they teach the child to read the word of God; that they instruct it in the principles of our holy religion, as contained in the Scriptures of the Old and New Testament; an excellent summary of which we have in the Confession of Faith of this Church, and in the Larger and Shorter Catechisms of the Westminster Assembly, which are to be recommended to them, as adopted by this Church, for their direction and assistance, in the discharge of this important duty; that they pray with and for it; that they set an example of piety and godliness before it;

and endeavor, by all the means of God's appointment, to bring up their child in the nurture and admonition of the Lord."

V. Then the minister is to pray for a blessing to attend this ordinance; after which, calling the child by its name, he shall say,

"I baptize thee, in the name of the Father, and of the Son, and of the Holy Ghost."

As he pronounces these words, he is to baptize the child with water, by pouring or sprinkling it, on the face of the child, without adding any other ceremony: and the whole shall be concluded with prayer.

Although it is proper that baptism be administered in the presence of the congregation; yet there may be cases when it will be expedient to administer this ordinance in private houses; of which the minister is to be the Judge.

CHAPTER VIII.

OF THE ADMINISTRATION OF THE LORD'S SUPPER.

I. THE communion, or supper of the Lord, is to be celebrated frequently; but how often, may be determined by the minister and eldership of each congregation, as they may judge most for edification.

II. The ignorant and scandalous are not to be admitted to the Lord's supper.

III. It is proper that public notice should be given to the congregation, at least, the Sabbath before the administration of this ordinance, and that, either then, or on some day of the week, the people be instructed in its nature, and a due preparation for it; that all may come in a suitable manner to this holy feast.

IV. When the sermon is ended, the minister shall show, "That this is an ordinance of Christ: by reading the words of institution, either from one of the Evangelists, or from 1 Cor. xi. *chapter*; which, as to him may appear expedient, he may explain and apply; that it is to be observed in remembrance of Christ, to show forth his death till he come; that it is of inestimable benefit, to strengthen his people against sin; to support them under troubles: to encourage and quicken them in duty; to inspire them with love and zeal; to increase their faith, and holy resolution; and to beget peace of conscience, and comfortable hopes of eternal life."

He is to warn the profane, the ignorant, and the scandalous, and those that secretly indulge themselves in any known sin, not to approach this holy table. On the other hand, he shall invite to this holy table, such as, sensible of their lost and helpless state by sin, depend upon the atonement of Christ for pardon and acceptance with God; such as, being instructed in the Gospel-doctrine, have a competent knowledge to discern the Lord's body, and such as desire to renounce their sins, and are determined to lead a holy and godly life.

V. The table, on which the elements are placed, being decently covered, the bread in convenient dishes, and the wine in cups, and the communicants orderly and gravely sitting around the table, (or in their seats before it,) in the presence of the minister; let him set the elements apart, by prayer and thanksgiving.

The bread and wine being thus set apart by prayer and thanksgiving, the minister is to take the bread, and break it, in the view of the people, saying, in expressions of this sort,

"Our Lord Jesus Christ, on the same night in which he was betrayed, having taken bread, and blessed, and broken it, gave it to his disciples; as I, ministering in his name, give this bread unto you, saying, [here the bread is to be distributed.] Take, eat: this is my body, which is broken for you: this do in remembrance of me."

After having given the bread, he shall take the cup, and say,

"After the same manner, our Saviour also took the cup; and, having given thanks, as hath been done in his name, he gave it to the disciples; saying, [while the minister is repeating these words, let him give the cup.] This cup is the new testament in my blood, which is shed for many, for the remission of sins: drink ye all of it."

The minister himself is to communicate, at such time as may appear to him most convenient.

The minister may, in a few words, put the communicants in mind,

"Of the grace of God, in Jesus Christ, held forth in this sacrament; and of their obligation to be the Lord's: and may exhort them to walk worthy of the vocation wherewith they are called; and, as they have professedly received Christ Jesus the Lord, that they be careful so to walk in him, and to maintain good works."

It may not be improper for the minister to give a word of exhortation also to those who have been only spectators, reminding them,

"Of their duty; stating their sin and danger, by living in disobedience to Christ, in neglecting this holy ordinance; and calling upon them to be earnest in making preparation for attending upon it, at the next time of its celebration."

Then the minister is to pray, and give thanks, to God,

"For his rich mercy, and invaluable goodness, vouchsafed to them in that sacred communion; to implore pardon for the defects of the whole service; and to pray for the acceptance of their persons and performances; for the gracious assistance of the Holy Spirit, to enable them, as they have received Christ Jesus the Lord, so to walk in him; that they may hold fast that which they have received, that no man take their crown; that their conversation may be as becometh the Gospel; that they may bear about with them, continually, the dying of the Lord Jesus, that the life also of Jesus may be manifested in their mortal body; that their light may so shine before men, that others, seeing their good works, may glorify their Father, who is in heaven."

The collection, for the poor, and to defray the expense of the elements, may be made after this: or at such other time as may seem meet to the eldership.

Now let a psalm or hymn be sung, and the congregation dismissed with the following, or some other, gospel-benediction:

"Now the God of peace, that brought again from the dead our Lord Jesus, that great Shepherd of the sheep, through the blood of the everlasting covenant, make you perfect in every good work to do his will, working in you that which is well-pleasing in his sight, through Jesus Christ; to whom be glory for ever and ever. Amen."

VI. As it has been customary, in some parts of our Church, to observe a fast before the Lord's supper; to have sermon on Saturday and Monday; and to invite two or three ministers, on such occasions; and as these seasons have been blessed to many souls, and may tend to keep up a stricter union of ministers and congregations; we think it not improper, that they, who choose it, may continue in this practice.

CHAPTER IX.

OF THE ADMISSION OF PERSONS TO SEALING ORDINANCES.

I. CHILDREN, born within the pale of the visible church, and dedicated to God in baptism, are under the inspection and government of the church; and are to be taught to read, and repeat the Catechism, the Apostles' Creed, and the Lord's Prayer. They are to be taught to pray, to abhor sin, to fear God, and to obey the Lord Jesus Christ. And, when they come to years of discretion, if they be free from scandal, appear sober and steady, and to have sufficient knowledge to discern the Lord's body, they ought to be informed, it is their duty, and their privilege, to come to the Lord's supper.

II. The years of discretion, in young Christians, cannot be precisely fixed. This must be left to the prudence of the eldership. The officers of the church are the judges of the qualifications of those to be admitted to sealing ordinances; and of the time when it is proper to admit young Christians to them.

III. Those who are to be admitted to sealing ordinances, shall be examined as to their knowledge and piety.

IV. When unbaptized persons apply for admission into the church, they shall, in ordinary cases, after giving satisfaction with respect to their knowledge and piety, make a public profession of their faith, in the presence of the congregation; and thereupon be baptized.

CHAPTER X.

OF THE MODE OF INFLICTING CHURCH-CENSURES.

I. THE power which Christ has given the rulers of his Church is for edification, and not for destruction. As, in the preaching of the word, the wicked are, doctrinally, separated from the good; so, by discipline, the church authoritatively makes a distinction between the holy and the profane. In this, she acts the part of a tender mother, correcting her children only for their good, that every one of them may be presented faultless, in the day of the Lord Jesus.

II. When any member of the church shall have been guilty of a fault, deserving censure, the judicatory shall proceed with all tenderness, and restore their offending brother in the spirit of meekness; considering themselves, lest they also be tempted. Censure ought to be inflicted with great solemnity; that it may be the means of impressing the mind of the delinquent with a proper sense of his danger, while he stands excluded from the privileges of the church of the living God, and that, with the divine blessing, it may lead him to repentance.

III. When the judicatory has resolved to pass sentence, suspending a member from church-privileges, the moderator shall address him, to the following purpose:

"Whereas you are guilty [by your own confession, or convicted by sufficient proof, as the case may be,] of the sin of [here mention the particular offence], we declare you suspended from the sacraments of the church, till you give satisfactory evidence of the sincerity of your repentance." To this shall be added such advice, admonition, or rebuke, as may be judged necessary; and the whole shall be concluded by prayer to almighty God, that he would follow this act of discipline with his blessing. We judge it prudent, in general, that such censures be inflicted in the presence of the judicatory only; but, if any church think it expedient to rebuke the offender publicly, this solemn suspension from the sacraments may be in the presence of the congregation.

IV. After any person has been thus suspended from the sacraments, it is proper that the minister, and elders, and other Christians, should frequently converse with him, as well as pray for him in private, that it would please God to give him repentance. And it may be requisite likewise, particularly on days preparatory to the dispensing of the Lord's supper, that the prayers of the church be offered up for those unhappy persons who, by their wickedness, have shut themselves out from this holy communion.

V. When the judicatory shall be satisfied as to the reality of the repentance of any offender, he shall be admitted to profess his repentance, and be restored to the privileges of the church. Which restoration shall be declared to the penitent, in the presence of the session, or of the congregation; and followed with prayer and thanksgiving.

VI. When any offender has been adjudged to be cut off from the communion of the church, it is proper that the sentence be publicly pronounced against him.

VII. The design of excommunication is, to operate upon the offender as a means of reclaiming him; to deliver the church from the scandal of his offence; and to inspire all with fear, by the example of his punishment.

The minister shall give the church, or congregation, a short narrative of the several steps, which have been taken, with respect to their offending brother, and inform them, that it has been found necessary to cut him off from the communion; and shall, in the presence of the church, or congregation, pronounce this sentence in the following or like form: viz.

He shall begin, by showing the authority of the church to cast out unworthy members, from Matt. xviii. 15, 16, 17, 18; 1 Cor. v. 1, 2, 3, 4, 5; and shall briefly explain the nature, use, and consequences of this censure; warning the people to avoid all unnecessary intercourse with him who is cast out.

Then he shall say,

"Whereas A. B. hath been, by sufficient proof, convicted of [here insert the sin], and after much admonition and prayer, obstinately refuseth to hear the church, and hath manifested no evidence of repentance; therefore, in the name, and by the authority, of the Lord Jesus Christ, I pronounce him to be excluded from the communion of the church."

After which, prayer shall be made, that the blessing of God may follow his ordinance, for the conviction and reformation of the excommunicated person, and for the establishment of all true believers.

VIII. When one who hath been excommunicated shall he so affected with his state, as to be brought to repentance, and to desire to be re-admitted to the privileges of the church; the session, having obtained sufficient evidence of his sincere repentance, shall, with the advice and concurrence of the Presbytery, restore him. In order to which, the minister shall, on two Lord's days previous thereto, inform the congregation of the measures which have been taken with the excommunicated person, and of the resolution of the session to receive him again to the communion of the church.

On the day appointed for his restoration, when the other parts of divine service are ended, before pronouncing the blessing, the minister shall call upon the excommunicated person, and propose to him, in the presence of the congregation, the following questions:

"Do you, from a deep sense of your great wickedness, freely confess your sin, in thus rebelling against God, and in refusing to hear his church: and do you acknowledge that you have been in justice and mercy cut off from the communion of the saints?" _Answer,_ "I do." "Do you now voluntarily profess your sincere repentance and deep contrition, for your sin and obstinacy; and do you humbly ask the forgiveness of God, and of his church?" _Answer,_ "I do." "Do you sincerely promise, through divine grace, to live in all humbleness of mind and circumspection; and to endeavor to adorn the doctrine of God our Saviour, by having your conversation as becometh the Gospel?" _Answer,_ "I do."

Here the minister shall give the penitent a suitable exhortation, addressing him in the bowels of brotherly love, encouraging and comforting him. Then he shall pronounce the sentence of restoration, in the following words:

"Whereas you, A. B., have been shut out from the communion of the faithful, but have now manifested such repentance as satisfies the church: In the name of the Lord Jesus Christ, and by his authority, I declare you absolved from the sentence of excommunication formerly denounced against you; and I do receive you into the communion of the church, that you may be a partaker of all the benefits of the Lord Jesus, to your eternal salvation."

The whole shall be concluded with prayer, and the people dismissed with the usual blessing.

CHAPTER XI.

OF THE SOLEMNIZATION OF MARRIAGE.

I. MARRIAGE is not a sacrament; nor peculiar to the church of Christ. It is proper that every commonwealth, for the good of society, make laws to regulate marriage; which all citizens are bound to obey.

II. Christians ought to marry in the Lord: therefore it is fit that their marriage be solemnized by a lawful minister; that special instruction may be given them, and suitable prayers made, when they enter into this relation.

III. Marriage is to be between one man and one woman only: and they are not to be within the degrees of consanguinity, or affinity, prohibited by the word of God.

IV. The parties ought to be of such years of discretion as to be capable of making their own choice: and, if they be under age, or live with their parents, the consent of the parents or others under whose care they are, ought to be previously obtained, and well certified to the minister, before he proceeds to solemnize the marriage.

V. Parents ought neither to compel their children to marry contrary to their inclinations, nor deny their consent without just and important reasons.

VI. Marriage is of a public nature. The welfare of civil society, the happiness of families, and the credit of religion, are deeply interested in it. Therefore the purpose

of marriage ought to be sufficiently published, a proper time previously to the solemnization of it. It is enjoined on all ministers, to be careful that, in this matter, they neither transgress the laws of God, nor the laws of the community: and, that they may not destroy the peace and comfort of families, they must be properly certified with respect to the parties applying to them, that no just objections lie against their marriage.

VII. Marriage must always be performed before a competent number of witnesses; and at any time, except in a day of public humiliation. And we advise that it be not on the Lord's day. And the minister is to give a certificate of the marriage when required.

VIII. When the parties present themselves, for marriage, the minister is to desire, if there is any person present, who knows any lawful reason, why these persons may not be joined together in the marriage-relation, that they will now make it known, or ever after hold their peace.

No objections being made, he is then severally to address himself to the parties to be married, in the following or like words:

"You, the man, declare, in the presence of God, that you do not know any reason, by pre-contract, or otherwise, why you may not lawfully marry this woman."

Upon his declaring he does not, the minister shall address himself to the bride, in the same or similar terms:

"You, the woman, declare, in the presence of God, that you do not know any reason, by pre-contract, or otherwise, why you may not lawfully marry this man."

Upon her declaring she does not, he is to begin with prayer for the presence and blessing of God.

The minister shall then proceed to give them some instruction from the Scriptures, respecting the institution and duties of this state, showing,

"That God has instituted marriage for the comfort and happiness of mankind, in declaring a man shall forsake his father and mother, and cleave unto his wife; and that marriage is honorable in all; that he hath appointed various duties, which are incumbent upon those who enter into this relation; such as, a high esteem and mutual love for one another; bearing with each other's infirmities and weaknesses, to which human nature is subject in its present lapsed state; to encourage each other under the various ills of life; to comfort one another in sickness; in honesty and industry to provide for each other's temporal support; to pray for and encourage one another in the things which pertain to God, and to their immortal souls; and to live together as the heirs of the grace of life."

Then the minister shall cause the bridegroom and bride to join their hands, and shall pronounce the marriage-covenant, first to the man, in these words:

"You take this woman, whom you hold by the hand, to be your lawful and married wife; and you promise, and covenant, in the presence of God and these witnesses, that you will be unto her a loving and faithful husband, until you shall be separated by death."

The bridegroom shall express his consent, by saying, "Yes, I do."

Then the minister shall address himself to the woman, in these words:

"You take this man, whom you hold by the hand, to be your lawful and married husband; and you promise, and covenant, in the presence of God and these witnesses, that you will be unto him a loving, faithful, and obedient wife, until you shall be separated by death."

The bride shall express her consent, by saying, "Yes, I do."

Then the minister is to say,

"I pronounce you husband and wife, according to the ordinance of God; whom therefore God hath joined together, let not man put asunder."

After this the minister may exhort them, in a few words, to the mutual discharge of their duty.

Then let him conclude with a prayer suitable to the occasion.

Let the minister keep a proper register of the names of all persons whom he marries, and of the time of their marriage, for the perusal of all whom it may concern.

CHAPTER XII.

OF THE VISITATION OF THE SICK.

I. WHEN persons are sick, it is their duty, before their strength and understanding fail them, to send for their minister, and to make known to him, with prudence, their spiritual state; or to consult him on the concerns of their precious souls. And it is his duty to visit them, at their request, and to apply himself, with all tenderness and love, to administer spiritual good to their immortal souls.

II. He shall instruct the sick, out of the Scriptures, that diseases arise not out of the ground, nor do they come by chance; but that they are directed and sent by a wise and holy God, either for correction of sin, for the trial of grace, for improvement in religion, or for other important ends: and that they shall work together for good, to all those who make a wise improvement of God's visitation, neither despising his chastening hand, nor fainting under his rebukes.

III. If the minister finds the sick person to be grossly ignorant, he shall instruct him in the nature of repentance and faith, and the way of acceptance with God, through the mediation and atonement of Jesus Christ.

IV. He shall exhort the sick to examine himself, to search his heart, and try his former ways, by the word of God; and shall assist him, by mentioning some of the obvious marks and evidences of sincere piety.

V. If the sick shall signify any scruple, doubt, or temptation, under which he labors, the minister must endeavor to resolve his doubts, and administer instruction and direction, as the case may seem to require.

VI. If the sick appear to be a stupid, thoughtless, and hardened sinner, he shall endeavor to awaken his mind; to arouse his conscience; to convince him of the evil and danger of sin; of the curse of the law, and the wrath of God due to sinners; to bring him to a humble and penitential sense of his iniquities; and to state before him the fullness of the grace and mercy of God, in and through the glorious Redeemer; the absolute necessity of faith and repentance, in order to his being interested in the favor of God, or his obtaining everlasting happiness.

VII. If the sick person shall appear to have knowledge, to be of a tender conscience, and to have been endeavoring to serve God in uprightness, though not without many failings and sinful infirmities; or if his spirit be broken with a sense of sin, or through apprehensions of the want of the divine favor; then it will be proper to administer consolation and encouragement to him, by setting before him the freeness and riches of the grace of God, the all-sufficiency of the righteousness of Christ, and the supporting promises of the Gospel.

VIII. The minister must endeavor to guard the sick person against ill-grounded persuasions of the mercy of God, without a vital union to Christ; and against unreasonable fears of death, and desponding discouragements; against presumption upon his own goodness and merit, upon the one hand, and against despair of the mercy and grace of God in Jesus Christ, on the other.

IX. In one word, it is the minister's duty to administer to the sick person, instruction, conviction, support, consolation, or encouragement, as his case may seem to require. At a proper time, when he is most composed, the minister shall pray with and for him.

X. Lastly, the minister may improve the present occasion, to exhort those about the sick, to consider their mortality; to turn to the Lord, and make their peace with him; in health to prepare for sickness, death, and judgment.

CHAPTER XIII.

OF THE BURIAL OF THE DEAD.

I. WHEN any person departs this life, let the corpse be taken care of in a decent manner: and be kept a proper and sufficient time before interment.

II. When the season for the funeral comes, let the dead body be decently attended to the grave, and interred. During such solemn occasions, let all who attend conduct themselves with becoming gravity; and apply themselves to serious meditation, or discourse: and the minis-

ter, if present, may exhort them to consider the frailty of life, and the importance of being prepared for death and eternity.

CHAPTER XIV.

OF FASTING, AND OF THE OBSERVATION OF THE DAYS OF THANKSGIVING.

I. THERE is no day, under the Gospel, commanded to be kept holy, except the Lord's Day, which is the Christian Sabbath.

II. Nevertheless, to observe days of fasting and thanksgiving, as the extraordinary dispensations of divine Providence may direct, we judge both scriptural and rational.

III. Fasts and thanksgivings may be observed by individual Christians; or families, in private; by particular congregations; by a number of congregations contiguous to each other; by the congregations under the care of a presbytery, or of a synod; or by all the congregations of our Church.

IV. It must be left to the judgment and discretion of every Christian and family, to determine when it is proper to observe a private fast, or thanksgiving; and to the church-sessions, to determine for particular congregations; and to the presbyteries or synods to determine for larger districts. When it is deemed expedient that a fast, or thanksgiving, should be general, the call for them must be judged of by the synod, or general assembly. And if, at any time, the civil power should think it proper to appoint a fast, or thanksgiving, it is the duty of the ministers and people of our communion, as we live under a Christian government, to pay all due respect to the same.

V. Public notice is to be given, a convenient time before the day of fasting, or thanksgiving, comes, that persons may so order their temporal affairs, that they may properly attend to the duties thereof.

VI. There shall be public worship upon all such days; and let the prayers, psalms, portions of Scripture to be read, and sermons, be all, in a special manner, adapted to the occasion.

VII. On fast-days, let the minister point out the authority, and providences, calling to the observation thereof; and let him spend a more than usual portion of time in solemn prayer, particular confession of sin, especially of the sins of the day and place, with their aggravations, which have brought down the judgments of heaven. And let the whole day be spent in deep humiliation and mourning before God.

VIII. On days of thanksgiving, he is to give the like information respecting the authority, and providences, which call to the observance of them; and to spend a more than usual part of the time in the giving of thanks, agreeably to the occasion, and in singing psalms or hymns of praise.

It is the duty of people, on these days, to rejoice with holy gladness of heart; but let trembling be so joined with our mirth, that no excess, or unbecoming levity, be indulged.

CHAPTER XV.

THE DIRECTORY FOR SECRET AND FAMILY WORSHIP.

I. BESIDES the public worship in congregations, it is the indispensable duty of each person, alone, in secret; and of every family, by itself, in private, to pray to, and worship God.

II. Secret worship is most plainly enjoined by our Lord. In this duty every one, apart by himself, is to spend some time in prayer, reading the Scriptures, holy meditation and serious self-examination. The many advantages arising from a conscientious discharge of these duties are best known to those who are found in the faithful discharge of them.

III. Family-worship, which ought to be performed by every family, ordinarily, morning and evening, consists in prayer, reading the Scriptures, and singing praises.

IV. The head of the family, who is to lead in this service, ought to be careful that all the members of his household duly attend; and that none withdraw themselves unnecessarily from any part of family-worship; and that all refrain from their common business, while the Scriptures are read, and gravely attend to the same, no less than when prayer or praise is offered up.

V. Let the heads of families be careful to instruct their children and servants in the principles of religion. Every proper opportunity ought to be embraced for such instruction. But we are of opinion, that the Sabbath-evenings, after public worship, should be sacredly preserved for this purpose. Therefore, we highly disapprove of paying unnecessary private visits on the Lord's day; admitting strangers into the families, except when necessity or charity requires it; or any other practices, whatever plausible pretences may be offered in their favor, if they interfere with the above important and necessary duty.

APPENDIX.

GENERAL RULES FOR JUDICATORIES.*

1. THE moderator shall take the chair, precisely at the hour to which the judicatory stands adjourned; shall immediately call the members to order; and, on the appearance of a quorum, shall open the session with prayer.

2. If a quorum be assembled at the hour appointed, and the moderator be absent, the last moderator present shall be requested to take his place without delay.

3. If a quorum be not assembled at the hour appointed, any two members shall be competent to adjourn, from time to time, that an opportunity may be given for a quorum to assemble.

4. After calling the roll, and marking the absentees, the minutes of the last sitting shall be read, and, if requisite, corrected.

5. It shall be the duty of the moderator, at all times, to preserve order, and to endeavor to conduct all business before the judicatory to a speedy and proper result.

6. It shall be the duty of the clerk, as soon as possible after the commencement of the sessions of every judicatory, to form a complete roll of the members present, and put the same into the hands of the moderator. And it shall, also, be the duty of the clerk, whenever any additional members take their seats, to add their names, in their proper places, to the said roll.

7. It shall be the duty of the clerk, immediately to file all papers, in the order in which they have been read with proper indorsements, and to keep them in perfect order.

8. It shall be the duty of the moderator, carefully to keep notes of the several articles of business, which may be assigned to particular days, and to call them up at the time appointed.

9. The moderator may speak to points of order, in preference to other members, rising from his seat for that purpose; and shall decide questions of order, subject to an appeal to the judicatory by any two members.

10. Business left unfinished at the last sitting is, ordinarily, to be taken up first.

11. A motion made must be seconded, and afterward repeated by the moderator, or read aloud, before it is debated; and every motion shall be reduced to writing, if the moderator, or any member, require it.

12. Any member, who shall have made a motion, shall have liberty to withdraw it, with the consent of his sec-

ond, before any debate has taken place thereon; but not afterward, without the leave of the judicatory.

13. On questions of order, adjournment, postponement, commitment, or the previous question, no member shall speak more than once. On all other questions, each member may speak twice, but not oftener, without express leave of the judicatory.

14. When a question is under debate, no motion shall be received, unless to amend it, to commit it, to postpone it, for the previous question, or to adjourn.

15. An amendment may be moved on any motion, and shall be decided before the original motion.

16. If a motion under debate contains several parts, any two members may have it divided, and a question taken on each part.

17. The previous question shall be in this form:—"Shall the main question be now put?" And, when demanded by a majority of the members present, shall be put without debate; and, until it is decided, shall preclude all amendment, and further debate on the main question.

18. If the previous question be decided in the affirmative, the main question shall be immediately put without debate; if in the negative, the debate may proceed.

19. A question shall not be again called up, or reconsidered, at the same sessions of the judicatory at which it has been decided, unless by the consent of two-thirds of the members who were present at the decision; and, unless the motion to reconsider be made, and seconded, by persons who voted with the majority.

20. A subject which has been indefinitely postponed, either by the operation of the previous question, or by a direct motion for indefinite postponement, shall not be again called up during the same sessions of the judicatory, unless by the consent of three-fourths of the members who were present at the decision.

21. Every member, when speaking, shall address himself to the moderator, and shall treat his fellow-members, and especially the moderator, with decorum and respect. Nor shall members address one another, nor any person present, but through the moderator.

22. Without express permission, no member of a judicatory, while business is going on, shall engage in private conversation.

23. No speaker shall be interrupted, unless he be out of order, or for the purpose of correcting mistakes or misrepresentations.

24. It is indispensable, that members of ecclesiastical judicatories maintain great gravity and dignity, while judicially convened; that they attend closely, in their speeches, to the subject under consideration, and avoid prolix and desultory harangues: and, when they deviate from the subject, it is the privilege of any member, and the duty of the moderator, to call them to order.

25. No member, in the course of debate, shall be allowed to indulge in personal reflections.

---

* The following rules, not having been submitted to the Presbyteries, make no part of the Constitution of the Presbyterian Church. Yet the General Assembly of 1821, considering uniformity in proceedings in all the subordinate judicatories, as greatly conducive to order and dispatch of business, and having revised and approved these rules, recommend them to the Synods, Presbyteries, and Sessions, as a system of regulations, which, *if they think proper*, may be advantageously adopted by them.

26. If more than one member rise to speak at the same time, the member who is most distant from the moderator's chair shall speak first.

27. When more than three members of the judicatory shall be standing at the same time, the moderator shall require all to take their seats, the person only excepted who may be speaking.

28. If any member act, in any respect, in a disorderly manner, it shall be the privilege of any member, and the duty of the moderator, to call him to order.

29. If any member consider himself as aggrieved by a decision of the moderator, it shall be his privilege to appeal to the judicatory; and the question on such appeal shall be taken without debate.

30. Members ought not, without weighty reasons, to decline voting, as this practice might leave the decision of very interesting questions to a small proportion of the judicatory. Silent members, unless excused from voting, must be considered as acquiescing with the majority.

31. It is the duty of the moderator to appoint all committees, except in those cases in which the judicatory shall decide otherwise.

32. The person first named on any committee shall be considered as the chairman thereof, whose duty it shall be to convene the committee, and, in case of his absence, or inability to act, the second named member shall take his place, and perform his duties.

33. When various motions are made, with respect to the filling of blanks with particular numbers, or times, the question shall always be first taken on the highest number, and the longest time.

34. When the moderator has commenced taking the vote, no further debate, or remark, shall be admitted, unless there has evidently been a mistake; in which case, the mistake shall be rectified, and the moderator shall recommence taking the vote.

35. When a vote is taken by ballot in any judicatory, the moderator shall vote with the other members; but he shall not vote in any other case, unless the judicatory be equally divided; when, if he do not choose to vote, the question shall be lost.

36. The yeas and nays on any question shall not be recorded, unless it be required by one-third of the members present.

37. All judicatories have a right to sit in private, on business which, in their judgment, ought not be matter of public speculation.

38. Besides the right to sit judicially in private, whenever they think it right to do so, all judicatories have a right to hold what are commonly called "*interlocutory meetings*," or a sort of committees of the whole judicatory, in which members may freely converse together, without the formalities which are usually necessary in judicial proceedings.

39. Whenever a judicatory is about to sit in a judicial capacity, it shall be the duty of the moderator, solemnly to announce from the chair, that the body is about to pass to the consideration of the business assigned for trial; and to enjoin on the members to recollect and regard their high character, as judges of a court of Jesus Christ, and the solemn duty in which they are about to act.

40. In all process before a judicatory, where there is an accuser, or prosecutor, it is expedient, that there be a committee of the judicatory appointed, (provided the number of members be sufficient to admit of it without inconvenience,) who shall be called the *Judicial Committee;* and whose duty it shall be, to digest and arrange all the papers, and to prescribe, under the direction of the judicatory, the whole order of the proceedings. The members of this committee shall be entitled, notwithstanding their performance of this duty, to sit and vote in the cause, as members of the judicatory.

41. But in cases of process on the ground of *general rumor*, where there is, of course, no particular accuser, there may be a committee appointed, (if convenient,) who shall be called the *Committee of Prosecution*, and who shall conduct the whole cause on the part of the prosecution. The members of this committee shall not be permitted to sit in judgment in the case.

42. No member shall retire from any judicatory, without the leave of the moderator, nor withdraw from it to return home, without the consent of the judicatory.

43. The moderator of every judicatory, above the church-session, in finally closing its sessions, in addition to prayer, may cause to be sung an appropriate psalm or hymn, and shall pronounce the apostolical benediction.

CPSIA information can be obtained
at www.ICGtesting.com
Printed in the USA
LVHW112136140722
723579LV00019B/327